Microsoft®
Access® 2013
ILLUSTRATED

Brief   Introductory   Complete

Microsoft®
Access® 2013
ILLUSTRATED

Brief   Introductory   Complete

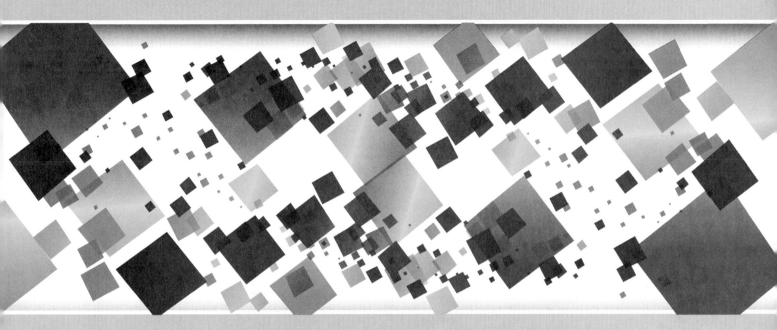

Lisa Friedrichsen

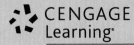
CENGAGE
Learning·

Australia • Brazil • Japan • Korea • Mexico • Singapore • Spain • United Kingdom • United States

Microsoft® Access® 2013—Illustrated Complete
Lisa Friedrichsen

Senior Product Manager: Marjorie Hunt

Associate Product Manager: Amanda Lyons

Senior Content Developer: Christina Kling-Garrett

Content Developer: Kim Klasner

Editorial Assistant: Brandelynn Perry

Brand Manager: Elinor Gregory

Print Buyer: Fola Orekoya

Developmental Editor: Lisa Ruffolo

Full-Service Project Management: GEX Publishing
Services

Copyeditor: Karen Annett

Proofreader: Vicki Zimmer

Indexer: Alexandra Nickerson

QA Manuscript Reviewers: John Freitas, Susan
Pedicini, Susan Whalen, Jeff Schwartz

Cover Designer: GEX Publishing Services

Cover Artist: © Tumanyan/Shutterstock

Composition: GEX Publishing Services

For product information and technology assistance, contact us at
Cengage Learning Customer & Sales Support, 1-800-354-9706

For permission to use material from this text or product, submit all
requests online at **www.cengage.com/permissions**
Further permissions questions can be emailed to
permissionrequest@cengage.com

Library of Congress Control Number: 2013942722
ISBN-13: 978-1-285-09327-7
ISBN-10: 1-285-09327-5

Cengage Learning
200 First Stamford Place, 4th Floor
Stamford, CT 06902
USA

Cengage Learning is a leading provider of customized learning solutions
with office locations around the globe, including Singapore, the United
Kingdom, Australia, Mexico, Brazil, and Japan. Locate your local office at:
www.cengage.com/global

Cengage Learning products are represented in Canada by
Nelson Education, Ltd.

For your course and learning solutions, visit **www.cengage.com**

Purchase any of our products at your local college store or at our
preferred online store **www.cengagebrain.com**

Printed in the United States of America
1 2 3 4 5 6 7 18 17 16 15 14 13

Brief Contents

Preface xviii

Windows 8

Unit A: Getting Started with Windows 8 .... Windows 1
Unit B: Understanding File Management .... Windows 25

Office 2013

Unit A: Getting Started with Microsoft Office 2013 .... Office 1

Access 2013

Unit A: Getting Started with Access 2013.. Access 1
Unit B: Building and Using Queries .... Access 27
Unit C: Using Forms .... Access 53
Unit D: Using Reports... Access 79
Unit E: Modifying the Database Structure.. Access 105
Unit F: Improving Queries .... Access 137
Unit G: Enhancing Forms.. Access 163
Unit H: Analyzing Data with Reports .... Access 189
Unit I: Importing and Exporting Data .... Access 217
Unit J: Analyzing Database Design Using Northwind .... Access 243
Unit K: Creating Advanced Queries.. Access 269
Unit L: Creating Advanced Reports... Access 297
Unit M: Creating Macros... Access 321
Unit N: Creating Modules and VBA... Access 345
Unit O: Administering the Database .... Access 369
Unit P: Access and the Web... Access 393

Cloud

Appendix: Working in the Cloud .... Cloud 1

Glossary.. Glossary 1
Index... Index 17

Contents

Preface xviii

Windows 8

Unit A: Getting Started with Windows 8 .... **Windows 1**

Start Windows 8.. Windows 2
    Using touch screens

Navigate the Start Screen and Desktop.. Windows 4

Point, Click, and Drag... Windows 6
    Using newer touch devices

Start an App... Windows 8
    Searching for apps and files

Work with a Window.. Windows 10
    Using the Quick Access toolbar

Manage Multiple Windows.. Windows 12

Use Command Buttons, Menus, and Dialog Boxes.. Windows 14

Get Help .... Windows 16
    Finding other ways to get help
    Using right-clicking

Exit Windows 8 .... Windows 18
    Installing updates when you exit Windows

Practice .... Windows 20

Unit B: Understanding File Management .... **Windows 25**

Understand Files and Folders... Windows 26
    Plan your file organization

Create and Save a File... Windows 28

Explore the Files and Folders on Your Computer .... Windows 30

Change File and Folder Views... Windows 32
    Snapping Windows 8 apps

Open, Edit, and Save Files.. Windows 34
    Comparing Save and Save As
    Using cloud storage
Copy Files.. Windows 36
    Copying files using Send to
Move and Rename Files .... Windows 38
    Using Windows 8 libraries
Search for Files, Folders, and Programs.. Windows 40
    Using the Search Tools tab in File Explorer
Delete and Restore Files .... Windows 42
    More techniques for selecting and moving files
Practice .... Windows 44

Office 2013

Unit A: Getting Started with Microsoft Office 2013 .... **Office 1**
Understand the Office 2013 Suite...Office 2
    What is Office 365?
Start an Office App...Office 4
    Starting an app using Windows 7
    Using shortcut keys to move between Office programs
    Using the Office Clipboard
Identify Office 2013 Screen Elements..Office 6
    Using Backstage view
Create and Save a File..Office 8
    Saving files to SkyDrive

Open a File and Save It with a New Name ....Office 10
  Exploring File Open options
  Working in Compatibility Mode
View and Print Your Work ....Office 12
  Customizing the Quick Access toolbar
  Creating a screen capture
Get Help, Close a File, and Exit an App...Office 14
  Enabling touch mode
  Recovering a document
Practice ....Office 16

Access 2013

Unit A: Getting Started with Access 2013...**Access 1**
Understand Relational Databases .... Access 2
Explore a Database .... Access 4
Create a Database .... Access 6
Create a Table... Access 8
  Creating a table in Datasheet View
Create Primary Keys .... Access 10
  Learning about field properties
Relate Two Tables .... Access 12
Enter Data... Access 14
  Changing from Navigation mode to Edit mode
  Cloud computing
Edit Data... Access 16
  Resizing and moving datasheet columns
Practice .... Access 18

Unit B: Building and Using Queries..**Access 27**

    Use the Query Wizard...Access 28

    Work with Data in a Query...Access 30
        Hiding and unhiding fields in a datasheet
        Freezing and unfreezing fields in a datasheet

    Use Query Design View...Access 32
        Adding or deleting a table in a query

    Sort and Find Data ....Access 34

    Filter Data...Access 36
        Using wildcard characters

    Apply AND Criteria..Access 38
        Searching for blank fields

    Apply OR Criteria ....Access 40

    Format a Datasheet ....Access 42

    Practice ....Access 44

Unit C: Using Forms...**Access 53**

    Use the Form Wizard..Access 54

    Create a Split Form...Access 56

    Use Form Layout View ....Access 58
        Table layouts

    Add Fields to a Form ....Access 60
        Bound versus unbound controls

    Modify Form Controls ....Access 62

    Create Calculations ....Access 64

    Modify Tab Order..Access 66
        Layout positioning

    Insert an Image ....Access 68
        Applying a background image

    Practice ....Access 70

Unit D: Using Reports ....**Access 79**

    Use the Report Wizard .... Access 80
        Changing page orientation
    Use Report Layout View .... Access 82
    Review Report Sections .... Access 84
    Apply Group and Sort Orders .... Access 86
    Add Subtotals and Counts .... Access 88
    Resize and Align Controls .... Access 90
        Precisely moving and resizing controls
    Format a Report .... Access 92
    Create Mailing Labels .... Access 94
    Practice .... Access 96

Unit E: Modifying the Database Structure ....**Access 105**

    Examine Relational Databases .... Access 106
        Enforcing referential integrity
        Using many-to-many relationships
    Design Related Tables .... Access 108
        Specifying the foreign key field data type
    Create One-to-Many Relationships .... Access 110
        More on enforcing referential integrity
    Create Lookup Fields .... Access 112
        Creating multivalued fields
    Modify Short Text Fields .... Access 114
        Working with the Input Mask property
    Modify Number and Currency Fields .... Access 116
        Modifying fields in Datasheet View

Modify Date/Time Fields .... Access 118

Using Smart Tags

Modify Validation Properties .... Access 120

Create Attachment Fields .... Access 122

Working with database file types

Practice .... Access 124

Unit F: Improving Queries .... **Access 137**

Create Multitable Queries .... Access 138

Deleting a field from the query grid

Apply Sorts and View SQL .... Access 140

Specifying a sort order different from the field order in the datasheet

Develop AND Criteria .... Access 142

Develop OR Criteria .... Access 144

Using wildcard characters in query criteria

Create Calculated Fields .... Access 146

Build Summary Queries .... Access 148

Build Crosstab Queries .... Access 150

Using query wizards

Create a Report on a Query .... Access 152

Practice .... Access 154

Unit G: Enhancing Forms .... **Access 163**

Use Form Design View .... Access 164

Add Subforms .... Access 166

Linking the form and subform

Align Control Edges .... Access 168

Anchoring, margins, and padding

Add a Combo Box for Data Entry .... Access 170

Choosing between a combo box and a list box

Add a Combo Box to Find Records .... Access 172

Add Command Buttons .... Access 174
    Shape effects

Add Option Groups.. Access 176
    Protecting data

Add Tab Controls .... Access 178

Practice .... Access 180

Unit H: Analyzing Data with Reports .... **Access 189**

Use Report Design View .... Access 190

Create Parameter Reports... Access 192
    Parameter criteria

Apply Conditional Formatting .... Access 194
    Conditional formatting using data bars

Add Lines... Access 196
    Line troubles

Use the Format Painter and Themes... Access 198

Add Subreports .... Access 200

Modify Section Properties .... Access 202

Create Summary Reports... Access 204

Practice .... Access 206

Unit I: Importing and Exporting Data .... **Access 217**

Use Database Templates .... Access 218
    Setting a startup form

Use Application Parts .... Access 220
    Referential integrity cascade options

Import Data from Excel .... Access 222
    Importing from another database

Link Data... Access 224

Export Data to Excel...Access 226

Publish Data to Word..Access 228

Merge Data with Word...Access 230

Export Data to PDF...Access 232

Practice..Access 234

Unit J: Analyzing Database Design Using Northwind...........................Access 243

Normalize Data..Access 244
Understanding third normal form

Analyze Relationships..Access 246
Multivalued fields
More about Cascade options

Evaluate Tables..Access 248
Modifying fields in Datasheet View

Improve Fields...Access 250
Using Long Text fields

Use Subqueries..Access 252
Using Expression Builder

Modify Joins..Access 254

Analyze Forms...Access 256

Analyze Reports...Access 258

Practice..Access 260

Unit K: Creating Advanced Queries...Access 269

Query for Top Values...Access 270

Create a Parameter Query..Access 272

Modify Query Properties..Access 274
Creating an Alias

Create a Make Table Query..Access 276

Create an Append Query..Access 278
1900 versus 2000 dates

Create a Delete Query .... Access 280

Create an Update Query.. Access 282
     Restoring hidden objects

Specify Join Properties.. Access 284
     Null and zero-length string values

Find Unmatched Records.. Access 286
     Reviewing referential integrity
     Find Duplicates Query Wizard

Practice .... Access 288

Unit L: Creating Advanced Reports .... **Access 297**

Apply Advanced Formatting.. Access 298

Control Layout.. Access 300

Set Advanced Print Layout.. Access 302

Create Multicolumn Reports.. Access 304

Use Domain Functions.. Access 306
     Adding page numbers or the date and time to a report

Create Charts.. Access 308
     Using the Blank Report button versus the Report Design button

Modify Charts .... Access 310

Apply Chart Types.. Access 312

Practice .... Access 314

Unit M: Creating Macros .... **Access 321**

Understand Macros.. Access 322

Create a Macro .... Access 324

Modify Actions and Arguments.. Access 326
     Assigning a macro to a key combination

Assign a Macro to a Command Button.. Access 328
     Using a trusted database and setting up a trusted folder

Use If Statements... Access 330

Work with Events... Access 332

Create a Data Macro.. Access 334

Troubleshoot Macros... Access 336

Practice .... Access 338

Unit N: Creating Modules and VBA..**Access 345**

Understand Modules and VBA... Access 346

Compare Macros and Modules .... Access 348

Create Functions .... Access 350

Use If Statements... Access 352

Document Procedures .... Access 354

Build Class Modules .... Access 356

Modify Sub Procedures.. Access 358

Troubleshoot Modules .... Access 360

Practice .... Access 362

Unit O: Administering the Database ....**Access 369**

Create a Navigation Form .... Access 370

Setting navigation options

Compact and Repair a Database .... Access 372

Trusting a database

Change Startup Options .... Access 374

Analyze Database Performance... Access 376

Viewing object dependencies

Set a Database Password... Access 378

Back Up a Database .... Access 380

Using portable storage media

Convert a Database .... Access 382

Split a Database .... Access 384
    Databases and client/server computing

Practice .... Access 386

Unit P: Access and the Web .... **Access 393**

Create a Hyperlink Field .... Access 394

Create a Hyperlink Control... Access 396

Use HTML Tags to Format Text.. Access 398
    HTML 5

Export to HTML and XML .... Access 400
    XML, XSD, and XSL files

Import from HTML and XML .... Access 402

Save and Share a Database with SkyDrive .... Access 404

Understand Access Web Apps .... Access 406

Create an Access Web App .... Access 408

Practice .... Access 410

Appendix: Working in the Cloud..Cloud 1

      Understand Office 2013 in the Cloud ....Cloud 2

      Work Online...Cloud 4

            Getting a Microsoft account

      Explore SkyDrive ....Cloud 6

            How to disable default saving to Skydrive

      Manage Files on SkyDrive ....Cloud 8

      Share Files..Cloud 10

            Co-authoring documents

      Explore Office Web Apps ....Cloud 12

            Exploring other Office Web Apps

      Team Project...Cloud 14

Glossary ....Glossary 1

Index .... Index 17

Preface

Welcome to *Microsoft Access 2013—Illustrated Complete*. This book has a unique design: each skill is presented on two facing pages, with steps on the left and screens on the right. The layout makes it easy to learn a skill without having to read a lot of text and flip pages to see an illustration.

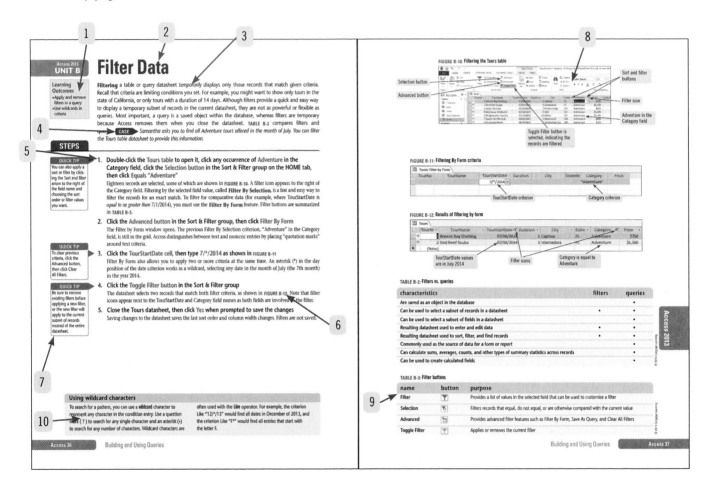

1　New! Learning Outcomes box lists measurable learning goals for which a student is accountable in that lesson.

2　Each two-page lesson focuses on a single skill.

3　Introduction briefly explains why the lesson skill is important.

4　A case scenario motivates the steps and puts learning in context.

5　Step-by-step instructions and brief explanations guide students through each hands-on lesson activity.

6　New! Figure references are now in red bold to help students refer back and forth between the steps and screenshots.

7　Tips and troubleshooting advice, right where you need it—next to the step itself.

8　New! Larger screenshots with green callouts now placed on top keep students on track as they complete steps.

9　Tables provide summaries of helpful information such as button references or keyboard shortcuts.

10　Clues to Use yellow boxes provide useful information related to the lesson skill.

This book is an ideal learning tool for a wide range of learners—the "rookies" will find the clean design easy to follow and focused with only essential information presented, and the "hotshots" will appreciate being able to move quickly through the lessons to find the information they need without reading a lot of text. The design also makes this a great reference after the course is over! See the illustration on the left to learn more about the pedagogical and design elements of a typical lesson.

What's New in this Edition

- **Coverage** — This book helps students learn to use Microsoft Access 2013, including step-by-step instructions on creating tables, queries, forms, and reports. Working in the Cloud appendix helps students learn to use SkyDrive to save, share, and manage files in the cloud and to use Office Web Apps.
- **New! Learning Outcomes** — Each lesson displays a green Learning Outcomes box that lists skills-based or knowledge-based learning goals for which students are accountable. Each Learning Outcome maps to a variety of learning activities and assessments. (See the *New! Learning Outcomes* section on page xxi for more information.)
- **New! Updated Design** — This edition features many new design improvements to engage students — including larger lesson screenshots with green callouts placed on top, and a refreshed Unit Opener page.
- **New! Independent Challenge 4: Explore** — This new case-based assessment activity allows students to explore new skills and use creativity to solve a problem or create a project.

Assignments

This book includes a wide variety of high quality assignments you can use for practice and assessment. Assignments include:

- **Concepts Review** — Multiple choice, matching, and screen identification questions.
- **Skills Review** — Step-by-step, hands-on review of every skill covered in the unit.
- **Independent Challenges 1-3** — Case projects requiring critical thinking and application of the unit skills. The Independent Challenges increase in difficulty. The first one in each unit provides the most hand-holding; the subsequent ones provide less guidance and require more critical thinking and independent problem solving.
- **Independent Challenge 4: Explore** — Case projects that let students explore new skills that are related to the core skills covered in the unit and are often more open ended, allowing students to use creativity to complete the assignment.
- **Visual Workshop** — Critical thinking exercises that require students to create a project by looking at a completed solution; they must apply the skills they've learned in the unit and use critical thinking skills to create the project from scratch.

Certification Prep Tool

This textbook was developed to instruct on the Microsoft® Office® 2013 certification objectives. Microsoft Corporation has developed a set of standardized, performance-based examinations that you can take to demonstrate your overall expertise with Microsoft Office 2013 programs. Microsoft Office 2013 certification provides a number of benefits for you:

- Differentiate yourself in the employment marketplace from those who are not Microsoft Office Specialist or Expert certified.
- Prove skills and expertise when using Microsoft Office 2013.
- Perform at a higher skill level in your job.
- Work at a higher professional level than those who are not certified.
- Broaden your employment opportunities and advance your career more rapidly.

For more information about Microsoft Office 2013 certification, including a complete list of certification objectives, visit the Microsoft web site, http://www.microsoft.com/learning. To see which Microsoft Office 2013 certification objectives are addressed by the contents of this text and where each is included in the text, visit the Certification resource on the Student Companion Site located on www.cengagebrain.com. For detailed instructions about accessing available resources, visit www.cengage.com/ct/student download or contact your instructor for information about accessing the required files.

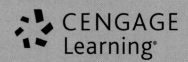

New! Learning Outcomes

Every 2-page lesson in this book now contains a green **Learning Outcomes box** that states the learning goals for that lesson.

- **What is a learning outcome?** A learning outcome states what a student is expected to know or be able to do after completing a lesson. Each learning outcome is skills-based or knowledge-based and is *measurable*. Learning outcomes map to learning activities and assessments.

- **How do students benefit from learning outcomes?** Learning outcomes tell students exactly what skills and knowledge they are *accountable* for learning in that lesson. This helps students study more efficiently and effectively and makes them more active learners.

- **How do instructors benefit from learning outcomes?** Learning outcomes provide clear, measurable, skills-based learning goals that map to various high-quality learning activities and assessments. A **Learning Outcomes Map**, available for each unit in this book, maps every learning outcome to the learning activities and assessments shown below.

Learning Outcomes Map to These Learning Activities:

1. **Book lessons:** Step-by-step tutorial on one skill presented in a two-page learning format
2. **SAM Training:** Short animations and hands-on practice activities in simulated environment

Learning Outcomes Map to These Assessments:

1. **End-of-Unit Exercises: Concepts Review** (screen identification, matching, multiple choice); **Skills Review** (hands-on review of each lesson); **Independent Challenges** (hands-on, case-based review of specific skills); **Visual Workshop** (activity that requires student to build a project by looking at a picture of the final solution).
2. **Exam View Test Banks:** Objective-based questions you can use for online or paper testing.
3. **SAM Assessment:** Performance-based assessment in a simulated environment.
4. **SAM Projects:** Auto-graded projects for Word, Excel, Access, and PowerPoint that students create live in the application.
5. **Extra Independent Challenges:** Extra case-based exercises available in the Instructor Resources that cover various skills.

Learning Outcomes Map

A **Learning Outcomes Map**, contained in the Instructor Resources, provides a listing of learning activities and assessments for each learning outcome in the book.

Learning Outcomes Map
Microsoft Access 2013 Illustrated
Unit A--Getting Started with Microsoft Office 2013

KEY:
IC=Independent Challenge   EIC=Extra Independent Challenge
VW=Visual Workshop

	Concepts Review	Skills Review	IC1	IC2	IC3	IC4	VW	EIC 1	EIC 2	Test Bank	SAM Assessment	SAM Projects	SAM Training	Illustrated Video
Understand the Office 2013 Suite														
Identify Office suite components	✓		✓							✓				✓
Describe the features of each program			✓							✓				✓
Start an Office App														
Start an Office App			✓							✓	✓	✓	✓	✓
Explain the purpose of a template														✓
Start a new blank document			✓											✓
Identify Office 2013														

Instructor Resources

This book comes with a wide array of high-quality technology-based teaching tools to help you teach and to help students learn. The following teaching tools are available for download at our Instructor Companion Site. Simply search for this text at *login.cengage.com.* An instructor login is required.

- **New! Learning Outcomes Map** — A detailed grid for each unit (in Excel format) shows the learning activities and assessments that map to each learning outcome in that unit.

- **Instructor's Manual** — Available as an electronic file, the Instructor's Manual includes lecture notes with teaching tips for each unit.

- **Sample Syllabus** — Prepare and customize your course easily using this sample course outline.

- **PowerPoint Presentations** — Each unit has a corresponding PowerPoint presentation covering the skills and topics in that unit that you can use in lectures, distribute to your students, or customize to suit your course.

- **Figure Files** — The figures in the text are provided on the Instructor Resources site to help you illustrate key topics or concepts. You can use these to create your own slide shows or learning tools.

- **MOS Exam Study Guide** — provides information on the Access 2013 Microsoft Office Sprecialist exam;

grid lists each exam objective and page numbers of where each is covered in the book.

- **Solution Files** — Solution Files are files that contain the finished project that students create or modify in the lessons or end-of-unit material.

- **Solutions Document** — This document outlines the solutions for the end-of-unit Concepts Review, Skills Review, Independent Challenges and Visual Workshops. An Annotated Solution File and Grading Rubric accompany each file and can be used together for efficient grading.

- **ExamView Test Banks** — ExamView is a powerful testing software package that allows you to create and administer printed, computer (LAN-based), and Internet exams. Our ExamView test banks include questions that correspond to the skills and concepts covered in this text, enabling students to generate detailed study guides that include page references for further review. The computer-based and Internet testing components allow students to take exams at their computers, and also save you time by grading each exam automatically.

Key Facts About Using This Book

Data Files are needed: To complete many of the lessons and end-of-unit assignments, students need to start from partially completed Data Files, which help students learn more efficiently. By starting out with a Data File, students can focus on performing specific tasks without having to create a file from scratch. All Data Files are available as part of the Instructor Resources. Students can also download Data Files themselves for free at cengagebrain.com. (For detailed instructions, go to www.cengage.com/ct/studentdownload.)

System requirements: This book was developed using Microsoft Office 2013 Professional running on Windows 8. Note that Windows 8 is not a requirement for the units on Microsoft Office; Office 2013 runs virtually the same on Windows 7 and Windows 8. Please see Important Notes for Windows 7 Users on the next page for more information.

Screen resolution: This book was written and tested on computers with monitors set at a resolution of 1366 x 768. If your screen shows more or less information than the figures in this book, your monitor is probably set at a higher or lower resolution. If you don't see something on your screen, you might have to scroll down or up to see the object identified in the figure.

Tell Us What You Think!

We want to hear from you! Please email your questions, comments, and suggestions to the Illustrated Series team at: **illustratedseries@cengage.com**

Important Notes for Windows 7 Users

The screenshots in this book show Microsoft Office 2013 running on Windows 8. However, if you are using Microsoft Windows 7, you can still use this book because Office 2013 runs virtually the same on both platforms. There are only two differences that you will encounter if you are using Windows 7. Read this section to understand the differences.

Dialog boxes

If you are a Windows 7 user, dialog boxes shown in this book will look slightly different than what you see on your screen. Dialog boxes for Windows 7 have a light blue title bar, instead of a medium blue title bar. However, beyond this superficial difference in appearance, the options in the dialog boxes across platforms are the same. For instance, the screenshots below show the Font dialog box running on Windows 7 and the Font dialog box running on Windows 8.

FIGURE 1: Font dialog box in Windows 7

FIGURE 2: Font dialog box in Windows 8

Alternate Steps for Starting an App in Windows 7

Nearly all of the steps in this book work exactly the same for Windows 7 users. However, starting an app (or program/application) requires different steps for Windows 7. The steps below show the Windows 7 steps for starting an app. (Note: Windows 7 alternate steps also appear in red Trouble boxes next to any step in the book that requires starting an app.)

Starting an app (or program/application) using Windows 7

1. Click the **Start button** on the taskbar to open the Start menu.
2. Click **All Programs**, then click the **Microsoft Office 2013 folder**. See Figure 3.
3. Click the app you want to use (such as **Access 2013**).

FIGURE 3: Starting an app using Windows 7

Acknowledgements

Author Acknowledgements

The Access portion is dedicated to my students, and all who are using this book to teach and learn about Access. Thank you. Also, thank you to all of the professionals who helped me create this book.

–Lisa Friedrichsen

Advisory Board Acknowledgements

We thank our Illustrated Advisory Board who gave us their opinions and guided our decisions as we developed all of the new editions for Microsoft Office 2013.

They are as follows:

Merlin Amirtharaj, Stanly Community College

Londo Andrews, J. Sargeant Reynolds Community College

Rachelle Hall, Glendale Community College

Terri Helfand, Chaffey Community College

Sheryl Lenhart, Terra Community College

Dr. Jose Nieves, Lord Fairfax Community College

Getting Started with Windows 8

CASE You are about to start a new job, and your employer has asked you to get familiar with Windows 8 to help boost your productivity. You'll need to start Windows 8 and Windows 8 apps, work with on-screen windows and commands, look for help, and exit Windows.

Unit Objectives

After completing this unit, you will be able to:

- Start Windows 8
- Navigate the Start screen and desktop
- Point, click, and drag
- Start an app
- Work with a window

- Manage multiple windows
- Use command buttons, menus, and dialog boxes
- Get help
- Exit Windows 8

Files You Will Need

No files needed.

Microsoft product screenshots used with permission from Microsoft Corporation.

Start Windows 8

Learning
Outcomes
• Power on a
  computer
• Log into
  Windows 8

Windows 8 is an **operating system**, a type of program that runs your computer and lets you use it. A **program** is a set of instructions written for a computer. When you turn on your computer, the Windows 8 operating system starts automatically. If your computer did not have an operating system, you wouldn't see anything on the screen after you turned it on. The operating system can reserve a special area called a **user account** where each user can keep his or her files. If your computer is set up for more than one user, you might need to **sign in**, or select your user account name when the computer starts, also called **logging in**. If you are the only user on your computer, you won't have to select an account. You might also need to enter a **password**, a special sequence of numbers and letters. Your password lets you enter and use the files in a secured user account area on your computer. Depending on how your user account is set up, your password might also let you access content you have stored online. Users cannot see each other's account areas without the other person's password, so passwords help keep your computer information secure. After you log in, you see the Windows 8 Start screen. You will learn about the Start screen in the next lesson. **CASE** ▶ *You're about to start a new job, so you decide to learn more about Windows 8, the operating system used at your new company.*

STEPS

1. **Press your computer's** power button, **which might look like** 🔘 **or** ▭⏻▭ **, then if the monitor is not turned on press its** power button

   On a desktop computer, the power button is probably on the front panel. On a laptop computer it's most likely at the top of the keys on your keyboard. After a few moments, a **lock screen** appears with the time and date. See **FIGURE A-1**. The lock screen appears when you first start your computer and also if you leave it unattended for a period of time.

QUICK TIP

To see the characters, move the mouse pointer over the eye icon 👁 on the right side of the password box, then press and hold down the mouse button. When you release the mouse button, the bullets reappear.

2. **Press [Spacebar]**

   The sign-in screen shows your Windows user account picture, name, and e-mail address, as well as a space to enter your user account password. The user account may have your name assigned to it, or it might have a general name like "Student" or "Lab User".

3. **Type your** password, **as shown in** FIGURE A-2, **using uppercase and lowercase letters as necessary**

   If necessary, ask your instructor or technical support person what password you should use. Passwords are **case sensitive**, which means that if you type any letter using capital letters when lowercase letters are needed, or vice versa, Windows will not let you use your account. For example, if your password is "book", typing "Book" or "BOOK," will not let you enter your account. For security, Windows substitutes bullets for the password characters you type.

TROUBLE

If you see a message saying your password is incorrect, click OK to redisplay the password entry box. Type your password carefully, then click ➡.

4. **Click the** Submit button ➡

   A welcome message appears, followed by the Windows 8 Start screen. See **FIGURE A-3**.

Using touch screens

The Windows 8 style UI was developed to work with touch-screen monitors and tablet computers, in addition to traditional laptops. So if you have a touch-screen device, like the one shown in **FIGURE A-4**, you'll find that many tasks are easier to accomplish because they are designed for use with gestures instead of a mouse. A **gesture** is an action you take with your fingertip directly on the screen, such as tapping or swiping. For example, when you sign into Windows, you can tap the Submit button on the screen, instead of clicking it. In general, mouse users can locate items by pointing to the screen corners, and touch-screen users can swipe from the screen edges. Touch screens are easy to use for many people because they use these same gestures with their other devices, such as mobile phones and tablet computers.

FIGURE A-4: A touch-screen device

vovan/Shutterstock.com

FIGURE A-1: Lock screen with time and date

FIGURE A-2: Typing your password

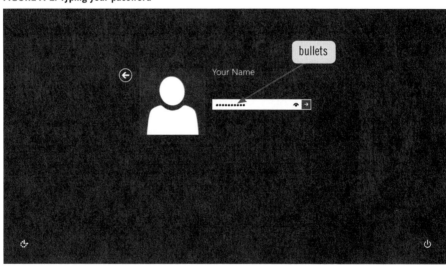

FIGURE A-3: Windows 8 Start screen

Navigate the Start Screen and Desktop

Learning Outcomes
• Scroll the Start screen
• Display the Charms bar
• Switch between Start screen and desktop

Every time you start Windows 8, the **Start screen** appears, containing controls that let you interact with the Windows 8 operating system. These controls are called its **user interface (UI)**. The Windows 8 user interface is called the **Windows 8 UI**. The Start screen contains many shaded rectangles called **tiles**. Each tile represents an **app**, short for **application program**, which lets you perform a certain type of task. For example, the Photos tile represents the **Photos app**, which lets you view and organize your pictures. Your user name and an optional picture appear in the upper-right corner. You can easily switch between the Start screen and the **Windows desktop**, an electronic work area that lets you organize and manage your information, much like your own physical desktop. **CASE** To become better acquainted with Windows 8, you decide to explore the Start screen and the desktop.

STEPS

1. **Move the mouse pointer to the bottom of the screen, then drag the light gray scroll bar to the right**
    If your Start screen contains additional apps that won't fit on the screen, a scroll bar appears when you move the mouse pointer toward the bottom of the screen. See **FIGURE A-5**.

2. **Scroll back to display the left side of the screen**
    The first set of apps reappears. These are **Windows 8 apps**, application programs that have a single purpose, such as Photos, News, or SkyDrive. Some Windows 8 app tiles show updated content using a feature called **live tile**; for example, the Weather app can show the current weather for any city you choose. (Note that the screens in this book do not show live tiles.)

3. **Move the mouse pointer to the lower-right corner of the screen, until you see a silhouette of a bar, then slowly move the mouse pointer upward into the bar**
    Pointing to the lower-right corner displays an outline of the Charms bar, and moving up into the outline displays the bar in full. The **Charms bar** is a set of buttons that let you find and send information, change your machine settings, and turn off your computer. When you point to the Charms bar, the time and date appear on the left side of the screen. See **FIGURE A-6**.

4. **Move the mouse pointer over the tile labeled Desktop, then click the left mouse button once**
    The Windows 8 desktop appears. You can use the desktop to manage the files and folders on your computer. A **file** is a collection of stored information, such as a letter, video, or program. A **folder** is a container that helps you organize your files. The desktop is where **desktop apps**, sometimes called **traditional apps**, like the productivity suite Microsoft Office, open in windows. Because desktop apps don't take up the whole screen, you can have several app windows open on the desktop at once, and you can move them around so you can easily go back and forth between them.

5. **If you don't see a blue bar at the bottom of the screen, move the mouse pointer to the bottom of the screen**
    The narrow blue bar, called the **taskbar**, displays icons for apps you use often. See **FIGURE A-7**. By default, the taskbar contains two icons: The [e] icon represents the Internet Explorer application program, and the [▢] icon represents an app called File Explorer you can use to view the contents of your computer.

6. **Move the mouse pointer back up over the desktop**
    Your desktop contains one or more small images called **icons** that represent items such as the **Recycle Bin**, an electronic wastepaper basket, on your computer. You can rearrange, add, and delete desktop icons. If you're using a new installation of Windows 8, the desktop might show only a Recycle Bin in the upper-left corner of the screen. If you are using a computer in a school or one that you purchased yourself, you might see other icons, files, and folders.

FIGURE A-5: Scrolling to display apps on the Start screen

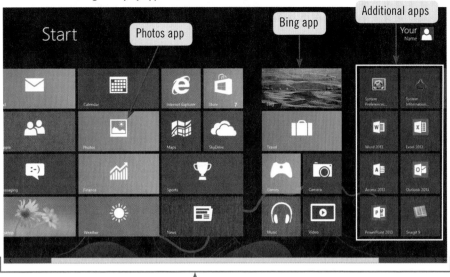

Photos app · Bing app · Additional apps · Your Name

Start

Scroll bar · Charms bar

FIGURE A-6: Displaying the Charms bar

Start · Your Name

4:30 Sunday October 16

Search · Share · Start · Devices · Settings

FIGURE A-7: Windows 8 desktop

Recycle Bin · Picture background · Notification area

Taskbar

Point, Click, and Drag

Learning Outcomes
• Point to, select, and deselect an item
• Move an item

As you learned in the last lesson, you communicate with Windows 8 using a pointing device or, if you have a touch screen, your fingertip. A **pointing device** controls the movement of the **mouse pointer**, a small arrow or other symbol that moves on the screen. Your pointing device could be a mouse, track-ball, touch pad, pointing stick, on-screen touch pointer, graphics tablet, or a touch-enabled mouse or touchpad. **FIGURE A-8** shows some common pointing devices. There are five basic **pointing device actions** you use to communicate with your computer: pointing, clicking, double-clicking, dragging, and right-clicking. **TABLE A-1** describes each action. **CASE** ▶ *You practice the basic pointing device actions.*

STEPS

QUICK TIP
A pointing device might be attached to your computer with a cable, connect wirelessly, or be built into your computer.

1. **Locate the mouse pointer on the desktop, then move your pointing device left, right, up, and down (or move your finger across a touch pad)**

   The mouse pointer moves in the same direction as your pointing device.

2. **Move your pointing device so the mouse pointer is over the Recycle Bin**

   You are pointing to the Recycle Bin. The pointer shape is the **Select pointer** ⮜ . The Recycle Bin becomes **highlighted**, looking as though it is framed in a box with a lighter color background.

QUICK TIP
The mouse pointer's shape changes depending on both where you point and on the options available to you when you point.

3. **While pointing to the Recycle Bin, press and quickly release the left mouse button once, then move the pointer away from the Recycle Bin**

   You click a desktop icon once to **select** it, which signals that you intend to perform an action. When an icon is selected, its background changes color and maintains the new color even when you point away from it.

4. **Point to (but do not click) the Internet Explorer button** 🅴 **on the taskbar**

   The button border appears and an informational message called a **ScreenTip** identifies the program the button represents. ScreenTips are useful because they identify screen items, helping you to learn about the tools available to you.

5. **Move the mouse pointer over the time and date in the notification area on the right side of the taskbar, read the ScreenTip, then click once**

   A pop-up window appears, containing a calendar and a clock displaying the current date and time.

TROUBLE
You need to double-click quickly, with a fast click-click, without moving the mouse. If a window didn't open, try again with a faster click-click.

6. **Place the tip of the mouse pointer over the Recycle Bin, then quickly click twice**

   You **double-clicked** the Recycle Bin. Touch screen users can quickly tap an item twice to double-click it. A window opens, showing the contents of the Recycle Bin, as shown in **FIGURE A-9**. The area at the top of the window is the title bar, which displays the name of the window. The area below the title bar is the **Ribbon**, which contains tabs, commands, and the Address bar. **Tabs** are electronic pages that contain groups of **buttons** you use to interact with an object or a program.

7. **Click any tab**

   The buttons on that tab appear; you can double-click to expand the Ribbon and keep the tab area open. (You'll expand the Ribbon in a later lesson.) Buttons act as commands that perform tasks, and **commands** are instructions to perform tasks. The **Address bar** shows the name and location of the item you have opened. If your Recycle Bin contains any discarded items, they appear in the window.

8. **Point to the Close button** ❎ **on the title bar, read the ScreenTip, then click once**

   Clicking the Close button issues the command to Windows to close the Recycle Bin window.

9. **Point to the Recycle Bin, press and hold down the left mouse button, move the mouse so the object moves right as shown in FIGURE A-10, release the mouse button, then drag the Recycle Bin back to its original location**

   You use dragging to move folders, files, and other objects to new locations.

FIGURE A-8: Pointing devices

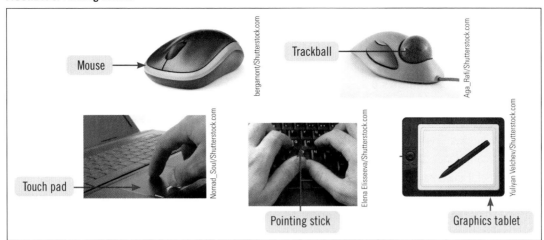

Mouse
Trackball
Touch pad
Pointing stick
Graphics tablet

FIGURE A-9: Recycle Bin window

Tabs
Title bar
Ribbon
Address bar
Any discarded items appear here

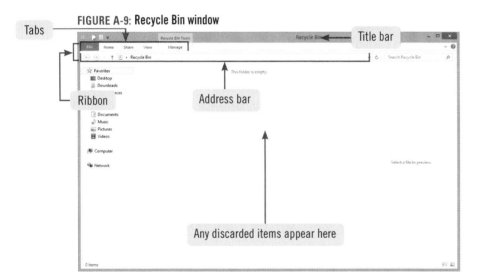

FIGURE A-10: Dragging the Recycle Bin

Recycle Bin
Recycle Bin

Releasing mouse
button moves object
to this location

TABLE A-1: Basic pointing device actions

action	mouse action	touch pad action	use to
Point	Move pointing device to position tip of pointer over an item	Move your finger over touch pad to position tip of pointer over an item	Highlight items or display small informational boxes called ScreenTips
Click	Quickly press and release left mouse button once	Tap touch pad surface once	Select objects or commands, opening menus or items on the taskbar
Double-click	Quickly press and release left mouse button twice	Tap twice in quick succession on touch pad	Open programs, folders, or files represented by desktop icons
Drag	Point to an object, press and hold down left mouse button, move object to a new location, then release mouse button	Slide finger over touch pad to point to an object, press and hold left touch pad button, drag across touch pad to move object to new location, then release button	Move objects, such as icons on the desktop
Right-click	Point to an object, then press and release right mouse button		Display a shortcut menu containing options specific to the object

Using newer touch devices

Since the arrival of Windows 8, manufacturers have started releasing new products that incorporate touch technology, such as a touch-enabled mouse and an external touch pad that recognizes gestures such as tapping and swiping. So even if your computer does not have a touch screen, you can still use gestures to take advantage of new Windows 8 features using one of these devices.

Start an App

Learning
Outcomes
• Start a Windows
  Accessory program
• Open the full apps
  listing
• Run an app

The Windows 8 operating system lets you operate your computer and see the files and folders it contains. But to do your work, you use apps. There are three kinds of apps: Windows 8 apps, desktop apps, and Windows accessories. **Windows 8 apps** fill the screen when you open them and are specially designed so they can stay open as you work without slowing down your computer. Examples include the Photos app, which lets you view your photographs, and the SkyDrive app, which lets you connect to files and programs on the Windows SkyDrive Web site. Windows 8 apps also work well on other devices, such as tablet computers or smartphones. **Desktop apps** such as Microsoft Office let you create letters, financial summaries, and other useful documents, as well as view Web pages on the Internet and send and receive e-mail. Still other apps, called Windows accessories, come with Windows 8. See **TABLE A-2** for some examples of Windows accessories. To use an app, you must start (or open) it so you can see and use its tools. **CASE** *To prepare for your new job, you start a Windows 8 app and an accessory.*

STEPS

1. **Point to the upper-right corner of the screen to display the Charms bar, move the pointer downward, then click Start**
   The Start screen opens.

2. **Point to the Weather app tile, click once, then click Allow if you are asked for permission**
   The Weather app opens to the weather **app window**, showing the weather for a location, as shown in **FIGURE A-11**. Note that Windows 8 apps are updated regularly, so your app screen may differ. To close the app, you will use dragging.

   > **TROUBLE**
   > Be sure to drag all the way to the bottom of the screen, or the app will not close.

3. **Move the mouse pointer to the top of the screen, until you see the hand pointer 🖑, then drag to the bottom of the screen to close the app**

4. **Right-click a blank area of the Start screen**
   The App bar appears at the bottom of the screen. Next, you'll open a desktop app called Paint.

   > **QUICK TIP**
   > To view all apps on one screen, click the Reduce screen button in the lower-right corner of the screen.

5. **Left-click the All apps button in the App bar**
   A list of the apps on your computer appears, as shown in **FIGURE A-12**. The Windows 8 apps are listed alphabetically on the left side of the screen, and all other applications are grouped on the right side.

6. **Scroll to the right until you can see the group called Windows Accessories**
   If you have a lot of apps, Windows categorizes them alphabetically and groups accessories and application suites.

   > **TROUBLE**
   > If your Paint window doesn't look like Figure A-13, point to the lower-right corner of the window until the pointer becomes ⬉, then drag until it matches the figure.

7. **Move the pointer over the Paint accessory, then click once**
   The Paint app window opens on your screen, as shown in **FIGURE A-13**. When Windows opens an application program, it starts it from your computer's hard disk, where it's permanently stored. Then it **loads**, or copies and places, the program in your computer's memory so you can use it.

8. **If your Paint window fills the screen completely, click the Restore Down button ❐ in the upper-right corner of the window**

Searching for apps and files

If you need to find an app, setting, or file from the Start screen, simply start typing the first few letters of the item you want to find; for example, the letters "P-a-i" for Microsoft Paint. A search box opens, and Windows lists on the left side of the screen all the items that contain the text you typed. Windows lists applications containing your search text, and the Apps category is highlighted below the Search box on the right side of the screen. To see results for a different category, click Settings, Files, or one of the apps in the list, such as Photos, to see matches in that category. For files, you'll also see each file's date, file size, and location. Point to an item in the Results list to see more information, including its location on your computer.

FIGURE A-11: Weather app

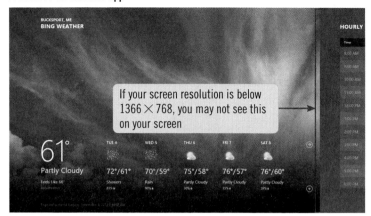

If your screen resolution is below 1366 × 768, you may not see this on your screen

FIGURE A-12: Apps list

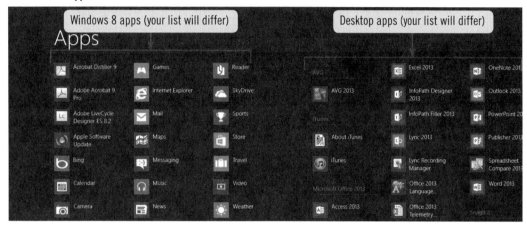

Windows 8 apps (your list will differ)   Desktop apps (your list will differ)

FIGURE A-13: Paint app window

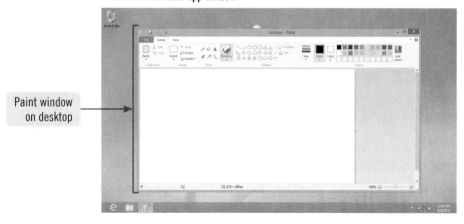

Paint window on desktop

TABLE A-2: Useful Windows 8 accessory programs

accessory name	use to
Notepad	Create text files with basic text formatting
Paint	Create and edit drawings using lines, shapes, and colors
Snipping Tool	Capture an image of any screen area that you can save to use in a document
Sound Recorder	With a computer microphone, make recordings of voice or music
Sticky Notes	Create short text notes that you can use to set reminders or create to-do lists for yourself
Windows Media Player	Play music, videos, recorded TV and show pictures

Work with a Window

Learning
Outcomes
• Minimize, restore,
  and maximize a
  window
• Scroll a window
• Move a window

When you start a desktop app, its **window**, a frame displaying the app's tools, opens. In many apps, a blank file also opens so you can start creating a new document. For example, in Paint, a drawing app, a blank document opens so you can start drawing right away. All windows in the Windows 8 operating system have similar window elements. Once you can use a window in one app, you will know how to work with windows in many other apps. **CASE** ▶ *To become more familiar with the Windows 8 user interface, you explore elements in the Paint window.*

DETAILS

Many windows have the following common elements. Refer to FIGURE A-14:

● At the top of the window, you see a **title bar**, a colored strip that contains the name of the document and app you opened. This document has not been saved, so it has the temporary name "Untitled" and the app name is "Paint."

● On the right side of the title bar, the **Window control icons** let you control the app window. The **Minimize button** ▭ temporarily hides it, making it a button on the taskbar. The app is still running, but its window is hidden until you reopen it. The **Maximize button** ▢ enlarges the window to fill the entire screen. If a window is already maximized, the Maximize button changes to the **Restore Down button** ▣, which reduces it to the last nonmaximized size. Clicking the **Close button** ✕ closes the app.

● Many windows have a **scroll bar** on the right side and/or the bottom of the window. You click the scroll bar elements to show additional parts of your document. See **TABLE A-3** to learn the parts of a scroll bar.

● Just below the title bar, at the top of the Paint window, is the Ribbon, the strip that contains tabs. The Paint window has three tabs, the File tab, the Home tab, and the View tab. Tabs are divided into **groups** of command buttons. The Home tab has five groups: Clipboard, Image, Tools, Shapes, and Colors. Many apps also include **menus** that display words you click to show lists of commands, as well as **toolbars** containing buttons.

● The **Quick Access toolbar**, in the upper-left corner of the window, lets you quickly perform common actions such as saving a file.

STEPS

1. **Click the Paint window** Minimize button ▭
   The app is minimized to a program button with a gradient shading, indicating the app is still open. See **FIGURE A-15**. Taskbar buttons representing closed programs are not shaded.

2. **Click the taskbar button representing the** Paint app 🖌
   The app window reappears.

3. **Drag the gray** scroll box **down, notice the lower edge of the work area that appears, then click the** Up scroll arrow ▲ **until you see the top edge of the work area**

4. **Point to the** View tab **with the tip of the mouse pointer, then click the** View tab **once**
   Clicking the View tab moved it in front of the Home tab. This tab has three groups, Zoom, Show or hide, and Display, containing buttons that let you change your view of the document window to work more easily.

5. **Click the** Home tab, **then click the Paint window** Maximize button ▢
   The window fills the screen, and the Maximize button becomes the Restore Down button ▣.

6. **Click the window's** Restore Down button
   The Paint window returns to its previous size on the screen.

FIGURE A-14: Typical app window elements

Quick Access toolbar · Untitled - Paint · Title bar · Window control icons

File Home View

Paste · Cut · Copy · Clipboard

Select · Crop · Resize · Rotate · Image

Brushes · Tools

Shapes · Outline · Fill

Size · Color 1 · Color 2 · Colors · Edit colors

+ ⌐ 819 × 460px 100% ⊖ ──── ⊕

Ribbon with tabs

Click arrow to display a menu

Groups

Scroll bar

Windows 8

FIGURE A-15: Taskbar on the desktop

Icons with solid backgrounds represent programs that are not open

Paint program button with gradient background indicates program is open

Your icons may differ

TABLE A-3: Parts of a scroll bar

name	looks like	use for
Scroll box	(Size may vary)	Drag to scroll quickly through a long document
Scroll arrows	∧ ∨	Click to scroll up, down, left, or right in small amounts
Shaded area	(Above, below, and to either side of scroll box)	Click to move up or down by one screen

---

Using the Quick Access toolbar

On the left side of the title bar, the Quick Access toolbar lets you perform common tasks with just one click. The Save button saves the changes you have made to a document. The Undo button lets you reverse (undo) the last action you performed.

The Redo button reinstates the change you just undid. Use the Customize Quick Access Toolbar button to add other frequently used buttons to the toolbar, move the toolbar below the Ribbon, or hide the Ribbon.

Manage Multiple Windows

Learning Outcomes
• Open a second app
• Activate a window
• Resize, snap, and close a window

You can work with more than one desktop app at a time by switching among open app windows. If you open two or more apps, a window opens for each one. You can work with each open app window, going back and forth between them. The window in front is called the **active window**. Any other open window behind the active window is called an **inactive window**. For ease in working with multiple windows, you can move, arrange, make them smaller or larger, minimize, or restore them so they're not in the way. To resize a window, drag a window's edge, called its **border**. You can also use the taskbar to switch between windows. See **TABLE A-4** for a summary of taskbar actions. ■ **CASE** ▶ *Keeping the Paint app open, you open the WordPad app and then work with both app windows.*

STEPS

1. **With the Paint window open, point to the lower-left corner of the screen until the Start thumbnail appears, click the Start thumbnail, then type word**

   The Apps screen appears, displaying apps that have "word" in them, such as WordPad.

2. **Click WordPad, then if the window is maximized, click its Restore Down button in the title bar**

   The WordPad window opens, as shown in **FIGURE A-16**. The WordPad window is in front, indicating that it is the active window. The Paint window is the inactive window. On the taskbar, the gradient backgrounds on the WordPad and Paint app buttons tell you both apps are open.

3. **Point to a blank part of the WordPad window title bar, then drag the WordPad window down slightly so you can see more of the Paint window**

4. **Click once on the Paint window's title bar**

   The Paint window is now the active window and appears in front of the WordPad window. You can make any window active by clicking it, or by clicking an app's icon in the taskbar.

5. **Point to the taskbar, then click the WordPad window button** 🗔

   The WordPad window becomes active. When you open multiple windows on the desktop, you may need to resize windows so they don't get in the way of other open windows.

6. **Point to the lower-right corner of the WordPad window until the pointer becomes ⤡, then drag up and to the left about an inch to make the window smaller**

   You can also point to any edge of a window until you see the ⟷ or ↕ pointer and drag to make it larger or smaller in one direction only.

7. **Point to the WordPad window title bar, drag the window to the left side of the screen until the mouse pointer reaches the screen edge and you see a vertical line down the middle of the screen, then release the mouse button**

   The WordPad window instantly fills the left side of the screen. This is called the **Snap feature**.

8. **Drag the Paint window title bar to the right side of the screen and release the mouse button**

   The Paint window fills the right side of the screen. Snapping makes it easy to view the contents of two windows at the same time. See **FIGURE A-17**.

9. **Click the WordPad window Close button** ▨✕ **, click Don't Save if prompted to save changes, then click the Maximize button** ▢ **in the Paint window's title bar**

   The WordPad app closes, so you can no longer use its tools unless you start it again. The Paint app window remains open.

Getting Started with Windows 8

FIGURE A-16: Working with multiple windows

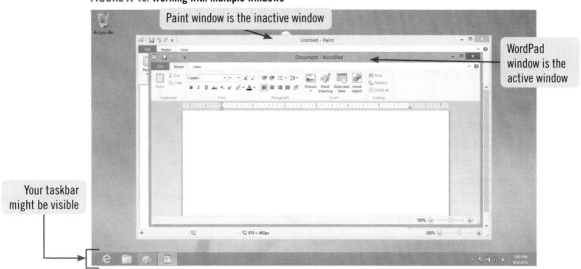

Paint window is the inactive window

WordPad window is the active window

Your taskbar might be visible

FIGURE A-17: WordPad and Paint windows snapped to each side of the screen

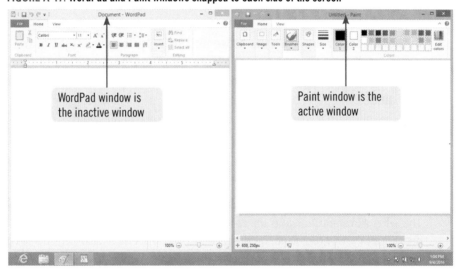

WordPad window is the inactive window

Paint window is the active window

TABLE A-4: Using the Desktop taskbar

to	do this
Add buttons to taskbar	Open an app, right-click its icon on the task bar, then click Pin this program to taskbar
Change order of taskbar buttons	Drag any icon to a new taskbar location
See a list of recent documents opened in a taskbar app	Right-click taskbar app button
Close a document using the taskbar	Point to taskbar button, point to document image, then click its Close button
Minimize all open windows	Click Show desktop button to the right of taskbar date and time
Redisplay all minimized windows	Click Show desktop button to the right of taskbar date and time
See preview of documents in taskbar	Point to taskbar button for open app

Learning
Outcomes
• Use a command
button and
a menu
• Work in a
dialog box

Use Command Buttons, Menus, and Dialog Boxes

When you work in an app, you communicate using command buttons, menus, and dialog boxes. **Command buttons** let you issue instructions to modify app objects. Command buttons are often organized on a Ribbon into tabs, and then into groups like those in the Paint window. Some command buttons have text on them, and others show only an icon that represents what they do. Other command buttons reveal **menus**, lists of commands you can choose. And some command buttons open up a **dialog box**, a window with controls that lets you tell Windows what you want. **TABLE A-5** lists the common types of controls you find in dialog boxes. **CASE** ▶ *You use command buttons, menus, and dialog boxes to communicate with the Paint app.*

STEPS

QUICK TIP
Depending on your
screen size, you might
see a Shapes button
instead of a gallery of
shapes. If so, simply
click the button, then
click ☆.

1. **In the Shapes group, click the More button ▼ just to the right of the shapes, then click the Five-point star button ☆**

2. **Click the Gold button in the Colors group, move the pointer over the white drawing area, then drag to draw a star similar to the one in FIGURE A-18**
   The white drawing area is called the **canvas.**

3. **In the Shapes group, click the More button ▼ just to the right of the shapes, click the down scroll arrow if necessary, click the Lightning button, click the Indigo color button in the Colors group, then drag a lightning bolt shape near the star, using FIGURE A-18 as a guide**
   Don't be concerned if your object isn't exactly like the one in the figure.

QUICK TIP
If you need to move
the selected object,
use the keyboard
arrow keys to move it
left, right, up,
or down.

4. **Click the Fill with color button 🖌 in the Tools group, click the Light turquoise color button in the Colors group, click inside the star, click the Lime color button, click inside the lightning bolt, then compare your drawing to FIGURE A-18**

5. **Click the Select list arrow in the Image group, then click Select all, as shown in FIGURE A-19**
   The Select all command selects the entire drawing, as indicated by the dotted line surrounding the white drawing area. Other commands on this menu let you select individual elements or change your selection.

6. **Click the Rotate button 🔄 in the Image group, then click Rotate 180°**
   You often need to use multiple commands to perform an action—in this case, you used one command to select the item you wanted to work with, and the next command rotated the item.

7. **Click the File tab, then click Print**
   The Print dialog box opens, as shown in **FIGURE A-20**. This dialog box lets you choose a printer, specify which part of your document or drawing you want to print, and choose how many copies you want to print. The **default**, or automatically selected, number of copies is 1, which is what you want.

8. **Click Print, or, if you prefer not to print, click Cancel**
   The drawing prints on your printer. You decide to close the app without saving your drawing.

9. **Click the File tab, click Exit, then click Don't Save**
   You closed the file without saving your changes, then exited the app. Most apps include a command for closing a document without exiting the program. However, Paint allows you to open only one document at a time, so it does not include a Close command.

FIGURE A-18: Star and lightning shapes filled with color

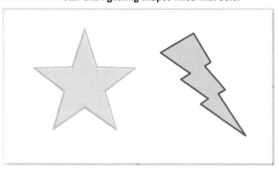

FIGURE A-19: Select menu options

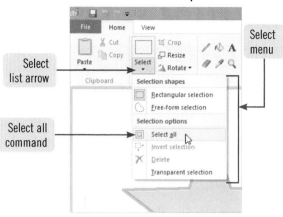

Select list arrow

Select all command

Select menu

FIGURE A-20: Print dialog box

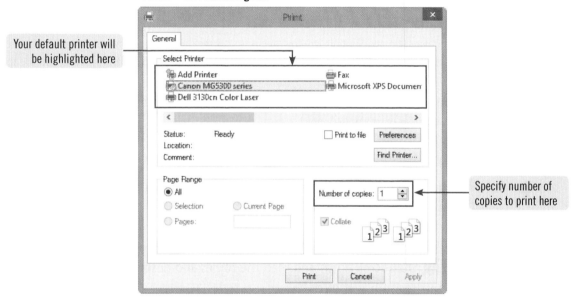

Your default printer will be highlighted here

Specify number of copies to print here

TABLE A-5: Common dialog box controls

element	example	description
Text box	132	A box in which you type text or numbers
Spin box	1	A box with up and down arrows; you can click arrows or type to increase or decrease value
Option button		A small circle you click to select the option; only one in a set can be selected at once
Check box		A small box that turns an option on when checked or off when unchecked; more than one can be selected at once
List box		A box that lets you select from a list of options
Command button	Save	A button you click to issue a command

Get Help

Learning
Outcomes
• Open the
  Help app
• Explore and search
  for help topics

As you use Windows 8, you might feel ready to learn more about it, or you might have a problem and need some advice. You can open the Windows 8 Help and Support to find the information you need. You can browse Help and Support topics by clicking a category, such as "Get started." Within this category, you see more specific topics. Each topic is represented by blue or purple text called **links** that you can click to learn more. You can also search Help and Support by typing one or more descriptive words called **keywords**, such as "taskbar," to find topics related to your keywords. **CASE** *You use Windows 8 help to learn more about Windows and the WordPad accessory.*

STEPS

1. **Point to the lower-left corner of the screen, click the Start thumbnail once to display the Start screen, then type** help

   The Help and Support app is listed in the found items area.

2. **Click** Help and Support, **then click the window's** Maximize button 🔲 **if the window does not fill the screen**

   The Windows Help and Support window opens and is maximized, as shown in **FIGURE A-21**. A search box appears near the top of the window. Three topics appear in blue boxes. Below them, you see text briefly describing each topic.

3. **Position the** hand pointer 🖑 **over** Get Started, **then click once**

   Several categories of Get Started topics appear.

4. **Click** Touch: swipe, tap, and beyond

   Help and Support information appears.

5. **Drag the** scroll box **down to view text and graphics about touch, then drag the** scroll box **back to the top of the scroll bar**

   You decide to learn more about the taskbar.

6. **Click in the** Search **text box near the top of the window, type** taskbar, **click the** Search button 🔍, **then scroll down and read the topics and descriptions**

   A list of links related to using the taskbar appears. See **FIGURE A-22**.

7. **Click** How to use the taskbar, **scroll down if necessary, then click** To move the taskbar

8. **Read the information, clicking any other** links **that interest you**

9. **When you are finished, click the** Close button [×] **in the upper-right corner of the Windows Help and Support window**

   The Windows Help and Support window closes.

Finding other ways to get help

The Windows Help and Support Home window includes a variety of resources for learning more about Windows 8 and solving problems. In the More to Explore section, click the **Windows website** link to locate **blogs** (Web logs, which are personal commentaries), downloads, video tours, and other current Windows 8 resources. You'll also find FAQs (Frequently Asked Questions) about current Windows topics. Click the **Microsoft Community website** (formerly called the **Microsoft Answers website**) link to find **forums**, electronic gathering places where anyone can read and add questions and answers on computer issues.

FIGURE A-21: Windows Help and Support window

FIGURE A-22: Getting help on the term "taskbar"

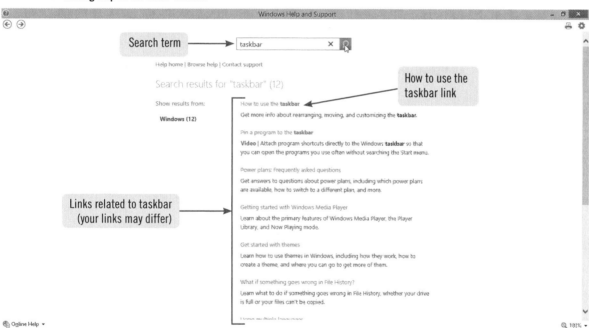

Using right-clicking

For some actions, you click items using the right mouse button, known as **right-clicking**. You can right-click almost any icon on your desktop to open a shortcut menu. A **shortcut menu** lists common commands for an object, such as emptying the Recycle Bin. The shortcut menu commands depend on the object you right-click. For example, **FIGURE A-23** shows the shortcut menu that appears if you right-click the Recycle Bin. Then you click (with the left mouse button) a shortcut menu command to issue that command.

FIGURE A-23: Shortcut menu

Exit Windows 8

When you finish working on your computer, you should close any open files, exit any open apps, close any open windows, and exit (or **shut down**) Windows 8. TABLE A-6 shows options for ending your Windows 8 sessions. Whichever option you choose, it's important to shut down your computer in an orderly way. If you turn off or unplug the computer while Windows 8 is running, you could lose data or damage Windows 8 and your computer. If you are working in a computer lab, follow your instructor's directions and your lab's policies for ending your Windows 8 session. **CASE** ▶ *You have examined the basic ways you can use Windows 8, so you are ready to end your Windows 8 session.*

STEPS

QUICK TIP

Pressing ⊞ [C] again hides the Charms bar.

1. **Press ⊞ [C] to display the Charms bar**

2. **Click Settings, then click Power, as shown in FIGURE A-24**
   The Power button menu lists shut down options.

QUICK TIP

If you are using a Windows 8 tablet, press the lock button on your tablet to bring up the lock screen, swipe the lock screen, then click the shutdown button to power off your computer.

3. **If you are working in a computer lab, follow the instructions provided by your instructor or technical support person for ending your Windows 8 session; if you are working on your own computer, click Shut down or the option you prefer for ending your Windows 8 session**

4. **After you shut down your computer, you may also need to turn off your monitor and other hardware devices, such as a printer, to conserve energy**

Installing updates when you exit Windows

Sometimes, after you shut down your machine, you might find that your machine does not shut down immediately. Instead, Windows might install software updates. If you see an option on your Power menu that lets you update, you can select it to update your software. A window indicating that updates are being installed, do not unplug or press the power switch to turn off your machine. Let the updates install completely. After the updates are installed, your computer will shut down, as you originally requested.

FIGURE A-24: Shutting down your computer

TABLE A-6: Power options

option	description
Sleep	Puts computer in a low-power state while keeping any open apps open so you can return immediately to where you left off
Shut down	Closes any open apps and completely turns off the computer
Restart	Closes any open apps, shuts down the computer, then restarts it

Practice

Concepts Review

Label the elements of the Windows 8 window shown in FIGURE A-25.

FIGURE A-25

Match each term with the statement that best describes it.

6. Accessory
7. Keyword
8. Windows 8 UI
9. Active window
10. Password
11. Operating system
12. App

a. A sequence of numbers and letters you enter to access a secure user account
b. The window in front of other windows
c. An application program
d. Name for the Windows 8 user interface
e. An application program that comes with Windows 8
f. Descriptive word you use to search Windows Help and Support
g. A program necessary to run your computer

Select the best answer from the list of choices.

13. You use the Maximize button to:
    a. Scroll down a window.
    b. Restore a window to a previous size.
    c. Temporarily hide a window.
    d. Expand a window to fill the entire screen.
14. Which of the following is not a Windows accessory?
    a. Sticky Notes
    b. Windows 8
    c. Sound Recorder
    d. Paint
15. Which button do you click to reduce an open window to a button on the taskbar?
    a. Close button
    b. Minimize button
    c. Restore Down button
    d. Maximize button

16. **The screen controls that let you interact with an operating system are called its:**
    a. Accessories.
    c. User interface.
    b. Application program.
    d. Taskbar.

17. **Which type of program runs your computer and lets you use it?**
    a. App.
    c. Accessory.
    b. Traditional app.
    d. Operating system.

18. **Which Windows 8 feature lets you find and share information, change your machine settings, and turn off your computer?**
    a. Charms bar.
    c. Application program.
    b. Operating system.
    d. Accessory program.

19. **What part of a window shows the name of an open app?**
    a. Scroll bar.
    c. Quick Access toolbar.
    b. Title bar.
    d. Ribbon.

Skills Review

1. **Start Windows 8.**
   a. If your computer and monitor are not running, press your computer's and (if necessary) your monitor's power buttons.
   b. If necessary, click the user name that represents your user account.
   c. Enter your password, using correct uppercase and lowercase letters.

2. **Navigate the Start screen and desktop.**
   a. Examine the Windows 8 Start screen, scroll to the right so you can display any hidden apps, then display the Charms bar.
   b. Display the Windows 8 desktop, and then display the taskbar.

3. **Point, click, and drag.**
   a. Use pointing and clicking to go to the Start screen, then return to the desktop.
   b. On the Windows 8 desktop, use clicking to select the Recycle Bin.
   c. Use pointing to display the ScreenTip for Internet Explorer in the taskbar, and then display the ScreenTips for any other icons on the taskbar.
   d. Use double-clicking to open the Recycle Bin window, then close it.
   e. Drag the Recycle Bin to the lower-right corner of the screen, then drag it back to the upper-left corner.
   f. Click the Date and Time area to display the calendar and clock, then click it again to close it.

4. **Start an app.**
   a. Return to the Start screen, then use the Apps bar to display all the apps on your computer.
   b. Open the Windows 8 accessory of your choice, then close it. (*Hint:* To close, drag from the top of the window all the way to the bottom.)
   c. Scroll if necessary to display the Windows accessories.
   d. Open the WordPad accessory, then if the window fills the screen, restore it down.

5. **Manage a window.**
   a. Minimize the WordPad window.
   b. Redisplay the window using a taskbar button.
   c. In the WordPad window, click the File tab on the Ribbon, then click the About WordPad command.
   d. Read the contents of the window, then close the About WordPad dialog box by clicking OK.
   e. Maximize the WordPad window, then restore it down.
   f. Display the View tab in the WordPad window.

6. **Manage multiple windows.**
   a. Leaving WordPad open, go to the Start screen and use typing to locate the Paint app, open Paint, then restore down the Paint window if necessary.

Skills Review (continued)

b. Make the WordPad window the active window.

c. Make the Paint window the active window.

d. Minimize the Paint window.

e. Drag the WordPad window so it's in the middle of the screen.

f. Redisplay the Paint window.

g. Drag the Paint window so it automatically fills the right side of the screen.

h. Close the WordPad window, maximize the Paint window, then restore down the Paint window.

7. Use command buttons, menus, and dialog boxes.

a. In the Paint window, draw a red right arrow shape, similar to the one shown in **FIGURE A-26**.

b. Use the Fill with color button to fill the arrow with a light turquoise color.

c. Draw an indigo rectangle to the right of the arrow shape, using the figure as a guide.

d. Use the Fill with color button to fill the blue rectangle with a lime color.

e. Fill the drawing background with lavender as shown in the figure.

f. Use the Select list arrow and menu to select the entire drawing, then use the Rotate command to rotate the drawing 180°.

g. If you wish, print a copy of the picture, then close the Paint app without saving the drawing.

FIGURE A-26

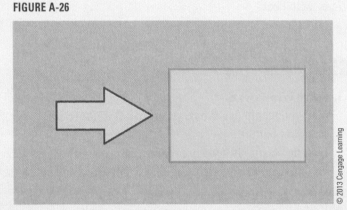

© 2013 Cengage Learning

8. Get help.

a. Start the Help and Support app, then maximize the window if it's not already maximized.

b. Open the Get started topic.

c. Open the Mouse and keyboard: What's new topic, then read the Help information on that topic.

d. In the Search Help text box, search for help about user accounts.

e. Find the link that describes how to create a user account, then click it.

f. Read the topic, clicking links as necessary, then close the Windows Help and Support window.

9. Exit Windows 8.

a. Shut down your computer using the Shut down command or the preferred command for your work or school setting.

b. Turn off your monitor if necessary.

Independent Challenge 1

You work for Will's Percussion, a Maine manufacturer of drums and drumsticks. The company ships percussion instruments and supplies to music stores and musicians in the United States and Canada. The owner, Will, wants to know an easy way for his employees to learn about the new features of Windows 8, and he has asked you to help.

a. Start your computer, log on to Windows 8 if necessary, then open Windows Help and Support.

b. Search Help for the text **what's new**.

c. Click the Get to know Windows 8 link.

d. Scroll the results window to see its contents, then scroll back to the top.

e. Using pencil and paper, or the WordPad app if you wish, write a short memo to Will summarizing, in your own words, three important new features in Windows 8. If you used WordPad to write the memo, use the Print button to print the document, then use the Exit command on the File tab to close WordPad without saving your changes to the document.

f. Close the Windows Help and Support window, then exit Windows and shut down.

Independent Challenge 2

You are the new manager for Katharine Anne's Designs, a business that supplies floral arrangements to New York businesses. The company maintains four delivery vans that supply flowers to various locations. Katharine asks you to investigate how the Windows 8 Calculator accessory can help her company be a responsible energy consumer.

a. Start your computer, log on to Windows 8 if necessary, then open the Windows 8 accessory called Calculator.

b. Click to enter the number 87 on the Calculator.

c. Click the division sign (/) button.

FIGURE A-27

d. Click the number 2.

e. Click the equals sign button (=), and write down the result shown in the Calculator window. (*Hint:* The result should be 43.5.) See **FIGURE A-27**.

f. Click the Help menu in the Calculator window, then click View Help. Locate the Calculator: Frequently asked questions topic, and scroll down to locate information on how to calculate fuel economy. Follow the instructions, and perform at least one calculation of fuel economy.

g. Start WordPad, write a short memo about how Calculator can help you calculate fuel consumption, print the document using the Print command on the File tab, then exit WordPad without saving.

h. Close the Help window.

i. Close the Calculator, then exit Windows.

Independent Challenge 3

You are the office manager for Eric's Pet Shipping, a service business in Seattle, Washington, that specializes in air shipping of cats and dogs across the United States and Canada. It's important to know the temperature in the destination city, so the animals won't be in danger from extreme temperatures when they are unloaded from the aircraft. Eric has asked you to find a way to easily monitor temperatures in destination cities. You decide to use a Windows app so you can see current temperatures in Celsius on your desktop. (*Note*: To complete the steps below, your computer must be connected to the Internet.)

a. Start your computer and sign in to Windows 8 if necessary, then at the Start screen, click the Weather app.

b. If multiple locations appear, click one of your choice.

c. Right-click the sky area above the weather information, then in the bar at the top of the screen, click Places.

d. Click the plus sign, click in the Enter Location text box if necessary, then type **Vancouver**.

e. Click Vancouver, British Columbia, Canada, in the drop-down list. Vancouver, Canada, is added to your Places Favorites.

f. Add another location that interests you.

g. Close the apps and return to the Start screen.

h. Open WordPad, write Eric a memo outlining how you can use the Windows Weather app to help keep pets safe, print the memo if you wish, close WordPad, then exit Windows.

Independent Challenge 4: Explore

As a professional photographer, you often evaluate pictures. You decide to explore the Windows Photo app so you can access pictures from various online sources. (*Note:* To complete the steps below, your computer must be connected to the Internet.)

a. Start your computer and sign in to Windows 8 if necessary, then click to open the Photos app.

b. Explore any picture that may have been downloaded from your Windows SkyDrive account, Facebook, or Flickr. (*Note:* You might need to sign into your Microsoft account in order to access some locations.)

c. Right-click any area of the Photo app screen, then explore what this allows you to do.

d. Add three pictures to your Pictures library.

e. Click OK.

Visual Workshop

Using the skills you've learned in this unit, open and arrange elements on your screen so it looks similar to **FIGURE A-28** (the date and time will differ). Note the position of the Recycle Bin, the size and location of the Paint window and the Help and Support window, and the presence of the Charms bar. Open WordPad and write a paragraph summarizing how you used pointing, clicking, and dragging to make your screen look like **FIGURE A-28**. Print your work if you wish, exit WordPad without saving changes to the document, then shut down Windows.

FIGURE A-28

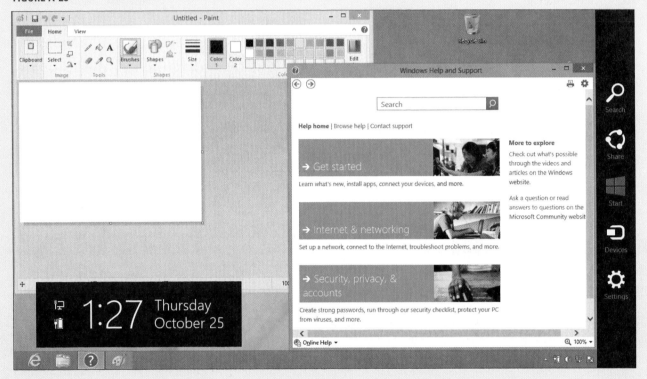

Understanding File Management

CASE ▶ Now that you are familiar with the Windows 8 operating system, your new employer has asked you to become familiar with **file management**, or how to create, save, locate and delete the files you create with Windows application programs. You begin by reviewing how files are organized on your computer, and then begin working with files you create in the WordPad app.

Unit Objectives

After completing this unit, you will be able to:

- Understand files and folders
- Create and save a file
- Explore the files and folders on your computer
- Change file and folder views

- Open, edit, and save files
- Copy files
- Move and rename files
- Search for files, folders, and programs
- Delete and restore files

Files You Will Need

No files needed.

Understand Files and Folders

Learning Outcomes
- Analyze a file hierarchy
- Examine files and folders

As you work with computer programs, you create and save files, such as letters, drawings, or budgets. When you save files, you usually save them inside folders to help keep them organized. The files and folders on your computer are organized in a **file hierarchy**, a system that arranges files and folders in different levels, like the branches of a tree. FIGURE B-1 shows a sample file hierarchy. **CASE** *You decide to use folders and files to organize the information on your computer.*

DETAILS

Use the following guidelines as you organize files using your computer's file hierarchy:

- **Use folders and subfolders to organize files**

  As you work with your computer, you can add folders to your hierarchy and name them to help you organize your work. As you've learned, folders are storage areas in which you can group related files. You should give folders unique names that help you easily identify them. You can also create **subfolders**, which are folders that are inside other folders. Windows 8 comes with several existing folders, such as My Documents, My Music, My Pictures, and My Videos, that you can use as a starting point.

- **View and manage files in File Explorer**

  You can view and manage your computer contents using a built-in program called **File Explorer**, shown in **FIGURE B-2**. A File Explorer window is divided into **panes**, or sections. The **Navigation pane** on the left side of the window shows the folder structure on your computer. When you click a folder in the Navigation pane, you see its contents in the **File list** on the right side of the window. To open File Explorer from the desktop, click the File Explorer button 📁 on the taskbar. To open it from the Start screen, begin typing File Explorer, and when you see the program name on the Apps screen, press [Enter].

QUICK TIP
The program name "File Explorer" doesn't appear in the title bar. Instead, you'll see the current folder name.

- **Understand file addresses**

  A window also contains an **Address bar**, an area just below the Ribbon that shows the address, or location, of the files that appear in the File list. An **address** is a sequence of folder names, separated by the ▶ symbol, which describes a file's location in the file hierarchy. An address shows the folder with the highest hierarchy level on the left and steps through each hierarchy level toward the right; this is sometimes called a **path**. For example, the My Documents folder might contain subfolders named Work and Personal. If you clicked the Personal folder in the File list, the Address bar would show My Documents ▶ Personal. Each location between the ▶ symbols represents a level in the file hierarchy. The same path appears in the window's title bar, but instead of ▶ between the hierarchy levels, you see the backslash symbol (\ ). If you see a file path written out, you'll most likely see it with backslashes. For example, in Figure B-1, if you wanted to write the path to the Honolulu Sunset photo file, you would write My Documents\Quest Specialty Travel\Photos\Honolulu Sunset.jpg. File addresses might look complicated if they may have many levels, but they are helpful because they always describe the exact location of a file or folder in a file hierarchy.

QUICK TIP
Remember that in the Address bar you single-click a folder or subfolder to show its contents, but in the File list you double-click it.

- **Navigate up and down using the Address bar and File list**

  You can use the Address bar and the File list to move up or down in the hierarchy one or more levels at a time. To **navigate up** in your computer's hierarchy, you can click a folder or subfolder name to the left of the current folder name in the Address bar. For example, in **FIGURE B-2**, you can move up in the hierarchy one level by clicking once on Users in the Address bar. Then the File list would show the subfolders and files inside the Users folder. To **navigate down** in the hierarchy, double-click a subfolder in the File list. The path in the Address bar then shows the path to that subfolder.

- **Navigate up and down using the Navigation pane**

  You can also use the Navigation pane to navigate among folders. Move the mouse pointer over the Navigation pane, then click the small triangles to the left of a folder name to show ▷ or hide ◢ the folder's contents under the folder name. Subfolders appear indented under the folders that contain them, showing that they are inside that folder.

FIGURE B-1: Sample file hierarchy

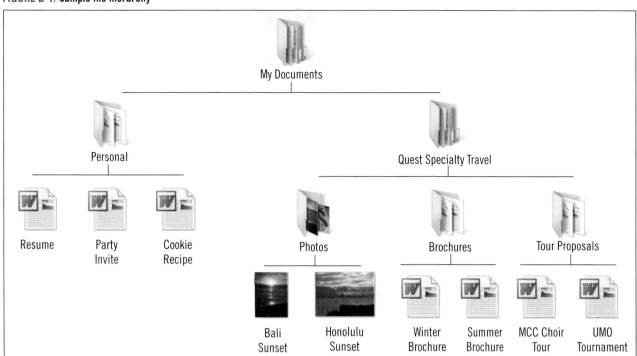

© 2013 Cengage Learning

FIGURE B-2: File Explorer window

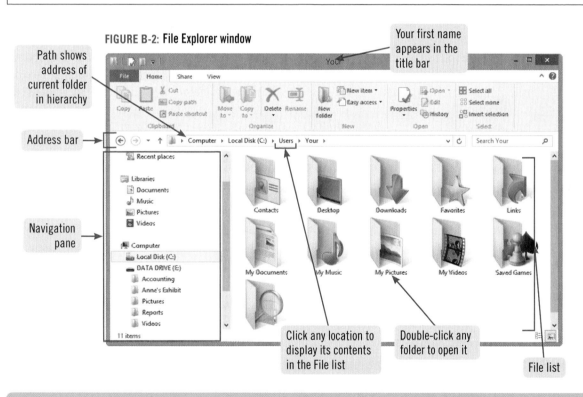

Path shows address of current folder in hierarchy

Your first name appears in the title bar

Address bar

Navigation pane

Click any location to display its contents in the File list

Double-click any folder to open it

File list

Plan your file organization

As you manage your files, you should plan how you want to organize them. First, identify the types of files you work with, such as images, music, and documents. Think about the content, such as personal, business, clients, or projects. Then think of a folder organization that will help you find them later. For example, you can use subfolders in the My Pictures folder to separate family photos from business photos or to group them by location

or by month. In the My Documents folder, you might group personal files in one subfolder and business files in another subfolder. Then create additional subfolders to further separate sets of files. You can always move files among folders and rename folders. You should periodically reevaluate your folder structure to make sure it continues to meet your needs.

Create and Save a File

After you start a program and create a new file, the file exists only in your computer's **random access memory (RAM)**, a temporary storage location. RAM contains information only when your computer is on. When you turn off your computer, it automatically clears the contents of RAM. So you need to save a new file onto a storage device that permanently stores the file so you can open, change, and use it later. One important storage device is your computer's hard drive built into your computer. Another popular option is a **USB flash drive**, a small, portable storage device. **CASE** *You create a document, then save it.*

STEPS

1. **At the Start screen, type word**
   Available apps with "word" in their names are listed. See **FIGURE B-3**.

2. **Click WordPad, then maximize the WordPad window if necessary**
   Near the top of the WordPad window you see the Ribbon containing command buttons, similar to those you used in Paint in Unit A. The Home tab appears in front. A new, blank document appears in the document window. The blinking insertion point shows you where the next character you type will appear.

TROUBLE
If you make a typing mistake, press [Backspace] to delete the character to the left of the insertion point.

3. **Type New Tours, then press [Enter] twice, type Thailand, press [Enter], type New Zealand, press [Enter], type Canada, press [Enter] twice, then type your name**
   See **FIGURE B-4**.

4. **Click the File tab, then click Save**
   The first time you save a file using the Save button, the Save As dialog box opens. You use this dialog box to name the file and choose a storage location for it. The Save As dialog box has many of the same elements as a File Explorer window, including an Address bar, a Navigation pane, and a File list. Below the Address bar, the **toolbar** contains command buttons you can click to perform actions. In the Address bar, you can see the Documents library (which includes the My Documents folder) is the **default**, or automatically selected, storage location. But you can easily change it.

QUICK TIP
On a laptop computer, the USB port is on the left or right side of your computer.

5. **Plug your USB flash drive into a USB port on your computer, if necessary**

TROUBLE
If you don't have a USB flash drive, you can save the document in the My Documents folder or ask your instructor which storage location is best.

6. **In the Navigation pane scroll bar, click the down scroll arrow ▼ as needed to see Computer and any storage devices listed under it**
   Under Computer, you see the storage locations available on your computer, such as Local Disk (C:) (your hard drive) and Removable Disk (F:) (your USB drive name and letter might differ). These storage locations are like folders in that you can open them and store files in them.

7. **Click the name for your USB flash drive**
   The files and folders on your USB drive, if any, appear in the File list. The Address bar shows the location where the file will be saved, which is now Computer ▶ Removable Disk (F:) (or the name of your drive). You need to give your document a meaningful name so you can find it later.

TROUBLE
If your Save As dialog box does not show the .rtf file extension, click Cancel, open File Explorer, click the View tab, then in the Show/hide group, click the File name extensions check box to select it.

8. **Click in the File name text box to select the default name Document.rtf, type New Tours, compare your screen to FIGURE B-5, then click Save**
   The document is saved as a file on your USB flash drive. The filename New Tours.rtf appears in the title bar. The ".rtf" at the end of the filename is the file extension that Windows 8 added automatically. A **file extension** is a three- or four-letter sequence, preceded by a period, which identifies a file to your computer, in this case **Rich Text Format**. The WordPad program creates files in RTF format.

9. **Click the Close button ☒ on the WordPad window**
   The WordPad program closes. Your New Tours document is now saved in the location you specified.

Understanding File Management

FIGURE B-3: Results list

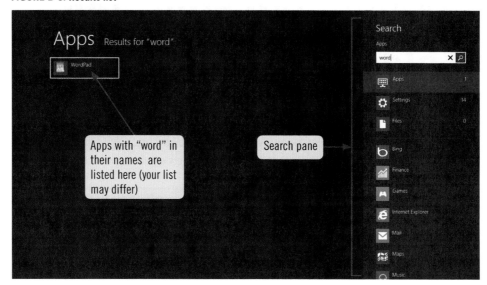

Apps with "word" in their names are listed here (your list may differ)

Search pane

FIGURE B-4: New document in WordPad

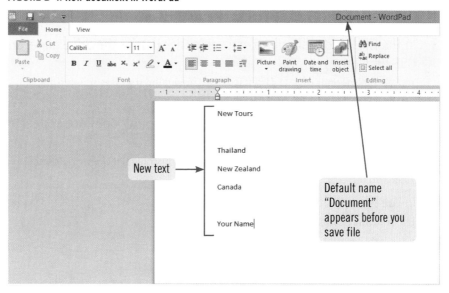

New text

Default name "Document" appears before you save file

FIGURE B-5: Save As dialog box

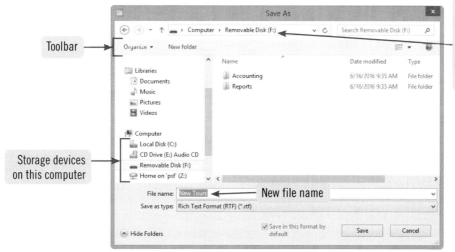

Toolbar

Storage devices on this computer

New file name

After you click Save, your New Tours.rtf document will be saved at this address (your drive name and letter will differ)

Understanding File Management

Explore the Files and Folders on Your Computer

In a File Explorer window, you can navigate through your computer contents using the File list, the Address bar, and the Navigation pane. Examining your computer and its existing folder and file structure helps you decide where to save files as you work with Windows 8 apps. **CASE** ▶ *In preparation for organizing documents at your new job, you look at the files and folders on your computer.*

STEPS

1. **If you see the Start screen, click the** Desktop tile **to display the Windows 8 desktop**

2. **On the taskbar, click the** File Explorer button 📁, **then in the File Explorer Navigation pane, click** Computer

   Your computer's storage devices appear in a window, as shown in **FIGURE B-6**. These include hard drives; devices with removable storage, such as CD and DVD drives or USB flash drives; portable devices such as personal digital assistants (PDAs); and any network storage locations. A colored bar shows you how much space has been taken up on your hard drive. You decide to move down a level in your computer's hierarchy and see what is on your USB flash drive.

3. **In the File list, double-click** Removable Disk (F:) **(or the drive name and letter for your USB flash drive)**

   You see the contents of your USB flash drive, including the New Tours.rtf file you saved in the last lesson. You decide to navigate one level up in the file hierarchy.

4. **In the Address bar, click** Computer, **or if Computer does not appear, click the far-left list arrow in the Address bar, then click** Computer

   You return to the Computer window showing your storage devices. You decide to look at the contents of your hard drive.

5. **In the File list, double-click** Local Disk (C:)

   The contents of your hard drive appear in the File list.

6. **In the File list, double-click the** Users folder

   The Users folder contains a subfolder for each user account on this computer. You might see a folder with your user account name on it. Each user's folder contains that person's documents. User folder names are the names that were used to log in when your computer was set up. When a user logs in, the computer allows that user access to the folder with the same user name. If you are using a computer with more than one user, you might not have permission to view other users' folders. There is also a Public folder that any user can open.

7. **Double-click the folder with your user name on it**

   Depending on how your computer is set up, this folder might be labeled with your name; however, if you are using a computer in a lab or a public location, your folder might be called Student or Computer User or something similar. You see a list of folders, such as My Documents, My Music, and others. See **FIGURE B-7**.

8. **Double-click** My Documents **in the File list**

   In the Address bar, the path to the My Documents folder is Computer ▶ Local Disk (C:) ▶ Users ▶ *Your User Name* ▶ My Documents.

9. **In the Navigation pane, click** Computer

   You once again see your computer's storage devices. You can also move up one level at a time in your file hierarchy by clicking the Up arrow ↑ on the toolbar, or by pressing [Backspace] on your keyboard. See **TABLE B-1** for a summary of techniques for navigating through your computer's file hierarchy.

Understanding File Management

FIGURE B-6: Computer window showing storage devices

Click this arrow if necessary to navigate to a different location

Colored bar shows how full the drive is

Storage devices

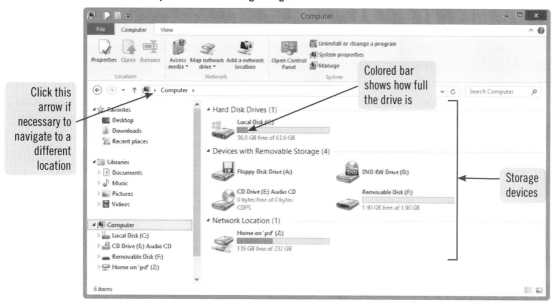

FIGURE B-7: Your user name folder

Path to your user name folder contents

Step 8

Your user name folder contents may differ

TABLE B-1: Navigating your computer's file hierarchy

to do this	Navigation pane	Address bar	File list	keyboard
Move up in hierarchy	Click a drive or folder name	Click an item to the left of ▶ or Click the **Up to** arrow ↑		Press [**Backspace**]
Move down in hierarchy	Click a drive or folder name that is indented from the left	Click an item to the right of ▶	Double-click a folder	Press ↑ or ↓ to select a folder, then press [**Enter**] to open the selected folder
Return to previously viewed location		Click the **Back to** button ← or **Forward to** button →		

Windows 8

Change File and Folder Views

Learning
Outcomes:
• View files as large
  icons
• Sort files
• Preview files

As you view your folders and files, you can customize your **view**, which is a set of appearance choices for files and folders. Changing your view does not affect the content of your files or folders, only the way they appear. You can choose from eight different **layouts** to display your folders and files as different sized icons, or as a list. You can also change the order in which the folders and files appear. You can also show a preview of a file in the window. **CASE** ▶ *You experiment with different views of your folders and files.*

STEPS

1. **In the File Explorer window's Navigation pane, click Local Disk (C:), in the File list double-click Users, then double-click the folder with your user name**
   You opened your user name folder, which is inside the Users folder.

2. **Click the View tab on the Ribbon, then click the More button ⬇ in the Layout group**
   The list of available layouts appears, as shown in **FIGURE B-8**.

3. **Click Extra large icons in the Layout list**
   In this view, the folder items appear as very large icons in the File list. This layout is especially helpful for image files, because you can see what the pictures are without opening each one.

QUICK TIP
You can scroll up and down in the Layout group to see views that are not currently visible.

4. **On the View tab, in the Layout list, point to the other layouts while watching the appearance of the File list, then click Details**
   In Details view, shown in **FIGURE B-9**, you can see each item's name, the date it was modified, and its file type. It shows the size of any files in the current folder, but it does not show sizes for folders.

5. **Click the Sort by button in the Current view group**
   The Sort by menu lets you **sort**, or reorder, your files and folders according to several criteria.

6. **Click Descending if it is not already selected**
   Now the folders are sorted in reverse alphabetical order.

QUICK TIP
Clicking Favorites in the Navigation pane displays folders you use frequently; to add a folder or location to Favorites, display it in the File list, then drag it to the Favorites list.

7. **Click Removable Disk (F:) (or the location where you store your Data Files) in the Navigation pane, then click the New Tours.rtf filename in the File list**

8. **Click the Preview pane button in the Panes group on the View tab if necessary**
   A preview of the selected New Tours.rtf file you created earlier in this unit appears in the Preview pane on the right side of the screen. The WordPad file is not open, but you can still see the file's contents. See **FIGURE B-10**.

9. **Click the Preview pane button again to close the pane, then click the window's Close button ✕**

Snapping Windows 8 apps

If your machine has a screen resolution of 1366 × 768 or higher, you can use snapping to view two Windows 8 apps side by side. Go to the Start screen and open the first app, then return to the Start screen and open the second app. Point to the upper-left corner of the screen until you can see a small square representing the first app, right-click the square, then click Snap left or Snap right. (Or you can drag the square to the right or left side of the screen.) One app then occupies one third of the screen and the other taking up two thirds of the screen. See **FIGURE B-11**.

FIGURE B-11: Using snapping to view Weather and SkyDrive apps

FIGURE B-8: Layout options for viewing folders and files

FIGURE B-9: Your user name folder contents in Details view

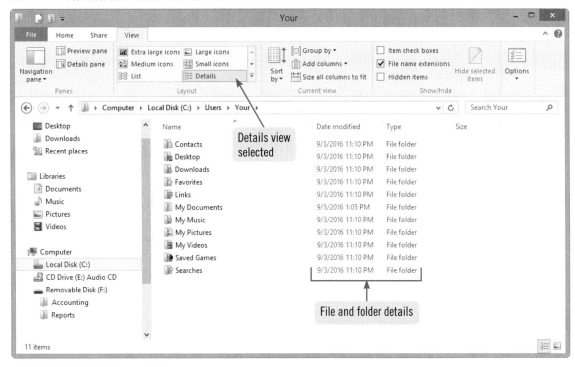

FIGURE B-10: Preview of selected New Tours.rtf file

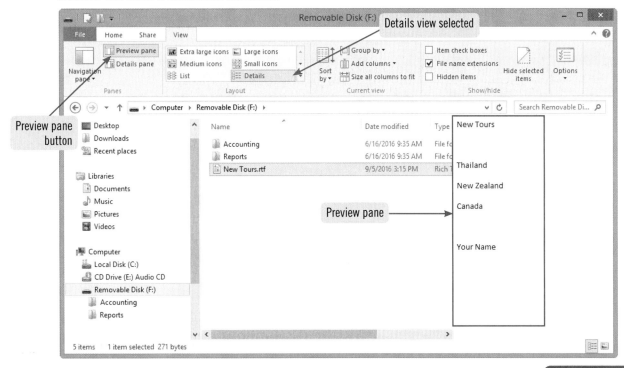

Understanding File Management

Open, Edit, and Save Files

Learning Outcomes:
• Open a file
• Edit a file
• Save a file

Once you have created a file and saved it with a name to a storage location, you can easily open it and **edit** (make changes to) it. For example, you might want to add or delete text or add a picture. Then you save the file again so the file contains your latest changes. Usually you save a file with the same filename and in the same location as the original, which replaces the existing file with the most up-to-date version. To save a file you have changed, you use the Save command. **CASE** ▶ *You need to complete the list of new tours, so you need to open the new Tours file you created earlier.*

STEPS

1. **Point to the lower-left corner of the screen, then click the Start thumbnail to display the Start screen**

2. **Begin typing wordpad, then click the WordPad program if it is not selected or, if it is, simply press [Enter]**

   The WordPad program opens on the desktop.

3. **Click the File tab, then click Open**

   The Open dialog box opens. It contains a Navigation pane and a File list like the Save As dialog box and the File Explorer window.

4. **Scroll down in the Navigation pane if necessary until you see Computer and the list of computer drives, then click Removable Disk (F:) (or the location where you store your Data Files)**

   The contents of your USB flash drive (or the file storage location you chose) appear in the File list, as shown in **FIGURE B-12**.

5. **Click New Tours.rtf in the File list, then click Open**

   The document you created earlier opens.

6. **Click to the right of the last "a" in Canada, press [Enter], then type Greenland**

   The edited document includes the text you just typed. See **FIGURE B-13**.

7. **Click the File tab, then click Save, as shown in FIGURE B-14**

   WordPad saves the document with your most recent changes, using the filename and location you specified when you previously saved it. When you save an existing file, the Save As dialog box does not open.

8. **Click the File tab, then click Exit**

Comparing Save and Save As

The WordPad menu has two save command options—Save and Save As. The first time you save a file, the Save As dialog box opens (whether you choose Save or Save As). Here you can select the drive and folder where you want to save the file and enter its filename. If you edit a previously saved file, you can save the file to the same location with the same filename using the Save command. The Save command updates the stored file using the same location and filename without opening the Save As dialog box. In some situations, you might want to save a copy of the existing document using a different filename or in a different storage location. To do this, open the document, click the Save As command on the File tab, navigate to the location where you want to save the copy if necessary, and/or edit the name of the file.

FIGURE B-12: Navigating in the Open dialog box

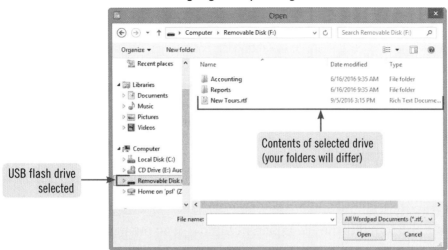

Contents of selected drive
(your folders will differ)

USB flash drive
selected

FIGURE B-13: Edited document

New Tours

Thailand

New Zealand

Canada

Greenland ◄─── Added text

Your Name

FIGURE B-14: Saving the updated document

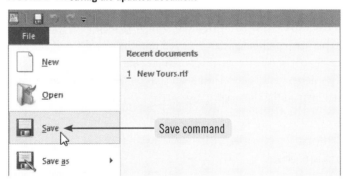

Save command

Using cloud storage

Many users store their files on special file storage locations on the World Wide Web, known as **cloud storage** locations. Examples of cloud storage locations include **Microsoft SkyDrive** and **DropBox**. By storing files in the cloud, your files are automatically updated when you make changes to them on your computer, and you can access them from different devices, including laptops, tablets, and smartphones. Microsoft Office programs such as Word and Excel show SkyDrive as a storage location when you open or save a file, making cloud storage a convenient option.

Copy Files

Learning
Outcomes:
• Create a new
  folder
• Copy and paste
  a file

Sometimes you need to make a copy of an existing file. For example, you might want to put a copy on a USB flash drive so you can open the file on another machine or share it with a friend or colleague. Or you might want to create a copy as a **backup**, or replacement, in case something happens to your original file. You can copy files and folders using the Copy command and then place the copy in another location using the Paste command. You cannot have two copies of a file with the same name in the same folder. If you try to do this, Windows 8 asks you if you want to replace the first one, and then gives you a chance to give the second copy a different name. **CASE** *You want to create a backup copy of the New Tours document that you can store in a folder for company newsletter items. First you need to create the folder, then you can copy the file.*

STEPS

1. **On the desktop, click the File Explorer button 📁 on the taskbar**

2. **In the Navigation pane, click Removable Disk (F:) (or the drive name and letter that represents the location where you store your Data Files)**
   First you create the new folder you plan to use for storing newsletter-related files.

3. **If you don't see the Ribbon, double-click the Home tab to open the Ribbon**

4. **In the New group on the Home tab, click the New folder button**
   A new folder appears in the File list, with its default name, New folder, selected.

5. **Type Newsletter Items, then press [Enter]**
   Because the folder name was selected, the text you typed, Newsletter Items, replaced it. Pressing [Enter] confirmed your entry, and the folder is now named Newsletter Items.

6. **In the File list, click the New Tours.rtf document you saved earlier, then click the Copy button in the Clipboard group, as shown in FIGURE B-15**
   When you use the Copy command, Windows 8 places a duplicate copy of the file in an area of your computer's random access memory called the **clipboard**, ready to paste, or place, in a new location. Copying and pasting a file leaves the file in its original location.

7. **In the File list, double-click the Newsletter Items folder**
   The folder opens. Nothing appears in the File list because the folder currently is empty.

8. **Click the Paste button in the Clipboard group**
   A copy of the New Tours.rtf file is pasted into the Newsletter Items folder. See **FIGURE B-16**. You now have two copies of the New Tours.rtf file: one on your USB flash drive in the main folder, and another in your new Newsletter Items folder. The file remains on the clipboard until you end your Windows session or place another item on the clipboard.

TABLE B-2: Selected Send to menu commands

menu option	use to
Compressed (zipped) folder	Create a new compressed (smaller) file with a .zip file extension
Desktop (create shortcut)	Create a shortcut (link) for the file on the desktop
Documents	Copy the file to the Documents library
Fax recipient	Send a file to a fax recipient
Mail recipient	Create an e-mail with the file attached to it (only if you have an e-mail program on your computer)
DVD RW Drive (D:)	Copy the file to your computer's DVD drive
Removable Disk (F:)	Copy the file to a removable disk drive (F:) (your drive letter may differ)

FIGURE B-15: Copying a file

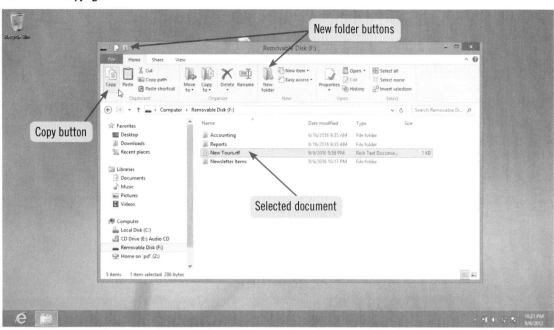

New folder buttons

Copy button

Selected document

Copy is pasted in Newsletter Items folder

FIGURE B-16: Duplicate file pasted into Newsletter Items folder

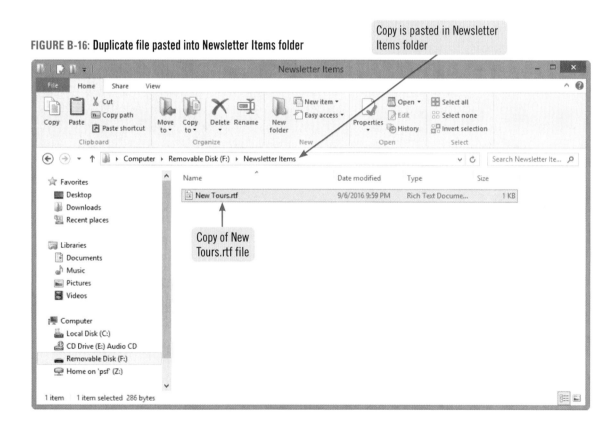

Copy of New Tours.rtf file

Copying files using Send to

You can also copy and paste a file using the Send to command. In File Explorer, right-click the file you want to copy, point to Send to, then in the shortcut menu, click the name of the device you want to send a copy of the file to. This leaves the original file on your hard drive and creates a copy on the external device. You can send a file to a compressed file, the desktop, a mail recipient, your Documents library, or a drive on your computer. See **TABLE B-2.**

Move and Rename Files

Learning
Outcomes:
• Cut and paste
  a file
• Rename a file

As you work with files, you might need to move files or folders to another location. You can move one or more files or folders at a time, and you can move them to a different folder on the same drive or to a different drive. When you **move** a file, the file is transferred to the new location, and unlike copying it no longer exists in its original location. You can move a file using the Cut and Paste commands. Before or after you move a file, you might find that you want to change its name. You can easily rename it to make the name more descriptive or accurate. **CASE** ▶ *You decide to move your original New Tours.rtf document to your Documents library. After you move it, you edit the filename so it better describes the file contents.*

STEPS

QUICK TIP

You can also cut a file by right-clicking it in the File list, then clicking Cut, or by clicking it, pressing and holding [Ctrl] on the keyboard, pressing [X], then releasing both keys.

1. **In the Address bar, click Removable Disk (F:) (or the drive name and letter for your USB flash drive)**

2. **Click the New Tours.rtf document to select it**

3. **Click the Cut button in the Clipboard group on the Ribbon**

   The icon representing the cut file becomes lighter in color, indicating you have cut it, as shown in **FIGURE B-17**.

4. **In the Navigation Pane, under Libraries, click Documents**

   You navigated to your Documents Library.

QUICK TIP

You can also paste a file by right-clicking an empty area in the File list and then clicking Paste, or by pressing and holding [Ctrl] on the keyboard, pressing [V], then releasing both keys.

5. **Click the Paste button in the Clipboard group**

   The New Tours.rtf document appears in your Documents library and remains selected. See **FIGURE B-18**. Documents you paste into your Documents library are automatically stored in your My Documents folder. The filename could be clearer, to help you remember that it contains a list of new tours.

6. **With the New Tours.rtf file selected, click the Rename button in the Organize group**

   The filename is highlighted. The file extension isn't highlighted because that part of the filename identifies the file to WordPad and should not be changed. If you deleted or changed the file extension, WordPad would be unable to open the file. You decide to add the word "List" to the end of the original filename.

7. **Move the I pointer after the "s" in "Tours", click to place the insertion point, press [Spacebar], type List as shown in FIGURE B-19, then press [Enter]**

   You changed the name of the pasted file in the Documents library. The filename now reads New Tours List.rtf.

8. **Close the window**

Using Windows 8 libraries

The Navigation pane contains not only files and folders, but also libraries. A **library** gathers file and folder locations from different locations on your computer and displays them in one location. For example, you might have pictures in several different folders on your storage devices. You can add these folder locations to your Pictures library. Then when you want to see all your pictures, you open your Pictures library instead of several different folders. The picture files stay in their original locations, but their names appear in the Pictures library. A library is not a folder that stores files, but rather a way of viewing similar types of documents that you have stored in multiple locations on your computer. **FIGURE B-20** shows the four libraries that come with Windows 8: Documents, Music, Pictures, and Videos. To help you distinguish between library locations and actual folder

locations, library names differ from actual folder names. For example, the My Documents folder is on your hard drive, but the library name is Documents. If you save a document to the Documents library, it is automatically saved to your My Documents folder.

FIGURE B-20: Libraries that come with Windows 8

Documents   Music   Pictures   Videos

FIGURE B-17: Cutting a file

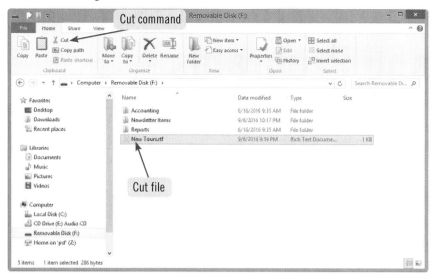

FIGURE B-18: Pasted file in Documents library

FIGURE B-19: Renaming a file

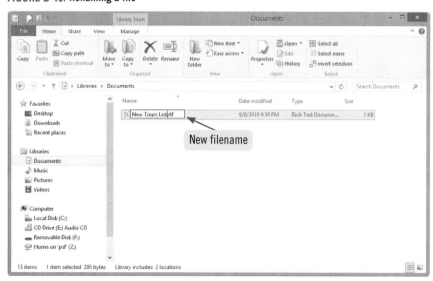

Understanding File Management

Learning
Outcomes:
• Search for a file
• Open a found file

Search for Files, Folders, and Programs

Windows Search helps you quickly find any program, folder, or file. You can search from the Start screen using the Charms bar to locate applications, settings, or files. To search a particular location on your computer, you can use the Search box in File Explorer. You enter search text by typing one or more letter sequences or words that help Windows identify the item you want. The search text you type is called your **search criteria.** Your search criteria can be a filename, part of a filename, or any other text. **CASE** ➤ *You want to locate the New Tours.rtf document so you can print it for a colleague.*

STEPS

1. **Move the pointer to the lower-left corner of the screen, then click the Start thumbnail**
   The Start screen opens.

2. **Point to the upper-right corner of the screen, then point to and click the Search charm**
   A listing of the apps on your computer appears, along with a Search pane on the right side of the screen. See **FIGURE B-21**. You can search for Apps, Settings, or Files. Apps is selected by default.

   QUICK TIP
   To immediately open File search in the Search charm, press ⊞ [F].

3. **Click Files in the Search panel, type new tour, then press [Enter]**
   Your New Tours List.rtf document appears under Files. By default, the Search charm finds only files located on your computer hard drive, not on any external drives.

   QUICK TIP
   If you navigated to a specific folder in your file hierarchy, Windows would search that folder and any subfolders below it.

4. **Point to the New Tours List.rtf file**
   The path in the ScreenTip, C:\Users\Your Name\My Documents, indicates the found file is in the My Documents folder on the C: drive, as shown in **FIGURE B-22**.

5. **Press ⊞ twice to display the desktop**

6. **Click the File Explorer button 📁 on the taskbar, then click Computer in the Navigation pane**

   QUICK TIP
   Windows search is not case-sensitive, meaning that you can type upper- or lowercase letters when you search, and obtain the same results.

7. **Click in the Search box to the right of the Address bar, type new tour, then press [Enter]**
   Windows searches your computer for files that contain the words "new tour". A green bar in the Address bar indicates the progress of your search. After a few moments, your search results, shown in **FIGURE B-23**, appear. Windows found both the renamed file, New Tours List.rtf, in your My Documents folder, and the original New Tours.rtf document on your removable drive, in the Newsletter Items folder.

8. **Double-click the New Tours.rtf document on your removable flash drive**
   The file opens in WordPad or in another word-processing program on your computer that reads RTF files.

9. **Click the Close button ✕ on the WordPad (or other word-processor) window**

Using the Search Tools tab in File Explorer

The **Search Tools tab** appears in the Ribbon as soon as you click the Search text box, and it lets you narrow your search criteria. Use the commands in the Location group to specify a particular search location. The Refine group lets you limit the search to files modified after a certain date, or to files of a particular kind, size, type, or other property. The Options group lets you repeat previous searches, save searches, and open the folder containing a found file. See **FIGURE B-24**.

FIGURE B-24: Search Tools tab

FIGURE B-21: Apps screen and search pane

FIGURE B-22: Viewing the location of a found file

FIGURE B-23: Search results in File Explorer

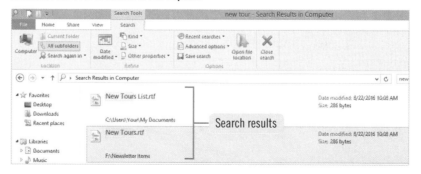

Delete and Restore Files

If you no longer need a folder or file, you can delete (or remove) it from the storage device. By regularly deleting files and folders you no longer need and emptying the Recycle Bin, you free up valuable storage space on your computer. Windows 8 places folders and files you delete from your hard drive in the Recycle Bin. If you delete a folder, Windows 8 removes the folder as well as all files and subfolders stored in it. If you later discover that you need a deleted file or folder, you can restore it to its original location, as long as you have not yet emptied the Recycle Bin. Emptying the Recycle Bin permanently removes deleted folders and files from your computer. However, files and folders you delete from a removable drive, such as a USB flash drive, do not go to the Recycle Bin. They are immediately and permanently deleted and cannot be restored. **CASE** ▶ *You decide to delete the New Tours document, but later you change your mind about this.*

STEPS

1. **Click the Documents library in the File Explorer Navigation pane**
   Your Documents library opens, along with the Library Tools Manage tab on the Ribbon.

2. **Click New Tours List.rtf to select it, then click the Delete list arrow in the Organize group on the Library Tools Manage tab; if the Show recycle confirmation command does not have a check mark next to it, click Show recycle confirmation (or if it does have a check mark, click the Delete list arrow again to close the menu)**
   Selecting the Show recycle confirmation command tells Windows that whenever you click the Delete button, you want to see a confirmation dialog box before Windows deletes the file. That way you can change your mind if you want, before deleting the file.

3. **Click the Delete button ⊠**
   The Delete File dialog box opens so you can confirm the deletion, as shown in **FIGURE B-25**.

4. **Click Yes**
   You deleted the file. Because the file was stored on your computer and not on a removable drive, it was moved to the Recycle Bin.

5. **Click the Minimize button ▬ on the window's title bar, examine the Recycle Bin icon, then double-click the Recycle Bin icon on the desktop**
   The Recycle Bin icon appears to contain crumpled paper, indicating that it contains deleted folders and/or files. The Recycle Bin window displays any previously deleted folders and files, including the New Tours List.rtf file.

6. **Click the New Tours List.rtf file to select it, then click the Restore the selected items button in the Restore group on the Recycle Bin Tools Manage tab, as shown in FIGURE B-26**
   The file returns to its original location and no longer appears in the Recycle Bin window.

7. **In the Navigation pane, click the Documents library**
   The Documents library window contains the restored file. You decide to permanently delete this file.

8. **Click the file New Tours List.rtf, click the Delete list arrow in the Organize group on the Library Tools Manage tab, click Permanently delete, then click Yes in the Delete File dialog box**

9. **Minimize the window, double-click the Recycle Bin, notice that the New Tours List.rtf file is no longer there, then close all open windows**

FIGURE B-25: Delete File dialog box

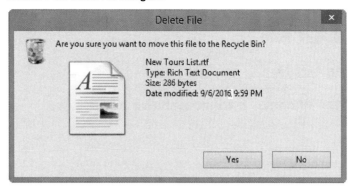

FIGURE B-26: Restoring a file from the Recycle Bin

Your Recycle Bin contents may differ

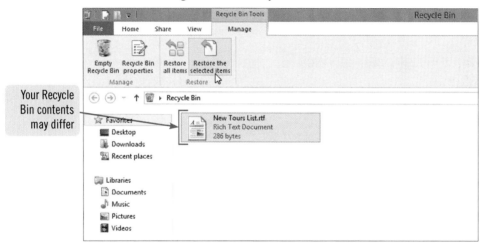

More techniques for selecting and moving files

To select a group of items that are next to each other in a window, click the first item in the group, press and hold [Shift], then click the last item in the group. Both items you click and all the items between them become selected. To select files that are not next to each other, click the first file, press and hold [Ctrl], then click the other items you want to select as a group. Then you can copy, cut, or delete the group of files or folders you selected. **Drag and drop** is a technique in which you use your pointing device to drag a file or folder into a different folder and then drop it, or let go of the mouse button, to place it in that folder. Using drag and drop does not copy your file to the clipboard. If you drag and drop a file to a folder on a different drive, Windows 8 *copies the file.* However, if you drag and drop a file to a folder on the same drive, Windows 8 *moves* the file into that

folder instead. See **FIGURE B-27**. If you want to move a file to another drive, hold down [Shift] while you drag and drop. If you want to copy a file to another folder on the same drive, hold down [Ctrl] while you drag and drop.

FIGURE B-27: Moving a file using drag and drop

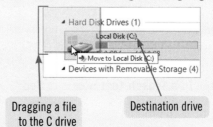

Dragging a file to the C drive

Destination drive

Understanding File Management

Practice

Concepts Review

Label the elements of the Windows 8 window shown in FIGURE B-28.

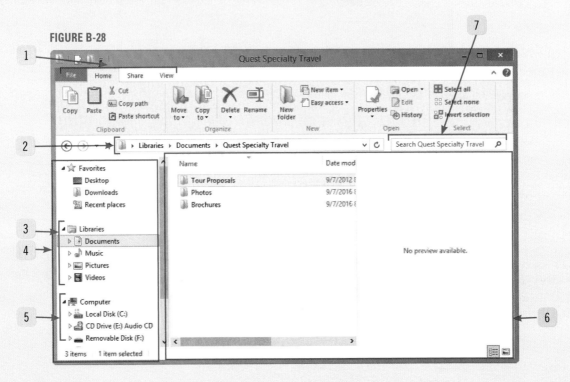

FIGURE B-28

Match each term with the statement that best describes it.

8. File management
9. File extension
10. Address bar
11. Path
12. Library
13. File hierarchy

a. An area above the Files list that contains a path
b. Structure of files and folders organized in different levels
c. A series of locations separated by small triangles or backslashes that describes a file's location in the file hierarchy
d. Skills that help you organize your files and folders
e. A three- or four-letter sequence, preceded by a period, that identifies the type of file
f. Gathers files and folders from different computer locations

Select the best answer from the list of choices.

14. **Which part of a window lets you see a file's contents without opening the file?**
   a. File list
   b. Preview pane
   c. Navigation pane
   d. Address bar

15. **When you move a file:**
   a. It remains in its original location.
   b. It is no longer in its original location.
   c. It is copied to another location.
   d. It is no longer in your file hierarchy.

16. **The text you type in a Search text box is called:**
   a. Search criteria.
   b. RAM.
   c. Sorting.
   d. Clipboard.

17. Which of the following is not a visible section in a File Explorer window?

a. Address bar   c. Navigation pane

b. File list   d. Clipboard

18. The way your files appear in the Files list is determined by the:

a. Path.   c. Subfolder.

b. View.   d. Criterion.

19. When you copy a file, it is automatically placed in the:

a. Preview pane.   c. Hierarchy.

b. My Documents folder.   d. Clipboard.

20. After you delete a file from your hard disk, it is automatically placed in the:

a. USB flash drive.   c. Recycle Bin.

b. Clipboard.   d. Search box.

Skills Review

1. Understand files and folders.

a. Create a file hierarchy for a property management business. The business manages three apartment buildings and two private homes. Activities include renting the properties and managing maintenance and repair. How would you organize your folders and files using a file hierarchy of at least three levels? How would you use folders and subfolders to keep the documents related to these activities distinct and easy to navigate? Draw a diagram and write a short paragraph explaining your answer.

b. Use tools in the File Explorer window to create the folder hierarchy in the My Documents folder on your computer.

2. Create and save a file.

a. Connect your USB flash drive to a USB port on your computer, then open WordPad from the Start screen.

b. Type **Tour Marketing Plan** as the title, then start a new line.

c. Type your name, then press [Enter] twice.

d. Create the following list:

Airline co-marketing

Email blasts

Web ads

Adult education partnership

e. Save the WordPad file with the filename **Tour Marketing Plan.rtf** on your USB flash drive.

f. View the filename in the WordPad title bar, then close WordPad.

3. Explore the files and folders on your computer.

a. Open a File Explorer window.

b. Use the Navigation pane to navigate to your USB flash drive or another location where you store your Data Files.

c. Use the Address bar to navigate to Computer.

d. Use the File list to navigate to your local hard drive (C:).

e. Use the File list to open the Users folder, and then open the folder that represents your user name.

f. Open the My Documents folder. (*Hint:* The path is Computer\Local Disk (C:) \Users \Your User Name\ My Documents.)

g. Use the Navigation pane to navigate back to your Computer contents.

4. Change file and folder views.

a. Navigate to your USB flash drive using the method of your choice.

b. Use the View tab to view its contents as large icons.

c. View the drive contents in the seven other views.

d. Sort the items on your USB flash drive by date modified in ascending order.

e. Open the Preview pane, then view the selected item's preview.

f. Close the Preview pane.

Skills Review (continued)

5. Open, edit, and save files.

   a. Open WordPad.

   b. Use the Open dialog box to open the Tour Marketing Plan.rtf document you created.

   c. After the text "Adult education partnership," add a line with the text **Travel conventions**.

   d. Save the document and close WordPad.

6. Copy files.

   a. In the File Explorer window, navigate to your USB flash drive if necessary.

   b. Copy the Tour Marketing Plan.rtf document.

   c. Create a new folder named **Marketing** on your USB flash drive or the location where you store your Data Files (*Hint:* Use the Home tab), then open the folder.

   d. Paste the document copy in the new folder.

7. Move and rename files.

   a. Navigate to your USB flash drive or the location where you store your Data Files.

   b. Select the Tour Marketing Plan.rtf document located there, then cut it.

   c. Navigate to your Documents library, then paste the file there.

   d. Rename the file **Tour Marketing Plan - Backup.rtf**.

8. Search for files, folders, and programs.

   a. Go to the Start screen, and use the Search charm to search for a file using the search text **backup**.

   b. Point to the found file, and notice its path.

   c. Open the Tour Marketing Plan - Backup document from the search results, then close WordPad. (*Hint:* Closing the program automatically closes any open documents.)

   d. Open a File Explorer window, click in the Search box, then use the Data Modified button on the Search Tools Search tab to find a file modified today. (*Hint:* Click the Date Modified button, then click Today.)

   e. Open the found document from the File list, then close WordPad.

9. Delete and restore files.

   a. Navigate to your Documents library.

   b. Verify that your Delete preference is Show recycle confirmation, then delete the Tour Marketing Plan Backup.rtf file.

   c. Open the Recycle Bin, and restore the document to its original location.

   d. Navigate to your Documents library, then move the Tour Marketing Plan-Backup.rtf file to your USB flash drive.

Independent Challenge 1

To meet the needs of pet owners in your town, you have opened a pet-sitting business named CritterCare. Customers hire you to care for their pets in their own homes when the pet owners go on vacation. To promote your new business, your Web site designer asks you to give her selling points to include in a Web ad.

   a. Connect your USB flash drive to your computer, if necessary.

   b. Create a new folder named **CritterCare** on your USB flash drive or the location where you store your Data Files.

   c. In the CritterCare folder, create two subfolders named **Print Ads** and **Web site**.

   d. Use WordPad to create a short paragraph or list that describes three advantages of your business. Use CritterCare as the first line, followed by the paragraph or list. Include an address and a phone number. Below the paragraph, type your name.

   e. Save the WordPad document with the filename **Selling Points.rtf** in the Web site folder, then close the document and exit WordPad.

   f. Open a File Explorer window, then navigate to the Web site folder.

   g. View the contents in at least three different views, then choose the view option that you prefer.

   h. Copy the Selling Points.rtf file, then paste a copy in the Document library.

   i. Rename the copied file **Selling Points Backup.rtf**.

   j. Close the folder.

Independent Challenge 2

As a freelance editor for several international publishers, you depend on your computer to meet critical deadlines. Whenever you encounter a computer problem, you contact a computer consultant who helps you resolve the problem. This consultant has asked you to document, or keep records of, your computer's current settings.

a. Connect your USB flash drive to your computer, if necessary.

b. Open the Computer window so you can view information on your drives and other installed hardware.

c. View the window contents using three different views, then choose the one you prefer.

d. Open WordPad and create a document with the title **My Hardware Documentation** and your name on separate lines.

e. List the names of the hard drive (or drives), devices with removable storage, and any other hardware devices installed on the computer you are using. Also include the total size and amount of free space on your hard drive(s) and removable storage drive(s). (*Hint:* If you need to check the Computer window for this information, use the taskbar button for the Computer window to view your drives, then use the WordPad taskbar button to return to WordPad.)

f. Save the WordPad document with the filename **My Hardware Documentation** on your USB flash drive or the location where you store your Data Files.

g. Close WordPad, then preview your document in the Preview pane.

Independent Challenge 3

You are an attorney at Garcia, Buck, and Sato, a large law firm. You participate in your firm's community outreach program by speaking at career days in area high schools. You teach students about career opportunities available in the field of law. You want to create a folder structure on your USB flash drive to store the files for each session.

a. Connect your USB flash drive to your computer, then open the window for your USB flash drive or the location where you store your Data Files.

b. Create a folder named **Career Days**.

c. In the Career Days folder, create a subfolder named **Nearwater High**, then open the folder.

d. Close the Nearwater High folder window.

e. Use WordPad to create a document with the title **Career Areas** and your name on separate lines, and the following list of items:
Current Opportunities:
Attorney
Paralegal
Police Officer
Judge

f. Save the WordPad document with the filename **Careers.rtf** in the Nearwater High folder. (*Hint:* After you switch to your USB flash drive in the Save As dialog box, open the Career Days folder, then open the Nearwater High folder before saving the file.)

g. Close WordPad.

h. Open WordPad and the Careers document again, add **Court Reporter** to the bottom of the list, then save the file and close WordPad.

i. Using pencil and paper, draw a diagram of your new folder structure.

j. Use the Search method of your choice to search for the Careers document, then open the file, to search your computer using the search criterion **car**. Locate the Careers.rtf document in the list, then use the link to open the file.

k. Close the file.

Independent Challenge 4: Explore

Think of a hobby or volunteer activity that you do now, or one that you would like to start. You will use your computer to help you manage your plans or ideas for this activity.

a. Using paper and pencil, sketch a folder structure with at least two subfolders to contain your documents for this activity.

b. Connect your USB flash drive to your computer, then open the window for your USB flash drive.

c. Create the folder structure for your activity, using your sketch as a reference.

d. Think of at least three tasks that you can do to further your work in your chosen activity.

e. Go to the Windows 8 Start screen, click the Store app tile and scroll to explore the available app categories. Choose a category that might relate to your activity, and click the Top Free tile to see if any of these apps might help you. Click an app name to read its description. (*Note:* You do not need to install any apps.)

f. Close the Store app by dragging its top border to the bottom of the screen.

g. Start a new WordPad document. Add the title **Next Steps** at the top of the page and your name on the next line.

h. Below your name, list the three tasks, then write a paragraph on how Windows 8 apps might help you accomplish your tasks. Save the file in one of the folders created on your USB flash drive, with the title **To Do.rtf**.

i. Close WordPad, then open a File Explorer window for the folder where you stored the document.

j. Create a copy of the file, place the copied file in your documents library, then rename this file with a name you choose.

k. Delete the copied file from your Documents library.

l. Open the Recycle Bin window, then restore the copied file to the Documents library.

Visual Workshop

Create the folder structure shown in FIGURE B-29 on your USB flash drive (or in another location if requested by your instructor). As you work, use WordPad to prepare a short summary of the steps you followed to create the folder structure. Add your name to the document, then save it as **Customer Support.rtf** on your USB Flash drive or the location where you store your Data Files.

FIGURE B-29

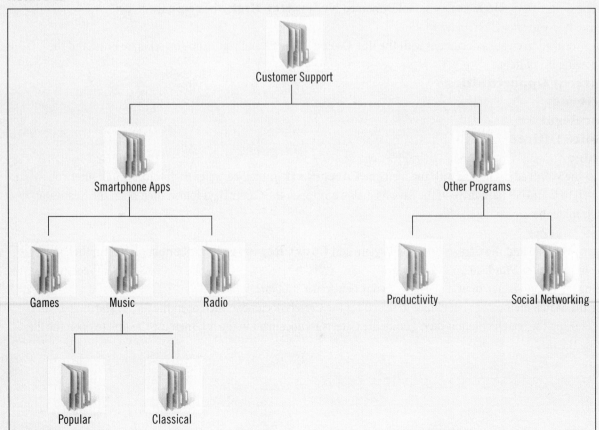

Getting Started with Microsoft Office 2013

CASE This unit introduces you to the most frequently used programs in Office, as well as common features they all share.

Unit Objectives

After completing this unit, you will be able to:

- Understand the Office 2013 suite
- Start an Office app
- Identify Office 2013 screen elements
- Create and save a file

- Open a file and save it with a new name
- View and print your work
- Get Help, close a file, and exit an app

File You Will Need

OFFICE A-1.xlsx

Dimec/Shutterstock

Learning
Outcomes
• Identify Office
  suite components
• Describe the
  features of each
  program

Understand the Office 2013 Suite

Microsoft Office 2013 is a group of programs--which are also called applications or apps--designed to help you create documents, collaborate with coworkers, and track and analyze information. You use different Office programs to accomplish specific tasks, such as writing a letter or producing a presentation, yet all the programs have a similar look and feel. Microsoft Office 2013 apps feature a common, context-sensitive user interface, so you can get up to speed faster and use advanced features with greater ease. The Office apps are bundled together in a group called a **suite**. The Office suite is available in several configurations, but all include Word, Excel, and PowerPoint. Other configurations include Access, Outlook, Publisher, and other programs. **CASE** *As part of your job, you need to understand how each Office app is best used to complete specific tasks.*

DETAILS

The Office apps covered in this book include:

- **Microsoft Word 2013**

  When you need to create any kind of text-based document, such as a memo, newsletter, or multipage report, Word is the program to use. You can easily make your documents look great by inserting eye-catching graphics and using formatting tools such as themes, which are available in most Office programs. **Themes** are predesigned combinations of color and formatting attributes you can apply to a document. The Word document shown in **FIGURE A-1** was formatted with the Organic theme.

- **Microsoft Excel 2013**

  Excel is the perfect solution when you need to work with numeric values and make calculations. It puts the power of formulas, functions, charts, and other analytical tools into the hands of every user, so you can analyze sales projections, calculate loan payments, and present your findings in a professional manner. The Excel worksheet shown in **FIGURE A-1** tracks personal expenses. Because Excel automatically recalculates results whenever a value changes, the information is always up to date. A chart illustrates how the monthly expenses are broken down.

- **Microsoft PowerPoint 2013**

  Using PowerPoint, it's easy to create powerful presentations complete with graphics, transitions, and even a soundtrack. Using professionally designed themes and clip art, you can quickly and easily create dynamic slide shows such as the one shown in **FIGURE A-1**.

- **Microsoft Access 2013**

  Access is a relational database program that helps you keep track of large amounts of quantitative data, such as product inventories or employee records. The form shown in **FIGURE A-1** was created for a grocery store inventory database. Employees use the form to enter data about each item. Using Access enables employees to quickly find specific information such as price and quantity.

Microsoft Office has benefits beyond the power of each program, including:

QUICK TIP
In Word, Excel, and
PowerPoint, the
interface can be
modified to auto-
matically open a
blank document,
workbook, or pre-
sentation. To do this,
click the FILE tab,
click Options, click
Show the Start
screen when this
application starts
(to deselect it), then
click OK. The next
time the program
opens, it will open a
blank document.

- **Common user interface: Improving business processes**

  Because the Office suite programs have a similar **interface**, or look and feel, your experience using one program's tools makes it easy to learn those in the other programs. In addition, Office documents are **compatible** with one another, meaning that you can easily incorporate, or **integrate**, an Excel chart into a PowerPoint slide, or an Access table into a Word document.

- **Collaboration: Simplifying how people work together**

  Office recognizes the way people do business today, and supports the emphasis on communication and knowledge sharing within companies and across the globe. All Office programs include the capability to incorporate feedback—called **online collaboration**—across the Internet or a company network.

FIGURE A-1: Microsoft Office 2013 documents

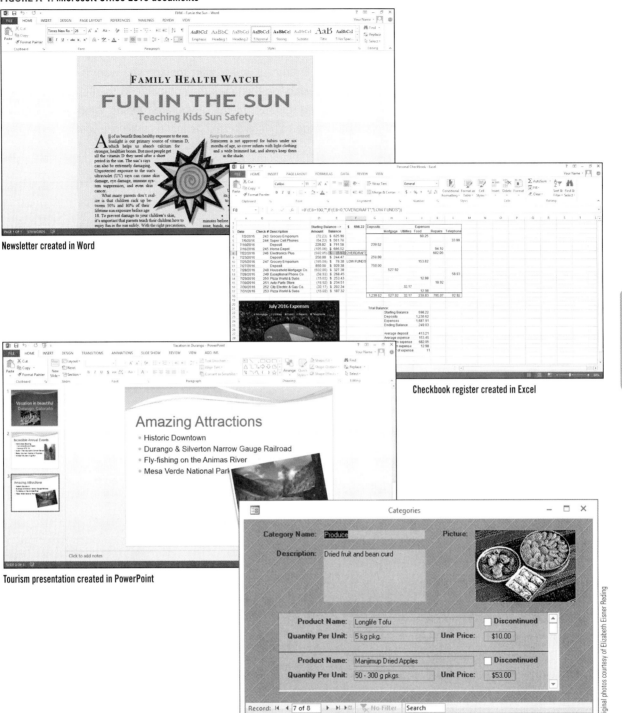

Newsletter created in Word

Checkbook register created in Excel

Tourism presentation created in PowerPoint

Store inventory form created in Access

What is Office 365?

Until the release of Microsoft Office 2013, most consumers purchased Microsoft Office in a traditional way: by buying a retail package from a store or downloading it from Microsoft.com. You can still purchase Microsoft Office 2013 in this traditional way--but you can also now purchase it as a subscription service called Microsoft Office 365 (for businesses) and Microsoft Office 365 Home Premium (for consumers). Office 365 requires businesses to pay a subscription fee for each user. Office 365 Home Premium Edition allows households to install Office on up to 5 devices. These subscription versions of Office provide extra services and are optimized for working in the cloud.

Start an Office App

To get started using Microsoft Office, you need to start, or **launch**, the Office app you want to use. If you are running Microsoft Office on Windows 8, an easy way to start the app you want is to go to the Start screen, type the app name you want to search for, then click the app name In the Results list. If you are running Windows 7, you start an app using the Start menu. (If you are running Windows 7, follow the Windows 7 steps at the bottom of this page.) **CASE** *You decide to familiarize yourself with Office by starting Microsoft Word.*

STEPS

1. **Go to the** Windows 8 Start screen

   Your screen displays a variety of colorful tiles for all the apps on your computer. You could locate the app you want to open by scrolling to the right until you see it, or you can type the app name to search for it.

2. **Type** word

   Your screen now displays "Word 2013" under "Results for 'word'", along with any other app that has "word" as part of its name (such as WordPad). See **FIGURE A-2**.

3. **Click** Word 2013

   Word 2013 launches, and the Word **start screen** appears, as shown in **FIGURE A-3**. The start screen is a landing page that appears when you first start an Office app. The left side of this screen displays recent files you have opened. (If you have never opened any files, then there will be no files listed under Recent.) The right side displays images depicting different templates you can use to create different types of documents. A **template** is a file containing professionally designed content that you can easily replace with your own. You can also start from scratch using the Blank Document option.

Starting an app using Windows 7

1. Click the Start button 🔘 on the taskbar
2. Click All Programs on the Start menu, click the Microsoft Office 2013 folder as shown in FIGURE A-4, then click Word 2013

Word 2013 launches, and the Word start screen appears, as shown previously in FIGURE A-3. The start screen is a landing page that appears when you first start an Office app. The left side of this

screen displays recent files you have opened. (If you have never opened any files, then there will be no files listed under Recent.) The right side displays images depicting different templates you can use to create different types of documents. A **template** is a file containing professionally designed content that you can easily replace with your own. Using a template to create a document can save time and ensure that your document looks great. You can also start from scratch using the Blank Document option.

Using shortcut keys to move between Office programs

You can switch between open apps using a keyboard shortcut. The [Alt][Tab] keyboard combination lets you either switch quickly to the next open program or file or choose one from a gallery. To switch immediately to the next open program or file, press [Alt][Tab]. To choose from all open programs and files, press and hold [Alt], then press and release [Tab] without releasing

[Alt]. A gallery opens on screen, displaying the filename and a thumbnail image of each open program and file, as well as of the desktop. Each time you press [Tab] while holding [Alt], the selection cycles to the next open file or location. Release [Alt] when the program, file, or location you want to activate is selected.

FIGURE A-2: Searching for Word app from the Start screen in Windows 8

FIGURE A-3: Word start screen

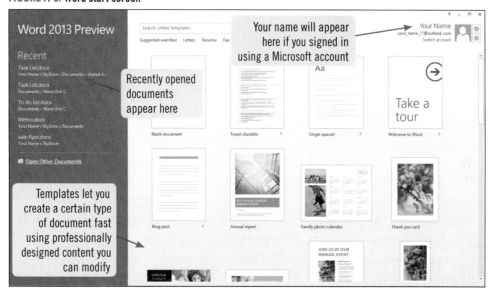

FIGURE A-4: Starting an app using Windows 7

Using the Office Clipboard

You can use the Office Clipboard to cut and copy items from one Office program and paste them into others. The Office Clipboard can store a maximum of 24 items. To access it, open the Office Clipboard task pane by clicking the dialog box launcher ⬜ in the Clipboard group on the HOME tab. Each time you copy a selection, it is saved in the Office Clipboard. Each entry in the Office Clipboard includes an icon that tells you the program it was created in. To paste an entry, click in the document where you want it to appear, then click the item in the Office Clipboard. To delete an item from the Office Clipboard, right-click the item, then click Delete.

Identify Office 2013 Screen Elements

One of the benefits of using Office is that the programs have much in common, making them easy to learn and making it simple to move from one to another. Individual Office programs have always shared many features, but the innovations in the Office 2013 user interface mean even greater similarity among them all. That means you can also use your knowledge of one program to get up to speed in another. A **user interface** is a collective term for all the ways you interact with a software program. The user interface in Office 2013 provides intuitive ways to choose commands, work with files, and navigate in the program window. **CASE** ▶ *Familiarize yourself with some of the common interface elements in Office by examining the PowerPoint program window.*

STEPS

1. **Go to the Windows 8** Start screen, **type** pow, **click** PowerPoint 2013, **then click** Blank Presentation

   PowerPoint becomes the active program displaying a blank slide. Refer to **FIGURE A-5** to identify common elements of the Office user interface. The **document window** occupies most of the screen. At the top of every Office program window is a **title bar** that displays the document name and program name. Below the title bar is the **Ribbon**, which displays commands you're likely to need for the current task. Commands are organized onto **tabs**. The tab names appear at the top of the Ribbon, and the active tab appears in front.

2. **Click the** FILE tab

   The FILE tab opens, displaying **Backstage view**. It is called Backstage view becausee the commands available here are for working with the files "behind the scenes." The navigation bar on the left side of Backstage view contains commands to perform actions common to most Office programs.

3. **Click the** Back button ⊖ **to close Backstage view and return to the document window, then click the** DESIGN tab **on the Ribbon**

   To display a different tab, click its name. Each tab contains related commands arranged into **groups** to make features easy to find. On the DESIGN tab, the Themes group displays available design themes in a **gallery**, or visual collection of choices you can browse. Many groups contain a **dialog box launcher**, which you can click to open a dialog box or pane from which to choose related commands.

4. **Move the mouse pointer** ⍩ **over the** Ion theme **in the Themes group as shown in** FIGURE A-6, **but** *do not click* **the mouse button**

   The Ion theme is temporarily applied to the slide in the document window. However, because you did not click the theme, you did not permanently change the slide. With the **Live Preview** feature, you can point to a choice, see the results, then decide if you want to make the change. Live Preview is available throughout Office.

5. **Move** ⍩ **away from the Ribbon and towards the slide**

   If you had clicked the Ion theme, it would be applied to this slide. Instead, the slide remains unchanged.

6. **Point to the** Zoom slider ▬─────┃─────+ 100% **on the status bar, then drag to the right until the Zoom level reads** 166%

   The slide display is enlarged. Zoom tools are located on the status bar. You can drag the slider or click the Zoom In or Zoom Out buttons to zoom in or out on an area of interest. **Zooming in** (a higher percentage), makes a document appear bigger on screen but less of it fits on the screen at once; **zooming out** (a lower percentage) lets you see more of the document at a reduced size.

7. **Click the** Zoom Out button ▬ **on the status bar to the left of the Zoom slider until the Zoom level reads** 120%

FIGURE A-5: PowerPoint program window

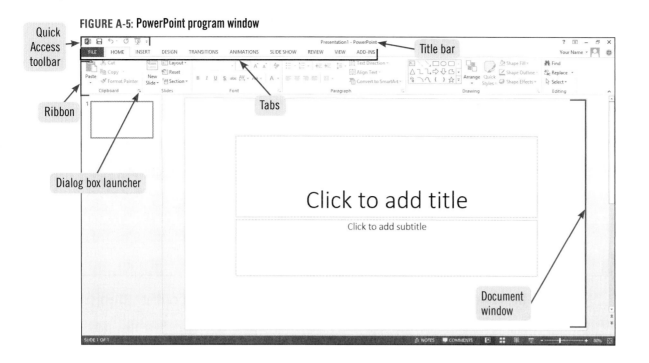

FIGURE A-6: Viewing a theme with Live Preview

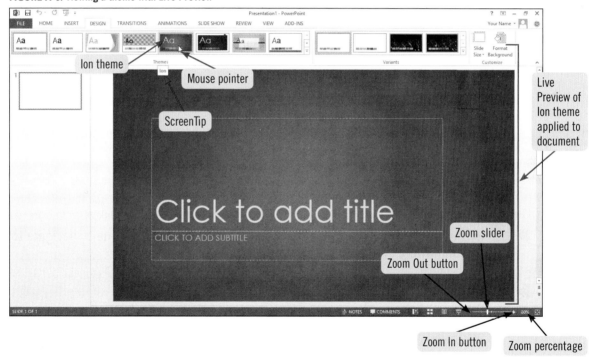

Using Backstage view

Backstage view in each Microsoft Office program offers "one stop shopping" for many commonly performed tasks, such as opening and saving a file, printing and previewing a document, defining document properties, sharing information, and exiting a program. Backstage view opens when you click the FILE tab in any Office program, and while features such as the Ribbon, Mini toolbar, and Live Preview all help you work *in* your documents, the FILE tab and Backstage view help you work *with* your documents. You can return to your active document by pressing the Back button.

Create and Save a File

When working in an Office program, one of the first things you need to do is to create and save a file. A **file** is a stored collection of data. Saving a file enables you to work on a project now, then put it away and work on it again later. In some Office programs, including Word, Excel, and PowerPoint, you can open a new file when you start the program, then all you have to do is enter some data and save it. In Access, you must create a file before you enter any data. You should give your files meaningful names and save them in an appropriate location, such as a folder on your hard drive or SkyDrive so they're easy to find. **SkyDrive** is the Microsoft cloud storage system that lets you easily save, share, and access your files from anywhere you have Internet access. See "Saving Files to SkyDrive" for more information on this topic. **CASE** ▶ *Use Word to familiarize yourself with creating and saving a document. First you'll type some notes about a possible location for a corporate meeting, then you'll save the information for later use.*

STEPS

1. **Click the** Word program button 📄 **on the taskbar, click** Blank document, **then click the** Zoom In button ➕ **until the level is 120%, if necessary**

2. **Type** Locations for Corporate Meeting, **then press [Enter] twice**
   The text appears in the document window, and the **insertion point** blinks on a new blank line. The insertion point indicates where the next typed text will appear.

3. **Type** Las Vegas, NV, **press [Enter], type** San Diego, CA, **press [Enter], type** Seattle, WA, **press [Enter] twice, then type your name**

4. **Click the** Save button 💾 **on the Quick Access toolbar**
   Backstage view opens showing various options for saving the file, as shown in **FIGURE A-7**.

5. **Click** Computer, **then click** Browse
   Because this is the first time you are saving this document, the Save As command is displayed. Once you choose a location where you will save the file, the Save As dialog box displays, as shown in **FIGURE A-8**. Once a file is saved, clicking 💾 saves any changes to the file *without* opening the Save As dialog box. The Address bar in the Save As dialog box displays the default location for saving the file, but you can change it to any location. The File name field contains a suggested name for the document based on text in the file, but you can enter a different name.

6. **Type** OF A-Potential Corporate Meeting Locations
   The text you type replaces the highlighted text. (The "OF A-" in the filename indicates that the file is created in Office Unit A. You will see similar designations throughout this book when files are named.)

7. **In the Save As dialog box, use the Address bar or Navigation Pane to navigate to the location where you store your Data Files**
   You can store files on your computer, a network drive, your SkyDrive, or any acceptable storage device.

8. **Click** Save
   The Save As dialog box closes, the new file is saved to the location you specified, and the name of the document appears in the title bar, as shown in **FIGURE A-9**. (You may or may not see the file extension ".docx" after the filename.) See **TABLE A-1** for a description of the different types of files you create in Office, and the file extensions associated with each.

TABLE A-1: Common filenames and default file extensions

file created in	is called a	and has the default extension
Word	document	.docx
Excel	workbook	.xlsx
PowerPoint	presentation	.pptx
Access	database	.accdb

FIGURE A-7: Save As screen in Backstage view

FIGURE A-8: Save As dialog box

FIGURE A-9: Saved and named Word document

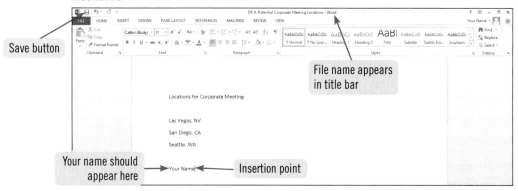

Saving files to SkyDrive

All Office programs include the capability to incorporate feedback—called **online collaboration**—across the Internet or a company network. Using **cloud computing** (work done in a virtual environment), you can take advantage of commonly shared features such as a consistent interface. Using SkyDrive, a free file storage service from Microsoft, you and your colleagues can create and store documents in the cloud and make the documents available anywhere there is Internet access to whomever you choose. To use SkyDrive, you need a free Microsoft Account, which you obtain at the signup.live.com website. You can find more information about SkyDrive in the "Working in the Cloud" appendix. When you are logged into your Microsoft account and you save a file in any of

the Office apps, the first option in the Save As screen is your SkyDrive. Double-click your SkyDrive option and the Save As dialog box opens displaying a location in the address bar unique to your SkyDrive account. Type a name in the File name text box, then click Save and your file is saved to your SkyDrive. To sync your files with SkyDrive, you'll need to download and install the SkyDrive for Windows app. Then, when you open Explorer, you'll notice a new folder called SkyDrive has been added to the Users folder. In this folder is a sub-folder called Documents, in which an updated copy of your Office app files resides. This means if your Internet connection fails, you can work on your files offline. The SkyDrive folder also displays Explorer in the list of Favorites folders.

Office 2013

Open a File and Save It with a New Name

Learning Outcomes
- Open an existing file
- Save a file with a new name

In many cases as you work in Office, you start with a blank document, but often you need to use an existing file. It might be a file you or a coworker created earlier as a work in progress, or it could be a complete document that you want to use as the basis for another. For example, you might want to create a budget for this year using the budget you created last year; instead of typing in all the categories and information from scratch, you could open last year's budget, save it with a new name, and just make changes to update it for the current year. By opening the existing file and saving it with the Save As command, you create a duplicate that you can modify to suit your needs, while the original file remains intact. **CASE** ▸ *Use Excel to open an existing workbook file, and save it with a new name so the original remains unchanged.*

STEPS

TROUBLE
If you are running WIndows 7, click the Start button on the taskbar, type excel, then click Excel 2013.

1. **Go to the Windows 8 Start screen, type exc, click Excel 2013, click Open Other Workbooks, click Computer on the navigation bar, then click Browse**

   The Open dialog box opens, where you can navigate to any drive or folder accessible to your computer to locate a file. You can click Recent Workbooks on the navigation bar to display a list of recent workbooks; click a file in the list to open it.

2. **In the Open dialog box, navigate to the location where you store your Data Files**

   The files available in the current folder are listed, as shown in **FIGURE A-10**. This folder displays one file.

TROUBLE
Click Enable Editing on the Protected View bar near the top of your document window if prompted.

3. **Click OFFICE A-1.xlsx, then click Open**

   The dialog box closes, and the file opens in Excel. An Excel file is an electronic spreadsheet, so the new file displays a grid of rows and columns you can use to enter and organize data.

4. **Click the FILE tab, click Save As on the navigation bar, then click Browse**

   The Save As dialog box opens, and the current filename is highlighted in the File name text box. Using the Save As command enables you to create a copy of the current, existing file with a new name. This action preserves the original file and creates a new file that you can modify.

5. **Navigate to the location where you store your Data Files if necessary, type OF A-Budget for Corporate Meeting in the File name text box, as shown in FIGURE A-11, then click Save**

   A copy of the existing workbook is created with the new name. The original file, Office A-1.xlsx, closes automatically.

6. **Click cell A19, type your name, then press [Enter], as shown in FIGURE A-12**

   In Excel, you enter data in cells, which are formed by the intersection of a row and a column. Cell A19 is at the intersection of column A and row 19. When you press [Enter], the cell pointer moves to cell A20.

7. **Click the Save button 🖫 on the Quick Access toolbar**

   Your name appears in the workbook, and your changes to the file are saved.

Exploring File Open options

You might have noticed that the Open button in the Open dialog box includes a list arrow to the right of the button. In a dialog box, if a button includes a list arrow you can click the button to invoke the command, or you can click the list arrow to see a list of related commands that you can apply to a selected file in the file list. The Open list arrow includes several related commands, including Open Read-Only and Open as Copy.

Clicking Open Read-Only opens a file that you can only save with a new name; you cannot make changes to the original file. Clicking Open as Copy creates and opens a copy of the selected file and inserts the word "Copy" in the file's title. Like the Save As command, these commands provide additional ways to use copies of existing files while ensuring that original files do not get changed by mistake.

FIGURE A-10: Open dialog box

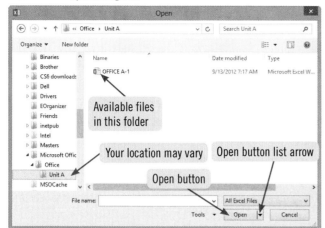

Available files in this folder

Your location may vary

Open button list arrow

Open button

FIGURE A-11: Save As dialog box

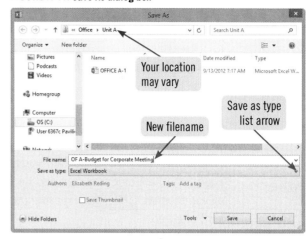

Your location may vary

Save as type list arrow

New filename

FIGURE A-12: Your name added to the workbook

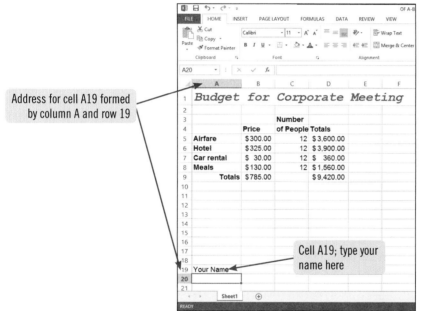

Address for cell A19 formed by column A and row 19

Cell A19; type your name here

Working in Compatibility Mode

Not everyone upgrades to the newest version of Office. As a general rule, new software versions are **backward compatible**, meaning that documents saved by an older version can be read by newer software. To open documents created in older Office versions, Office 2013 includes a feature called Compatibility Mode. When you use Office 2013 to open a file created in an earlier version of Office, "Compatibility Mode" appears in the title bar, letting you know the file was created in an earlier but usable version of the program. If you are working with someone who may not be using the newest version of the software, you can avoid possible incompatibility problems by saving your file in another, earlier format. To do this in an Office program, click the FILE tab, click Save As on the navigation bar, click the location where you want to save the file, then click Browse. In the Save As dialog box, click the Save as type list arrow in the Save As dialog box, then click an option on the list. For example, if you're working in Excel, click Excel 97-2003 Workbook format in the Save as type list to save an Excel file so it can be opened in Excel 97 or Excel 2003.

View and Print Your Work

Learning Outcomes
• Describe and change views in an app
• Print a document

Each Microsoft Office program lets you switch among various **views** of the document window to show more or fewer details or a different combination of elements that make it easier to complete certain tasks, such as formatting or reading text. Changing your view of a document does not affect the file in any way, it affects only the way it looks on screen. If your computer is connected to a printer or a print server, you can easily print any Office document using the Print button on the Print tab in Backstage view. Printing can be as simple as **previewing** the document to see exactly what a document will look like when it is printed and then clicking the Print button. Or, you can customize the print job by printing only selected pages. The Backstage view can also be used to share your document with others, or to export it in a different format. **CASE** *Experiment with changing your view of a Word document, and then preview and print your work.*

STEPS

1. **Click the Word program button [icon] on the taskbar**

   Word becomes the active program, and the document fills the screen.

QUICK TIP

To minimize the display of the buttons and commands on tabs, click the Collapse the Ribbon button (>) on the lower-right end of the Ribbon.

2. **Click the VIEW tab on the Ribbon**

   In most Office programs, the VIEW tab on the Ribbon includes groups and commands for changing your view of the current document. You can also change views using the View buttons on the status bar.

3. **Click the Read Mode button in the Views group on the VIEW tab**

   The view changes to Read Mode view, as shown in **FIGURE A-13**. This view shows the document in an easy-to-read, distraction-free reading mode. Notice that the Ribbon is no longer visible on screen.

4. **Click the Print Layout button [icon] on the Status bar**

   You return to Print Layout view, the default view in Word.

5. **Click the FILE tab, then click Print on the navigation bar**

   The Print tab opens in Backstage view. The preview pane on the right side of the window displays a preview of how your document will look when printed. Compare your screen to **FIGURE A-14**. Options in the Settings section enable you to change margins, orientation, and paper size before printing. To change a setting, click it, and then click a new setting. For instance, to change from Letter paper size to Legal, click Letter in the Settings section, then click Legal on the menu that opens. The document preview updates as you change the settings. You also can use the Settings section to change which pages to print. If your computer is connected to multiple printers, you can click the current printer in the Printer section, then click the one you want to use. The Print section contains the Print button and also enables you to select the number of copies of the document to print.

QUICK TIP

You can add the Quick Print button [icon] to the Quick Access toolbar by clicking the Customize Quick Access Toolbar button, then clicking Quick Print. The Quick Print button prints one copy of your document using the default settings.

6. **If your school allows printing, click the Print button in the Print section (otherwise, click the Back button [icon])**

   If you chose to print, a copy of the document prints, and Backstage view closes.

Customizing the Quick Access toolbar

You can customize the Quick Access toolbar to display your favorite commands. To do so, click the Customize Quick Access Toolbar button [icon] in the title bar, then click the command you want to add. If you don't see the command in the list, click More Commands to open the Quick Access Toolbar tab of the current program's Options dialog box. In the Options dialog box, use the Choose commands from list to choose a category, click the desired command in the list on the left, click Add to add it to the Quick Access toolbar, then click OK. To remove a button from the toolbar, click the name in the list on the right in the Options dialog box, then click Remove. To add a command to the Quick Access toolbar as you work, simply right-click the button on the Ribbon, then click Add to Quick Access Toolbar on the shortcut menu. To move the Quick Access toolbar below the Ribbon, click the Customize Quick Access Toolbar button, and then click Show Below the Ribbon.

FIGURE A-13: Web Layout view

FIGURE A-14: Print settings on the FILE tab

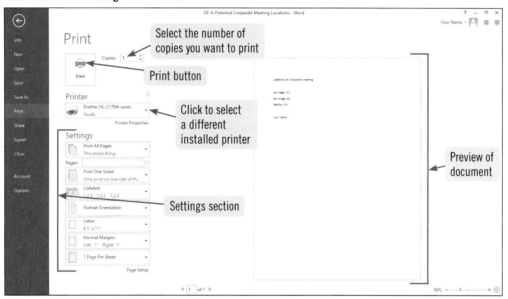

Creating a screen capture

A **screen capture** is a digital image of your screen, as if you took a picture of it with a camera. For instance, you might want to take a screen capture if an error message occurs and you want a Technical Support person to see exactly what's on the screen. You can create a screen capture using features found in Windows 8 or Office 2013. Both Windows 7 and Windows 8 come with the Snipping Tool, a separate program designed to capture whole screens or portions of screens. To open the Snipping Tool, click the Start screen thumbnail, type "sni", then click the Snipping Tool when it appears in the left panel. After opening the Snipping Tool, click New, then drag the pointer on the screen to select the area of the screen you want to capture. When you release the mouse button, the screen capture opens in the Snipping Tool window, and you can save, copy, or send it in an email. In Word, Excel, and PowerPoint 2013, you can capture screens or portions of screens and insert them in the current document using the Screenshot button in the Illustrations group on the INSERT tab. And finally, you can create a screen capture by pressing [PrtScn]. (Keyboards differ, but you may find the [PrtScn] button in or near your keyboard's function keys.) Pressing this key places a digital image of your screen in the Windows temporary storage area known as the **Clipboard**. Open the document where you want the screen capture to appear, click the HOME tab on the Ribbon (if necessary), then click the Paste button in the Clipboard group on the HOME tab. The screen capture is pasted into the document.

Office 2013

Get Help, Close a File, and Exit an App

Learning
Outcomes
• Display a
ScreenTip
• Use Help
• Close a file
• Exit an app

You can get comprehensive help at any time by pressing [F1] in an Office app or clicking the Help button on the right end of the title bar. You can also get help in the form of a ScreenTip by pointing to almost any icon in the program window. When you're finished working in an Office document, you have a few choices regarding ending your work session. You close a file by clicking the FILE tab, then clicking Close; you exit a program by clicking the Close button on the title bar. Closing a file leaves a program running, while exiting a program closes all the open files in that program as well as the program itself. In all cases, Office reminds you if you try to close a file or exit a program and your document contains unsaved changes. **CASE** ▶ *Explore the Help system in Microsoft Office, and then close your documents and exit any open programs.*

STEPS

1. **Point to the Zoom button in the Zoom group on the VIEW tab of the Ribbon**
   A ScreenTip appears that describes how the Zoom button works and explains where to find other zoom controls.

QUICK TIP
You can also open Help (in any of the Office apps) by pressing [F1].

2. **Click the Microsoft Word Help (F1) button ⁇ in the upper-right corner of the title bar**
   The Word Help window opens, as shown in **FIGURE A-15**, displaying the home page for help in Word. Each entry is a hyperlink you can click to open a list of topics. The Help window also includes a toolbar of useful Help commands such as printing and increasing the font size for easier readability, and a Search field. If you are not connected to Office.com, a gold band is displayed telling you that you are not connected. Office.com supplements the help content available on your computer with a wide variety of up-to-date topics, templates, and training. If you are not connected to the Internet, the Help window displays only the help content available on your computer.

3. **Click the Learn Word basics link in the Getting started section of the Word Help window**
   The Word Help window changes, and a list of basic tasks appears below the topic.

4. **If necessary, scroll down until the Choose a template topic fills the Word Help window**
   The topic is displayed in the pane of the Help window, as shown in **FIGURE A-16**. The content in the window explains that you can create a document using a template (a pre-formatted document) or just create a blank document.

QUICK TIP
You can print the entire current topic by clicking the Print button 🖶 on the Help toolbar, then clicking Print in the Print dialog box.

5. **Click in the Search online help text box, type Delete, then press [Enter]**
   The Word Help window now displays a list of links to topics about different types of deletions that are possible within Word.

6. **Click the Keep Help on Top button 📌 in the upper-right corner (below the Close button)**
   The Pin Help button rotates so the pin point is pointed towards the bottom of the screen: this allows you to read the Help window while you work on your document.

7. **Click the Word document window, then notice the Help window remains visible**

8. **Click a blank area of the Help window, click 📌 to Unpin Help, click the Close button ✕ in the Help window, then click the Close button ✕ in the upper-right corner of the screen**
   Word closes, and the Excel program window is active.

9. **Click the Close button ✕ to exit Excel, click the Close button ✕ to exit the remaining Excel workbook, click the PowerPoint program button 📰 on the taskbar if necessary, then click the Close button ✕ to exit PowerPoint**
   Excel and PowerPoint both close.

FIGURE A-15: Word Help window

FIGURE A-16: Create a document Help topic

Enabling touch mode

If you are using a touch screen with any of the Office 2013 apps, you can enable the touch mode to give the user interface a more spacious look. Enable touch mode by clicking the Quick Access toolbar list arrow, then clicking Touch/Mouse Mode to select it. Then you'll see the Touch Mode button in the Quick Access toolbar. Click , and you'll see the interface spread out.

Recovering a document

Each Office program has a built-in recovery feature that allows you to open and save files that were open at the time of an interruption such as a power failure. When you restart the program(s) after an interruption, the Document Recovery task pane opens on the left side of your screen displaying both original and recovered versions of the files that were open. If you're not sure which file to open (original or recovered), it's usually better to open the recovered file because it will contain the latest information. You can, however, open and review all versions of the file that were recovered and save the best one. Each file listed in the Document Recovery task pane displays a list arrow with options that allow you to open the file, save it as is, delete it, or show repairs made to it during recovery.

Office 2013

Practice

Concepts Review

Label the elements of the program window shown in FIGURE A-17.

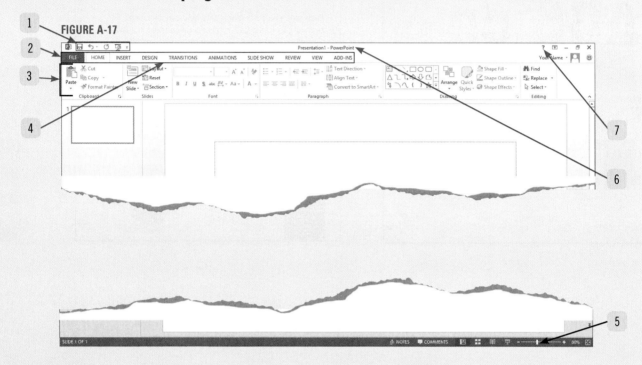

FIGURE A-17

Match each project with the program for which it is best suited.

8. Microsoft Access
9. Microsoft Excel
10. Microsoft Word
11. Microsoft PowerPoint

a. Corporate convention budget with expense projections
b. Presentation for city council meeting
c. Business cover letter for a job application
d. Department store inventory

Independent Challenge 1

You just accepted an administrative position with a local independently owned produce vendor that has recently invested in computers and is now considering purchasing Microsoft Office for the company. You are asked to propose ways Office might help the business. You produce your document in Word.

a. Start Word, create a new Blank document, then save the document as **OF A-Microsoft Office Document** in the location where you store your Data Files.

b. Change the zoom factor to 120%, type **Microsoft Word**, press [Enter] twice, type **Microsoft Excel**, press [Enter] twice, type **Microsoft PowerPoint**, press [Enter] twice, type **Microsoft Access**, press [Enter] twice, then type your name.

c. Click the line beneath each program name, type at least two tasks you can perform using that program (each separated by a comma), then press [Enter].

d. Save the document, then submit your work to your instructor as directed.

e. Exit Word.

Getting Started with Access 2013

> **CASE** ▶ Samantha Hooper is the tour developer for United States group travel at Quest Specialty Travel (QST), a tour company that specializes in customized group travel packages. Samantha uses Microsoft Access 2013 to store, maintain, and analyze customer and tour information.

Unit Objectives

After completing this unit, you will be able to:

- Understand relational databases
- Explore a database
- Create a database
- Create a table

- Create primary keys
- Relate two tables
- Enter data
- Edit data

Files You Will Need

QuestTravel-A.accdb
RealEstate-A.accdb
Recycle-A.accdb
BusinessContacts-A.accdb
Basketball-A.accdb

Access 2013

UNIT A

Learning
Outcomes
• Describe relational
database concepts
• Explain when to
use a database

Understand Relational Databases

Microsoft Access 2013 is relational database software that runs on the Windows operating system. You use **relational database software** to manage data that is organized into lists, such as information about customers, products, vendors, employees, projects, or sales. Many small companies track customer, inventory, and sales information in a spreadsheet program such as Microsoft Excel. Although Excel offers some list management features and is more commonly used than Access, Access provides many more tools and advantages for managing data. The advantages are mainly due to the "relational" nature of the lists that Access manages. **TABLE A-1** compares the two programs. **CASE** *You and Samantha Hooper review the advantages of database software over spreadsheets for managing lists of information.*

DETAILS

The advantages of using Access for database management include:

- **Duplicate data is minimized**

  FIGURES A-1 and **A-2** compare how you might store sales data in a single Excel spreadsheet list versus three related Access tables. With Access, you do not have to reenter information such as a customer's name and address or tour name every time a sale is made, because lists can be linked, or "related," in relational database software.

- **Information is more accurate, reliable, and consistent because duplicate data is minimized**

  The relational nature of data stored in an Access database allows you to minimize duplicate data entry, which creates more accurate, reliable, and consistent information. For example, customer data in a Customers table is entered only once, not every time a customer makes a purchase.

- **Data entry is faster and easier using Access forms**

  Data entry forms (screen layouts) make data entry faster, easier, and more accurate than entering data in a spreadsheet.

- **Information can be viewed and sorted in many ways using Access queries, forms, and reports**

  In Access, you can save queries (questions about the data), data entry forms, and reports, allowing you to use them over and over without performing extra work to re-create a particular view of the data.

- **Information is more secure using Access passwords and security features**

  Access databases can be encrypted and password protected.

- **Several users can share and edit information at the same time**

  Unlike spreadsheets or word-processing documents, more than one person can enter, update, and analyze data in an Access database at the same time.

FIGURE A-1: Using a spreadsheet to organize sales data

	A	B	C	D	E	F	G	H	I
1	CustNo	FName	LName	SalesNo	SaleDate	TourName	TourStartDate	City	Price
2	1	Gracita	Mayberry	35	7/1/2014	Red Reef Scuba	7/6/2014	Islamadora	1,500.00
3	2	Jacob	Alman	34	7/1/2014	Red Reef Scuba	7/6/2014	Islamadora	1,500.00
4	3	Julia	Bouchart	33	7/1/2014	Red Reef Scuba	7/6/2014	Islamadora	1,500.00
5	3	Julia	Bouchart	7	5/1/2014	Piper-Heitman Wedding	5/30/2014	Captiva	825.00
6	4	Jane	Taylor	13	5/11/2014	Red Reef Scuba	7/6/2014	Islamadora	1,500.00
7	4	Jane	Taylor	20	6/1/2014	American Heritage Tour	8/24/2014	Philadelphia	1,200.00
8	5	Samantha	Braven	30	7/1/2014	Red Reef Scuba	7/6/2014	Islamadora	1,500.00
9	5	Samantha	Braven	52	7/11/2014	Bright Lights Expo	12/1/2014	Branson	200.00
10	6	Kristen	Collins	3	4/30/2014	Ames Ski Club	1/2/2015	Breckenridge	850.00
11	6	Kristen	Collins	21	6/1/2014	Yosemite National Park Great Cleanup	7/20/2014	Sacramento	1,100.00
12	6	Kristen	Collins	29	7/1/2014	American Heritage Tour	8/24/2014	Philadelphia	1,200.00
13	6	Kristen	Collins	40	7/7/2014	Bright Lights Expo	12/1/2014	Branson	200.00
14	7	Tom	Camel	41	7/7/2014	Bright Lights Expo	12/1/2014	Branson	200.00
15	7	Tom	Camel	36	7/1/2014	American Heritage Tour	8/24/2014	Philadelphia	1,200.00
16	7	Tom	Camel	8	5/1/2014	Ames Ski Club	1/2/2015	Breckenridge	850.00
17	7	Tom	Camel	19	6/1/2014	Yosemite National Park Great Cleanup	7/20/2014	Sacramento	1,100.00
18	8	Dick	Tracy	43	7/8/2014	Bright Lights Expo	12/1/2014	Branson	200.00
19	9	Daniel	Cabriella	45	7/9/2014	American Heritage Tour	8/24/2014	Philadelphia	1,200.00
20	9	Daniel	Cabriella	46	7/9/2014	Bright Lights Expo	12/1/2014	Branson	200.00
21	10	Brad	Eahlie	66	7/14/2014	Boy Scout Jamboree	1/13/2015	Vail	1,900.00
22	11	Nancy	Diverman	32	7/1/2014	Red Reef Scuba	7/6/2014	Islamadora	1,500.00

Customer information is duplicated when the same customer purchases multiple tours

Tour information is duplicated when the same tour is purchased by multiple customers

FIGURE A-2: Using a relational database to organize sales data

Customers table

Cust No	First	Last	Street	City	State	Zip	Phone
1	Gracita	Mayberry	52411 Oakmont Rd	Kansas City	MO	64144	(555) 444-1234
2	Jacob	Alman	2505 McGee St	Des Moines	IA	50288	(555) 111-6931
3	Julia	Bouchart	5200 Main St	Kansas City	MO	64105	(555) 111-3081

Sales table

Cust No	TourNo	Date	SalesNo
1	2	7/1/14	35
2	2	7/1/14	34
3	2	7/1/14	33

Tours table

TourNo	TourName	TourStartDate	Duration	City	Cost
1	Stanley Bay Shelling	07/06/2014	3	Captiva	$750.00
2	Red Reef Scuba	07/06/2014	3	Islamadora	$1,500.00
3	Ames Ski Club	01/02/2015	7	Breckenridge	$850.00

TABLE A-1: Comparing Excel with Access

feature	Excel	Access
Layout	Provides a natural tabular layout for easy data entry	Provides a natural tabular layout as well as the ability to create customized data entry screens called forms
Storage	Restricted to a file's limitations	Virtually unlimited when coupled with the ability to use Microsoft SQL Server to store data
Linked tables	Manages single lists of information—no relational database capabilities	Relates lists of information to reduce data redundancy and create a relational database
Reporting	Limited	Provides the ability to create an unlimited number of reports
Security	Limited to file security options such as marking the file "read-only" or protecting a range of cells	When used with SQL Server, provides extensive security down to the user and data level
Multiuser capabilities	Not allowed	Allows multiple users to simultaneously enter and update data
Data entry	Provides limited data entry screens	Provides the ability to create an unlimited number of data entry forms

© 2014 Cengage Learning

Explore a Database

Learning
Outcomes
• Start Access and
open a database
• Identify Access
components
• Open and define
Access objects

You can start Access in many ways. If you double-click an existing Access *database* icon or shortcut, that specific database will open directly within Access. This is the fastest way to open an *existing* Access database. If you start Access on its own, however, you see a window that requires you to make a choice between opening a database and creating a new database. **CASE** *Samantha Hooper has developed a database called QuestTravel-A, which contains tour information. She asks you to start Access 2013 and review this database.*

STEPS

1. **Start Access**

   Access starts, as shown in **FIGURE A-3**. This window allows you to open an existing database, create a new database from a template, or create a new blank database.

   TROUBLE
   If a yellow Security
   Warning bar appears
   below the Ribbon,
   click Enable Content.

2. **Click the Open Other Files link, navigate to the location where you store your Data Files, click the QuestTravel-A.accdb database, click Open, then click the Maximize button ☐ if the Access window is not already maximized**

   The QuestTravel-A.accdb database contains five tables of data named Customers, Sales, States, TourCategories, and Tours. It also contains six queries, six forms, and four reports. Each of these items (table, query, form, and report) is a different type of **object** in an Access database and is displayed in the **Navigation Pane**. The purpose of each object is defined in **TABLE A-2**. To learn about an Access database, you explore its objects.

   TROUBLE
   If the Navigation
   Pane is not open,
   click the Shutter Bar
   Open/Close button
   ⏩ to open it and
   view the database
   objects.

3. **In the Navigation Pane, double-click the Tours table to open it, then double-click the Customers table to open it**

   The Tours and Customers tables open to display the data they store. A **table** is the fundamental building block of a relational database because it stores all of the data. You can enter or edit data in a table.

4. **In the Navigation Pane, double-click the TourSales query to open it, double-click any occurrence of Heritage (as in American Heritage Tour), type Legacy, then click any other row**

   A **query** selects a subset of data from one or more tables. In this case, the TourSales query selects data from the Tours, Sales, and Customers tables. Editing data in one object changes that information in every other object of the database, demonstrating the power and productivity of a relational database.

5. **Double-click the CustomerRoster form to open it, double-click Tour in "American Legacy Tour," type Rally, then click any name in the middle part of the window**

   An Access **form** is a data entry screen. Users prefer forms for data entry (rather than editing and entering data in tables and queries) because information can be presented in an easy-to-use layout.

6. **Double-click the TourSales report to open it**

   An Access **report** is a professional printout. A report is for printing purposes only, not data entry. As shown in **FIGURE A-4**, the edits made to the American Legacy Rally tour name have carried through to the report.

7. **Click the Close button ☒ in the upper-right corner of the window**

   Clicking the Close button in the upper-right corner of the window closes Access as well as the database on which you are working. Changes to data, such as the edits you made to the American Legacy Rally tour, are automatically saved as you work. Access will prompt you to save *design* changes to objects before it closes.

FIGURE A-3: Opening Microsoft Access 2013 window

Use Custom web app to create a Web-enabled database

Click a database name to open a recently used database; your list will differ

Click to browse for an Access database

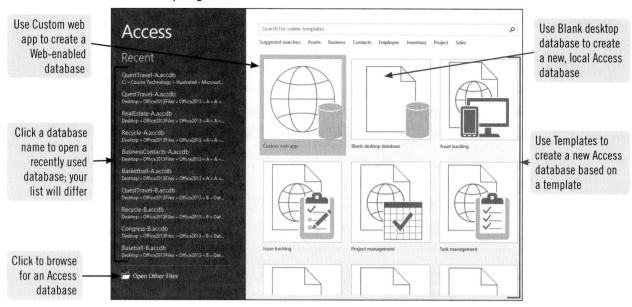

Use Blank desktop database to create a new, local Access database

Use Templates to create a new Access database based on a template

FIGURE A-4: Objects in the QuestTravel-A database

Shutter Bar Open/ Close button

Navigation Pane

Tours table tab

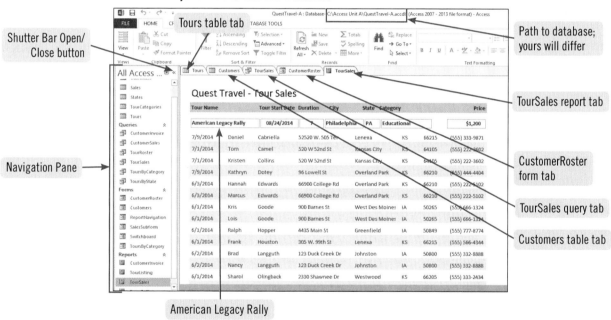

American Legacy Rally

Path to database; yours will differ

TourSales report tab

CustomerRoster form tab

TourSales query tab

Customers table tab

TABLE A-2: Access objects and their purpose

object	icon	purpose
Table		Contains all of the raw data within the database in a spreadsheet-like view; tables are linked with a common field to create a relational database, which minimizes redundant data
Query		Allows you to select a subset of fields or records from one or more tables; queries are created when you have a question about the data
Form		Provides an easy-to-use data entry screen
Report		Provides a professional printout of data that can contain enhancements such as headers, footers, graphics, and calculations on groups of records

© 2014 Cengage Learning

Create a Database

Learning
Outcomes
• Create a database
• Create a table
• Define key data-
  base terms

You can create a database using an Access **template**, a sample database provided within the Microsoft Access program, or you can start with a blank database to create a database from scratch. Your decision depends on whether Access has a template that closely resembles the type of data you plan to manage. If it does, building your own database from a template might be faster than creating the database from scratch. Regardless of which method you use, you can always modify the database later, tailoring it to meet your specific needs. **CASE** ▶ *Samantha Hooper reasons that the best way for you to learn Access is to start a new database from scratch, so she asks you to create a new database that will track customer communication.*

STEPS

1. **Start Access**

2. **Click the** Blank desktop database icon, **click the** Browse button 📁, **navigate to the location where you store your Data Files, type** Quest **in the File name box, click** OK, **then click the** Create button

   A new, blank database file with a single table named Table1 is created, as shown in **FIGURE A-5**. Although you might be tempted to start entering data into the table, a better way to build a table is to first define the columns, or **fields**, of data that the table will store. **Table Design View** provides the most options for defining fields.

3. **Click the** View button ☑ **on the FIELDS tab to switch to Design View, type** Customers **in the Save As dialog box as the new table name, then click** OK

   The table name changes from Table1 to Customers, and you are positioned in Table Design View, a window you use to name and define the fields of a table. Access created a field named ID with an AutoNumber data type. The **data type** is a significant characteristic of a field because it determines what type of data the field can store such as text, dates, or numbers. See **TABLE A-3** for more information about data types.

4. **Type** CustID **to rename ID to CustID, press** [↓] **to move to the first blank Field Name cell, type** FirstName, **press** [↓], **type** LastName, **press** [↓], **type** Phone, **press** [↓], **type** Birthday, **then press** [↓]

   Be sure to separate the first and last names into two fields so that you can easily sort, find, and filter on either part of the name later. The Birthday field will only contain dates, so you should change its data type from Short Text (the default data type) to Date/Time.

5. **Click** Short Text **in the Birthday row, click the** list arrow, **then click** Date/Time

   With these five fields properly defined for the new Customers table, as shown in **FIGURE A-6**, you're ready to enter data. You switch back to Datasheet View to enter or edit data. **Datasheet View** is a spreadsheet-like view of the data in a table. A **datasheet** is a grid that displays fields as columns and records as rows. The new **field names** you just defined are listed at the top of each column.

6. **Click the** View button 🔲 **to switch to Datasheet View, click** Yes **when prompted to save the table, press** [Tab] **to move to the FirstName field, type** *your* **first name, press** [Tab] **to move to the LastName field, type** *your* **last name, press** [Tab] **to move to the Phone field, type** 111-222-3333, **press** [Tab], **type** 1/32/1980, **then press** [Tab]

   Because 1/32/1980 is not a valid date, Access does not allow you to make that entry and displays an error message, as shown in **FIGURE A-7**. This shows that selecting the best data type for each field in Table Design View before entering data in Datasheet View helps prevent data entry errors.

TROUBLE
Tab through the
CustID field rather
than typing a value.
The CustID value
automatically incre-
ments to the next
number.

7. **Press** [Esc], **edit the Birthday entry for the first record to** 1/31/1980, **press** [Tab], **enter two more sample records using realistic data, right-click the** Customers **table tab, then click** Close **to close the Customers table**

FIGURE A-5: Creating a database with a new table

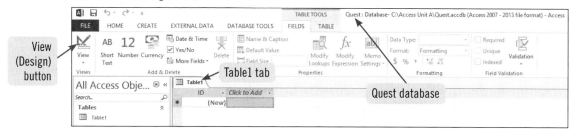

FIGURE A-6: Defining field names and data types for the Customers table in Table Design View

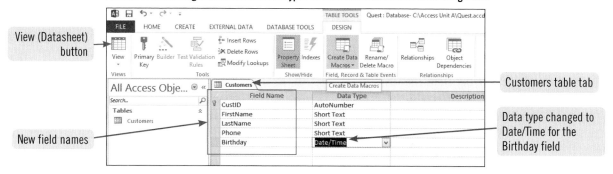

FIGURE A-7: Entering your first record in the Customers table

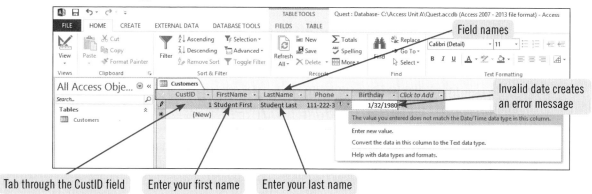

TABLE A-3: Data types

data type	description of data
Short Text	Text or numbers not used in calculations such as a name, zip code, or phone number
Long Text	Lengthy text greater than 255 characters, such as comments or notes
Number	Numeric data that can be used in calculations, such as quantities
Date/Time	Dates and times
Currency	Monetary values
AutoNumber	Sequential integers controlled by Access
Yes/No	Only two values: Yes or No
OLE Object	OLE (Object Linking and Embedding) objects such as an Excel spreadsheet or Word document
Hyperlink	Web and e-mail addresses
Attachment	External files such as .jpg images, spreadsheets, and documents
Calculated	Result of a calculation based on other fields in the table
Lookup Wizard	The Lookup Wizard helps you set Lookup properties, which display a drop-down list of values for the field; after using the Lookup Wizard, the final data type for the field is either Short Text or Number depending on the values in the drop-down list

Create a Table

Learning Outcomes
• Create a table in Table Design View
• Set appropriate data types for fields

After creating your database and first table, you need to create new, related tables to build a relational database. Creating a table consists of these essential tasks: defining the fields in the table, selecting an appropriate data type for each field, naming the table, and determining how the table will participate in the relational database. **CASE** ▶ *Samantha Hooper asks you to create another table to store customer comments. The new table will eventually be connected to the Customers table so each customer record in the Customers table may be related to many records in the Comments table.*

STEPS

1. **Click the CREATE tab on the Ribbon, then click the Table Design button in the Tables group**
   Design View is a view in which you create and manipulate the structure of an object.

2. **Enter the field names and data types, as shown in FIGURE A-8**
   The Comments table will contain four fields. CommentID is set with an AutoNumber data type so each record is automatically numbered by Access. The Comment field has a Long Text data type so a long comment can be recorded. CommentDate is a Date/Time field to identify the date of the comment. CustID has a Number data type and will be used to link the Comments table to the Customers table later.

   TROUBLE
   To rename an object, close it, right-click it in the Navigation Pane, and then click Rename.

3. **Click the View button 🔲 to switch to Datasheet View, click Yes when prompted to save the table, type Comments as the table name, click OK, then click No when prompted to create a primary key**
   A **primary key field** contains unique data for each record. You'll identify a primary key field for the Comments table later. For now, you'll enter the first record in the Comments table in Datasheet View. A **record** is a row of data in a table. Refer to **TABLE A-4** for a summary of important database terminology.

4. **Press [Tab] to move to the Comment field, type Interested in future tours to New Zealand, press [Tab], type 1/7/15 in the CommentDate field, press [Tab], then type 1 in the CustID field**
   You entered 1 in the CustID field to connect this comment with the customer in the Customers table that has a CustID value of 1. Knowing which CustID value to enter for each comment is difficult. After you relate the tables properly (a task you have not yet performed), Access can make it easier to link each comment to the correct customer.

   TROUBLE
   The CommentID field is an AutoNumber field, which will automatically increment to provide a unique value. If the number has already incremented beyond 1 for the first record, AutoNumber still works as intended.

5. **Point to the divider line between the Comment and CommentDate field names, and then drag the ↔ pointer to the right to widen the Comment field to read the entire comment, as shown in FIGURE A-9**

6. **Right-click the Comments table tab, click Close, then click Yes if prompted to save the table**

Creating a table in Datasheet View

You can also create a new table in Datasheet View using the commands on the FIELDS tab of the Ribbon. But if you use Design View to design your table before starting the data entry process, you will probably avoid some common data entry errors. Design View helps you focus on the appropriate data type for each field.

Selecting the best data type for each field before entering any data into that field helps prevent incorrect data and unintended typos. For example, if a field is given a Number, Currency, or Date/Time data type, you will not be able to enter text into that field by mistake.

FIGURE A-8: Creating the Comments table

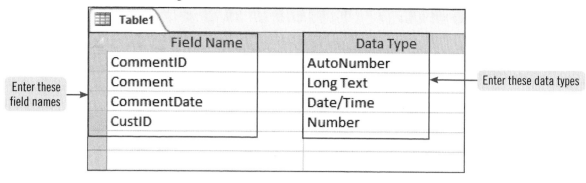

Enter these field names →

← Enter these data types

FIGURE A-9: Entering the first record in the Comments table

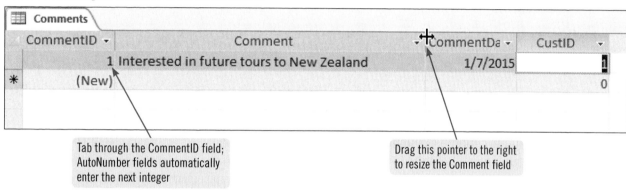

Tab through the CommentID field; AutoNumber fields automatically enter the next integer

Drag this pointer to the right to resize the Comment field

TABLE A-4: Important database terminology

term	description
Field	A specific piece or category of data such as a first name, last name, city, state, or phone number
Record	A group of related fields that describes a person, place, thing, or transaction such as a customer, location, product, or sale
Key field	A field that contains unique information for each record, such as a customer number for a customer
Table	A collection of records for a single subject such as Customers, Products, or Sales
Relational database	Multiple tables that are linked together to address a business process such as managing tours, sales, and customers at Quest Specialty Travel
Objects	The parts of an Access database that help you view, edit, manage, and analyze the data: **tables, queries, forms, reports, macros,** and **modules**

Access 2013

Create Primary Keys

Learning Outcomes
• Set the primary key field
• Define one-to-many relationships

The **primary key field** of a table serves two important purposes. First, it contains data that uniquely identifies each record. No two records can have the exact same entry in the field designated as the primary key field. Second, the primary key field helps relate one table to another in a **one-to-many relationship**, where one record from one table may be related to many records in the second table. For example, one record in the Customers table may be related to many records in the Comments table. (One customer may have many comments.) The primary key field is always on the "one" side of a one-to-many relationship between two tables. **CASE** ▶ *Samantha Hooper asks you to check that a primary key field has been appropriately identified for each table in the new Quest database.*

STEPS

1. **Right-click the** Comments table **in the Navigation Pane, then click** Design View

   Table Design View for the Comments table opens. The field with the AutoNumber data type is generally the best candidate for the primary key field in a table because it automatically contains a unique number for each record.

> **TROUBLE**
> Make sure the DESIGN tab is selected on the Ribbon.

2. **Click the** CommentID field **if it is not already selected, then click the** Primary Key button **in the Tools group on the DESIGN tab**

   The CommentID field is now set as the primary key field for the Comments table, as shown in **FIGURE A-10**.

> **QUICK TIP**
> You can also click the Save button 🔲 on the Quick Access toolbar to save a table.

3. **Right-click the** Comments table tab**, click** Close**, then click** Yes **to save the table**

   Any time you must save design changes to an Access object such as a table, Access displays a dialog box to remind you to save the object.

4. **Right-click the** Customers table **in the Navigation Pane, then click** Design View

   Access has already set CustID as the primary key field for the Customers table, as shown in **FIGURE A-11**.

5. **Right-click the** Customers table tab**, then click** Close

   You were not prompted to save the Customers table because you did not make any design changes. Now that you're sure that each table in the Quest database has an appropriate primary key field, you're ready to link the tables. The primary key field plays a critical role in this relationship.

FIGURE A-10: Creating a primary key field for the Comments table

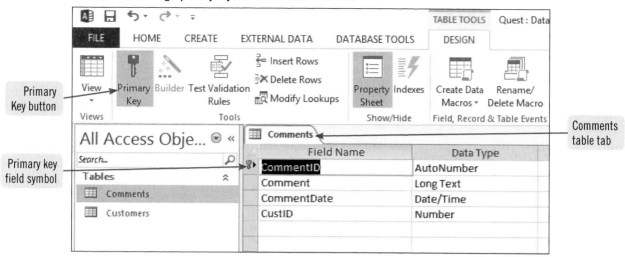

FIGURE A-11: Confirming the primary key field for the Customers table

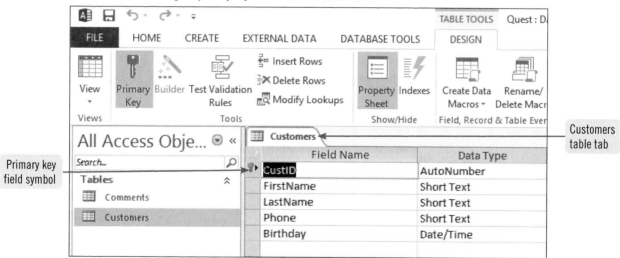

Learning about field properties

Properties are the characteristics that define the field. Two properties are required for every field: Field Name and Data Type. Many other properties, such as Field Size, Format, Caption, and Default Value, are defined in the Field Properties pane in the lower half of a table's Design View. As you add more property entries, you are generally restricting the amount or type of data that can be entered in the field, which increases data entry accuracy. For example, you might change the Field Size property for a State field to 2 to eliminate an incorrect entry such as FLL. Field properties change depending on the data type of the selected field. For example, date fields do not have a Field Size property because Access controls the size of fields with a Date/Time data type.

Relate Two Tables

Learning
Outcomes
• Define common
field and foreign
key field
• Create one-to-
many relationships
• Set referential
integrity

After you create tables and set primary key fields, you must connect the tables in one-to-many relation-ships to enjoy the benefits of a relational database. A one-to-many relationship between two tables means that one record from the first table is related to many records in the second table. You use a common field to make this connection. The common field is always the primary key field in the table on the "one" side of the relationship. **CASE** *Samantha Hooper explains that she has new comments to enter into the Quest database. To identify which customer is related to each comment, you define a one-to-many relationship between the Customers and Comments tables.*

STEPS

1. Click the DATABASE TOOLS tab on the Ribbon, then click the Relationships button

> **TROUBLE**
> If the Show Table dialog box doesn't appear, click the Show Table button on the DESIGN tab.

2. In the Show Table dialog box, double-click Customers, double-click Comments, then click Close

Each table is represented by a small **field list** window that displays the table's field names. A key sym-bol identifies the primary key field in each table. To relate the two tables in a one-to-many relationship, you connect them using a common field, which is always the primary key field on the "one" side of the relationship.

> **QUICK TIP**
> Drag a table's title bar to move the field list.

3. Drag CustID in the Customers field list to the CustID field in the Comments field list

The Edit Relationships dialog box opens, as shown in **FIGURE A-12**. **Referential integrity**, a set of Access rules that governs data entry, helps ensure data accuracy.

> **TROUBLE**
> If you need to delete an incorrect relation-ship, right-click a relationship line, then click Delete.

4. Click the Enforce Referential Integrity check box in the Edit Relationships dialog box, then click Create

The **one-to-many line** shows the link between the CustID field of the Customers table (the "one" side) and the CustID field of the Comments table (the "many" side, indicated by the **infinity symbol**), as shown in **FIGURE A-13**. The linking field on the "many" side is called the **foreign key field**. Now that these tables are related, it is much easier to enter comments for the correct customer.

> **QUICK TIP**
> To print the Relationships window, click the Relationship Report button on the DESIGN tab, then click Print.

5. Right-click the Relationships tab, click Close, click Yes to save changes, then double-click the Customers table in the Navigation Pane to open it in Datasheet View

When you relate two tables in a one-to-many relationship, expand buttons [+] appear to the left of each record in the table on the "one" side of the relationship. In this case, the Customers table is on the "one" side of the relationship.

6. Click the expand button [+] to the left of the first record

A **subdatasheet** shows the related comment records for each customer. In other words, the subdatasheet shows the records on the "many" side of a one-to-many relationship. The expand button [+] also changed to the collapse button [−] for the first customer. Widening the Comment field allows you to see the entire entry in the Comments subdatasheet. Now the task of entering comments for the correct customer is much more straightforward.

> **TROUBLE**
> Be careful to enter complete comments for the correct customer, as shown in **FIGURE A-14**.

7. Enter two more comments, as shown in FIGURE A-14

Interestingly, the CustID field in the Comments table (the foreign key field) is not displayed in the subdata-sheet. Behind the scenes, Access is entering the correct CustID value in the Comments table, which is the glue that ties each comment to the correct customer.

8. Close the Customers table, then click Yes if prompted to save changes

FIGURE A-12: Edit Relationships dialog box

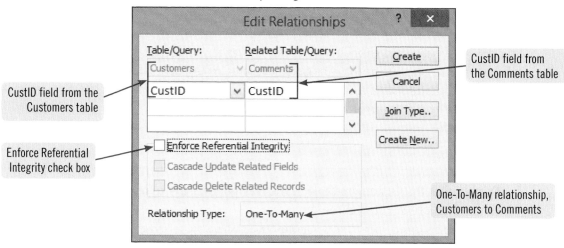

CustID field from the Customers table

Enforce Referential Integrity check box

CustID field from the Comments table

One-To-Many relationship, Customers to Comments

FIGURE A-13: Linking the Customers and Comments tables

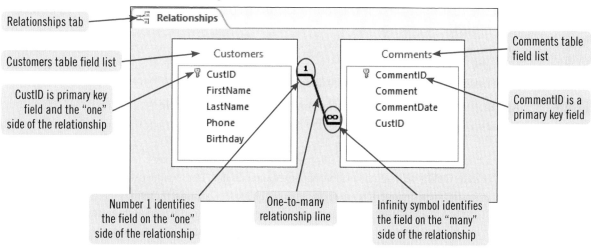

Relationships tab

Customers table field list

CustID is primary key field and the "one" side of the relationship

Comments table field list

CommentID is a primary key field

Number 1 identifies the field on the "one" side of the relationship

One-to-many relationship line

Infinity symbol identifies the field on the "many" side of the relationship

FIGURE A-14: Entering comments using the subdatasheet

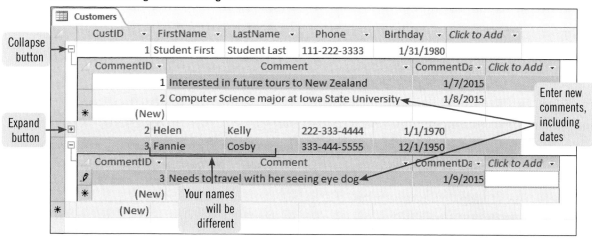

Collapse button

Expand button

Enter new comments, including dates

Your names will be different

Enter Data

Your skill in navigating and entering new records is a key to your success with a relational database. You can use many techniques to navigate through the records in the table's datasheet. **CASE** ▶ *Even though you have already successfully entered some records, Samantha Hooper asks you to master this essential skill by entering several more customers in the Quest database.*

STEPS

1. **Double-click the Customers table in the Navigation Pane to open it, press [Tab] three times, then press [Enter] three times**

   The Customers table reopens. The Comments subdatasheets are collapsed. Both the [Tab] and [Enter] keys move the focus to the next field. The **focus** refers to which data you would edit if you started typing. When you navigate to the last field of the record, pressing [Tab] or [Enter] advances the focus to the first field of the next record. You can also use the Next record ▶ and Previous record ◀ **navigation buttons** on the navigation bar in the lower-left corner of the datasheet to navigate through the records. The **Current record** text box on the navigation bar tells you the number of the current record as well as the total number of records in the datasheet.

2. **Click the FirstName field of the fourth record to position the insertion point to enter a new record**

   You can also use the New (blank) record button ▶✳ on the navigation bar to move to a new record. You enter new records at the end of the datasheet. You learn how to sort and reorder records later. A complete list of navigation keystrokes is shown in **TABLE A-5**.

3. **At the end of the datasheet, enter the three records shown in FIGURE A-15**

   The **edit record symbol** 🖉 appears to the left of the record you are currently editing. When you move to a different record, Access saves the data. Therefore, Access never prompts you to save *data* because it performs that task automatically. Saving data automatically allows Access databases to be **multiuser** databases, which means that more than one person can enter and edit data in the same database at the same time.

   Your CustID values might differ from those in **FIGURE A-15**. Because the CustID field is an **AutoNumber** field, Access automatically enters the next consecutive number into the field as it creates the record. If you delete a record or are interrupted when entering a record, Access discards the value in the AutoNumber field and does not reuse it. Therefore, AutoNumber values do not represent the number of records in your table. Instead, they provide a unique value per record, similar to check numbers.

Changing from Navigation mode to Edit mode

If you navigate to another area of the datasheet by clicking with the mouse pointer instead of pressing [Tab] or [Enter], you change from **Navigation mode** to Edit mode. In **Edit mode**, Access assumes that you are trying to make changes to the current field value, so keystrokes such as [Ctrl][End], [Ctrl][Home], [◀], and [▶] move the insertion point within the field. To return to Navigation mode, press [Tab] or [Enter] (thus moving the focus to the next field), or press [▲] or [▼] (thus moving the focus to a different record).

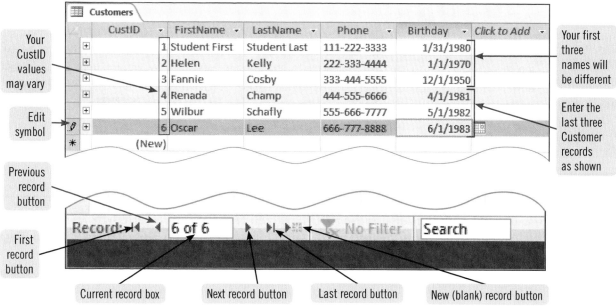

FIGURE A-15: New records in the Customers table

Your CustID values may vary

Your first three names will be different

Edit symbol

Enter the last three Customer records as shown

Previous record button

First record button

Record: 6 of 6   No Filter   Search

Current record box   Next record button   Last record button   New (blank) record button

TABLE A-5: Navigation mode keyboard shortcuts

shortcut key	moves to the
[Tab], [Enter], or [→]	Next field of the current record
[Shift][Tab] or [←]	Previous field of the current record
[Home]	First field of the current record
[End]	Last field of the current record
[Ctrl][Home] or [F5]	First field of the first record
[Ctrl][End]	Last field of the last record
[↑]	Current field of the previous record
[↓]	Current field of the next record

Cloud computing

Using SkyDrive, a free service from Microsoft, you can store files in the "cloud" and retrieve them anytime you are connected to the Internet. Saving your files to the SkyDrive is one example of cloud computing. **Cloud computing** means you are using an Internet resource to complete your work. You can find more information in the "Working in the Cloud" appendix.

Edit Data

Learning
Outcomes
• Edit data in a data-sheet
• Delete records in a datasheet
• Preview and print a datasheet

Updating existing data in a database is another critical database task. To change the contents of an exist-ing record, navigate to the field you want to change and type the new information. You can delete unwanted data by clicking the field and using [Backspace] or [Delete] to delete text to the left or right of the insertion point. Other data entry keystrokes are summarized in **TABLE A-6**. **CASE** *Samantha Hooper asks you to correct two records in the Customers table.*

STEPS

1. **Double-click the name in the FirstName field of the second record, type Kelsey, press [Enter], type Barker, press [Enter], type 111-222-4444, press [Enter], type 2/15/84, then press [Enter]**

   You changed the name, telephone number, and birth date of the second customer. When you entered the last two digits of the year value, Access inserted the first two digits after you pressed [Enter]. You'll also change the third customer.

2. **Press [Enter] to move to the FirstName field of the third record, type Joshua, press [Enter], type Lang, press [Enter], type 222-333-4444, then press [Esc]**

   Pressing [Esc] once removes the current field's editing changes, so the Phone value changes back to the pre-vious entry. Pressing [Esc] twice removes all changes to the current record. When you move to another record, Access saves your edits, so you can no longer use [Esc] to remove editing changes to the current record. You can, however, click the Undo button ↺ on the Quick Access toolbar to undo changes to a previous record.

3. **Retype 222-333-4444, press [Enter], type 12/1/50 in the Birthday field, press [Enter], click the 12/1/50 date you just entered, click the Calendar icon ▦, then click April 14, 1951, as shown in FIGURE A-16**

   When you are working in the Birthday field, which has a Date/Time data type, you can enter a date from the keyboard or use the **Calendar Picker**, a pop-up calendar to find and select a date.

4. **Click the record selector for the last record (Oscar Lee), click the Delete button in the Records group on the HOME tab, then click Yes**

   A message warns that you cannot undo a record deletion. The Undo button is dimmed, indicating that you cannot use it. The Customers table now has five records, as shown in **FIGURE A-17**. Keep in mind that your CustID values might differ from those in the figure because they are controlled by Access.

5. **Click the FILE tab, click Print, then click Print Preview to review the printout of the Customers table before printing**

6. **Click the Close Print Preview button, click the Close button in the upper-right corner of the window to close the Quest.accdb database and Access 2013, then click Yes if prompted to save design changes to the Customers table**

FIGURE A-16: Editing customer records

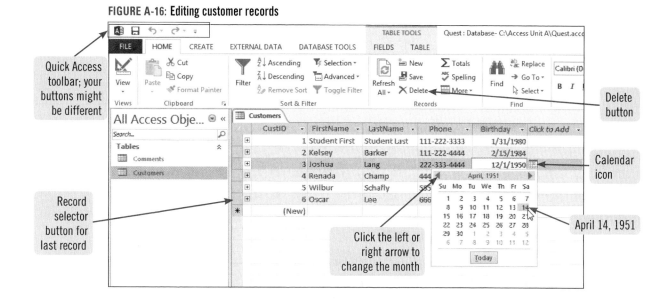

FIGURE A-17: Final Customers datasheet

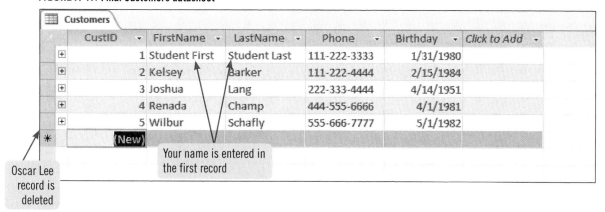

TABLE A-6: Edit mode keyboard shortcuts

editing keystroke	action
[Backspace]	Deletes one character to the left of the insertion point
[Delete]	Deletes one character to the right of the insertion point
[F2]	Switches between Edit and Navigation mode
[Esc]	Undoes the change to the current field
[Esc][Esc]	Undoes all changes to the current record
[F7]	Starts the spell-check feature
[Ctrl][']	Inserts the value from the same field in the previous record into the current field
[Ctrl][;]	Inserts the current date in a Date field

© 2014 Cengage Learning

Resizing and moving datasheet columns

You can resize the width of a field in a datasheet by dragging the column separator, the thin line that separates the field names to the left or right. The pointer changes to ✛ as you make the field wider or narrower. Release the mouse button when you have resized the field. To adjust the column width to accommodate the widest entry in the field, double-click the column separator. To move a column, click the field name to select the entire column, then drag the field name left or right.

Practice

Concepts Review

Label each element of the Access window shown in FIGURE A-18.

FIGURE A-18

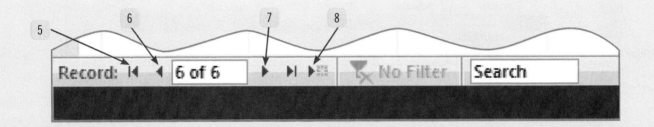

Match each term with the statement that best describes it.

10. Field
11. Record
12. Table
13. Datasheet
14. Query
15. Form
16. Report

a. A subset of data from one or more tables
b. A collection of records for a single subject, such as all the customer records
c. A professional printout of database information
d. A spreadsheet-like grid that displays fields as columns and records as rows
e. A group of related fields for one item, such as all of the information for one customer
f. A category of information in a table, such as a company name, city, or state
g. An easy-to-use data entry screen

Select the best answer from the list of choices.

17. Which of the following is *not* a typical benefit of relational databases?
   a. Minimized duplicate data entry
   b. More accurate data
   c. Faster information retrieval
   d. More common than spreadsheets

Getting Started with Access 2013

18. **Which of the following is *not* an advantage of managing data with relational database software such as Access versus spreadsheet software such as Excel?**
    a. Allows multiple users to enter data simultaneously
    b. Uses a single table to store all data
    c. Provides data entry forms
    d. Reduces duplicate data entry

19. **When you create a new database, which object is created first?**
    a. Form
    b. Query
    c. Module
    d. Table

Skills Review

1. **Understand relational databases.**
    a. Write down five advantages of managing database information in Access versus using a spreadsheet.
    b. Write a sentence to explain how the terms *field*, *record*, *table*, and *relational database* relate to one another.

2. **Explore a database.**
    a. Start Access.
    b. Open the RealEstate-A.accdb database from the location where you store your Data Files. Click Enable Content if a yellow Security Warning message appears.
    c. Open each of the four tables to study the data they contain. Complete the following table:

table name	number of records	number of fields

    d. Double-click the ListingsByRealtor query in the Navigation Pane to open it. Change any occurrence of Gordon Bono to *your* name. Move to another record to save your changes.
    e. Double-click the RealtorsMainForm in the Navigation Pane to open it. Use the navigation buttons to navigate through the 11 realtors to observe each realtor's listings.
    f. Double-click the RealtorListingReport in the Navigation Pane to open it. The records are listed in ascending order by last name. Scroll through the report to make sure your name is positioned correctly.
    g. Close the RealEstate-A database, and then close Access 2013.

3. **Create a database.**
    a. Start Access, click the Blank desktop database icon, use the Browse button to navigate to the location where you store your Data Files, type **RealEstateMarketing** as the filename, click OK, and then click Create to create a new database named RealEstateMarketing.accdb.

Skills Review (continued)

b. Switch to Table Design View, name the table **Prospects**, then enter the following fields and data types:

field name	data type
ProspectID	AutoNumber
ProspectFirst	Short Text
ProspectLast	Short Text
Phone	Short Text
Email	Hyperlink
Street	Short Text
City	Short Text
State	Short Text
Zip	Short Text

c. Save the table, switch to Datasheet View, and enter two records using *your* name in the first record and your instructor's name in the second. Tab through the ProspectID field, an AutoNumber field.

d. Enter **TX** (Texas) as the value in the State field for both records. Use school or fictitious (rather than personal) data for all other field data, and be sure to fill out each record completely.

e. Widen each column in the Prospects table so that all data is visible, then save and close the Prospects table.

4. Create a table.

a. Click the CREATE tab on the Ribbon, click the Table Design button in the Tables group, then create a new table with the following two fields and data types:

field name	data type
StateAbbrev	Short Text
StateName	Short Text

b. Save the table with the name **States**. Click No when asked if you want Access to create the primary key field.

5. Create primary keys.

a. In Table Design View of the States table, set the StateAbbrev as the primary key field.

b. Save the States table and open it in Datasheet View.

c. Enter one state record, using **TX** for the StateAbbrev value and **Texas** for the StateName value to match the State value of TX that you entered for both records in the Prospects table.

d. Close the States table.

6. Relate two tables.

a. From the DATABASE TOOLS tab, open the Relationships window.

b. Add the States, then the Prospects table to the Relationships window.

c. Drag the bottom edge of the Prospects table to expand the field list to display all of the fields.

d. Drag the StateAbbrev field from the States table to the State field of the Prospects table.

e. In the Edit Relationships dialog box, click the Enforce Referential Integrity check box, then click Create. Your Relationships window should look similar to **FIGURE A-19**. If you connect the wrong fields by mistake, right-click the line connecting the two fields, click Delete, then try again.

f. Close the Relationships window, and save changes when prompted.

FIGURE A-19

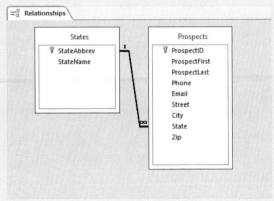

Skills Review (continued)

7. Enter data.

a. Open the States table and enter the following records:

StateAbbrev field	StateName field
CO	Colorado
IA	Iowa
KS	Kansas
MO	Missouri
NE	Nebraska
OK	Oklahoma
WI	Wisconsin

b. Add three more state records of your choice for a total of 11 records in the States table using the correct two-character abbreviation for the state and the correctly spelled state name.

c. Close and reopen the States table. Notice that Access automatically sorts the records by the values in the primary key field, the StateAbbrev field.

8. Edit data.

a. Click the Expand button for the TX record to see the two related records from the Prospects table.

b. Enter two more prospects in the TX subdatasheet using any fictitious but realistic data, as shown in **FIGURE A-20**. Notice that you are not required to enter a value for the State field, the foreign key field in the subdatasheet.

FIGURE A-20

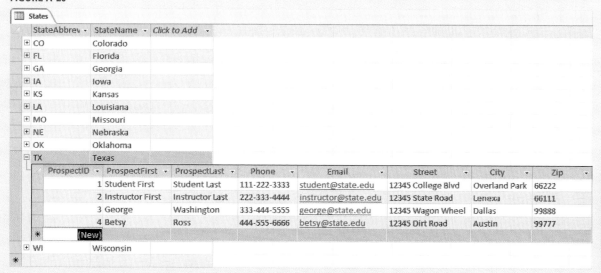

c. If required by your instructor, print the States datasheet and the Prospects datasheet.

d. Click the Close button in the upper-right corner of the Access window to close all open objects as well as the RealEstateMarketing.accdb database and Access 2013. If prompted to save any design changes, click Yes.

Access 2013

Independent Challenge 1

Consider the following twelve subject areas:

- Telephone directory
- College course offerings
- Restaurant menu items
- Vehicles
- Movie listings

- Islands of the Caribbean
- Physical activities
- Shopping catalog items
- Conventions
- Party guest list

- Members of the U.S. House
- Ancient wonders of the world of Representatives

a. For each subject, build a Word table with 4–7 columns and three rows. In the first row, enter field names that you would expect to see in a table used to manage that subject.

b. In the second and third rows of each table, enter two realistic records. The first table, Telephone Directory, is completed as an example to follow.

TABLE: Telephone Directory

FirstName	LastName	Street	Zip	Phone
Marco	Lopez	100 Main Street	88715	555-612-3312
Christopher	Stafford	253 Maple Lane	77824	555-612-1179

Independent Challenge 2

You are working with several civic groups to coordinate a community-wide cleanup effort. You have started a database called Recycle-A, which tracks the clubs, their trash deposits, and the trash collection centers that are participating.

a. Start Access, then open the Recycle-A.accdb database from the location where you store your Data Files. Enable content if prompted.

b. Open each table's datasheet to study the number of fields and records per table. Notice that there are no expand buttons to the left of any records because relationships have not yet been established between these tables.

c. In a Word document, re-create the following table and fill in the blanks:

d. Close all table datasheets, then open the Relationships window and create the following one-to-many relationships. Drag the tables from the Navigation Pane to the Relationships window, and drag the title bars and borders of the field lists to position them as shown in FIGURE A-21.

table name	number of fields	number of records

field on the "one" side of the relationship	field on the "many" side of the relationship
ClubNumber in Clubs table	ClubNumber in Deposits table
CenterNumber in Centers table	CenterNumber in Deposits table

e. Be sure to enforce referential integrity on all relationships. If you create an incorrect relationship, right-click the line linking the fields, click Delete, and try again. Your final Relationships window should look like FIGURE A-21.

f. Click the Relationship Report button on the DESIGN tab, and if required by your instructor, click Print to print a copy of the Relationships for Recycle-A report. To close the report, right-click the Relationships for Recycle-A tab and click Close. Click Yes when prompted to save changes to the report with the name **Relationships for Recycle-A**. Save and close the Relationships window.

FIGURE A-21

g. Open the Clubs table and add a new record with fictitious but realistic data in all of the fields. Enter **8** as the ClubNumber value and *your* name in the FName (first name) and LName (last name) fields.

h. Expand the subdatasheets for each record in the Clubs table to see the related records from the Deposits table. Which club made the most deposits? Be ready to answer in class. Close the Clubs table.

i. Open the Centers table and add a new record with fictitious but realistic data in all of the fields. Enter *your* first and last names in the CenterName field and **5** as the CenterNumber.

j. Expand the subdatasheets for each record in the Centers table to see the related records from the Deposits table. Which center made the most deposits? Be ready to answer in class. Close the Centers table.

k. Close the Recycle-A.accdb database, then exit Access 2013.

Independent Challenge 3

You are working for an advertising agency that provides advertising media for small and large businesses in the midwestern United States. You have started a database called BusinessContacts-A, which tracks your company's customers. (*Note: To complete this Independent Challenge, make sure you are connected to the Internet.*)

a. Start Access and open the BusinessContacts-A.accdb database from the location where you store your Data Files. Enable content if prompted.

b. Add a new record to the Customers table, using any local business name, *your* first and last names, **$7,788.99** in the YTDSales field, and fictitious but reasonable entries for the rest of the fields.

c. Edit the Sprint Systems record (ID 1). The Company name should be changed to **MTB Mobile**, and the Street value should be changed to **4455 College St**.

d. Delete the record for St Luke's Hospital (ID 20), then close the Customers table.

e. Create a new table with two fields, **State2** and **StateName**. Assign both fields a Short Text data type. The State2 field will contain the two-letter abbreviation for state names. The StateName field will contain the full state name.

f. Set the State2 field as the primary key field, then save the table as **States**.

g. Enter at least three records into the States table, making sure that all of the states used in the Customers datasheet are entered in the States table. This includes **KS Kansas**, **MO Missouri**, and any other state you entered in Step b when you added a new record to the Customers table.

h. Close all open tables. Open the Relationships window, add both the States and Customers field lists to the window, then expand the size of the Customers field list so that all fields are visible.

i. Build a one-to-many relationship between the States and Customers tables by dragging the State2 field from the States table to the State field of the Customers table to create a one-to-many relationship between the two tables. Enforce referential integrity on the relationship. If you are unable to enforce referential integrity, it means that a value in the State field of the Customers table doesn't have a perfect match in the State2 field of the States table. Open both table datasheets, making sure every state in the State field of the Customers table is also represented in the State2 field of the States table, close all datasheets, then reestablish the one-to-many relationship between the two tables with referential integrity.

j. Click the Relationship Report button on the DESIGN tab, then if requested by your instructor, click Print to print the report.

k. Right-click the Relationships for BusinessContacts-A tab, then click Close. Click Yes when prompted to save the report with the name **Relationships for BusinessContacts-A**.

l. Close the Relationships window, saving changes as prompted.

m. Close BusinessContacts-A.accdb database, and exit Access 2013.

Independent Challenge 4: Explore

Now that you've learned about Microsoft Access and relational databases, brainstorm how you might use an Access database in your daily life or career. Start by visiting the Microsoft Web site, and explore what's new about Access 2013.

(*Note:* To complete this Independent Challenge, make sure you are connected to the Internet.)

a. Using your favorite search engine, look up the keywords *benefits of a relational database* or *benefits of Microsoft Access* to find articles that discuss the benefits of organizing data in a relational database.

b. Read several articles about the benefits of organizing data in a relational database such as Access, identifying three distinct benefits. Use a Word document to record those three benefits. Also, copy and paste the Web site address of the article you are referencing for each benefit you have identified.

c. In addition, as you read the articles that describe relational database benefits, list any terminology unfamiliar to you, identifying at least five new terms.

d. Using a search engine or a Web site that provides a computer glossary such as *www.whatis.com* or *www.webopedia.com*, look up the definition of the new terms, and enter both the term and the definition of the term in your document as well as the Web site address where your definition was found.

e. Finally, based on your research and growing understanding of Access 2013, list three ways you could use an Access database to organize, enhance, or support the activities and responsibilities of your daily life or career. Type your name at the top of the document, and submit it to your instructor as requested.

Visual Workshop

Open the Basketball-A.accdb database from the location where you store your Data Files, then enable content if prompted. Open the Offense query datasheet, which lists offensive statistics by player by game. Modify any of the Ellyse Howard records to contain *your* first and last names, then move to a different record, observing the power of a relational database to modify every occurrence of that name throughout the database. Close the Offense query, then open the Players table. Note that there are no expand buttons to the left of the records indicating that this table does not participate on the "one" side of a one-to-many relationship. Close the Players table and open the Relationships window. Drag the tables from the Navigation Pane and create the relationships with referential integrity, as shown in **FIGURE A-22**. Note the one-to-many relationship between the Players and Stats table. Print the Relationships report if requested by your instructor and save it with the name **Relationships for Basketball-A**. Close the report and close and save the Relationships window. Now reopen the Players table noting the expand buttons to the left of each record. Expand the subdatasheet for your name and for several other players to observe the "many" records from the Stats table that are now related to each record in the Players table.

FIGURE A-22

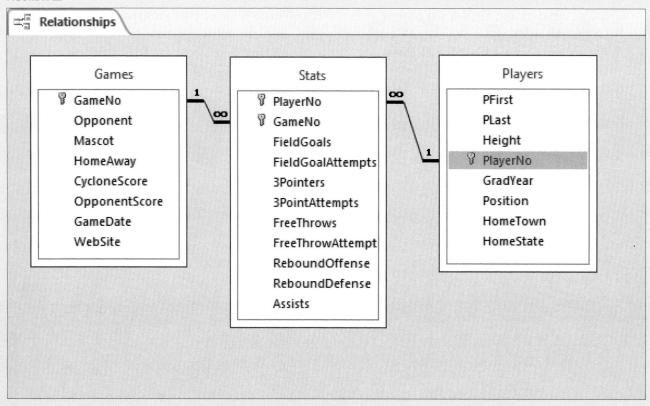

Building and Using Queries

CASE ▶ Samantha Hooper, tour developer for U.S. group travel at Quest Specialty Travel, has several questions about the customer and tour information in the Quest database. You'll develop queries to provide Samantha with up-to-date answers.

Unit Objectives

After completing this unit, you will be able to:

- Use the Query Wizard
- Work with data in a query
- Use Query Design View
- Sort and find data

- Filter data
- Apply AND criteria
- Apply OR criteria
- Format a datasheet

Files You Will Need

QuestTravel-B.accdb
Recycle-B.accdb
Membership-B.accdb
Congress-B.accdb
Vet-B.accdb
Baseball-B.accdb

Use the Query Wizard

Learning
Outcomes
• Describe the
  purpose for
  a query
• Create a query
  with the Simple
  Query Wizard

A **query** answers a question about the information in the database. A query allows you to select a subset of fields and records from one or more tables and then present the selected data as a single datasheet. A major benefit of working with data through a query is that you can focus on only the specific informa- tion you need to answer a question, rather than navigating through all the fields and records from many large tables. You can enter, edit, and navigate data in a query datasheet just like a table datasheet. However, keep in mind that Access data is physically stored only in tables, even though you can select, view, and edit it through other Access objects such as queries and forms. Because a query doesn't physically store the data, a query datasheet is sometimes called a **logical view** of the data. Technically, a query is a set of **SQL (Structured Query Language)** instructions, but because you can use Access query tools such as Query Design View to create and modify the query, you are not required to know SQL to build or use Access queries. **CASE** ➤ *You use the Simple Query Wizard to create a query that displays fields from the Tours and Customers tables in one datasheet.*

STEPS

1. **Start Access, open the** QuestTravel-B.accdb database, **enable content if prompted, then maximize the window**

   Access provides several tools to create a new query. One way is to use the **Simple Query Wizard**, which prompts you for the information it needs to create a new query.

2. **Click the** CREATE **tab on the Ribbon, click the** Query Wizard button **in the Queries group, then click** OK **to start the Simple Query Wizard**

   The Simple Query Wizard dialog box opens, prompting you to select the fields you want to view in the new query. You can select fields from one or more existing tables or queries.

3. **Click the** Tables/Queries list arrow, **click** Table: Tours, **double-click** TourName, **double-click** City, **double-click** Category, **then double-click** Price

   So far, you've selected four fields from the Tours table to display basic tour information in this query. You also want to add the first and last name information from the Customers table so you know which customers purchased each tour.

TROUBLE
Click the Remove
Single Field button
`<` if you need
to remove a field
from the Selected
Fields list.

4. **Click the** Tables/Queries list arrow, **click** Table: Customers, **double-click** FName, **then double-click** LName

   You've selected four fields from the Tours table and two from the Customers table for your new query, as shown in **FIGURE B-1**.

5. **Click** Next, **click** Next **to select Detail, select** Tours Query **in the title text box, type** TourCustomerList **as the name of the query, then click** Finish

   The TourCustomerList datasheet opens, displaying four fields from the Tours table and two from the Customers table, as shown in **FIGURE B-2**. The query can show which customers have purchased which tours because of the one-to-many table relationships established in the Relationships window.

FIGURE B-1: Selecting fields using the Simple Query Wizard

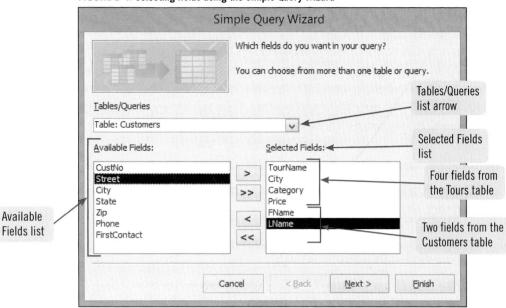

FIGURE B-2: TourCustomerList datasheet

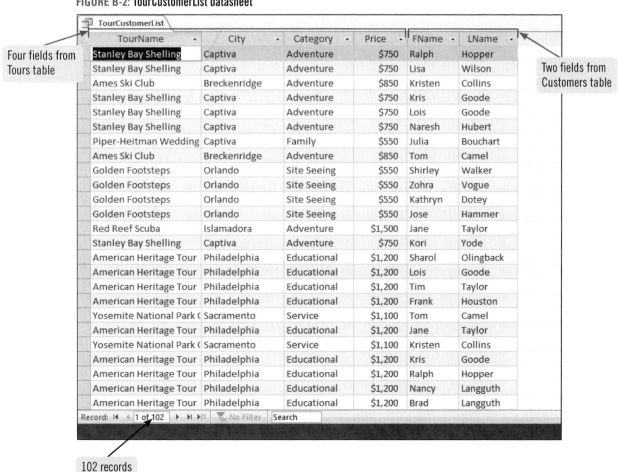

Work with Data in a Query

Learning
Outcomes
• Edit records in
  a query
• Delete records in
  a query

You enter and edit data in a query datasheet the same way you do in a table datasheet. Because all data is stored in tables, any edits you make to data in a query datasheet are actually stored in the underlying tables and are automatically updated in all views of the data in other queries, forms, and reports. **CASE** ➤ *You want to change the name of one tour and update a customer name. You can use the TourCustomerList query datasheet to make these edits.*

STEPS

1. **Double-click Stanley in the TourName field of the first or second record, type Breeze, then click any other record**

   All occurrences of Stanley Bay Shelling automatically update to Breeze Bay Shelling because this tour name value is stored only once in the Tours table. See **FIGURE B-3**. The tour name is selected from the Tours table and displayed in the TourCustomerList query for each customer who purchased this tour.

2. **Double-click Orlando in the City field of any record for the Golden Footsteps tour, type Kissimmee, then click any other record**

   All occurrences of Orlando automatically update to Kissimmee because this value is stored only once in the City field of the Tours table for the Golden Footsteps record. The Golden Footsteps tour is displayed in the TourCustomerList query for each customer who purchased the tour.

3. **Click the record selector button to the left of the first record, click the HOME tab, click the Delete button in the Records group, then click Yes**

   You can delete records from a query datasheet the same way you delete them from a table datasheet. Notice that the navigation bar now indicates you have 101 records in the datasheet, as shown in **FIGURE B-4**.

4. **Right-click the TourCustomerList query tab, then click Close**

   Each time a query is opened, it shows a current view of the data. This means that as new tours, customers, or sales are recorded in the database, the next time you open this query, the information will include all updates.

FIGURE B-3: Working with data in a query datasheet

Record selector button for first record

Updating Stanley to Breeze in one record updates all records

TourName	City	Category	Price	FName	LName
Breeze Bay Shelling	Captiva	Adventure	$750	Ralph	Hopper
Breeze Bay Shelling	Captiva	Adventure	$750	Lisa	Wilson
Ames Ski Club	Breckenridge	Adventure	$850	Kristen	Collins
Breeze Bay Shelling	Captiva	Adventure	$750	Kris	Goode
Breeze Bay Shelling	Captiva	Adventure	$750	Lois	Goode
Breeze Bay Shelling	Captiva	Adventure	$750	Naresh	Hubert
Piper-Heitman Wedding	Captiva	Family	$550	Julia	Bouchart
Ames Ski Club	Breckenridge	Adventure	$850	Tom	Camel
Golden Footsteps	Orlando	Site Seeing	$550	Shirley	Walker
Golden Footsteps	Orlando	Site Seeing	$550	Zohra	Vogue
Golden Footsteps	Orlando	Site Seeing	$550	Kathryn	Dotey
Golden Footsteps	Orlando	Site Seeing	$550	Jose	Hammer
Red Reef Scuba	Islamadora	Adventure	$1,500	Jane	Taylor
Breeze Bay Shelling	Captiva	Adventure	$750	Kori	Yode
American Heritage Tour	Philadelphia	Educational	$1,200	Sharol	Olingback

FIGURE B-4: Final TourCustomerList datasheet

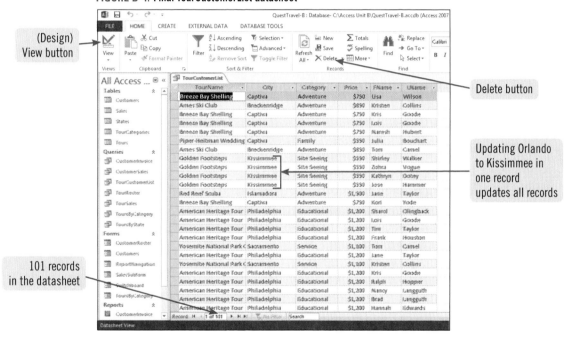

(Design) View button

Delete button

Updating Orlando to Kissimmee in one record updates all records

101 records in the datasheet

Hiding and unhiding fields in a datasheet

To hide a field in a datasheet, right-click the field name at the top of the datasheet and click the Hide Fields option on the shortcut menu. To unhide a field, right-click any field name, click Unhide Fields, and check the hidden field's check box in the Unhide Columns dialog box.

Freezing and unfreezing fields in a datasheet

In large datasheets, you may want to freeze certain fields so that they remain on the screen at all times. To freeze a field, right-click its field name in the datasheet, and then click Freeze Fields. To unfreeze a field, right-click any field name and click Unfreeze All Fields.

Use Query Design View

Learning Outcomes
- Work in Query Design View
- Add criteria to a query

You use **Query Design View** to add, delete, or move the fields in an existing query; to specify sort orders; or to add **criteria** to limit the number of records shown in the resulting datasheet. You can also use Query Design View to create a new query from scratch. Query Design View presents the fields you can use for that query in small windows called **field lists**. If you use the fields of two or more related tables in the query, the relationship between two tables is displayed with a **join line** (also called a **link line**) identifying which fields are used to establish the relationship. **CASE** *Samantha Hooper asks you to produce a list of tours in Florida. You use Query Design View to modify the existing ToursByState query to meet her request.*

STEPS

1. **Double-click the ToursByState query in the Navigation Pane to review the datasheet**

   The ToursByState query contains the StateName field from the States table and the TourName, TourStartDate, and Price fields from the Tours table. This query contains two ascending sort orders: StateName and TourName. All records in California, for example, are further sorted by the TourName value.

   QUICK TIP
   Drag the lower edge of the field list to view more fields.

2. **Click the View button 🗹 on the HOME tab to switch to Query Design View**

   Query Design View displays the tables used in the query in the upper pane of the window. The link line shows that one record in the States table may be related to many records in the Tours table. The lower pane of the window, called the **query design grid** (or query grid for short), displays the field names, sort orders, and criteria used within the query.

   QUICK TIP
   Query criteria are not case sensitive, so Florida equals FLORIDA equals florida.

3. **Click the first Criteria cell for the StateName field, then type Florida as shown in FIGURE B-5**

   Criteria are limiting conditions you set in the query design grid. In this case, the condition limits the selected records to only those with "Florida" in the StateName field.

4. **Click the View button ▦ in the Results group to switch to Datasheet View**

   Now only nine records are selected, because only nine of the tours have "Florida" in the StateName field, as shown in FIGURE B-6. You want to save this query with a different name.

5. **Click the FILE tab, click Save As, click Save Object As, click the Save As button, type FloridaTours, then click OK**

   In Access, the **Save As command** on the FILE tab allows you to save the entire database (and all objects it contains) or just the current object with a new name. Recall that Access saves *data* automatically as you move from record to record.

6. **Right-click the FloridaTours query tab, then click Close**

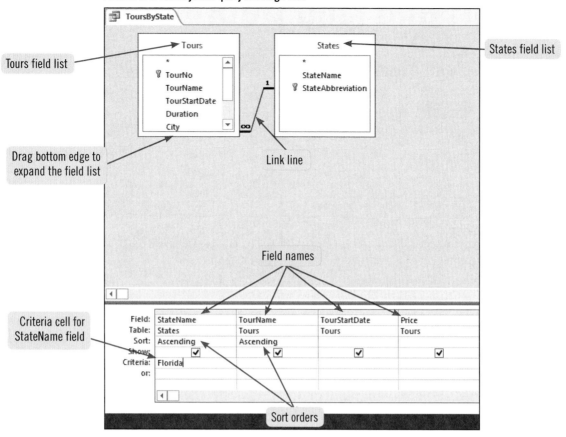

FIGURE B-5: ToursByState query in Design View

Tours field list

Drag bottom edge to expand the field list

States field list

Link line

Field names

Criteria cell for StateName field

Sort orders

FIGURE B-6: ToursByState query with Florida criterion

StateName	TourName	TourStartDate	Price
Florida	Breeze Bay Shelling	07/06/2014	$750
Florida	Golden Footsteps	05/23/2014	$550
Florida	Gulfside Birdwatchers	06/29/2014	$700
Florida	High Adventurers	06/05/2014	$575
Florida	Hummer Trail	05/30/2014	$725
Florida	Patriot Debate Club	06/12/2014	$605
Florida	Piper-Heitman Wedding	05/30/2014	$550
Florida	Red Reef Scuba	07/06/2014	$1,500
Florida	Tropical Sailboats	06/19/2014	$655

TourName values are in ascending order

Only nine Florida records are selected

Adding or deleting a table in a query

You might want to add a table's field list to the upper pane of Query Design View to select fields from that table for the query. To add a new table to Query Design View, drag it from the Navigation Pane to Query Design View, or click the Show Table button on the Design tab, then add the desired table(s). To delete an unneeded table from Query Design View, click its title bar, then press [Delete].

Sort and Find Data

Learning Outcomes
• Apply sort orders to a query
• Find and replace data in a query
• Undo edits in a query

The Access sort and find features are handy tools that help you quickly organize and find data in a table or query datasheet. TABLE B-1 describes the Sort and Find buttons on the HOME tab. Besides using these buttons, you can also click the list arrow on the field name in a datasheet, and then click a sorting option. **CASE** ▶ *Samantha asks you to provide a list of tours sorted by TourStartDate, and then by Price. You'll modify the ToursByCategory query to answer this query.*

STEPS

1. **Double-click the ToursByCategory query in the Navigation Pane to open its datasheet**

   The ToursByCategory query currently sorts tours by Category, then by TourName. You'll add the Duration field to this query, then change the sort order for the records.

   > **QUICK TIP**
   > Drag a selected field selector right or left to move the column to a new position in the query grid.

2. **Click the View button ▨ in the Views group to switch to Design View, then double-click the Duration field in the Tours field list**

   When you double-click a field in a field list, Access inserts it in the next available column in the query grid. You can also drag a field from a field list to a specific column of the query grid. To select a field in the query grid, you click its field selector. The **field selector** is the thin gray bar above each field in the query grid. If you want to delete a field from a query, click its field selector, then press [Delete]. Deleting a field from a query does not delete it from the underlying table; the field is only deleted from the query's logical view.

   Currently, the ToursByCategory query is sorted by Category and then by TourName. Access evaluates sort orders from left to right. You want to change the sort order so that the records sort first by TourStartDate then by Price.

3. **Click Ascending in the Category Sort cell, click the list arrow, click (not sorted), click Ascending in the TourName Sort cell, click the list arrow, click (not sorted), double-click the TourStartDate Sort cell to specify an Ascending sort, then double-click the Price Sort cell to specify an Ascending sort**

   The records are now set to be sorted in ascending order, first by TourStartDate, then by the values in the Price field, as shown in FIGURE B-7. Because sort orders always work from left to right, you might need to rearrange the fields before applying a sort order that uses more than one field. To move a field in the query design grid, click its field selector, then drag it left or right.

4. **Click the View button ▦ in the Results group**

   The new datasheet shows the Duration field in the fifth column. The records are now sorted in ascending order by the TourStartDate field. If two records have the same TourStartDate, they are further sorted by Price. Your next task is to replace all occurrences of "Site Seeing" with "Cultural" in the Category field.

5. **Click the Find button on the HOME tab, type Site Seeing in the Find What box, click the Replace tab, click in the Replace With box, then type Cultural**

   The Find and Replace dialog box is shown in FIGURE B-8.

   > **TROUBLE**
   > If your find-and-replace effort did not work correctly, click the Undo button ↺ and repeat Steps 5 and 6.

6. **Click the Replace All button in the Find and Replace dialog box, click Yes to continue, then click Cancel to close the Find and Replace dialog box**

   Access replaced all occurrences of "Site Seeing" with "Cultural" in the Category field, as shown in FIGURE B-9.

7. **Right-click the ToursByCategory query tab, click Close, then click Yes to save changes**

FIGURE B-7: Changing sort orders for the ToursByCategory query

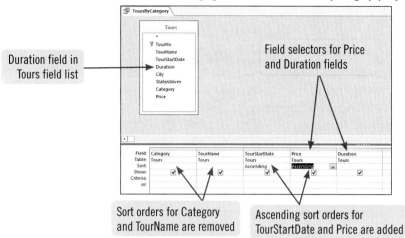

Duration field in Tours field list

Field selectors for Price and Duration fields

Sort orders for Category and TourName are removed

Ascending sort orders for TourStartDate and Price are added

FIGURE B-8: Find and Replace dialog box

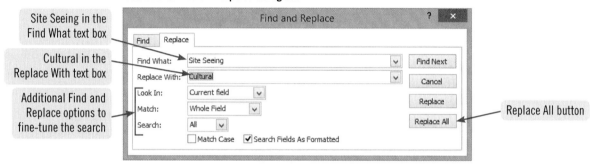

Site Seeing in the Find What text box

Cultural in the Replace With text box

Additional Find and Replace options to fine-tune the search

Replace All button

FIGURE B-9: Final ToursByCategory datasheet with new sort orders

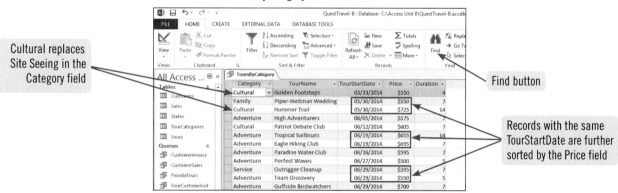

Cultural replaces Site Seeing in the Category field

Find button

Records with the same TourStartDate are further sorted by the Price field

TABLE B-1: Sort and Find buttons

name	button	purpose
Ascending		Sorts records based on the selected field in ascending order (0 to 9, A to Z)
Descending		Sorts records based on the selected field in descending order (Z to A, 9 to 0)
Remove Sort		Removes the current sort order
Find		Opens the Find and Replace dialog box, which allows you to find data in a single field or in the entire datasheet
Replace		Opens the Find and Replace dialog box, which allows you to find and replace data
Go To		Helps you navigate to the first, previous, next, last, or new record
Select		Helps you select a single record or all records in a datasheet

Access 2013

Filter Data

Learning Outcomes
• Apply and remove filters in a query
• Use wildcards in criteria

Filtering a table or query datasheet *temporarily* displays only those records that match given criteria. Recall that criteria are limiting conditions you set. For example, you might want to show only tours in the state of California, or only tours with a duration of 14 days. Although filters provide a quick and easy way to display a temporary subset of records in the current datasheet, they are not as powerful or flexible as queries. Most important, a query is a saved object within the database, whereas filters are temporary because Access removes them when you close the datasheet. TABLE B-2 compares filters and queries. **CASE** *Samantha asks you to find all Adventure tours offered in the month of July. You can filter the Tours table datasheet to provide this information.*

STEPS

QUICK TIP
You can also apply a sort or filter by clicking the Sort and filter arrow to the right of the field name and choosing the sort order or filter values you want.

1. **Double-click the Tours table to open it, click any occurrence of Adventure in the Category field, click the Selection button in the Sort & Filter group on the HOME tab, then click Equals "Adventure"**
   Eighteen records are selected, some of which are shown in **FIGURE B-10**. A filter icon appears to the right of the Category field. Filtering by the selected field value, called **Filter By Selection**, is a fast and easy way to filter the records for an exact match. To filter for comparative data (for example, where TourStartDate is *equal to* or *greater than* 7/1/2014), you must use the **Filter By Form** feature. Filter buttons are summarized in **TABLE B-3**.

2. **Click the Advanced button in the Sort & Filter group, then click Filter By Form**
   The Filter by Form window opens. The previous Filter By Selection criterion, "Adventure" in the Category field, is still in the grid. Access distinguishes between text and numeric entries by placing "quotation marks" around text criteria.

QUICK TIP
To clear previous criteria, click the Advanced button, then click Clear All Filters.

3. **Click the TourStartDate cell, then type 7/*/2014 as shown in FIGURE B-11**
   Filter By Form also allows you to apply two or more criteria at the same time. An asterisk (*) in the day position of the date criterion works as a wildcard, selecting any date in the month of July (the 7th month) in the year 2014.

QUICK TIP
Be sure to remove existing filters before applying a new filter, or the new filter will apply to the current subset of records instead of the entire datasheet.

4. **Click the Toggle Filter button in the Sort & Filter group**
   The datasheet selects two records that match both filter criteria, as shown in **FIGURE B-12**. Note that filter icons appear next to the TourStartDate and Category field names as both fields are involved in the filter.

5. **Close the Tours datasheet, then click Yes when prompted to save the changes**
   Saving changes to the datasheet saves the last sort order and column width changes. Filters are not saved.

Using wildcard characters

To search for a pattern, you can use a **wildcard** character to represent any character in the condition entry. Use a question mark (?) to search for any single character and an asterisk (*) to search for any number of characters. Wildcard characters are often used with the **Like** operator. For example, the criterion Like "12/*/13" would find all dates in December of 2013, and the criterion Like "F*" would find all entries that start with the letter F.

FIGURE B-10: Filtering the Tours table

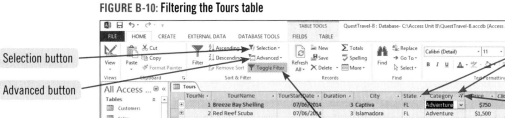

Selection button

Advanced button

Sort and filter buttons

Filter icon

Adventure in the Category field

Toggle Filter button is selected, indicating the records are filtered

FIGURE B-11: Filtering By Form criteria

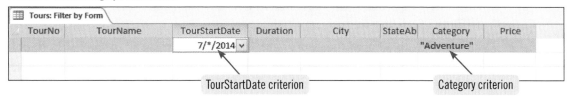

TourStartDate criterion

Category criterion

FIGURE B-12: Results of filtering by form

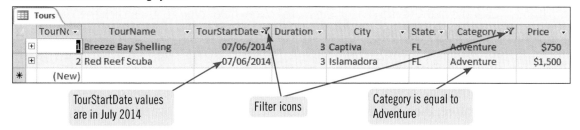

TourStartDate values are in July 2014

Filter icons

Category is equal to Adventure

TABLE B-2: Filters vs. queries

characteristics	filters	queries
Are saved as an object in the database		•
Can be used to select a subset of records in a datasheet	•	•
Can be used to select a subset of fields in a datasheet		•
Resulting datasheet used to enter and edit data	•	•
Resulting datasheet used to sort, filter, and find records	•	•
Commonly used as the source of data for a form or report		•
Can calculate sums, averages, counts, and other types of summary statistics across records		•
Can be used to create calculated fields		•

TABLE B-3: Filter buttons

name	button	purpose
Filter	▼	Provides a list of values in the selected field that can be used to customize a filter
Selection	▼⚡	Filters records that equal, do not equal, or are otherwise compared with the current value
Advanced	▼⋯	Provides advanced filter features such as Filter By Form, Save As Query, and Clear All Filters
Toggle Filter	▼	Applies or removes the current filter

Apply AND Criteria

Learning Outcomes
• Enter AND criteria in a query
• Define criteria syntax
• Use comparison operators with criteria

You can limit the number of records that appear on a query datasheet by entering criteria in Query Design View. Criteria are tests, or limiting conditions, for which the record must be true to be selected for the query datasheet. To create **AND criteria**, which means that *all* criteria must be true to select the record, enter two or more criteria on the *same* Criteria row of the query design grid. **CASE** ▶ *Samantha Hooper asks you to provide a list of all Adventure tours in the state of Florida with a duration of 7 days or less. Use Query Design View to create the query with AND criteria to meet her request.*

STEPS

1. **Click the CREATE tab on the Ribbon, click the Query Design button, double-click Tours, then click Close in the Show Table dialog box**

   You want four fields from the Tours table in this query.

2. **Drag the bottom edge of the Tours field list down to display all of the fields, double-click TourName, double-click Duration, double-click StateAbbrev, then double-click Category to add these fields to the query grid**

   First add criteria to select only those records in Florida. Because you are using the StateAbbrev field, you need to use the two-letter state abbreviation for Florida, FL, as the Criteria entry.

3. **Click the first Criteria cell for the StateAbbrev field, type FL, then click the View button 🔲 to display the results**

   Querying for only those tours in the state of Florida selects nine records. Next, you add criteria to select only the tours in Florida in the Adventure category.

4. **Click the View button 🔲, click the first Criteria cell for the Category field, type Adventure, then click the View button 🔲 in the Results group**

   Criteria added to the same line of the query design grid are AND criteria. When entered on the same line, each criterion must be true for the record to appear in the resulting datasheet. Querying for both FL and Adventure tours narrows the selection to five records. Every time you add AND criteria, you *narrow* the number of records that are selected because the record must be true for *all* criteria.

5. **Click the View button 🔲, click the first Criteria cell for the Duration field, then type <=7, as shown in FIGURE B-13**

   Access assists you with **criteria syntax**, rules that specify how to enter criteria. Access automatically adds "quotation marks" around text criteria in Short Text and Long Text fields ("FL" and "Adventure") and pound signs (#) around date criteria in Date/Time fields. The criteria in Number, Currency, and Yes/No fields are not surrounded by any characters. See **TABLE B-4** for more information about comparison operators such as > (greater than).

TROUBLE
If your datasheet doesn't match FIGURE B-14, return to Query Design View and compare your criteria with that of FIGURE B-13.

6. **Click the View button 🔲**

   The third AND criterion further narrows the number of records selected to four, as shown in **FIGURE B-14**.

7. **Click the Save button 🔲 on the Quick Access toolbar, type AdventureFL as the query name, click OK, then close the query**

   The query is saved with the new name, AdventureFL, as a new object in the QuestTravel-B database. Criteria entered in Query Design View are permanently saved with the query (as compared with filters in the previous lesson, which are temporary and not saved with the object).

FIGURE B-13: Query Design View with AND criteria

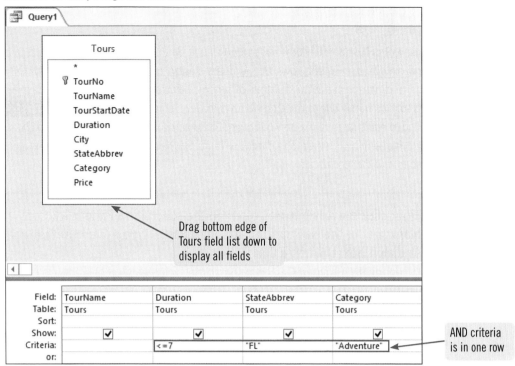

FIGURE B-14: Final datasheet of AdventureFL query

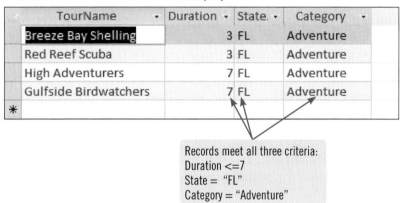

TABLE B-4: Comparison operators

operator	description	expression	meaning
>	Greater than	>500	Numbers greater than 500
>=	Greater than or equal to	>=500	Numbers greater than or equal to 500
<	Less than	<"Braveheart"	Names from A to Braveheart, but not Braveheart
<=	Less than or equal to	<="Bridgewater"	Names from A through Bridgewater, inclusive
<>	Not equal to	<>"Fontanelle"	Any name except for Fontanelle

Searching for blank fields

Is Null and Is Not Null are two other types of common criteria. The **Is Null** criterion finds all records where no entry has been made in the field. **Is Not Null** finds all records where there is any entry in the field, even if the entry is 0. Primary key fields cannot have a null entry.

Access 2013

Apply OR Criteria

Learning
Outcomes
• Enter OR criteria in
  a query
• Rename a query

You use **OR criteria** when *any one* criterion must be true in order for the record to be selected. Enter OR criteria on *different* Criteria rows of the query design grid. As you add rows of OR criteria to the query design grid, you *increase* the number of records selected for the resulting datasheet because the record needs to match *only one* of the Criteria rows to be selected for the datasheet. **CASE** ▶ *Samantha Hooper asks you to add criteria to the previous query. She wants to include Cultural tours in the state of Florida that are shorter than or equal to 7 days in duration. To do this, you modify a copy of the AdventureFL query to use OR criteria to add the records.*

STEPS

1. **Right-click the AdventureFL query in the Navigation Pane, click Copy, right-click a blank spot in the Navigation Pane, click Paste, type AdventureCulturalFL in the Paste As dialog box, then click OK**

   By copying the AdventureFL query before starting your modifications, you avoid changing the AdventureFL query by mistake.

2. **Right-click the AdventureCulturalFL query in the Navigation Pane, click Design View, click the second Criteria cell in the Category field, type Cultural, then click the View button ▦ to display the query datasheet**

   The query selected 11 records including all of the tours with Cultural in the Category field. Note that some of the Duration values are greater than 7 and some of the StateAbbrev values are not FL. Because each row of the query grid is evaluated separately, all Cultural tours are selected regardless of criteria in any other row. In other words, the criteria in one row have no effect on the criteria of other rows. To make sure that the Cultural tours are also in Florida and have a duration of less than or equal to 7 days, you need to modify the second row of the query grid (the "or" row) to specify that criteria.

   QUICK TIP
   The Datasheet, Design, and other view buttons are also located in the lower-right corner of the Access window.

3. **Click the View button ☒, click the second Criteria cell in the Duration field, type <=7, click the second Criteria cell in the StateAbbrev field, type FL, then click in any other cell of the grid**

   Query Design View should look like **FIGURE B-15**.

4. **Click the View button ▦**

   Six records are selected that meet all three criteria as entered in row one *or* row two of the query grid, as shown in **FIGURE B-16**.

5. **Right-click the AdventureCulturalFL query tab, click Close, then click Yes to save and close the query datasheet**

FIGURE B-15: Query Design View with OR criteria

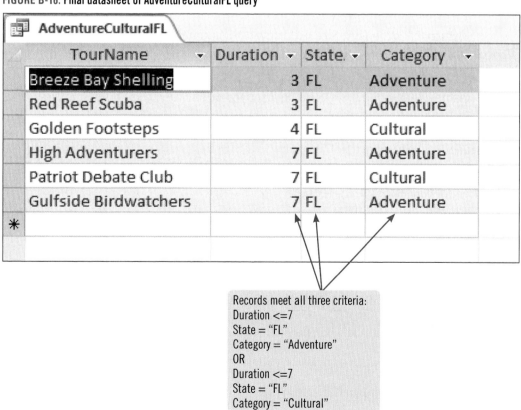

AdventureCulturalFL

Tours

*
🔑 TourNo
TourName
TourStartDate
Duration
City
StateAbbrev
Category
Price

◀ ▮

Field:	TourName	Duration	StateAbbrev	Category
Table:	Tours	Tours	Tours	Tours
Sort:				
Show:	✔	✔	✔	✔
Criteria:		<=7	"FL"	"Adventure"
or:		<=7	"FL"	"Cultural"

OR criteria is on
multiple rows

FIGURE B-16: Final datasheet of AdventureCulturalFL query

AdventureCulturalFL

TourName	Duration	State	Category
Breeze Bay Shelling	3	FL	Adventure
Red Reef Scuba	3	FL	Adventure
Golden Footsteps	4	FL	Cultural
High Adventurers	7	FL	Adventure
Patriot Debate Club	7	FL	Cultural
Gulfside Birdwatchers	7	FL	Adventure
✱			

Records meet all three criteria:
Duration <=7
State = "FL"
Category = "Adventure"
OR
Duration <=7
State = "FL"
Category = "Cultural"

Format a Datasheet

Learning
Outcomes
• Zoom in print
  preview
• Format a datasheet
• Change page
  orientation

A report is the primary Access tool to create a professional printout, but you can print a datasheet as well. A datasheet allows you to apply some basic formatting modifications such as changing the font size, font face, colors, and gridlines. **CASE** ➤ *Samantha Hooper asks you to print a list of customers. You decide to format the Customers table datasheet before printing it for her.*

STEPS

1. **In the Navigation Pane, double-click the Customers table to open it in Datasheet View**
   Before applying new formatting enhancements, you preview the default printout.

2. **Click the FILE tab, click Print, click Print Preview, then click the header of the printout to zoom in**
   The preview window displays the layout of the printout, as shown in **FIGURE B-17**. By default, the printout of a datasheet contains the object name and current date in the header. The page number is in the footer.

3. **Click the Next Page button ▶ in the navigation bar to move to the next page of the printout**
   The last two fields print on the second page because the first is not wide enough to accommodate them. You decide to switch the report to landscape orientation so that all of the fields print on one page, and then increase the size of the font before printing to make the text easier to read.

4. **Click the Landscape button on the PRINT PREVIEW tab to switch the report to landscape orientation, then click the Close Print Preview button**
   You return to Datasheet View where you can make font face, font size, font color, gridline color, and background color choices.

5. **Click the Font list arrow** Calibri (Body) ▾ **in the Text Formatting group, click Times New Roman, click the Font Size list arrow** 11 ▾ **, then click 12**
   With the larger font size applied, you need to resize some columns to accommodate the widest entries.

6. **Use the ✛ pointer to double-click the field separator between the Street and City field names, then double-click the field separator between the Phone and FirstContact field names**
   Double-clicking the field separators widens the columns as needed to display every entry in those fields, as shown in **FIGURE B-18**.

QUICK TIP
If you need a print-out of this datasheet, click the Print button on the PRINT PREVIEW tab, then click OK.

7. **Click the FILE tab, click Print, click Print Preview, then click the preview to zoom in and out to review the information**
   All of the fields now fit across a page in landscape orientation. The preview of the printout is still two pages, but with the larger font size, it is easier to read.

8. **Right-click the Customers table tab, click Close, click Yes when prompted to save changes, then click the Close button on the title bar to close the QuestTravel-B.accdb database and Access 2013**

FIGURE B-17: Preview of Customers datasheet

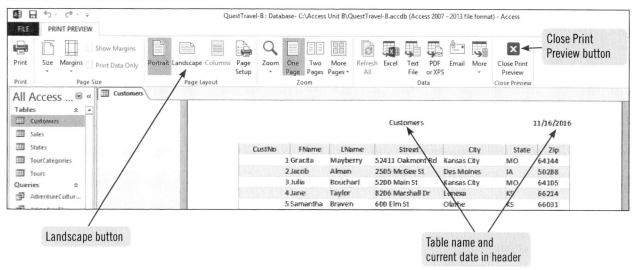

Landscape button

Close Print Preview button

Table name and current date in header

FIGURE B-18: Formatting the Customers datasheet

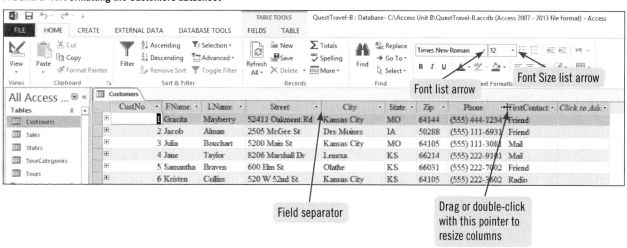

Font list arrow

Font Size list arrow

Field separator

Drag or double-click with this pointer to resize columns

Access 2013

Practice

Concepts Review

Label each element of the Access window shown in FIGURE B-19.

FIGURE B-19

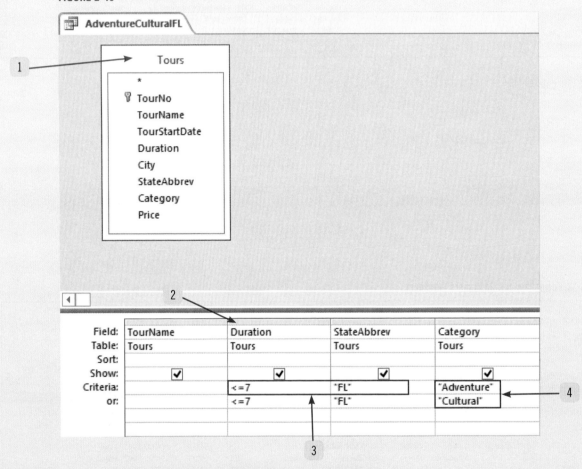

Match each term with the statement that best describes it.

5. **Query grid**
6. **Field selector**
7. **Filter**
8. **Filter By Selection**
9. **Field lists**
10. **Sorting**
11. **Join line**
12. **Is Null**
13. **Criteria**
14. **Syntax**
15. **Wildcard**

a. Putting records in ascending or descending order based on the values of a field
b. Limiting conditions used to restrict the number of records that are selected in a query
c. Creates a temporary subset of records
d. Small windows that display field names
e. Rules that determine how criteria are entered
f. Used to search for a pattern of characters
g. Criterion that finds all records where no entry has been made in the field
h. The lower pane in Query Design View
i. Identifies which fields are used to establish a relationship between two tables
j. A fast and easy way to filter the records for an exact match
k. The thin gray bar above each field in the query grid

Select the best answer from the list of choices.

16. **AND criteria:**
    a. Determine sort orders.
    b. Must all be true for the record to be selected.
    c. Determine fields selected for a query.
    d. Help set link lines between tables in a query.

17. **SQL stands for which of the following?**
    a. Structured Query Language
    b. Standard Query Language
    c. Special Query Listing
    d. Simple Query Listing

18. **A query is sometimes called a logical view of data because:**
    a. You can create queries with the Logical Query Wizard.
    b. Queries contain logical criteria.
    c. Query naming conventions are logical.
    d. Queries do not store data—they only display a view of data.

19. **Which of the following describes OR criteria?**
    a. Selecting a subset of fields and/or records to view as a datasheet from one or more tables
    b. Using two or more rows of the query grid to select only those records that meet given criteria
    c. Reorganizing the records in either ascending or descending order based on the contents of one or more fields
    d. Using multiple fields in the query design grid

20. **Which of the following is *not* true about a query?**
    a. A query is the same thing as a filter.
    b. A query can select fields from one or more tables in a relational database.
    c. A query can be created using different tools.
    d. An existing query can be modified in Query Design View.

Skills Review

1. Use the Query Wizard.

   a. Open the Recycle-B.accdb database from the location where you store your Data Files. Enable content if prompted.

   b. Create a new query using the Simple Query Wizard. Select the CenterName field from the Centers table, the DepositDate and Weight fields from the Deposits table, and the ClubName field from the Clubs table. Select Detail, and enter **CenterDeposits** as the name of the query.

   c. Open the query in Datasheet View, then change any record with the Barker Trash value to a center name that includes *your* last name.

2. Work with data in a query.

   a. Delete the first record (Hugo Trash Can with a DepositDate value of 2/4/2014).

   b. Change any occurrence of Lions of Fontanelle in the ClubName field to **Lions of Bridgewater**.

   c. Click any value in the DepositDate field, then click the Descending button on the HOME tab to sort the records in descending order on the DepositDate field.

   d. Use the Calendar Picker to choose the date of **12/16/2016** for the first record.

   e. Save and close the CenterDeposits query.

3. Use Query Design View.

   a. Click the CREATE tab, click the Query Design button, double-click Clubs, double-click Deposits, and then click Close to add the Clubs and Deposits tables to Query Design View.

   b. Drag the bottom edge of both field lists down to display all of the field names in both tables.

   c. Add the following fields from the Clubs table to the query design grid in the following order: FName, LName, ClubName. Add the following fields from the Deposits table in the following order: DepositDate, Weight. View the results in Datasheet View observing the number of records that are selected.

   d. In Design View, enter criteria to display only those records with a Weight value of **greater than or equal to 100**, then observe the number of records that are selected in Datasheet View.

   e. Save the query with the name **HeavyDeposits**.

4. Sort and find data.

   a. In Query Design View of the HeavyDeposits query, choose an ascending sort order for the ClubName field and a descending sort order for the Weight field.

   b. Display the query in Datasheet View noting how the records have been resorted.

   c. In the ClubName field, change any occurrence of Jaycees to **Dallas Jaycees**.

   d. In the FName field, change any occurrence of Tara to *your* initials.

5. Filter data.

   a. Filter the HeavyDeposits datasheet for only those records where the ClubName equals **Dallas Jaycees**.

   b. Apply an advanced Filter By Form and use the >= operator to further narrow the records so that only the deposits with a DepositDate value on or after 1/1/2015 are selected.

   c. Apply the filter to see the datasheet and if requested by your instructor, print the filtered HeavyDeposits datasheet.

   d. Save and close the HeavyDeposits query. Reopen the HeavyDeposits query to confirm that filters are temporary (not saved), and then close the HeavyDeposits query again.

Skills Review (continued)

6. **Apply AND criteria.**

   a. Right-click the HeavyDeposits query, copy it, and then paste it as **Heavy2014Deposits**.

   b. Open the Heavy2014Deposits query in Query Design View.

   c. Modify the criteria to select all of the records with a DepositDate in **2014** and a Weight value **greater than or equal to 100**.

   d. If requested by your instructor, print the Heavy2014Deposits datasheet, then save and close it.

7. **Apply OR criteria.**

   a. Right-click the HeavyDeposits query, copy it, then paste it as **HeavyDeposits2Clubs**.

   b. Open the HeavyDeposits2Clubs query in Design View, then add criteria to select the records with a ClubName of **Ice Kings** and a Weight value **greater than or equal to 100**.

   c. Add criteria to also include the records with a ClubName of **Junior League** with a Weight value **greater than or equal to 100**. FIGURE B-20 shows the results.

   d. If requested by your instructor, print the HeavyDeposits2Clubs datasheet, then save and close it.

8. **Format a datasheet.**

   a. In the Clubs table datasheet, apply an Arial Narrow font and a 14-point font size.

   b. Resize all columns so that all data and field names are visible.

   c. Display the Clubs datasheet in Print Preview, switch the orientation to landscape, click the Margins button in the Page Size group, then click Narrow to fit the printout on a single sheet of paper.

   d. If requested by your instructor, print the Clubs datasheet.

   e. Save and close the Clubs table, then close Access 2013.

FIGURE B-20

FName	LName	ClubName	DepositDate	Weight
SI	Jackson	Ice Kings	2/13/2014	200
SI	Jackson	Ice Kings	2/18/2015	185
SI	Jackson	Ice Kings	2/13/2015	185
SI	Jackson	Ice Kings	3/7/2015	145
SI	Jackson	Ice Kings	4/19/2015	115
SI	Jackson	Ice Kings	5/1/2015	105
SI	Jackson	Ice Kings	2/22/2016	100
SI	Jackson	Ice Kings	1/30/2015	100
SI	Jackson	Ice Kings	2/26/2014	100
Lottie	Moon	Junior League	9/24/2015	200
Lottie	Moon	Junior League	3/2/2015	150
Lottie	Moon	Junior League	2/8/2015	150
Lottie	Moon	Junior League	3/4/2014	150
Lottie	Moon	Junior League	3/1/2014	150
Lottie	Moon	Junior League	2/8/2014	150

Your initials in the FName field

Access 2013

Independent Challenge 1

You have built an Access database to track membership in a community service club. The database tracks member names and addresses as well as their community service hours.

a. Open the Membership-B.accdb database from the location where you store your Data Files, enable content if prompted, then open the Activities, Members, and Zips tables to review their datasheets.

b. In the Zips table, click the expand button to the left of the 64131, Overland Park, KS, record to display the two members linked to that zip code. Click the expand button to the left of the Gabriel Hammer record to display the three activity records linked to Gabriel.

c. Close all three datasheets, click the DATABASE TOOLS tab, then click the Relationships button. The Relationships window also shows you that one record in the Zips table is related to many records in the Members table through the common ZipCode field, and that one record in the Members table is related to many records in the Activities table through the common MemberNo field.

d. Click the Relationship Report button, then if requested by your instructor, print the Relationship report. Close and save the report with the default name **Relationships for Membership-B**. Close the Relationships window.

e. Using Query Design View, build a query with the following fields: FirstName and LastName from the Members table and ActivityDate and HoursWorked from the Activities table.

f. View the datasheet, observe the number of records selected, then return to Query Design View.

g. Add criteria to select only those records where the ActivityDate is in March of 2014.

h. In Query Design View, apply an ascending sort order to the LastName and ActivityDate fields, then view the datasheet.

i. Change the name Quentin Garden to *your* name, widen all columns so that all data and field names are visible, and save the query with the name **March2014**, as shown in **FIGURE B-21**.

j. If requested by your instructor, print the March2014 datasheet, then close the March2014 query and close Access 2013.

FIGURE B-21

FirstName	LastName	ActivityDate	HoursWorked
Bart	Bouchart	3/29/2014	4
Golga	Collins	3/31/2014	8
Martha	Duman	3/27/2014	4
Allie	Eahlie	3/29/2014	4
Jana	Eckert	3/29/2014	5
Student First	Student Last	3/29/2014	4
Student First	Student Last	3/30/2014	8
Loraine	Goode	3/29/2014	5
Gabriel	Hammer	3/29/2014	5
Jeremiah	Hopper	3/27/2014	4
Helen	Hubert	3/29/2014	5
Heidi	Kalvert	3/29/2014	4
Harvey	Mackintosh	3/30/2014	4
Jon	Maxim	3/30/2014	4
Micah	Mayberry	3/29/2014	4
Patch	Mullins	3/30/2014	8
Patch	Mullins	3/31/2014	8
Young	Nelson	3/30/2014	10
Mallory	Olson	3/31/2014	8
Su	Vogue	3/30/2014	8
Sherry	Walker	3/29/2014	4
Taney	Wilson	3/30/2014	8

Record: ◄ ◄ 7 of 22 ► ►I ►⊟ No Filter Search

Independent Challenge 2

You work for a nonprofit agency that tracks the voting patterns of Congress. You have developed an Access database with contact information for members of the House of Representatives. The director of the agency has asked you to create several state lists of representatives. You will use queries to extract this information.

a. Open the Congress-B.accdb database from the location where you store your Data Files, then enable content if prompted.

b. Open the Representatives and the States tables. Notice that one state is related to many representatives as evidenced by the expand buttons to the left of the records in the States tables.

c. Close both datasheets, then using Query Design View, create a query with the StateAbbrev, StateName, and Capital fields from the States table (in that order) as well as the LName field from the Representatives table.

d. Sort the records in ascending order on the StateName field, then in ascending order on the LName field.

e. Add criteria to select the representatives from Arizona or New Mexico. Use the StateAbbrev field to enter your criteria, using the two-character state abbreviations of **AZ** and **NM**.

f. Save the query with the name **ArizonaAndNewMexico** as shown in FIGURE B-22, view the results, then change the last name of Upton in the last record to *your* last name. Resize the columns as needed to view all the data and field names.

g. Print the ArizonaAndNewMexico datasheet if requested by your instructor, then close it and exit Access 2013.

FIGURE B-22

StateAbbrev	StateName	Capital	LName
AZ	Arizona	Phoenix	Christian
AZ	Arizona	Phoenix	Drake
AZ	Arizona	Phoenix	Gohmert
AZ	Arizona	Phoenix	Gonzalez
AZ	Arizona	Phoenix	Matheson
AZ	Arizona	Phoenix	McCaul
AZ	Arizona	Phoenix	Sanders
AZ	Arizona	Phoenix	Wolf
NM	New Mexico	Santa Fe	Miller
NM	New Mexico	Santa Fe	Student Last Name
NM	New Mexico	Santa Fe	Stupak

Independent Challenge 3

You have built an Access database to track the veterinarians and clinics in your area.

a. Open the Vet-B.accdb database from the location where you store your Data Files, then enable content if prompted.

b. Open the Vets table and then the Clinics table to review the data in both datasheets.

c. Click the expand button next to the Veterinary Specialists record in the Clinics table, then add *your* name as a new record to the Vets subdatasheet.

d. Close both datasheets.

e. Using the Simple Query Wizard, select the VetLast and VetFirst fields from the Vets table, and select the ClinicName and Phone fields from the Clinics table. Title the query **ClinicListing**, then view the datasheet.

f. Update any occurrence of Leawood Animal Clinic in the ClinicName field by changing Leawood to **Emergency** so the ClinicName is **Emergency Animal Clinic**.

g. In Query Design View, add criteria to select only **Emergency Animal Clinic** or **Veterinary Specialists** in the ClinicName field, then view the datasheet.

h. In Query Design View, move the ClinicName field to the first column, then add an ascending sort order on the ClinicName and VetLast fields.

i. Display the ClinicListing query in Datasheet View, resize the fields as shown in **FIGURE B-23**, then print the datasheet if requested by your instructor.

j. Save and close the ClinicListing datasheet, then exit Access 2013.

FIGURE B-23

ClinicName	VetLast	VetFirst	Phone
Emergency Animal Clinic	Ridwelll	Kiirk	(555) 555-1311
Emergency Animal Clinic	Rosenheim	Howard	(555) 555-1311
Emergency Animal Clinic	Salamander	Stephen	(555) 555-1311
Veterinary Specialists	Garver	Mark	(555) 555-4000
Veterinary Specialists	Major	Mark	(555) 555-4000
Veterinary Specialists	Manheim	Thomas	(555) 555-4000
Veterinary Specialists	Stewart	Frank	(555) 555-4000
Veterinary Specialists	Student Last	Student First	(555) 555-4000

Independent Challenge 4: Explore

An Access database is an excellent tool to help record and track job opportunities. For this exercise, you'll create a database from scratch that you can use to enter, edit, and query data in pursuit of a new job or career.

a. Create a new desktop database named **Jobs.accdb**.

b. Create a table named **Positions** with the following field names, data types, and descriptions:

Field name	Data type	Description
PositionID	AutoNumber	Primary key field
Title	Short Text	Title of position such as Accountant, Assistant Court Clerk, or Web Developer
CareerArea	Short Text	Area of the career field such as Accounting, Government, or Information Systems
AnnualSalary	Currency	Annual salary
Desirability	Number	Desirability rating of 1 = low to 5 = high to show how desirable the position is to you
EmployerID	Number	Foreign key field to the Employers table

c. Create a table named **Employers** with the following field names, data types, and descriptions:

Field name	Data type	Description
EmployerID	AutoNumber	Primary key field
CompanyName	Short Text	Company name of the employer
EmpStreet	Short Text	Employer's street address
EmpCity	Short Text	Employer's city
EmpState	Short Text	Employer's state
EmpZip	Short Text	Employer's zip code
EmpPhone	Short Text	Employer's phone, such as 913-555-8888

d. Be sure to set EmployerID as the primary key field in the Employers table and the PositionID as the primary key field in the Positions table.

e. Link the Employers and Positions tables together in a one-to-many relationship using the common EmployerID field. One employer record will be linked to many position records. Be sure to enforce referential integrity.

f. Using any valid source of potential employer data, enter five records into the Employers table.

g. Using any valid source of job information, enter five records into the Positions table by using the subdatasheets from within the Employers datasheet.
Because one employer may have many positions, all five of your Positions records may be linked to the same employer, you may have one position record per employer, or any other combination.

h. Build a query that selects CompanyName from the Employers table, and the Title, CareerArea, AnnualSalary, and Desirability fields from the Positions table. Sort the records in descending order based on Desirability. Save the query as **JobList**, and print it if requested by your instructor.

i. Close the JobList datasheet, then exit Access 2013.

Visual Workshop

Open the Baseball-B.accdb database from the location where you store your Data Files, and enable content if prompted. Create a query based on the Players and Teams tables, as shown in **FIGURE B-24**. Add criteria to select only those records where the PlayerPosition field values are equal to 1 or 2 (representing pitchers and catchers). In Query Design View, set an ascending sort order on the TeamName and PlayerPosition fields. In the results, change the name of Roy Campanella to *your* name. Save the query with the name **PitchersAndCatchers**, then compare the results with **FIGURE B-24**, making changes and widening columns to see all of the data. Print the datasheet if requested by your instructor. Save and close the query and the Baseball-B.accdb database, then exit Access 2013.

FIGURE B-24

TeamName	PlayerLast	PlayerFirst	Position
Brooklyn Beetles	Student Last Name	Student First Name	1
Brooklyn Beetles	Young	Cycylie	2
Mayfair Monarchs	Durocher	Luis	1
Mayfair Monarchs	Mathewson	Carl	2
Rocky's Rockets	Spalding	Andrew	1
Rocky's Rockets	Koufax	Sanford	2
Snapping Turtles	Ford	Charles	1
Snapping Turtles	Perry	Greg	2

Using Forms

CASE Samantha Hooper, a tour developer at Quest Specialty Travel, asks you to create forms to make tour information easier to access, enter, and update.

Unit Objectives

After completing this unit, you will be able to:

- Use the Form Wizard
- Create a split form
- Use Form Layout View
- Add fields to a form

- Modify form controls
- Create calculations
- Modify tab order
- Insert an image

Files You Will Need

QuestTravel-C.accdb	Membership-C.accdb
QuestLogo.bmp	People.jpg
RealEstate-C.accdb	Recycle-C.accdb
ForSale.bmp	Jobs-C.accdb
Dives-C.accdb	Baseball-C.accdb

©Tumanyan/Shutterstock

Use the Form Wizard

Learning Outcomes
• Create a form with the Form Wizard
• Sort data in a form
• Describe form terminology and views

A **form** is an easy-to-use data entry and navigation screen. A form allows you to arrange the fields of a record in any layout so a **database user** can quickly and easily find, enter, edit, and analyze data. The **database designer** is the person responsible for building and maintaining tables, queries, forms, and reports for all of the database users. **CASE** ▸ *Samantha Hooper asks you to build a form to enter and maintain tour information.*

STEPS

1. **Start Access, open the QuestTravel-C.accdb database from the location where you store your Data Files, then enable content if prompted**

   You can use many methods to create a new form, but the Form Wizard is a fast and popular tool that helps you get started. The **Form Wizard** prompts you for information it needs to create a form, such as the fields, layout, and title for the form.

2. **Click the CREATE tab on the Ribbon, then click the Form Wizard button in the Forms group**

   The Form Wizard starts, prompting you to select the fields for this form. You want to create a form to enter and update data in the Tours table.

3. **Click the Tables/Queries list arrow, click Table: Tours, then click the Select All Fields button** >>

   You could now select fields from other tables, if necessary, but in this case, you have all of the fields you need.

4. **Click Next, click the Columnar option button, click Next, type Tours Entry Form as the title, then click Finish**

   The Tours Entry Form opens in **Form View**, as shown in **FIGURE C-1**. Access provides three different views of forms, as summarized in **TABLE C-1**. Each item on the form is called a **control**. A **label control** is used to *describe* the data shown in other controls such as text boxes. A label is also used for the title of the form, Tours Entry Form. A **text box** is used to *display* the data as well as enter, edit, find, sort, and also filter the data. A **combo box** is a combination of two controls: a text box and a list. The Category data is displayed in a combo box control. You click the arrow button on a combo box control to display a list of values, or you can edit data directly in the combo box itself.

QUICK TIP
Click in the text box of the field you want to sort *before* clicking a sort button.

5. **Click Breeze Bay Shelling in the TourName text box, click the Ascending button in the Sort & Filter group, then click the Next record button ▶ in the navigation bar to move to the second record**

   The Ames Ski Club is the second record when the records are sorted in ascending order on the TourName data. Information about the current record number and total number of records appears in the navigation bar, just as it does in a datasheet.

6. **Click the Previous record button ◀ in the navigation bar to move back to the first record, click the TourName text box, then change American Heritage Tour to Washington DC History Tour**

   Your screen should look like **FIGURE C-2**. Forms displayed in Form View are the primary tool for database users to enter, edit, and delete data in an Access database.

7. **Right-click the Tours Entry Form tab, then click Close**

   When a form is closed, Access automatically saves any edits made to the current record.

FIGURE C-1: Tours Entry Form in Form View

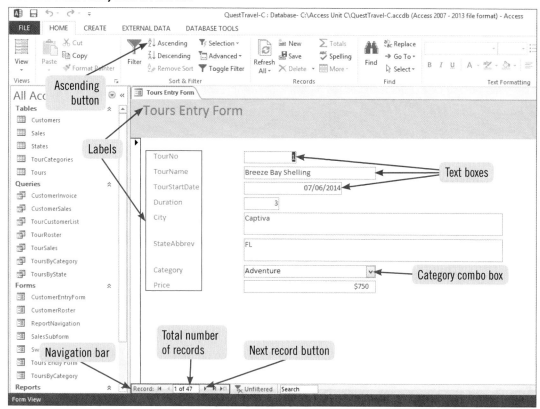

FIGURE C-2: Displaying the results of a calculation in Form View

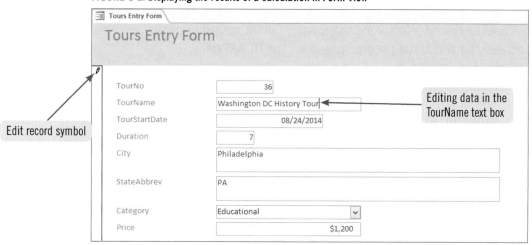

TABLE C-1: Form views

view	primary purpose
Form	To find, sort, enter, and edit data
Layout	To modify the size, position, or formatting of controls; shows data as you modify the form, making it the tool of choice when you want to change the appearance and usability of the form while viewing live data
Design	To modify the Form Header, Detail, and Footer section, or to access the complete range of controls and form properties; Design View does not display data

Access 2013

Create a Split Form

Learning
Outcomes
• Create a split form
• Enter and edit
  data in a form

In addition to the Form Wizard, you should be familiar with several other form creation tools. **TABLE C-2** identifies those tools and the purpose for each. **CASE** ▶ *Samantha Hooper asks you to create another form to manage customer data. You'll work with the Split Form tool for this task.*

STEPS

QUICK TIP
Layout View allows you to view and filter the data, but not edit it.

1. **Click the Customers table in the Navigation Pane, click the CREATE tab, click the More Forms button, click Split Form, then click the Add Existing Fields button in the Tools group on the DESIGN tab to close the Field List if it opens**

   The Customers data appears in a split form with the top half in **Layout View**, as shown in **FIGURE C-3**. The benefit of a **split form** is that the upper pane allows you to display the fields of one record in any arrangement, and the lower pane maintains a datasheet view of the first few records. If you edit, sort, or filter records in the upper pane, the lower pane is automatically updated, and vice versa.

2. **Click MO in the State text box in the upper pane, click the HOME tab, click the Selection button in the Sort & Filter group, then click Does Not Equal "MO"**

   Thirty-seven records are filtered where the State field is not equal to MO. You also need to change a value in the Jacob Alman record.

TROUBLE
Make sure you edit the record in the datasheet in the lower pane.

3. **In the lower pane, select Des Moines in the City field of the first record, edit the entry to read Dallas Center, click any other record in the lower pane, then click Jacob in the first record of the lower pane**

   Moving from record to record automatically saves data. Note that "Dallas Center" is now the entry in the City field in both the upper and lower panes, as shown in **FIGURE C-4**.

4. **Click the record selector for the Kristen Collins record in the lower pane, then click the Delete button in the Records group on the HOME tab**

   You cannot delete this record because it contains related records in the Sales table. This is a benefit of referential integrity on the one-to-many relationship between the Customers and Sales tables. Referential integrity prevents the creation of **orphan records**, records on the *many* side of a relationship (in this case, the Sales table) that do not have a match on the *one* side (in this case, the Customers table).

5. **Click OK, right-click the Customers form tab, click Close, click Yes when prompted to save changes, then click OK to save the form with the name Customers**

TABLE C-2: Form creation tools

tool	icon	creates a form
Form		with one click based on the selected table or query
Form Design		from scratch in Form Design View
Blank Form		from scratch in Form Layout View
Form Wizard		by answering a series of questions provided by the Form Wizard dialog boxes
Navigation		used to navigate or move between different areas of the database
More Forms		based on Multiple Items, Datasheet, Split Form, Modal Dialog, PivotChart, or PivotTable arrangements
Split Form		with two panes, the upper showing one record at a time and the lower displaying a datasheet of many records

FIGURE C-3: Customers table in a split form

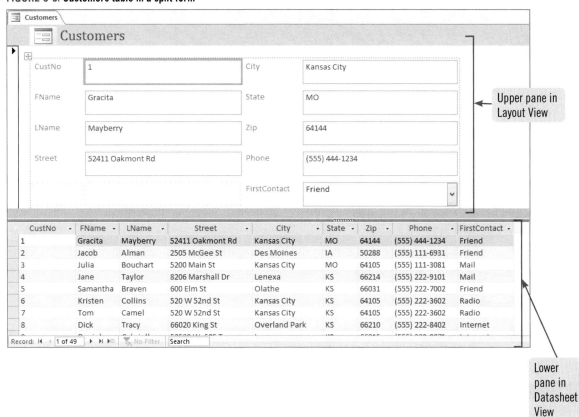

FIGURE C-4: Editing data in a split form

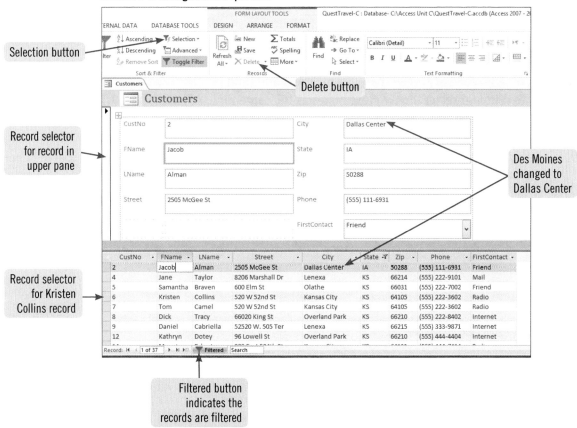

Use Form Layout View

Learning
Outcomes
• Resize controls in
  Layout View
• Format controls in
  Layout View

Layout View lets you make some design changes to a form while you are browsing the data. For example, you can move and resize controls, add or delete a field on the form, filter and sort data, or change formatting characteristics, such as fonts and colors. **CASE** ▶ *Samantha Hooper asks you to make several design changes to the Tours Entry Form. You can make these changes in Layout View.*

STEPS

1. **Right-click** Tours Entry Form **in the Navigation Pane, then click** Layout View

   In Layout View, you can move through the records, but you cannot enter or edit the data as you can in Form View.

2. **Click the** Next record button **in the navigation bar twice to move to the third record, Bigfoot Rafting Club**

   You often use Layout View to make minor design changes, such as editing labels and changing formatting characteristics.

3. **Click the** TourNo label **to select it if it is not already selected, click between the words Tour and No, then press** [Spacebar]

   You also want to edit a few more labels.

4. **Continue editing the labels, as shown in** FIGURE C-5

   You also want to change the text color of the first two labels, Tour No and Tour Name, to red to make them more noticeable.

5. **Click the** Tour No label**, click the** HOME tab**, click the** Font Color button ▲ **in the Text Formatting group, click the** Tour Name label**, then click** ▲

   Often, you want to apply the same formatting enhancement to multiple controls. For example, you decide to narrow the City and StateAbbrev text boxes. Select the text boxes at the same time to make the same change to both.

6. **Click** Placerville **in the City text box, press and hold** [Shift]**, click** CA **in the StateAbbrev text box to select the two text boxes at the same time, release** [Shift]**, then use the ↔ pointer to drag the** right edge of the selection **to the left to make the text boxes approximately half as wide**

   Layout View for the Tours Entry Form should look like **FIGURE C-6**. Mouse pointers in Form Layout and Form Design View are very important as they indicate what happens when you drag the mouse. Mouse pointers are described in **TABLE C-3**.

TABLE C-3: Mouse pointer shapes

shape	when does this shape appear?	action
▷	When you point to any unselected control on the form (the default mouse pointer)	Single-clicking with this mouse pointer *selects* a control
⁺↖	When you point to the upper-left corner or edge of a selected control in Form Design View or the middle of the control in Form Layout View	Dragging with this mouse pointer *moves* the selected control(s)
↕↔⤡	When you point to any sizing handle (except the larger one in the upper-left corner in Form Design View)	Dragging with one of these mouse pointers *resizes* the control

Using Forms

FIGURE C-5: Using Layout View to modify form labels on the Tours Entry Form

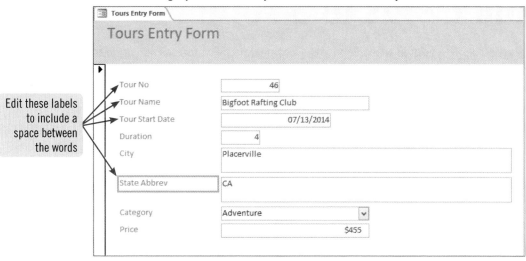

Edit these labels to include a space between the words

FIGURE C-6: Layout View for the Tours Entry Form

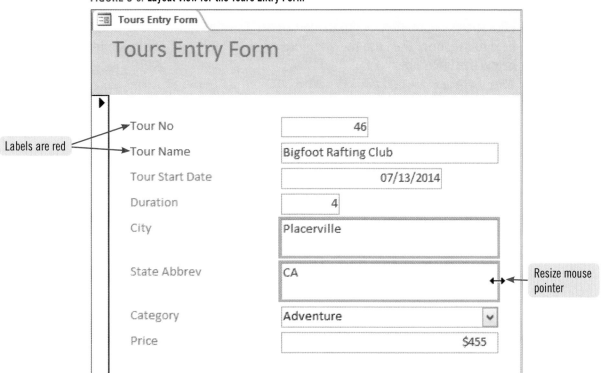

Labels are red

Resize mouse pointer

Table layouts

Layouts provide a way to group several controls together on a form or report to more quickly add, delete, rearrange, resize, or align controls. To insert a layout into a form or report, select the controls you want to group together, then choose the Stacked or Tabular button on the ARRANGE tab. Each option applies a table layout to the controls so that you can insert, delete, merge, or split the cells in the layout to quickly rearrange or edit the controls in the layout. To remove a layout, use the Remove Layout button on the ARRANGE tab in Form Design View.

Add Fields to a Form

Learning
Outcomes
• Add fields to a
  form
• Align controls
• Resize controls

Adding and deleting fields in an existing form is a common activity. You can add or delete fields in a form in either Layout View or Design View using the Field List. The **Field List** lists the database tables and the fields they contain. To add a field to the form, drag it from the Field List to the desired location on the form. To delete a field on a form, click the field to select it, then press the [Delete] key. Deleting a field from a form does not delete it from the underlying table or have any effect on the data contained in the field. You can toggle the Field List on and off using the Add Existing Fields button on the DESIGN tab. **CASE** ▶ *Samantha Hooper asks you to add the tour description from the TourCategories table to the Tours Entry Form. You can use Layout View and the Field List to accomplish this goal.*

STEPS

1. **Click the** DESIGN **tab on the Ribbon, click the** Add Existing Fields **button in the Tools group, then click the** Show all tables **link in the Field List**

    The Field List opens in Layout View, as shown in **FIGURE C-7**. Notice that the Field List is divided into sections. The upper section shows the tables currently used by the form, the middle section shows directly related tables, and the lower section shows other tables in the database. The expand/collapse button to the left of the table names allows you to expand (show) the fields within the table or collapse (hide) them. The Description field is in the TourCategories table in the middle section.

    If you make a mistake, click the Undo button ↶ and try again.

2. **Click the** expand button ⊞ **to the left of the TourCategories table, drag the** Description **field to the form, then use the** 🕏 **pointer to drag the new Description text box and label below the Price label**

    When you add a new field to a form, two controls are usually created: a label and a text box. The label contains the field name and the text box displays the data in the field. The TourCategories table moved from the middle to the top section of the Field List. You also want to align and size the new controls with others already on the form. Form Design View works well for alignment activities.

3. **Right-click the** Tours Entry Form **tab, click** Design View, **click the** Description label, **press and hold** [Shift], **click the** Price label **to select both labels, release** [Shift], **click the** ARRANGE **tab, click the** Align **button in the Sizing & Ordering group, then click** Left

    Now resize the labels.

4. **With the two labels still selected, click the** Size/Space **button in the Sizing & Ordering group, then click** To Widest

    With the new controls in position, you want to enter a new record. You must switch to Form View to edit, enter, or delete data.

    Don't worry if your Tour No value doesn't match **FIGURE C-8**. As an AutoNumber value, the value is inserted automatically and is controlled by Access.

5. **Click the** HOME **tab, click the** View **button** 🖼 **to switch to Form View, click the** New (blank) record button ▶✱ **in the navigation bar, click the** TourName text box, **then enter a new record in the updated form, as shown in** FIGURE C-8

    Note that when you select a value in the Category combo box, the Description is automatically updated. This is due to the one-to-many relationship between the TourCategories and Tours tables in the Relationships window.

FIGURE C-7: Field List in Form Layout View

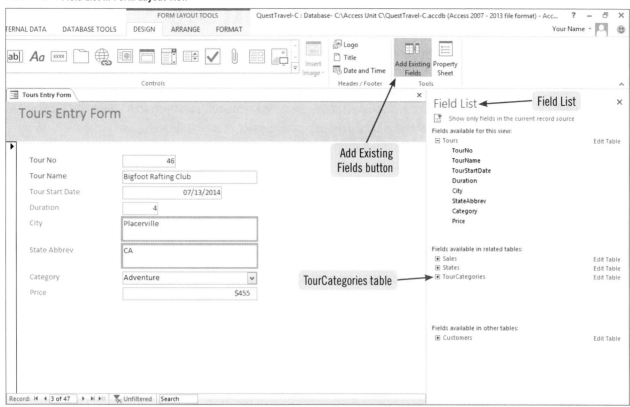

FIGURE C-8: Entering a record in the updated Tours Entry Form in Form View

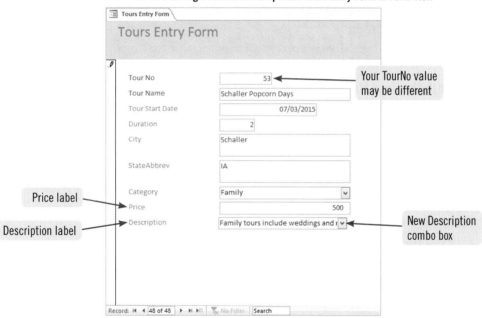

Bound versus unbound controls

Controls are either bound or unbound. **Bound controls** display values from a field such as text boxes and combo boxes. **Unbound controls** do not display data; unbound controls describe data or enhance the appearance of the form. Labels are the most common type of unbound control, but other types include lines, images, tabs, and command buttons. Another way to distinguish bound from unbound controls is to observe the form as you move from record to record. Because bound controls display data, their contents change as you move through the records, displaying the entry in the field of the current record. Unbound controls such as labels and lines do not change as you move through the records in a form.

Modify Form Controls

Learning
Outcomes
• Modify control
  properties
• Define bound and
  unbound controls

You have already made many modifications to form controls, such as changing the font color of labels and the size of text boxes. Labels and text boxes are the two most popular form controls. Other common controls are listed in **TABLE C-4**. When you modify controls, you change their **properties** (characteristics). All of the control characteristics you can modify are stored in the control's **Property Sheet**. **CASE** ▶ *Because Quest offers more Adventure tours than any other type of tour, you decide to use the Property Sheet of the Category field to modify the default value to be "Adventure." You also use the Property Sheet to make other control modifications to better size and align the controls.*

STEPS

1. **Click the** Layout View button ▦ **on the HOME tab, then click the** Property Sheet button **in the Tools group**

   The Property Sheet opens, showing you all of the properties for the selected item.

2. **Click the** Category combo box, **click the** Data tab **in the Property Sheet (if it is not already selected), click the** Default Value box, **type** Adventure, **then press** [Enter]

   The Property Sheet should look like **FIGURE C-9**. Access often helps you with the **syntax** (rules) of entering property values. In this case, Access added quotation marks around "Adventure" to indicate that the default entry is text. Properties are categorized in the Property Sheet with the Format, Data, Event, and Other tabs. The All tab is a complete list of all the control's properties. You can use the Property Sheet to make all control modifications, although you'll probably find that some changes are easier to make using the Ribbon. The property values change in the Property Sheet as you modify a control using the Ribbon.

TROUBLE
Be sure to click the
Tour No label on the
left, not the TourNo
text box on the right.

3. **Click the** Format tab **in the Property Sheet, click the** Tour No label **in the form to select it, click the** HOME tab **on the Ribbon, then click the** Align Right button ≡ **in the Text Formatting group**

   Notice that the **Text Align property** on the Format tab in the Property Sheet is automatically updated from Left to Right even though you changed the property using the Ribbon instead of within the Property Sheet.

4. **Click the** Tour Name label, **press and hold** [Shift], **then click** each other label **in the first column on the form**

   With all the labels selected, you can modify their Text Align property at the same time.

TROUBLE
You may need to
click ≡ twice.

5. **Click** ≡ **in the Text Formatting group**

   Don't be overwhelmed by the number of properties available for each control on the form or the number of ways to modify each property. Over time, you will learn about most of these properties. At this point, it's only important to know the purpose of the Property Sheet and understand that properties are modified in various ways.

TROUBLE
Don't worry if your
Tour No value
doesn't match
FIGURE C-10. It
is an AutoNumber
value, controlled
by Access.

6. **Click the** Save button ▦ **on the Quick Access toolbar, click the** Form View button ▦ **to switch to Form View, click the** New (blank) record button � **in the navigation bar, then enter the record shown in** FIGURE C-10

   For new records, "Adventure" is provided as the default value for the Category combo box, but you can change it by typing a new value or selecting one from the list. With the labels right-aligned, they are much closer to the data in the text boxes that they describe.

FIGURE C-9: Using the Property Sheet

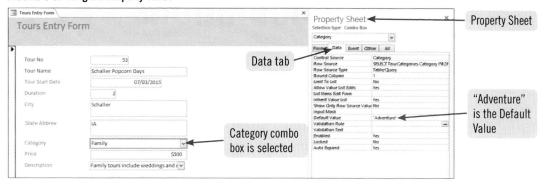

FIGURE C-10: Modified Tours Entry Form

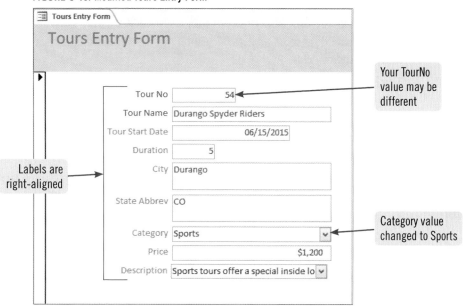

TABLE C-4: Common form controls

name	used to	bound	unbound
Label	Provide consistent descriptive text as you navigate from record to record; the label is the most common type of unbound control and can also be used as a hyperlink to another database object, external file, or Web page		•
Text box	Display, edit, or enter data for each record from an underlying record source; the text box is the most common type of bound control	•	
List box	Display a list of possible data entries	•	
Combo box	Display a list of possible data entries for a field, and provide a text box for an entry from the keyboard; combines the list box and text box controls	•	
Tab control	Create a three-dimensional aspect on a form		•
Check box	Display "yes" or "no" answers for a field; if the box is checked, it means "yes"	•	
Toggle button	Display "yes" or "no" answers for a field; if the button is pressed, it means "yes"	•	
Option button	Display a choice for a field	•	
Option group	Display and organize choices (usually presented as option buttons) for a field	•	
Line and Rectangle	Draw lines and rectangles on the form		•
Command button	Provide an easy way to initiate a command or run a macro		•

Create Calculations

Learning Outcomes
• Build calculations on a form
• Move controls on a form

Text boxes are generally used to display data from underlying fields. The connection between the text box and field is defined by the **Control Source property** on the Data tab of the Property Sheet for that text box. A text box control can also display a calculation. To create a calculation in a text box, you enter an expression instead of a field name in the Control Source property. An **expression** is a combination of field names, operators (such as +, –, /, and *), and functions (such as Sum, Count, or Avg) that results in a single value. Sample expressions are shown in TABLE C-5. **CASE** ▶ *Samantha Hooper asks you to add a text box to the Tours Entry Form to calculate the tour end date. You can add a text box in Form Design View to accomplish this.*

STEPS

1. **Right-click the Tours Entry Form tab, then click Design View**

   You want to add the tour end date calculation just below the Duration text box. First, you'll resize the City and StateAbbrev fields.

2. **Click the City label, press and hold [Shift], click the City text box, click the State Abbrev label, click the StateAbbrev text box to select the four controls together, release [Shift], click the ARRANGE tab, click the Size/Space button, then click To Shortest**

   With the City and StateAbbrev fields resized, you're ready to move them to make room for the new control to calculate the tour end date.

3. **Click a blank spot on the form to deselect the four controls, click the StateAbbrev text box, use the ⬚ pointer to move it down, click the City text box, then use the ⬚ pointer to move it down**

   To add the calculation to determine the tour end date (the tour start date plus the duration), start by adding a new text box to the form between the Duration and City text boxes.

4. **Click the DESIGN tab, click the Text Box button ⌑ in the Controls group, then click between the Duration and City text boxes to insert the new text box**

   Adding a new text box automatically adds a new label to the left of the text box.

5. **Click the new Text20 label on the left, double-click Text20, type Tour End Date, then press [Enter]**

   With the label updated to correctly identify the text box to the right, you're ready to enter the expression to calculate the tour end date.

6. **Click the new text box to select it, click the Data tab in the Property Sheet, click the Control Source property, type =[TourStartDate]+[Duration], then press [Enter] to update the form, as shown in FIGURE C-11**

   All expressions entered in a control start with an equal sign (=). When referencing a field name within an expression, [square brackets]—(not parentheses) and not {curly braces}—surround the field name. In an expression, you must type the field name exactly as it was created in Table Design View, but you do not need to match the capitalization.

7. **Click the View button ⬚ to switch to Form View, click the value in the Tour Name text box, click the Ascending button, select 7 in the Duration text box, type 5, then press [Enter]**

   Note that the tour end date, calculated by an expression, automatically changed to five days after the tour start date to reflect the new duration value. The updated Tours Entry Form with the tour date end calculation for the Ames Ski Club is shown in FIGURE C-12.

FIGURE C-11: Adding a text box to calculate a value

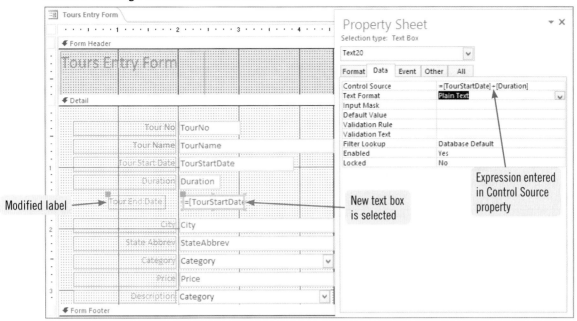

FIGURE C-12: Displaying the results of a calculation in Form View

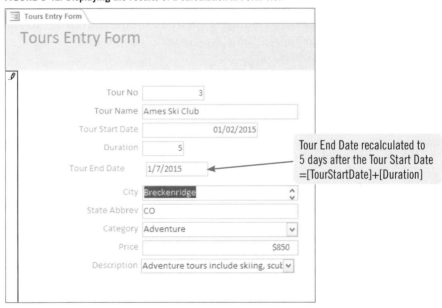

TABLE C-5: Sample expressions

sample expression	description
=Sum([Salary])	Uses the **Sum function** to add the values in the Salary field
=[Price] * 1.05	Multiplies the Price field by 1.05 (adds 5% to the Price field)
=[Subtotal] + [Shipping]	Adds the value of the Subtotal field to the value of the Shipping field
=Avg([Freight])	Uses the **Avg function** to display an average of the values in the Freight field
=Date()	Uses the **Date function** to display the current date in the form of mm-dd-yy
="Page " &[Page]	Displays the word Page, a space, and the result of the [Page] field, an Access field that contains the current page number
=[FirstName]& " " &[LastName]	Displays the value of the FirstName and LastName fields in one control, separated by a space
=Left([ProductNumber],2)	Uses the **Left function** to display the first two characters in the ProductNumber field

© 2014 Cengage Learning

Modify Tab Order

After positioning all of the controls on the form, you should check the tab order and tab stops. **Tab order** is the order the focus moves as you press [Tab] in Form View. A **tab stop** refers to whether a control can receive the focus in the first place. By default, the Tab Stop property for all text boxes and combo boxes is set to Yes, but some text boxes, such as those that contain expressions, will not be used for data entry. Therefore, the Tab Stop property for a text box that contains a calculation should be set to No. Unbound controls such as labels and lines do not have a Tab Stop property because they cannot be used to enter or edit data. **CASE** ▶ *You plan to check the tab order of the Tours Entry Form, then change tab stops and tab order as necessary.*

STEPS

1. **Press [Tab] enough times to move through several records, watching the focus move through the bound controls of the form**

   Because the Tour End Date text box is a calculated field, you don't want it to receive the focus. To prevent the Tour End Date text box from receiving the focus, you set its Tab Stop property to No using its Property Sheet. You can work with the Property Sheet in either Layout or Design View.

2. **Right-click the Tours Entry Form tab, click Design View, click the text box with the Tour End Date calculation if it is not selected, click the Other tab in the Property Sheet, double-click the Tab Stop property to toggle it from Yes to No, then change the Name property to TourEndDate, as shown in FIGURE C-13**

   The Other tab of the Property Sheet contains the properties you need to change the tab stop and tab order. The **Tab Stop property** determines whether the field accepts focus, and the **Tab Index property** indicates the numeric tab order for all controls on the form that have the Tab Stop property set to Yes. The **Name property** on the Other tab is also important as it identifies the name of the control, which is used in other areas of the database. To review your tab stop changes, return to Form View.

3. **Click the View button ▦ to switch to Form View, then press [Tab] nine times to move to the next record**

   Now that the tab stop has been removed from the TourEndDate text box, the tab order flows correctly from the top to the bottom of the form, but skips the calculated field. To review the tab order for the entire form in one dialog box, you must switch to Form Design View.

4. **Right-click the Tours Entry Form tab, click Design View, then click the Tab Order button in the Tools group to open the Tab Order dialog box, as shown in FIGURE C-14**

   The Tab Order dialog box allows you to view and change the tab order by dragging fields up or down using the **field selector** to the left of the field name. Moving fields up and down in this list also renumbers the Tab Index property for the controls in their respective Property Sheets. If you want Access to create a top-to-bottom and left-to-right tab order, click **Auto Order**.

5. **Click OK to close the Tab Order dialog box, click the Property Sheet button to toggle it off, then click the Save button ▤ on the Quick Access toolbar to save your work**

FIGURE C-13: Using the Property Sheet to set tab properties

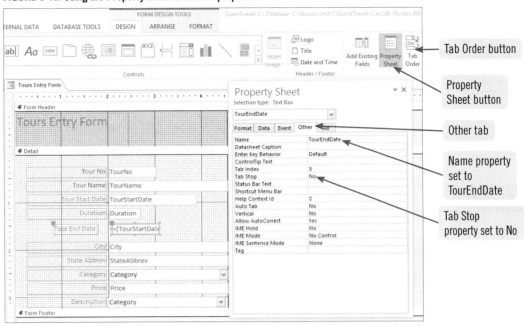

Tab Order button

Property Sheet button

Other tab

Name property set to TourEndDate

Tab Stop property set to No

FIGURE C-14: Tab Order dialog box

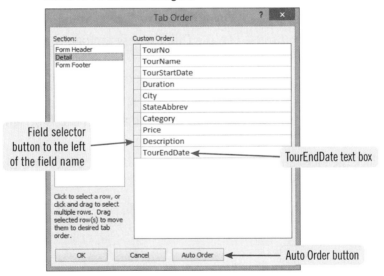

Field selector button to the left of the field name

TourEndDate text box

Auto Order button

Layout positioning

If the controls on a form are organized in a layout, you can quickly modify that layout by modifying the margins, padding, and anchoring options of the layout. Each of these features is found in the Position group on the ARRANGE tab in Form Design View. **Margin** refers to the space between the outer edge of the control and the data displayed inside the control. **Padding** is the space between the controls. **Anchoring** allows you to tie controls together so you can work with them as a group.

Insert an Image

Learning
Outcomes
• Insert an image on
  a form
• Modify form
  sections
• Print a selected
  record

Graphic images, such as pictures, logos, or clip art, can add style and professionalism to a form. The form section in which you place the images is significant. **Form sections** determine where controls are displayed and printed; they are described in TABLE C-6. For example, if you add a company logo to the Form Header section, the image appears at the top of the form in Form View as well as at the top of a printout. If you add the same image to the Detail section, it prints next to each record in the printout because the Detail section is printed for every record. **CASE** ▶ Samantha Hooper suggests that you add the Quest logo to the top of the Tours Entry Form. You can add the control in either Layout or Design View, but if you want to place it in the Form Header section, you have to work in Design View.

STEPS

1. **Click the** Form Header section bar, **click the** Insert Image button **in the Controls group, click** Browse, **then navigate to the location where you store your Data Files**
   The Insert Picture dialog box opens, prompting you for the location of the image.

2. **Double-click** QuestLogo.bmp, **then click in the Form Header section at about the 3" mark on the horizontal ruler**
   The QuestLogo image is added to the right side of the Form Header. You want to resize it to about 1" × 1".

TROUBLE
The lower-right
corner of the image
touches the top
edge of the Detail
section. To resize the
Quest logo, click it
to select it.

3. **With the QuestLogo image still selected, use the** ↖ **pointer to drag the** lower-right corner **of the image up and to the left so that the image is about 1" × 1", then drag the** top edge **of the Detail section up using the** ✛ **pointer, as shown in** FIGURE C-15
   When an image or control is selected in Design View, you can use **sizing handles,** which are small squares at the corners of the selection box. Drag a handle to resize the image or control. With the form completed, you open it in Form View to observe the changes.

4. **Click the** Save button 🖫 **on the Quick Access toolbar, then click the** View button 📄 **to switch to Form View**
   You decide to add one more record with your final Tours Entry Form.

5. **Click the** New (blank) record button ▶※ **in the navigation bar, then enter the new record shown in** FIGURE C-16, **using your last name in the TourName field**
   Now print only this single new record.

TROUBLE
If you do not click
the Selected
Record(s) option
button, you will print
all records, which
creates a very long
printout.

6. **Click the** FILE tab, **click** Print **in the navigation bar, click** Print, **click the** Selected Record(s) option button, **then click** OK

7. **Close the Tours Entry Form, click** Yes **if prompted to save it, close the QuestTravel-C.accdb database, then exit Access 2013**

TABLE C-6: Form sections

section	controls placed in this section print:
Form Header	Only once at the top of the first page of the printout
Detail	Once for every record
Form Footer	Only once at the end of the last page of the printout

FIGURE C-15: Adding an image to the Form Header section

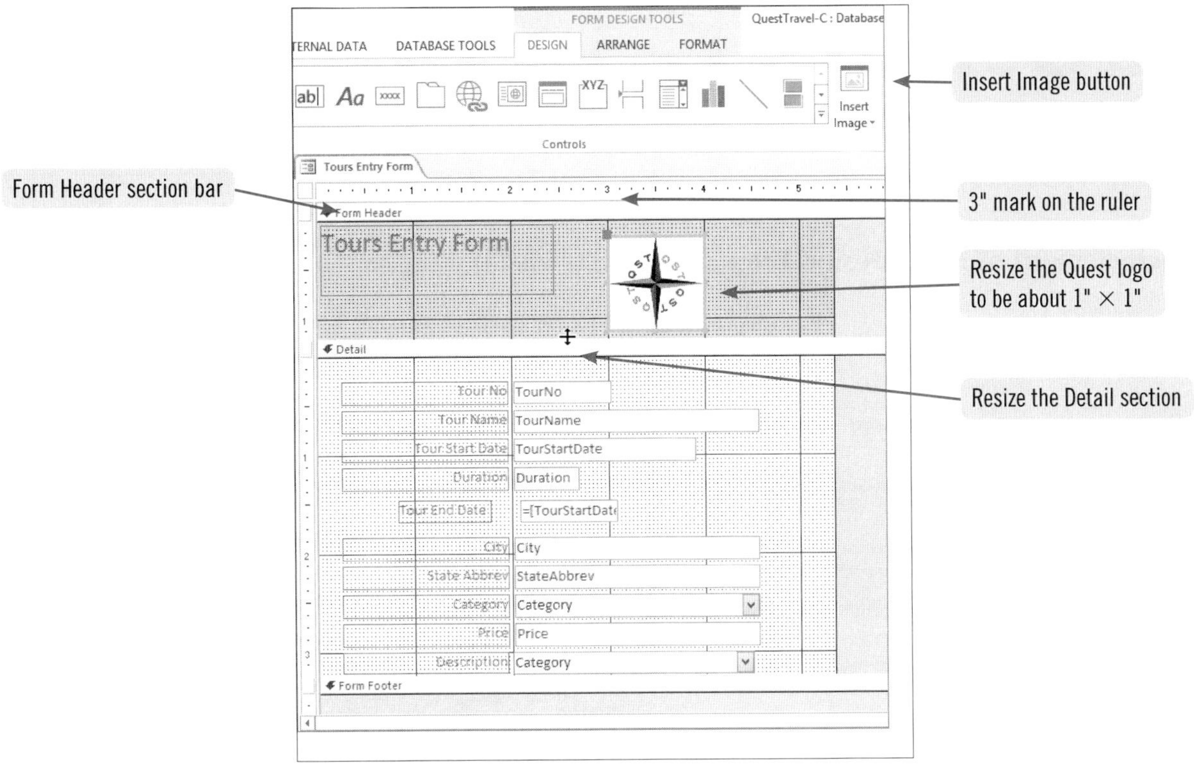

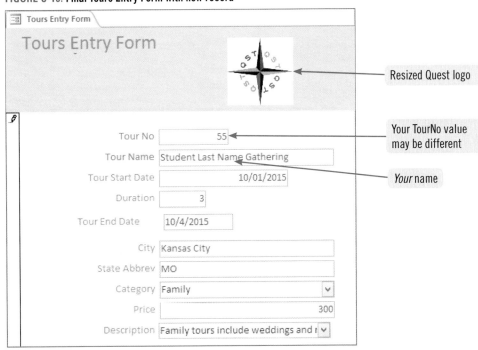

Insert Image button

Form Header section bar

3" mark on the ruler

Resize the Quest logo to be about 1" × 1"

Resize the Detail section

FIGURE C-16: Final Tours Entry Form with new record

Resized Quest logo

Your TourNo value may be different

Your name

Applying a background image

A **background image** is an image that fills the entire form or report, appearing "behind" the other controls. A background image is sometimes called a watermark image. To add a background image, use the Picture property for the form or report to browse for the image that you want to use in the background.

Practice

Put your skills into practice with **SAM Projects**! SAM Projects for this unit can be found online. If you have a SAM account, go to www.cengage.com/sam2013 to download the most recent Project Instruction and Start Files.

Concepts Review

Label each element of Form Design View shown in FIGURE C-17.

FIGURE C-17

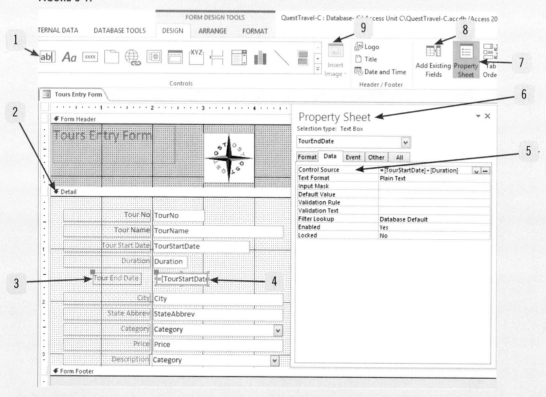

Match each term with the statement that best describes it.

10. **Bound control**
11. **Calculated control**
12. **Detail section**
13. **Database designer**
14. **Tab order**
15. **Form Footer section**

a. Created by entering an expression in a text box
b. Controls placed here print once for every record in the underlying record source
c. Used on a form to display data from a field
d. Controls placed here print only once at the end of the printout
e. The way the focus moves from one bound control to the next in Form View
f. Responsible for building and maintaining tables, queries, forms, and reports

Select the best answer from the list of choices.

16. **Every element on a form is called a(n):**
   a. Property.
   b. Control.
   c. Item.
   d. Tool.

17. **Which of the following is probably *not* a graphic image?**
   a. Logo
   b. Calculation
   c. Clip art
   d. Picture

18. The most common bound control is the:
- **a.** Text box.
- **b.** Label.
- **c.** Combo box.
- **d.** List box.

19. The most common unbound control is the:
- **a.** Combo box.
- **b.** Command button.
- **c.** Label.
- **d.** Text box.

20. Which form view *cannot* be used to view data?
- **a.** Datasheet
- **b.** Layout
- **c.** Preview
- **d.** Design

Skills Review

1. Use the Form Wizard.
- **a.** Start Access and open the RealEstate-C.accdb database from the location where you store your Data Files. Enable content if prompted.
- **b.** Click the CREATE tab, then use the Form Wizard to create a form based on all of the fields in the Realtors table. Use a Columnar layout and type **Realtor Entry Form** to title the form.
- **c.** Add a *new* record with *your* name in the RFirst and RLast text boxes. Note that the RealtorNo field is an AutoNumber field that is automatically incremented as you enter your first and last names. Enter your school's telephone number for the RPhone field value, and enter **4** as the AgencyNo field value.
- **d.** Save and close the Realtor Entry Form.

2. Create a split form.
- **a.** Click the Agencies table in the Navigation Pane, click the CREATE tab, click the More Forms button, then click Split Form.
- **b.** Switch to Form View and close the Property Sheet if it opens.
- **c.** Click the record selector in the lower pane for AgencyNo 3, Emerald Point Realtors, then click the Delete button in the Records group to delete this realtor. Click OK when prompted that you cannot delete this record because there are related records in the Realtors table.
- **d.** Navigate to the AgencyNo 4, Hollister Real Estate, record in either the upper or lower pane of the split form. Change 7744 Pokeberry Lane to **12345 Amanda Drive**.
- **e.** Right-click the Agencies form tab, click Close, click Yes when prompted to save changes, type **Agencies Split Form** as the name of the form, then click OK.

3. Use Form Layout View.
- **a.** Open the Realtor Entry Form in Layout View.
- **b.** Modify the labels on the left to read: **Realtor Number**, **Realtor First Name**, **Realtor Last Name**, **Realtor Phone**, **Agency Number**.
- **c.** Modify the text color of the labels to be black.
- **d.** Resize the RFirst, RLast, and RPhone text boxes on the right to be the same width as the RealtorNo and AgencyNo text boxes.
- **e.** Save the Realtor Entry Form.

4. Add fields to a form.
- **a.** Open the Field List, show all the tables, then expand the Agencies table to display its fields.
- **b.** Drag the AgencyName field to the form, then move the AgencyName label and combo box below the Agency Number controls.
- **c.** Modify the AgencyName label to read **Agency Name**.
- **d.** Modify the text color of the Agency Name label to black.
- **e.** Close the Field List and save and close the Realtor Entry Form.

Skills Review (continued)

5. Modify form controls.

   a. Reopen the Realtor Entry Form in Layout View, then use the Align Right button on the HOME tab to right-align each of the labels in the left column.

   b. Save the form, switch to Form View, then use the Agency Name combo box to change the Agency Name to **Marvin and Pam Realtors** for Realtor Number 1.

   c. If the combo box is not wide enough to display the entire entry for Marvin and Pam Realtors, switch back to Layout View and widen the combo box as much as needed to display the entire entry.

   d. In Layout View, resize and move all controls so that the labels are lined up on the left and the text boxes are lined up on the right, as shown in **FIGURE C-18**.

FIGURE C-18

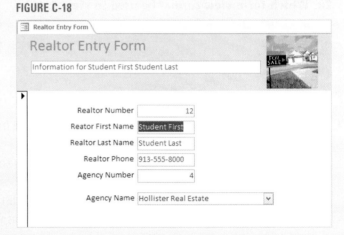

6. Create calculations.

   a. Switch to Form Design View, then add a text box below the Realtor Entry Form label in the Form Header section. Delete the Text14 label that is created when you add a new text box. The number in your label is based on previous work done to the form, so it might vary.

   b. Widen the text box to be almost as wide as the entire form, then enter the following expression into the text box, which will add the words *Information for* to the realtor's first name, a space, and then the realtor's last name.
  ="Information for "&[RFirst]&" "&[RLast]

   c. Save the form, then view it in Form View. Be sure the new text box correctly displays spaces in the text. Return to Design View to edit the expression if #Name? appears, which indicates that the expression was entered incorrectly.

   d. In Form View, change the Realtor Last Name for Realtor Number 1 from West to **South**. Tab to the RPhone text box to observe how the expression in the Form Header automatically updates.

   e. Tab through several records, observing the expression in the Form Header section.

7. Modify tab order.

   a. Switch to Form Design View, then open the Property Sheet.

   b. Select the new text box with the expression in the Form Header section, then change the Tab Stop property from Yes to No.

   c. Select the RealtorNo text box in the Detail section, then change the Tab Stop property from Yes to No. (AutoNumber fields cannot be edited, so they do not need to have a tab stop.)

   d. Close the Property Sheet.

   e. Save the form and view it in Form View. Tab through the form to make sure that the tab order is sequential and skips the expression in the Form Header as well as the Realtor Number text box. Use the Tab Order button on the DESIGN tab in Form Design View to modify tab order, if necessary.

8. Insert an image.

   a. Switch to Design View, then click the Form Header section bar.

   b. Add the ForSale.bmp image to the right side of the Form Header, then resize the image to be about 1" × 1".

   c. Remove extra blank space in the Form Header section by dragging the top edge of the Detail section up as far as possible.

   d. Drag the right edge of the form as far as possible to the left.

   e. Save the form, then switch to Form View. Move through the records, observing the calculated field from record to record to make sure it is calculating correctly.

   f. Find the record with your name, as shown in **FIGURE C-18**, and if requested by your instructor, print only that record.

   g. Close the Realtor Entry Form, close the RealEstate-C.accdb database, then exit Access.

Independent Challenge 1

As the manager of the scuba divers branch of the Quest Specialty Travel tour company, you have developed a database to help manage scuba dives. In this exercise, you'll create a data entry form to manage the dive trips.

a. Start Access, then open the Dives-C.accdb database from the location where you store your Data Files. Enable content if prompted.

b. Using the Form Wizard, create a form that includes all the fields in the DiveTrips table and uses the Columnar layout, then type **Dive Trip Entry** as the title of the form.

c. Switch to Layout View, then delete the ID text box and label.

d. Using Form Design View, use the [Shift] key to select all of the text boxes except the last one for TripReport, then resize them to the shortest size using the To Shortest option on the Size/Space button on the ARRANGE tab.

e. Using Form Design View, resize the Location, City, State/Province, Country, and Lodging text boxes to be no wider than the Rating text box.

f. Using Form Design View, move and resize the controls, as shown in FIGURE C-19. Once the controls are resized, drag the top of the Form Footer section up to remove the extra blank space in the Detail section.

g. Using Form Layout View, modify the labels and alignment of the labels, as shown in FIGURE C-19. Note that there are spaces between the words in the labels, the labels are right-aligned, and the text boxes are left-aligned. Use a dark blue color for the labels and black for the text in the text boxes.

h. In Form View, find the Great Barrier Reef tour. Edit the State/Province, Certification Diving, and Trip Report fields, as shown in FIGURE C-19 for the TripReport field using *your* name.

i. Save the form, then if requested by your instructor, print only the record with your name.

j. Close the Dive Trip Entry form, close the Dives-C.accdb database, then exit Access 2013.

FIGURE C-19

Dive Master ID	1
Location	Great Barrier Reef
City	Cairns
State/Province	QLD
Country	Australia
Trip Start Date	5/14/2015
Lodging	Royal Palm
Rating	4
Certification Diving	✔
Participants	5
Trip Report	Excellent trip with friendly locals and wonderful weather. Your Name

Dive Trip Entry

Independent Challenge 2

You have built an Access database to track membership in a community service club. The database tracks member names and addresses as well as their status in the club, which moves from rank to rank as the members contribute increased hours of service to the community.

a. Start Access, then open the Membership-C.accdb database from the location where you store your Data Files. Enable content if prompted.

b. Using the Form Wizard, create a form based on all of the fields of the Members table and only the DuesOwed field in the Status table.

c. View the data by Members, use a Columnar layout, then enter **Member Information** as the title of the form.

d. Enter a new record with *your* name and the school name, address, and phone number of your school for the Company and address fields. Give yourself a StatusNo entry of **1**. In the DuesPaid field, enter **75**. DuesOwed automatically displays 100 because that value is pulled from the Status table and is based on the entry in the StatusNo field, which links the Members table to the Status table.

e. In Layout View, add a text box to the form and move it below the DuesOwed text box.

f. Open the Property Sheet for the new text box, display the Data tab, and in the Control Source property of the new text box, enter the expression that calculates the balance between DuesOwed and DuesPaid: **=[DuesOwed]-[DuesPaid]**.

g. Open the Property Sheet for the new label, and change the Caption property on the Format tab for the new label to **Balance**.

h. Right-align all of the labels in the first column.

i. Set the Tab Stop property for the text box that contains the calculated Balance to **No**, then close the Property Sheet.

j. In Layout or Design View, resize DuesPaid and DuesOwed text boxes to be the same width as the new Balance text box, then right-align all data within the three text boxes.

FIGURE C-20

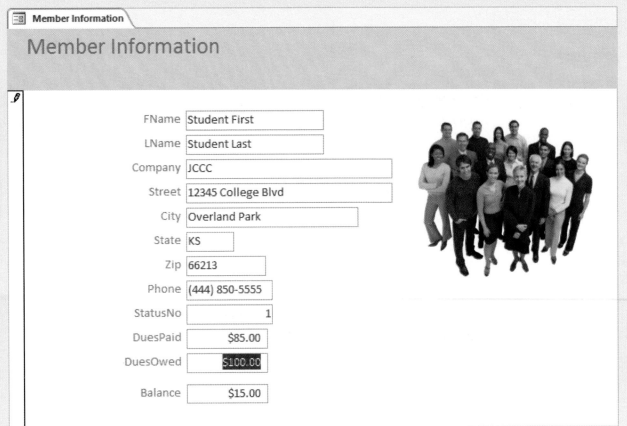

Independent Challenge 2 (continued)

k. Open the Property Sheet for the text box that contains the expression, and change the Format property on the Format tab to Currency. Close the Property Sheet.

l. Switch to Form Design View, then drag the right edge of the form to the 7" mark on the horizontal ruler. The horizontal ruler is located just above the Form Header section.

m. Click a blank spot on the right edge of the form, click the Insert Image button on the DESIGN tab, browse for the People.jpg image, then insert it on the right side of the form in the Detail section. (*Hint*: You will need to change the Web-Ready Image Files list in the Insert Picture dialog box to All Files to find .jpg images.)

n. Resize the picture to be about 2" × 2", then drag the right edge of the form to the left as far as possible. Also drag the top edge of the Form Footer up as far as possible to eliminate blank space in the Detail section.

o. Save the form, find the record with your name, change the DuesPaid value to **85**, then move and resize controls as necessary to match **FIGURE C-20**.

p. If requested by your instructor, print only the record with your name.

q. Save and close the Member Information form, then close the Membership-C.accdb database and exit Access 2013.

Independent Challenge 3

You have built an Access database to organize the deposits at a recycling center. Various clubs regularly deposit recyclable material, which is measured in pounds when the deposits are made.

a. Open the Recycle-C.accdb database from the location where you store your Data Files. Enable content if prompted.

b. Using the Form Wizard, create a form based on all of the fields in the CenterDeposits query. View the data by Deposits, use the Columnar layout, and title the form **Deposit Listing**.

c. Switch to Layout View, then make each label bold.

d. Modify the labels so that CenterName is **Center Name**, DepositDate is **Deposit Date**, and ClubName is **Club Name**.

e. Switch to Form Design View and resize the CenterName and ClubName text boxes so they are the same height and width as the Weight text box, as shown in **FIGURE C-21**.

f. Switch to Form View, find and change any entry of Dallas Jaycees in the ClubName field to *your* last name, then print one record with your name if requested by your instructor.

g. Using Form View of the Deposit Listing form, filter for all records with your last name in the ClubName field.

h. Using Form View of the Deposit Listing form, sort the filtered records in descending order on the DepositDate field.

i. Preview the first record, as shown in **FIGURE C-21**. If requested by your instructor, print the first record.

j. Save and close the Deposit Listing form, close the Recycle-C.accdb database, then exit Access.

FIGURE C-21

Independent Challenge 4: Explore

One way you can use an Access database on your own is to record and track your job search efforts. In this exercise, you will develop a form to help you enter data into your job-tracking database.

   a. Start Access and open the Jobs-C.accdb database from the location where you store your Data Files. Enable content if prompted.

   b. Click the CREATE tab, then use the Form Wizard to create a new form based on all the fields of both the Employers and Positions tables.

   c. View the data by Employers, use a Datasheet layout for the subform, accept the default names for the form and subform, then open the form to view information.

   d. Use Layout View and Design View to modify the form labels, text box positions, alignment, and sizes, as shown in FIGURE C-22. Note that the columns within the subform have been resized to display all of the data in the subform.

   e. Change the CompanyName of IBM in the first record to *Your* **Last Name's Software**, and if instructed to create a printout, print only that record. Close the Employers form.

   f. Click the Employers table in the Navigation Pane, then use the Split Form option on the More Forms button of the CREATE tab to create a split form on the Employers table. Close and save the split form with the name **Employers Split Form**.

FIGURE C-22

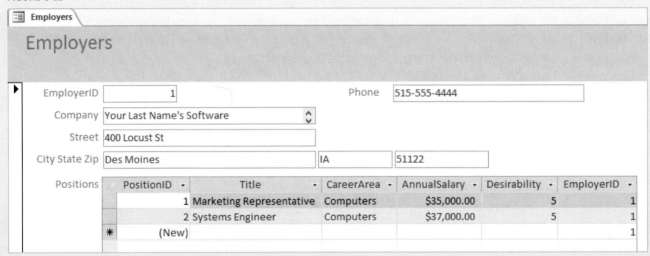

Independent Challenge 4: Explore (continued)

g. Open the Employers Split Form in Form View, and change the address and phone number information for EmployerID 1 to *your* school's address and phone information, as shown in **FIGURE C-23**.

h. Navigate through all five records, then back to EmployerID 1, observing both the upper and lower panes of the split form as you move from record to record.

i. Open the Employers form and navigate forward and backward through all five records to study the difference between the Employers form, which uses a form/subform versus the Employers Split Form. Even though both the Employers form and Employers Split Form show datasheets in the bottom halves of the forms, they are fundamentally very different. The split form is displaying the records of only the Employers table, whereas the Employers form is using a subform to display related records from the Positions table in the lower datasheet. You will learn more about forms and subforms in later units.

j. Close the Jobs-C.accdb database, then exit Access.

FIGURE C-23

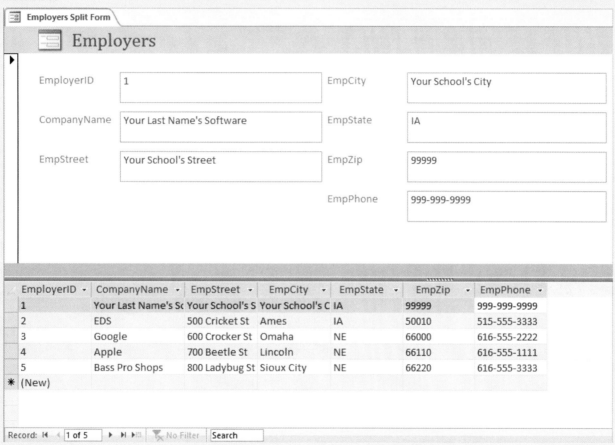

Access 2013

Visual Workshop

Open the Baseball-C.accdb database, enable content if prompted, then use the Split Form tool to create a form named **Players**, as shown in FIGURE C-24, based on the Players table. Resize the PlayerLast text box as shown. Modify the labels as shown. View the data in Form View, and sort the records in ascending order by last name. Change the first, last, and nickname of the Henry Aaron record in the first record to *your* name, and if instructed to create a printout, print only that record. Save and close the Players form, close the Baseball-C.accdb database, then exit Access.

FIGURE C-24

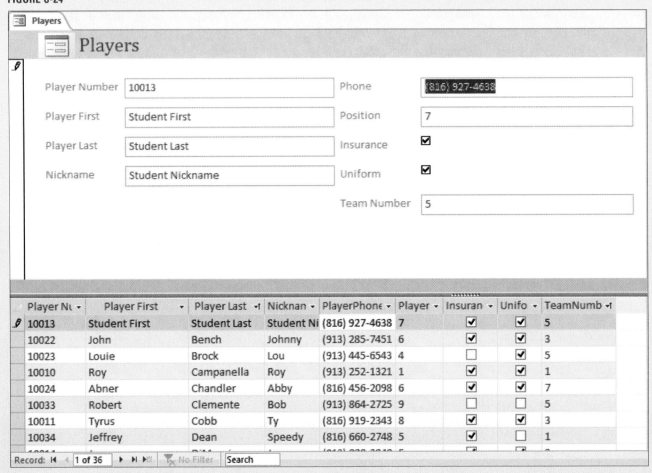

Using Reports

CASE ▶ Samantha Hooper, a tour developer at Quest Specialty Travel, asks you to produce some reports to help her share and analyze data. A report is an Access object that creates a professional looking printout.

Unit Objectives

After completing this unit, you will be able to:

- Use the Report Wizard
- Use Report Layout View
- Review report sections
- Apply group and sort orders
- Add subtotals and counts
- Resize and align controls
- Format a report
- Create mailing labels

Files You Will Need

QuestTravel-D.accdb
RealEstate-D.accdb
Conventions-D.accdb
Membership-D.accdb

Recycle-D.accdb
JobSearch-D.accdb
Basketball-D.accdb

Use the Report Wizard

Learning
Outcomes
• Create a report
with the Report
Wizard
• Change page
orientation

A **report** is the primary object you use to print database content because it provides the most formatting, layout, and summary options. A report may include various fonts and colors, clip art and lines, and multiple headers and footers. A report can also calculate subtotals, averages, counts, and other statistics for groups of records. You can create reports in Access by using the **Report Wizard**, a tool that asks questions to guide you through the initial development of the report. Your responses to the Report Wizard determine the record source, style, and layout of the report. The **record source** is the table or query that defines the fields and records displayed on the report. The Report Wizard also helps you sort, group, and analyze the records. **CASE** *You use the Report Wizard to create a report to display the tours within each state.*

STEPS

1. **Start Access, open the** QuestTravel-D.accdb database, **enable content if prompted, click the** CREATE tab **on the Ribbon, then click the** Report Wizard button **in the Reports group**

   The Report Wizard starts, prompting you to select the fields you want on the report. You can select fields from one or more tables or queries.

TROUBLE
If you select a field by mistake, click the unwanted field in the Selected Fields list, then click the Remove Field button [<].

2. **Click the** Tables/Queries list arrow, **click** Table: States, **double-click the** StateName field, **click the** Tables/Queries list arrow, **click** Table: Tours, **click the** Select All Fields button [>>], **click** StateAbbrev **in the Selected Fields list, then click the** Remove Field button [<]

   By selecting the StateName field from the States table, and all fields from the Tours table except the StateAbbrev field, you have all of the fields you need for the report, as shown in **FIGURE D-1**.

3. **Click** Next, **then click** by States **if it is not already selected**

   Choosing "by States" groups together the records for each state. In addition to record-grouping options, the Report Wizard later asks if you want to sort the records within each group. You can use the Report Wizard to specify up to four fields to sort in either ascending or descending order.

QUICK TIP
Click Back to review previous dialog boxes within a wizard.

4. **Click** Next, **click** Next **again to include no additional grouping levels, click the** first sort list arrow, **click** TourStartDate, **then click** Next

   The last questions in the Report Wizard deal with report appearance and the report title.

5. **Click the** Stepped option button, **click the** Landscape option button, **click** Next, **type** Tours by State **for the report title, then click** Finish

   The Tours by State report opens in **Print Preview**, which displays the report as it appears when printed, as shown in **FIGURE D-2**. The records are grouped by state, the first state being California, and then sorted in ascending order by the TourStartDate field within each state. Reports are **read-only objects**, meaning you can use them to read and display data but not to change (write to) data. As you change data using tables, queries, or forms, reports constantly display those up-to-date edits just like all of the other Access objects.

6. **Scroll down to see the second grouping section on the report for the state of Colorado, then click the** Next Page button [▶] **in the navigation bar to see the second page of the report**

   Even in **landscape orientation** (11" wide by 8.5" tall as opposed to **portrait orientation**, which is 8.5" wide by 11" tall), the fields on the Tours by State report may not fit on one sheet of paper. The labels in the column headings and the data in the columns need to be resized to improve the layout. Depending on your monitor, you might need to scroll to the right to display all the fields on this page.

FIGURE D-1: Selecting fields for a report using the Report Wizard

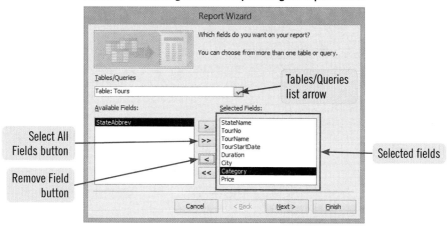

Select All Fields button

Remove Field button

Tables/Queries list arrow

Selected fields

FIGURE D-2: Tours by State report in Print Preview

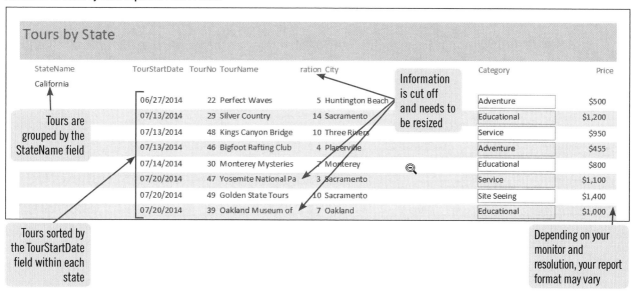

Tours are grouped by the StateName field

Information is cut off and needs to be resized

Tours sorted by the TourStartDate field within each state

Depending on your monitor and resolution, your report format may vary

Changing page orientation

To change page orientation from Portrait (8.5" wide by 11" tall) to Landscape (11" wide by 8.5" tall) and vice versa, click the Portrait or Landscape button on the PRINT PREVIEW tab when viewing the report in Print Preview. To switch to Print Preview, right-click the report in the Navigation Pane, and then choose Print Preview on the shortcut menu.

Use Report Layout View

Learning Outcomes
- Move and resize controls in Layout View
- Modify labels

Reports have multiple views that you use for various report-building and report-viewing activities. Although some tasks can be accomplished in more than one view, each view has a primary purpose to make your work with reports as easy and efficient as possible. The different report views are summarized in **TABLE D-1.** **CASE** ▸ *Samantha Hooper asks you to modify the Tours by State report so that all of the fields fit comfortably across one sheet of paper in landscape orientation.*

STEPS

TROUBLE
If the Field List window opens, close it.

1. **Right-click the** Tours by State report tab, **then click** Layout View
   Layout View opens and applies a grid to the report that helps you resize, move, and position controls. You decide to narrow the City column to make room for the Price data.

2. **Click** Huntington Beach **(or any value in the City column), then use the ←→ pointer to drag the right edge of the City column to the left to narrow it to about half of its current size, as shown in** FIGURE D-3
   By narrowing the City column, you create extra space in the report.

3. **Click** $500 **(or any value in the Price column), use the ⁺ₖ pointer to drag the Price values to the left of the Category column, click the** Price label, **then use ⁺ₖ to move the Price label to the left of the Category label**
   All the columns are now within the boundaries of a single sheet of paper in landscape orientation. You also notice that centering some data would make it easier to read.

4. **Click** 22 **(or any value in the TourNo column), click the** HOME tab, **then click the** Center **button ☰ in the Text Formatting group**
   The TourName column needs more space to completely display the tour names.

QUICK TIP
Resizing with ←→ instead of moving with ⁺ₖ maintains the vertical alignment of the controls.

5. **Use ←→ to resize both sides of the** TourStartDate, TourNo, **and** TourName **columns and their labels to the left, then use ←→ to resize the** Category, Price, City, **and** Duration **columns and their labels to the right**
   Now the report has enough room to resize the TourName column and the Duration label.

QUICK TIP
You can use the Undo button arrow ↺ ▾ to undo many actions in Layout View.

6. **Resize the** TourName column **so that all of the data is visible, paying special attention to the longest value, Yosemite National Park Great Cleanup, then resize the** Duration label **to display the complete text**
   You can also rename labels in Report Layout View.

7. **Click the** StateName label, **click between the words** State **and** Name, **press the [Spacebar] so that the label reads State Name, then modify the** TourStartDate, TourNo, **and** TourName **labels to contain spaces as well**

8. **Continue resizing the columns so that all of the data is visible and your report looks like** FIGURE D-4

FIGURE D-3: Modifying the column width in Report Layout View

Resizing the City field to make room for other information

FIGURE D-4: Final Tours by State report in Report Layout View

Duration label is completely displayed

Labels have spaces

TourNo field values are centered

Longest tour name is clearly displayed

Price column is moved

TABLE D-1: Report views

view	primary purpose
Report View	To quickly review the report without page breaks
Print Preview	To review each page of an entire report as it will appear if printed
Layout View	To modify the size, position, or formatting of controls; shows live data as you modify the report, making it the tool of choice when you want to change the appearance and positioning of controls on a report while also reviewing live data
Design View	To work with report sections or to access the complete range of controls and report properties; Design View does not display data

Review Report Sections

Learning
Outcomes
• Navigate through
  report sections
  and pages
• Resize the width of
  the report
• Work with error
  indicators

Report **sections** determine where and how often controls in that section print in the final report. For example, controls in the Report Header section print only once at the beginning of the report, but controls in the Detail section print once for every record the report displays. **TABLE D-2** describes report sections. **CASE** ▶ *You and Samantha Hooper preview the Tours by State report to review and understand report sections.*

STEPS

1. **Right-click the** Tours by State tab, **click** Print Preview, **then scroll up and click the light blue bar at the top of the report if you need to zoom in to display the first page of the report, as shown in** FIGURE D-5

   The first page shows four sections: Report Header, Page Header, StateAbbreviation Header, and Detail.

2. **Click the** Next Page button ▶ **on the navigation bar to move to the second page of the report**

   If the second page of the report does not contain data, it means that the report may be too wide to fit on a single sheet of paper. You fix that problem in Report Design View.

QUICK TIP
If your report is too wide, you will see a green **error indicator** in the upper-left corner of the report. Pointing to the error icon ◈ displays a message about the error.

3. **Right-click the** Tours by State tab, **click** Design View, **scroll to the far right using the bottom horizontal scroll bar, then use the** ↔ **pointer to drag the** right edge of the report **as far as you can to the left, as shown in** FIGURE D-6

   In Report Design View, you can work with the report sections and make modifications to the report that you cannot make in other views, such as narrowing the width. Report Design View does not display any data, though. For your report to fit on one page in landscape orientation, you need to move all of the controls within the 10.5" mark on the horizontal **ruler** using the default 0.25" left and right margins. You will practice fixing this problem by moving all controls within the 10" mark on the ruler to make sure they all fit on the landscape printout.

TROUBLE
Be sure that the right edge of the page calculation is within the 10" mark on the ruler.

4. **Use the** ⬚ **pointer to drag the** page calculation **about 0.5" to the left, then use** ↔ **to drag the** right edge of the report **as far as you can to the left**

   To review your modifications, show the report in Print Preview.

QUICK TIP
You can also use the View buttons in the lower-right corner of a report to switch views.

5. **Right-click the** Tours by State tab, **click** Print Preview, **click** ▶ **to navigate to the last page of the report, then click the report to zoom in and out to examine the page, as shown in** FIGURE D-7

   Previewing each page of the report helps you confirm that no blank pages are created and allows you to examine how the different report sections print on each page.

TABLE D-2: Report sections

section	where does this section print?
Report Header	At the top of the first page
Page Header	At the top of every page (but below the Report Header on the first page)
Group Header	Before every group of records
Detail	Once for every record
Group Footer	After every group of records
Page Footer	At the bottom of every page
Report Footer	At the end of the report

© 2014 Cengage Learning

FIGURE D-5: Tours by State in Print Preview

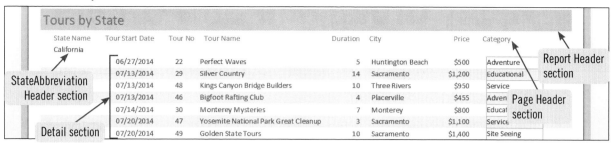

FIGURE D-6: Tours by State report in Design View

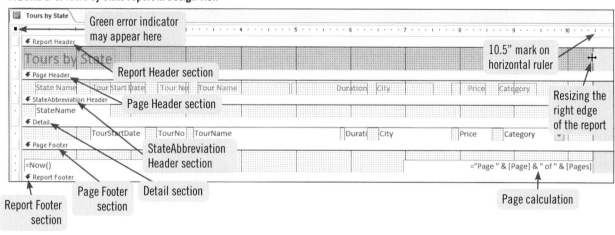

FIGURE D-7: Last page of Tours by State report in Print Preview

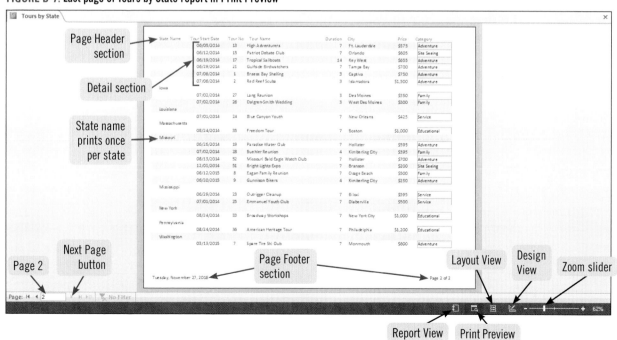

Apply Group and Sort Orders

Learning Outcomes
• Group and sort records in a report
• Copy and paste controls

Grouping means to sort records by a particular field *plus* provide a header and/or footer section before or after each group of sorted records. For example, if you group records by the StateName field, the Group Header is called the StateName Header and the Group Footer is called the StateName Footer. The StateName Header section appears once for each state in the report, immediately before the records in that state. The StateName Footer section also appears once for each state in the report, immediately after the records for that state. **CASE** *The records in the Tours by State report are currently grouped by the StateAbbreviation field. Samantha Hooper asks you to further group the records by the Category field (Adventure, Educational, and Family, for example) within each state.*

STEPS

1. **Click the Close Print Preview button to return to Report Design View, then click the Group & Sort button in the Grouping & Totals group to open the Group, Sort, and Total pane**

   Currently, the records are grouped by the StateAbbreviation field and further sorted by the TourStartDate field. To add the Category field as a grouping field within each state, you work with the Group, Sort, and Total pane in Report Design View.

2. **Click the Add a group button in the Group, Sort, and Total pane, click Category, then click the Move up button ⬆ on the right side of the Group, Sort, and Total pane so that Category is positioned between StateAbbreviation and TourStartDate**

   A Category Header section is added to Report Design View just below the StateAbbreviation Header section. You move the Category control from the Detail section to the Category Header section so it prints only once for each new Category instead of once for each record in the Detail section.

QUICK TIP
Use the Move up and Move down buttons as needed to make sure your Group, Sort, and Total pane looks exactly like **FIGURE D-8**.

3. **Right-click the Category combo box in the Detail section, click Cut on the shortcut menu, right-click the Category Header section, click Paste, then use the 🖐 pointer to drag the Category combo box to the right to position it as shown in FIGURE D-8**

   Now that you've moved the Category combo box to the Category Header, it will print only once per category within each state. You no longer need the Category label in the Page Header section.

4. **Click the Category label in the Page Header section, press [Delete], then switch to Print Preview and zoom to 100%**

   The Tours by State report should look like **FIGURE D-9**. Notice that the records are now grouped by category within state. Detail records are further sorted in ascending order by the tour start date.

FIGURE D-8: Group, Sort, and Total pane and new Category Header section

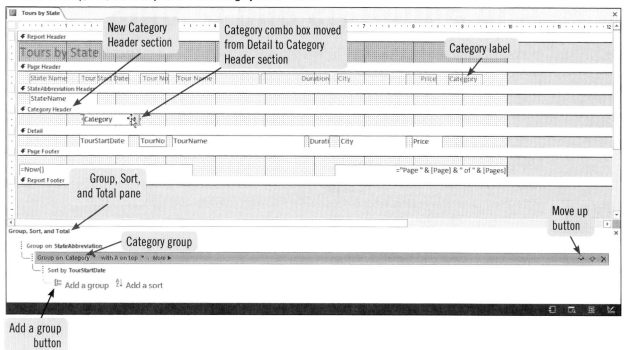

FIGURE D-9: Tours by State report grouped by category within state

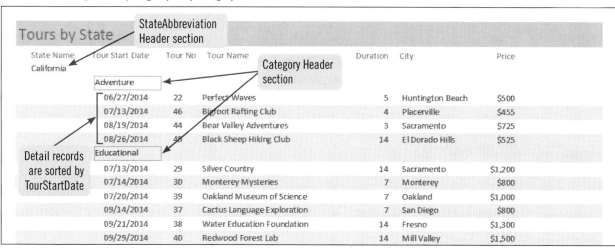

Add Subtotals and Counts

In a report, you create a **calculation** by entering an expression into a text box. When a report is previewed or printed, the expression is evaluated and the resulting calculation is placed on the report. An **expression** is a combination of field names, operators (such as +, –, /, and *), and functions that results in a single value. A **function** is a built-in formula, such as Sum or Count, that helps you quickly create a calculation. Notice that every expression starts with an equal sign (=), and when it uses a function, the arguments for the function are placed in (parentheses). **Arguments** are the pieces of information that the function needs to create the final answer. When an argument is a field name, the field name must be surrounded by [square brackets]. **CASE** *Samantha Hooper asks you to add a calculation to the Tours by State report to sum the total number of tour days within each category and within each state.*

STEPS

1. **Switch to Report Design View**

   A logical place to add subtotals for each group is right after that group of records prints, in the Group Footer section. You use the Group, Sort, and Total pane to open Group Footer sections.

2. **Click the More button for the StateAbbreviation field in the Group, Sort, and Total pane, click the without a footer section list arrow, click with a footer section, then do the same for the Category field, as shown in FIGURE D-10**

   With the StateAbbreviation Footer and Category Footer sections open, you're ready to add controls to calculate the total number of tour days within each category and within each state. You use a text box control with an expression to make this calculation.

3. **Click the Text Box button ab| in the Controls group, then click just below the Duration text box in the Category Footer section**

   Adding a new text box automatically adds a new label to its left. First, you modify the label to identify the information, then you modify the text box to contain the correct expression to sum the number of tour days for that category.

4. **Click the Text19 label to select it, double-click Text19, type Total days:, click the Unbound text box to select it, click Unbound again, type =Sum([Duration]), press [Enter], then widen the text box to view the entire expression**

   The expression =Sum([Duration]) uses the Sum function to add the days in the Duration field. Because the expression is entered in the Category Footer section, it will sum all Duration values for that category within that state. To sum the Duration values for each state, the expression needs to be inserted in the StateAbbreviation Footer.

5. **Right-click the =Sum([Duration]) text box, click Copy, right-click the StateAbbreviation Footer section, click Paste, then press [→] enough times to position the controls in the StateAbbreviation Footer section just below those in the Category Footer section, as shown in FIGURE D-11**

   With the expression copied to the StateAbbreviation Footer section, you're ready to preview your work.

6. **Switch to Print Preview, navigate to the last page of the report, then click to zoom so you can see all of the Washington tours**

   As shown in **FIGURE D-12**, 21 tour days are totaled for the Adventure category, and 3 for the Site Seeing category, which is a total of 24 tour days for the state of Washington. The summary data would look better if it were aligned more directly under the tour Duration values. You resize and align controls in the next lesson.

FIGURE D-10: Opening group footer sections

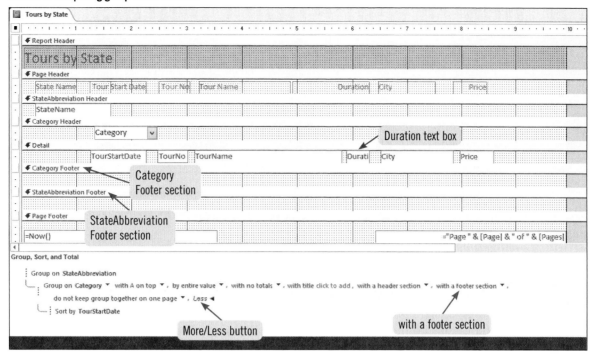

FIGURE D-11: Adding subtotals to group footer sections

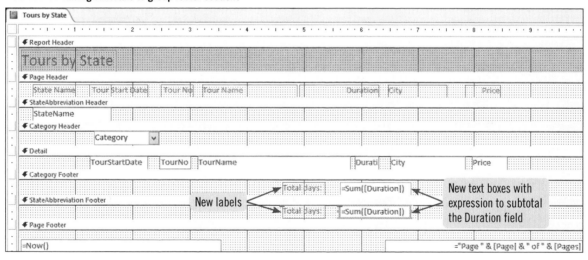

FIGURE D-12: Previewing the new group footer calculations

Access 2013

Resize and Align Controls

Learning Outcomes
• Align data within a control
• Align the borders of controls

After you add information to the appropriate section of a report, you might also want to align the data in precise columns and rows to make the information easier to read. To do so, you can use two different types of **alignment** commands. You can left-, right-, or center-align a control *within its own border* using the Align Left ☰, Center ☰, and Align Right ☰ buttons on the HOME tab. You can also align the edges of controls *with respect to one another* using the Left, Right, Top, and Bottom commands on the Align button of the ARRANGE tab in Report Design View. **CASE** *You decide to resize and align several controls to improve the readability of the Tours by State report. Layout View is a good choice for these tasks.*

STEPS

1. Switch to Layout View, click the DESIGN tab on the Ribbon, then click the Group & Sort button to toggle off the Group, Sort, and Total pane

QUICK TIP
You can also use the buttons on the FORMAT tab to align and format text, including applying number formats and increasing or decreasing decimals.

You decide to align the expressions that subtotal the number of tour days for each category within the Duration column.

2. Click the Total days text box in the Category Footer, click the HOME tab, click the Align Right button ☰ in the Text Formatting group, then use the ↔ pointer to resize the text box so that the data is aligned in the Duration column, as shown in FIGURE D-13

With the calculation formatted as desired in the Category Footer, you can quickly apply those modifications to the calculation in the StateAbbreviation Footer as well.

TROUBLE
If you make a mistake, click the Undo button ↺ on the Quick Access toolbar.

3. Scroll down the report far enough to find and then click the Total days text box in the StateAbbreviation Footer, click ☰, then use the ↔ pointer to resize the text box so that it is the same width as the text box in the Category Footer section

With both expressions right-aligned and resized so they line up under the Duration values in the Detail section, they are easier to read on the report.

4. Scroll the report so you can see all of the Colorado tours, as shown in FIGURE D-14

You can apply resize, alignment, or formatting commands to more than one control at a time. **TABLE D-3** provides techniques for selecting more than one control at a time in Report Design View.

Precisely moving and resizing controls

You can move and resize controls using the mouse or other pointing device, but you can move controls more precisely using the keyboard. Pressing the arrow keys while holding [Ctrl] moves selected controls one **pixel (picture element)** at a time in the direction of the arrow. Pressing the arrow keys while holding [Shift] resizes selected controls one pixel at a time.

FIGURE D-13: Resizing controls in Layout View

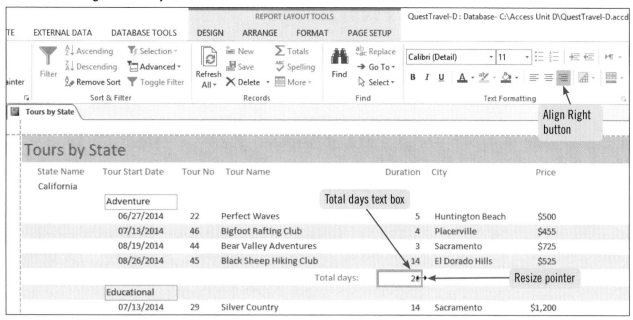

FIGURE D-14: Reviewing the aligned and resized controls

Colorado					
Adventure					
06/19/2014	18	Eagle Hiking Club	7	Aspen	$695
06/29/2014	20	Team Discovery	5	Breckenridge	$550
01/02/2015	3	Ames Ski Club	7	Breckenridge	$850
01/13/2015	4	Boy Scout Jamboree	7	Vail	$1,900
02/15/2015	5	Bridgewater Country	10	Aspen	$1,200
		Total days:	36		
Family					
03/11/2015	6	Franklin Family Reunion	3	Breckenridge	$700
		Total days:	3		
		Total days:	39		

Data is right-aligned and text boxes are resized

TABLE D-3: Selecting more than one control at a time in Report Design View

technique	description
Click, [Shift]+click	Click a control, then press and hold [Shift] while clicking other controls; each one is selected
Drag a selection box	Drag a selection box (an outline box you create by dragging the pointer in Report Design View); every control that is in or is touched by the edges of the box is selected
Click in the ruler	Click in either the horizontal or vertical ruler to select all controls that intersect the selection line
Drag in the ruler	Drag through either the horizontal or vertical ruler to select all controls that intersect the selection line as it is dragged through the ruler

Format a Report

Learning
Outcomes
• Format controls
and sections of a
report
• Add labels to a
report

Formatting refers to enhancing the appearance of the information. TABLE D-4 lists several of the most popular formatting commands found on the FORMAT tab when you are working in Layout or Report Design View. Although the Report Wizard automatically applies many formatting embellishments, you often want to change the appearance of the report to fit your particular needs. **CASE** *When reviewing the Tours by State report with Samantha, you decide to change the background color of some of the report sections to make the data easier to read. Your first change will be to shade each Category Header and Footer section (rather than alternating sections, the format initially provided by the Report Wizard). To make changes to entire report sections, you work in Report Design View.*

STEPS

QUICK TIP
The quick keystroke
for Undo is [Ctrl][Z].
The quick keystroke
for Redo is [Ctrl][Y].

1. **Switch to Design View, click the Category Header section bar, click the FORMAT tab on the Ribbon, click the Alternate Row Color button arrow, click No Color, click the Shape Fill button, then click the Maroon 2 color square, as shown in FIGURE D-15**

   Make a similar modification by applying a different fill color to the Category Footer section.

2. **Click the Category Footer section bar, click the Alternate Row Color button arrow, click No Color, click the Shape Fill button, then click the Green 2 color square (just to the right of Maroon 2 in the Standard Colors section)**

   When you use the Alternate Row Color and Shape Fill buttons, you're actually modifying the **Back Color** and **Alternate Back Color** properties in the Property Sheet of the section or control you selected. Background shades can help differentiate parts of the report, but be careful with dark colors as they may print as solid black on some printers and fax machines.

3. **Switch to Layout View to review your modifications**

   The category sections are clearer, but you decide to make one more modification to emphasize the report title.

4. **Click the Tours by State label in the Report Header section, click the HOME tab, then click the Bold button B in the Text Formatting group**

   The report in Layout View should look like FIGURE D-16. You also want to add a label to the Report Footer section to identify yourself.

5. **Switch to Report Design View, drag the bottom edge of the Report Footer down about 0.5", click the Label button Aa in the Controls group, click at the 1" mark in the Report Footer, type Created by your name, press [Enter], click the HOME tab, then click B in the Text Formatting group**

6. **Save and preview the Tours by State report**

7. **If required by your instructor, print the report, and then close it**

FIGURE D-15: Formatting section backgrounds

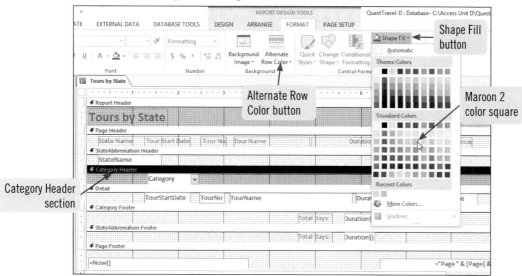

FIGURE D-16: Final formatted Tours by State report

TABLE D-4: Useful formatting commands

button	button name	description
B	Bold	Toggles bold on or off for the selected control(s)
I	Italic	Toggles italic on or off for the selected control(s)
U	Underline	Toggles underline on or off for the selected control(s)
≣	Align Left	Left-aligns the selected control(s) within its own border
≣	Center	Centers the selected control(s) within its own border
≣	Align Right	Right-aligns the selected control(s) within its own border
⬛	Background Color or Shape Fill	Changes the background color of the selected control(s)
▦	Alternate Row Color	Changes the background color of alternate records in the selected section
A	Font Color	Changes the text color of the selected control(s)
✎	Shape Outline Line Thickness option Line Type option	Changes the border color of the selected control(s) Changes the border style of the selected control(s) Changes the special visual effect of the selected control(s)

Access 2013

Create Mailing Labels

Learning Outcomes
• Create a report of labels
• Print specific pages of a report

Mailing labels are often created to apply to envelopes, postcards, or letters when assembling a mass mailing. They have many other business purposes too, such as applying them to paper file folders or name tags. Any data in your Access database can be converted into labels using the **Label Wizard**, a special report wizard that precisely positions and sizes information for hundreds of standard business labels. **CASE** ➤ *Samantha Hooper asks you to create mailing labels for all of the addresses in the Customers table. You use the Label Wizard to handle this request.*

STEPS

1. **Click the Customers table in the Navigation Pane, click the CREATE tab, then click the Labels button in the Reports group**

   The first Label Wizard dialog box opens. The Filter by manufacturer list box provides over 30 manufacturers of labels. Because Avery is the most common, it is the default choice. With the manufacturer selected, your next task is to choose the product number of the labels you will feed through the printer. The cover on the box of labels you are using provides this information. In this case, you'll be using Avery 5160 labels, a common type of sheet labels used for mailings and other purposes.

2. **Scroll through the Product number list, then click 5160 (if not already selected), as shown in FIGURE D-17**

   Note that by selecting a product number, you also specify the dimensions of the label and number of columns.

3. **Click Next, then click Next again to accept the default font and color choices**

   The third question of the Label Wizard asks how you want to construct your label. You'll add the fields from the Customers table with spaces and line breaks to pattern a standard mailing format.

4. **Double-click FName, press [Spacebar], double-click LName, press [Enter], double-click Street, press [Enter], double-click City, type a comma (,) and press [Spacebar], double-click State, press [Spacebar], then double-click Zip**

   If your prototype label doesn't look exactly like **FIGURE D-18**, delete the fields in the Prototype label box and try again. Be careful to put a space between the FName and LName fields in the first row, a comma and a space between the City and State fields, and a space between the State and Zip fields.

   > **QUICK TIP**
   > In this case, all data is displayed. This message reminds you to carefully preview the data to make sure long names and addresses fully display within the constraints of the 5160 label dimensions.

5. **Click Next, double-click LName to select it as a sorting field, click Next, click Finish to accept the name Labels Customers for the new report, then click OK if prompted that some data may not be displayed**

   A portion of the new report is shown in **FIGURE D-19**. It is generally a good idea to print the first page of the report on standard paper to make sure everything is aligned correctly before printing on labels.

   > **QUICK TIP**
   > To include your name on the printout, change Aaron Alito's name to *your* own name in the Customers table, then close and reopen the Labels Customers report.

6. **If requested by your instructor, click the Print button on the PRINT PREVIEW tab, click the From box, type 1, click the To box, type 1, then click OK to print the first page of the report**

7. **Close the Labels Customers report, close the QuestTravel-D.accdb database, then exit Access 2013**

FIGURE D-17: Label Wizard dialog box

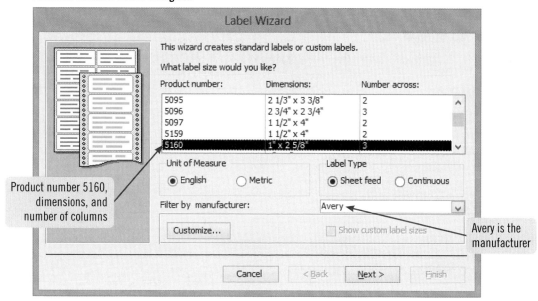

Label Wizard
This wizard creates standard labels or custom labels.
What label size would you like?
Product number:
Dimensions:
Number across:
5095
2 1/3" x 3 3/8"
2
5096
2 3/4" x 2 3/4"
3
5097
1 1/2" x 4"
2
5159
1 1/2" x 4"
2
5160
1" x 2 5/8"
3
Unit of Measure
English
Metric
Label Type
Sheet feed
Continuous
Filter by manufacturer:
Avery
Customize...
Show custom label sizes
Cancel
< Back
Next >
Finish
Product number 5160, dimensions, and number of columns
Avery is the manufacturer

FIGURE D-18: Building a prototype label

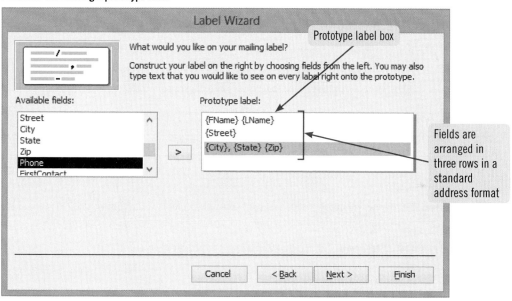

Label Wizard
Prototype label box
What would you like on your mailing label?
Construct your label on the right by choosing fields from the left. You may also type text that you would like to see on every label right onto the prototype.
Available fields:
Street
City
State
Zip
Phone
Prototype label:
{FName} {LName}
{Street}
{City}, {State} {Zip}
>
Fields are arranged in three rows in a standard address format
Cancel
< Back
Next >
Finish

FIGURE D-19: Labels Customers report

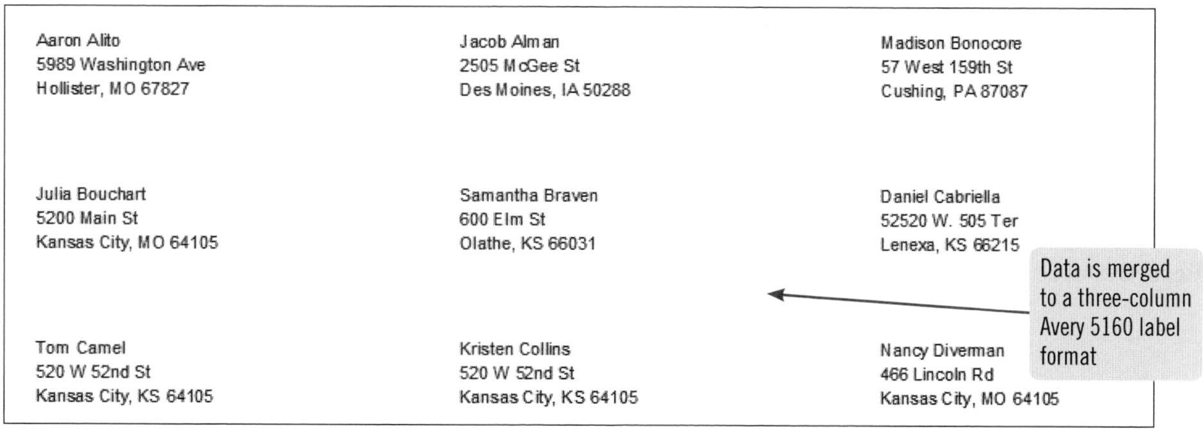

Aaron Alito
5989 Washington Ave
Hollister, MO 67827
Jacob Alman
2505 McGee St
Des Moines, IA 50288
Madison Bonocore
57 West 159th St
Cushing, PA 87087
Julia Bouchart
5200 Main St
Kansas City, MO 64105
Samantha Braven
600 Elm St
Olathe, KS 66031
Daniel Cabriella
52520 W. 505 Ter
Lenexa, KS 66215
Tom Camel
520 W 52nd St
Kansas City, KS 64105
Kristen Collins
520 W 52nd St
Kansas City, KS 64105
Nancy Diverman
466 Lincoln Rd
Kansas City, MO 64105
Data is merged to a three-column Avery 5160 label format

Practice

Concepts Review

Label each element of the Report Design View window shown in FIGURE D-20.

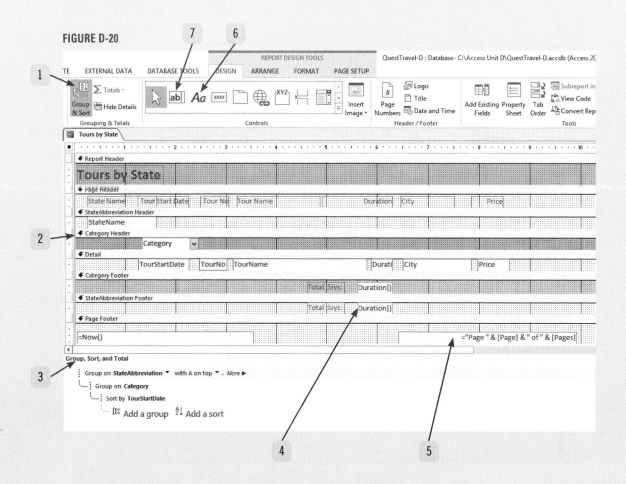

FIGURE D-20

Match each term with the statement that best describes it.

8. **Alignment**
9. **Expression**
10. **Grouping**
11. **Section**
12. **Detail section**
13. **Formatting**
14. **Record source**

a. Left, center, or right are common choices

b. Prints once for every record

c. Used to identify which fields and records are passed to the report

d. Sorting records *plus* providing a header or footer section

e. Determines how controls are positioned on the report

f. A combination of field names, operators, and functions that results in a single value

g. Enhancing the appearance of information displayed in the report

Select the best answer from the list of choices.

15. **Which of the following is *not* a valid report view?**
    a. Print Preview
    b. Section View
    c. Layout View
    d. Design View

16. **Which type of control is most commonly placed in the Detail section?**
    a. Image
    b. Line
    c. Text box
    d. Label

17. **A title for a report would most commonly be placed in which report section?**
    a. Group Footer
    b. Detail
    c. Report Header
    d. Report Footer

18. **A calculated expression that presents page numbering information would probably be placed in which report section?**
    a. Report Header
    b. Detail
    c. Group Footer
    d. Page Footer

19. **Which of the following expressions counts the number of records using the FirstName field?**
    a. =Count([FirstName])
    b. =Count[FirstName]
    c. =Count((FirstName))
    d. =Count{FirstName}

20. **To align the edges of several controls with each other, you use the alignment commands on the:**
    a. FORMATTING tab.
    b. DESIGN tab.
    c. PRINT PREVIEW tab.
    d. ARRANGE tab.

Skills Review

1. **Use the Report Wizard.**
   a. Start Access and open the RealEstate-D.accdb database from the location where you store your Data Files. Enable content if prompted.
   b. Use the Report Wizard to create a report based on the RLast and RPhone fields from the Realtors table, and the Type, SqFt, BR, Bath, and Asking fields from the Listings table.
   c. View the data by Realtors, do not add any more grouping levels, and sort the records in descending order by the Asking field. (*Hint*: Click the Ascending button to toggle it to Descending.)
   d. Use a Stepped layout and a Landscape orientation. Title the report **Realtor Listings**.
   e. Preview the first and second pages of the new report.

2. **Use Report Layout View.**
   a. Switch to Layout View and close the Field List and Property Sheet if they are open.
   b. Narrow the RLast, RPhone, and Bath columns enough so they are only as wide as needed to display all data.
   c. Modify the RLast label to read **Realtor**, the RPhone label to read **Phone**, the SqFt label to read **Square Feet**, the BR label to read **Bedrooms**, and the Bath label to read **Baths**.
   d. Switch to Print Preview to review your changes.

3. **Review report sections.**
   a. Switch to Report Design View.
   b. Drag the text box that contains the Page calculation in the lower-right corner of the Page Footer section to the left so that it is to the left of the 9" mark on the horizontal ruler.
   c. Drag the right edge of the entire report to the left so it ends within the 10" mark on the horizontal ruler. You may need to move or narrow the Baths label and Bath text box more than you did in Step 2b in order to accomplish this.

4. **Apply group and sort orders.**
   a. Open the Group, Sort, and Total pane.
   b. Add the Type field as a grouping field between the RealtorNo grouping field and Asking sort field. Make sure the sort order on the Asking field is in descending order (from largest to smallest).
   c. Cut and paste the Type combo box from its current position in the Detail section to the Type Header section.
   d. Move the Type combo box in the Type Header section so its left edge is at about the 1" mark on the horizontal ruler.
   e. Delete the Type label in the Page Header section.
   f. Switch to Layout View, and resize the Asking, Square Feet, Bedrooms, and Baths columns as needed so they are more evenly spaced across the page.

5. **Add subtotals and counts.**
   a. Switch to Report Design View, then open the RealtorNo Footer section.
   b. Add a text box control to the RealtorNo Footer section, just below the Asking text box in the Detail section. Change the label to read **Subtotal:**, and enter the expression **=Sum([Asking])** in the text box.
   c. Drag the bottom edge of the Report Footer down about 0.25" to add space to the Report Footer.
   d. Copy and paste the new expression in the RealtorNo Footer section to the Report Footer section. Position the new controls in the Report Footer section directly below the controls in the RealtorNo Footer section.
   e. Modify the Subtotal: label in the Report Footer section to read **Grand Total:**.
   f. Preview the last page of the report to view the new subtotals in the RealtorNo Footer and Report Footer sections.

6. **Resize and align controls.**
   a. Switch to Layout View, click the Group & Sort button on the DESIGN tab to close the Group, Sort, and Total pane if it is open, and move to the last page of the report to view the Subtotal and Grand Total calculations at the same time.
   b. Right-align the text within the Subtotal and Grand Total labels.

   c. Switch to Design View, click the Asking text box, press and hold [Shift], and then click the text box in the RealtorNo and also the Report Footer sections to select all three text boxes at the same time. Click the ARRANGE tab, click the Align button, then click Right to right-align the edges of the Subtotal and Grand Total text boxes.

   d. With all three text boxes still selected, click the FORMAT tab on the Ribbon, click the Apply Comma Number Format button, and click the Decrease Decimals button twice.

   e. Preview the report to view the alignment and format on the Asking data and subtotals.

7. Format a report.

   a. In Report Design View, change the Alternate Row Color of the Detail section to No Color.

   b. Change the Alternate Row Color of the Type Header section as well as the RealtorNo Header section to No Color.

   c. Change the Shape Fill color of the RealtorNo Header section to Green 2.

   d. Select the RLast text box in the RealtorNo Header section, and change the Shape Fill color to Green 2 to match the RealtorNo Header section. Apply the Green 2 background color to the RPhone text box as well.

FIGURE D-21

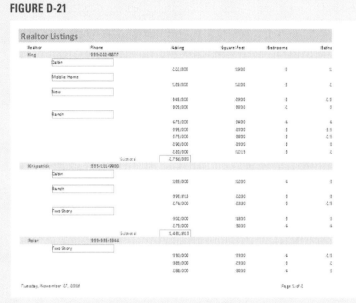

   e. Bold the title of the report, the **Realtor Listings** label in the Report Header, and resize it to make it a little wider to accommodate the bold text.

   f. Change the font color of each label in the Page Header section to black.

   g. Save and preview the report in Report View. It should look like **FIGURE D-21**. The report should fit on two pages and the grand total for all Asking values should be 7,771,513. If there are blank pages between printed pages, return to Report Design View and drag the right edge of the report to the left.

   h. In Report Design View, add a label to the left side of the Report Footer section with your name.

   i. Return to Print Preview, print the report if requested by your instructor, then save and close the Realtor Listings report.

8. Create mailing labels.

   a. Click the Agencies table in the Navigation Pane, then start the Label Wizard.

   b. Choose Avery 5160 labels and the default text appearance choices.

   c. Build a prototype label with the AgencyName on the first line, Street on the second line, and City, State, and Zip on the third line with a comma and space between City and State, and a space between State and Zip.

   d. Sort by AgencyName, and name the report **Labels Agencies**.

   e. Preview then save and close the report. Click OK if a warning dialog box appears regarding horizontal space. The data in your label report does not exceed the dimensions of the labels.

   f. If your instructor asks you to print the Labels Agencies report, open the Agencies table and change the name of Four Lakes Realtors to *Your* **LastName Realtors**. Close the Agencies table, reopen the Labels Agencies report, then print it.

   g. Close the Labels Agencies report, close the RealEstate-D.accdb database, then exit Access 2013.

Independent Challenge 1

As the office manager of an international convention planning company, you have created a database to track convention, enrollment, and company data. Your goal is to create a report of up-to-date attendee enrollments.

a. Start Access, then open the Conventions-D.accdb database from the location where you store your Data Files. Enable content if prompted.

b. Use the Report Wizard to create a report with the AttendeeFirst and AttendeeLast fields from the Attendees table, the CompanyName field from the Companies table, and the ConventionName and CountryName from the Conventions table.

c. View your data by Conventions, do not add any more grouping levels, and sort in ascending order by CompanyName, then AttendeeLast.

d. Use the Block layout and Portrait orientation, then name the report **Convention Listing**.

e. In Layout View, change the labels in the Page Header section from ConventionName to **Convention** and AttendeeLast to **Attendee**. Delete the CountryName, CompanyName, and AttendeeFirst labels in the Page Header section.

f. In Report Design View, open the Group, Sort, and Total pane, then open the CompanyName Header and CompanyName Footer sections.

g. In Report Design View, expand the ConventionNo Header section about 0.25", then use the Cut and Paste commands to move the ConventionName text box from the Detail section to the left edge of the ConventionNo Header section.

h. Cut and paste the CountryName text box from the Detail section to the ConventionNo Header section. Move it to the right of the ConventionName text box.

i. Drag the top edge of the CompanyName Header section up to remove any extra blank space in the ConventionNo Header section.

j. Cut and paste the CompanyName text box from the Detail section to the CompanyName Header section. Move it to the right of the ConventionName text box in the ConventionNo Header section and to the left of the AttendeeLast text box in the Detail section.

k. Remove any extra blank space in the CompanyName Header section by dragging the top edge of the Detail section up as far as possible. Close the Group, Sort, and Total pane.

l. In Layout View, scroll through the entire report and resize the ConventionName, CountryName, and CompanyName text boxes as needed to show all of the data. Be careful, however, to not expand the report beyond the width of the portrait orientation of the report.

m. In Design View, expand the CompanyName Footer about 0.5", and add a new text box positioned below the AttendeeLast text box in the Detail section. Modify the new label in the Company Name Footer to read **Count:**. Enter an expression in a new text box to count the values in the AttendeeLast field, **=Count([AttendeeLast])**.

n. Format the text color of the Count: label to black and right-align the text within the label.

o. Change the color of the report title and the labels in the Page Header section to black. Preview the report. The subtotal count for the first convention should be 21.

p. Add a label with your name to the right side of the Report Header section, then print the first page if required by your instructor.

q. Save and close the Convention Listing report, close the Conventions-D.accdb database, then exit Access 2013.

Independent Challenge 2

You have built an Access database to track membership in a community service club. The database tracks member names and addresses as well as their status and rank in the club, and their hours of service to the community.

a. Start Access and open the Membership-D.accdb database from the location where you store your Data Files. Enable content if prompted.

b. Open the Members table, find and change the name of Traci Kalvert to *your* name, then close the Members table.

c. Use the Report Wizard to create a report using the Status and DuesOwed fields from the Status table, and the FName, LName, and DuesPaid fields from the Members table.

d. View the data by Status. Do not add any more grouping fields, and sort the records in ascending order by LName then FName.

e. Use a Stepped layout and Portrait orientation, title the report **Dues Report**, then preview the report.

f. Switch to Report Design View, then use the Group, Sort, and Total pane to open the StatusNo Footer section.

g. Add a text box to the StatusNo Footer section, just below the DuesPaid text box in the Detail section. Change the label to **Count:** and the expression in the text box to **=Count([DuesPaid])**.

h. Expand the StatusNo Footer section to provide more space, and add a second text box to the StatusNo Footer section, just below the first. Change the label to **Subtotal:** and the expression in the text box to **=Sum([DuesPaid])**.

i. Expand the StatusNo Footer section to provide more space, and add a third text box to the StatusNo Footer section, just below the second. Change the accompanying label to **Balance:**.

j. Change the text box expression to **=Count([DuesPaid])*[DuesOwed]–Sum([DuesPaid])**. This expression counts the number of values in the DuesPaid field, and multiplies it by the DuesOwed field. From that value, the sum of the DuesPaid field is subtracted. This calculates the balance between dues owed and dues paid.

k. Open the Property Sheet for the =Sum([DuesPaid]) text box. On the Format tab, set the Format property to **Currency** and the Decimal Places property to **2**. Repeat these property changes for the text box with the balance calculation.

l. Select the DuesPaid text box in the Detail section, press and hold [Shift], then select all three text boxes in the StatusNo Footer section. Align the right edges of all four controls using the Align button, then Right command on the ARRANGE tab of the Ribbon. Also, right-align the contents within the text boxes of the StatusNo Footer section using the Align Right button on the HOME tab of the Ribbon. Right-align the right edges of the three new labels in the StatusNo Footer section.

m. Save, then preview the Dues Report. Make sure the report does not contain blank pages and fix that in Report Design View if needed. Print the first page of the Dues Report if requested by your instructor. The StatusNo Footer section for the first status, New, is shown in **FIGURE D-22**.

n. Close the Dues Report, close the Membership-D.accdb database, then exit Access.

FIGURE D-22

Count:	7
Subtotal:	$375.00
Balance:	$325.00

Independent Challenge 3

You have built an Access database to organize the deposits at a recycling center. Various clubs regularly deposit recyclable material, which is measured in pounds when the deposits are made.

a. Start Access and open the Recycle-D.accdb database from the location where you store your Data Files. Enable content if prompted.

b. Open the Centers table, change **Trash Can** to *Your* **Last Name Recycling**, then close the table.

c. Use the Report Wizard to create a report with the CenterName field from the Centers table, the DepositDate and Weight fields from the Deposits table, and the ClubName field from the Clubs table.

d. View the data by Centers, do not add any more grouping levels, and sort the records in ascending order by DepositDate.

e. Use a Stepped layout and a Portrait orientation, then title the report **Deposit Listing**.

f. In Layout View, center the Weight label and Weight data within their controls. Resize the DepositDate label and data by dragging the left edge of the control farther to the left so the label text and all dates are clearly displayed.

g. Add spaces to the labels so that CenterName becomes **Center Name**, DepositDate becomes **Deposit Date**, and ClubName becomes **Club Name**.

h. In Report Design View, open the Group, Sort, and Total pane and then open the CenterNumber Footer section.

i. Add a text box to the CenterNumber Footer section just below the Weight text box with the expression **=Sum([Weight])**.

j. Rename the new label to be **Total Center Weight** and move and resize it as needed so that it doesn't overlap the text box.

k. Resize the =Sum([Weight]) text box in the CenterNumber Footer section to be the same size as the Weight text box in the Detail section. Align the right edges of the Weight text box in the Detail section with the =Sum([Weight]) text box in the CenterNumber Footer section. Center the data in the =Sum([Weight]) text box.

l. Expand the Report Footer section, then copy and paste the =Sum([Weight]) text box from the CenterNumber Footer section to the Report Footer section.

m. Move and align the controls in the Report Footer section to be positioned directly under their counterparts in the CenterNumber Footer section.

n. Change the label in the Report Footer section to **Grand Total Weight**.

o. Remove extra blank space in the report by dragging the bottom of the report as well as the section bars up, then preview a portion of the last page of the report, as shown in FIGURE D-23. The last Total Center Weight and Grand Total Weight values on your report should match the figure.

p. Save and close the Deposit Listing report, close the Recycle-D.accdb database, then exit Access.

FIGURE D-23

6/4/2013	90	Lions
6/20/2013	85	Junior League
8/31/2013	50	Girl Scouts #11
10/2/2013	90	Lions
Total Center Weight	2720	
Grand Total Weight	9365	

Independent Challenge 4: Explore

One way you can use an Access database on your own is to record and track your job search efforts. In this exercise, you create a report to help read and analyze data into your job-tracking database.

a. Start Access and open the JobSearch-D.accdb database from the location where you store your Data Files. Enable content if prompted.

b. Open the Employers table, and enter five more records to identify five more potential employers.

c. Use subdatasheets in the Employers table to enter five more potential jobs. You may enter all five jobs for one employer, one job for five different employers, or any combination thereof. Be sure to check the spelling of all data entered. For the Desirability field, enter a value from **1** to **5**, 1 being the least desirable and 5 the most desirable. Close the Employers table.

d. Use the Report Wizard to create a report that lists the CompanyName, EmpCity, and EmpState fields from the Employers table, and the Title, AnnualSalary, and Desirability fields from the Positions table.

e. View the data by Employers, do not add any more grouping levels, and sort the records in ascending order by Title.

f. Use an Outline layout and a Landscape orientation, then title the report **Job Opportunities**.

g. In Design View, revise the labels in the EmployerID Header section from CompanyName to **Company**, EmpCity to **City**, EmpState to **State**, and AnnualSalary to **Salary**.

h. In Design View, right-align the text within the Company, City, and State labels so they are closer to the text boxes they describe.

i. In Report Design View, move the Page expression in the Page Footer section and the right edge of the report to the left, within the 10.5" mark on the horizontal ruler, and then drag the right edge of the report to the left to make sure that the report fits within the margins of one sheet of paper in landscape orientation.

j. Open the EmployerID Footer section and use the Line control in the Controls group on the DESIGN tab to add a horizontal line across the width of the report in the EmployerID Footer section. (*Hint*: The Line control may be on the second row of the Controls box. Also, press and hold [Shift] while dragging the line to create a perfectly horizontal line.)

k. Click a green error indicator that appears on the labels in the EmployerID Header section, point to the warning button to read the ScreenTip, then click the drop-down arrow on the error indicator and click Ignore Error.

l. Preview and save the Job Opportunities report making sure that the report fits within one page wide, then print the first page if requested by your instructor.

m. Close the Job Opportunities report, close the JobSearch-D.accdb database, then exit Access 2013.

Visual Workshop

Open the Basketball-D.accdb database from the location where you store your Data Files and enable content if prompted. Open the Players table, enter *your* name instead of Kelsey Douglas, then close the table. Your goal is to create the report shown in FIGURE D-24. Use the Report Wizard, and select the PFirst, PLast, HomeTown, and HomeState fields from the Players table. Select the FieldGoals, 3Pointers, and FreeThrows fields from the Stats table. View the data by Players, do not add any more grouping levels, and do not add any more sorting levels. Use a Block layout and a Portrait orientation, then title the report **Scoring Report**. In Layout View, resize all of the columns so that they fit on a single piece of portrait paper, and change the labels in the Page Header section as shown. In Design View, open the PlayerNo Footer section and add text boxes with expressions to sum the FieldGoals, 3Pointers, and FreeThrow fields. Move, modify, align, and resize all controls as needed to match FIGURE D-24. Be sure to print preview the report to make sure that it fits within the width of one sheet of paper. Modify the report to narrow it in Report Design View if needed.

FIGURE D-24

Scoring Report

Player Name		Home Town	State	Field Goals	3 Pointers	Free Throws
Student First	Student Last	Linden	IA	4	1	3
				5	2	2
				5	3	3
				6	3	5
				4	1	1
				4	2	2
				3	2	1
				4	2	3
				4	2	3
				3	2	1
		Subtotals		42	20	24

Modifying the Database Structure

CASE Working with Samantha Hooper, the tour developer for U.S. group travel at Quest Specialty Travel, you are developing an Access database to track tours, customers, sales, and payments. The database consists of multiple tables that you link, modify, and enhance to create a relational database.

Unit Objectives

After completing this unit, you will be able to:

- Examine relational databases
- Design related tables
- Create one-to-many relationships
- Create Lookup fields
- Modify Short Text fields

- Modify Number and Currency fields
- Modify Date/Time fields
- Modify validation properties
- Create Attachment fields

Files You Will Need

QuestTravel-E.accdb   JobSearch-E.accdb
GMayberry.jpg   Training-E.accdb
Member1.jpg

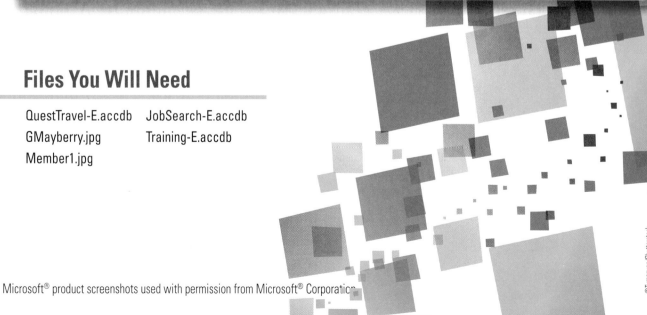

Examine Relational Databases

Learning
Outcomes
• Design tables and
  fields
• Design primary
  and foreign key
  fields
• Analyze one-to-
  many relationships

The purpose of a relational database is to organize and store data in a way that minimizes redundancy and maximizes your flexibility when querying and analyzing data. To accomplish these goals, a relational database uses related tables rather than a single large table of data. **CASE** At one time, the Sales Department at Quest Specialty Travel tracked information about their tour sales and payments using a single Access table called Sales, shown in FIGURE E-1. This created data redundancy problems because of the duplicate tour, customer, and payment information entered into a single table. You decide to study the principles of relational database design to help Quest Specialty Travel reorganize these fields into a correctly designed relational database.

DETAILS

To redesign a list into a relational database, follow these principles:

• **Design each table to contain fields that describe only one subject**

Currently, the table in FIGURE E-1 contains four subjects—tours, sales, customers, and payments—which creates redundant data. For example, the tour name must be duplicated for each sale of that tour. The customer's name must be reentered every time that customer purchases a tour or makes a payment. The problems of redundant data include extra data entry work; more data entry inconsistencies and errors; larger physical storage requirements; and limitations on your ability to search for, analyze, and report on the data. You minimize these problems by implementing a properly designed relational database.

• **Identify a primary key field for each table**

A **primary key field** is a field that contains unique information for each record. For example, in a customer table, the customer number field usually serves this purpose. Although using the customer's last name as the primary key field might work in a small database, names are generally a poor choice for a primary key field because the primary key could not accommodate two customers who have the same name.

• **Build one-to-many relationships**

To tie the information from one table to another, a field must be common to each table. This linking field is the primary key field on the "one" side of the relationship and the **foreign key field** on the "many" side of the relationship. Recall that a primary key field stores unique information for each record in that table. For example, a CustomerNo field acting as the primary key field in the Customers table would link to a CustomerNo foreign key field in a Sales table to join one customer to many sales. You are not required to give the primary and foreign key fields the same name, although doing so does clarify which fields are used to link two tables in a one-to-many relationship.

The revised design for the database is shown in FIGURE E-2. One customer can purchase many tours, so the Customers and Sales tables have a one-to-many relationship based on the linking CustNo field. One tour can be purchased many times, so the Tours and Sales tables have a one-to-many relationship (TourID in the Sales table and TourNo in the Tours table). One sale may have many payments, creating a one-to-many relationship between the Sales and Payments tables based on the common SalesNo field.

Enforcing referential integrity

Referential integrity is a set of rules that helps reduce invalid entries and orphan records. An **orphan record** is a record in the "many" table that doesn't have a matching entry in the linking field of the "one" table. With referential integrity enforced on a one-to-many relationship, you cannot enter a value in a foreign key field of the "many" table that does not have a match in the linking field of the "one" table. Referential integrity also prevents you from deleting a record in the "one" table if a matching entry exists in the foreign key field of the "many" table. You should enforce referential integrity on all one-to-many relationships if possible. If you are working with a database that already contains orphan records, you cannot enforce referential integrity on that relationship.

FIGURE E-1: Single Sales table results in duplicate data

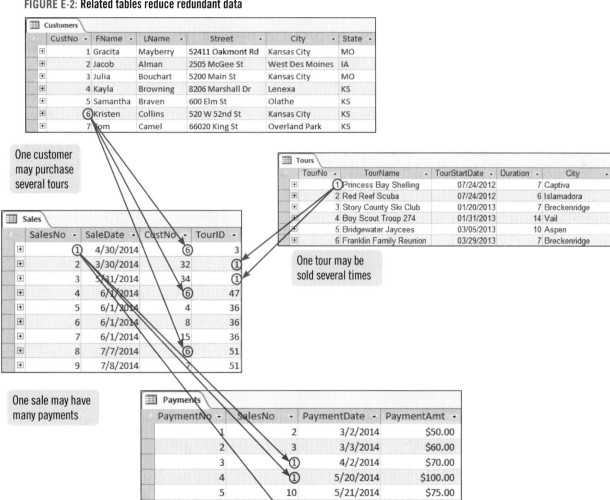

TourName	City	Price	SalesNo	SaleDate	FName	LName	PaymentDate	PaymentAmt
Princess Bay Shelling	Captiva	$750	2	3/30/2014	Lisa	Wilson	3/2/2014	$50.00
Princess Bay Shelling	Captiva	$750	3	5/31/2014	Kori	Yode	3/3/2014	$60.00
Story County Ski Club	Breckenridge	$850	1	4/30/2014	Kristen	Collins	4/2/2014	$70.00
Story County Ski Club	Breckenridge	$850	1	4/30/2014	Kristen	Collins	5/20/2014	$100.00
Bright Lights Expo	Branson	$200	10	7/9/2014	Mark	Custard	5/21/2014	$75.00
American Heritage Tour	Philadelphia	$1,200	5	6/1/2014	Kayla	Browning	5/22/2014	$150.00
Story County Ski Club	Breckenridge	$850	1	4/30/2014	Kristen	Collins	6/2/2014	$200.00

Tour information is duplicated for each sale or payment

Sales information is duplicated for each payment

Customer information is duplicated for each sale or payment

Payment fields

FIGURE E-2: Related tables reduce redundant data

Customers

CustNo	FName	LName	Street	City	State
1	Gracita	Mayberry	52411 Oakmont Rd	Kansas City	MO
2	Jacob	Alman	2505 McGee St	West Des Moines	IA
3	Julia	Bouchart	5200 Main St	Kansas City	MO
4	Kayla	Browning	8206 Marshall Dr	Lenexa	KS
5	Samantha	Braven	600 Elm St	Olathe	KS
6	Kristen	Collins	520 W 52nd St	Kansas City	KS
7	Tom	Camel	66020 King St	Overland Park	KS

One customer may purchase several tours

Tours

TourNo	TourName	TourStartDate	Duration	City
1	Princess Bay Shelling	07/24/2012	7	Captiva
2	Red Reef Scuba	07/24/2012	6	Islamadora
3	Story County Ski Club	01/20/2013	7	Breckenridge
4	Boy Scout Troop 274	01/31/2013	14	Vail
5	Bridgewater Jaycees	03/05/2013	10	Aspen
6	Franklin Family Reunion	03/29/2013	7	Breckenridge

Sales

SalesNo	SaleDate	CustNo	TourID
1	4/30/2014	6	3
2	3/30/2014	32	1
3	5/31/2014	34	1
4	6/1/2014	6	47
5	6/1/2014	4	36
6	6/1/2014	8	36
7	6/1/2014	15	36
8	7/7/2014	6	51
9	7/8/2014	7	51

One tour may be sold several times

One sale may have many payments

Payments

PaymentNo	SalesNo	PaymentDate	PaymentAmt
1	2	3/2/2014	$50.00
2	3	3/3/2014	$60.00
3	1	4/2/2014	$70.00
4	1	5/20/2014	$100.00
5	10	5/21/2014	$75.00
6	5	5/22/2014	$150.00
7	1	6/2/2014	$200.00

Using many-to-many relationships

As you design your database, you might find that two tables have a **many-to-many relationship**, which means that a record in one table may be related to many records in the other table and vice versa. To join them, you must establish a third table called a **junction table**, which contains two foreign key fields to serve on the "many" side of separate one-to-many relationships

with the two original tables. The Customers and Tours tables have a many-to-many relationship because one customer can purchase many tours and one tour can have many customers purchase it. The Sales table serves as the junction table to link the three tables together.

Access 2013

Design Related Tables

Learning
Outcomes:
• Set field data types
  in Table Design
  View
• Set field descrip-
  tions in Table
  Design View

After you develop a valid relational database design, you are ready to create the tables in Access. Using **Table Design View**, you can specify all characteristics of a table, including field names, data types, field descriptions, field properties, Lookup properties, and primary key field designations. **CASE** *Using the new database design, you are ready to create the Payments table for Quest Specialty Travel.*

STEPS

1. **Start Access, open the QuestTravel-E.accdb database, then enable content if prompted**
   The Customers, Sales, and Tours tables have already been created in the database. You need to create the Payments table.

2. **Click the CREATE tab on the Ribbon, then click the Table Design button in the Tables group**
   Table Design View opens, where you can enter field names and specify data types and field properties for the new table. Field names should be as short as possible, but long enough to be descriptive. The field name you enter in Table Design View is used as the default name for the field in all later queries, forms, and reports.

   QUICK TIP
   When specifying field data types, you can type the first letter of the data type to quickly select it.

3. **Type PaymentNo, press [Enter], click the Data Type list arrow, click AutoNumber, press [Tab], type Unique payment number and primary key field, then press [Enter]**
   The AutoNumber data type automatically assigns the next available integer in the sequence to each new record. The AutoNumber data type is often used as the primary key field for a table because it always contains a unique value for each record.

4. **Type the other field names, data types, and descriptions, as shown in FIGURE E-3**
   Field descriptions entered in Table Design View are optional, but provide a way to add helpful information about the field.

   TROUBLE
   If you set the wrong field as the primary key field, click the Primary Key button again to toggle it off.

5. **Click PaymentNo in the Field Name column, then click the Primary Key button in the Tools group**
   A **key symbol** appears to the left of PaymentNo to indicate that this field is defined as the primary key field for this table. Primary key fields have two roles: They uniquely define each record, and they may also serve as the "one" side of a one-to-many relationship between two tables. **TABLE E-1** describes common examples of one-to-many relationships.

   QUICK TIP
   To delete or rename an existing table, right-click it in the Navigation Pane, then click Delete or Rename.

6. **Click the Save button on the Quick Access toolbar, type Payments in the Table Name text box, click OK, then close the table**
   The Payments table is now displayed as a table object in the QuestTravel-E.accdb database Navigation Pane, as shown in **FIGURE E-4**.

FIGURE E-3: Table Design View for the new Payments table

Field Name	Data Type	Description (Optional)
PaymentNo	AutoNumber	Unique payment number and primary key field
PaymentDate	Date/Time	Date the payment is made
PaymentAmt	Currency	Amount of the payment
SalesNo	Number	Foreign key field to the Sales table

Field names — *Data types* — *Descriptions*

FIGURE E-4: Payments table in the Navigation Pane of the QuestTravel-E database

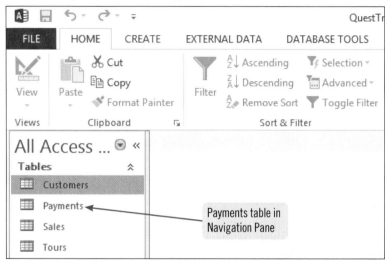

Payments table in Navigation Pane

TABLE E-1: Common one-to-many relationships

table on "one" side	table on "many" side	linking field	description
Products	Sales	ProductID	A ProductID field must have a unique entry in a Products table, but it is listed many times in a Sales table
Students	Enrollments	StudentID	A StudentID field must have a unique entry in a Students table, but it is listed many times in an Enrollments table as the student enrolls in multiple classes
Employees	Promotions	EmployeeID	An EmployeeID field must have a unique entry in an Employees table, but it is listed many times in a Promotions table as the employee is promoted over time

Specifying the foreign key field data type

A foreign key field in the "many" table must have the same data type (Short Text or Number) as the primary key it is related to in the "one" table. An exception to this rule is when the primary key field in the "one" table has an AutoNumber data type. In this case, the linking foreign key field in the "many" table must have a Number data type. Also note that a Number field used as a foreign key field must have a Long Integer Field Size property to match the Field Size property of the AutoNumber primary key field.

Create One-to-Many Relationships

Learning
Outcomes
• Enforce referential
integrity on a
one-to-many
relationship
• Create a
Relationship report

After creating the tables you need, you link them together in appropriate one-to-many relationships using the primary key field in the "one" table and the foreign key field in the "many" table. To avoid time-consuming rework, be sure that your table relationships are finished before building queries, forms, or reports using fields from multiple tables. **CASE** ➤ *You are ready to define the one-to-many relationships between the tables of the QuestTravel-E.accdb database.*

STEPS

QUICK TIP
Drag the table's title
bar to move the
field list.

1. **Click the DATABASE TOOLS tab on the Ribbon, click the Relationships button, click the Show Table button, double-click Customers, double-click Sales, double-click Tours, double-click Payments, then click Close in the Show Table dialog box**

   The four table field lists appear in the Relationships window. The primary key fields are identified with a small key symbol to the left of the field name. With all of the field lists in the Relationships window, you're ready to link them in proper one-to-many relationships.

QUICK TIP
Drag the bottom
border of the field
list to display all of
the fields.

2. **Click CustNo in the Customers table field list, then drag it to the CustNo field in the Sales table field list**

   Dragging a field from one table to another in the Relationships window links the two tables by the selected fields and opens the Edit Relationships dialog box, as shown in **FIGURE E-5**. Recall that referential integrity helps ensure data accuracy.

TROUBLE
Right-click a relation-
ship line, then click
Delete if you need to
delete a relationship
and start over.

3. **Click the Enforce Referential Integrity check box in the Edit Relationships dialog box, then click Create**

   The **one-to-many line** shows the link between the CustNo field of the Customers table and the CustNo field of the Sales table. The "one" side of the relationship is the unique CustNo value for each record in the Customers table. The "many" side of the relationship is identified by an infinity symbol pointing to the CustNo field in the Sales table. You also need to link the Tours table to the Sales table.

4. **Click TourNo in the Tours table field list, drag it to TourNo in the Sales table field list, click the Enforce Referential Integrity check box, then click Create**

   Finally, you need to link the Payments table to the Sales table.

5. **Click SalesNo in the Sales table field list, drag it to SalesNo in the Payments table field list, click the Enforce Referential Integrity check box, click Create, then drag the Tours title bar down so all links are clear**

   The updated Relationships window should look like **FIGURE E-6**.

TROUBLE
Click the Landscape
button on the PRINT
PREVIEW tab if the
report is too wide for
portrait orientation.

6. **Click the Relationship Report button in the Tools group, click the Print button on the PRINT PREVIEW tab, then click OK**

   A printout of the Relationships window, called the **Relationship report**, shows how your relational database is designed and includes table names, field names, primary key fields, and one-to-many relationship lines. This printout is helpful as you later create queries, forms, and reports that use fields from multiple tables. Note that it is not necessary to directly link each table to every other table.

7. **Right-click the Relationships for QuestTravel-E report tab, click Close, click Yes to save the report, then click OK to accept the default report name**

   The Relationships for QuestTravel-E report is saved in your database, as shown in the Navigation Pane.

8. **Close the Relationships window, then click Yes if prompted to save changes**

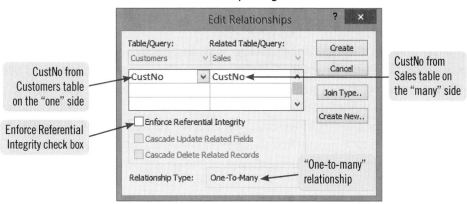

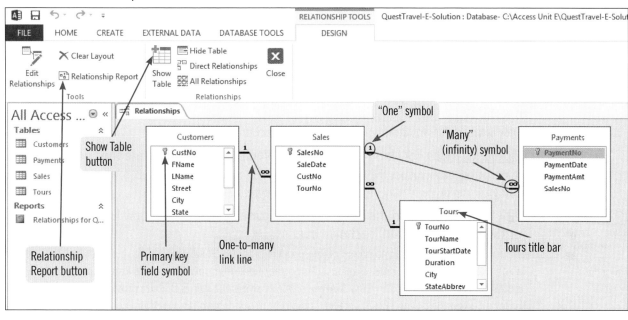

More on enforcing referential integrity

Recall that referential integrity is a set of rules to help ensure that no orphan records are entered or created in the database. An orphan record is a record in the "many" table (also called the **child table**) that doesn't have a matching entry in the linking field of the "one" table (also called the **parent table**). Referential integrity prevents orphan records in multiple ways. Referential integrity will not allow you to make an entry in the foreign key field of the child table that does not have a matching value in the linking field of the parent table. (So you can't make a sale to a customer who doesn't first exist in the Customers table, for example.) Referential integrity also prevents you from deleting a record in the parent table that has related records in the child table. (So you can't delete a customer from the Customers table who already has related sales records in the Sales table, for example.) You should enforce referential integrity on all one-to-many relationships if possible. Unfortunately, if you are working with a database that already contains orphan records, you cannot enforce this powerful set of rules unless you find and fix the data so that orphan records no longer exist. The process of removing and fixing orphan records is commonly called **scrubbing the database**.

Create Lookup Fields

A **Lookup field** is a field that contains Lookup properties. **Lookup properties** are field properties that supply a drop-down list of values for a field. The values can be stored in another table or directly stored in the **Row Source** Lookup property of the field. Fields that are good candidates for Lookup properties are those that contain a defined set of appropriate values such as State, Gender, or Department. You can set Lookup properties for a field in Table Design View using the **Lookup Wizard**. CASE ▶ *The FirstContact field in the Customers table identifies how the customer first made contact with Quest Specialty Travel such as being referred by a friend (Friend), finding the company through the Internet (Internet), or responding to a radio advertisement (Radio). Because the FirstContact field has only a handful of valid entries, it is a good Lookup field candidate.*

STEPS

1. **Right-click the Customers table in the Navigation Pane, then click Design View**
   The Lookup Wizard is included in the Data Type list.

2. **Click the Short Text data type for the FirstContact field, click the Data Type list arrow, then click Lookup Wizard**
   The Lookup Wizard starts and prompts you for information about where the Lookup column will get its values.

3. **Click the I will type in the values that I want option button, click Next, click the first cell in the Col1 column, type Friend, press [Tab], then type the rest of the values, as shown in FIGURE E-7**
   These are the values for the drop-down list for the FirstContact field.

4. **Click Next, then click Finish to accept the default label and complete the Lookup Wizard**
   Note that the data type for the FirstContact field is still Short Text. The Lookup Wizard is a process for setting Lookup property values for a field, not a data type itself.

5. **Click the Lookup tab in the Field Properties pane to observe the new Lookup properties for the FirstContact field, as shown in FIGURE E-8**
   The Lookup Wizard helped you enter Lookup properties for the FirstContact field, but you can always enter or edit them directly, too. Some of the most important Lookup properties include Row Source, Limit To List, and Allow Value List Edits. The **Row Source** property stores the values that are provided in the drop-down list for a Lookup field. The **Limit To List** Lookup property determines whether you can enter a new value into a field with other Lookup properties, or whether the entries are limited to the drop-down list. The **Allow Value List Edits** property determines whether users can add or edit the list of items.

6. **Click the View button 🔲 to switch to Datasheet View, click Yes when prompted to save the table, press [Tab] eight times to move to the FirstContact field, then click the FirstContact list arrow, as shown in FIGURE E-9**
   The FirstContact field now provides a list of four values for this field. To edit the list in Datasheet View, click the **Edit List Items button** 📝 below the list.

7. **Close the Customers table**

Modifying the Database Structure

FIGURE E-7: Entering a list of values in the Lookup Wizard

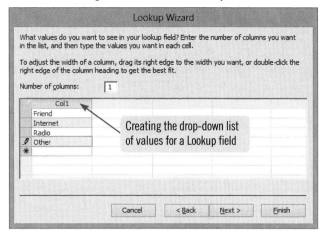

FIGURE E-8: Viewing Lookup properties

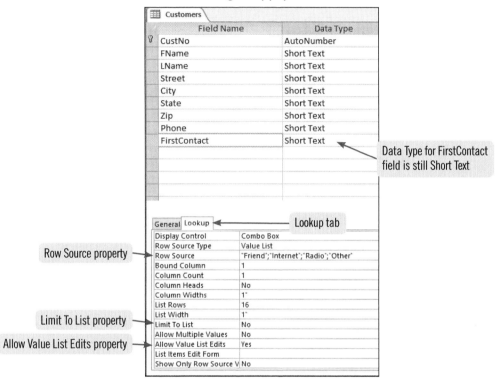

FIGURE E-9: Using a Lookup field in a datasheet

	CustNo	FName	LName	Street	City	State	Zip	Phone	FirstContact	Click to Add
⊞	1	Gracita	Mayberry	52411 Oakmont Rd	Kansas City	MO	64144	(555) 444-1234	Friend	
⊞	2	Jacob	Alman	2505 McGee St	Des Moines	IA	50288	(555) 111-6931	Friend	
⊞	3	Julia	Bouchart	5200 Main St	Kansas City	MO	64105	(555) 111-3081	Internet	
⊞	4	Jane	Taylor	8206 Marshall Dr	Lenexa	KS	66214	(555) 222-9101	Radio	
⊞	5	Samantha	Braven	600 Elm St	Olathe	KS	66031	(555) 222-7002	Other	
⊞	6	Kristen	Collins	520 W 52nd St	Kansas City	KS	64105	(555) 222-3602	Radio	
⊞	7	Tom	Camel	520 W 52nd St	Kansas City	KS	64105	(555) 222-3602	Radio	

Drop-down list for Lookup field

Edit List Items button

Creating multivalued fields

Multivalued fields allow you to make more than one choice from a drop-down list for a field. As a database designer, multivalued fields allow you to select and store more than one choice without having to create a more advanced database design. To create a multivalued field, enter Yes in the **Allow Multiple Values** Lookup property.

Modify Short Text Fields

Learning
Outcomes
• Modify the Field
Size property for
Short Text fields
• Modify the Input
Mask property
• Enter data using
an input mask

Field properties are the characteristics that describe each field, such as Field Size, Default Value, Caption, or Row Source. These properties help ensure database accuracy and clarity because they restrict the way data is entered, stored, and displayed. You modify field properties in Table Design View. See **TABLE E-2** for more information on Short Text field properties. (*Note*: The "Short Text" data type was called the "Text" data type in previous versions of Access.) **CASE** *After reviewing the Customers table with Samantha Hooper, you decide to change field properties for several Short Text fields in that table.*

STEPS

1. **Right-click the** Customers table **in the Navigation Pane, then click** Design View **on the shortcut menu**

    The Customers table opens in Design View. Field properties appear on the General tab on the lower half of the Table Design View window, the **Field Properties pane**, and apply to the selected field. Field properties change depending on the field's data type. For example, when you select a field with a Short Text data type, you see the **Field Size property**, which determines the number of characters you can enter in the field. However, when you select a field with a Date/Time data type, Access controls the size of the data, so the Field Size property is not displayed. Many field properties are optional, but for those that require an entry, Access provides a default value.

2. **Press [↓] to move through each field while viewing the field properties in the lower half of the window**

    The **field selector button** to the left of the field indicates which field is currently selected.

3. **Click the** FirstContact field name, **double-click** 255 **in the Field Size property text box, type** 8, **click the** Save button 🖫 **on the Quick Access toolbar, then click** Yes

    The maximum and the default value for the Field Size property for a Short Text field is 255. In general, however, you want to make the Field Size property for Short Text fields only as large as needed to accommodate the longest entry. You can increase the size later if necessary. In some cases, shortening the Field Size property helps prevent typographical errors. For example, you should set the Field Size property for a State field that stores two-letter state abbreviations to 2 to prevent errors such as TXX. For the FirstContact field, your longest entry is "Internet"—8 characters.

4. **Change the Field Size property to** 30 **for the FName and LName fields, click** 🖫, **then click** Yes

    No existing entries are greater than 30 characters for either of these fields, so no data is lost. The **Input Mask** property provides a visual guide for users as they enter data. It also helps determine what types of values can be entered into a field.

QUICK TIP
If the Input Mask
Wizard is not
installed on your
computer, type
!(999) 000-0000;;_
for the Input Mask
property for the
Phone field.

5. **Click the** Phone field name, **click the** Input Mask property text box, **click the** Build button **[...], click the** Phone Number input mask, **click** Next, **click** Next, **click** Finish, **then click to the right of the Input Mask property value so you can read it**

    Table Design View of the Customers table should look like **FIGURE E-10**, which shows the Input Mask property created for the Phone field by the Input Mask Wizard.

6. **Right-click the** Customers table tab, **click** Datasheet View, **click** Yes **to save the table, press [Tab] enough times to move to the Phone field for the first record, type** 5552223333, **then press [Enter]**

    The Phone Input Mask property creates an easy-to-use visual guide to facilitate accurate data entry.

7. **Close the Customers table**

FIGURE E-10: Changing Short Text field properties

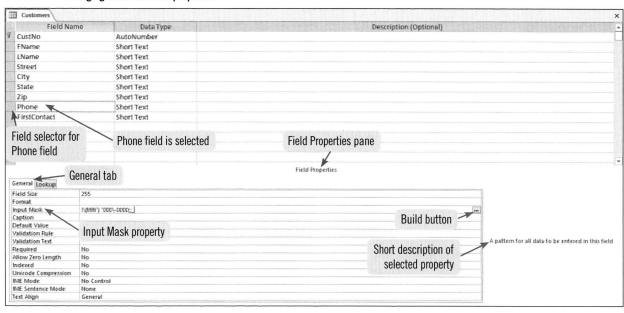

TABLE E-2: Common Short Text field properties

property	description	sample field	sample property entry
Field Size	Controls how many characters can be entered into the field	State	2
Format	Controls how information will be displayed and printed	State	> (displays all characters in uppercase)
Input Mask	Provides a pattern for data to be entered	Phone	!(999) 000-0000;1;_
Caption	Describes the field in the first row of a datasheet, form, or report; if the Caption property is not entered, the field name is used to label the field	EmpNo	Employee Number
Default Value	Displays a value that is automatically entered in the given field for new records	City	Des Moines
Required	Determines if an entry is required for this field	LastName	Yes

Working with the Input Mask property

The Input Mask property provides a pattern for data to be entered, using three parts separated by semicolons. The first part provides a pattern for what type of data can be entered. For example, 9 represents an optional number, 0 a required number, ? an optional letter, and L a required letter. The second part determines whether all displayed characters (such as dashes in a phone number) are stored in the field. For the second part of the input mask, a 0 entry stores all characters such as 555-7722, and a 1 entry stores only the entered data, 5557722. The third part of the input mask determines which character Access uses to guide the user through the mask. Common choices are the asterisk (*), underscore (_), or pound sign (#).

Modify Number and Currency Fields

Learning
Outcomes
• Modify the Field
 Size property for
 Number fields
• Modify the
 Decimal Places
 property

Although some properties for Number and Currency fields are the same as the properties of Short Text fields, each data type has its own list of valid properties. Number and Currency fields have similar properties because they both contain numeric values. Currency fields store values that represent money, and Number fields store values that represent values such as quantities, measurements, and scores. **CASE** *The Tours table contains both a Number field (Duration) and a Currency field (Price). You want to modify the properties of these two fields.*

STEPS

1. **Right-click the Tours table in the Navigation Pane, click Design View on the shortcut menu, then click the Duration field name**

   The default Field Size property for a Number field is **Long Integer**. See **TABLE E-3** for more information on the Field Size property and other common properties for a Number field. Access sets the size of Currency fields to control the way numbers are rounded in calculations, so the Field Size property isn't available for Currency fields.

2. **Click Long Integer in the Field Size property text box, click the Field Size list arrow, then click Byte**

   Choosing a **Byte** value for the Field Size property allows entries from 0 to 255, so it greatly restricts the possible values and the storage requirements for the Duration field.

3. **Click the Price field name, click Auto in the Decimal Places property text box, click the Decimal Places list arrow, click 0, then press [Enter]**

   Your Table Design View should look like **FIGURE E-11**. Because all of Quest's tours are priced at a round dollar value, you do not need to display cents in the Price field.

4. **Save the table, then switch to Datasheet View**

   You won't lose any data because none of the current entries in the Duration field is greater than 255, the maximum value allowed by a Number field with a Byte Field Size property. You want to test the new property changes.

5. **Press [Tab] three times to move to the Duration field for the first record, type 800, then press [Tab]**

   Because 800 is larger than what the Byte Field Size property allows (0–255), an Access error message appears indicating that the value isn't valid for this field.

6. **Press [Esc] twice to remove the inappropriate entry in the Duration field, then press [Tab] four times to move to the Price field**

   The Price field is set to display zero digits after the decimal point.

7. **Type 750.25 in the Price field of the first record, press [Tab], then click $750 in the Price field of the first record to see the full entry**

   Although the Decimal Places property for the Price field specifies that entries in the field are *formatted* to display zero digits after the decimal point, 750.25 is the actual value stored in the field. Modifying the Decimal Places property does not change the actual data. Rather, the Decimal Places property only changes the way the data is *presented*.

8. **Close the Tours table**

FIGURE E-11: Changing Currency and Number field properties

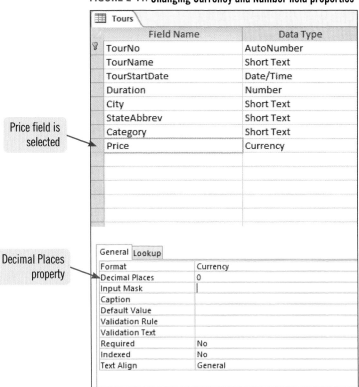

Price field is selected →

Decimal Places property →

TABLE E-3: Common Number field properties

property	description
Field Size	Determines the largest number that can be entered in the field, as well as the type of data (e.g., integer or fraction)
Byte	Stores numbers from 0 to 255 (no fractions)
Integer	Stores numbers from –32,768 to 32,767 (no fractions)
Long Integer	Stores numbers from –2,147,483,648 to 2,147,483,647 (no fractions)
Single	Stores numbers (including fractions with six digits to the right of the decimal point) times 10 to the –38th to +38th power
Double	Stores numbers (including fractions with over 10 digits to the right of the decimal point) in the range of 10 to the –324th to +324th power
Decimal Places	The number of digits displayed to the right of the decimal point

© 2014 Cengage Learning

Modifying fields in Datasheet View

When you work in Table *Datasheet* View, the FIELDS tab on the Ribbon provides many options to modify fields and field properties. For example, you can add and delete fields, change a field name or data type, and modify many field properties such as Caption, Default Value, and Format. Table *Design* View, however, gives you full access to *all* field properties such as all of the Lookup properties. In Datasheet View, an **Autofilter** arrow is displayed to the right of each field name. Click the Autofilter arrow to quickly sort or filter by that field.

Modify Date/Time Fields

Many properties of the Date/Time field, such as Input Mask, Caption, and Default Value, work the same way as they do in fields with a Short Text or Number data type. One difference, however, is the **Format** property, which helps you format dates in various ways such as January 25, 2013; 25-Jan-13; or 01/25/2013. **CASE** *You want to change the format of Date/Time fields in the Tours table to display two digits for the month and day values and four digits for the year, as in 05/05/2015.*

STEPS

1. **Right-click the Tours table in the Navigation Pane, click Design View on the shortcut menu, then click the TourStartDate field name**

   You want the tour start dates to appear with two digits for the month and day, such as 07/05/2015, instead of the default presentation of dates, 7/5/2015.

QUICK TIP

Click any property box, then press [F1] to open a page on the Microsoft Web site where you can enter the property name in the Search box to display an explanation of how to use the property.

2. **Click the Format property box, then click the Format list arrow**

   Although several predefined Date/Time formats are available, none matches the format you want. To define a custom format, enter symbols that represent how you want the date to appear.

3. **Type mm/dd/yyyy then press [Enter]**

   The updated Format property for the TourStartDate field shown in **FIGURE E-12** sets the date to appear with two digits for the month, two digits for the day, and four digits for the year. The parts of the date are separated by forward slashes.

4. **Save the table, display the datasheet, then click the New (blank) record button 📑 on the navigation bar**

   To test the new Format property for the TourStartDate field, you can add a new record to the table.

QUICK TIP

Access assumes that years entered with two digits from 30 to 99 refer to the years 1930 through 1999, and 00 to 29 refers to the years 2000 through 2029. To enter a year before 1930 or after 2029, enter all four digits of the year.

5. **Press [Tab] to move to the TourName field, type Missouri Eagle Watchers, press [Tab], type 9/1/15, press [Tab], type 7, press [Tab], type Hollister, press [Tab], type MO, press [Tab], type Adventure, press [Tab], type 700, then press [Tab]**

   The new record you entered into the Tours table should look like **FIGURE E-13**. The Format property for the TourStartDate field makes the entry appear as 09/01/2015, as desired.

Modifying the Database Structure

FIGURE E-12: Changing Date/Time field properties

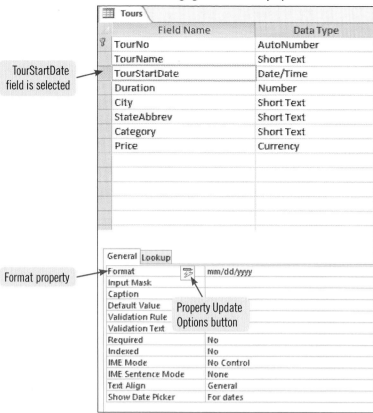

TourStartDate field is selected →

Format property →

Property Update Options button

FIGURE E-13: Testing the Format property

Custom mm/dd/yyyy Format property applied to TourStartDate field

Using Smart Tags

Smart Tags are buttons that automatically appear in certain conditions. They provide a small menu of options to help you work with the task at hand. Access provides the **Property Update Options** Smart Tag to help you quickly apply property changes to other objects of the database that use the field. The

Error Indicator Smart Tag helps identify potential design errors. For example, if you are working in Report Design View and the report is too wide for the paper, the Error Indicator appears in the upper-left corner by the report selector button to alert you to the problem.

Access 2013

Modify Validation Properties

Learning Outcomes
• Modify the Validation Rule property
• Modify the Validation Text property
• Define Validation Rule expressions

The **Validation Rule** property determines what entries a field can accept. For example, a validation rule for a Date/Time field might require date entries on or after a particular date. A validation rule for a Currency field might indicate that valid entries fall between a minimum and maximum value. You use the **Validation Text** property to display an explanatory message when a user tries to enter data that breaks the validation rule. Therefore, the Validation Rule and Validation Text field properties help you prevent unreasonable data from being entered into the database. **CASE** ▶ *Samantha Hooper reminds you that all new Quest tours start on or after May 1, 2014. You can use the validation properties to establish this rule for the TourStartDate field in the Tours table.*

STEPS

1. **Right-click the** Tours table tab, **click** Design View, **click the** TourStartDate field, **click the** Validation Rule property box, **then type** >=5/1/2014

   This entry forces all dates in the TourStartDate field to be greater than or equal to 5/1/2014. See **TABLE E-4** for more examples of Validation Rule expressions. The Validation Text property provides a helpful message to the user when the entry in the field breaks the rule entered in the Validation Rule property.

2. **Click the** Validation Text box, **then type** Date must be on or after 5/1/2014

   Design View of the Tours table should now look like **FIGURE E-14**. Access modifies a property to include additional syntax by changing the entry in the Validation Rule property to >=#5/1/2014#. Pound signs (#) are used to surround date criteria.

3. **Save the table, then click** Yes **when asked to test the existing data with new data integrity rules**

   Because no dates in the TourStartDate field are earlier than 5/1/2014, Access finds no date errors in the current data and saves the table. You now want to test that the Validation Rule and Validation Text properties work when entering data in the datasheet.

4. **Click the** View button ▦ **to display the datasheet, press [Tab] twice to move to the** TourStartDate field, **type** 5/1/13, **then press** [Tab]

   Because you tried to enter a date that was not true for the Validation Rule property for the TourStartDate field, a dialog box opens and displays the Validation Text entry, as shown in **FIGURE E-15**.

5. **Click** OK **to close the validation message**

   You now know that the Validation Rule and Validation Text properties work properly.

6. **Press** [Esc] **to reject the invalid date entry in the TourStartDate field**

7. **Close the Tours table**

FIGURE E-14: Entering Validation properties

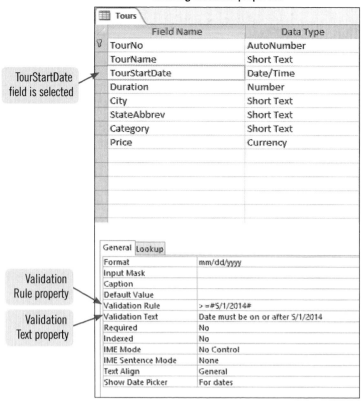

TourStartDate field is selected

Validation Rule property

Validation Text property

FIGURE E-15: Validation Text message

TourNo	TourName	TourStartDate	Duration	City	State	Category	Price
1	Breeze Bay Shelling	5/1/13	3	Captiva	FL	Autofilter button	$750
2	Red Reef Scuba	07/06/2014	3	Islamadora	FL	Adventure	$1,500
3	Ames Ski Club	01/02/2015	7	Breckenridge	CO	Adventure	$850
4	Boy Scout Jamboree	01/13/2015	7	Vail	CO	Adventure	$1,900
5	Bridgewater Country	02/15/2015	10	Aspen	CO	Adventure	$1,200
6	Franklin Family Reunion	03/11/2015	3	Breckenridge	CO	Family	$700
7	Spare Tire Ski Club	03/13/2015	7	Monmouth	WA	Adventure	$600
8	Eagan Family Reunion	06/12/2015					$500
9	Gunnison Bikers	06/20/2015				ure	$250
10	Golden Footsteps	05/23/2014				eing	$550
11	Hummer Trail	05/30/2014				eing	$725
12	Piper-Heitman Wedding	05/30/2014					$550
13	High Adventurers	06/05/2014				ure	$575
15	Patriot Debate Club	06/12/2014	7	Orlando	FL	Site Seeing	$605

Entering a TourStartDate that breaks the Validation Rule

Microsoft Access

Date must be on or after 5/1/2014

OK   Help

Validation Text message when Validation Rule is broken

TABLE E-4: Validation Rule expressions

data type	validation rule expression	description
Number or Currency	>0	The number must be positive
Number or Currency	>10 And <100	The number must be greater than 10 and less than 100
Number or Currency	10 Or 20 Or 30	The number must be 10, 20, or 30
Short Text	"IA" Or "NE" Or "MO"	The entry must be IA, NE, or MO
Date/Time	>=#7/1/93#	The date must be on or after 7/1/1993
Date/Time	>#1/1/10# And <#1/1/18#	The date must be greater than 1/1/2010 and less than 1/1/2018

Create Attachment Fields

Learning
Outcomes
• Create an
Attachment field
• Attach and view a
file in an
Attachment field

An **Attachment field** allows you to attach an external file such as a picture, Word document, PowerPoint presentation, or Excel workbook to a record. Earlier versions of Access allowed you to link or embed external data using the **OLE** (object linking and embedding) data type. The Attachment data type stores more file formats such as JPEG images, requires no additional software to view the files from within Access, and allows you to attach more than one file to the Attachment field. **CASE** *Samantha Hooper asks you to incorporate images on forms and reports to help describe and market each tour. You can use an Attachment field to store JPEG images for customer photo identification.*

STEPS

QUICK TIP
You can drag the
field selectors to the
left of the field name
to reorder your fields
in Table Design View.

1. **Right-click the Customers table in the Navigation Pane, then click Design View**

   You can insert a new field anywhere in the list.

2. **Click the Street field selector, click the Insert Rows button on the DESIGN tab, click the Field Name cell, type Photo, press [Tab], click the Data Type list arrow, then click Attachment, as shown in FIGURE E-16**

   Now that you've created the new Attachment field named Photo, you're ready to add data to it in Datasheet View.

3. **Click the Save button on the Quick Access toolbar, click the View button on the DESIGN tab to switch to Datasheet View, then press [Tab] three times to move to the new Photo field**

   An Attachment field cell displays a small paper clip icon with the number of files attached to the field in parentheses. You have not attached any files to this field yet, so each record shows zero (0) file attachments. You can attach files to this field directly from Datasheet View.

4. **Double-click the attachment icon for the Gracita Mayberry record to open the Attachments dialog box, click Add, navigate to the location where you store your Data Files, double-click GMayberry.jpg, then click OK**

   The GMayberry.jpg file is now included with the first record, and the datasheet reflects that one (1) file is attached to the Photo field of the first record. You can add more than one file attachment and different types of files to the same field. You can view file attachments directly from the datasheet, form, or report.

5. **Double-click the attachment icon for the Gracita Mayberry record to open the Attachments dialog box shown in FIGURE E-17, then click Open**

   The image opens in the program that is associated with the .jpg extension on your computer such as Windows Photo Viewer. The **.jpg** file extension is short for **JPEG**, an acronym for **Joint Photographic Experts Group**. This group defines the standards for the compression algorithms that make JPEG files very efficient to use in databases and on Web pages.

6. **Close the window that displays the GMayberry.jpg image, click Cancel in the Attachments dialog box, close the Customers table, close the QuestTravel-E.accdb database, then exit Access**

Modifying the Database Structure

FIGURE E-16: Adding an Attachment field

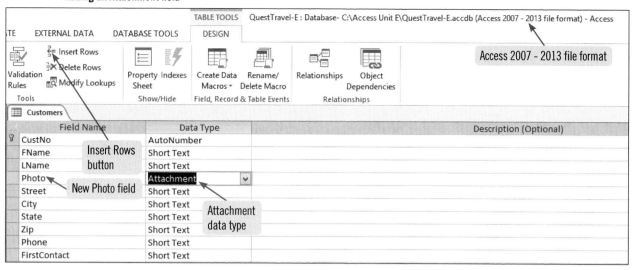

FIGURE E-17: Opening an attached file

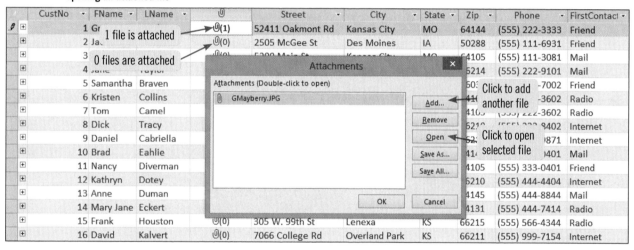

Working with database file types

When you create a new database in Microsoft Access 2013, Access gives the file an **.accdb** extension, and saves it as an Access 2007-2013 database file type. Saving the database as an Access 2007-2013 file type allows users of Access 2007, 2010, and 2013 to share the same database. Access 2007 databases are *not* readable by earlier versions of Access such as Access 2000, Access 2002 (XP), or Access 2003. If you need to share your database with people using Access 2000, 2002, or 2003, you can use the Save As command on the FILE tab to save the database with an Access 2000 or 2002-2003 file type, which applies an **.mdb** file extension to the database. Databases with an Access 2000 file type can be used by any version of Access from Access 2000 through 2013, but some features such as multivalued fields and Attachment fields are only available when working with an Access 2007-2013 database.

Practice

Concepts Review

Identify each element of the Relationships window shown in FIGURE E-18.

FIGURE E-18

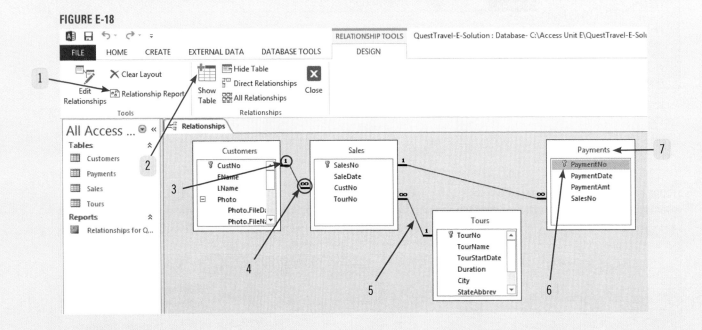

Match each term with the statement that best describes it.

8. **Validation Rule**

9. **Table Design View**

10. **Row Source**

11. **Attachment field**

12. **Limit To List**

13. **Input Mask**

14. **Lookup properties**

15. **Primary key field**

16. **Multivalued field**

a. Field that allows you to store external files such as a Word document, PowerPoint presentation, Excel workbook, or JPEG image

b. Field that holds unique information for each record in the table

c. Field that allows you to make more than one choice from a drop-down list

d. Determines whether you can enter a new value into a field

e. Field properties that allow you to supply a drop-down list of values for a field

f. Access window where all characteristics of a table, such as field names and field properties, are defined

g. Field property that provides a visual guide as you enter data

h. Field property that prevents unreasonable data entries for a field

i. Lookup property that determines where the Lookup field gets its list of values

Select the best answer from the list of choices.

17. **Which of the following problems most clearly indicates that you need to redesign your database?**
    a. Referential integrity is enforced on table relationships.
    b. The Input Mask Wizard has not been used.
    c. There is duplicated data in several records of a table.
    d. Not all fields have Validation Rule properties.

18. **Which of the following is *not* done in Table Design View?**
    a. Defining field data types
    b. Specifying the primary key field
    c. Setting Field Size properties
    d. Creating file attachments

19. **What is the purpose of enforcing referential integrity?**
    a. To require an entry for each field of each record
    b. To prevent incorrect entries in the primary key field
    c. To prevent orphan records from being created
    d. To force the application of meaningful validation rules

20. **To create a many-to-many relationship between two tables, you must create:**
    a. Foreign key fields in each table.
    b. A junction table.
    c. Two primary key fields in each table.
    d. Two one-to-one relationships between the two tables, with referential integrity enforced.

21. **The linking field in the "many" table is called the:**
    a. Attachment field.
    b. Child field.
    c. Foreign key field.
    d. Primary key field.

22. **The default filename extension for a database created in Access 2013 is:**
    a. .accdb.   c. .acc13.
    b. .mdb.   d. .mdb13.

23. **If the primary key field in the "one" table is an AutoNumber data type, the linking field in the "many" table will have which data type?**
    a. Number   c. Short Text
    b. AutoNumber   d. Attachment

24. **Which symbol is used to identify the "many" field in a one-to-many relationship in the Relationships window?**
    a. Arrow   c. Triangle
    b. Key   d. Infinity

25. **The process of removing and fixing orphan records is commonly called:**
    a. Relating tables.   c. Designing a relational database.
    b. Scrubbing the database.   d. Analyzing performance.

Skills Review

1. Examine relational databases.

a. List the fields needed to create an Access relational database to manage volunteer hours for the members of a philanthropic club or community service organization.

b. Identify fields that would contain duplicate values if all of the fields were stored in a single table.

c. Group the fields into subject matter tables, then identify the primary key field for each table.

d. Assume that your database contains two tables: Members and ServiceRecords. If you did not identify these two tables earlier, regroup the fields within these two table names, then identify the primary key field for each table, the foreign key field in the ServiceRecords table, and how the tables would be related using a one-to-many relationship.

2. Design related tables.

a. Start Access 2013, then create a new blank desktop database named **Service-E** in the location where you store your Data Files.

b. Use Table Design View to create a new table with the name **Members** and the field names, data types, descriptions, and primary key field, as shown in **FIGURE E-19**. Close the Members table.

FIGURE E-19

Field Name	Data Type	Description
MemberNo	AutoNumber	Member Number. Unique number for each member
FirstName	Short Text	Member's first name
LastName	Short Text	Member's last name
City	Short Text	Member's city
Phone	Short Text	Member's best phone number
Email	Short Text	Member's best email address
Birthdate	Date/Time	Member's birthdate
Gender	Short Text	Member's gender: male, female, unknown

c. Use Table Design View to create a new table named **ServiceHours** with the field names, data types, descriptions, and primary key field shown in **FIGURE E-20**. Close the ServiceHours table.

FIGURE E-20

Field Name	Data Type	Description (Optional)
ServiceNo	AutoNumber	Unique number to identify each ServiceHours record
MemberNo	Number	Foreign key field to Members table. One member may have many ServiceHours records
ServiceDate	Date/Time	Date that the service occurred
Location	Short Text	Location where the service occurred
Description	Short Text	Description of the service activity
ServiceHours	Number	Number of hours spent on service activity
ServiceValue	Currency	Monetary value of the service activity

3. Create one-to-many relationships.

a. Open the Relationships window, double-click Members, then double-click ServiceHours to add the two tables to the Relationships window. Close the Show Table dialog box.

b. Resize all field lists by dragging the bottom border down so that all fields are visible, then drag the MemberNo field from the Members table to the MemberNo field in the ServiceHours table.

Skills Review (continued)

c. Enforce referential integrity, and create the one-to-many relationship between Members and ServiceHours. See **FIGURE E-21**.

d. Create a Relationship report for the Service-E database, add your name as a label to the Report Header section of the report in Report Design View, save the Relationship report with the default name, **Relationships for Service-E**, then preview it.

e. Print the report if requested by your instructor, close the Relationship report, then save and close the Relationships window.

FIGURE E-21

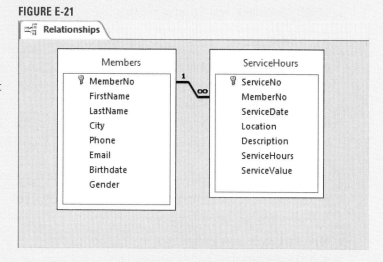

4. **Create Lookup fields.**

a. Open the Members table in Design View, then start the Lookup Wizard for the Gender field.

b. Select the option that allows you to enter your own values, then enter **Female**, **Male**, and **Unknown** as the values for the Lookup column in the Col1 list.

c. Use the default **Gender** label, click the Limit To List check box, then click Finish to finish the Lookup Wizard.

d. Save the Members table, display it in Datasheet View, and enter *your* name in the FirstName and LastName fields for the first record. Enter your school's city, **5556667777** in the Phone field, *your* school email address in the Email field, **1/1/1990** in the Birthdate field, and any valid choice in the Gender field.

e. Type **Test** in the Gender field, then press [Tab] to test the Limit To List property. If it worked properly, you should receive an error message that states that the text you entered isn't an item on the list. Click OK in that dialog box, make a choice from the Gender drop-down list, then press [Tab] to finish the record. (*Hint*: If you were allowed to enter Test in the Gender field, it means that the Limit To List property is set to No instead of Yes. If that's the case, delete the Test entry, then switch to Table Design View. Modify the Limit To List Lookup property in the Lookup properties for the Gender field from No to Yes, save the table, then switch back to Datasheet View. Retest the property change by repeating Step e.)

f. Resize fields in Datasheet View as needed to clearly see all entries.

5. **Modify Short Text fields.**

a. Open the Members table in Design View.

b. Use the Input Mask Wizard to create an Input Mask property for the Phone field. Choose the Phone Number Input Mask. Accept the other default options provided by the Input Mask Wizard. (*Hint*: If the Input Mask Wizard is not installed on your computer, type **!(999) 000-0000;;_** for the Input Mask property for the Phone field.)

c. Change the Field Size property of the FirstName, LastName, and City fields to **30**. Change the Field Size property of the Phone field to **10**. Change the Field Size property of the Gender field to **7**. Save the Members table. None of these fields has data greater in length than the new Field Size properties, so click OK when prompted that some data may be lost.

d. Open the Members table in Datasheet View, and enter a new record with *your* instructor's name in the FirstName and LastName fields and *your* school's City and Phone field values. Enter *your* instructor's email address, **1/1/1980** for the Birthdate field, and an appropriate choice for the Gender field. Close the Members table.

Skills Review (continued)

6. **Modify Number and Currency fields.**
   a. Open the ServiceHours table in Design View.
   b. Change the Decimal Places property of the ServiceHours field to **0**.
   c. Change the Decimal Places property of the ServiceValue field to **2**.
   d. Save and close the ServiceHours table.

7. **Modify Date/Time fields.**
   a. Open the ServiceHours table in Design View.
   b. Change the Format property of the ServiceDate field to **mm/dd/yyyy**.
   c. Save and close the ServiceHours table.
   d. Open the Members table in Design View.
   e. Change the Format property of the Birthdate field to **mm/dd/yyyy**.
   f. Save and close the Members table.

8. **Modify validation properties.**
   a. Open the Members table in Design View.
   b. Click the Birthdate field name, click the Validation Rule text box, then type **<1/1/2000**. (Note that Access automatically adds pound signs around date criteria in the Validation Rule property.)
   c. Click the Validation Text box, then type **Birthdate must be before 1/1/2000**.
   d. Save and accept the changes, then open the Members table in Datasheet View.
   e. Test the Validation Text and Validation Rule properties by tabbing to the Birthdate field and entering a date after 1/1/2000 such as **1/1/2001**. Click OK when prompted with the Validation Text message, press [Esc] to remove the invalid Birthdate field entry, then close the Members table. (*Note*: Be sure your Validation Text message is spelled properly. If not, correct it in Table Design View.)

9. **Create Attachment fields.**
   a. Open the Members table in Design View, then add a new field after the Gender field with the field name **Picture** and an Attachment data type. Enter **Member's picture** for the Description. Save the Members table.
   b. Display the Members table in Datasheet View, then attach a .jpg file of yourself to the record. If you do not have a .jpg file of yourself, use the **Member1.jpg** file provided in the location where you store your Data Files.
   c. Close the Members table.
   d. Use the Form Wizard to create a form based on all of the fields in the Members table. Use a Columnar layout, and title the form **Member Entry Form**.
   e. If requested by your instructor, print the first record in the Members Entry Form that shows the picture you just entered in the Picture field, then close the form.
   f. Close the Service-E.accdb database, then exit Access.

Independent Challenge 1

As the manager of a music store's instrument rental program, you decide to create a database to track rentals to school-children. The fields you need to track are organized with four tables: Instruments, Rentals, Customers, and Schools.

a. Start Access, then create a new blank desktop database called **Music-E** in the location where you store your Data Files.

b. Use Table Design View or the FIELDS tab on the Ribbon of Table Datasheet View to create the four tables in the MusicStore-E database using the field names, data types, descriptions, and primary keys shown in FIGURES E-22, E-23, E-24, and E-25.

FIGURE E-22

Schools

Field Name	Data Type	Description (Optional)
SchoolName	Short Text	Full name of school
SchoolCode	Short Text	Unique three character code for each school

FIGURE E-23

Customers

Field Name	Data Type	Description (Optional)
FirstName	Short Text	Customer's first name
LastName	Short Text	Customer's last name
Street	Short Text	Customer's street
City	Short Text	Customer's city
State	Short Text	Customer's state
Zip	Short Text	Customer's zip code
CustNo	AutoNumber	Unique number to identify each customer
SchoolCode	Short Text	Three character school code for that customer

FIGURE E-24

Instruments

Field Name	Data Type	Description (Optional)
Description	Short Text	Description of the instrument
SerialNo	Short Text	Unique serial number on each instrument
MonthlyFee	Currency	Monthly rental fee

FIGURE E-25

Rentals

Field Name	Data Type	Description (Optional)
RentalNo	AutoNumber	Unique rental number for each record
CustNo	Number	Foreign key field to Customers table. One customer can be linked to many rental records
SerialNo	Short Text	Foreign key field to Instruments table. One instrument can be linked to many rental records
RentalStartDate	Date/Time	Date the rental starts

Independent Challenge 1 (continued)

c. In Design View of the Rentals table, enter **>1/1/2014** as the Validation Rule property for the RentalStartDate field. This change allows only dates later than 1/1/2014, the start date for this business, to be entered into this field.

d. Enter **Rental start dates must be after January 1, 2014** as the Validation Text property to the RentalStartDate field of the Rentals table. Note that Access adds pound signs (#) to the date criteria entered in the Validation Rule as soon as you tab out of the Validation Text property.

e. Save and close the Rentals table.

f. Open the Relationships window, then add the Schools, Customers, Rentals, and Instruments tables to the window. Expand the Customers field list to view all fields. Create one-to-many relationships, as shown in **FIGURE E-26**. Be sure to enforce referential integrity on each relationship.

FIGURE E-26

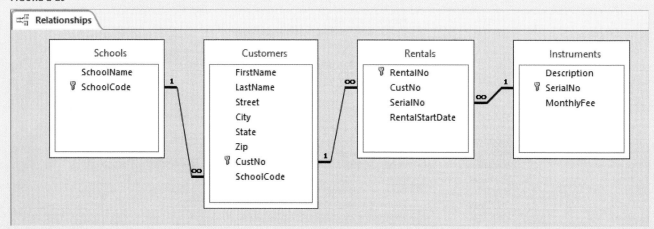

g. Preview the Relationship report, add *your* name as a label to the Report Header section, then save the report with the default name **Relationships for Music-E**. If requested by your instructor, print the report then close it.

h. Save and close the Relationships window.

i. Close the Music-E.accdb database, then exit Access.

Independent Challenge 2

You want to create a database that documents blood bank donations by the employees of your company. You want to track information such as employee name, blood type, date of donation, and the hospital where the employee chooses to make the donation. You also want to track basic hospital information, such as the hospital name and address.

a. Start Access, then create a new, blank desktop database called **BloodDrive-E** in the location where you store your Data Files.

b. Create an **Employees** table with appropriate field names, data types, and descriptions to record the automatic employee ID, employee first name, employee last name, and blood type. Make the EmployeeID field the primary key field. Use **FIGURE E-27** as a guide for appropriate field names.

c. Add Lookup properties to the blood type field in the Employees table to provide only valid blood type entries of **A+**, **A−**, **B+**, **B−**, **O+**, **O−**, **AB+**, and **AB−** for this field.

d. Create a **Donations** table with appropriate field names, data types, and descriptions to record an automatic donation ID, date of the donation, employee ID field, and hospital code field. Make the donation ID the primary key field. Use **FIGURE E-27** as a guide for appropriate field names.

e. Create a **Hospitals** table with fields and appropriate field names, data types, and descriptions to record a hospital code, hospital name, street, city, state, and zip. Make the hospital code field the primary key field. Use **FIGURE E-27** as a guide for appropriate field names.

f. In the Relationships window, create one-to-many relationships with referential integrity between the tables in the database, as shown in **FIGURE E-27**. One employee may make several donations over time. Each donation is marked for a particular hospital so each hospital may receive many donations over time.

FIGURE E-27

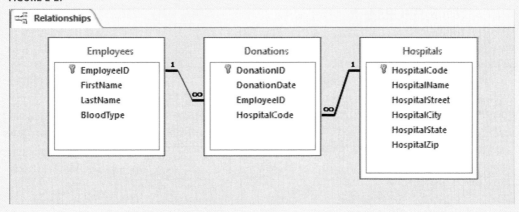

g. Preview the Relationship report, add *your* name as a label to the Report Header section, then save the report with the default name **Relationships for BloodDrive-E**. If requested by your instructor, print the report then close it.

h. Save and close the Relationships window.

i. Close the BloodDrive-E.accdb database, then exit Access.

Independent Challenge 3

You're a member and manager of a recreational baseball team and decide to create an Access database to manage player information, games, and batting statistics.

a. Start Access, then create a new, blank desktop database called **Baseball-E** in the location where you store your Data Files.

b. Create a **Players** table with appropriate field names, data types, and descriptions to record the player first name, last name, and uniform number. Make the uniform number field the primary key field. Use **FIGURE E-28** as a guide for appropriate field names.

c. Create a **Games** table with appropriate field names, data types, and descriptions to record an automatic game number, date of the game, opponent's name, home score, and visitor score. Make the game number field the primary key field. Use **FIGURE E-28** as a guide for appropriate field names.

d. Create an **AtBats** table with appropriate field names, data types, and descriptions to record hits, at bats, the game number, and the uniform number of each player. The game number and uniform number fields will both be foreign key fields. This table does not need a primary key field. Use **FIGURE E-28** as a guide for appropriate field names.

e. In the Relationships window, create one-to-many relationships with referential integrity between the tables shown in **FIGURE E-28**. The AtBats table contains one record for each player that plays in each game to record his hitting statistics, hits and at bats, for each game. Therefore, one player record is related to many records in the AtBats table and one game record is related to many records in the AtBats table.

f. Preview the Relationship report, add *your* name as a label to the Report Header section, then save the report with the default name **Relationships for Baseball-E**. If requested by your instructor, print the report then close it.

g. Save and close the Relationships window.

h. Close the Baseball-E.accdb database, then exit Access.

FIGURE E-28

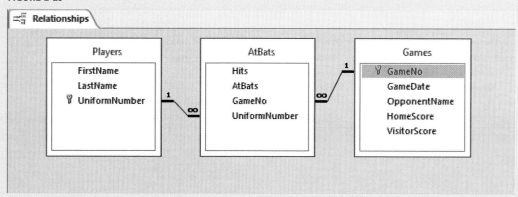

Independent Challenge 4: Explore

An Access database can help record and track your job search efforts. In this exercise, you will modify two fields in the Positions table in your JobSearch database with Lookup properties to make data entry easier, more efficient, and more accurate.

a. Start Access, open the JobSearch-E.accdb database from the location where you store your Data Files, then enable content if prompted.

b. Open the Positions table in Design View. Click the EmployerID field, then start the Lookup Wizard.

c. In this situation, you want the EmployerID field in the Positions table to look up both the EmployerID and the CompanyName fields from the Employers table, so leave the "I want the lookup field to get the values from another table or query" option button selected.

d. The Employers table contains the fields you want to display in this Lookup field. Select both the EmployerID field and the CompanyName fields. Sort the records in ascending order by the CompanyName field.

e. Deselect the "Hide key column" check box so that you can see the data in both the EmployerID and CompanyName fields.

f. Choose EmployerID as the field in which to store values, **EmployerID** as the label for the Lookup field, click the Enable Data Integrity check box, then click Finish to finish the Lookup Wizard. Click Yes when prompted to save the table.

g. Switch to Datasheet View of the Positions table and tab to the EmployerID field for the first record. Click the EmployerID list arrow. You should see both the EmployerID value as well as the CompanyName in the drop-down list, as shown in FIGURE E-29.

FIGURE E-29

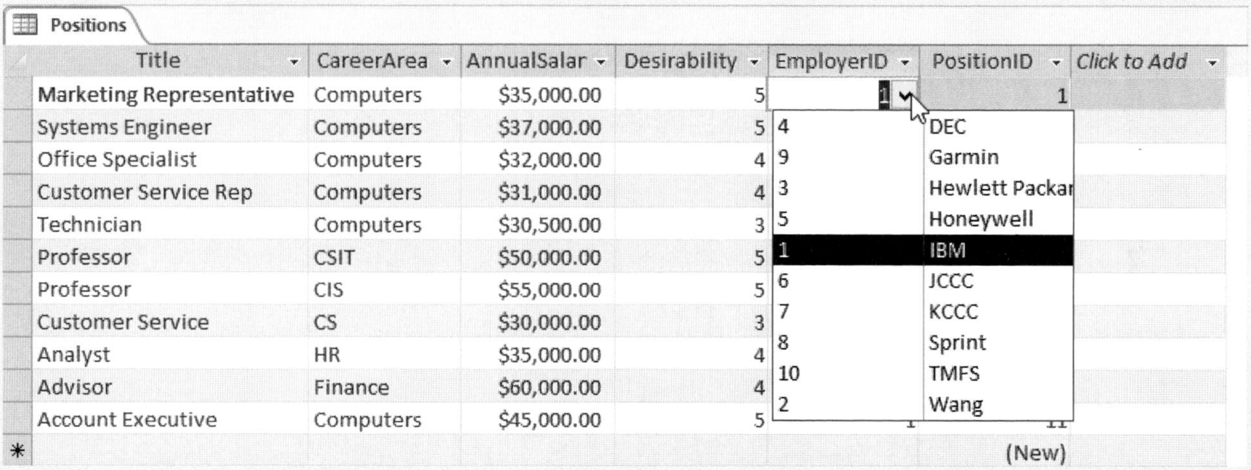

h. Return to Design View of the Positions table, click the Desirability field, and start the Lookup Wizard. This field stores the values 1 through 5 as a desirability rating. You will manually enter those values, so choose the "I will type in the values that I want" option button.

i. Enter 1, 2, 3, 4, and 5 in the Col1 column; accept the Desirability label for the Lookup field; click the Limit To List check box; then click Finish to finish the Lookup Wizard.

Independent Challenge 4: Explore (continued)

j. Save the table, and test the Desirability field for the first record in Datasheet View. You should see a drop-down list with the values 1, 2, 3, 4, and 5 in the list, as shown in **FIGURE E-30**.

FIGURE E-30

Title	CareerArea	AnnualSalar	Desirability	EmployerID	PositionID	Click to Add
Marketing Representative	Computers	$35,000.00		1	1	
Systems Engineer	Computers	$37,000.00	1	1	2	
Office Specialist	Computers	$32,000.00	2	2	3	
Customer Service Rep	Computers	$31,000.00	3	2	4	
Technician	Computers	$30,500.00	4	2	5	
Professor	CSIT	$50,000.00	5	6	6	
Professor	CIS	$55,000.00	5	7	7	
Customer Service	CS	$30,000.00	3	8	8	
Analyst	HR	$35,000.00	4	9	9	
Advisor	Finance	$60,000.00	4	10	10	
*					(New)	

k. Save the table, and test the Desirability and EmployerID fields. You should not be able to make any entries in those fields that are not presented in the list.

l. Close the Positions table, and open the Relationships window. Your Relationships window should look like **FIGURE E-31**. The Lookup Wizard created the relationship between the Employers and Positions table when you completed Step f. Save and close the Relationships window.

FIGURE E-31

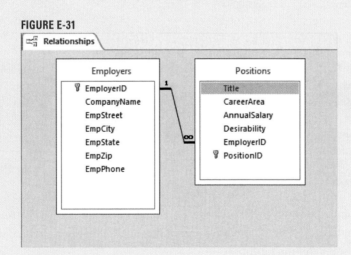

Independent Challenge 4: Explore (continued)

m. Use the Form Wizard and select all of the fields from both the Employers and Positions tables. View the data by Employers, and use a Datasheet layout for the subform.

n. Title the form **Employers Entry Form** and the subform **Positions Subform**. View the form in Form View.

o. In Form Design View, use your skills to move, resize, align, and edit the controls, as shown in **FIGURE E-32**.

p. Add a new record to the subform for the first company, IBM. Use realistic but fictitious data. Note that the EmployerID and PositionID values are automatically entered.

q. Save and close the Employers Entry Form, close the JobSearch-E.accdb database, and exit Access.

FIGURE E-32

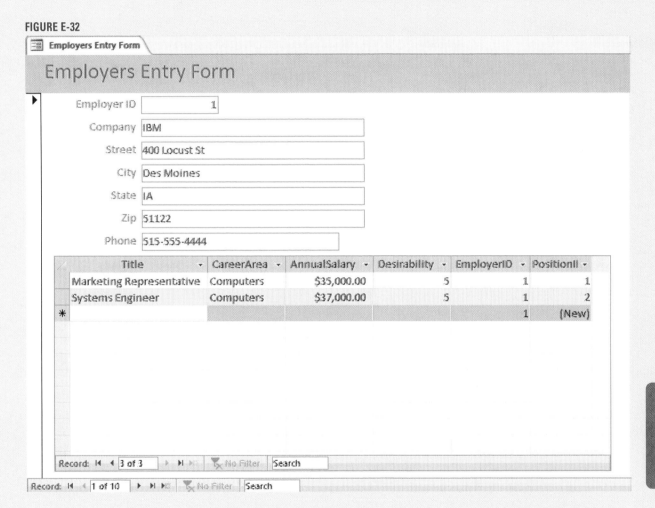

Visual Workshop

Open the Training-E.accdb database from the location where you store your Data Files, then enable content if prompted. Create a new table called **Vendors** using the Table Design View shown in FIGURE E-33 to determine field names, data types, and descriptions. Make the following property changes: Change the Field Size property of the VState field to **2**, the VZip field to **9**, and VPhone field to **10**. Change the Field Size property of the VendorName, VStreet, and VCity fields to **30**. Apply a Phone Number Input Mask to the VPhone field. Be sure to specify that the VendorID field is the primary key field. Relate the tables in the Training-E database, as shown in FIGURE E-34, then view the Relationship report in landscape orientation. Add *your* name as a label to the Report Header section to document the Relationship report, then print it if requested by your instructor. Save the Relationship report with the default name of **Relationships for Training-E**, close the report, save and close the Relationships window, close the Training-E database, and exit Access.

FIGURE E-33

Vendors		
Field Name	Data Type	
VendorID	AutoNumber	Unique vendor identification number
VendorName	Short Text	Vendor full name
VStreet	Short Text	Vendor street address
VCity	Short Text	Vendor city
VState	Short Text	Vendor State
VZip	Short Text	Vendor Zip code
VPhone	Short Text	Vendor phone

FIGURE E-34

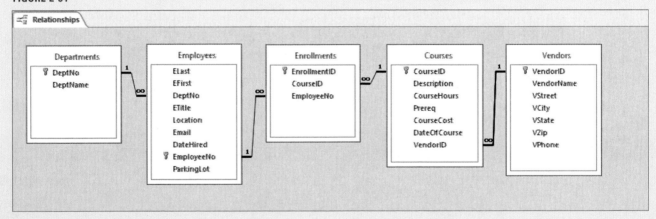

Improving Queries

CASE
The Quest database has been updated to contain more customers, tours, and sales. You help Samantha Hooper, a Quest tour developer for U.S. travel, create queries to analyze this information.

Unit Objectives

After completing this unit, you will be able to:

- Create multitable queries
- Apply sorts and view SQL
- Develop AND criteria
- Develop OR criteria

- Create calculated fields
- Build summary queries
- Build crosstab queries
- Create a report on a query

Files You Will Need

QuestTravel-F.accdb	RealEstate-F.accdb
Service-F.accdb	Scholarships-F.accdb
MusicStore-F.accdb	Training-F.accdb

© Tumanyan/Shutterstock

Create Multitable Queries

Learning Outcomes
- Create a multitable query in Query Design View
- Add and delete fields in Query Design View

A **select query**, the most common type of query, selects fields from related tables and displays records in a datasheet where you can view, enter, edit, or delete data. You can create select queries by using the Simple Query Wizard, or you can start from scratch in Query Design View. **Query Design View** gives you more options for selecting and presenting information. When you open (or **run**) a query, the fields and records that you selected for the query are presented in **Query Datasheet View**, also called a **logical view** of the data. **CASE** *Samantha Hooper asks you to create a query to analyze customer payments. You select fields from the Customers, Tours, Sales, and Payments tables to complete this analysis.*

STEPS

1. **Start Access, open the QuestTravel-F.accdb database from the location where you store your Data Files, then enable content if prompted**

2. **Click the CREATE tab on the Ribbon, then click the Query Design button in the Queries group**

   The Show Table dialog box opens and lists all the tables in the database.

   > **TROUBLE**
   > If you add a table to Query Design View twice by mistake, click the title bar of the extra field list, then press [Delete].

3. **Double-click Customers, double-click Sales, double-click Tours, double-click Payments, then click Close**

   Recall that the upper pane of Query Design View displays the fields for each of the selected tables in field lists. The name of the table is shown in the field list title bar. Primary key fields are identified with a small key icon. Relationships between tables are displayed with **one-to-many join lines** that connect the linking fields. You select the fields you want by adding them to the query design grid.

   > **TROUBLE**
   > Drag the bottom edge of the Tours field list down to resize it.

4. **Double-click the FName field in the Customers table field list to add this field to the first column of the query design grid, double-click LName, double-click TourName in the Tours field list, scroll then double-click Price in the Tours field list, double-click PaymentDate in the Payments field list, then double-click PaymentAmt, as shown in FIGURE F-1**

   When you *double-click* a field in a field list, it is automatically added as the next field in the query grid. When you *drag* a field to the query design grid, any existing fields move to the right to accommodate the new field.

5. **Click the View button ⊞ in the Results group to run the query and display the query datasheet**

   The resulting datasheet looks like **FIGURE F-2**. The datasheet shows the six fields selected in Query Design View: FName and LName from the Customers table, TourName and Price from the Tours table, and PaymentDate and PaymentAmt from the Payments table. The datasheet displays 78 records because 78 different payments have been made. Some of the payments are from the same customer. For example, Kristen Collins has made payments on multiple tours (records 2 and 20). Kristen's last name has changed to Bayes.

6. **Double-click Collins in the LName field of the second record, type Bayes, then click any other record**

   Because Kristen's data is physically stored in only one record in the Customers table (but selected multiple times in this query because Kristen has made more than one payment), changing any occurrence of her last name automatically updates all other selections of that data in this query and throughout all other queries, forms, and reports in the database, too. Note that Kristen's name has been updated to Kristen Bayes in record 20, as shown in **FIGURE F-2**.

FIGURE F-1: Query Design View with six fields in the query design grid

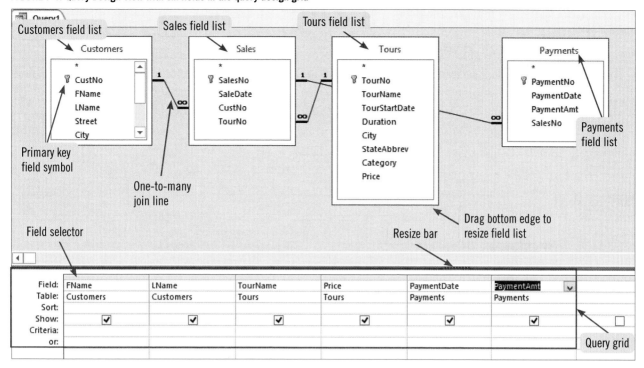

FIGURE F-2: Query datasheet

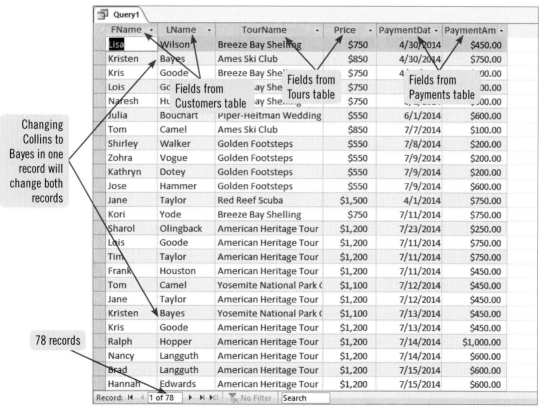

Deleting a field from the query grid

If you add the wrong field to the query design grid, you can delete it by clicking the **field selector**, the thin gray bar above each field name, then pressing [Delete]. Deleting a field from the query design grid removes it from the logical view of this query's datasheet, but does not delete the field from the database. A field is defined and the field's contents are stored in a table object only.

Apply Sorts and View SQL

Sorting refers to reordering records in either ascending or descending order based on the values in a field. You can specify more than one sort field in Query Design View. Sort orders are evaluated from left to right, meaning that the sort field on the far left is the primary sort field. Sort orders defined in Query Design View are saved with the query object. **CASE** ▶ *You want to list the records in alphabetical order based on the customer's last name. If the customer has made more than one payment, you further sort the records by the payment date.*

STEPS

1. **Click the** View button ⬜ **on the HOME tab to return to Query Design View**

   To sort the records by last name then by payment date, the LName field must be the primary sort field, and the PaymentDate field must be the secondary sort field.

2. **Click the** LName field Sort cell **in the query design grid, click the** Sort list arrow, **click** Ascending, **click the** PaymentDate field Sort cell **in the query design grid, click the** Sort list arrow, **then click** Ascending

   The resulting query design grid should look like **FIGURE F-3**.

3. **Click the** View button ⬛ **in the Results group to display the query datasheet**

   The records of the datasheet are now listed in ascending order based on the values in the LName field. When the same value appears in the LName field, the records are further sorted by the secondary sort field, PaymentDate, as shown in **FIGURE F-4**. Jacob Alman made two payments, one on 7/26/2014 and the next on 9/1/2014. Kristen Bayes made many payments.

4. **Click the** Save button 🖫 **on the Quick Access toolbar, type** CustomerPayments **in the Save As dialog box, then click** OK

   When you save a query, you save a logical view of the data, a selection of fields and records from underlying tables. Technically, when you save a query, you are saving a set of instructions written in **Structured Query Language (SQL)**. You can view the SQL code for any query by switching to **SQL View**.

5. **Click the** View button list arrow, **click** SQL View, **then click in the** lower part of the SQL window **to deselect the code**

   The SQL statements shown in **FIGURE F-5** start with the **SELECT** keyword. Field names follow SELECT, and how the tables are joined follow the **FROM** keyword. The **ORDER BY** keyword determines how records are sorted. Fortunately, you do not have to write or understand SQL to use Access or select data from multiple tables. The easy-to-use Query Design View gives you a way to select and sort data from underlying tables without being an SQL programmer.

6. **Close the CustomerPayments query**

FIGURE F-3: Specifying multiple sort orders in Query Design View

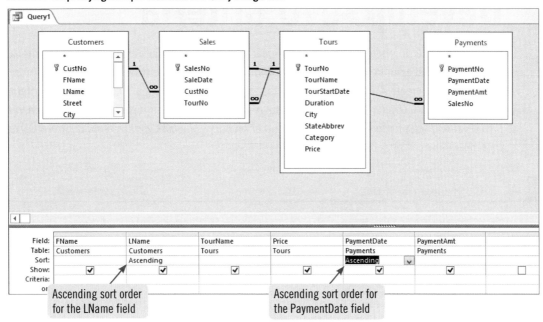

Field:	FName	LName	TourName	Price	PaymentDate	PaymentAmt	
Table:	Customers	Customers	Tours	Tours	Payments	Payments	
Sort:		Ascending			Ascending		
Show:	✓	✓	✓	✓	✓	✓	☐
Criteria:							
or:							

Ascending sort order for the LName field

Ascending sort order for the PaymentDate field

FIGURE F-4: Records sorted by LName, then by PaymentDate

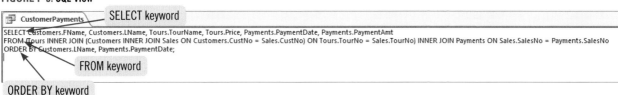

FName ▾	LName ▾	TourName ▾	Price ▾	PaymentDat ▾	PaymentAm ▾
Jacob	Alman	Red Reef Scuba	$1,500	7/26/2014	$300.00
Jacob	Alman	Red Reef Scuba	$1,500	9/1/2014	$100.00
Kristen	Bayes	Ames Ski Club	$850	4/30/2014	$750.00
Kristen	Bayes	Yosemite National Park (	$1,100	7/13/2014	$450.00
Kristen	Bayes	ge Tour	$1,200	7/20/2014	$400.00
Kristen	Bayes	American Heritage Tour	$1,200	8/20/2014	$100.00

Secondary sort order

Primary sort order

FIGURE F-5: SQL View

SELECT keyword

```
SELECT Customers.FName, Customers.LName, Tours.TourName, Tours.Price, Payments.PaymentDate, Payments.PaymentAmt
FROM Tours INNER JOIN (Customers INNER JOIN Sales ON Customers.CustNo = Sales.CustNo) ON Tours.TourNo = Sales.TourNo) INNER JOIN Payments ON Sales.SalesNo = Payments.SalesNo
ORDER BY Customers.LName, Payments.PaymentDate;
```

FROM keyword

ORDER BY keyword

Specifying a sort order different from the field order in the datasheet

If your database has several customers with the same last name, you can include a secondary sort on the first name field to distinguish the customers. If you want to display the fields in a different order from which they are sorted, you can use the solution shown in **FIGURE F-6**. Add a field to the query design grid twice, once to select for the datasheet, and once to use as a sort order. Use the Show check box to deselect the field used as a sort order.

FIGURE F-6: Sorting on a field that is not displayed

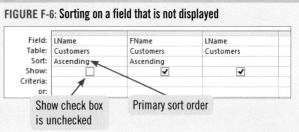

Field:	LName	FName	LName
Table:	Customers	Customers	Customers
Sort:	Ascending	Ascending	
Show:	☐	✓	✓
Criteria:			
or:			

Show check box is unchecked

Primary sort order

Develop AND Criteria

Learning
Outcomes
• Use the Like
  operator in query
  criteria
• Define advanced
  comparison
  operators

You can limit the number of records that appear on the resulting datasheet by entering criteria in Query Design View. **Criteria** are tests, or limiting conditions, that must be true for the record to be selected for a datasheet. To create **AND criteria**, which means the query selects a record only if *all* criteria are true, enter two or more criteria on the *same* Criteria row of the query design grid. **CASE** *Samantha Hooper predicts strong sales for family tours that start in or after July. She asks you to create a list of the existing tours that meet those criteria.*

STEPS

1. **Click the CREATE tab, click the Query Design button, double-click Tours, then click Close in the Show Table dialog box**

   To query for family tours, you need to add the Category field to the query grid. In addition, you want to know the tour name and start date.

2. **Drag the bottom edge of the Tours field list down to resize it to display all fields, double-click the TourName field, double-click the TourStartDate field, then double-click the Category field**

   To find tours in the Family category, you need to add a criterion for this field in the query grid.

QUICK TIP
Criteria are not case
sensitive, so *family*,
Family, and *FAMILY*
are equivalent
criteria entries.

3. **Click the first Criteria cell for the Category field, then type Family**

   To find all tours that start after July 1st, use the > (greater than) operator.

4. **Click the first Criteria cell for the TourStartDate field, type >7/1/2014, then press [↓]**

   As shown in **FIGURE F-7**, Access assists you with criteria syntax, rules by which criteria need to be entered. Access automatically adds quotation marks around text criteria in Short Text fields, such as "Family" in the Category field, and pound signs around date criteria in Date/Time fields, such as #7/1/2014# in the TourStartDate field. The criteria in Number, Currency, and Yes/No fields are not surrounded by any characters. See **TABLE F-1** for more information on common Access comparison operators and criteria syntax.

5. **Click the Save button 🖫 on the Quick Access toolbar, type FamilyJuly in the Save As dialog box, click OK, then click the View button 🏢 to view the query results**

   The query results are shown in **FIGURE F-8**.

6. **Close the FamilyJuly datasheet**

FIGURE F-7: Entering AND criteria on the same row

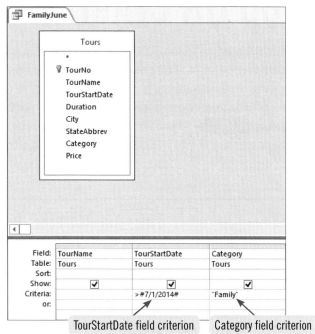

TourStartDate field criterion   Category field criterion

FIGURE F-8: Datasheet for FamilyJuly records

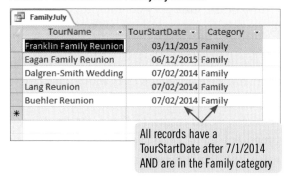

All records have a
TourStartDate after 7/1/2014
AND are in the Family category

TABLE F-1: Common comparison operators

operator	description	example	result
>	Greater than	>50	Value exceeds 50
>=	Greater than or equal to	>=50	Value is 50 or greater
<	Less than	<50	Value is less than 50
<=	Less than or equal to	<=50	Value is 50 or less
<>	Not equal to	<>50	Value is any number other than 50
Between...And	Finds values between two numbers or dates	Between #2/2/2014# And #2/2/2015#	Dates between 2/2/2014 and 2/2/2015, inclusive
In	Finds a value that is one of a list	In ("IA","KS","NE")	Value equals IA or KS or NE
Null	Finds records that have no entry in a particular field	Null	No value has been entered in a field
Is Not Null	Finds records that have any entry in a particular field	Is Not Null	Any value has been entered in a field
Like	Finds records that match the criterion, used with the * (asterisk) wildcard character	Like "A*"	Value starts with A
Not	Finds records that do not match the criterion	Not 2	Numbers other than 2

Develop OR Criteria

As you experienced in the previous lesson, AND criteria *narrow* the number of records in the datasheet by requiring that a record be true for multiple criteria. You also learned that AND criteria are entered on the *same* row. OR criteria work in the opposite way. **OR criteria** expand the number of records in the datasheet because a record needs to be true for *only one* of the criteria. You enter OR criteria in the query design grid on *different* criteria rows. **CASE** *Samantha Hooper asks you to modify the FamilyJuly query to expand the number of records to include tours in the Adventure category that start after 7/1/2014 as well.*

STEPS

1. **Right-click the** FamilyJuly query **in the Navigation Pane, click** Copy, **right-click a blank spot in the** Navigation Pane, **click** Paste, **type** FamilyAdventureJuly **in the Paste As dialog box, then click** OK

   By making a copy of the FamilyJuly query before modifying it, you won't change the FamilyJuly query by mistake. To add OR criteria, you have to enter criteria in the next available "or" row of the query design grid. By default, the query grid displays eight rows for additional OR criteria, but you can add even more rows using the Insert Rows button on the DESIGN tab.

2. **Right-click the** FamilyAdventureJuly query, **click** Design View, **type** Adventure **in the next row (the "or" row) of the Category column, then click the** View button ▦ **to display the datasheet**

   The datasheet expands from 5 to 26 records because 21 tours with a Category of Adventure were added to the datasheet. But notice that many of the TourStartDate values for the Adventure records are prior to 7/1/2014. To select only those Adventure tours with a TourStartDate after 7/1/2014, you need to add more criteria to Query Design View.

3. **Click the** View button ⬆ **to return to Query Design View, click the next** TourStartDate Criteria cell, **type** >7/1/2014, **then click elsewhere in the grid, as shown in** FIGURE F-9

   Criteria in one row do not affect criteria in another row. Therefore, to select only those tours that start after 7/1/2014, you must put the same TourStartDate criterion in *both* rows of the query design grid.

4. **Click** ▦ **to return to Datasheet View**

   The resulting datasheet selects 18 records, as shown in **FIGURE F-10**. When no sort order is applied, the records are sorted by the primary key field of the first table in the query (in this case, TourNo, which is not selected for this query). All of the records have a Category of Family or Adventure and a TourStartDate value greater than 7/1/2014.

5. **Save and close the FamilyAdventureJuly query**

   The QuestTravel-F.accdb Navigation Pane displays the three queries you created plus the StateAnalysis query that was already in the database.

FIGURE F-9: Entering OR criteria on different rows

FIGURE F-10: Datasheet for FamilyAdventureJuly query

Using wildcard characters in query criteria

To search for a pattern, use a **wildcard character** to represent any character in the criteria entry. Use a **question mark (?)** to search for any single character, and an **asterisk (*)** to search for any number of characters. Wildcard characters are often used with the Like operator. For example, the criterion Like "10/*/2015" finds all dates in October of 2015, and the criterion Like "F*" finds all entries that start with the letter F.

Create Calculated Fields

Learning
Outcomes
• Create calculated
  fields in queries
• Define functions
  and expressions

A **calculated field** is a field of data that can be created based on the values of other fields. For example, you can calculate the value for a Tax field by multiplying the value of the Sales field by a percentage. To create a calculated field, define it in Query Design View using an expression that describes the calculation. An **expression** is a combination of field names, operators (such as +, –, /, and *), and functions that result in a single value. A **function** is a predefined formula that returns a value such as a subtotal, count, or the current date. See **TABLE F-2** for more information on arithmetic operators and **TABLE F-3** for more information on functions. **CASE** *Samantha Hooper asks you to find the number of days between the sale date and the tour start date. To determine this information, you create a calculated field called LeadTime that subtracts the SaleDate from the TourStartDate. You create another calculated field to determine the commission on each tour sale.*

STEPS

1. **Click the CREATE tab on the Ribbon, click the Query Design button, double-click Tours, double-click Sales, then click Close in the Show Table dialog box**

   First, you add the fields to the grid that you want to display in the query.

QUICK TIP
Drag the bottom edge of the Tours field list down to display all fields.

2. **Double-click the TourName field, double-click the TourStartDate field, double-click the Price field, then double-click the SaleDate field**

   You create a calculated field in the Field cell of the design grid by entering a new descriptive field name followed by a colon, followed by an expression. Field names used in an expression must be surrounded by square brackets.

QUICK TIP
To display a long entry in a field cell, right-click the cell, then click Zoom.

3. **Click the blank Field cell in the fifth column, type LeadTime:[TourStartDate]-[SaleDate], then drag the ✛ pointer on the right edge of the fifth column selector to the right to display the entire entry**

   You create another calculated field to determine the commission paid on each sale, which is calculated as 11% of the Price field.

TROUBLE
Field names in expressions are surrounded by [square brackets] not {curly braces} and not (parentheses).

4. **Click the blank Field cell in the sixth column, type Commission:[Price]*0.11, then widen the column, as shown in FIGURE F-11**

   You view the datasheet to see the resulting calculated fields.

5. **Click the View button 🔲, press [Tab], type 8/1/14 in the TourStartDate field for the first record, press [Tab], type 1000 in the Price field for the first record, then press [↓]**

   A portion of the resulting datasheet, with two calculated fields, is shown in **FIGURE F-12**. The LeadTime field is automatically recalculated, showing the number of days between the SaleDate and the TourStartDate. The Commission field is also automatically recalculated, multiplying the Price value by 11%.

6. **Click the Save button 🖫 on the Quick Access toolbar, type LeadTimesAndCommissions in the Save As dialog box, click OK, then close the datasheet**

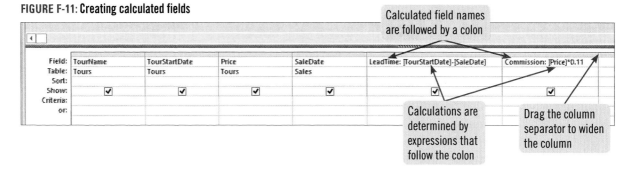

FIGURE F-11: Creating calculated fields

- Calculated field names are followed by a colon
- Calculations are determined by expressions that follow the colon
- Drag the column separator to widen the column

Field:	TourName	TourStartDate	Price	SaleDate	LeadTime: [TourStartDate]-[SaleDate]	Commission: [Price]*0.11
Table:	Tours	Tours	Tours	Sales		
Sort:						
Show:	✓	✓	✓	✓	✓	✓
Criteria:						
or:						

FIGURE F-12: Viewing and testing calculated fields

TourName	TourStartDate	Price	SaleDate	LeadTime	Commission
Breeze Bay Shelling	08/01/2014	$1,000	4/30/2014	93	110
Breeze Bay Shelling	08/01/2014	$1,000	4/30/2014	93	110
Breeze Bay Shelling	08/01/2014	$1,000	4/30/2014	93	110
Breeze Bay Shelling	08/01/2014	$1,000	4/30/2014	93	110
Breeze Bay Shelling	08/01/2014	$1,000	5/31/2014	62	110
Breeze Bay Shelling	08/01/2014	$1,000	6/30/2014	32	110
Red Reef Scuba	07/06/2014	$1,500	5/11/2014	56	165
Red Reef Scuba	07/06/2014	$1,500	7/1/2014	5	165
Red Reef Scuba	07/06/2014	$1,500	7/1/2014	5	165
Red Reef Scuba	07/06/2014	$1,500	7/1/2014	5	165
Red Reef Scuba	07/06/2014	$1,500	7/1/2014	5	165
Red Reef Scuba	07/06/2014	$1,500	7/1/2014	5	165
Red Reef Scuba	07/06/2014	$1,500	7/1/2014	5	165
Red Reef Scuba	07/06/2014	$1,500	7/2/2014	4	165
Red Reef Scuba	07/06/2014	$1,500	7/2/2014	4	165
Ames Ski Club	01/02/2015	$850	4/30/2014	247	93.5
Ames Ski Club	01/02/2015	$850	5/1/2014	246	93.5
Ames Ski Club	01/02/2015	$850	7/11/2014	175	93.5

- Commission equals Price * 11%
- LeadTime equals the days between the SaleDate and TourStartDate

TABLE F-2: Arithmetic operators

operator	description
+	Addition
–	Subtraction
*	Multiplication
/	Division
^	Exponentiation

TABLE F-3: Common functions

function	sample expression and description
DATE	DATE()-[BirthDate] Calculates the number of days between today and the date in the BirthDate field; Access expressions are not case sensitive, so DATE()-[BirthDate] is equivalent to date()-[birthdate] and DATE()-[BIRTHDATE]; therefore, use capitalization in expressions in any way that makes the expression easier to read
PMT	PMT([Rate],[Term],[Loan]) Calculates the monthly payment on a loan where the Rate field contains the monthly interest rate, the Term field contains the number of monthly payments, and the Loan field contains the total amount financed
LEFT	LEFT([LastName],2) Returns the first two characters of the entry in the LastName field
RIGHT	RIGHT([PartNo],3) Returns the last three characters of the entry in the PartNo field
LEN	LEN([Description]) Returns the number of characters in the Description field

Access 2013

Build Summary Queries

Learning
Outcomes
• Create a summary
  query
• Define aggregate
  functions

A **summary query** calculates statistics for groups of records. To create a summary query, you add the **Total row** to the query design grid to specify how you want to group and calculate the records using aggregate functions. **Aggregate functions** calculate a statistic such as a subtotal, count, or average on a field in a group of records. Some aggregate functions, such as Sum or Avg (Average), only work on fields with Number or Currency data types. Other functions, such as Min (Minimum), Max (Maximum), or Count, also work on Short Text fields. TABLE F-4 provides more information on aggregate functions. A key difference between the statistics displayed by a summary query and those displayed by calculated fields is that summary queries provide calculations that describe a *group of records*, whereas calculated fields provide a new field of information for *each record*. **CASE** ▶ *Samantha Hooper asks you to calculate total sales for each tour category. You build a summary query to provide this information.*

STEPS

QUICK TIP
In Query Design
View, drag a table
from the Navigation
Pane to add it to
the query.

1. **Click the CREATE tab on the Ribbon, click the Query Design button, double-click Sales, double-click Tours, then click Close in the Show Table dialog box**

   It doesn't matter in what order you add the field lists to Query Design View, but it's important to move and resize the field lists as necessary to clearly see all field names and relationships.

2. **Double-click the SalesNo field in the Sales field list, double-click the Category field in the Tours field list, double-click the Price field in the Tours field list, then click the View button 🔲 to view the datasheet**

   One hundred and one records are displayed, representing all 101 records in the Sales table. You can add a Total row to any datasheet to calculate grand total statistics for that datasheet.

3. **Click the Totals button in the Records group, click the Total cell below the Price field, click the Total list arrow, click Sum, then use ↔ to widen the Price column to display the entire total**

   The Total row is added to the bottom of the datasheet and displays the sum total of the Price field, $85,510. Other Total row statistics you can select include Average, Count, Maximum, Minimum, Standard Deviation, and Variance. To create subtotals per Category, you need to modify the query in Query Design View.

4. **Click the View button 🔲 to return to Query Design View, click the Totals button in the Show/Hide group, click Group By in the SalesNo column, click the list arrow, click Count, click Group By in the Price column, click the list arrow, then click Sum**

   The Total row is added to the query grid below the Table row. To calculate summary statistics for each category, the Category field is the Group By field, as shown in **FIGURE F-13**. With the records grouped together by Category, you will subtotal the Price field using the Sum operator to calculate a subtotal of revenue for each Category of tour sales.

5. **Click 🔲 to display the datasheet, widen each column as necessary to view all field names, click in the Total row for the SumOfPrice field, click the list arrow, click Sum, then click another row in the datasheet to remove the selection**

   The Adventure category leads all others with a count of 55 sales totaling $52,560. The total revenue for all sales is $85,510, as shown in **FIGURE F-14**.

TROUBLE
To delete or rename
any object, close it,
then right-click it in
the Navigation Pane
and click Delete or
Rename on the
shortcut menu.

6. **Click the Save button 🔲 on the Quick Access toolbar, type CategorySummary, click OK, then close the datasheet**

FIGURE F-13: Summary query in Design View

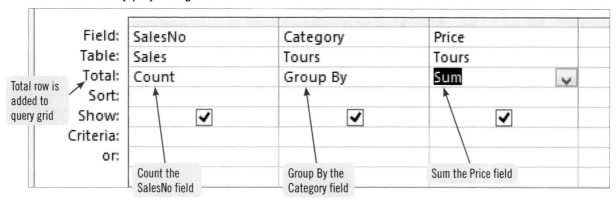

Total row is added to query grid →

Field:	SalesNo	Category	Price	
Table:	Sales	Tours	Tours	
Total:	Count	Group By	Sum	▾
Sort:				
Show:	✔	✔	✔	
Criteria:				
or:				

Count the SalesNo field — Group By the Category field — Sum the Price field

FIGURE F-14: Summary query datasheet

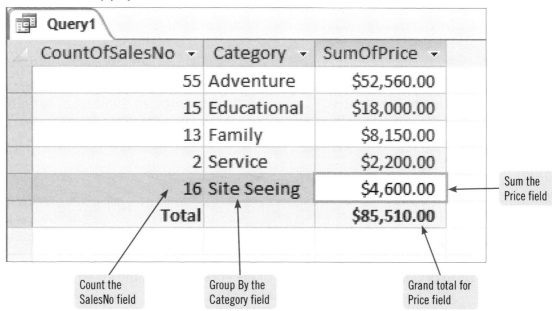

Query1

CountOfSalesNo ▾	Category ▾	SumOfPrice ▾
55	Adventure	$52,560.00
15	Educational	$18,000.00
13	Family	$8,150.00
2	Service	$2,200.00
16	Site Seeing	$4,600.00
Total		$85,510.00

Sum the Price field

Count the SalesNo field — Group By the Category field — Grand total for Price field

TABLE F-4: Aggregate functions

aggregate function	used to find the
Sum	Total of values in a field
Avg	Average of values in a field
Min	Minimum value in a field
Max	Maximum value in a field
Count	Number of values in a field (not counting null values)
StDev	Standard deviation of values in a field
Var	Variance of values in a field
First	Field value from the first record in a table or query
Last	Field value from the last record in a table or query

Build Crosstab Queries

Learning Outcomes
- Create a crosstab query
- Describe the Find Duplicates and Find Unmatched Query Wizards

A **crosstab query** subtotals one field by grouping records using two other fields that are placed in the column heading and row heading positions. You can use the **Crosstab Query Wizard** to guide you through the steps of creating a crosstab query, or you can build the crosstab query from scratch using Query Design View. **CASE** ▶ *Samantha Hooper asks you to continue your analysis of prices per category by summarizing the price values for each tour within each category. A crosstab query works well for this request because you want to subtotal the Price field as summarized by two other fields, TourName and Category.*

STEPS

1. **Click the CREATE tab on the Ribbon, click the Query Design button, double-click Tours, double-click Sales, then click Close in the Show Table dialog box**

   The fields you need for your crosstab query come from the Tours table, but you also need to include the Sales table in this query to select tour information for each record (sale) in the Sales table.

2. **Double-click the TourName field, double-click the Category field, then double-click the Price field**

   The first step in creating a crosstab query is to create a select query with the three fields you want to use in the crosstabular report.

3. **Click the View button ⊞ to review the unsummarized datasheet of 101 records, then click the View button ⊠ to return to Query Design View**

   To summarize these 101 records in a crosstabular report, you need to change the current select query into a crosstab query.

4. **Click the Crosstab button in the Query Type group**

   Note that two new rows are added to the query grid—the Total row and the Crosstab row. The **Total row** helps you determine which fields group or summarize the records, and the **Crosstab row** identifies which of the three positions each field takes in the crosstab report: Row Heading, Column Heading, or Value. The **Value field** is typically a numeric field, such as Price, that can be summed or averaged.

5. **Click Group By in the Total cell of the Price field, click the list arrow, click Sum, click the Crosstab cell for the TourName field, click the list arrow, click Row Heading, click the Crosstab cell for the Category field, click the list arrow, click Column Heading, click the Crosstab cell for the Price field, click the list arrow, then click Value**

   The completed Query Design View should look like **FIGURE F-15**. Note the choices made in the Total and Crosstab rows of the query grid.

6. **Click ⊞ to review the crosstab datasheet**

   The final crosstab datasheet is shown in **FIGURE F-16**. The datasheet summarizes all 101 sales records by the Category field used as the column headings and by the TourName field used in the row heading position. Although you can switch the row and column heading fields without changing the numeric information on the crosstab datasheet, you should generally place the field with the most entries (in this case, TourName has more values than Category) in the row heading position so that the printout is taller than it is wide.

7. **Click the Save button 🖫 on the Quick Access toolbar, type TourCrosstab as the query name, click OK, then close the datasheet**

   Crosstab queries appear with a crosstab icon to the left of the query name in the Navigation Pane.

FIGURE F-15: Query Design View of crosstab query

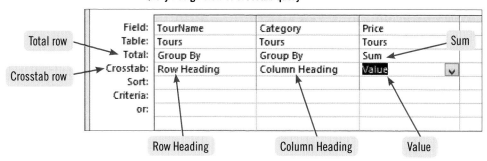

FIGURE F-16: Crosstab query datasheet

TourName	Adventure	Educational	Family	Service	Site Seeing
American Heritage Tour		$18,000.00			
Ames Ski Club	$11,050.00				
Bear Valley Adventures	$1,450.00				
Bigfoot Rafting Club	$910.00				
Black Sheep Hiking Club	$1,050.00				
Boy Scout Jamboree	$3,800.00				
Breeze Bay Shelling	$6,000.00				
Bridgewater Country	$9,600.00				
Bright Lights Expo					$2,400.00
Eagan Family Reunion			$2,000.00		
Franklin Family Reunion			$5,600.00		
Golden Footsteps					$2,200.00
Gunnison Bikers	$1,000.00				
Piper-Heitman Wedding			$550.00		
Red Reef Scuba	$13,500.00				
Spare Tire Ski Club	$4,200.00				
Yosemite National Park (				$2,200.00	

Category field values are column headings

TourName field values are row headings

Price field values are subtotaled

Using query wizards

Four query wizards are available to help you build queries including the Simple (which creates a select query), Crosstab, Find Duplicates, and Find Unmatched Query Wizards. Use the **Find Duplicates Query Wizard** to determine whether a table contains duplicate values in one or more fields. Use the **Find Unmatched Query Wizard** to find records in one table that do not have related records in another table. To use the query wizards, click the Query Wizard button on the CREATE tab.

Create a Report on a Query

Learning
Outcomes
• Create a report on
  a query
• Modify a report's
  Record Source
  property

When you want a more professional printout of the information than can be provided by a query datasheet, you use a report object. By first selecting the fields and records you want in a query and then basing the report on that query, you can easily add new fields and calculations to the report by adding them to the underlying query. When you base a report on a query, the query name is identified in the **Record Source** property of the report. **CASE** *Samantha Hooper asks you to create a report to subtotal the revenue for each tour.*

STEPS

1. **Double-click the StateAnalysis query in the Navigation Pane to open its datasheet**

   The StateAnalysis query contains the customer state, tour name, and price of each tour sold. Analyzing which tours are the most popular in various states will help focus marketing expenses. Creating a query to select the fields and records needed on a report is the first step in creating a report that can be easily modified later.

2. **Close the StateAnalysis query, click the CREATE tab on the Ribbon, click the Report Wizard button, click the Tables/Queries list arrow, click Query: StateAnalysis, click the Select All button `>>`, then click Next**

   The Report Wizard wants to group the records by the State field. This is also how you want to analyze the data.

3. **Click Next, click TourName, then click the Select Field button `>` to add the TourName field as a second grouping level, click Next, click Next to not choose any sort orders, click Next to accept a Stepped layout and Portrait orientation, type State Revenue Report as the title for the report, then click Finish**

   The report lists each tour sold within each state as many times as it has been sold. You decide to add the name of the customers who have purchased these tours to the report. First, you will need to add them to the StateAnalysis query. Given that the State Revenue Report is based on the StateAnalysis query, you can access the StateAnalysis query from Report Design View of the State Revenue Report.

QUICK TIP
You can also double-click the report selector button to open the Property Sheet for the report.

4. **Right-click the State Revenue Report tab, click Design View, close the Field List if it is open, then click the Property Sheet button in the Tools group on the DESIGN tab**

   The Property Sheet for the State Revenue Report opens.

5. **Click the Data tab, click StateAnalysis in the Record Source property, then click the Build button `...`, as shown in FIGURE F-17**

   The StateAnalysis query opens in Query Design View.

6. **Close the Property Sheet, double-click the FName field, double-click the LName field, click the Close button on the DESIGN tab, then click Yes when prompted to save the changes**

   Now that the FName and LName fields have been added to the StateAnalysis query, they are available to the report.

TROUBLE
The number in the Text13 label varies based on previous activity in the report.

7. **Click the DESIGN tab, click the Text Box button `ab|`, click to the left of the Price text box in the Detail section, click the Text13 label, press [Delete], click Unbound in the text box, type =[FName] &" "&[LName], then press [Enter]**

   You could have added the FName and LName fields directly to the report but the information looks a little more professional as the result of one expression that calculates the entire name.

8. **Switch to Layout View, resize the new text box as shown in FIGURE F-18 to see the entire name, save and close the State Revenue Report, close the QuestTravel-F.accdb database, then exit Access**

FIGURE F-17: Modifying a query from the Record Source property

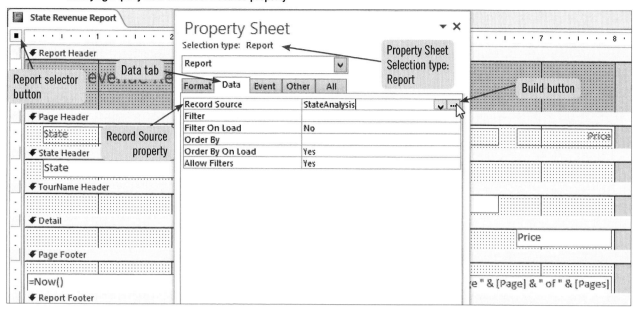

FIGURE F-18: Final State Revenue Report

Practice

Concepts Review

Identify each element of Query Design View shown in FIGURE F-19.

FIGURE F-19

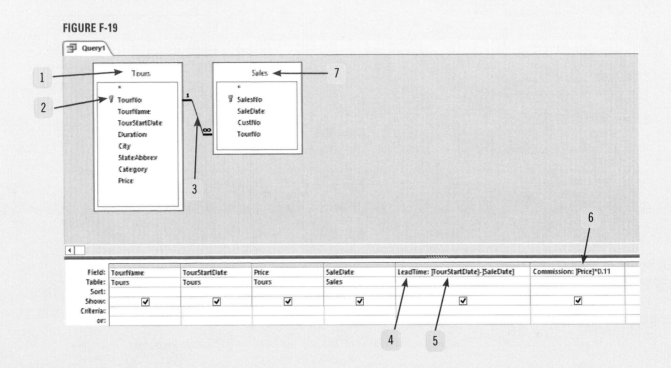

Match each term with the statement that best describes it.

8. Record Source
9. Select query
10. Wildcard character
11. AND criteria
12. Sorting
13. OR criteria

a. Placing the records of a datasheet in a certain order
b. Entered on more than one row of the query design grid
c. Report property that determines what fields and records the report will display
d. Asterisk (*) or question mark (?) used in query criteria
e. Retrieves fields from related tables and displays records in a datasheet
f. Entered on one row of the query design grid

Select the best answer from the list of choices.

14. The query datasheet can best be described as a:
   a. Logical view of the selected data from underlying tables.
   b. Duplication of the data in the underlying table's datasheet.
   c. Separate file of data.
   d. Second copy of the data in the underlying tables.

15. Queries may *not* be used to:

  a. Calculate new fields of data.   **c.** Enter or update data.

  b. Set the primary key field for a table.   **d.** Sort records.

16. When you update data in a table that is also selected in a query:

  a. You must relink the query to the table to refresh the data.

  b. The updated data is automatically displayed in the query.

  c. You must also update the data in the query datasheet.

  d. You can choose whether to update the data in the query.

17. Which of the following is *not* an aggregate function available to a summary query?

  a. Avg   **c.** Count

  b. Subtotal   **d.** Max

18. The order in which records in a query are sorted is determined by:

  a. The order in which the fields are defined in the underlying table.

  b. The importance of the information in the field.

  c. The alphabetic order of the field names.

  d. The left-to-right position of the fields in the query design grid that contain a sort order choice.

19. A crosstab query is generally constructed with how many fields?

  a. 1   **c.** 2

  b. 3   **d.** More than 5

20. In a crosstab query, which field is the most likely candidate for the Value position?

  a. FName   **c.** Cost

  b. Department   **d.** Country

Skills Review

1. Create multitable queries.

  a. Start Access and open the Service-F.accdb database from the location where you store your Data Files, then enable content if prompted.

  b. Create a new select query in Query Design View using the Names and Zips tables.

  c. Add the following fields to the query design grid in this order:

     • FirstName, LastName, and Street from the Names table

     • City, State, and Zip from the Zips table

  d. In Datasheet View, replace the LastName value in the Martin Chen record with *your* last name.

  e. Save the query as **AddressList**, print the datasheet if requested by your instructor, then close the query.

2. Apply sorts and view SQL.

  a. Open the AddressList query in Query Design View.

  b. Drag the FirstName field from the Names field list to the third column in the query design grid to make the first three fields in the query design grid FirstName, LastName, and FirstName.

  c. Add an ascending sort to the second and third fields in the query design grid, and uncheck the Show check box in the third column. The query is now sorted in ascending order by LastName, then by FirstName, though the order of the fields in the resulting datasheet still appears as FirstName, LastName.

  d. Click the FILE tab, click Save As, then use Save Object As to save the query as **SortedAddressList**. View the datasheet, print the datasheet if requested by your instructor, then close the SortedAddressList query.

3. Develop AND criteria.

  a. Right-click the SortedAddressList query in the Navigation Pane, click Copy, right-click a blank spot in the Navigation Pane, click Paste, then type **KansasC** as the name for the new query.

  b. Open the KansasC query in Design View, then type **C*** (the asterisk is a wildcard) in the LastName field Criteria cell to choose all people whose last name starts with *C*. Access assists you with the syntax for this type of criterion and enters Like "C*" in the cell when you click elsewhere in the query design grid.

Skills Review (continued)

c. Enter **KS** as the AND criterion for the State field. Be sure to enter the criterion on the same line in the query design grid as the Like "C*" criterion.

d. View the datasheet. It should select only those people from Kansas with a last name that starts with the letter C.

e. Enter *your* hometown in the City field of the first record to uniquely identify the printout.

f. Save the KansasC query, print the datasheet if requested by your instructor, then close the KansasC query.

4. Develop OR criteria.

a. Right-click the KansasC query in the Navigation Pane, click Copy, right-click a blank spot in the Navigation Pane, click Paste, then type **KansasCD** as the name for the new query.

b. Open the KansasCD query in Design View, then enter **D*** in the second Criteria row (the or row) of the LastName field.

c. Enter **KS** as the criterion in the second Criteria row (the or row) of the State field so that those people from KS with a last name that starts with the letter D are added to this query.

d. View the datasheet. It should select only those people from Kansas with a last name that starts with the letter C or D. Print the datasheet if requested by your instructor, then save and close the query.

5. Create calculated fields.

a. Create a new select query in Query Design View using only the Names table.

b. Add the following fields to the query design grid in this order: FirstName, LastName, Birthday.

c. Create a calculated field called Age in the fourth column of the query design grid by entering the expression: **Age: Int((Now()-[Birthday])/365)** to determine the age of each person in years based on the information in the Birthday field. The Now() function returns today's date. Now()-[Birthday] determines the number of days a person has lived. Dividing that value by 365 determines the number of years a person has lived. The Int() function is used to return the integer portion of the answer. So if a person has lived 23.5 years, Int(23.5) = 23.

d. Sort the query in descending order on the calculated Age field.

e. Save the query with the name **AgeCalculation**, view the datasheet, print the datasheet if requested by your instructor, then close the query.

6. Build summary queries.

a. Create a new select query in Query Design View using the Names and Activities tables.

b. Add the following fields: FirstName and LastName from the Names table, and Hours from the Activities table.

c. Add the Total row to the query design grid, then change the aggregate function for the Hours field from Group By to Sum.

d. Sort in descending order by Hours.

e. Save the query as **HoursSummary**, view the datasheet, widen all columns so that all data is clearly visible, print the datasheet if requested by your instructor, then save and close the query.

7. Build crosstab queries.

a. Use Query Design View to create a select query with the City and State fields from the Zips table and the Dues field from the Names table. Save the query as **DuesCrosstab**, then view the datasheet.

b. Return to Query Design View, then click the Crosstab button to add the Total and Crosstab rows to the query design grid.

Skills Review (continued)

   c. Specify City as the crosstab row heading, State as the crosstab column heading, and Dues as the summed value field within the crosstab datasheet.

   d. View the datasheet as shown in **FIGURE F-20**, print the datasheet if requested by your instructor, then save and close the DuesCrosstab query.

8. Create a report on a query.

   a. Use the Report Wizard to create a report on all of the fields of the SortedAddressList query. View the data by Names, add State as a grouping level, add LastName then FirstName as the ascending sort orders, use a Stepped layout and Landscape orientation, then title the report **Names by State**.

   b. In Design View, open the Property Sheet for the report, then open the SortedAddressList query in Design View using the Build button on the Record Source property.

   c. Add the Birthday field to the SortedAddressList query then close the query.

   d. To the left of the LastName field in the Detail section, add a text box bound to the Birthday field. (*Hint*: Type **Birthday** in place of Unbound or modify the text box's Control Source property to be Birthday.) Delete the label that is automatically created to the left of the text box.

   e. In Layout View, resize the City and Zip columns so that all data is clearly visible, as shown in **FIGURE F-21**. Be sure to preview the report to make sure it fits on the paper.

   f. If requested by your instructor, print the first page of the Names by State report, save and close it, close the Service-F.accdb database, then exit Access.

FIGURE F-20

City	IA	KS	MO
Blue Springs			$50.00
Bridgewater	$50.00		
Buehler		$50.00	
Des Moines	$25.00		
Dripping Spring		$25.00	
Flat Hills		$50.00	
Fontanelle	$50.00		
Greenfield	$50.00		
Kansas City		$50.00	$100.00
Langguth		$25.00	
Leawood			$50.00
Lee's Summit			$75.00
Lenexa		$25.00	
Manawatta		$25.00	
Manhattan		$25.00	
Overland Park		$100.00	
Red Bridge		$425.00	
Running Deer			$25.00
Shawnee		$200.00	
Student Home		$100.00	

FIGURE F-21

Names by State

State		LastName	FirstName	Street	City	Zip
IA						
	10/6/1961	Goode	Loraine	900 Barnes Road	Greenfield	50265
	7/16/1963	Martin	Benjamin	5253 Duck Creek Dr	Des Moines	52240
	9/30/1960	May	Jaye	1515 Maple St	Fontanelle	50033
	8/19/1980	StudentLastName	Martin	1010 Green St	Bridgewater	50022
KS						
	6/4/1979	Alman	Josiah	2505 McGee St	Flat Hills	64141
	10/1/1989	Bovier	Mary	110 College Blvd	Manhattan	66031
	9/4/1961	Browning	Forrest	8206 Marshall Drive	Dripping Springs	66214
	1/1/1954	Cabriella	Holly	52520 W. 505 Terr	Student Home Town	66215
	6/19/1960	Camel	Mark	66020 King Street	Red Bridge	66210
	6/12/1958	Custard	Mildred	66900 College Blvd	Red Bridge	66210

Independent Challenge 1

As the manager of a music store's instrument rental program, you have created a database to track rentals to schoolchildren. Now that several rentals have been made, you want to query the database for several different datasheet printouts to analyze school information.

a. Start Access and open the MusicStore-F.accdb database from the location where you store your Data Files, then enable content if prompted.

b. In Query Design View, create a query with the following fields in the following order:
   - SchoolName field from the Schools table
   - RentalDate field from the Rentals table
   - Description field from the Instruments table

   (*Hint*: Although you don't use any fields from the Customers table, you need to add the Customers table to this query to make the connection between the Schools table and the Rentals table.)

c. Sort in ascending order by SchoolName, then in ascending order by RentalDate.

d. Save the query as **SchoolRentals**, view the datasheet, replace Lincoln Elementary with *your* elementary school name, print the datasheet if requested by your instructor, then close the datasheet.

e. Copy and paste the SchoolRentals query as **SchoolCount**, then open the SchoolCount query in Query Design View.

f. Modify the SchoolCount query by deleting the Description field. Use the Totals button to group the records by SchoolName and to count the RentalDate field. Print the datasheet if requested by your instructor, then save and close the SchoolCount query.

g. Create a crosstab query named **SchoolCrosstab** based on the SchoolRentals query. (*Hint*: Select the SchoolRentals query in the Show Table dialog box.) Use Description as the column heading position and SchoolName in the row heading position. Count the RentalDate field.

h. View the SchoolCrosstab query in Datasheet View. Resize each column to best fit the data in that column, then print the datasheet if requested by your instructor. Save and close the SchoolCrosstab query.

i. Copy and paste the SchoolRentals query as **ElementaryRentals**. Modify the ElementaryRentals query in Query Design View so that only those schools with the word **Elementary** in the SchoolName field are displayed. (*Hint*: You have to use wildcard characters in the criteria.)

j. View the ElementaryRentals query in Datasheet View, print it if requested by your instructor, then save and close the datasheet.

k. Close the MusicStore-F.accdb database, then exit Access.

Independent Challenge 2

As the manager of a music store's instrument rental program, you have created a database to track rentals to schoolchildren. You can use queries to analyze customer and rental information.

a. Start Access and open the MusicStore-F.accdb database from the location where you store your Data Files, then enable content if prompted.

b. In Query Design View, create a query with the following fields in the following order:
   - Description and MonthlyFee fields from the Instruments table
   - LastName, Zip, and City fields from the Customers table

   (*Hint*: Although you don't need any fields from the Rentals table in this query's datasheet, you need to add the Rentals table to this query to make the connection between the Customers table and the Instruments table.)

Independent Challenge 2 (continued)

c. Add the Zip field to the first column of the query grid, and specify an ascending sort order for this field. Uncheck the Show check box for the first Zip field so that it does not appear in the datasheet.

d. Add an ascending sort order to the Description field.

e. Save the query as **ZipAnalysis**.

f. View the datasheet, replace Johnson with *your* last name in the LastName field, print the datasheet if requested by your instructor, then save and close the datasheet. (*Note*: If you later view this query in Design View, note that Access changes the way the sort orders are specified but in a way that gives you the same results in the datasheet.)

g. In Query Design View, create a query with the following fields in the following order:
  - Description and MonthlyFee fields from the Instruments table
  - LastName, Zip, and City fields from the Customers table
  (*Hint*: You'll need to add the Rentals table.)

h. Add criteria to find the records where the Description is equal to **viola**. Sort in ascending order based on the Zip then City fields. Save the query as **Violas**, view the datasheet, print it if requested by your instructor, then close the datasheet.

i. Copy and paste the Violas query as **DesMoinesViolas**, then modify the DesMoinesViolas query with AND criteria to further specify that the City must be **Des Moines**. View the datasheet, print it if requested by your instructor, then save and close the datasheet.

j. Copy and paste the DesMoinesViolas query as **DesMoinesOrViolas**, then modify the DesMoinesOrViolas query so that all records with a Description equal to Violas or a City value of **Des Moines** are selected. View the datasheet, print it if requested by your instructor, then save and close the datasheet.

k. Close the MusicStore-F.accdb database, then exit Access.

Independent Challenge 3

As a real estate agent, you use an Access database to track residential real estate listings in your area. You can use queries to answer questions about the real estate properties and to analyze home values.

a. Start Access and open the RealEstate-F.accdb database from the location where you store your Data Files, then enable content if prompted.

b. In Query Design View, create a query with the following fields in the following order:
  - AgencyName from the Agencies table
  - RFirst and RLast from the Realtors table
  - SqFt and Asking from the Listings table

c. Sort the records in descending order by the Asking field.

d. Save the query as **AskingPrice**, view the datasheet, enter *your* last name instead of Dell for the most expensive listing, then print the datasheet if requested by your instructor.

e. In Query Design View, modify the AskingPrice query by creating a calculated field that determines price per square foot. The new calculated field's name should be **SquareFootCost**, and the expression should be the asking price divided by the square foot field, or **[Asking]/[SqFt]**.

f. Remove any former sort orders, sort the records in descending order based on the SquareFootCost calculated field, and view the datasheet. Save and close the AskingPrice query. ###### means the data is too wide to display in the column. You can make the data narrower and also align it by applying a Currency format.

g. Reopen the AskingPrice query in Query Design View, right-click the calculated SquareFootCost field, click Properties, then change the Format property to Currency. View the datasheet, print it if requested by your instructor, then save and close the AskingPrice query.

h. Copy and paste the AskingPrice query as **CostSummary**.

Independent Challenge 3 (continued)

i. In Design View of the CostSummary query, delete the RFirst, RLast, and SqFt fields.

j. View the datasheet, then change the Sun and Ski Realtors agency name to *your* last name followed by **Realtors**.

k. In Design View, add the Total row, then sum the Asking field and use the Avg (Average) aggregate function for the SquareFootCost calculated field.

l. In Datasheet View, add the Total row and display the sum of the SumOfAsking field. Widen all columns as needed, as shown in FIGURE F-22.

m. If requested by your Instructor, print the CostSummary query, then save and close it.

n. Close the RealEstate-F.accdb database, then exit Access.

FIGURE F-22

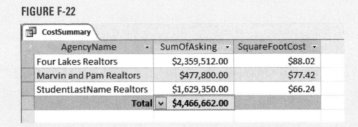

AgencyName	SumOfAsking	SquareFootCost
Four Lakes Realtors	$2,359,512.00	$88.02
Marvin and Pam Realtors	$477,800.00	$77.42
StudentLastName Realtors	$1,629,350.00	$66.24
Total	$4,466,662.00	

Independent Challenge 4: Explore

You're working with the local high school guidance counselor to help him with an Access database used to record college scholarship opportunities. You help him with the database by creating several queries. (*Note: To complete this Independent Challenge, make sure you are connected to the Internet.*)

a. Start Access, open the Scholarships-F.accdb database from the location where you store your Data Files, then enable content if prompted.

b. Conduct research on the Internet or at your school to find at least five new scholarships relevant to your major, and enter them into the Scholarships table.

c. Conduct research on the Internet or at your school to find at least one new scholarship relevant to a Business major as well as a Science major, and enter the two records into the Scholarships table.

d. Create a query called **Business** that displays all fields from the Scholarships table that selects all records with a Business major. If requested by your instructor, print the Business query then save and close it.

e. Copy and paste the Business query as **BusinessOrScience**. Add OR criteria to the BusinessOrScience query to select all scholarships in the Business or Science majors. If requested by your instructor, print the BusinessOrScience query then save and close it.

Independent Challenge 4: Explore (continued)

f. Create a new query that selects the ScholarshipName, DueDate, and Amount from the Scholarships table, and sorts the records in ascending order by DueDate, then descending order by Amount. Name the query **ScholarshipMasterList**. If requested by your instructor, print the ScholarshipMasterList query then save and close it.

g. Use the Report Wizard to create a report on the ScholarshipMasterList, do not add any grouping levels, sort the records in ascending order by ScholarshipName, use a Tabular layout and a Portrait orientation, and title the report **Scholarship Master List**.

h. In Design View of the Scholarship Master List report, open the Property Sheet, and use the Record Source Build button to open the ScholarshipMasterList query in Design View. Add the Major field to the query, save and close it.

i. In Report Design View, open the Group, Sort, and Total pane, add the Major field as a grouping field, then move it above the Sort by ScholarshipName sort field.

j. Add a text box to the Major Header section, and bind it to the Major field. (*Hint*: Type **Major** in place of Unbound or modify the text box's Control Source property to be Major.) Delete the label that is automatically created to the left of the text box. Preview the report, as shown in FIGURE F-23, then print it if requested by your instructor.

k. Save and close the Scholarship Master List report, close the Scholarships-F.accdb database, then exit Access.

FIGURE F-23

ScholarshipName	DueDate	Amount
Scholarship Master List		
All Majors		
Achievement Community Scholarship	2/16/2013	$2,000.00
Alpha Kappa Alpha	3/30/2013	$1,000.00
Balanced Man Scholarship Sigma Phi	3/29/2014	$1,000.00
Delta Sigma Phi Fraternity at K-State Scholarship	3/26/2013	$500.00
Great Plains Associations of College Admissions Counseling	2/27/2013	$1,000.00
Hispanic Scholarship of Greater Kansas City	3/1/2014	$1,000.00
Kohl's Kids Who Care	3/13/2014	$1,000.00
Masonic Grand Lodge of AF & AM of Kansas	10/30/2013	$500.00

Visual Workshop

Open the Training-F.accdb database from the location where you store your Data Files, then enable content if prompted. In Query Design View, create a new select query with the DeptName field from the Departments table, the CourseCost field from the Courses table, and the Description field from the Courses table. (*Hint*: You will also have to add the Employees and Enrollments tables to Query Design View to build relationships from the Departments table to the Courses table.) Save the query with the name **DepartmentCrosstab,** then display it as a crosstab query, as shown in **FIGURE F-24**. Print the DepartmentCrosstab query if requested by your instructor, save and close it, then close the Training-F.accdb database.

FIGURE F-24

Description	Accounting	Engineering	Executive	Human Resc	Information	Legal	Marketing	Operations	Research	Shipping	Training
Access Case Problems	$400.00	$200.00	$200.00			$600.00	$200.00	$200.00			$200.00
Computer Fundamentals	$200.00	$200.00	$200.00	$400.00	$200.00	$800.00	$600.00		$400.00	$400.00	$400.00
Dynamite Customer Service Skills			$100.00	$100.00	$100.00	$100.00	$200.00		$100.00		
Employee Benefits Made Clear		$50.00	$50.00	$100.00	$50.00	$150.00	$150.00	$50.00	$100.00	$100.00	$50.00
Excel Case Problems	$200.00		$200.00	$200.00				$400.00	$200.00	$400.00	$200.00
Intermediate Access	$800.00	$400.00	$400.00			$1,200.00	$400.00	$400.00			$400.00
Intermediate Excel	$400.00		$200.00	$200.00		$200.00		$400.00	$200.00	$400.00	$200.00
Intermediate Internet Explorer	$400.00		$400.00	$400.00	$200.00	$800.00	$400.00	$200.00	$200.00	$200.00	$400.00
Intermediate Phone Skills	$300.00		$150.00			$300.00		$300.00	$150.00		$150.00
Intermediate PowerPoint	$400.00	$200.00	$200.00	$200.00		$600.00	$200.00	$200.00	$200.00	$200.00	$400.00
Intermediate Tax Planning	$100.00		$100.00	$50.00	$50.00	$50.00		$50.00	$100.00	$100.00	$50.00
Intermediate Windows		$200.00	$400.00	$200.00	$200.00	$200.00	$400.00		$400.00	$400.00	$200.00
Intermediate Word			$200.00	$200.00	$200.00	$200.00	$400.00		$200.00		
Internet Fundamentals		$200.00	$200.00	$400.00	$200.00	$600.00	$600.00		$400.00	$400.00	$400.00
Introduction to Access	$400.00	$200.00	$200.00	$200.00		$600.00	$400.00	$200.00			$200.00
Introduction to Excel	$400.00		$400.00	$200.00		$200.00		$400.00	$400.00	$400.00	$200.00
Introduction to Insurance Planning	$150.00	$75.00	$75.00	$75.00		$225.00	$75.00	$75.00	$75.00	$150.00	$150.00
Introduction to Internet Explorer	$400.00	$200.00	$400.00	$400.00	$200.00	$800.00	$600.00	$200.00	$400.00	$200.00	$400.00
Introduction to Networking		$200.00	$200.00	$400.00	$200.00	$400.00	$600.00		$400.00	$400.00	$200.00
Introduction to Outlook	$400.00	$200.00		$400.00		$600.00	$400.00	$400.00	$200.00	$400.00	$400.00
Introduction to Phone Skills	$300.00	$150.00	$150.00			$450.00	$150.00	$300.00	$150.00	$150.00	$150.00
Introduction to PowerPoint	$400.00	$200.00	$200.00	$400.00	$200.00	$800.00	$600.00	$200.00	$200.00	$200.00	$400.00
Introduction to Project	$1,200.00	$800.00	$1,200.00	$400.00		$2,000.00	$1,600.00	$1,600.00	$1,200.00	$1,600.00	$1,200.00
Introduction to Tax Planning	$100.00		$100.00	$50.00	$50.00	$100.00	$50.00	$50.00	$100.00	$100.00	$50.00
Introduction to Windows		$200.00	$200.00	$400.00	$200.00	$600.00	$600.00	$200.00	$400.00	$400.00	$400.00

Record: 1 of 31 — No Filter — Search

Enhancing Forms

CASE Samantha Hooper wants to improve the usability of the forms in the QuestTravel database. You will build and improve forms by working with subforms, combo boxes, option groups, and command buttons to enter, find, and filter data.

Unit Objectives

After completing this unit, you will be able to:

- Use Form Design View
- Add subforms
- Align control edges
- Add a combo box for data entry

- Add a combo box to find records
- Add command buttons
- Add option groups
- Add tab controls

Files You Will Need

QuestTravel-G.accdb	RealEstate-G.accdb
Service-G.accdb	Scholarships-G.accdb
MusicStore-G.accdb	Baseball-G.accdb

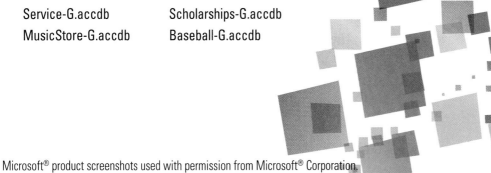

Use Form Design View

Learning
Outcomes
• Create a form in
  Form Design View
• Modify the Record
  Source property
• Add fields to a
  form with the
  Field List

A **form** is a database object designed to make data easy to find, enter, and edit. You create forms by using **controls**, such as labels, text boxes, combo boxes, and command buttons, which help you manipulate data more quickly and reliably than working in a datasheet. A form that contains a **subform** allows you to work with related records in an easy-to-use screen arrangement. For example, using a form/subform combination, you can display customer data and all of the orders placed by that customer at the same time. **Design View** of a form is devoted to working with the detailed structure of a form. The purpose of Design View is to provide full access to all of the modifications you can make to the form. **CASE** *Samantha Hooper has asked you to create a customer entry form. You create this form from scratch in Form Design View.*

STEPS

1. **Start Access, then open the** QuestTravel-G.accdb database **from the location where you store your Data Files, enable content if prompted, click the** CREATE tab **on the Ribbon, then click the** Form Design button **in the Forms group**

   A blank form is displayed in Design View. Your first step is to connect the blank form to an underlying **record source**, a table or query that contains the data you want to display on the form. The fields in the record source populate the **Field List**, a small window that lists the fields in the record source. The Customers table should be the record source for the CustomerEntry form.

QUICK TIP
Click the Build button [...] in the Record Source property to build or edit a query as the record source for this form.

2. **Double-click the** form selector button ■ **to open the form's Property Sheet, click the** Data tab **in the Property Sheet, click the** Record Source list arrow, **then click** Customers

   The Record Source property lists all existing tables and queries. With the record source selected, you're ready to add controls to the form. Recall that bound controls, such as text boxes and combo boxes, display data from the record source, and unbound controls, such as labels and lines, clarify information for the person using the form.

3. **Click the** Add Existing Fields button **in the Tools group to open the Field List, click** CustNo **in the Field List, press and hold** [Shift], **click** Photo **in the Field List, then drag the selection to the form at about the** 1" **mark on the horizontal ruler**

   The fields of the Customers table are added to the form, as shown in **FIGURE G-1**. The FirstContact field is added as a combo box because it has Lookup properties. The other fields are text boxes except for the Photo field, which is inserted as an **Attachment** control given the Photo field has an Attachment data type. Labels are created for each bound control and are captioned with the field name. You can rearrange the controls by moving them.

QUICK TIP
In a column of controls, labels are on the left and text boxes are on the right.

4. **Click the** form **to deselect all controls, click the** Phone text box, **press and hold** [Ctrl], **click the** FirstContact combo box **and** Photo Attachment box **to add them to the selection, then release** [Ctrl]

   Selected controls will move as a group.

5. **Use the** ⬧ **pointer to drag the selected controls up and to the right to position them about** 0.25" **to the right of the name and address controls, then click the** View button ▤ **to switch to Form View**

   The new form in Form View is shown in **FIGURE G-2**. You will improve and enhance it in later lessons.

6. **Click the** Save button 🖫 **on the Quick Access toolbar, type** CustomerEntry **as the form name, click** OK, **then close the CustomerEntry form**

FIGURE G-1: Adding fields in Form Design View

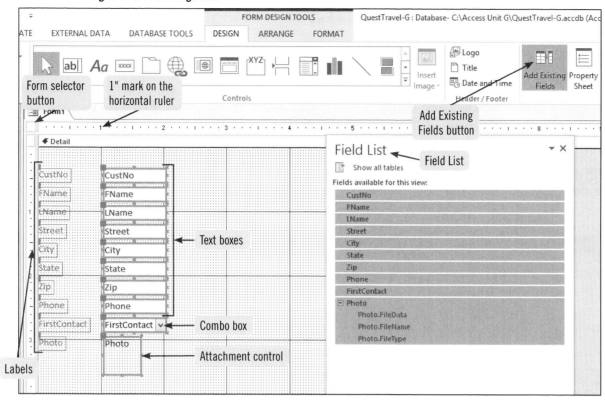

FIGURE G-2: New form in Form View

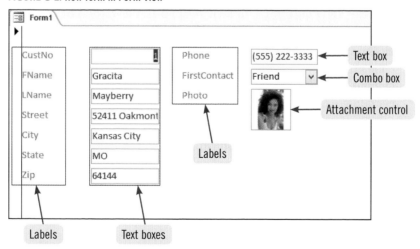

Add Subforms

Learning
Outcomes
• Add a subform to
a form
• Resize columns in
a subform
• Define form layouts

A **subform** is a form within a form. The form that contains the subform is called the **main form**. A main form/subform combination displays the records of two tables that are related in a one-to-many relationship. The main form shows data from the table on the "one" side of the relationship, and the subform shows the records from the table on the "many" side of the relationship. **CASE** *You decide to add a subform to the CustomerEntry form to show related sales for each customer.*

STEPS

TROUBLE
If the SubForm Wizard doesn't start, click the More button in the Controls group, then click Use Control Wizards to toggle it on.

1. **Open the CustomerEntry form in Design View, then close the Field List and Property Sheet if they are open**

   You add new controls to a form by dragging fields from the Field List or selecting the control on the DESIGN tab of the Ribbon.

2. **Click the More button in the Controls group to view all of the form controls, click the Subform/Subreport button , then click below the Zip label in the form, as shown in FIGURE G-3**

   The Subform Wizard opens to help you add a subform control to the form.

QUICK TIP
To remove a form layout, you must work in Form Design View.

3. **Click Next to use existing Tables and Queries as the data for the subform, click the Tables/Queries list arrow, click Query: SalesInfo, click the Select All Fields button >> , click Next, click Next to accept the option Show SalesInfo for each record in Customers using CustNo, then click Finish to accept SalesInfo subform as the name for the new subform control**

   A form **layout** is the general way that the data and controls are arranged on the form. By default, subforms display their controls in a columnar layout in Design View, but their **Default View property** is set to Datasheet. See **TABLE G-1** for a description of form layouts. The difference in form layout is apparent when you view the form in Form View.

4. **Click the View button to switch to Form View, then navigate to CustNo 6, Kristen Collins, who has purchased four different tours, as shown in the subform**

   Sales information appears in the subform in a datasheet layout. As you move through the customer records of the main form, the information changes in the subform to reflect sales for each customer. The main form and subform are linked by the common CustNo field. Resize the columns of the subform to make the information easier to read.

QUICK TIP
Double-click the line between field names to automatically adjust the width of the column to the widest field entry.

5. **Point to the line between field names in the subform and use the ✛ pointer to resize the column widths of the subform, as shown in FIGURE G-4**

   The CustomerEntry form displays two navigation bars. The inside bar is for the subform records, and the outside bar is for the main form records.

6. **Right-click the CustomerEntry form tab, click Close, then click Yes when prompted to save changes to both form objects**

FIGURE G-3: Adding a subform control

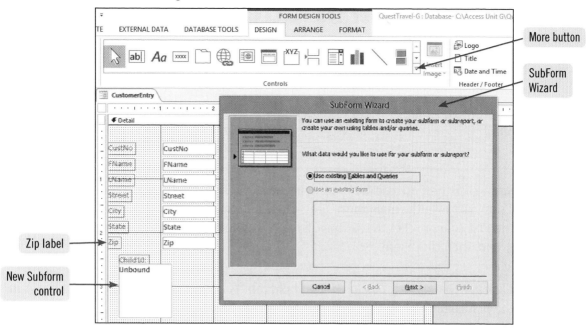

FIGURE G-4: CustomerEntry form and SalesInfo subform

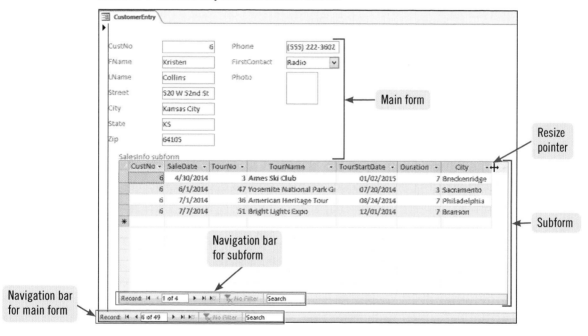

TABLE G-1: Form layouts

layout	description
Columnar	Default view for main forms; each field appears on a separate row with a label to its left
Tabular	Each field appears as an individual column, and each record is presented as a row
Datasheet	Default view for subforms; fields and records are displayed as they appear in a table or query datasheet

Linking the form and subform

If the form and subform do not appear to be correctly linked, examine the subform's Property Sheet, paying special attention to the **Link Child Fields** and **Link Master Fields** properties on the Data tab. These properties tell you which field serves as the link between the main form and subform.

Align Control Edges

Well-designed forms are logical, easy to read, and easy to use. Aligning the edges of controls can make a big difference in form usability. To align the left, right, top, or bottom edges of two or more controls, use the Align button on the ARRANGE tab of the Ribbon. **CASE** ▶ *Samantha Hooper asks you to align and rearrange the controls in the main form to make it easier to read, and to resize the Photo box so it is much larger.*

STEPS

1. **Right-click the CustomerEntry form in the Navigation Pane, click Design View, click the CustNo label in the main form, press and hold [Shift] while clicking the other labels in the first column, click the ARRANGE tab, click the Align button in the Sizing & Ordering group, then click Right**

   Aligning the right edges of these labels makes them easier to read and closer to the data they describe.

2. **Click the CustNo text box, press and hold [Shift] while clicking the other text boxes in the first column, then drag a middle-left sizing handle to the left**

   Leave only a small amount of space between the labels in the first column and the bound controls in the second column, as shown in **FIGURE G-5**.

3. **Click the form to deselect the selected controls, press and hold [Shift] to select the three labels in the third column of the main form, click the Align button in the Sizing & Ordering group, then click Right**

   With the main form's labels and text boxes better sized and aligned, you decide to delete the Photo label, and move and resize the Photo box to make it much larger.

4. **Click the form to deselect any selected controls, click the Photo label, press [Delete], click the Photo box to select it, use the ⁺ₖ pointer to move it to the upper-right corner of the form, use the ⤢ pointer to drag the lower-left sizing handle to fill the space, right-click the CustomerEntry form tab, then click Form View to review the changes**

   The final CustomerEntry form should look like **FIGURE G-6**. Use the subform to enter a new sale to Gracita Mayberry.

5. **Click the SaleDate field in the second record of the subform, use the Calendar Picker to choose 8/1/14, press [Tab], enter 3 for the TourNo, then press [Tab]**

   Once you identify the correct TourNo, the rest of the fields describing that tour are automatically added to the record. Continue to make additional enhancements in Form Design View as needed to match **FIGURE G-6**.

6. **Save and close the CustomerEntry form**

Anchoring, margins, and padding

Anchoring means to position and tie a control to other controls so they move or resize together. The control **margin** is the space between the content inside the control and the outside border of the control. Control **padding** is the space between the outside borders of adjacent controls. To apply anchoring, margins, or padding, work in Form Design View. Click the ARRANGE tab, select the control(s) you want to modify, and choose the Control Margins, Control Padding, or Anchoring buttons in the Position group.

Enhancing Forms

FIGURE G-5: Aligning and resizing controls

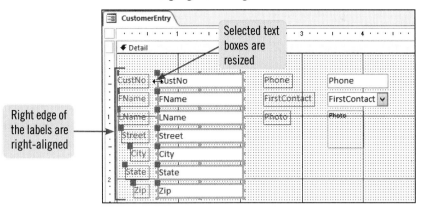

Selected text boxes are resized

Right edge of the labels are right-aligned

FIGURE G-6: Final CustomerEntry form

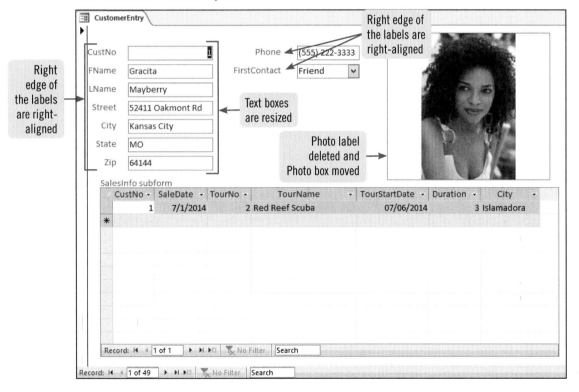

Right edge of the labels are right-aligned

Right edge of the labels are right-aligned

Text boxes are resized

Photo label deleted and Photo box moved

Access 2013

Add a Combo Box for Data Entry

Learning Outcomes
• Add a combo box to a form
• Modify combo box properties
• Use a combo box for data entry

If a finite set of values can be identified for a field, using a combo box instead of a text box control on a form allows the user to select a value from the list, which increases data entry accuracy and speed. Both the **list box** and **combo box** controls provide a list of values from where the user can choose an entry. A combo box also allows the user to type an entry from the keyboard; therefore, it is a "combination" of the list box and text box controls. You can create a combo box by using the **Combo Box Wizard**, or you can change an existing text box or list box into a combo box. Fields with Lookup properties are automatically created as combo boxes on new forms. Foreign key fields are also good candidates for combo boxes. **CASE** *Samantha Hooper asks you to change the TourNo field in the subform of the CustomerEntry form into a combo box so that when a customer purchases a new tour, users can choose the tour from a list instead of entering the TourNo value from the keyboard.*

STEPS

1. **Open the CustomerEntry form in Design View, click the TourNo text box in the subform to select it, right-click the TourNo text box, point to Change To on the shortcut menu, then click Combo Box**

   Now that the control has been changed from a text box to a combo box, you need to populate the list with the appropriate values.

QUICK TIP
A brief description of the property appears in the status bar.

2. **Click the Property Sheet button in the Tools group, click the Data tab in the Property Sheet, click the Row Source property box, then click the Build button [...]**

   Clicking the Build button for the **Row Source property** opens the Query Builder window, which allows you to select the field values you want to display in the combo box list. You want to select the TourNo and TourName fields for the list, which are both stored in the Tours table.

3. **Double-click Tours, then click Close in the Show Table dialog box**

4. **Double-click TourNo in the Tours field list to add it to the query grid, double-click TourName, click the Sort list arrow for the TourName field, click Ascending, click the Close button on the DESIGN tab, then click Yes to save the changes**

   The beginning of a SELECT statement is displayed in the Row Source property, as shown in **FIGURE G-7**. This is an SQL (Structured Query Language) statement and can be modified by clicking the Build button [...]. If you save the query with a name, the query name will appear in the Row Source property.

QUICK TIP
The title bar of the Property Sheet identifies the name of the control with which you are currently working.

5. **With the TourNo combo box still selected, click the Format tab in the Property Sheet, click the Column Count property, change 1 to 2, click the Column Widths property, type 0.5;2, click the List Width property and change Auto to 2.5, save the form, then display it in Form View**

   Entering 0.5;2 sets the width of the first column to 0.5 inches and the width of the second column to 2 inches. To test the new combo box, you add another new sales record in the subform.

6. **Move to the second record for CustNo 2, click the TourNo list arrow in the second record in the subform, scroll as needed and click Franklin Family Reunion on the list, press [Tab], enter 9/1/14 as the SaleDate value, then press [Enter]**

   The new record is entered as shown in **FIGURE G-8**. Selecting a specific TourNo automatically fills in the correct Tour fields for that TourNo number.

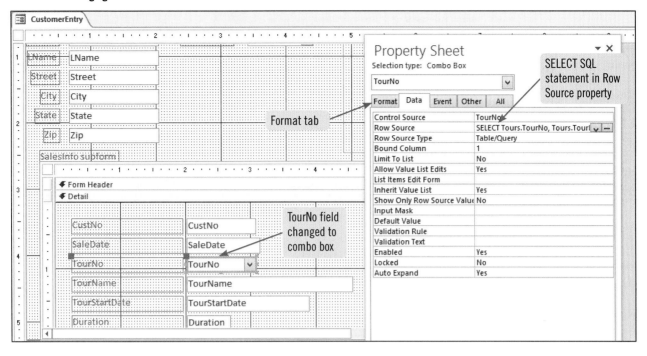

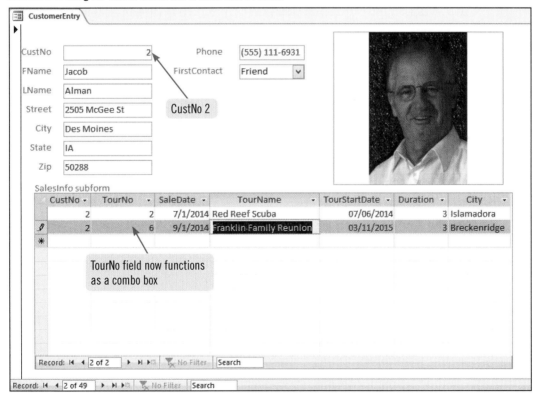

Choosing between a combo box and a list box

The list box and combo box controls are very similar, but the combo box is more popular for two reasons. While both provide a list of values from which the user can choose to make an entry in a field, the combo box also allows the user to make a unique entry from the keyboard (unless the **Limit To List property** is set to Yes). More important, however, is that most users like the drop-down list action of the combo box.

Add a Combo Box to Find Records

Learning
Outcomes
• Add a combo box
  to find records
• Modify the Row
  Source property
• Search for data
  with a combo box

Most combo boxes are used to enter data; however, you can also use a combo box to find records. Often, controls used for navigation are placed in the Form Header section to make them easy to find. **Sections** determine where controls appear on the screen and print on paper. See **TABLE G-2** for more information on form sections. **CASE** ▶ *You decide to add a combo box to the Form Header section to quickly locate customers in the CustomerEntry form.*

STEPS

1. **Right-click the CustomerEntry form tab, click Design View, close the Property Sheet if it is open, then click the Title button in the Header/Footer group on the DESIGN tab**

   The **Form Header** section opens and displays a label captioned with the name of the form. You modify and resize the label.

2. **Click between the words Customer and Entry in the label in the Form Header, press the [Spacebar], then use the ↔ pointer to drag the middle-right sizing handle to the left to about the 3" mark on the horizontal ruler**

   Now you have space on the right side of the Form Header section to add a combo box to find records.

3. **Click the Combo Box button 📧 in the Controls group, click in the Form Header at about the 5" mark on the horizontal ruler, click the Find a record option button in the Combo Box Wizard, click Next, double-click LName, double-click FName, click Next, click Next to accept the column widths and hide the key column, type Find Customer: as the label for the combo box, then click Finish**

   The new combo box is placed in the Form Header section, as shown in **FIGURE G-9**. The accompanying label is hard to read because of the text color. You modify the label and widen the combo box.

4. **Click the Find Customer: label, click the HOME tab, click the Font Color button arrow 🅰️ ▾, click the Dark Blue, Text 2 color box (top row, fourth from the left), click the Unbound combo box, use the ↔ pointer to drag the middle-right sizing handle to the right edge of the form to widen the combo box, then click the View button 📧**

   You test the combo box in Form View.

5. **Click the Find Customer: list arrow, then click Braven, Samantha**

   The combo box works to find the customer named Samantha Braven as intended, but the combo box list entries are not in alphabetical order. You fix this in Form Design View by working with the Property Sheet of the combo box.

6. **Right-click the CustomerEntry form tab, click Design View, double-click the edge of the Unbound combo box in the Form Header to open its Property Sheet, click the Data tab, click SELECT in the Row Source property, then click the Build button ⋯**

   The Query Builder opens, allowing you to modify the fields or sort order of the values in the combo box list.

7. **Click the Sort cell for LName, click Ascending, click Ascending in the Sort cell for FName, click the Close button on the DESIGN tab, click Yes when prompted to save changes, click the View button 📧, then click the Find Customer: list arrow**

   This time, the combo box list is sorted in ascending order by last name, then by first name, as shown in **FIGURE G-10**.

8. **Scroll and click Taylor, Tim to test the combo box again, then save and close the CustomerEntry form**

   To modify the number of items displayed in the list, use the **List Rows property** on the Format tab.

FIGURE G-9: Adding a combo box to find records

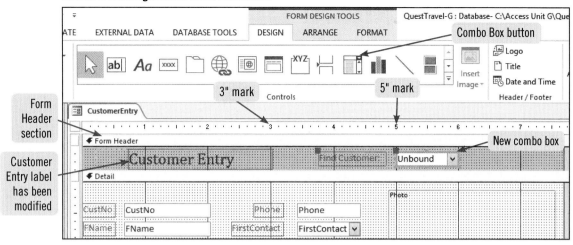

FIGURE G-10: Using a combo box to find customers

TABLE G-2: Form sections

section	description
Detail	Appears once for every record
Form Header	Appears at the top of the form and often contains command buttons or a label with the title of the form
Form Footer	Appears at the bottom of the form and often contains command buttons or a label with instructions on how to use the form
Page Header	Appears at the top of a printed form with information such as page numbers or dates
Page Footer	Appears at the bottom of a printed form with information such as page numbers or dates

Add Command Buttons

Learning
Outcomes
• Add a command
button to a form
• Expand form
sections

You use a **command button** to perform a common action in Form View such as printing the current record, opening another form, or closing the current form. Command buttons are often added to the Form Header or Form Footer sections. **CASE** *You add command buttons to the Form Footer section of the CustomerEntry form to help other Quest Specialty Travel employees print the current record and close the form.*

STEPS

1. **Right-click the CustomerEntry form in the Navigation Pane, click Design View, close the Property Sheet if it is open, then scroll to the bottom of the form to display the Form Footer section**

   Good form design gives users everything they need in a logical location. You decide to use the Form Footer section for all of your form's command buttons.

2. **Click the Button button ⌗ in the Controls group, then click in the Form Footer at the 1" mark**

   The Command Button Wizard opens, listing 28 of the most popular actions for the command button, organized within six categories, as shown in **FIGURE G-11**.

3. **Click Record Operations in the Categories list, click Print Record in the Actions list, click Next, click the Text option button, click Next to accept the default text of Print Record, type PrintRecord as the meaningful button name, then click Finish**

   Adding a command button to print only the current record prevents the user from using the Print option on the File tab, which prints *all* records. You also want to add a command button to close the form.

4. **Click the Button button ⌗ in the Controls group, then click to the right of the Print Record button in the Form Footer section**

5. **Click Form Operations in the Categories list, click Close Form in the Actions list, click Next, click the Text option button, click Next to accept the default text of Close Form, type CloseForm as the meaningful button name, then click Finish**

   To test your command buttons, you switch to Form View.

6. **Click the Save button ⊟ on the Quick Access toolbar, click the View button ⊞ to review the form, as shown in FIGURE G-12, click the Print Record button you added in the Form Footer section, then click OK to confirm that only one record prints**

7. **Click the Close Form button in the Form Footer section to close the form**

Shape effects

Shape effects provide a special visual impact (such as shadow, glow, soft edges, and bevel) to command buttons. To apply a shape effect, work in Form Design View. Click the FORMAT tab, select the command button you want to modify, then click the Shape Effects button in the Control Formatting group to display the options.

FIGURE G-11: Command Button Wizard

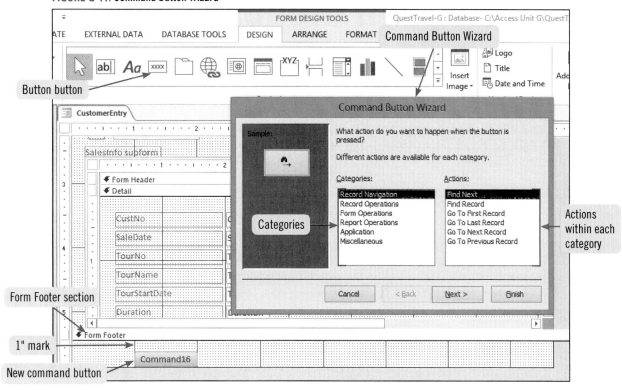

FIGURE G-12: Final Customer Entry form with two command buttons

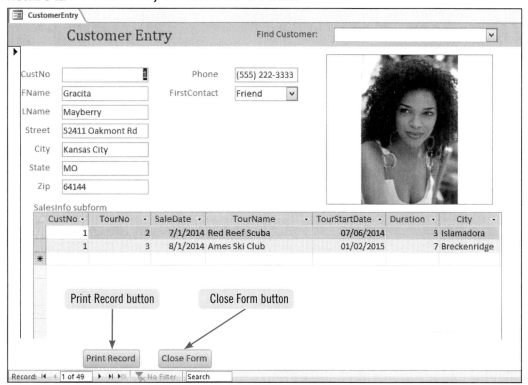

Add Option Groups

Learning
Outcomes
• Add an option
  group to a form
• Add option buttons
  to an option group
• Use option buttons
  to edit data

An **option group** is a bound control used in place of a text box when only a *few* values are available for a field. You add one **option button** control within the option group box for each possible field value. Option buttons within an option group are mutually exclusive; only one can be chosen at a time. **CASE** ▸ *Samantha Hooper asks you to build a new form to view tours and sales information. You decide to use an option group to work with the data in the Duration field because there are only a handful of possible duration values for Quest tours.*

STEPS

1. **Click the Tours table in the Navigation Pane, click the CREATE tab, then click the Form button in the Forms group**

   A form/subform combination is created and displayed in Layout View, showing tour information in the main form and sales records in the subform. You delete the Duration text box and resize the controls to provide room for an option group.

   > **TROUBLE**
   > The blank place-holder is where the Duration text box formerly appeared.

2. **Click the Duration text box, press [Delete], click the blank placeholder, press [Delete], click the right edge of any text box, then use the ↔ pointer to drag the right edge of the controls to the left so they are about half as wide**

   You add the Duration field back to the form as an option group control using the blank space on the right that you created.

3. **Right-click the Tours form tab, click Design View, click the DESIGN tab on the Ribbon, click the Option Group button [XYZ] in the Controls group, then click to the right of the TourNo text box**

   The Option Group Wizard starts and prompts for label names. All the tours sold by Quest Specialty Travel have a duration of 3, 4, 5, 7, 10, or 14 days, so the labels and values will describe this data.

   > **TROUBLE**
   > FIGURE G-13 shows the completed Label Names and Values in the Option Group Wizard at the end of Step 4.

4. **Enter the Label Names shown in FIGURE G-13, click Next, click the No, I don't want a default option button, click Next, then enter the Values to correspond with their labels, as shown in FIGURE G-13**

   The Values are the actual data that are entered into the field and correspond with the **Option Value property** of each option button. The Label Names are clarifying text.

5. **Click Next, click the Store the value in this field list arrow, click Duration, click Next, click Next to accept Option buttons in an Etched style, type Duration as the caption for the option group, then click Finish**

   View and work with the new option group in Form View.

6. **Click the View button [icon] to switch to Form View, click the Next record button [▶] in the navigation bar for the main form twice to move to the Ames Ski Club tour, then click the 5 days option button**

   Your screen should look like FIGURE G-14. You changed the duration of this tour from 7 to 5 days.

7. **Right-click the Tours form tab, click Close, click Yes when prompted to save changes, then click OK to accept Tours as the form name**

FIGURE G-13: Option Group Label Names and Values

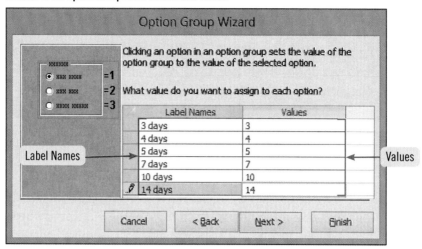

FIGURE G-14: Tours form with option group for Duration field

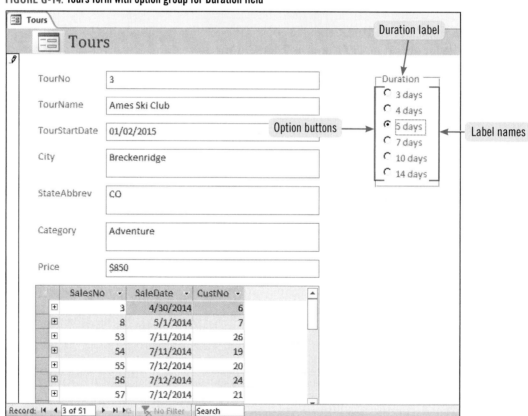

Protecting data

You may not want to allow all users who view a form to change all the data that appears on that form. You can design forms to limit access to certain fields by changing the Enabled and Locked properties of a control. The **Enabled property** specifies whether a control can have the focus in Form View. The **Locked property** specifies whether you can edit data in a control in Form View.

Add Tab Controls

Learning
Outcomes
• Add a tab control
  to a form
• Modify tab control
  properties

You use the **tab control** to create a three-dimensional aspect to a form so that many controls can be organized and displayed by clicking the tabs. You have already used tab controls because many Access dialog boxes use tabs to organize information. For example, the Property Sheet uses tab controls to organize properties identified by categories: Format, Data, Event, Other, and All. **CASE** Samantha Hooper asks *you to organize database information based on two categories: Tours and Customers. You create a new form with tab controls to organize command buttons for easy access to tour and customer information.*

STEPS

1. **Click the CREATE tab, click the Blank Form button in the Forms group, close the Field List if it is open, click the Tab Control button ☐ in the Controls group, then click the form**

   A new tab control is automatically positioned in the upper-left corner of the new form with two tabs. You rename the tabs to clarify their purpose.

2. **Click the Page1 tab to select it, click the Property Sheet button in the Tools group, click the Other tab in the Property Sheet, double-click Page1 in the Name property, type Customers, then press [Enter]**

   You also give Page2 a meaningful name.

3. **Click Page2 to open its Property Sheet, click the Other tab (if it is not already selected), double-click Page2 in the Name property text box, type Tours, then press [Enter]**

   Now that the tab names are meaningful, you're ready to add controls to each page. In this case, you add command buttons to each page.

4. **Click the Customers tab, click the Button button ⌷ˣˣˣˣ in the Controls group, click in the middle of the Customers page, click the Form Operations category, click the Open Form action, click Next, click CustomerEntry, click Next, then click Finish**

   You add a command button to the Tours tab to open the Tours form.

5. **Click the Tours tab, click the Button button ⌷ˣˣˣˣ, click in the middle of the Tours page, click the Form Operations category, click the Open Form action, click Next, click Tours, click Next, then click Finish**

   Your new form should look like **FIGURE G-15**. To test your command buttons, you must switch to Form View.

6. **Click the View button ▦ to switch to Form View, click the command button on the Tours tab, right-click the Tours form tab, click Close, click the Customers tab in Form1, click the command button on the Customers tab, then click the Close Form command button at the bottom of the CustomerEntry form**

   Your screen should look like **FIGURE G-16**. The two command buttons opened the CustomerEntry and Tours forms and are placed on different pages of a tab control in the form. In a fully developed database, you would add many more command buttons to make all of the database objects (tables, queries, forms, and reports) that users need to access very easy to find and open.

7. **Right-click the Form1 form tab, click Close, click Yes to save changes, type Form Navigation as the form name, click OK, then close the QuestTravel-G.accdb database**

   To add or delete a page, right-click a tab and choose Insert Page or Delete Page.

Enhancing Forms

FIGURE G-15: Adding command buttons to a tab control

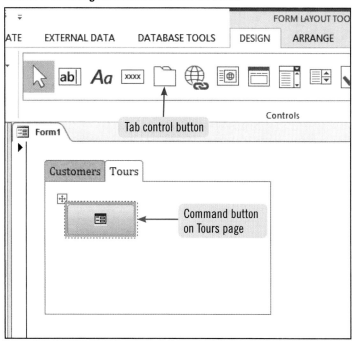

FIGURE G-16: Form Navigation form

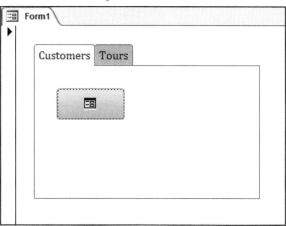

Practice

Concepts Review

Identify each element of Form Design View shown in FIGURE G-17.

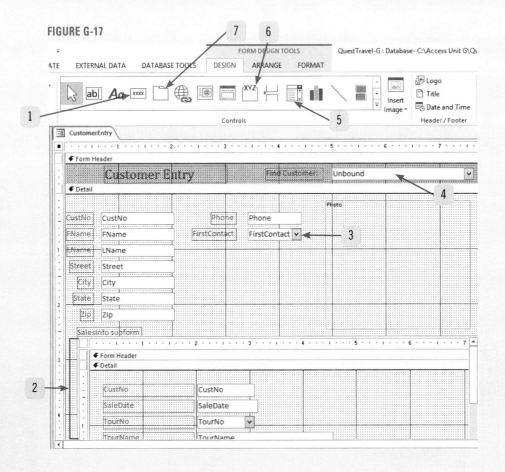

FIGURE G-17

Match each term with the statement that best describes it.

8. **Command button**
9. **Subform**
10. **Tab control**
11. **Option group**
12. **Combo box**

a. A bound control that displays a few mutually exclusive entries for a field
b. A control that provides a three-dimensional aspect to a form used to organize other controls
c. A bound control that is really both a list box and a text box
d. A control that shows records that are related to one record shown in the main form
e. An unbound control that executes an action when it is clicked

Select the best answer from the list of choices.

13. **Which control works best to display three choices—1, 2, or 3—for a Rating field?**
    a. Option group
    b. Label
    c. Text box
    d. Command button

14. **Which control would you use to initiate a print action?**
    a. Option group
    b. Command button
    c. Text box
    d. List box

15. **Which control would you use to display a drop-down list of 50 states?**
    a. Check box
    b. Field label
    c. Combo box
    d. List box

16. **To view many related records within a form, use a:**
    a. Subform.
    b. List box.
    c. Design template.
    d. Link control.

17. **Which of the following form properties defines the fields and records that appear on a form?**
    a. Record Source
    b. Default View
    c. Row Source
    d. List Items Edit Form

18. **Which is a popular layout for a main form?**
    a. Datasheet
    b. Global
    c. Columnar
    d. Justified

19. **Which is a popular layout for a subform?**
    a. Columnar
    b. Justified
    c. Global
    d. Datasheet

20. **To align controls on their left edges, first:**
    a. Click the LAYOUT tab on the Ribbon.
    b. Select the controls whose edges you want to align.
    c. Click the DESIGN tab on the Ribbon.
    d. Align the data within the controls.

21. **Which control is most commonly used within an option group?**
    a. Command button
    b. Toggle button
    c. Option button
    d. Check box

Skills Review

1. **Use Form Design View.**
   a. Start Access and open the Service-G.accdb database from the location where you store your Data Files. Enable content if prompted.
   b. Create a new form in Form Design View, open the Property Sheet for the new form, then choose Names as the Record Source.
   c. Open the Field List, then add all fields from the Names table to Form Design View.
   d. Move the Birthday, Dues, MemberNo, CharterMember, and StatusNo controls to a second column, about an inch to the right of the FirstName, LastName, Street, and Zip fields.
   e. Save the form with the name **MemberActivity**.

2. **Add subforms.**
   a. In Form Design View of the MemberActivity form, use the SubForm Wizard to create a subform below the Zip label.
   b. Use all three fields in the Activities table for the subform. Show Activities for each record in Names using MemberNo, and name the subform **Activities**.
   c. Drag the bottom edge of the form up to just below the subform control.
   d. View the MemberActivity form in Form View, and move through several records. Note that the form could be improved with better alignment, and that the Street text box is too narrow to display the entire value in the field.

Skills Review (continued)

3. Align control edges.

   a. Switch to Form Design View, then edit the FirstName, LastName, MemberNo, CharterMember, and StatusNo labels in the main form to read **First Name**, **Last Name**, **Member No**, **Charter Member**, and **Status No**.

   b. Select the four labels in the first column (First Name, Last Name, Street, and Zip) together, and align their right edges.

   c. Move the Charter Member label between the Member No and Status No labels. (*Hint*: Point to the upper-left corner of the Charter Member label to move the label without moving the label and its associated check box.)

   d. Select the five labels in the third column (Birthday, Dues, Member No, Charter Member, and Status No) together, and align their right edges.

   e. Select the First Name label, the FirstName text box, the Birthday label, and the Birthday text box together. Align their top edges.

   f. Select the Last Name label, the LastName text box, the Dues label, and the Dues text box together. Align their top edges.

   g. Select the Street label, the Street text box, the Member No label, and the MemberNo text box together. Align their top edges.

   h. Select the Zip label, the Zip text box, the Charter Member label, and the CharterMember check box together. Align their top edges.

   i. Select the FirstName text box, the LastName text box, the Street text box, and the Zip text box together. Align their left edges and resize them to be wider and closer to the corresponding labels in the first column.

   j. Align the left edges of the Birthday, Dues, MemberNo, and StatusNo text box controls.

   k. Resize the Street text box to be about twice as wide as its current width.

   l. Save the MemberActivity form.

4. Add a combo box for data entry.

   a. In Form Design View, right-click the Zip text box, then change it to a combo box control.

   b. In the Property Sheet of the new combo box, click the Row Source property, then click the Build button.

   c. Select only the Zips table for the query, then double-click the Zip field and the City field to add them to the query grid.

   d. Close the Query Builder window, and save the changes.

   e. On the Format tab of the Property Sheet for the Zip combo box, change the Column Count property to **2**, the Column Widths property to **0.5;2**, and the List Width property to **2.5**.

   f. Close the Property Sheet, then save and view the MemberActivity form in Form View.

   g. In the first record for Micah Mayberry, change the Zip to **64153** using the new combo box.

5. Add a combo box to find records.

   a. Display the MemberActivity form in Design View.

   b. Open the Form Header section by clicking the Title button in the Header/Footer section on the DESIGN tab.

   c. Modify the label to read **Member Activity**, then narrow the width of the label to be only as wide as needed.

   d. Add a combo box to the right side of the Form Header, and choose the "Find a record on my form..." option in the Combo Box Wizard.

   e. Choose the MemberNo, LastName, and FirstName fields in that order.

   f. Hide the key column.

   g. Label the combo box **FIND MEMBER:**.

   h. Move and widen the new combo box to be at least 2" wide, change the FIND MEMBER: label text color to black so it is easier to read, save the MemberActivity form, then view it in Form View.

   i. Use the FIND MEMBER combo box to find the Patch Mullins record. Notice that the entries in the combo box are not alphabetized on last name.

   j. Return to Form Design View, and use the Row Source property and Build button for the FIND MEMBER combo box to open the Query Builder. Add an ascending sort order to the LastName and FirstName fields.

   k. Close the Query Builder, saving changes. View the MemberActivity form in Form View, and find the record for Benjamin Martin. Note that the entries in the combo box list are now sorted in ascending order first by the LastName field, then by the FirstName field.

Skills Review (continued)

6. Add command buttons.

a. Display the MemberActivity form in Design View.

b. Use the Command Button Wizard to add a command button to the middle of the Form Footer section.

c. Choose the Print Record action from the Record Operations category.

d. Choose the Text option button, type **Print Current Record**, then name the button **PrintButton**.

e. Use the Command Button Wizard to add a command button to the right side of the Form Footer section.

f. Choose the Close Form action from the Form Operations category.

g. Choose the Text option button, type **Close**, then name the button **CloseButton**.

h. Select both command buttons then align their top edges.

i. Save the form, display it in Form View, navigate through the first few records, then close the MemberActivity form using the new Close command button.

7. Add option groups.

a. Open the MemberActivity form in Form Design View.

b. Because the dues are always $25 or $50, the Dues field is a good candidate for an option group control. Delete the existing Dues text box and label.

c. Click the Option Group button in the Controls group on the DESIGN tab, then click the form just to the right of the Birthday text box.

d. Type **$25** and **$50** for Label Names, do not choose a default value, and enter **25** and **50** for corresponding Values.

e. Store the value in the Dues field, use option buttons, use the etched style, and caption the option group **Initiation Dues:**.

f. Save the MemberActivity form, and view it in Form View. Move and align the other form controls as needed to match **FIGURE G-18**.

g. Use the FIND MEMBER: combo box to find the record for Roberto Maxim, change his first and last names to *your* name, then change the Initiation Dues to $50 using the new option group. Print this record if requested by your instructor.

h. Use the Close command button to close the MemberActivity form.

FIGURE G-18

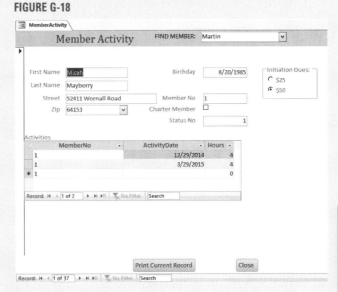

8. Add tab controls.

a. Create a new blank form, and add a tab control to it.

b. Open the Property Sheet, then use the Name property to rename Page1 to **Member Info** and Page2 to **Activity Info**.

c. Right-click the Activity Info tab, click Insert Page, and use the Name property to rename the third page to **Dues Info**.

d. On the Member Info tab, add a command button with the Preview Report action from the Report Operations category. Choose the MemberListing report, choose Text on the button, type **Preview Member Listing Report** as the text, and name the button **MemberListingButton**.

e. On the Activity Info tab, add a command button with the Open Form action from the Form Operations category. Choose the MemberActivity form, choose to open the form and show all the records, choose Text on the button, type **Open Member Activity Form** as the text, and name the button **MemberActivityButton**.

f. On the Activity Info tab, add a second command button with the Preview Report action from the Report Operations category. Choose the ActivityAnalysis report, choose Text on the button, type **Preview Activity Analysis Report** as the text, and name the button **ActivityAnalysisButton**.

Skills Review (continued)

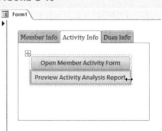

g. Widen the command buttons on the Activity Info tab as needed so that all of the text on the command buttons is clearly visible, as shown in FIGURE G-19.

h. On the Dues Info tab, add a command button with the Preview Report action from the Report Operations category. Choose the DuesAnalysis report, choose Text on the button, type **Preview Dues Analysis Report** as the text, and name the button **DuesAnalysisButton**.

i. Save the form with the name **Database Navigation**, then view it in Form View.

j. Test each button on each tab of the Navigation form to make sure it works as intended.

k. Close all open objects, then close the Service-G.accdb database.

Independent Challenge 1

As the manager of a music store's instrument rental program, you have created a database to track instrument rentals to schoolchildren. You want to build an enhanced form for data entry.

a. Start Access, then open the database MusicStore-G.accdb from the location where you store your Data Files. Enable content if prompted.

b. Using the Form Wizard, create a new form based on all of the fields in the Customers and Rentals tables.

c. View the data by Customers, choose a Datasheet layout for the subform, then accept the default form titles of **Customers** for the main form and **Rentals Subform** for the subform.

d. Add another record to the rental subform for Amanda Smith by typing **888335** as the SerialNo entry and **10/1/15** as the RentalDate entry. Note that no entry is necessary in the RentalNo field because it is an AutoNumber field. No entry is necessary in the CustNo field as it is the foreign key field that connects the main form to the subform and is automatically populated when the forms are in this arrangement.

e. Change Amanda Smith's name to *your* name.

f. Open the Customers form in Design View. Right-align the text within each label control in the first column of the main form. (*Hint*: Use the Align Right button on the HOME tab.)

g. Resize the Zip, CustNo, and SchoolNo text boxes to as wide as the State text box.

h. Move the CustNo and SchoolNo text boxes and their accompanying labels to the upper-right portion of the form, directly to the right of the FirstName and LastName text boxes.

i. Modify the FirstName, LastName, CustNo, and SchoolNo labels to read First Name, Last Name, Cust No, and School No.

j. Delete the RentalNo and CustNo fields from the subform.

FIGURE G-20

k. Open the Field List, and drag the Description field from the Instruments table to the subform above the existing text boxes. (*Hint*: Show all tables, then look in the Fields available in related tables section of the Field List.)

l. Move the subform up, and continue moving and resizing fields as needed so that your form in Form View looks similar to FIGURE G-20.

m. Save and close the Customers form, close the MusicStore-G.accdb database, then exit Access.

Customers

First Name	Student First Name		Cust No	1
Last Name	Student Last Name		School No	1
Street	9 Popular Street			
City	Des Moines			
State	IA			
Zip	50309			

Rentals

SerialNo	RentalDate	Description
1234567	2/26/2015	Cello
1234569	5/26/2015	Cello
888335	10/1/2015	Saxophone

Record: I◄ ◄ 1 of 18 ► ►I ►G No Filter Search

Independent Challenge 2

As the manager of a community effort to provide better access to residential real estate listings across a regional area, you have developed a database to track listings by realtor and real estate agency. You want to develop a form/subform system to see all listings within each realtor as well as within each real estate agency.

a. Start Access, then open the database RealEstate-G.accdb from the location where you store your Data Files. Enable content if prompted.

b. Using the Form Wizard, create a new form based on all of the fields in the Agencies, Realtors, and Listings tables.

c. View the data by Agencies, choose a Datasheet layout for each of the subforms, and accept the default titles of **Agencies**, **Realtors Subform**, and **Listings Subform**.

d. In Form Design View, use the Combo Box Wizard to add a combo box to the Form Header to find a record. Choose the AgencyName field, hide the key column, and enter the label **FIND AGENCY:**.

e. Change the text color of the FIND AGENCY: label to black, and widen the combo box to about twice its current size.

f. Add a command button to a blank spot on the main form to print the current record. Use the Print Record action from the Record Operations category. Use a picture on the button, and give the button the meaningful name of **PrintButton**.

g. Use your skills to modify, move, resize, align text, and align control edges, as shown in **FIGURE G-21**. Note that several labels have been modified, resized, and aligned. Note that the subforms have also been resized and moved.

h. Save the form, view it in Form View, then use the combo box to find Four Lakes Realtors.

i. Resize the columns of the subforms to view as much data as possible, as shown in **FIGURE G-21**, change Tom Hall's name in the first record of the Realtors subform to *your* name, then if requested by your instructor, print only the current record using the new command button.

FIGURE G-21

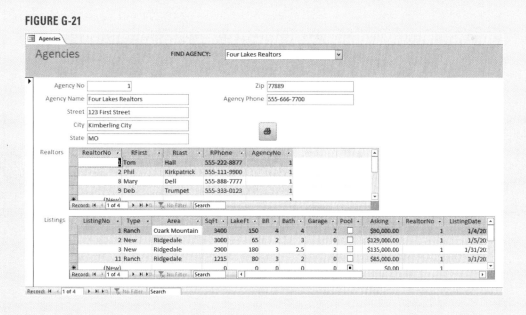

j. Save and close the Agencies form, close the RealEstate-G.accdb database, and exit Access.

Access 2013

Independent Challenge 3

As the manager of a community effort to provide better access to residential real estate listings across a regional area, you have developed a database to track listings by realtor and real estate agency. You want to develop a navigation form to help find queries and reports in your database much faster.

a. Start Access, then open the database RealEstate-G.accdb from the location where you store your Data Files. Enable content if prompted.

b. Create a new blank form, and add a tab control to it.

c. Open the Property Sheet and use the Name property to rename Page1 to **Realtors** and Page2 to **Listings**.

d. On the Realtors tab, add a command button with the Preview Report action from the Report Operations category. Choose the CurrentRealtors report, choose Text on the button, type **Preview Current Realtors** as the text, and name the button **cmdCurrentRealtors**. (Note that *cmd* is the three-character prefix sometimes used to name command buttons.)

e. On the Listings tab, add a command button with the Run Query action from the Miscellaneous category. Choose the AllListings query, choose Text on the button, type **Open All Listings query** as the text, and name the button **cmdAllListings**.

f. On the Listings tab, add a second command button with the Preview Report action from the Report Operations category. Choose the ListingReport report, choose Text on the button, type **Preview Listing Report** as the text, and name the button **cmdListingReport**.

g. Save the form with the name **Real Estate Navigation System**, then view it in Form View. The new form with the Listings tab selected should look like **FIGURE G-22**.

h. Test each command button on both the Realtors and Listings tabs.

i. Close all open objects, then close the RealEstate-G.accdb database and exit Access.

FIGURE G-22

Independent Challenge 4: Explore

You have created an Access database to help manage college scholarship opportunities. You can keep the database updated more efficiently by creating some easy-to-use forms.

a. Start Access and open the Scholarships-G.accdb database from the location where you store your Data Files. Enable content if prompted.

b. Create a split form for the Scholarships table. Save and name the form **Scholarships**.

c. In Form Design View, narrow the label in the Form Header section to about half of its current size, then use the Combo Box Wizard to add a combo box to the Form Header section to find a scholarship based on the ScholarshipName field. Hide the key column, and use the label **FIND SCHOLARSHIP:**.

d. In Form Design View, widen the combo box as necessary so that all of the scholarship names in the list are clearly visible in Form View. Change the color of the FIND SCHOLARSHIP: text to black, and move and resize the label and combo box as necessary to clearly view them. Switch between Form View and Form Design View to test the new combo box control.

e. In Form Design View, change the combo box's List Rows property (on the Format tab) to **50** and use the Build button to modify the Row Source property to add an ascending sort order based on the ScholarshipName field.

f. Save the form, and in Form View, use the combo box to find the Papa Johns Scholarship. Change Papa Johns to *your* name as shown in **FIGURE G-23**, then, if requested by your instructor, print only that record by using the Selected Record(s) option on the Print dialog box.

FIGURE G-23

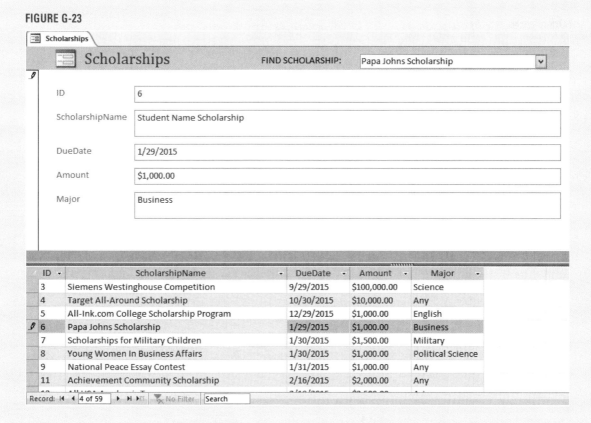

g. Save and close the Scholarships form, close the Scholarships-G.accdb database, then exit Access.

Visual Workshop

Open the Baseball-G.accdb database from the location where you store your Data Files. Enable content if prompted. Use Form Design View to create a form based on the Players table named **PlayersEntry**. Use your skills to modify, move, resize, align text, and align control edges as shown in FIGURE G-24. Note that both the PlayerPosition as well as the TeamNo fields are presented as option groups. The values that correspond with each Position label can be found in the Field Description of the PlayerPosition field in Table Design View of the Players table. The Position option group is tied to the PlayerPosition field. The values that correspond with each Team label can be found by reviewing the TeamNo and TeamName fields of the Teams table. The Team option group is tied to the TeamNo field. Do not choose default values for either option group. Change Louis Gehrig's name to *your* name, change the Position value to Pitcher, and change the Team to Yellow Jackets. If requested by your instructor, print only that record.

FIGURE G-24

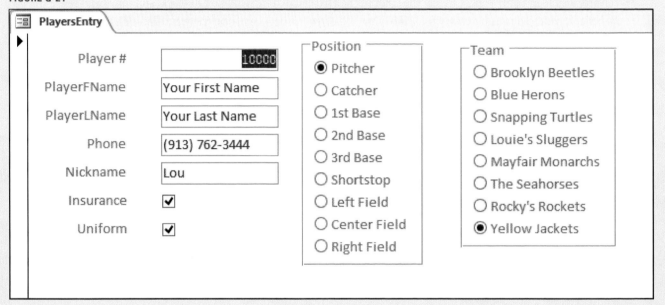

Analyzing Data with Reports

CASE ▶ Samantha Hooper asks you to create and enhance reports to analyze, clarify, and format important information at Quest Specialty Travel.

Unit Objectives

After completing this unit, you will be able to:

- Use Report Design View
- Create parameter reports
- Apply conditional formatting
- Add lines

- Use the Format Painter and themes
- Add subreports
- Modify section properties
- Create summary reports

Files You Will Need

QuestTravel-H.accdb   Scholarships-H.accdb
RealEstate-H.accdb   Baseball-H.accdb
MusicStore-H.accdb

Use Report Design View

Learning
Outcomes
• Modify report
properties
• Modify group and
sort orders

Although you can print data in forms and datasheets, **reports** give you more control over how data is printed and greater flexibility in presenting summary information. To create a report, you include text boxes to display data and use calculations and labels, lines, and graphics to clarify the data. **Report Design View** allows you to work with a complete range of report, section, and control properties. Because Report Design View gives you full control of all aspects of a report, it is well worth your time to master. **CASE** *Samantha Hooper asks you to build a report that shows all tours grouped by category and sorted in descending order by price. You use Report Design View to build this report.*

STEPS

1. **Start Access, open the QuestTravel-H.accdb database from the location where you store your Data Files, enable content if prompted, click the CREATE tab, then click the Report Design button in the Reports group**

   The first step to building a report in Report Design View is identifying the record source.

2. **If the Property Sheet is not open, click the Property Sheet button in the Tools group, click the Data tab in the Property Sheet, click the Record Source list arrow, then click Tours**

   The Record Source can be an existing table, query, or SQL SELECT statement. The **Record Source** identifies the fields and records that the report can display. To build a report that shows tours grouped by category, you'll need to add a Category Header section. See **TABLE H-1** for a review of report sections.

3. **Scroll down in the report to view the Page Footer section, use the ✛ pointer to drag the top edge of the Page Footer section up to about the 1" mark on the vertical ruler, then click the Group & Sort button in the Grouping & Totals group to open the Group, Sort, and Total pane if it is not already open**

   The Group, Sort, and Total pane gives you the ability to specify grouping and sorting fields and open group headers and footers.

4. **Click the Add a group button in the Group, Sort, and Total pane; click Category; click the Add a sort button in the Group, Sort, and Total pane; click Price; click the from smallest to largest button arrow; then click from largest to smallest, as shown in FIGURE H-1**

   With the grouping and sorting fields specified, you're ready to add controls to the report.

5. **Click the Add Existing Fields button in the Tools group, click TourNo in the Field List, press and hold [Shift] as you click Price in the Field List to select all fields in the Tours table, drag the selected fields to the Detail section of the report, then close the Field List window**

   Next, you move the Category controls to the Category Header section.

6. **Click the report to remove the current selection, right-click the Category text box, click Cut on the shortcut menu, right-click the Category Header section, then click Paste on the shortcut menu**

   If the data is self-explanatory, it doesn't need descriptive labels. Delete the labels, and position the text boxes across the page to finalize the report.

7. **Click each label and press [Delete] to delete each label in the first column of the Detail section, then move and resize the remaining text boxes and shorten the Detail section, as shown in FIGURE H-2**

8. **Click the Save button 🖫 on the Quick Access toolbar, type ToursByCategory as the new report name, click OK, preview the first page of the report, as shown in FIGURE H-3, then close the report**

FIGURE H-1: Creating a report in Report Design View

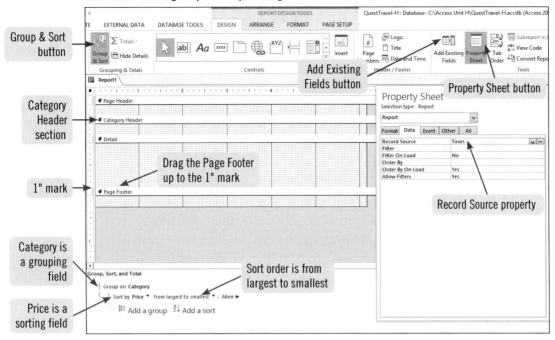

Group & Sort button

Category Header section

1" mark

Category is a grouping field

Price is a sorting field

Add Existing Fields button

Property Sheet button

Record Source property

FIGURE H-2: Moving and resizing the text box controls in the Detail section

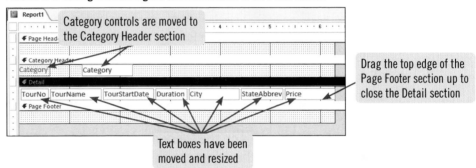

Category controls are moved to the Category Header section

Drag the top edge of the Page Footer section up to close the Detail section

Text boxes have been moved and resized

FIGURE H-3: Previewing the ToursByCategory report

Records are grouped by Category

Records are sorted in descending order by Price

TABLE H-1: Review of report sections

section	where does this section print?	what is this section most commonly used for?
Report Header	At the top of the first page of the report	To print a title or logo
Page Header	At the top of every page (but below the Report Header on page 1)	To print titles, dates, or page numbers
Group Header	Before every group of records	To display the grouping field value
Detail	Once for every record	To display data for every record
Group Footer	After every group of records	To calculate summary statistics on groups of records
Page Footer	At the bottom of every page	To print dates or page numbers

Create Parameter Reports

Learning
Outcomes
• Enter parameter
  criteria
• Create a
  parameter report

A **parameter report** prompts you for criteria to determine the records to use for the report. To create a parameter report, you base it on a parameter query. The report's **Record Source** property determines what table or query provides the fields and records for the report. **CASE** ▶ *Samantha Hooper requests a report that shows all tour sales for a given period. You use a parameter query to prompt the user for the dates, then build the report on that query.*

STEPS

1. **Click the CREATE tab, click the Query Design button in the Queries group, double-click Customers, double-click Sales, double-click Tours, then click Close**

   You want fields from all three tables in the report, so you add them to the query.

2. **Double-click FName in the Customers field list, LName in the Customers field list, and SaleDate in the Sales field list; resize the Tours field list; then double-click Price and TourName in the Tours field list**

   To select only those tours sold in a given period, you add parameter criteria to the SaleDate field.

3. **Click the Criteria cell for the SaleDate field, type Between [Enter start date] and [Enter end date], then widen the SaleDate column to see the entire entry, as shown in FIGURE H-4**

   To test the query, run it and enter dates in the parameter prompts. **Parameter criteria** are text entered in [square brackets] that prompt the user for an entry each time the query is run. In this case, the user will be prompted for the start and end date.

4. **Click the View button ⊞ on the DESIGN tab to run the query, type 6/1/15 in the Enter start date box, click OK, type 6/30/15 in the Enter end date box, then click OK**

   Eight records are displayed in the datasheet, each with a SaleDate value in June 2015.

5. **Click the Save button ⊟ on the Quick Access toolbar, type SalesParameter as the new query name, click OK, then close the SalesParameter query**

   You use the Report button on the CREATE tab to quickly build a report on the SalesParameter query.

6. **Click the SalesParameter query in the Navigation Pane, click the CREATE tab, click the Report button in the Reports group, type 6/1/15 in the Enter start date box, click OK, type 6/30/15 in the Enter end date box, then click OK**

   The report is displayed in Layout View with records in June 2015. You decide to preview and save the report.

QUICK TIP
Use Design View to narrow the report by dragging the right edge of the report to the left.

7. **Work in Layout and Design View to narrow the report so that it fits within the margins of a single page and to increase the height of the calculated field in the Report Footer, save the report with the name SalesDateParameter, then preview it, as shown in FIGURE H-5, entering 6/1/15 as the start date and 6/30/15 as the end date**

FIGURE H-4: Entering parameter criteria in a query

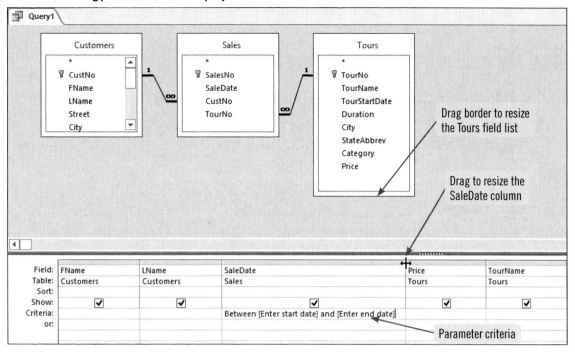

FIGURE H-5: Previewing the SalesDateParameter report

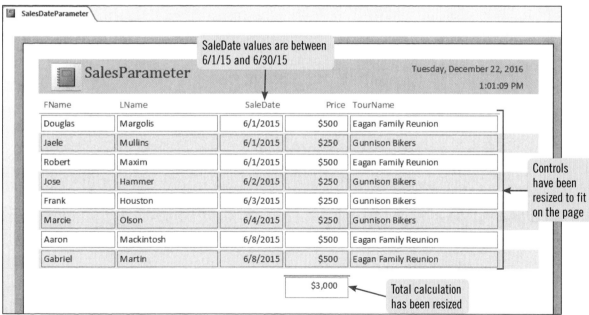

Parameter criteria

In Query Design View, you must enter parameter criteria within [square brackets]. Each parameter criterion you enter appears as a prompt in the Enter Parameter Value dialog box. The entry you make in the Enter Parameter Value box is used as the criterion for the field that contains the parameter criteria.

Learning
Outcomes
• Enter conditional
formats

Apply Conditional Formatting

Conditional formatting allows you to change the appearance of a control on a form or report based on criteria you specify. Conditional formatting helps you highlight important or exceptional data on a form or report. **CASE** *You want to apply conditional formatting to the SalesDateParameter report to emphasize different tour Price levels.*

STEPS

1. **Right-click the** SalesDateParameter report tab, **then click** Design View

TROUBLE
Be sure the Price text box (not Price label) is selected.

2. **Click the** Price text box **in the Detail section, click the** FORMAT tab, **then click the** Conditional Formatting button **in the Control Formatting group**

   The Conditional Formatting Rules Manager dialog box opens, asking you to define the conditional formatting rules. You want to format Price values between 500 and 1000 with a yellow background color.

3. **Click** New Rule, **click the** text box to the right of the between arrow, **type** 500, **click the** and box, **type** 999, **click the** Background color button arrow ⬛▾, **click the** Yellow box **on the bottom row, then click** OK

   You add the second conditional formatting rule to format Price values greater than or equal to 1000 with a light green background color.

4. **Click** New Rule, **click the** between list arrow, **click** greater than or equal to, **click the** value box, **type** 1000, **click the** Background color button arrow ⬛▾, **click the** Light Green box **on the bottom row, then click** OK

   The Conditional Formatting Rules Manager dialog box with two rules should look like **FIGURE H-6**.

5. **Click** OK **in the Conditional Formatting Rules Manager dialog box, right-click the** SalesDateParameter report tab, **click** Print Preview, **type** 7/1/15 **in the Enter start date box, click** OK, **type** 7/31/15 **in the Enter end date box, then click** OK

   Conditional formatting rules applied a light green background color to the Price text box for two tours because the Price value is greater than 1000, as shown in **FIGURE H-7**. Conditional formatting applied a yellow background color to the Price text box for one tour because the Price value is between 500 and 1000. Default formatting was not applied to the Price text box for two tours because they do not meet any of the conditions in the Conditional Formatting Rules Manager dialog box.

6. **Save then close the SalesDateParameter report**

FIGURE H-6: Conditional Formatting Rules Manager dialog box

New Rule button

First rule

Second rule

Formatting for first rule

Formatting for second rule

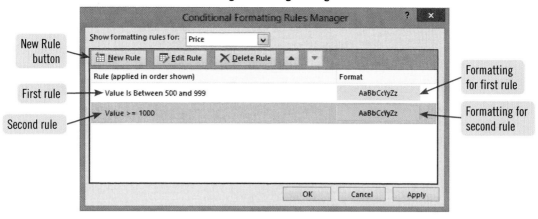

FIGURE H-7: Conditional formatting applied to SalesDateParameter report

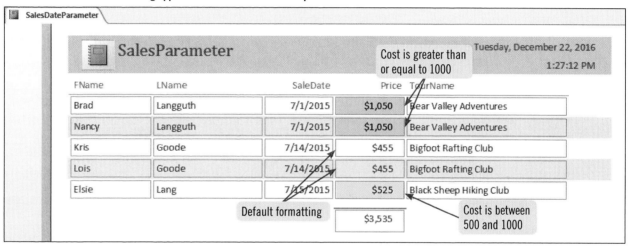

Cost is greater than or equal to 1000

Default formatting

Cost is between 500 and 1000

Conditional formatting using data bars

A recent feature of Access allows you to compare the values of one column to another with small data bars. To use this feature, use the "Compare to other records" rule type option in the New Formatting Rule dialog box, as shown in FIGURE H-8.

FIGURE H-8: Conditional formatting with data bars

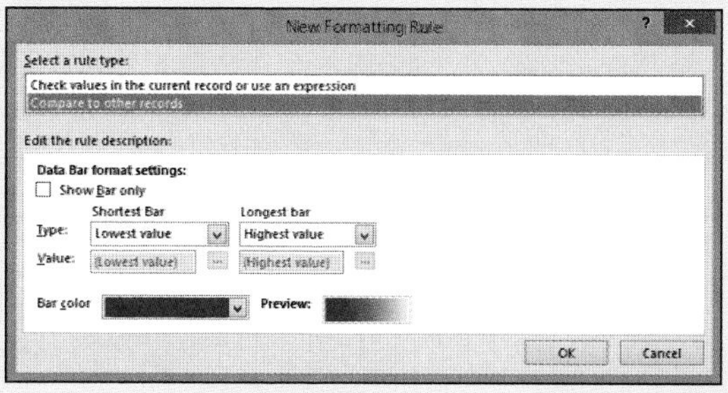

Add Lines

Learning
Outcome
• Add lines to a
  report

Lines are often added to a report to highlight information or enhance its clarity. For example, you might want to separate the Report Header and Page Header information from the rest of the report with a horizontal line. You can also use short lines to indicate subtotals and grand totals. **CASE** ▸ *Samantha Hooper likes the data on the CategoryRevenue report, which has already been created in the QuestTravel-H database, but she asks you to enhance the report by adding a grand total calculation and separating the categories more clearly. Lines will help clarify the information.*

STEPS

QUICK TIP
Recall that Report View does not show page margins or individual pages of the report.

1. **Double-click the CategoryRevenue report in the Navigation Pane to open it in Report View, then scroll to the end of the report**

   The report needs lines separating the tour categories and a new grand total calculation on the last page of the report. You use Report Design View to make these improvements.

2. **Right-click the CategoryRevenue report tab, click Design View, right-click the =Sum([Revenue]) text box in the Category Footer section, click Copy, right-click the Report Footer section, click Paste, press [→] enough times to position the expression directly under the one in the Category Footer, click Subtotal: in the Report Footer section to select it, double-click Subtotal: in the label to select it, type Grand Total:, then press [Enter]**

   The =Sum([Revenue]) expression in the Report Footer section sums the Revenue values in the entire report, whereas the same expression in the Category Footer section sums Revenue values in each category. With the calculations in place, you add clarifying lines.

TROUBLE
Lines can be difficult to find in Report Design View. See the "Line troubles" box in this lesson for tips on working with lines.

3. **Click the More button ⊽ in the Controls group to show all controls, click the Line button ◺, press and hold [Shift], drag from the upper-left edge of =Sum([Revenue]) in the Category Footer section to its upper-right edge, press [Ctrl][C] to copy the line, click the Report Footer section, press [Ctrl][V] two times to paste the line twice, then move the lines just below the =Sum([Revenue]) expression in the Report Footer section**

   Pressing [Shift] while drawing a line makes sure that the line remains perfectly horizontal or vertical. The single line above the calculation in the Category Footer section indicates that the calculation is a subtotal. Double lines below the calculation in the Report Footer section indicate that it is a grand total. You also want to add a line to visually separate the categories.

QUICK TIP
Use the Rectangle ☐ button to insert a rectangle control on a form or report.

4. **Click the More button ⊽ in the Controls group to show all controls, click the Line button ◺, press and hold [Shift], then drag along the bottom of the Category Footer section**

   The final CategoryRevenue report in Report Design View is shown in **FIGURE H-9**.

QUICK TIP
As a final report creation step, print preview a report to make sure it fits on the paper.

5. **Right-click the CategoryRevenue report tab, click Print Preview, then navigate to the last page of the report**

   The last page of the CategoryRevenue report shown in **FIGURE H-10** displays the Category Footer section line as well as the subtotal and grand total lines.

FIGURE H-9: Adding lines to a report

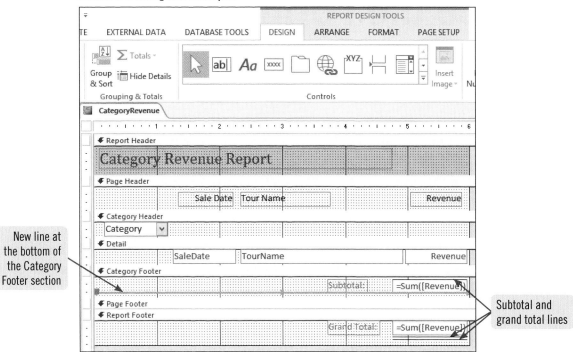

New line at the bottom of the Category Footer section

Subtotal and grand total lines

FIGURE H-10: Previewing the last page of the CategoryRevenue report

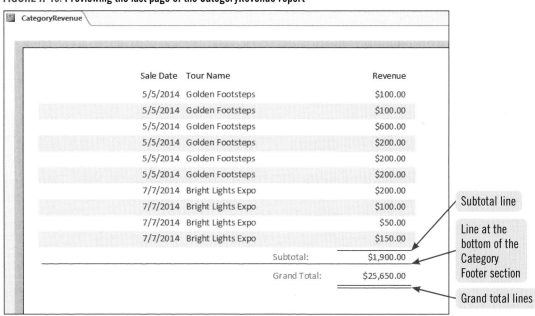

Sale Date	Tour Name	Revenue
5/5/2014	Golden Footsteps	$100.00
5/5/2014	Golden Footsteps	$100.00
5/5/2014	Golden Footsteps	$600.00
5/5/2014	Golden Footsteps	$200.00
5/5/2014	Golden Footsteps	$200.00
5/5/2014	Golden Footsteps	$200.00
7/7/2014	Bright Lights Expo	$200.00
7/7/2014	Bright Lights Expo	$100.00
7/7/2014	Bright Lights Expo	$50.00
7/7/2014	Bright Lights Expo	$150.00
	Subtotal:	$1,900.00
	Grand Total:	$25,650.00

Subtotal line

Line at the bottom of the Category Footer section

Grand total lines

Line troubles

Sometimes lines are difficult to find in Report Design View because they are placed against the edge of a section or the edge of other controls. To find lines that are positioned next to the edge of a section, drag the section bar to expand the section and expose the line. Recall that to draw a perfectly horizontal line, you hold [Shift] while creating or resizing the line. It is easy to accidentally widen a line beyond the report margins, thus creating extra unwanted pages in your printout. To fix this problem, narrow any controls that extend beyond the margins of the printout, and drag the right edge of the report to the left. Note that the default left and right margins for an 8.5 × 11-inch sheet of paper are often 0.25 inches each, so a report in portrait orientation must be no wider than 8 inches, and a report in landscape orientation must be no wider than 10.5 inches.

Use the Format Painter and Themes

The **Format Painter** is a tool you use to copy multiple formatting properties from one control to another in Design or Layout View for forms and reports. **Themes** are predefined formats that you apply to the database to set all of the formatting enhancements, such as font, color, and alignment on all forms and reports. **CASE** *You think the CategoryRevenue report can be improved with a few formatting embellishments. You can use the Format Painter to quickly change the characteristics of labels in the Page Header section, then apply a built-in theme to the entire report.*

STEPS

1. **Right-click the** CategoryRevenue report tab, **click** Design View, **click the** Category Revenue Report label **in the Report Header, click the** HOME tab, **click the** Format Painter button, **then click the** Sale Date label **in the Page Header section**

   The Format Painter applied several formatting characteristics, including font face, font color, and font size from the label in the Report Header section to the Sale Date label in the Page Header section. You like the new font face and color, but the font size is too large.

2. **Click the** Sale Date label, **click the Font Size list arrow** `18 ▾` **in the Text Formatting group, click** 12, **double-click the** Format Painter button, **click the** Tour Name label **in the Page Header section, click the** Revenue label **in the Page Header section, then press** [Esc] **to release the Format Painter pointer**

   Now that you've mastered the Format Painter, you're ready to see how themes affect the formatting of the report.

3. **Click the** DESIGN tab, **click the** Themes button, **point to several themes to observe the changes in the report, then click** Organic, **as shown in** FIGURE H-11

   The Organic theme gives the Report Header section a gray background. All text now has a consistent font face, controls in the same section are the same font size, and all controls have complementary font colors. You preview the report to review the changes as they will appear on a printout.

4. **Right-click the** CategoryRevenue report tab, **click** Layout View, **then resize the left edge of the Tour Name label and text box, as shown in** FIGURE H-12, **to better position the data on the newly formatted report**

   The first page of the CategoryRevenue report is shown in **FIGURE H-12**.

5. **Save and close the CategoryRevenue report**

FIGURE H-11: Applying a theme to a report

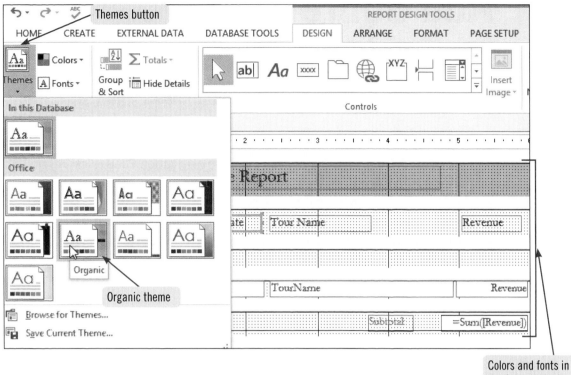

FIGURE H-12: Organic theme applied to the CategoryRevenue report

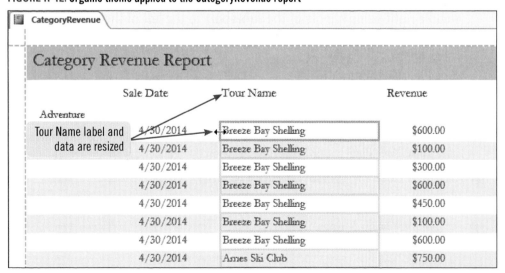

Add Subreports

A **subreport** control displays a report within another report. The report that contains the subreport control is called the **main report**. You can use a subreport control when you want to connect two reports together. **CASE** ▸ *You want the CategoryRevenue report to automatically print at the end of the ToursByCategory report. You use a subreport in the Report Footer section to accomplish this.*

STEPS

1. **Right-click the ToursByCategory report in the Navigation Pane, click Design View, right-click the Page Header section bar, then click Report Header/Footer on the shortcut menu to open the Report Header and Footer sections**

   With the Report Footer section open, you're ready to add the CategoryRevenue subreport.

2. **Click the More button ⊽ in the Controls group, click the Subform/Subreport button ▦, then click the left side of the Report Footer to start the SubReport Wizard, as shown in FIGURE H-13**

   The first question of the SubReport Wizard asks what data you want to use for the subreport.

3. **Click the Use an existing report or form option button in the SubReport Wizard, click CategoryRevenue if it is not already selected, click Next, click None when asked how you want the reports to be linked, click Next, then click Finish to accept the default name**

   The Report Footer section contains the CategoryRevenue report as a subreport. Therefore, the CategoryRevenue report will print after the ToursByCategory report prints. You don't need the label that accompanies the subreport so you delete it.

4. **Click the new CategoryRevenue label associated with the subreport, then press [Delete]**

   If the subreport pushes the right edge of the main report beyond the 8" mark on the ruler, you may see a green error indicator in the report selector button because the report width is greater than the page width. Narrow the subreport and main report to make sure the right edge is to the left of the 8" mark.

5. **Click the edge of the subreport control to select it, use the ◄─► pointer to drag the middle-right sizing handle of the subreport to the left of the 8" mark on the main ruler, then use the ⊹ pointer to drag the right edge of the main report to the left of the 8" mark on the main ruler**

   Report Design View should look similar to FIGURE H-14. Preview your changes.

6. **Right-click the ToursByCategory report tab, click Print Preview, then navigate through the pages of the report**

   The ToursByCategory report fills the first two pages. The CategoryRevenue subreport starts at the top of page three. There should be no blank pages between the printed pages of the report.

7. **Save and close the ToursByCategory report**

FIGURE H-13: SubReport Wizard dialog box

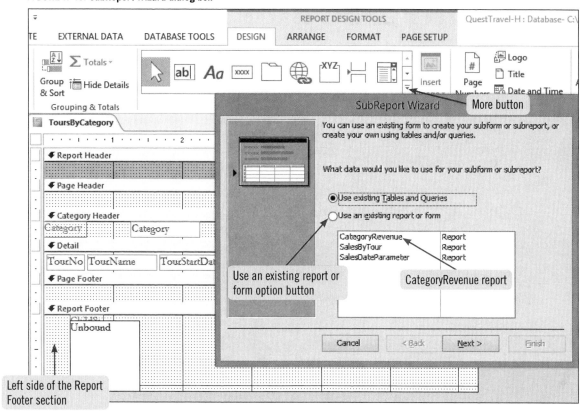

FIGURE H-14: Subreport in Report Design View

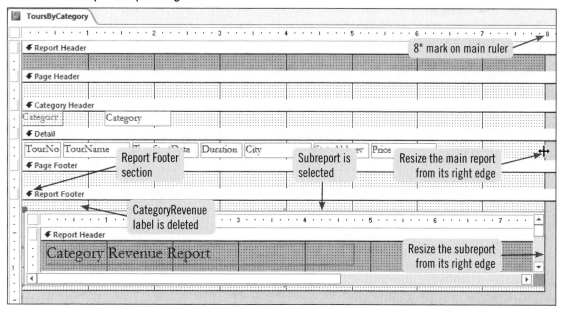

Modify Section Properties

Report **section properties**, the characteristics that define each section, can be modified to improve report printouts. For example, you might want each new Group Header to print at the top of a page. Or, you might want to modify section properties to format that section with a background color. **CASE** ▶ Samantha Hooper asks you to modify the SalesByTour report so that each tour prints at the top of a page.

STEPS

1. **Right-click the SalesByTour report in the Navigation Pane, then click Design View**

   To force each new tour to start printing at the top of a page, you open and modify the TourName Footer.

2. **Click the Group & Sort button to open the Group, Sort, and Total pane if it is not open; click the TourName More Options button in the Group, Sort, and Total pane; click the without a footer section list arrow; click with a footer section; then double-click the TourName Footer section bar to open its Property Sheet**

   You modify the **Force New Page** property of the TourName Footer section to force each tour to start printing at the top of a new page.

3. **Click the Format tab in the Property Sheet, click the Force New Page property list arrow, then click After Section, as shown in FIGURE H-15**

   You also move the Report Header controls into the Page Header so they print at the top of every page. First, you need to create space in the upper half of the Page Header section to hold the controls.

4. **Close the Property Sheet, drag the top edge of the TourName Header down to expand the Page Header section to about twice its height, click the vertical ruler to the left of the TourName label in the Page Header section to select all of the controls in that section, then use ⊹ to move the labels down to the bottom of the Page Header section**

   With space available in the top half of the Page Header section, you cut and paste the controls from the Report Header section to that new space.

5. **Drag down the vertical ruler to the left of the Report Header section to select all controls in that section, click the HOME tab, click the Cut button in the Clipboard group, click the Page Header section bar, click the Paste button, then drag the top of the Page Header section up to close the Report Header section, as shown in FIGURE H-16**

   Preview the report to make sure that each page contains the new header information and that each tour prints at the top of its own page.

6. **Right-click the SalesByTour report tab, click Print Preview, navigate back and forth through several pages to prove that each new TourName value prints at the top of a new page, then navigate and zoom into the second page, as shown in FIGURE H-17**

   Each tour now starts printing at the top of a new page, and the former Report Header section controls now print at the top of each page too, because they were moved to the Page Header section.

7. **Save and close the SalesByTour report**

FIGURE H-15: Changing section properties

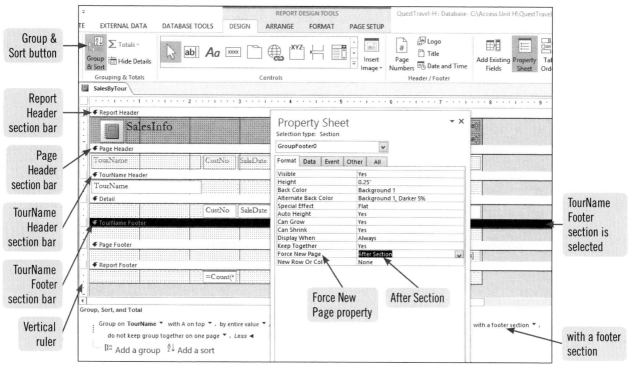

Group & Sort button
Report Header section bar
Page Header section bar
TourName Header section bar
TourName Footer section bar
Vertical ruler

Force New Page property
After Section

TourName Footer section is selected
with a footer section

FIGURE H-16: Moving controls from the Report Header to the Page Header

Report Header section is closed
Controls moved from the Report Header section to the Page Header section

FIGURE H-17: Second page of SalesByTour report

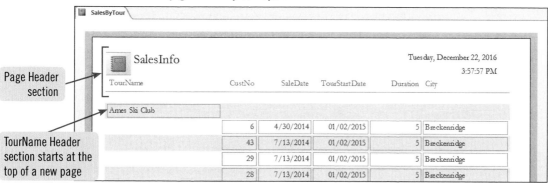

Page Header section
TourName Header section starts at the top of a new page

Create Summary Reports

Learning
Outcomes
• Use rulers to select
  controls in Report
  Design View

Summary reports are reports that show statistics on groups of records rather than details for each record. You create summary reports by using Access functions such as Sum, Count, or Avg in expressions that calculate the desired statistic. These expressions are entered in text boxes most commonly placed in the Group Footer section. **CASE** ▶ *Samantha Hooper asks for a report to summarize the revenue for each tour category. You create a copy of the CategoryRevenue report and modify it to satisfy this request.*

STEPS

1. **Right-click the CategoryRevenue report in the Navigation Pane, click Copy on the short-cut menu, right-click below the report objects in the Navigation Pane, click Paste, type CategorySummary as the report name, then click OK**

   Summary reports may contain controls in the Group Header and Group Footer sections, but because they provide summary statistics instead of details, they do not contain controls in the Detail section. You delete the controls in the Detail section and close it.

2. **Right-click the CategorySummary report in the Navigation Pane, click Design View, click the vertical ruler to the left of the Detail section to select all controls in the Detail section, press [Delete], then drag the top of the Category Footer section up to close the Detail section**

   You can also delete the labels in the Page Header section.

3. **Click the vertical ruler to the left of the Page Header section to select all controls in the Page Header section, press [Delete], then drag the top of the Category Header section up to close the Page Header section**

   Because the Page Header and Page Footer sections do not contain any controls, those section bars can be toggled off to simplify Report Design View.

4. **Right-click the Report Header section bar, then click Page Header/Footer on the shortcut menu to remove the Page Header and Page Footer section bars from Report Design View**

   With the unneeded controls and sections removed, as shown in **FIGURE H-18**, you preview the final summary report.

5. **Right-click the CategorySummary report tab, then click Print Preview**

   You could make this report look even better by moving the Category text box into the Category Footer section and deleting the Subtotal label and line.

6. **Right-click the CategorySummary report tab, click Design View, drag the Category text box down from the Category Header section to the Category Footer section, click the Subtotal label in the Category Footer section, press [Delete], click the subtotal line just above the =Sum([Revenue]) text box in the Category Footer section, press [Delete], right-click the CategorySummary report tab, then click Print Preview**

   The summarized revenue for each category is shown in the one-page summary report in **FIGURE H-19**.

7. **Save and close the CategorySummary report, then close QuestTravel-H.accdb and exit Access**

FIGURE H-18: Design View of the CategorySummary report

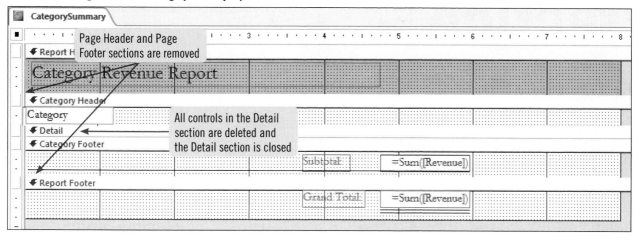

FIGURE H-19: Preview of the CategorySummary report

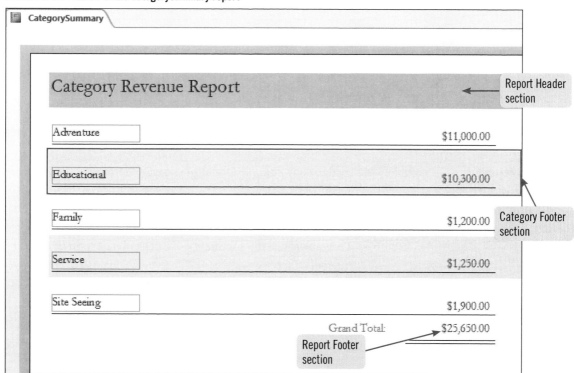

Practice

Concepts Review

Identify each element of Report Design View shown in FIGURE H-20.

FIGURE H-20

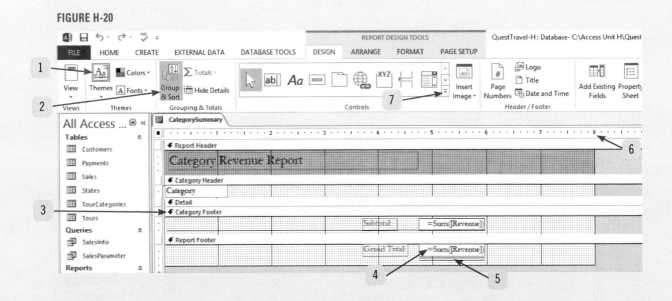

Match each term with the statement that best describes it.

8. **Summary report**
9. **Parameter report**
10. **Conditional formatting**
11. **Format Painter**
12. **Theme**

a. Used to copy multiple formatting properties from one control to another in Report Design View
b. Provides predefined formats that you apply to an entire form or report
c. Prompts the user for the criteria for selecting the records for the report
d. A way to change the appearance of a control on a form or report based on criteria you specify
e. Used to show statistics on groups of records

Select the best answer from the list of choices.

13. **Which control would you use to visually separate groups of records on a report?**
    a. Line
    b. Bound Object Frame
    c. Option group
    d. Image

14. **Which property would you use to force each group of records to print at the top of the next page?**
    a. Paginate
    b. Calculate
    c. Display When
    d. Force New Page

15. **What feature allows you to apply the formatting characteristics of one control to another?**
    a. Theme
    b. AutoContent Wizard
    c. Report Layout Wizard
    d. Format Painter

16. **Which key do you press when creating a line to make it perfectly horizontal?**
    a. [Ctrl]
    b. [Alt]
    c. [Shift]
    d. [Home]

17. **Which feature allows you to apply the same formatting characteristics to all the controls in a report at once?**
    a. Format Wizard
    b. AutoPainting
    c. Themes
    d. Palletizing

18. **In a report, an expression used to calculate values is entered in which type of control?**
    a. Text Box
    b. Label
    c. Combo Box
    d. Command Button

19. **Which section most often contains calculations for groups of records?**
    a. Page Header
    b. Detail
    c. Page Footer
    d. Group Footer

20. **Which control would you use to combine two reports?**
    a. Subreport
    b. List Box
    c. Combo Box
    d. Group & Sort Control

Skills Review

1. Use Report Design View.

a. Open the RealEstate-H.accdb database from the location where you store your Data Files and enable content if prompted.

b. Open the RealtorList query, and then change the RLast value for Sara Johnson to *your* last name. Close the query.

c. Create a new report in Report Design View based on the RealtorList query.

d. Select AgencyName as a grouping field and RLast as a sort field.

e. Add the AgencyName field to the AgencyName Header. Delete the accompanying AgencyName label, position the AgencyName text box on the left side of the AgencyName Header, then resize it to be about 3" wide.

f. Add the RealtorNo, RFirst, RLast, and RPhone fields to the Detail section. Delete all labels and position the text boxes horizontally across the top of the Detail section.

g. Drag the top edge of the Page Footer section up to remove the blank space in the Detail section.

h. Save the report with the name **RealtorList**, then preview it, as shown in FIGURE H-21. The width and spacing of the controls in your report may differ. Use Layout View to resize each control so it is wide enough to view all data.

i. Save and close the RealtorList report.

FIGURE H-21

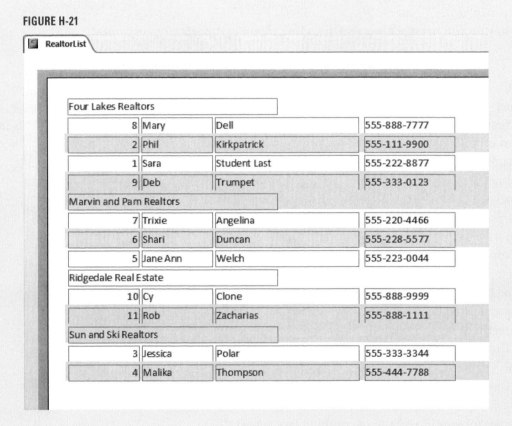

2. Create parameter reports.

a. Create a query in Query Design View, including the RFirst, RLast, and RPhone fields from the Realtors table. Include the Type, Area, SqFt, and Asking fields from the Listings table.

b. In the Asking field, include the following parameter criteria: **<[Enter maximum asking price]**.

Skills Review (continued)

   c. Test the query by switching to Datasheet View, enter **200,000** in the Enter maximum asking price box, then click OK. The query should display 21 records, all with an AskingPrice of less than $200,000. Save the query as **AskingParameter**, then close it.

   d. Click the AskingParameter query in the Navigation Pane, then click Report on the CREATE tab. Enter **250,000** in the Enter maximum asking price box, then click OK.

   e. Work in Layout View to narrow each column to be only as wide as necessary and to fit all columns across a single sheet of paper in portrait orientation.

   f. In Report Design View, add a label with *your* name to the Report Header section.

   g. In Report Design View, drag the right edge of the report to the left to make sure the report is no wider than 8 inches. This may include moving controls in the Page Footer or Report Footer to the left as well.

   h. Preview the report again to make sure it is not too wide to fit on the paper, enter **250,000** in the prompt, then print the report if requested by your instructor.

   i. Save the report with the name **AskingParameter**, then close it.

3. Apply conditional formatting.

   a. Open the AskingParameter report in Report Design View, click the Asking text box, then open the Conditional Formatting Rules Manager dialog box.

   b. Add a rule to format all Asking field values between **0** and **99999** with a light green background color.

   c. Add a rule to format all Asking field values between **100000** and **199999** with a yellow background color.

   d. Add a rule to format all Asking field values greater than or equal to **200000** with a red background color.

   e. Test the report in Print Preview, entering a value of **400,000** when prompted.

4. Add lines.

   a. Open the AskingParameter report in Design View, then use the Group, Sort, and Total pane to add a sort order. Sort the fields in descending (largest to smallest) order on the Asking field.

   b. Add a label to the Report Footer section directly to the left of the =Sum([Asking]) text box. Enter **Grand Total:** as the label text.

   c. Expand the vertical size of the Report Footer section to about twice its current height and resize the =Sum([Asking]) text box in the Report Footer to better read the contents.

   d. Draw two short horizontal lines just below the =Sum([Asking]) calculation in the Report Footer section to indicate a grand total.

   e. Save the report, then switch to Print Preview to review the changes using a value of **150,000** when prompted.

5. Use the Format Painter and themes.

   a. Open the AskingParameter report in Layout View.

   b. Change the AskingParameter label in the Report Header section to **Asking Price Analysis**.

   c. Apply the Retrospect theme. Review and resize the columns and the calculated field in the Report Footer to see all data as needed.

   d. Change the font color of the RFirst label in the Page Header section to Automatic (black).

   e. Use the Format Painter to copy the format from the RFirst label to the RLast, RPhone, Type, and Area labels in the Page Header section.

   f. Change the font color of the SqFt label in the Page Header section to red.

   g. Use the Format Painter to copy the format from the SqFt label to the Asking label.

   h. Save and close the AskingParameter report.

Skills Review (continued)

6. **Add subreports.**

   a. Open the ListingReport in Layout View, and resize any text boxes that are not wide enough to show all data. Be careful to not extend the right edge of the report beyond one sheet of paper. Resize and align the SqFt, LakeFt, and BR labels to better fit above the columns of data they describe.

   b. Open the RealtorList report in Layout View, and resize any text boxes that are not wide enough to show all data. Again be careful to not extend the right edge of the report beyond one sheet of paper. Save and close the RealtorList report.

   c. Display the ListingReport in Design View. Expand the Report Footer section, and add the RealtorList report as a subreport using the SubReport Wizard. Choose None when asked to link the main form to the subform (you may have to scroll), and accept the default name of RealtorList.

   d. Delete the extra RealtorList label in the Report Footer. (*Hint*: It will be positioned near the upper-left corner of the subreport, but it may be mostly hidden by the subreport.)

   e. Preview each page of the report to make sure all data is clearly visible. Widen any controls that do not clearly display information, again being careful not to extend the report beyond the right margin.

   f. Narrow the width of the report if necessary in Report Design View, then save and close it.

7. **Modify section properties.**

   a. In Report Design View of the ListingReport, modify the Realtors.RealtorNo Footer section's Force New Page property to After Section. (*Note*: The RealtorNo field is included in two tables, Realtors and Listings. Access uses the *tablename.fieldname* convention to specify that the RealtorNo grouping field is from the Realtors table.)

   b. Open the Page Footer section, and add a label, **Created by *Your* Name**.

   c. Save and preview the ListingReport to make sure that the new section property forces each new realtor group of records to print on its own page, as shown in **FIGURE H-22**. Also check that a label identifying you as the report creator appears at the bottom of each page. Remember that you must print preview the report (rather than display it in Report View) to see how the report prints on each page.

   d. Print the report if requested by your instructor, then save and close the report.

FIGURE H-22

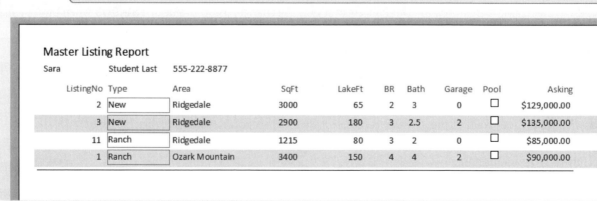

ListingReport										

Master Listing Report

Sara   Student Last   555-222-8877

ListingNo	Type	Area	SqFt	LakeFt	BR	Bath	Garage	Pool	Asking
2	New	Ridgedale	3000	65	2	3	0	☐	$129,000.00
3	New	Ridgedale	2900	180	3	2.5	2	☐	$135,000.00
11	Ranch	Ridgedale	1215	80	3	2	0	☐	$85,000.00
1	Ranch	Ozark Mountain	3400	150	4	4	2	☐	$90,000.00

Skills Review (continued)

8. Create summary reports.

a. Right-click the ListingReport, click Copy, right-click the Navigation Pane, click Paste, then type **ListingSummary**.

b. Open the ListingSummary report in Design View, then delete the subreport from the Report Footer, all the controls in the Detail section, and all the labels in the Realtors.RealtorNo Header section. (*Note:* Be careful not to delete the three text boxes for RFirst, RLast, and RPhone in the Realtors.RealtorNo Header section.)

c. Close the extra space in the Detail and Realtors.RealtorNo Header sections.

d. Expand the size of the Realtors.RealtorNo Footer section, move the line to the bottom of that section, then add a text box to the right side of the section with the following expression: **=Sum([Asking])**.

e. Modify the new label to read **Subtotal of Asking Price:**, then move and resize the controls as needed so that both the label and text box can be clearly read in Report Design View.

f. Open the Property Sheet for the =Sum([Asking]) text box, click the Format tab, then choose **Currency** for the Format property, and **0** for the Decimal Places property.

g. Copy the =Sum([Asking]) text box to the Report Footer section, move it directly under the =Sum([Asking]) text box in the Realtors.RealtorNo Footer section, then change the label to be **Grand Total:**.

h. Draw two short lines under the =Sum([Asking]) text box in the Report Footer section to indicate a grand total.

i. Change the Force New Page property of the Realtors.RealtorNo Footer section to None.

j. Position all controls within the 8" mark on the ruler so that the width of the paper is no wider than 8". Drag the right edge of the report as far to the left as possible so that it does not extend beyond 8".

k. Preview the report. Switch to Portrait orientation, and resize sections and move controls in Design View so the report matches FIGURE H-23. Print the report if requested by your instructor, then save and close the report.

l. Close the RealEstate-H.accdb database, and exit Access.

FIGURE H-23

Master Listing Report				
Sara	Student Last	555-222-8877		
			Subtotal of Asking Price:	$439,000
Phil	Kirkpatrick	555-111-9900		
			Subtotal of Asking Price:	$1,158,613
Jessica	Polar	555-333-3344		
			Subtotal of Asking Price:	$584,350
Malika	Thompson	555-444-7788		
			Subtotal of Asking Price:	$1,045,000
Jane Ann	Welch	555-223-0044		
			Subtotal of Asking Price:	$252,800
Shari	Duncan	555-228-5577		
			Subtotal of Asking Price:	$120,000
Trixie	Angelina	555-220-4466		
			Subtotal of Asking Price:	$105,000
Mary	Dell	555-888-7777		
			Subtotal of Asking Price:	$761,899
			Grand Total:	$4,466,662

Independent Challenge 1

As the manager of a music store's instrument rental program, you created a database to track instrument rentals to school-children. Now that several instruments have been rented, you need to create a report listing the rental transactions for each instrument.

a. Start Access, open the MusicStore-H.accdb database from the location where you store your Data Files, and enable content if prompted.

b. Use the Report Wizard to create a report based on the FirstName and LastName fields in the Customers table, the RentalDate field from the Rentals table, and the Description and MonthlyFee fields from the Instruments table.

c. View the data by Instruments, do not add any more grouping levels, sort the data in ascending order by RentalDate, use a Stepped layout and Portrait orientation, and title the report **Instrument Rental Report**.

d. Open the report in Design View, change the first grouping level from SerialNo to Description so that all instruments with the same description are grouped together, and open the Description Footer section.

e. Add a new text box to the Description Footer section with the expression **=Count([LastName])**. Change the label to **Customers:**.

f. Change the Force New Page property of the Description Footer section to After Section.

g. Add *your* name as a label to the Report Header section, and use the Format Painter to copy the formatting from the Instrument Rental Report label to your name. Double-click a corner sizing handle of the label with your name to resize it to show your entire name.

h. Save and preview the report, as shown in FIGURE H-24. Move, resize, and align controls as needed to match the figure, make sure all controls fit within the margins of one sheet of paper, then print the report if requested by your instructor.

i. Save and close the Instrument Rental Report, close the MusicStore-H.accdb database, then exit Access.

FIGURE H-24

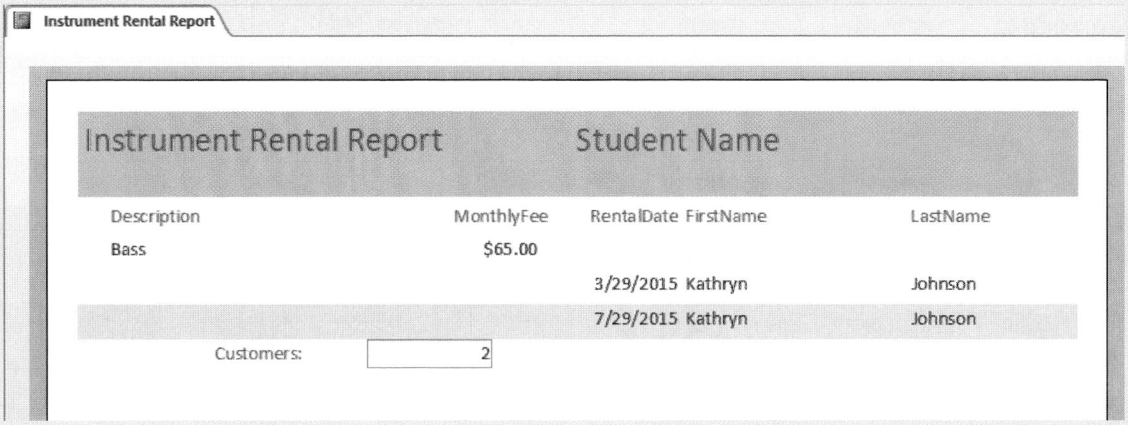

| Instrument Rental Report | | | | | |

Instrument Rental Report			Student Name		
Description		MonthlyFee	RentalDate	FirstName	LastName
Bass		$65.00			
			3/29/2015	Kathryn	Johnson
			7/29/2015	Kathryn	Johnson
	Customers:	2			

Independent Challenge 2

As the manager of a music store's instrument rental program, you have created a database to track instrument rentals to schoolchildren. Now that the rental program is under way, you need to create a summary report that shows how many instruments have been rented by each school.

a. Start Access, open the MusicStore-H.accdb database from the location where you store your Data Files, and enable content if prompted.

b. Build a query in Query Design View with the following fields: SchoolName from the Schools table and RentalDate from the Rentals table. (*Hint*: Include the Customers table to build the proper relationships between the Schools and the Rentals table.) Save the query with the name **SchoolSummary**, then close it.

c. Create a new report in Report Design View. Use the SchoolSummary query as the Record Source property.

d. Add SchoolName as a grouping field, and add the SchoolName field to the left side of the SchoolName Header section. Delete the SchoolName label, and widen the SchoolName text box to about 4".

e. Drag the top edge of the Page Footer section up to completely close the Detail section.

f. Add a label to the Page Header section with *your* name. Format the label with an Arial Black font and 14-point font size. Resize the label to display all the text.

g. Add a label to the Report Header section that reads **New student musicians per school**.

h. Add a text box to the right side of the SchoolName Header section with the expression **=Count([RentalDate])**. Delete the accompanying label.

i. Align the top edges of the two text boxes in the SchoolName Header.

j. Use the Format Painter to copy the formatting from the label with your name to the new label in the Report Header section, the SchoolName text box, and the =Count([RentalDate]) expression in the SchoolName Header section. Switch back and forth between Print Preview and Design View to resize the text boxes in the SchoolName Header section as needed to show all information in each box.

k. Open the Report Footer section, then copy and paste the =Count([RentalDate]) text box to the same position in the Report Footer section.

l. Add one short line above and two short lines below the =Count([RentalDate]) text box in the Report Footer section to indicate a subtotal and grand total.

m. Save the report with the name **SchoolSummary**, then preview it, as shown in FIGURE H-25.

n. Close the SchoolSummary report, close the MusicStore-H.accdb database, then exit Access.

FIGURE H-25

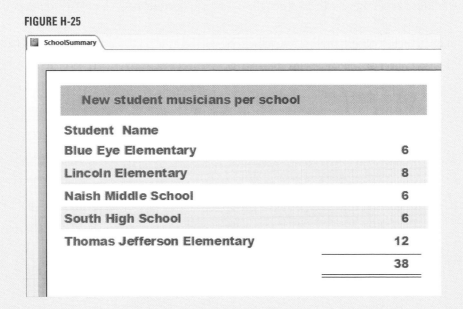

Independent Challenge 3

As the manager of a music store's instrument rental program, you have created a database to track instrument rentals to schoolchildren. Now that the rental program is under way, you need to create a parameter report for each instrument type.

a. Start Access, open the MusicStore-H.accdb database from the location where you store your Data Files, and enable content if prompted.

b. Create a query with the RentalDate field from the Rentals table, the Description and MonthlyFee fields from the Instruments table, and the FirstName and LastName fields from the Customers table.

c. Enter the parameter criteria **Between [Enter start date] And [Enter end date]** for the RentalDate field and **[Enter instrument type such as cello]** for the Description field.

d. Save the query with the name **RentalParameter**, test it with the dates **3/1/15** and **3/31/15** and the type **bass**. These criteria should select one record. Close the RentalParameter query.

e. Use the Report Wizard to create a report on all fields in the RentalParameter query. View the data by Instruments, do not add any more grouping levels, sort the records in ascending order by RentalDate, and use an Outline layout and a Portrait orientation. Title the report **Instrument Lookup**.

f. To respond to the prompts, enter **1/1/15** for the start date and **6/30/15** for the end date. Enter **viola** for the instrument type prompt.

g. In Report Design View, apply the Ion Boardroom theme. Resize the report title in the Report Header to display all the text.

h. Add *your* name as a label to the Report Header section. Change the font color to black so that it is clearly visible.

i. Add spaces between all words in the labels in the Description Header section: MonthlyFee, RentalDate, FirstName, and LastName to change them to **Monthly Fee**, **Rental Date**, **First Name**, and **Last Name**. Be sure to change the *labels* control and not the *text box* controls.

j. Open the Description Footer section.

k. Add a text box to the Description Footer section that contains the expression **=Count([LastName])*[MonthlyFee]**. Change the accompanying label to read **Monthly Revenue:**, then move the text box with the expression below the LastName text box and resize both so that their contents are clearly visible.

l. Open the Property Sheet for the new expression. On the Format tab, change the Format property to **Currency** and the Decimal Places property to **0**.

m. Display the report for RentalDates **1/1/15** through **3/31/15**, instrument type **cello**. Your report should look like **FIGURE H-26**.

n. Save the Instrument Lookup report, print it if requested by your instructor, close the MusicStore-H.accdb database, then exit Access.

FIGURE H-26

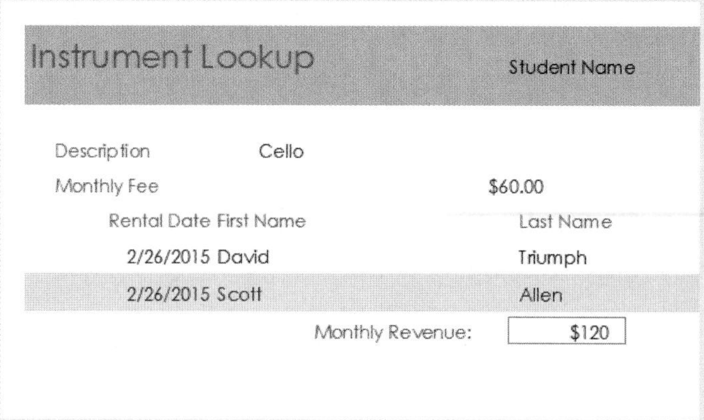

Independent Challenge 4: Explore

You have created an Access database to help manage college scholarship opportunities. You analyze scholarships by building a report with conditional formatting.

a. Start Access and open the Scholarships-H.accdb database from the location where you store your Data Files. Enable content if prompted.

b. Use the Report Wizard to create a report based on the Scholarships table. Include all of the fields. Add Major then Amount as the grouping levels, then click the Grouping Options button in the Report Wizard. Choose 5000s as the Grouping interval for the Amount field. Sort the records by DueDate in a descending order. Use a Stepped layout and a Landscape orientation. Title the report **Scholarships By Major**.

c. Preview the report, then add *your* name as a label next to the report title.

d. In Layout View, add spaces to the DueDate and ScholarshipName labels to read **Due Date** and **Scholarship Name**.

e. Delete the ID column.

f. Resize and narrow the columns to fit on a single sheet of landscape paper, then drag the right edge of the report to the left in Report Design View to make sure it is within the 10.5" mark on the horizontal ruler.

g. Expand the Page Header section to about twice its height, move the labels in the Page Header section to the bottom of the Page Header section, move the labels from the Report Header section to the top of the Page Header section, then close up the Report Header section.

h. Open the Major Footer section, then change the Force New Page property of the Major Footer section to After Section.

i. Click the Amount text box in the Detail section, then apply a new rule of conditional formatting. Use the Compare to other records rule type, and change the Bar color to green.

j. Preview page 3 of the report for the Business majors, as shown in **FIGURE H-27**.

k. Save and close the Scholarships By Major report and the Scholarships-H.accdb database.

FIGURE H-27

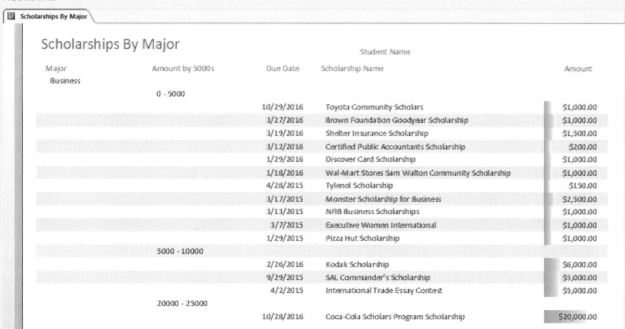

Visual Workshop

Open the Baseball-H.accdb database from the location where you store your Data Files and enable content if prompted. Using the Report Wizard, build a report on the PlayerLName field from the Players table, and the AtBats and Hits fields from the Player Stats table. View the data by Players, do not add any more grouping or sorting fields, and use a Stepped layout and Portrait orientation. Enter **Batting Average** as the name of the report. In Report Design View, open the PlayerNo Footer section and move the PlayerLName text box to the same position in the PlayerNo Footer section. Add new text boxes to the PlayerNo Footer section to sum the AtBats, sum the Hits, and calculate the overall batting average per player. The expression to find the batting average is **=Sum([Hits])/Sum([AtBats])**. Delete any extra labels that are created when you add the text boxes, and delete all of the controls in the Detail section. Close the PlayerNo Header and Detail sections and resize the PlayerNo Footer section to remove blank space. Modify the Decimal Places property of the batting average calculation to show **3** digits to the right of the decimal point, and modify the Format property to be Standard. Apply a conditional format to the batting average expression so that if it is greater than or equal to **0.5**, the background color is yellow. Add a label to the Page Header section to identify the batting average, add a label to the Report Header section with *your* name, and then edit the labels and align the controls, as shown in **FIGURE H-28**. As a final step, change the Group on field from PlayerNo to PlayerLName so the records are sorted by player last name, as shown in **FIGURE H-28**. Save the Batting Average report, print the report if requested by your instructor, and then close it.

FIGURE H-28

Batting Average			
Batting Average		Student Name	
PlayerLName	AtBats	Hits	Batting Average
Arno	6	2	0.333
Campanella	8	5	0.625
Dean	8	3	0.375
Douglas	8	8	1.000
Friedrichsen	6	3	0.500
Hammer	8	4	0.500
Kelsey	8	4	0.500
Langguth	8	4	0.500
Mantle	8	2	0.250

Importing and Exporting Data

CASE ▶ At Quest Specialty Travel, Jacob Thomas, director of staff development, has asked you to develop an Access database that tracks professional staff continuing education. First, you will explore the Access templates for creating a new database. Then, you will work with Access tools that allow you to share Access data with other software programs so that each Quest department can have the necessary data in a format they can use.

Unit Objectives

After completing this unit, you will be able to:

- Use database templates
- Use Application Parts
- Import data from Excel
- Link data

- Export data to Excel
- Publish data to Word
- Merge data with Word
- Export data to PDF

Files You Will Need

Education-I.accdb
DepartmentData.xlsx
CourseMaterials.xlsx
Machinery-I.accdb
MachineryEmp.xlsx

Vendors.xlsx
Basketball-I.accdb
2015-2016Schedule.xlsx
Languages-I.accdb

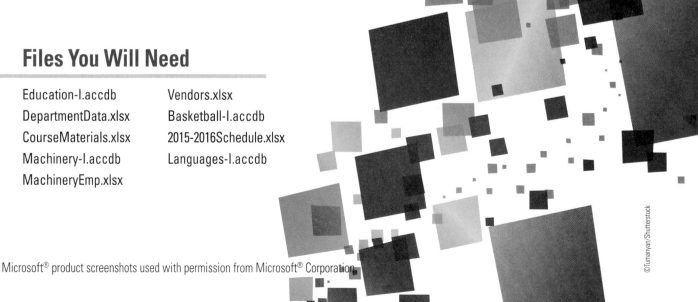

© Tumanyan/Shutterstock

Use Database Templates

Learning
Outcomes
• Create a database
  from a template
• Set a startup form

A **database template** is a tool that you use to quickly create a new database based on a particular subject, such as assets, contacts, events, or projects. When you install Access 2013 on your computer, Microsoft provides many database templates for you to use. Additional templates are available from Microsoft Office Online, where they are organized by category, such as business, personal, and education. **CASE** *Jacob Thomas, director of staff development, asks you to develop a new Access database to track the continuing education of Quest employees. You explore Microsoft database templates to fill this request.*

STEPS

QUICK TIP
Database templates are also called database wizards.

1. **Start Access 2013**

   As shown in **FIGURE I-1**, Microsoft provides many Web and desktop database templates to help you create a new database. A custom **Web app** is an Access database that you publish to a Web server so that it is available to users who work with a browser over the Internet. Web apps will be covered in Unit P.

   A **desktop database** is a traditional Access database available to users who work with Access on their computers over a local area network and is identified by the word *desktop* in the template name. All templates are **online**, meaning they are available to download from the Microsoft Office Online Web site. Templates change over time as more are added and enhancements to existing templates are provided by Microsoft. The database you want to create should track employees and the continuing education courses they have completed, so you search for database templates using Education as the search phrase.

QUICK TIP
To review the video later, open the Getting Started form.

2. **Click the** Search for online templates box, **type** education, **click the** Start searching **button** 🔍, **then double-click the** Desktop student database

   The Desktop student database template builds a new database that includes several sample tables, queries, forms, reports, macros, and a module object. You can use or modify these objects to meet your needs.

QUICK TIP
When using a template, the database is created in the default file location shown in the title bar.

3. **Click the** Enable Content button **(if it is presented), then close the** Getting Started window **to explore the actual database, as shown in** FIGURE I-2

   The Student List form opens automatically, and the other objects in the database are presented in the Navigation Pane.

4. **Right-click the** Student List form tab, **click** Close, **then double-click the** Student Details form **in the Navigation Pane**

   Objects created by database templates are rich in functionality and can be modified for your specific needs or analyzed to learn more about Access.

5. **Close the Student Details form, then double-click the** Guardian Details form **to open it**

   If you wanted to use this database, your next step would be to enter data and continue exploring the other objects in the database.

6. **Close the Guardian Details form, then open, explore, and close the other objects of the** Desktop student database

   Because this database is designed for a traditional school rather than a corporate educational environment, you won't be using it at Quest. However, you can still learn a great deal by exploring the objects that the template created. You will also keep using this sample database to learn about Application Parts.

FIGURE I-1: Creating a database from a template

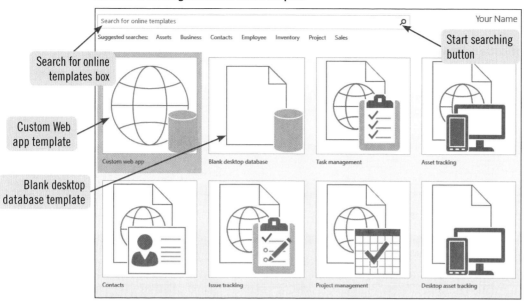

FIGURE I-2: Desktop student database template

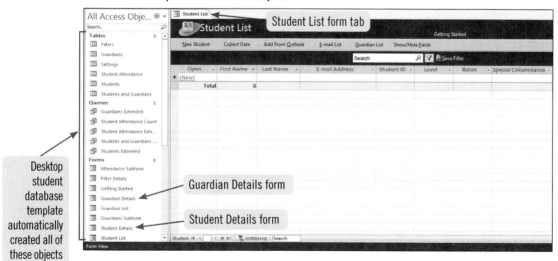

Setting a startup form

To specify that a particular form automatically opens when the database opens, click the FILE tab, click Options, then click the Current Database category in the Access Options dialog box. Use the Display Form drop-down list to specify which form should automatically open when the database is started. Another way to set startup options is to create an AutoExec macro. Macros will be covered in Unit M.

Use Application Parts

Learning Outcomes
• Create objects from Application Parts
• Describe referential integrity options

Application Parts are object templates that create objects such as tables and forms. Application Parts include several table, form, and report templates, tools you can use to quickly create these individual objects within an existing database. As with database templates, Microsoft is constantly updating and improving this part of Access. **CASE** ▶ *You continue your study of templates by exploring the Access 2013 Application Parts in the new database.*

STEPS

1. **Click the CREATE tab, then click the Application Parts button, as shown in FIGURE I-3, click Contacts, click the There is no relationship option button, click Create, then close the Getting Started window**

   The Contacts Application Part created a new table named Contacts; a new query named ContactsExtended; three new forms named ContactDetails, ContactDS, and ContactList; and four new reports named ContactAddressBook, ContactList, ContactPhoneBook, and Label that you can modify and relate to the other tables in the database as needed.

   Anytime you create a database or objects using Access templates, it's a good practice to check the Relationships window to make sure the objects are related correctly and that you understand the relationships.

2. **Close the Student List form, click the DATABASE TOOLS tab, then click the Relationships button**

   The Desktop student database template did not create relationships between the tables. You'll connect four of the main tables.

3. **Double-click Guardians, Students and Guardians, Students, and Student Attendance; click Close; then resize the Guardians and Students field lists to view as many fields as possible**

   With the four field lists for the main tables in the database positioned in the Relationships window so that you can see nearly all of the fields, you will build the one-to-many relationships between the tables.

4. **Drag the ID field from the Guardians table to the GuardianID field in the Students and Guardians table, click the Enforce Referential Integrity check box, then click Create**

5. **Create the other two relationships, as shown in FIGURE I-4**

   Note that in this database, the linking fields do not have the same name in both the "one" and "many" tables. Also recall that referential integrity helps prevent orphan records—records in the "many" table that don't have a matching record in the "one" table.

6. **Save and close the Relationships window, click the FILE tab, click Save As, click the Save As button, navigate to the location where you store your Data Files, enter Students as the filename, click Save, then close the Getting Started dialog box and exit Access 2013**

   Access database templates and Application Parts provide powerful tools to build databases and objects quickly. Templates are also an exciting way to learn more about Access features and possibilities.

FIGURE I-3: Application Parts list

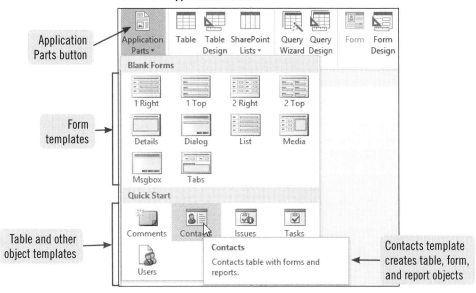

Application Parts button

Form templates

Table and other object templates

Contacts template creates table, form, and report objects

FIGURE I-4: Major relationships for the Students database

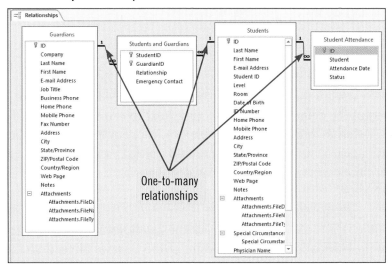

One-to-many relationships

Referential integrity cascade options

When connecting tables in one-to-many relationships, apply referential integrity whenever possible. This feature prevents orphan records from being created in the database and lets you select cascade options. **Cascade Update Related Fields** means that if a value in the primary key field (the field on the "one" side of a one-to-many relationship) is modified, all values in the foreign key field (the field on the "many" side of a one-to-many relationship) are automatically updated as well.

Cascade Delete Related Records means that if a record on the "one" side of a one-to-many relationship is deleted, all related records in the "many" table are also deleted. Because both of these options automatically change or delete data in the "many" table behind the scenes, they should be used carefully. Often these features are not employed as standard options, but are used temporarily to correct a problem in the database.

Import Data from Excel

Learning
Outcomes
• Import data
  from Excel
• Describe other data
  import options

Access can share data with many other Microsoft Office programs. **Importing** enables you to quickly copy data from an external file into an Access database. You can import data from many sources, such as another Access database; Excel spreadsheet; SharePoint site; Outlook email; or text files in an HTML, XML, or delimited text file format. A **delimited text file** stores one record on each line. Field values are separated by a common character, the **delimiter**, such as a comma, tab, or dash. A **CSV (comma-separated value)** file is a common example of a delimited text file. An **XML file** is a text file containing **Extensible Markup Language (XML)** tags that identify field names and data. One of the most common file formats from which to import data into an Access database is **Microsoft Excel**, the spreadsheet program in the Microsoft Office suite. **CASE** *Jacob Thomas gives you an Excel spreadsheet that contains a list of supplemental materials used for various courses, and asks you to import the information in the new internal training database.*

STEPS

1. **Start Access, open the Education-I.accdb database from the location where you store your Data Files, enable content if prompted, click the EXTERNAL DATA tab, click the Excel button in the Import & Link group, click the Browse button, navigate to the location where you store your Data Files, then double-click CourseMaterials.xlsx**

   The **Get External Data - Excel Spreadsheet** dialog box opens. You can import the records, **append** the records (add the records to an existing table), or link to the data source. In this case, you want to import the records into a new table.

2. **Click OK**

   The **Import Spreadsheet Wizard** helps you import data from Excel into Access and presents a sample of the data to be imported, as shown in **FIGURE I-5**.

3. **Click Next, click the First Row Contains Column Headings check box, click Next, click Next to accept the default field options, click Next to allow Access to add a primary key field, type Materials in the Import to Table box, click Finish, then click Close**

   To save the import steps so that they can be easily repeated, click the Save import steps check box on the last step of the import process. You run a saved import process by clicking the **Saved Imports** button on the EXTERNAL DATA tab.

   One record in the Courses table can be related to many records in the Materials table.

4. **Click the DATABASE TOOLS tab, click the Relationships button, drag the Materials table from the Navigation Pane to the right of the Courses table, drag the CourseID field in the Courses table to the CourseID field in the Materials table, click the Enforce Referential Integrity check box, then click Create**

   The final Relationships window is shown in **FIGURE I-6**. One employee record is related to many enrollments. One course record is related to many enrollments and to many materials.

5. **Click the Close button, then click Yes to save the changes to the database relationships**

Importing from another database

If you import from an Access database using the Access button on the EXTERNAL DATA tab, you are presented with a dialog box that allows you to import selected objects from the database. This provides an excellent way to develop new queries, forms, and reports in an external "development" database, and then import them into the "production" database only after they have been fully developed and tested.

FIGURE I-5: Import Spreadsheet Wizard

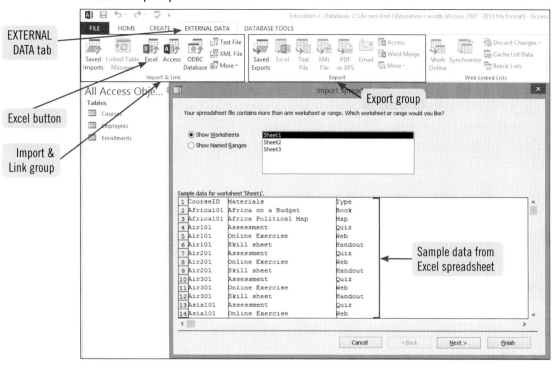

FIGURE I-6: Relationships window with imported Materials table

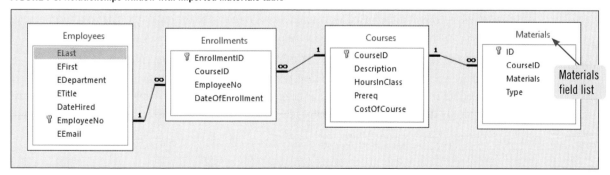

Link Data

Learning
Outcomes
• Link data from
  Excel
• Describe linking
  versus importing

Linking connects an Access database to data in an external file such as another Access database, Excel spreadsheet, text file, HTML file, XML file, or other data sources that support **ODBC (Open Database Connectivity)** standards. Linking is different from importing in that linked data is not copied into the database. If you link, data is only stored and updated in the original file. Importing, in contrast, makes a copy of the data in the Access database. **CASE** *Jacob Thomas has created a small spreadsheet with information about the departments at Quest. He wants to use the information in the Education-I database while maintaining it in Excel. He asks you to help create a link to this Excel file from the Education-I database.*

STEPS

1. **Click the EXTERNAL DATA tab, then click the Excel button in the Import & Link group**

   The Get External Data - Excel Spreadsheet dialog box opens. This dialog box allows you to choose whether you want to import, append, or link to the data source.

2. **Click Browse, navigate to the location where you store your Data Files, double-click DepartmentData.xlsx, click the Link to the data source by creating a linked table option button, as shown in FIGURE I-7, click OK, click Next to accept the default range selection, click Next to accept the default column headings, type Departments as the linked table name, click Finish, then click OK**

   The **Link Spreadsheet Wizard** guides you through the process of linking to a spreadsheet. The linked Departments table appears in the Navigation Pane with a linking Excel icon, as shown in **FIGURE I-8**. Like any other table, in order for the linked table to work with the rest of a database, a one-to-many relationship between it and another table should be created.

3. **Click the DATABASE TOOLS tab, click the Relationships button, drag the Departments table from the Navigation Pane to the left of the Employees table, then drag a border of the Departments table to display all fields**

   The Dept field in the Departments table is used to create a one-to-many relationship with the EDepartment field in the Employees table. One department may be related to many employees.

4. **Drag the Dept field in the Departments table to the EDepartment field in the Employees table, then click Create in the Edit Relationships dialog box**

   Your Relationships window should look like **FIGURE I-9**. A one-to-many relationship is established between the Departments and Employees tables, but because referential integrity is not enforced, the one and many symbols do not appear on the link line. You cannot establish referential integrity when one of the tables is a linked table. Now that the linked Departments table is related to the rest of the database, it can participate in queries, forms, and reports that select fields from multiple tables.

5. **Click the Close button, then click Yes when prompted to save changes**

   You work with a linked table just as you work with any other table. The data in a linked table can be edited through either the source program (in this case, Excel) or in the Access database, even though the data is only physically stored in the original source file.

FIGURE I-7: Get External Data - Excel Spreadsheet dialog box

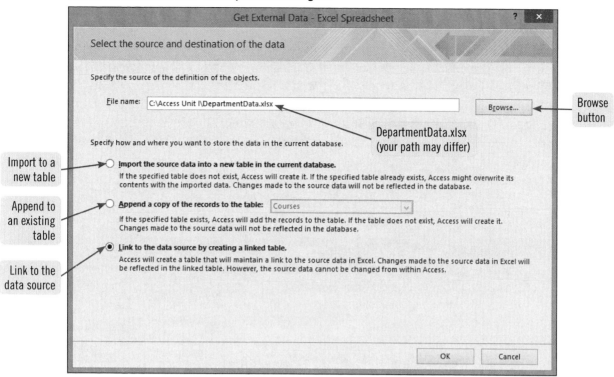

Import to a new table

Append to an existing table

Link to the data source

DepartmentData.xlsx (your path may differ)

Browse button

FIGURE I-8: Departments table is linked from Excel

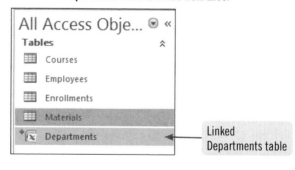

Linked Departments table

FIGURE I-9: Relationships window with linked Departments table

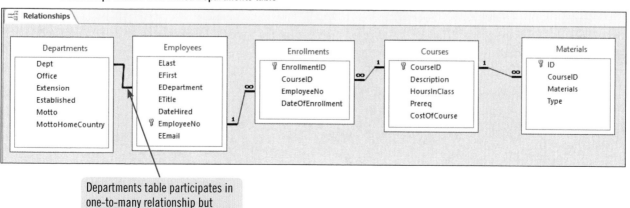

Departments table participates in one-to-many relationship but referential integrity is not enforced

Access 2013

Export Data to Excel

Learning
Outcomes
• Export data to
  Excel
• Describe other data
  export options

Exporting is a way to copy Access information to another database, spreadsheet, or file format. Exporting is the opposite of importing. You can export data from an Access database to other file types, such as those used by Excel or Word, and in several general file formats, including text, HTML, and XML. Given the popularity of analyzing numeric data in Excel, it is common to export Access data to an Excel spread-sheet for further analysis. **CASE** ▶ *The Finance Department asks you to export some Access data to an Excel spreadsheet so the finance personnel can use Excel to analyze how increases in the cost of the courses would affect departments. You can gather the fields needed in an Access query, then export the query to an Excel spreadsheet.*

STEPS

1. **Click the CREATE tab, click the Query Design button, double-click Employees, double-click Enrollments, double-click Courses, then click Close**

   The fields you want to export to Excel—EDepartment and CostOfCourse—are in the Employees and Courses tables. You also need to include the Enrollments table in this query because it provides the connection between the Employees and Courses tables.

2. **Double-click EDepartment in the Employees field list, double-click CostOfCourse in the Courses field list, click the Sort cell for the EDepartment field, click the Sort cell list arrow, click Ascending, then click the View button ▦ to display the query datasheet**

   The resulting datasheet has 403 records. You want to summarize the costs by department before exporting this to Excel.

3. **Click the View button ◩ to return to Design View, click the Totals button in the Show/Hide group, click Group By for the CostOfCourse field, click the Group By list arrow, click Sum, click ▦ to display the query datasheet, then widen the SumOfCostOfCourse column, as shown in FIGURE I-10**

   Save the query with a meaningful name to prepare to export it to Excel.

4. **Click the Save button 🖫 on the Quick Access toolbar, type DepartmentCosts, click OK, right-click the DepartmentCosts tab, then click Close**

   Before you start an export process, be sure to select the object you want to export in the Navigation Pane.

5. **Click the DepartmentCosts query in the Navigation Pane, click the EXTERNAL DATA tab, click the Excel button in the Export group, click Browse, navigate to the location where you store your Data Files, click Save to accept the default filename, click OK, then click Close**

   The data in the DepartmentCosts query has now been exported to an Excel spreadsheet file named DepartmentCosts and saved in the location where you store your Data Files. As with imports, you can save and then repeat the export process by saving the export steps when prompted by the last dialog box in the Export Wizard. Run the saved export process using the **Saved Exports** button on the EXTERNAL DATA tab or by assigning the export process to an Outlook task.

   Access can work with data in a wide variety of file formats. Other file formats that Access can import from, link with, and export to are listed in **TABLE I-1**.

FIGURE I-10: New query selects and summarizes data to be exported to Excel

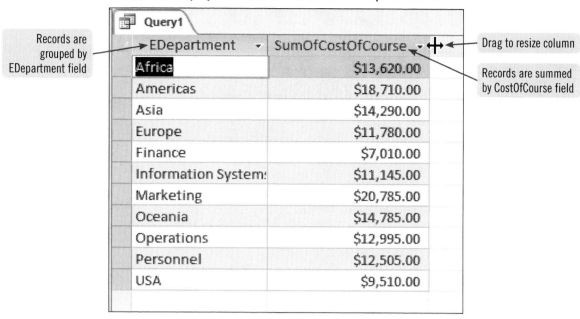

Records are grouped by EDepartment field

Drag to resize column

Records are summed by CostOfCourse field

EDepartment	SumOfCostOfCourse
Africa	$13,620.00
Americas	$18,710.00
Asia	$14,290.00
Europe	$11,780.00
Finance	$7,010.00
Information Systems	$11,145.00
Marketing	$20,785.00
Oceania	$14,785.00
Operations	$12,995.00
Personnel	$12,505.00
USA	$9,510.00

TABLE I-1: File formats that Access can link to, import, and export

file format	import	link	export
Access	•	•	•
Excel	•	•	•
Word			•
SharePoint site	•	•	•
Email file attachments			•
Outlook folder	•	•	
ODBC database (such as SQL Server)	•	•	•
dBASE	•	•	•
HTML document	•	•	•
PDF or XPS file			•
Text file (delimited or fixed width)	•	•	•
XML file	•		•

Publish Data to Word

Learning
Outcomes
• Export data to
  Word
• Describe techni-
  ques to share
  Access data

Microsoft Word, the word-processing program in the Microsoft Office suite, is a premier program for entering, editing, and formatting text. You can easily export data from an Access table, query, form, or report into a Word document. This is helpful when you want to use Word's superior text-editing features to combine the information in a Word document with Access data. **CASE** ▶ *You are asked to write a memo to the management committee describing departmental costs for continuing education. You export an Access query with this data to a Word document where you finish the memo.*

STEPS

1. **Click the DepartmentCosts query in the Navigation Pane, click the EXTERNAL DATA tab, click the More button in the Export group, click Word, click Browse, navigate to the location where you store your Data Files, click Save to accept the default filename DepartmentCosts.rtf, click OK, then click Close**

   The data in the DepartmentCosts query is exported as an **RTF (Rich Text Format)** file, which can be opened and edited in Word.

2. **Start Word, then open DepartmentCosts.rtf from the location where you store your Data Files**

   Currently, the document contains only a table of information, the data you exported from the DepartmentCosts query. Use Word to add the memo information.

3. **Press [Enter], then type the following text, pressing [Tab] after typing each colon**

To:	Management Committee
From:	*Your* Name
Re:	Analysis of Continuing Education Courses
Date:	*Today's date*

   The following information shows the overall cost for continuing education subtotaled by department. The information shows that the Americas and Marketing departments are the highest consumers of continuing education.

4. **Proofread your document, which should now look like FIGURE I-11, then preview and print it**

   The **word wrap** feature in Word determines when a line of text extends into the right margin of the page and automatically forces the text to the next line without you needing to press [Enter]. This allows you to enter and edit large paragraphs of text in Word very efficiently.

5. **Save and close the document, then exit Word**

   In addition to exporting data, **TABLE I-2** lists other techniques you can use to copy Access data to other applications.

FIGURE I-11: Word document with Access data

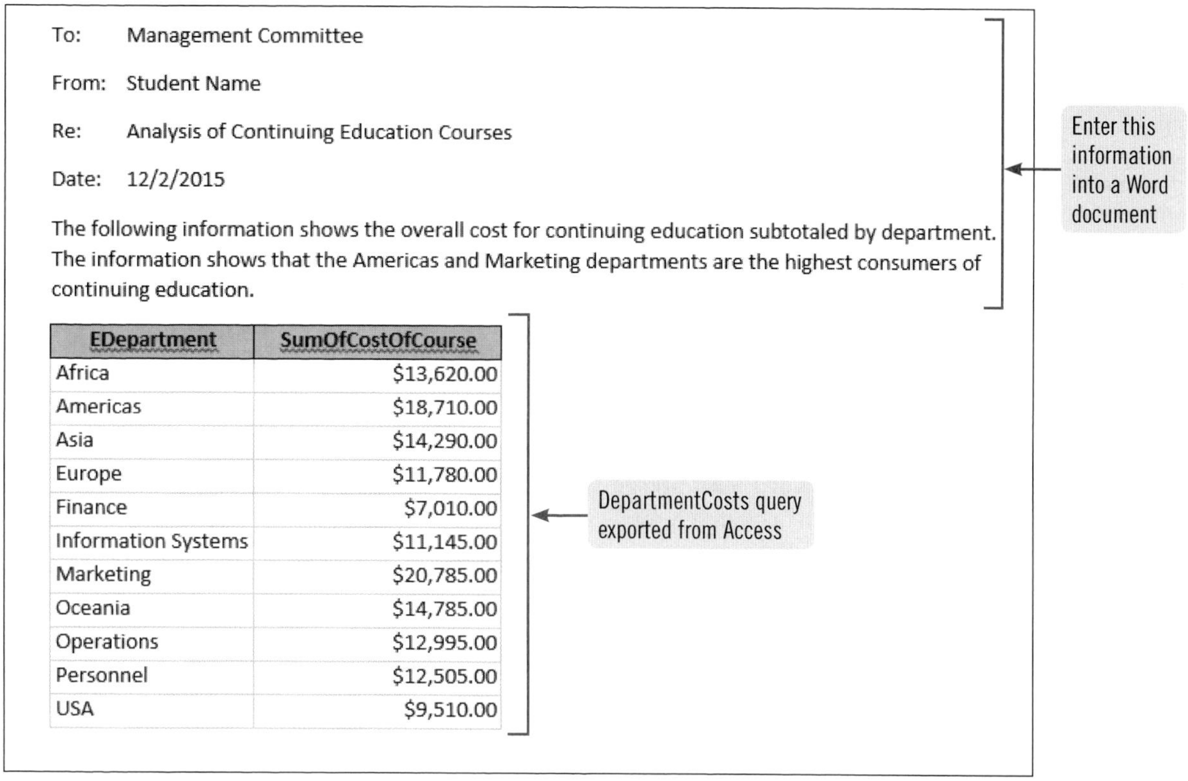

To: Management Committee

From: Student Name

Re: Analysis of Continuing Education Courses

Date: 12/2/2015

The following information shows the overall cost for continuing education subtotaled by department. The information shows that the Americas and Marketing departments are the highest consumers of continuing education.

EDepartment	SumOfCostOfCourse
Africa	$13,620.00
Americas	$18,710.00
Asia	$14,290.00
Europe	$11,780.00
Finance	$7,010.00
Information Systems	$11,145.00
Marketing	$20,785.00
Oceania	$14,785.00
Operations	$12,995.00
Personnel	$12,505.00
USA	$9,510.00

Enter this information into a Word document

DepartmentCosts query exported from Access

Access 2013

TABLE I-2: Techniques to copy Access data to other applications

technique	button or menu option	description
Drag and drop	Resize the Access window so that the target location (Word or Excel, for example) can also be seen on the screen	With both windows visible, drag the Access table, query, form, or report object icon from the Access window to the target (Excel or Word) window
Export	Use the buttons in the Export group on the EXTERNAL DATA tab	Copy information from an Access object into a different file format
Office Clipboard	Copy and Paste	Click the Copy button to copy selected data to the Office Clipboard (the Office Clipboard can hold multiple items); open a Word document or Excel spreadsheet, click where you want to paste the data, then click the Paste button

© 2014 Cengage Learning

Merge Data with Word

Learning Outcomes
- Merge data to a Word document
- Save a main document with merge fields

Another way to export Access data is to merge it to a Word document as the data source for a mail-merge process. In a **mail merge**, data from an Access table or query is combined into a Word form letter, label, or envelope to create mass mailing documents. **CASE** *Jacob Thomas wants to send Quest employees a letter announcing two new continuing education courses. You merge Access data to a Word document to customize a letter to each employee.*

STEPS

1. **Click the Employees table in the Navigation Pane, click the EXTERNAL DATA tab, then click the Word Merge button in the Export group**

   The **Microsoft Word Mail Merge Wizard** dialog box opens asking whether you want to link to an existing document or create a new one.

2. **Click the Create a new document and then link the data to it option button, click OK, then click the Word button on the taskbar**

   Word starts and opens the **Mail Merge task pane**, which steps you through the mail-merge process. Before you merge the Access data with the Word document, you must create the **main document**, the Word document that contains the standard text for each form letter.

   > **TROUBLE**
   > The "Next" links are at the bottom of the Mail Merge task pane.

3. **Type the standard text shown in FIGURE I-12, click the Next: Starting document link in the bottom of the Mail Merge task pane, click the Next: Select recipients link to use the current document, click the Next: Write your letter link to use the existing list of names, press [Tab] after To: in the letter, then click the Insert Merge Field arrow button in the Write & Insert Fields group on the MAILINGS tab**

   The Insert Merge Field drop-down list shows all of the fields in the original data source, the Employees table. You use this list to insert **merge fields**, codes that are replaced with the values in the field that the code represents when the mail merge is processed.

   > **TROUBLE**
   > You cannot type the merge codes directly into the document. You must use the Insert Merge Field button.

4. **Click EFirst, press [Spacebar], click the Insert Merge Field arrow button, click ELast, then click the Next: Preview your letters link**

   With the main document and merge fields inserted, you are ready to complete the mail merge.

5. **Click the Next: Complete the merge link as shown in FIGURE I-13, click the Edit individual letters link to view the letters on the screen, then click OK to complete the merge**

   The mail-merge process combines the EFirst and ELast field values from the Employees table with the main document, creating a 24-page document, as shown in the Word status bar. Each page is a customized letter for each record in the Employees table. The first page is a letter to Ron Dawson. "Ron" is the field value for the EFirst field in the first record in the Employees table, and "Dawson" is the field value for the ELast field.

   > **QUICK TIP**
   > The total number of pages in the document is displayed in the lower-left corner of the Word window.

6. **Press [Page Down] several times to view several pages of the final merged document, then close the merged document, Letters1, without saving it**

   You generally don't need to save the final, large merged document. Saving the one-page main document, however, is a good idea in case you need to repeat the merge process.

7. **Click the Save button 💾 on the Quick Access toolbar, navigate to the location where you store your Data Files, enter Employees in the File name text box, click Save, then close Word**

FIGURE I-12: Creating the main document in Word

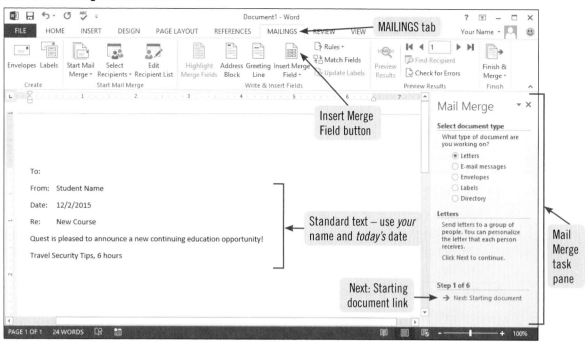

FIGURE I-13: Inserting merge fields

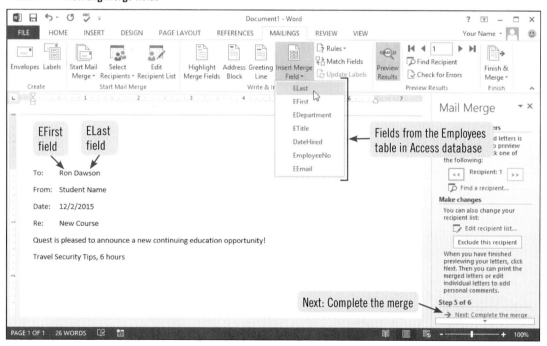

Export Data to PDF

Learning
Outcomes
• Publish data to PDF
• Export a report
as an email
attachment

Access data can be exported to a PDF document. **PDF** stands for **Portable Document Format**, a file format developed by Adobe that has become a standard format for exchanging documents. By sharing information in a PDF format, anyone can read the document using free **Adobe Reader software**, but they cannot edit or change the information. PDF files look on the screen just like they would look if printed. **CASE** ▶ *Jacob Thomas asks you to export the Courses table to a PDF document for later distribution to employees as an email attachment.*

STEPS

1. **Click the CourseRosters report in the Navigation Pane, click the EXTERNAL DATA tab, then click the PDF or XPS button in the Export group**

   The Publish as PDF or XPS dialog box opens asking you to choose a name and location for the file. **XPS** (structured XML) is a file format that is similar to a PDF file, but is based on the **XML** (Extensible Markup Language) instead of the PostScript language used by PDF files.

2. **Navigate to the location where you store your Data Files, as shown in FIGURE I-14**

   The Publish as PDF or XPS dialog box provides a check box to automatically open the file after publishing so you can double-check the results.

   TROUBLE
   If you do not have the free Adobe PDF Reader software installed on your computer, you may be prompted to download it.

3. **Click Publish to save the file with the default name CourseRosters.pdf**

   The CourseRosters.pdf file automatically opens, as shown in **FIGURE I-15**.

4. **Press [Alt][Tab] to return to the Access window, then click Close to close the Export - PDF dialog box**

   The CourseRosters.pdf file is now available for you to attach to an email. Because it is a PDF file, users can open, view, and print the report even if they don't have Access on their computers. PDF files are common because they provide an easy way to share information that cannot be modified.

   Another way to email an Access report (or any other Access object) as a PDF file is to click the report in the Navigation Pane, then click the Email button in the Export group of the EXTERNAL DATA tab on the Ribbon. You are presented with the Send Object As dialog box that allows you to choose the desired file format, such as .xlsx, .pdf, .htm, or .rtf, for the report. Once you select the desired file format and click OK, Outlook opens with the report attached to the email in the chosen file format. You must have Microsoft Outlook installed and configured to use this option.

5. **Close the Education-I.accdb database and Access 2013, then close the CourseRosters.pdf file**

FIGURE I-14: Publish as PDF or XPS dialog box

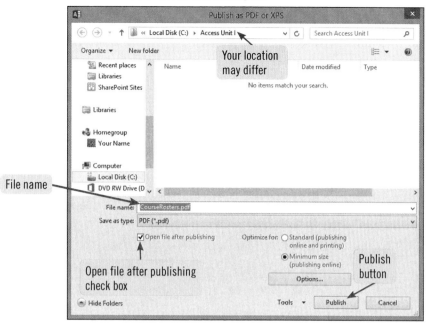

File name →

Open file after publishing check box

Publish button

FIGURE I-15: Previewing the CourseRosters.pdf file

Course Rosters by Deparment

Africa

PDF files can be viewed and printed but not modified

Employee	Description	Hours
Boyd Hosta	Air Reservations I	12
	Air Reservations II	12
	Air Reservations III	12
	Corporate Sales I	12
	Cruising I	24
	Ecological Tours I	12
	Ecological Tours II	12
	European Travel I	12
	European Travel II	12
	European Travel III	12
	Hotel Reservations I	12
	Time Management I	16
	Travel Sales and Trends	16
	USA Biking I	12
	USA Biking II	12
	USA Hiking I	12
	USA Hiking II	12
		224
Gail Owen	African Travel I	16
	African Travel II	16
	African Travel III	16
	Air Reservations I	12
	All Inclusives I	12
	Asian Travel I	12
	Asian Travel II	12
	Bus Travel I	12
	Cruising I	24
	Cruising II	12
	Customer Service Skills I	16
	Customer Service Skills II	16

Access 2013

Practice

Concepts Review

Identify each element of the EXTERNAL DATA tab shown in FIGURE I-16.

FIGURE I-16

Education-I : Database- C:\Users\Lisa\Desktop\Office2013Files\I\Data\Education-I.accdb (Access 2007 - 2013 file f

FILE HOME CREATE **EXTERNAL DATA** DATABASE TOOLS

Saved Imports | Linked Table Manager | Excel | Access | ODBC Database | Text File | XML File | More ▾
Import & Link

Saved Exports | Excel | Text File | XML File | PDF or XPS | Email | Access | Word Merge | More ▾
Export

Work Online | Synchronize | Discard Changes ▾ | Cache List Data | Relink Lists
Web Linked Lists

1   2 3   4 5   6

Match each term with the statement that best describes its function.

7. **Table template**
8. **Database template**
9. **Exporting**
10. **Main document**
11. **Linking**
12. **Delimited text file**
13. **Mail merge**
14. **Importing**

a. A tool used to quickly create a single table within an existing database
b. A file used to determine how a letter and Access data will be combined
c. A file that stores one record on each line, with the field values separated by a common character such as a comma, tab, or dash
d. A way to copy Access information to another database, spreadsheet, or file format
e. The process of converting data from an external source into an Access database
f. A way to connect to data in an external source without copying it
g. A tool used to quickly create a new database based on a particular subject, such as assets, contacts, events, or projects
h. To combine data from an Access table or query into a Word form letter, label, or envelope to create mass mailing documents

Select the best answer from the list of choices.

15. **Which of the following is *not* true about database templates?**
    a. They cover a wide range of subjects, including assets, contacts, events, or projects.
    b. Microsoft provides online templates in areas such as business and personal database applications.
    c. They create multiple database objects.
    d. They analyze the data on your computer and suggest database applications.

16. Which of the following is *not* true about exporting?

   a. Access data can be exported into Excel.

   b. Access data can be exported to Word.

   c. Exporting creates a copy of data.

   d. Exporting retains a link between the original and target data files.

17. Which of the following is *not* a file format that Access can import?

   a. Word   **c.** Access

   b. Excel   **d.** HTML

18. Which of the following file formats allows you to send information that cannot be modified?

   a. XLS   **c.** RTF

   b. HTM   **d.** PDF

19. Which is *not* true about enforcing referential integrity?

   a. It is required for all one-to-many relationships.

   b. It prevents records from being deleted on the "one" side of a one-to-many relationship that have matching records on the "many" side.

   c. It prevents records from being created on the "many" side of a one-to-many relationship that do not have a matching record on the "one" side.

   d. It prevents orphan records.

20. Which of the following is *not* true about linking?

   a. Linking copies data from one data file to another.

   b. Access can link to data in an HTML file.

   c. Access can link to data in an Excel spreadsheet.

   d. You can edit linked data in Access.

Skills Review

1. Use database templates.

   a. Start Access 2013 and use the Desktop asset tracking template to build a new Access database. (*Hint*: Be sure to use the *Desktop* asset tracking database, and not the Asset tracking database, which is a Web app.) Save the database with the name **Assets-I** in the location where you store your Data Files.

   b. Enable content if prompted, close the Getting Started with Assets dialog box, then explore the forms in the database by opening and closing the Asset Details form, the Contact Details form, the Contact List form, and the Getting Started form.

   c. Close all open forms, and then explore the relationships between tables by opening the Relationships window. Expand field lists as needed to view all fields.

   d. Note the arrow on the "one" side of the one-to-many relationship between Contacts and Assets. Double-click the link line to open the Edit Relationships dialog box, click Join Type, click option 1 Only include rows where the joined fields from both tables are equal, click OK, and then click OK in the Edit Relationships dialog box. Because there are no records in the Assets or Contacts tables yet, you do not need a modified relationship. Given referential integrity is applied to this relationship, no records can be entered in the Assets table without a matching record in the Contacts table. Save and close the Relationships window.

   e. Close all objects but leave the new Assets-I.accdb database open.

Skills Review (continued)

2. Use Application Parts.

a. Use the Issues table template in Application Parts to create a new table in the Assets-I.accdb database named Issues. Choose the One 'Assets' to many 'Issues' relationship, choose the ID field from 'Assets', do not choose a sorting field, and name the lookup column as **AssetID**.

b. Close all open forms, reopen the Relationships window then click the All Relationships button to show the new relationship you just created between the new Issues table and the Assets table.

c. Double-click the link line between the Assets and Issues tables, click the Enforce Referential Integrity check box, then click OK.

d. Click the Relationship Report button to create a relationships report for this database, then print it if requested by your instructor.

e. Save and close the **Relationships for Assets-I** report with that name.

f. Save and close the Relationships window, and then close the Assets-I.accdb database.

3. Import data from Excel.

a. Open the Machinery-I.accdb database from the location where you store your Data Files. Enable content if prompted.

b. Import the MachineryEmp.xlsx spreadsheet from the location where you store your Data Files to a new table in the current database using the Import Spreadsheet Wizard to import the data. Make sure that the first row is specified as the column headings.

c. Choose the EmployeeNo field as the primary key, and import the data to a table named **Employees**. Do not save the import steps.

d. In Table Design View for the Employees table, change the Data Type of the EmployeeNo field to Number. Save the table and click Yes when prompted. The EmployeeNo field values are from 1 to 6. No data will be lost. Close the Employees table.

4. Link data from Excel.

a. Link to the Vendors.xlsx Excel file in the location where you store your Data Files.

b. In the Link Spreadsheet Wizard, specify that the first row contains column headings.

c. Name the linked table **Vendors**.

d. Open the Relationships window and display all five field lists in the window. Link the tables together with one-to-many relationships, as shown in FIGURE I-17. Be sure to enforce referential integrity on all relationships except for the relationship between Products and the linked Vendors table.

e. Save and close the Relationships window.

FIGURE I-17

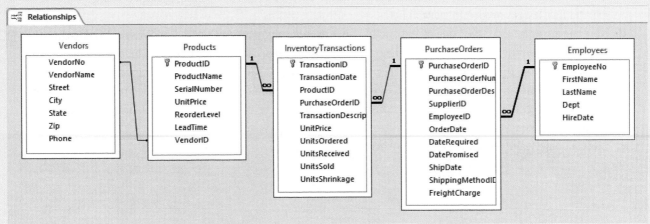

Skills Review (continued)

5. Export data to Excel.

   a. Open the Products table to view the datasheet, then close it.

   b. Export the Products table data to an Excel spreadsheet named **Products.xlsx**. Save the spreadsheet to the location where you store your Data Files. Do not save the export steps.

6. Publish data to Word.

   a. In the Machinery-I.accdb database, export the Products table to a Word document named **Products.rtf**. Save the Products.rtf file in the location where you store your Data Files. Do not save the export steps.

   b. Start Word, then open the Products.rtf document from the location where you store your Data Files. Press [Enter] twice, press [Ctrl][Home] to return to the top of the document, then type the following text:

INTERNAL MEMO

From:	***Your* Name**
To:	**Sales Staff**
Date:	***Today's* date**

Do not forget to check the lead times on the Back Hoe, Thatcher, and Biodegrader when you get an order for these items. We usually do not keep these items in stock.

   c. Proofread the document, then save and print it. Close the document, then exit Word.

7. Merge data with Word.

   a. In the Machinery-I.accdb database, merge the data from the Employees table to a new Word document.

   b. Use the "Create a new document and then link the data to it" option in the Microsoft Word Mail Merge Wizard dialog box. In the Word document, enter the following text as the main document for the mail merge:

Date:	***Today's* date**
To:	
From:	***Your* Name**
Re:	**CPR Training**

The annual CPR Training session will be held on Friday, February 26, 2016. Please sign up for this important event in the lunchroom. Friends and family who are at least 18 years old are also welcome.

   c. To the right of To:, press [Tab] to position the insertion point at the location for the first merge field.

   d. Click the Insert Merge Field button arrow, click FirstName, press [Spacebar], click the Insert Merge Field button arrow, then click LastName.

   e. Click the links at the bottom of the Mail Merge task pane to move through the steps of the mail-merge process, Steps 1 through 6, click Edit individual letters, then click OK to make sure that your final document has six pages for the six records in your Access Employees table.

   f. Print the first page of the merged document if required by your instructor (the letter to Melissa Lenox), then close the six-page final merged document without saving changes.

   g. Save the main document with the name **CPR.docx**, then exit Word.

8. Export data to PDF.

   a. Use the Report Wizard to create a new report based on all of the fields in the Products table. Do not specify any grouping levels, choose an ascending sort order on ProductName, choose a Tabular layout and a Landscape orientation, and title the report **Product List**.

   b. Use Layout View to resize the columns so that all data is clearly visible, then save and close the report.

   c. Export the Product List report with the name **Product List.pdf** to the location where you store your Data Files.

   d. Close the Product List report, close the Machinery-I database, then exit Access 2013.

Independent Challenge 1

As the manager of a women's college basketball team, you have created a database called Basketball-I that tracks the players, games, and player statistics. You want to export a report to a Word document.

a. Open the database Basketball-I.accdb from the location where you store your Data Files. Enable content if prompted.

b. In the Relationships window, connect the Games and Stats tables with a one-to-many relationship based on the common GameNo field. Connect the Players and Stats tables with a one-to-many relationship based on the common PlayerNo field. Be sure to enforce referential integrity on both relationships. Save and close the Relationships window.

c. Export the Player Statistics report to a Word file with the name **Player Statistics.rtf**. Save the Player Statistics.rtf document in the location where you store your Data Files. Do not save the export steps.

d. Start Word, then open the Player Statistics.rtf document.

e. Press [Enter] three times to enter three blank lines at the top of the document, then press [Ctrl][Home] to position the insertion point at the top of the document.

f. Type *your* name on the first line of the document, enter *today's* date as the second line, then write a sentence or two that explains the Player Statistics data that follows. Save, print, and close the Player Statistics document.

g. Exit Word. Close the Basketball-I.accdb database, then exit Access.

Independent Challenge 2

As the manager of a women's college basketball team, you have created a database called Basketball-I that tracks the players, games, and player statistics. The 2015–2016 basketball schedule has been provided to you as an Excel spreadsheet file. You will import that data and append it to the current Games table.

a. Open the database Basketball-I.accdb from the location where you store your Data Files. Enable content if prompted.

b. If the relationships haven't already been established in this database, create relationships as described in Step b of Independent Challenge 1.

c. Open the Games table to observe the datasheet. It currently contains 22 records with scores for the 2014–2015 basketball season.

d. Start Excel and open the 2015-2016Schedule.xlsx file from the location where you store your Data Files. Note that it contains 22 rows of data indicating the opponent, mascot, home or away status, and date of the games for the 2015–2016 season. You have been told that the data will import more precisely if it is identified with the same field names as have already been established in the Games table in Access, so you'll insert those field names as a header row in the Excel spreadsheet.

e. Click anywhere in row 1 of the 2015-2016Schedule.xlsx spreadsheet, click the Insert button arrow in the Cells group, then click Insert Sheet Rows to insert a new blank row.

f. In the new blank row 1, enter the field names that correspond to the field names in the Games table for the same data above each column: **Opponent**, **Mascot**, **Home-Away**, and **GameDate**. Be careful to enter the names precisely as shown.

g. Save and close the 2015-2016Schedule.xlsx spreadsheet, exit Excel, and return to the Basketball-I.accdb database.

h. Close the Games table, click the EXTERNAL DATA tab, click the Excel button in the Import & Link group, browse for the 2015-2016Schedule.xlsx spreadsheet in your Data Files, then choose the Append a copy of the records to the table option button. Be sure that Games is selected as the table to use for the append process.

i. Follow the steps of the Import Spreadsheet Wizard process through completion (do not save the import steps), then open the Games table. It should contain the original 22 records for the 2014–2015 season plus 22 more from the 2015-2016Schedule.xlsx spreadsheet with default values of 0 for both the CycloneScore and OpponentScore fields.

j. Change the Opponent value in the first record to *your* last name's College, then print the first page of the Games table if requested by your instructor.

k. Save and close the Games table, close the Basketball-I.accdb database, then exit Access.

Independent Challenge 3

You have been asked by a small engineering firm to build a database that tracks projects. You decide to explore Microsoft database templates to see if there is a template that could help you get started.

a. Start Access and start a new database with the Desktop project management template. Save and name the database **Project Tracking.accdb**, store it in the location where you store your Data Files, then enable content if prompted.

b. Click the Navigation Pane title bar, then choose Object Type to organize the objects in this database by type.

c. Open and review the Relationships window. Rearrange the field lists as shown in FIGURE I-18, then print the Relationships report in landscape orientation. Save the report with the default name, **Relationships for Project Tracking**, then close it.

FIGURE I-18

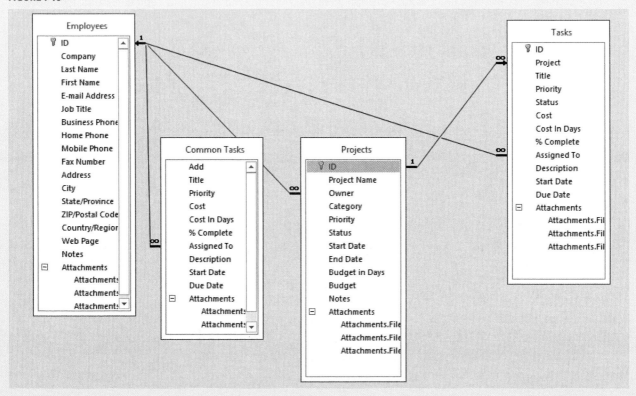

d. Save and close the Relationships window.

e. Open the Project List form (if it's not already open), and enter the following data: Project Name: **Web Site Update**, Owner: *Your* **Name**.

f. Click Yes to add your name to the list, then enter the Street, City, State/Province, Zip/Postal Code, and Country/Region information for your school in the Employee Details form.

g. Close the Employee Details form and the Project List form.

h. Open the Employee List form and add another record for your instructor. Enter your instructor's school email address, school phone, and school name for the E-mail Address, Business Phone, and Company fields. Enter **Professor** in the Job Title field for your instructor.

i. Close the Employee List form, then open the Employee Address Book report. If requested by your instructor, print the report and then close it.

j. Explore the other objects of the Project Tracking database, close the database, then exit Access.

Independent Challenge 4: Explore

Learning common phrases in a variety of foreign languages is extremely valuable if you travel or interact with people from other countries. As a volunteer with the foreign student exchange program at your college, you have created a database that documents the primary and secondary languages used by foreign countries. The database also includes a table of common words and phrases that you can use to practice basic conversation skills. (*Note: To complete this Independent Challenge, make sure you are connected to the Internet.*)

a. Open the Languages-I.accdb database from the location where you store your Data Files. Enable content if prompted.

b. Open the datasheets for each of the three tables to familiarize yourself with the fields and records. The Primary and Secondary fields in the Countries table represent the primary and secondary languages for that country. Close the datasheets for each of the three tables.

c. Open the Relationships window, then create a one-to-many relationship between the Languages and Countries table using the LanguageID field in the Languages table and the Primary field in the Countries table. Enforce referential integrity on the relationship.

d. Create a one-to-many relationship between the Languages and Countries tables using the LanguageID field in the Languages table and the Secondary field in the Countries table. Click No when prompted to edit the existing relationship, and enforce referential integrity on the new relationship. The field list for the Languages table will appear twice in the Relationships window with Languages_1 as the title for the second field list, as shown in FIGURE I-19. The Words table is used for reference and does not have a direct relationship to the other tables.

FIGURE I-19

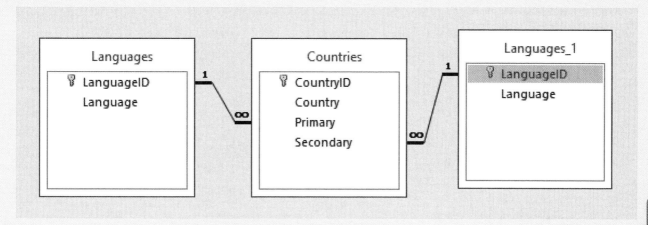

e. Create a Relationships report, then display it in Design View.

f. Add a label to the Report Header section with *your* name, change the font color of the new label to black, then save the report with the name **Relationships for Language-I**.

g. Print the report if requested by your instructor, then close it.

h. Save and close the Relationships window.

i. Connect to the Internet and go to www.ask.com, www.about.com, or any search engine. Your goal is to find a Web site that translates English to other languages, and to print the home page of that Web site.

j. Add a new field to the Words table with a new language that isn't already represented. Use the Web site to translate the existing six words into the new language.

k. Add three new words or phrases to the Words table, making sure that the translation is made in all of the represented languages: English, French, Spanish, German, Italian, Portuguese, Polish, and the new language you added.

l. If requested by your instructor, print the updated datasheet for the Words table, close the Words table, close the Languages-I.accdb database, then exit Access.

Visual Workshop

Start Access and open the Basketball-I.accdb database from the location where you store your Data Files. Enable content if prompted. Merge the information from the Players table to a new Word form letter. The first page of the merged document is shown in **FIGURE I-20**. Notice that the player's first and last names have been merged to the first line and that the player's first name is merged a second time in the first sentence of the letter. Be very careful to correctly add spaces as needed around the merge fields. Print the last page of the merged document if requested by your instructor, close the 13-page final merged document without saving it, save the main document as **Champs.docx**, then close it.

FIGURE I-20

To: Sydney Freesen

From: *Your* Name

Date: *Current Date*

Re: Conference Champions!

Congratulations, Sydney, for an outstanding year at State University! Your hard work and team contribution have helped secure the conference championship for State University for the second year in a row.

Thank you for your dedication!

Analyzing Database Design Using Northwind

CASE ▶ You work with Jacob Thomas, director of staff development at Quest Specialty Travel, to examine the Microsoft Northwind database and determine what features and techniques could be applied to improve the Education database.

Unit Objectives

After completing this unit, you will be able to:

- Normalize data
- Analyze relationships
- Evaluate tables
- Improve fields

- Use subqueries
- Modify joins
- Analyze forms
- Analyze reports

Files You Will Need

Education-J.accdb
Northwind.mdb
Northwind2.mdb
Basketball-J.accdb

RealEstate-J.accdb
JobSearch-J.accdb
Dives-J.accdb

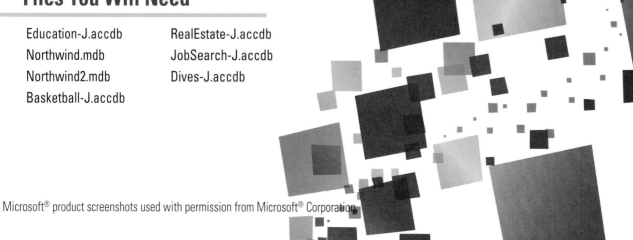

Normalize Data

Learning Outcomes
• Describe normalization
• Create Lookup fields

Normalizing data means to structure and link the tables in a well-designed relational database. A normalized database reduces inaccurate and redundant data, decreases storage requirements, improves database speed and performance, and simplifies overall database maintenance. **CASE** ▶ *Jacob Thomas asks you to study and improve the Education-J database.*

STEPS

1. Open the Education-J.accdb database from the location where you store your Data Files, then enable content if prompted

2. Double-click the Employees table in the Navigation Pane

   The EDepartment and ETitle fields both contain repeating data. You decide to further normalize the database by creating lookup tables for these fields. A **lookup table** is a small table that stores values used in a field of another table.

3. Close the Employees datasheet, click the CREATE tab, click the Table Design button in the Tables group, type Department as the field name, press [Tab], click the Primary Key button in the Tools group, save the table with the name Departments, then open it in Datasheet View and enter the values shown in FIGURE J-1

QUICK TIP

Use the ✛ pointer to resize columns.

4. Close the Departments datasheet, click the CREATE tab, click the Table Design button in the Tables group, type Titles as the field name, press [Tab], click the Primary Key button in the Tools group, save the table with the name Titles, then open it in Datasheet View and enter the values shown in FIGURE J-2

5. Save and close the Titles datasheet, right-click the Employees table in the Navigation Pane, then click Design View

   Next, you use the Lookup Wizard to establish a one-to-many relationship between the Department field in the Departments table and the EDepartment field in the Employees table. The Lookup Wizard also creates a drop-down list of values for the Lookup field.

TROUBLE

If you receive an error message, compare the values in your Departments table to **FIGURE J-1**, then redo Step 6.

6. Click Short Text in the Data Type column for the EDepartment field, click the list arrow, click Lookup Wizard, click Next to look up values in a table, click Table: Departments, click Next, double-click Department as the selected field, click Next, click the first sort arrow, click Department, click Next, click Next, click the Enable Data Integrity check box, click Finish, then click Yes

   The Departments and Employees tables are now linked in a one-to-many relationship with referential integrity enforced.

TROUBLE

If you receive an error message, compare the values in your Titles table to **FIGURE J-2**, then redo Step 7.

7. Click Short Text in the Data Type column for the ETitle field, click the list arrow, click Lookup Wizard, click Next to look up values in a table, click Table: Titles, click Next, double-click Titles as the selected field, click Next, click the first sort arrow, click Titles, click Next, click Next, click the Enable Data Integrity check box, click Finish, click Yes, then click Yes again

   The Titles and Employees tables are now linked in a one-to-many relationship with referential integrity enforced.

8. Click the View button 🏢 to switch to Datasheet View, click any value in the EDepartment field, click the list arrow, as shown in FIGURE J-3, click any value in the ETitle field, then click its list arrow to test its Lookup properties as well

   Lookup properties mean that data entry will be faster, more consistent, and more accurate.

FIGURE J-1: Departments datasheet

FIGURE J-2: Titles datasheet

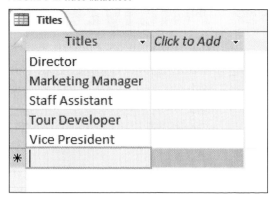

FIGURE J-3: EDepartment field of the Employees table has Lookup properties

ELast	EFirst	EDepartment	ETitle	DateHired	EmployeeNo
Dawson	Ron	Marketing	Vice President	2/15/2000	11-55-77
Lane	Keisha	Africa	Vice President	3/22/2000	13-47-88
Wong	Grace	Americas	Vice President	8/20/2002	17-34-22
Ramirez	Juan	Asia	Director	8/6/2003	22-33-44
	Gail	Europe	Tour Developer	1/3/2007	23-45-67
	Ellen	Finance	Tour Developer	7/1/2004	32-10-68
		Info Systems			
Hoppengarth	Wim	Marketing	Tour Developer	1/1/2005	33-38-37
McDonald	Nancy	Operations	Tour Developer	9/23/2010	33-44-09
Opazo	Derek	Pacific	Tour Developer	4/8/2003	34-58-99
Long	Jessica	Personnel	Marketing Manager	3/1/2004	34-78-13
Rock	Mark	USA	Tour Developer	2/25/2007	42-42-42
Rice	Julia	Personnel	Vice President	1/10/2001	45-99-11

List arrow for EDepartment

ETitle is now a Lookup field

EDepartment is now a Lookup field

Understanding third normal form

The process of normalization can be broken down into degrees, which include **first normal form (1NF)**, a single two-dimensional table with rows and columns; **second normal form (2NF)**, where redundant data in the original table is extracted, placed in a new table, and related to the original table; and **third normal form (3NF)**, where calculated fields (also called derived fields) such as totals or taxes are removed. In an Access database, calculated fields can be created "on the fly" using a query, which means that the information in the calculation is automatically produced and is always accurate based on the latest updates to the database. Strive to create databases that adhere to the rules of third normal form.

Analyze Relationships

Learning
Outcomes
• Analyze table
  relationships
• Analyze junction
  tables

One of the best ways to teach yourself advanced database skills is to study a well-developed database. Microsoft provides a fully developed, well-designed database example called **Northwind** that tracks world-wide orders for a specialty food wholesale business. Northwind was created in the 1990s but is still used to learn about Access today. The relationships between tables determine the health and effectiveness of a database because the Relationships window shows how well the data has been normalized. **CASE** ▶ *You study the Relationships window of the Education-J and the Northwind databases.*

STEPS

1. **Close the Employees table, click the DATABASE TOOLS tab, click the Relationships button, then click the All Relationships button**

   You used the Lookup Wizard to create a one-to-many relationship with referential integrity between the Departments and Employees tables using the Department and EDepartment fields. You also used the Lookup Wizard to create a one-to-many relationship with referential integrity between the Titles and Employees tables using the Titles and ETitle fields. Move the field lists to better view the relationships.

   QUICK TIP
   Move field lists
   by dragging their
   title bars.

2. **Drag and resize the field lists in the Relationships window to look like** FIGURE J-4

   When the relationship lines are clear, the database design is easier to read. A **many-to-many relationship** exists when two tables are related to the same intermediate table, called the **junction table**, with one-to-many relationships. The Employees and Courses tables have a many-to-many relationship (one employee can take many courses and one course can be taken by many employees). This relationship is resolved with the junction table, Enrollments.

3. **Save and close the Relationships window, close the Education-J database, open the Northwind.mdb database from the location where you store your Data Files, click the Close button to close the welcome message, enable content if prompted, read the welcome message, then click OK**

   Northwind.mdb is a database in the Access 2000 file format. Access 2013 can open and work with an Access database in a 2000 or 2002-2003 file format, both of which have the **.mdb** file extension. Databases with a 2007 through 2013 file format have an **.accdb** file extension.

4. **Double-click the Categories table in the Navigation Pane; note the number of fields and records in the table; then open, observe, and close each of the eight tables**

   Now that you're familiar with the data in each table, view their relationships.

   QUICK TIP
   Double-click the link
   line between two
   tables to open the
   Edit Relationships
   dialog box, which
   shows all aspects of a
   relationship,
   including the
   referential integrity
   and cascade options.

5. **Click the DATABASE TOOLS tab, click the Relationships button, scroll to the top of the window as needed, then resize and move the field lists so that all fields are visible, as shown in** FIGURE J-5

   Note that the Employees and Shippers tables have a many-to-many relationship, as do the Employees and Customers and the Shippers and Customers tables in the Northwind database. In each case, the Orders table is the junction table.

   Also note that the Order Details table has a **multifield primary key** that consists of the OrderID and ProductID fields. In other words, the combination of a particular OrderID value plus a ProductID value should be unique for each record.

Multivalued fields

Access allows you to store multiple values in one field by setting the **Allow Multiple Values property** to Yes. This property is found on the Lookup tab in Table Design View. For example, you might be tempted to create an Ingredients field in a Products table to list all of the major ingredients for each product. A better way to handle this, however, is to create an Ingredients table and relate it to the Products table using a one-to-many relationship. The latter approach may take a little more time up front, but it respects fundamental database design rules and gives you the most flexibility in the long run.

FIGURE J-4: Education-J.accdb relationships

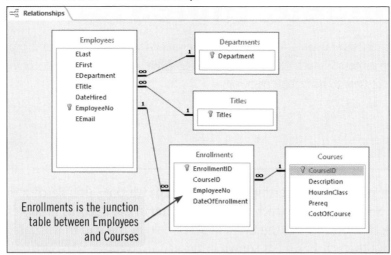

Enrollments is the junction table between Employees and Courses

FIGURE J-5: Northwind.mdb relationships

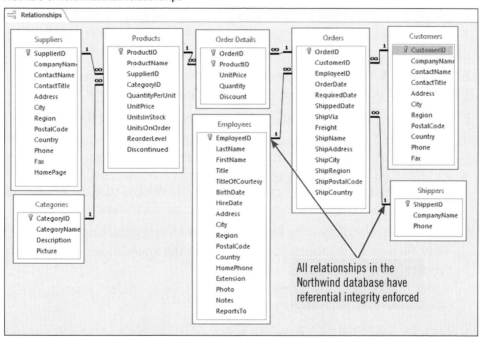

All relationships in the Northwind database have referential integrity enforced

More about Cascade options

When referential integrity is enforced on a relationship, two options become available in the Edit Relationships dialog box, as shown in **FIGURE J-6**: Cascade Update Related Fields and Cascade Delete Related Records. Checking the **Cascade Update Related Fields** check box means that if you change the primary key field value in the table on the "one" side of a one-to-many relationship, all foreign key field values in the "many" table automatically update as well. Checking the **Cascade Delete Related Records** check box means that if you delete a record in the table on the "one" side of a relationship, all related records in the "many" table are automatically deleted as well. Therefore, the cascade options both automatically change data in the "many" table based on changes in the "one" table.

FIGURE J-6: Edit Relationships dialog box

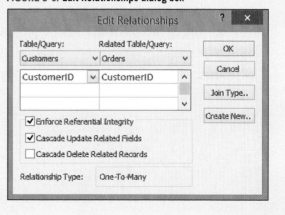

Evaluate Tables

Learning
Outcomes
• Apply the Totals
  row in a datasheet
• Modify table
  properties

Access offers several table features that make analyzing existing data and producing results, such as datasheet subtotals, much easier and faster. **CASE** ➤ *You review the tables of the Northwind database to analyze data and to study table properties.*

STEPS

QUICK TIP
Scroll to the right to find the Units In Stock field. Scroll to the bottom of the datasheet to find the Totals row.

1. **Save and close the Northwind Relationships window, double-click the Products table in the Navigation Pane, click the Totals button in the Records group on the HOME tab, click the Total cell for the Units In Stock field at the end of the datasheet, click the list arrow, then click Sum, as shown in FIGURE J-7**

   A subtotal of the units in stock, 3119, appears in the Total cell for the Units In Stock field. As shown in the Totals list, a numeric field allows you to calculate the Average, Sum, Count, Maximum, Minimum, Standard Deviation, or Variance statistic for the field. If you were working in the Total cell of a Text field, you could choose only the Count statistic. Notice that the Current Record box displays the word "Totals" to indicate that you are working in the Total row. You can use the Current Record box to quickly move to a record.

2. **Double-click Totals in the Current Record box, type 6, then press [Enter]**

   Access moves the focus to the Units In Stock field of the sixth record.

3. **Click the record selector button of the sixth record to select the entire record, then press [Delete]**

   Working with a well-defined relational database with referential integrity enforced on all relationships, you are prevented from deleting a record in a "one" (parent) table if the record is related to many records in a "many" (child) table. In this case, the sixth record in the Products table is related to records in the Order Details table, and therefore it cannot be deleted. Next, you examine table properties.

4. **Click OK, save and close the Products table, right-click the Employees table, click Design View, then click the Property Sheet button in the Show/Hide group to open the Property Sheet if it is not already open**

   For the Products table, you can prevent data entry errors by specifying that the HireDate field value is always greater than the BirthDate field value.

5. **Click the Validation Rule box, type [HireDate]>[BirthDate], click the Validation Text box, type Hire date must be greater than birth date, as shown in FIGURE J-8, click the Save button 🖫 on the Quick Access toolbar, click Yes, then click the View button 🎛 to switch to Datasheet View**

   Test the new table validation rule.

6. **Tab to the Hire Date field, type 4/4/40, then press [↓]**

   A dialog box opens, displaying the text entered in the Validation Text property.

7. **Click OK, then press [Esc] to remove the incorrect hire date entry for the first record**

FIGURE J-7: Products datasheet with Total row

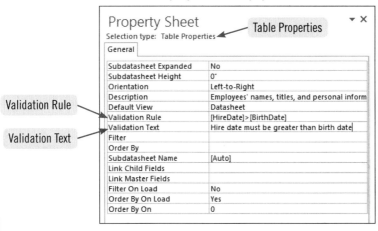

FIGURE J-8: Property Sheet for Employees table

Modifying fields in Datasheet View

When working in Table Datasheet View, the FIELDS tab on the Ribbon contains buttons that allow you to add or delete a field, or change the name or data type of an existing field. You can also modify certain field properties such as Caption, Field Size, Format, Required, Validation Rule, and Validation Text. For full access to all of the properties for a field, however, work in Table Design View.

Improve Fields

Learning Outcomes

- Modify the Caption property
- Modify the Index property
- Modify the Allow Zero Length property

To improve and enhance database functionality, the Northwind database also employs several useful field properties, such as Caption, Allow Zero Length, and Index. **CASE** *You review the Northwind database to study how lesser-used field properties have been implemented in the Employees table.*

STEPS

1. **Click the View button ☒ to switch to Design View, close the Property Sheet, click the EmployeeID field, then press [↓] to move through the fields of the Employees table while observing the Caption property in the Field Properties pane**

   The **Caption** property text is displayed as the default field name in datasheets and labels.

2. **Select Reports To in the Caption property of the ReportsTo field, then type Manager**

   Use the Caption property when you want to clarify a field for the users, but prefer not to change the actual field name.

3. **Click the HireDate field, then change the Indexed property to Yes (Duplicates OK)**

   An **index** keeps track of the order of the values in the indexed field as data is being entered and edited. The **Indexed property** is used to improve database performance when a field is often used for sorting. Fields that are not often used for sorting should have their Indexed property set to No, but you can still sort on any field at any time, whether the Indexed property is set to Yes or No.

4. **Click the HomePhone field and examine the Allow Zero Length property**

   Currently, the **Allow Zero Length property** is set to No, meaning zero-length strings ("") are not allowed. A zero-length string is an *intentional* "nothing" entry (as opposed to a **null** entry, which also means that the field contains nothing, but doesn't indicate intent). For example, some employees might *intentionally* not want to provide a home phone number. In those instances, a zero-length string entry is appropriate. Note that you query for zero-length strings using "" criteria, whereas you query for null values using the operator **Is Null**.

5. **Double-click the Allow Zero Length property to switch the choice from No to Yes, as shown in FIGURE J-9**

   With the field changes in place, you test them in Datasheet View.

6. **Click the View button ▦ to switch to Datasheet View, click Yes to save the table, tab to the Home Phone field, enter "" (two quotation marks without a space), tab to the Extension field, enter "", then press [Tab]**

   An error message appears, as shown in **FIGURE J-10**, indicating that you cannot enter a zero-length string in the Extension field.

7. **Click OK to acknowledge the error message, press [Esc], press [Tab] three more times to observe the Manager caption for the ReportsTo field, then save and close the Employees table**

FIGURE J-9: Changing field properties in the Employees table

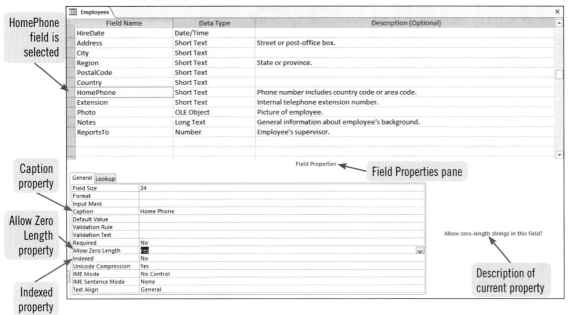

HomePhone field is selected

Field Properties pane

Caption property

Allow Zero Length property

Indexed property

Allow zero-length strings in this field?

Description of current property

FIGURE J-10: Testing field properties in the Employees table

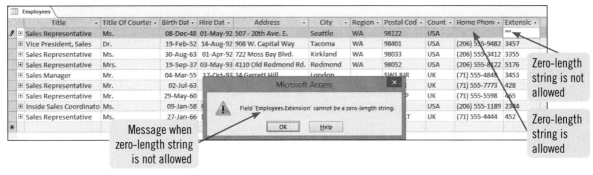

Zero-length string is not allowed

Message when zero-length string is not allowed

Zero-length string is allowed

Field 'Employees.Extension' cannot be a zero-length string.

Access 2013

Using Long Text fields

Use Long Text fields when you need to store more than 256 characters in a field, which is the maximum Field Size value for a Short Text field. Fields that store comments, reviews, notes, or other ongoing conversational information are good candidates for the Long Text data type. Set the **Append Only** property to Yes to allow users to add data to a Memo field, but not to change or remove existing data. The Append Only property is available for Memo or Long Text fields in Access 2007 databases created in Access 2007, 2010, or Access 2013.

Use Subqueries

Learning Outcomes
- Use subqueries
- Use advanced functions

The Northwind database contains several interesting queries that demonstrate advanced query techniques, such as grouping on more than one field, using functions in calculated fields, and developing subqueries, which you might not have studied yet. **CASE** ▶ *You work in the Northwind database to learn how to use advanced query techniques, including subqueries.*

STEPS

1. **Double-click the Product Sales for 1995 query to view the datasheet**

   This query summarizes product sales by product name for the year 1995. The datasheet includes 77 records, and each record represents one product name. The third column summarizes product sales for that product. To analyze the construction of the query, switch to Design View.

   QUICK TIP
   Right-click a field in the query grid, then click Build on the shortcut menu to open the Expression Builder dialog box.

2. **Click the View button 🖉, then resize the columns in the query grid to better view the data, as shown in FIGURE J-12**

   Several interesting techniques have been used in the construction of this query. The records are grouped by both the CategoryName and the ProductName fields. A calculated field, ProductSales, is computed by first multiplying the UnitPrice field from the Order Details table by the Quantity field, then subtracting the Discount. The result of this calculation is subtotaled using the Sum function. In addition, the ShippedDate field contains criteria so that only those sales between the dates of 1/1/1995 and 12/31/1995 are selected.

3. **Save and close the Product Sales for 1995 query, then double-click the Category Sales for 1995 query in the Navigation Pane to open the query datasheet**

   This query contains only eight records because the sales are summarized (grouped) by the Category field and there are only eight unique categories. The Category Sales field summarizes total sales by category. To see how this query was constructed, switch to Design View.

4. **Click 🖉 to switch to Design View, then resize the field list and the columns in the query grid to display all of the fields**

   Note that the field list for the query is based on the Product Sales for 1995 query, as shown in **FIGURE J-13**. When a query is based on another query's field list, the field list is called a **subquery**. In this case, the Category Sales for 1995 query used the Product Sales for 1995 as its subquery to avoid having to re-create the long ProductSales calculated field.

5. **Save and close the Category Sales for 1995 query**

Using Expression Builder

The **Expression Builder** is a dialog box that helps you evaluate and create expressions. The full expression is displayed at the top of the dialog box. The three panes at the bottom of the dialog box help you find and enter parts of the expression. The left pane shows all objects and built-in functions in the database. The middle and right panes further break down the options for the element selected in the left pane. FIGURE J-11 shows how to find the built-in CCur function used in the ProductSales calculated field. The **CCur** function is used to convert an expression to Currency.

FIGURE J-11: Expression Builder dialog box

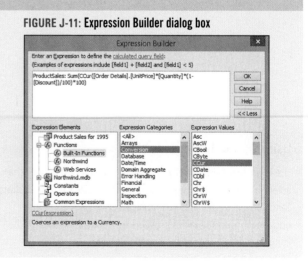

Analyzing Database Design Using Northwind

FIGURE J-12: Design View of the Product Sales for 1995 query

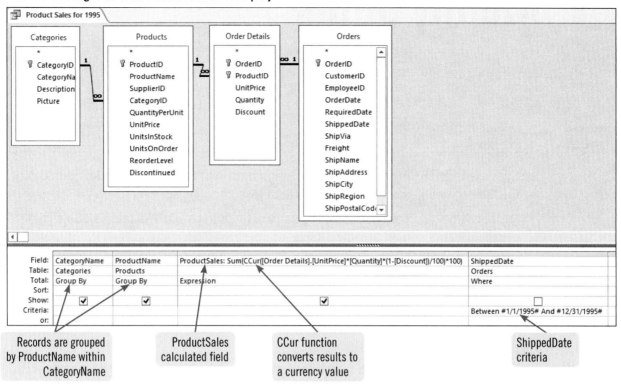

Records are grouped by ProductName within CategoryName

ProductSales calculated field

CCur function converts results to a currency value

ShippedDate criteria

FIGURE J-13: Using a subquery

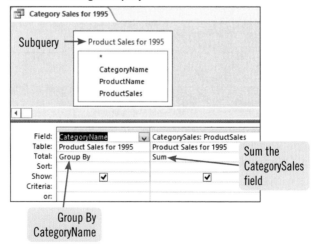

Subquery → Product Sales for 1995

Sum the CategorySales field

Group By CategoryName

Modify Joins

Learning
Outcomes
• Create an
  outer join
• Use Is Null criteria

STEPS

When you create a query based on multiple tables, only records that have matching data in each of the field lists present in the query are selected. This is due to the default **inner join** operation applied to the one-to-many relationship between two tables. Other join types are described in TABLE J-1. They help select records that do not have a match in a related table. **CASE** *You use the Northwind database and modify the join operation to find records in the Customers table that do not have a matching record in the Orders table.*

1. Click the CREATE tab, click the Query Design button in the Queries group, double-click Customers, double-click Orders, then click Close

2. Resize the field list so that you can see all the fields in the Orders table, double-click CompanyName in the Customers table, double-click OrderDate in the Orders table, double-click Freight in the Orders table, then click the View button 🔲 to view the datasheet

   This query selects 830 records using the default inner join between the tables. An inner join means that records are selected only if a matching value is present in both tables. Therefore, any records in the Customers table that did not have a related record in the Orders table would not be selected. You modify the join operation to find those customers.

3. Click the View button 🔲 to switch to Design View, then double-click the middle of the one-to-many relationship line between the tables to open the Join Properties dialog box shown in FIGURE J-14

   The Join Properties dialog box provides information regarding how the two tables are joined and allows you to change from the default inner join (option 1) to a left outer join (2) or right outer join (3).

4. Click the 2 option button, then click OK as shown in FIGURE J-15

   The arrow pointing to the Orders table indicates that the join line has been modified to be a left outer join. With join operations, "left" always refers to the "one" table of a one-to-many relationship regardless of where the table is physically positioned in Query Design View. A **left outer join** means that all of the records in the "one" table will be selected for the query regardless of whether they have matching records in the "many" table.

5. Click 🔲 to view the datasheet

   The datasheet now shows 832 records, two more than when an inner join operation was used. To find the two new records quickly, use Is Null criteria.

6. Click 🔲 to return to Design View, click the Criteria cell for the OrderDate field, type Is Null, then click 🔲 to view the datasheet again

   The datasheet now contains only two records, as shown in FIGURE J-16, the two customers who do not have any matching order records. Left outer joins are very useful for finding records on the "one" side of a relationship (parent records) that do not have matching records on the "many" side (child records).

   When referential integrity is enforced on a relationship before data is entered, it is impossible to create new records on the "many" side of a relationship that do not have matching records on the "one" side (orphan records). Therefore, a **right outer join** is very useful to help find orphan records in a poorly designed database, but a right outer join operation would not be useful in the Northwind database because referential integrity was applied on all relationships before any records were entered.

7. Close the query and save with the name CustomersWithoutOrders

FIGURE J-14: Join Properties dialog box

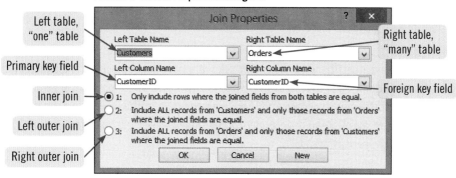

Left table, "one" table

Right table, "many" table

Primary key field

Inner join

Left outer join

Right outer join

Foreign key field

FIGURE J-15: Left outer join line

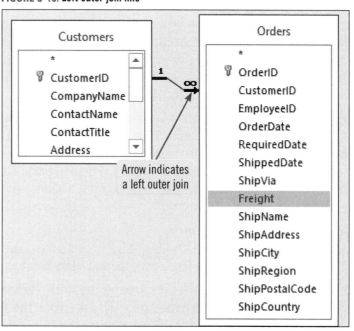

Arrow indicates a left outer join

FIGURE J-16: Customers without orders

Select All button

Order Date field value is null

TABLE J-1: Join operations

join operation	description
inner	Default join; selects records from two related tables in a query that have matching values in a field common to both tables
left outer	Selects all the records from the left table (the "one" table in a one-to-many relationship) even if the "one" table doesn't have matching records in the related "many" table
right outer	Selects all the records from the right table (the "many" table in a one-to-many relationship) even if the "many" table doesn't have matching records in the related "one" table

Analyze Forms

**Learning
Outcomes**
• Work with form
  properties
• Work with a splash
  screen form
• Work with a
  switchboard form

Database developers create forms to provide a fast and easy-to-use interface for database users. In a fully developed database, users generally do not work with individual objects or the Navigation Pane. Rather, they use forms to guide all of their activities. The Northwind database provides several examples of sophisticated forms used to easily navigate and work with the data in the underlying database. **CASE** *You examine Northwind forms to gain an understanding of how well-designed forms could be applied to the databases at Quest Specialty Travel.*

STEPS

1. **Double-click the Startup form in the Navigation Pane**

   The Startup form opens, as shown in **FIGURE J-17**. The Startup form is a **splash screen**, a special form used to announce information. To create a splash screen, you create a new form in Form Design View with the labels, graphics, and command buttons desired, plus you set the **Border Style** property of the form to None. You also set the following form properties to No: **Record Selectors**, **Navigation Buttons**, **Scroll Bars** (Neither), **Control Box**, and **Min Max Buttons** (None).

2. **Click OK, then double-click the Main Switchboard form in the Navigation Pane**

   The Main Switchboard form opens, as shown in **FIGURE J-18**. A **switchboard** is a special form used to help users navigate throughout the rest of the database. A switchboard contains command buttons to give users fast and easy access to the database objects they use. A switchboard form is created in Form Design View using many of the same form properties used to create a splash screen. Also note that the Record Source property for the splash screen and switchboard forms is not used because neither form is used for data entry.

3. **Click the Orders command button**

   The Orders form opens for the first of 830 orders. This form shows the attractiveness and sophistication of a well-developed form. You modify the first order to learn about the form's capabilities.

4. **Click the Bill To: combo box arrow, click Around the Horn, click the Salesperson combo box arrow, click King, Robert, click the Spegesild list arrow (the first product in the order), click Steeleye Stout, press [Tab], type 20 for the Quantity value, press [Tab], enter 50 for the Discount value, then press [Tab]**

   The first order in the Orders form should look like **FIGURE J-19**. The Orders form is a traditional Access form in that it is used to enter and edit data. The form uses combo boxes and calculations to make data entry fast, easy, and accurate. Also notice the Print Invoice command button used to print the current record, the current invoice. Well-designed forms contain a command button to print the *current* record because the regular Print button will print *all* records (in this case, all 830 orders).

5. **Right-click the Orders tab, then click Close**

   Northwind contains many other forms you can explore later to learn more about form design and construction.

FIGURE J-17: Northwind splash screen form, Startup

Welcome to Northwind Traders, a sample database you can use to learn about Microsoft Access. You can experiment with the data stored in Northwind, and use the forms, reports, and other database objects as models for your own database.

All the objects in Northwind are available from the Database window, which will be displayed when you click OK. In the Database window, you can display descriptions of the objects by clicking Details on the View menu.

OK

The names of companies, products, people, characters, and/or data mentioned herein are fictitious and are in no way intended to represent any real individual, company, product, or event, unless otherwise noted.

FIGURE J-18: Northwind startup form, Main Switchboard

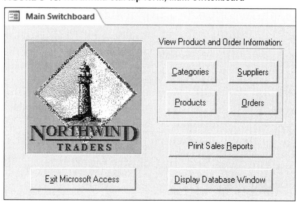

Main Switchboard

View Product and Order Information:

Categories   Suppliers

Products   Orders

Print Sales Reports

Exit Microsoft Access   Display Database Window

FIGURE J-19: Northwind Orders form

Salesperson combo box

Spegesild changed to Steeleye Stout

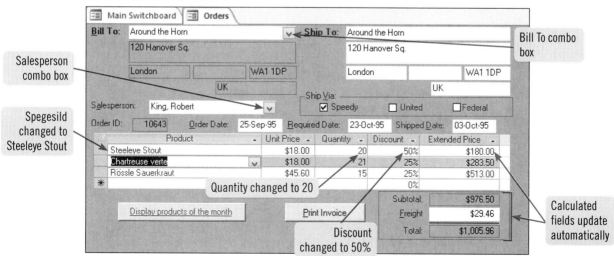

Main Switchboard   Orders

Bill To: Around the Horn
120 Hanover Sq.
London   WA1 1DP
UK

Ship To: Around the Horn
120 Hanover Sq.
London   WA1 1DP
UK

Bill To combo box

Salesperson: King, Robert

Ship Via: ☑ Speedy ☐ United ☐ Federal

Order ID: 10643   Order Date: 25-Sep-95   Required Date: 23-Oct-95   Shipped Date: 03-Oct-95

Product	Unit Price	Quantity	Discount	Extended Price
Steeleye Stout	$18.00	20	50%	$180.00
Chartreuse verte	$18.00	21	25%	$283.50
Rössle Sauerkraut	$45.60	15	25%	$513.00
*			0%	

Quantity changed to 20

Display products of the month   Print Invoice

Discount changed to 50%

Subtotal:	$976.50
Freight	$29.46
Total:	$1,005.96

Calculated fields update automatically

Analyze Reports

In a fully developed database, the database designer creates reports for the printed information needs of the users. In a well-designed database, the user can select what data he or she wants the report to display by making choices in a dialog box or by using parameter criteria in a query on which the report is based. **CASE** ▶ *You study some reports in the Northwind database to gain new ideas and skills.*

STEPS

1. **Click the Print Sales Reports command button on the Main Switchboard form**

   A form, the Sales Reports dialog box shown in **FIGURE J-20**, opens. A **dialog box** is a type of form used to make choices to modify the contents of another query, form, or report. In this case, the selections you make in the Sales Reports dialog box will help you create a specific report.

2. **Click the Sales by Category option button to enable the Category list box**

   In a well-designed form, controls are often enabled and disabled based on choices the user makes. In this case, the Category list box is enabled only if the Sales by Category option button is selected. You will learn how to modify a form to respond to user interaction when you work with Visual Basic for Applications (VBA).

3. **Click the Employee Sales by Country option button, click Preview, type 1/1/1995 in the Beginning Date text box, click OK, type 12/31/1995 in the Ending Date text box, click OK, then click the report to display it at 100% zoom**

   The Employee Sales by Country report opens in Print Preview, as shown in **FIGURE J-21**. It is based on the Employee Sales by Country query, which contains parameter criteria that prompted you for the beginning and ending dates to select the desired data for this report.

   The Employee Sales by Country report presents several advanced report techniques, including a calculated date expression in the Report Header section, multiple grouping levels, and a background picture also called a watermark. The **watermark** is achieved by specifying the desired watermark image, in this case Confidential.bmp, in the report's **Picture** property.

4. **Right-click the Employee Sales by Country report tab, click Design View, click the Property Sheet button to open the property sheet for the report, click the Data tab to observe Employee Sales by Country in the Record Source property, then click the Format tab to observe Confidential.bmp in the Picture property**

   By studying the Design View of Northwind's advanced tables, queries, and reports, you can reverse engineer the enhancements and apply them to your own database.

5. **Right-click the Employee Sales by Country report tab, click Close All, then close the Northwind.mdb database and exit Access**

   Northwind.mdb is the most common database in the history of Access. Experienced database developers often use Northwind to discuss and share database ideas.

Analyzing Database Design Using Northwind

FIGURE J-20: Sales Reports dialog box

Main Switchboard | Sales Reports ← Sales Reports dialog box form tab

Employee Sales by Country option button →

Report to Print

- ● Employee Sales by Country
- ○ Sales Totals by Amount
- ○ Sales by Category

To print only one category's sales, select a category in the list. To print all categories, make no selection.

Categories list box →

Beverages
Condiments
Confections
Dairy Products
Grains/Cereals

Preview ← Preview command button
Print
Cancel

FIGURE J-21: Report with background picture and date criteria

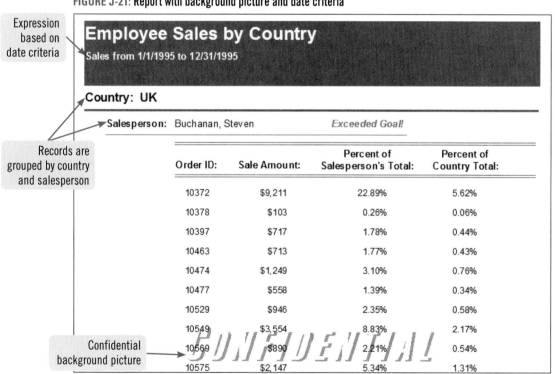

Expression based on date criteria →

Employee Sales by Country
Sales from 1/1/1995 to 12/31/1995

Country: UK

Records are grouped by country and salesperson →

Salesperson: Buchanan, Steven   *Exceeded Goal!*

Order ID:	Sale Amount:	Percent of Salesperson's Total:	Percent of Country Total:
10372	$9,211	22.89%	5.62%
10378	$103	0.26%	0.06%
10397	$717	1.78%	0.44%
10463	$713	1.77%	0.43%
10474	$1,249	3.10%	0.76%
10477	$558	1.39%	0.34%
10529	$946	2.35%	0.58%
10549	$3,554	8.83%	2.17%
10569	$890	2.21%	0.54%
10575	$2,147	5.34%	1.31%

Confidential background picture →

Practice

Put your skills into practice with SAM! If you have a SAM account, go to www.cengage.com/sam2013 to access SAM assignments for this unit.

Concepts Review

Identify each element of the Join Properties dialog box in FIGURE J-22.

FIGURE J-22

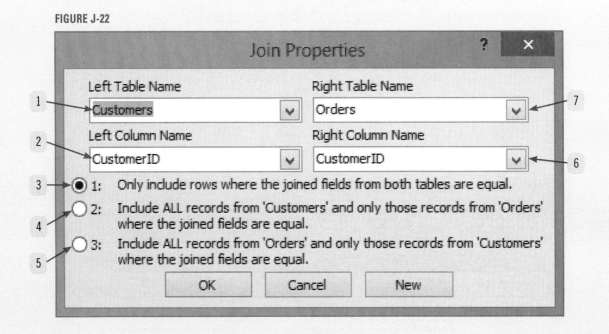

Match each term with the statement that best describes it.

8. **Normalization**
9. **Caption**
10. **Index**
11. **Zero-length string**

a. An *intentional* "nothing" entry
b. Displayed as the default field name at the top of the field column in datasheets as well as in labels that describe fields on forms and reports
c. Keeps track of the order of the values in the indexed field as data is entered and edited
d. The process of structuring data into a well-formed relational database

Select the best answer from the list of choices.

12. **Which of the following is *not* a benefit of a well-designed relational database?**
    a. Reduces redundant data
    b. Has lower overall storage requirements
    c. Improves reporting flexibility
    d. Is easier to create than a single-table database

13. **First normal form can be described as:**
    a. A well-functioning, fully developed relational database.
    b. Any collection of data in any form.
    c. A single two-dimensional table with rows and columns.
    d. A series of queries and subqueries.

14. **Which of the following activities occurs during the creation of second normal form?**
    a. Redundant data is removed from one table, and relationships are created.
    b. Calculated fields are removed from tables.
    c. Additional calculated fields are added to tables.
    d. All data is organized in one master table.

15. **Which of the following activities occurs during the creation of third normal form?**
    a. All data is organized in one master table.
    b. Calculated fields are removed from tables.
    c. Additional calculated fields are added to tables.
    d. Redundant data is removed from one table, and relationships are created.

16. **Which report property is used to add a watermark to a report?**
    a. Record Source
    c. Default View
    b. Caption
    d. Picture

17. **A multifield primary key consists of:**
    a. Two or more fields.
    c. An AutoNumber field.
    b. One field.
    d. A primary key field that also serves as a foreign key field.

18. **Which of the following is *not* true for the Caption property?**
    a. It is the default field name at the top of the field column in datasheets.
    b. The value of the Caption property is the default label that describes a field on a report.
    c. The value of the Caption property is the default label that describes a field on a form.
    d. It is used instead of the field name when you build expressions.

19. **Which of the following fields would most likely be used for an index?**
    a. MiddleName
    c. ApartmentNumber
    b. FirstName
    d. LastName

20. **Which of the following phrases best describes the need for both null values and zero-length strings?**
    a. They represent two different conditions.
    b. Having two different choices for "nothing" clarifies data entry.
    c. Null values speed up calculations.
    d. They look different on a query datasheet.

Skills Review

1. **Normalize data.**
    a. Start Access, open the Northwind2.mdb database from the location where you store your Data Files, close the splash screen, enable content if prompted, then click OK to close the splash screen again.
    b. Double-click the Employees table to view its datasheet. Notice the repeated data in the Title of Courtesy field. Close the Employees datasheet. You will build a lookup table to better manage the values in this field.

Skills Review (continued)

c. Click the CREATE tab, click Table Design, then create a table with one field, **TitleName**. Give it a Short Text data type, and set it as the primary key field.

d. Save the table with the name **TitlesOfCourtesy**, and enter the data in the datasheet, as shown in FIGURE J-23. Be very careful to type the data exactly as shown. Save and close the TitlesOfCourtesy table when you are finished.

e. Open the Employees table in Design View, click the TitlesOfCourtesy field, then choose Lookup Wizard using the Data Type list arrow.

f. Choose the "I want the lookup field to get the values…" option, choose Table: TitlesOfCourtesy, select the TitleName field for the list and specify an ascending sort order on the TitleName field, accept the column width, accept the TitlesOfCourtesy label, then click Yes to save the table.

g. Switch to Datasheet View, and then click the Title Of Courtesy field's list arrow to make sure all four values from the TitlesOfCourtesy table are listed as values.

h. Close the Employees table, open the Relationships window, click the All Relationships button, then double-click the link line between the TitlesOfCourtesy and Employees tables to open the Edit Relationships dialog box. Click the Enforce Referential Integrity check box, then click OK.

i. Move and resize the field lists to match FIGURE J-24.

FIGURE J-23

FIGURE J-24

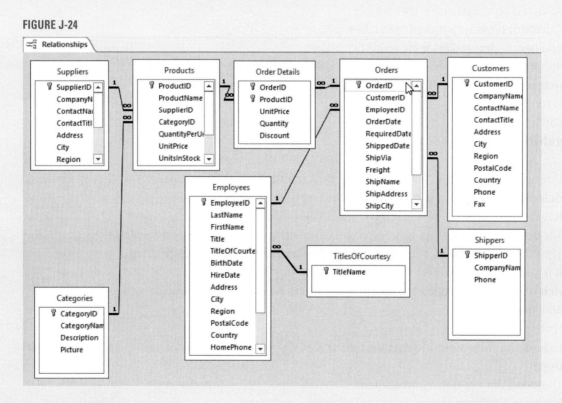

2. Analyze relationships.

a. It is easy to see that all of the relationships in the Northwind2.mdb database are one-to-many relationships with referential integrity enforced due to the presence of the "1" and "infinity" symbols. When two parent tables both have a one-to-many relationship with the same child table, they are said to have a many-to-many relationship with each other. This database has five many-to-many relationships. Use the following table to identify the tables involved. One many-to-many relationship is provided as an example.

Table 1	Junction Table	Table 2
Employees	Orders	Customers

Analyzing Database Design Using Northwind

Skills Review (continued)

b. Create a Relationship report. Use landscape orientation so that the report is only one page long, and insert your name as a label in the Report Header using black text and a 12-point font size. Save and close the report using the default name, **Relationships for Northwind2**.

c. Save and close the Relationships window.

3. Evaluate tables.

a. Open the datasheet for the Order Details table.

b. Tab to the Quantity field, then click the Totals button to open the Total row at the end of the datasheet.

c. Use the Total row to find the sum of the Quantity field, 51317, which represents the total quantity of products sold for this database.

d. Save and close the Order Details table.

4. Improve fields.

a. Open the Products table in Design View.

b. Change the Caption property for the UnitPrice field to **Retail Price**.

c. At the end of the field list, add a new field named **StandardQuantity** with a Number data type and a Caption property of **Standard Quantity**.

d. At the end of the field list, add a new field named **UnitOfMeasure** with a Short Text data type and a Caption property of **Unit of Measure**.

e. Save the table, then display it in Datasheet View.

f. Referring to the existing data in the Quantity Per Unit field, enter the correct information into the new Standard Quantity and Unit of Measure fields for the first 10 records. The first five records are completed for you in FIGURE J-25.

FIGURE J-25

Category	Quantity Per Unit	Retail Pr	Units In Stoc	Units On Orde	Reorder Leve	Discontinue	Standard Qu	Unit of Meas
⊞ Beverages	10 boxes x 20 bags	$18.00	39	0	10	☐	10	boxes x 20 bag:
⊞ Beverages	24 - 12 oz bottles	$19.00	17	40	25	☐	24	12 oz bottles
⊞ Condiments	12 - 550 ml bottles	$10.00	13	70	25	☐	12	550 ml bottles
⊞ Condiments	48 - 6 oz jars	$22.00	53	0	0	☐	48	6 oz jars
⊞ Condiments	36 boxes	$21.35	0	0	0	☑	36	boxes
⊞ Condiments	12 - 8 oz jars	$25.00	120	0	25	☐		
⊞ Produce	12 - 1 lb pkgs.	$30.00	15	0	10	☐		
⊞ Condiments	12 - 12 oz jars	$40.00	6	0	0	☐		
⊞ Meat/Poultry	18 - 500 g pkgs.	$97.00	29	0	0	☑		
⊞ Seafood	12 - 200 ml jars	$31.00	31	0	0	☐		
⊞ Dairy Products	1 kg pkg.	$21.00	22	30	30	☐		
⊞ Dairy Products	10 - 500 g pkgs.	$38.00	86	0	0	☐		
⊞ Seafood	2 kg box	$6.00	24	0	5	☐		

g. Explain the benefits of separating quantities from their units of measure. (*Hint*: Think about how you find, filter, sort, and calculate data.) If these benefits were significant to your company, you would want to convert the rest of the data from the Quantity Per Unit field to the new Standard Quantity and Unit of Measure fields, too. Once all of the new data was in place, you could delete the original Quantity Per Unit field.

h. Close the Products table datasheet.

5. Use subqueries.

a. Click the CREATE tab, then click the Query Design button.

b. Double-click Orders, Order Details, and Products, then click Close.

c. Double-click the OrderDate field in the Orders table, the Quantity and UnitPrice fields in the Order Details table, and the ProductName field in the Products table.

Skills Review (continued)

d. In the fifth column, enter the following calculated field: **GrossRevenue:[Quantity]*[Products].** **[UnitPrice]**. Because the UnitPrice field is given the same name in two tables present in this query, you use the [TableName].[FieldName] syntax to specify which table supplies this field.

e. Save the query with the name **GrossRevenueCalculation**, open it in Datasheet View to test and review the results, and then close it.

f. Click the CREATE tab, then click the Query Design button.

g. Click the Queries tab in the Show Table dialog box, double-click GrossRevenueCalculation, then click Close.

h. Double-click the ProductName and GrossRevenue fields, then click the Totals button.

i. Change Group By in the GrossRevenue field to Sum.

j. Open the Property Sheet for the GrossRevenue field, change the Format property to Currency, change the Caption property to **Total Gross Revenue**, then view the resulting datasheet.

k. Save the query with the name **GrossRevenueByProduct**, then close it.

6. Modify joins.

a. Open the Suppliers table in Datasheet View, and enter a record using your own last name as the company name. Enter realistic but fictitious data for the rest of the record, then close the Suppliers table.

b. Click the CREATE tab, click the Query Design button, double-click Suppliers, double-click Products, then click Close.

c. Double-click CompanyName from the Suppliers table and ProductName from the Products table. Add an ascending sort order for both fields, then view the datasheet. Note that there are 77 records in the datasheet.

d. Return to Query Design View, then change the join properties to option 2, which will select all Suppliers records even if they don't have matching data in the Products table.

e. View the datasheet, and note it now contains 78 records.

f. Return to Query Design View, and add **Is Null** criteria to the ProductName field.

g. View the datasheet noting that the only supplier without matching product records is the one you entered in Step a. That tells you that every other supplier in the database is related to at least one record in the Products table.

h. Save the query with the name **SuppliersWithoutProducts**, then close it.

7. Analyze forms.

a. Open the Customer Orders form in Form View.

b. Notice that this form contains customer information in the main form and in two subforms. The first subform is for order information, and the second subform shows order details. Navigate to the fourth company name in the main form, which shows the orders for the company named Around the Horn.

c. Click the Order ID value 10692 in the upper subform, and notice that the order details automatically change in the lower subform as you move from order to order.

d. Explore the form by moving through customer and order records, then answer this question: How would someone use this form? As navigation, information, data entry, or as a dialog box?

e. Continue exploring the rest of the forms in the Northwind2 database and identify at least one form that is used as a navigation form, an information form, a data entry form, and a dialog box form.

f. Close all open forms.

8. Analyze reports.

a. Double-click the Sales by Year report.

b. The Sales by Year dialog form appears. Enter **1/1/95** in the Enter beginning date text box, enter **6/30/95** in the Enter ending date text box, then click OK.

c. The Sales by Year report for the first two quarters of 1995 appears, indicating that 186 orders were shipped during this period. A subreport is used in the ShippedDate Header section to provide summary information for the entire report before the Detail section prints.

d. Continue to explore the other reports in the Northwind2 database and identify at least three new features or techniques that you would like to learn more about.

e. Close all open reports, close the Northwind2 database, and exit Access.

Analyzing Database Design Using Northwind

Independent Challenge 1

As the manager of a basketball team, you have created an Access database called Basketball-J.accdb to track players, games, and statistics. You have recently learned how to create lookup tables to better control the values of a field that contain repeated data and to apply your new skills to your database.

a. Start Access, open the Basketball-J.accdb database from the location where you store your Data Files, and enable content if prompted.

b. Double-click the Players table to view its datasheet. Notice the repeated data in the YearInSchool and Position fields. You will build lookup tables to better describe and manage the values in those fields. Close the Players datasheet.

c. Click the CREATE tab, click Table Design, then create a two-field table with the field names **PositionDescription** and **PositionID**. Both fields should have a Short Text data type. Set PositionID as the primary key field. Save the table with the name **Positions**, and enter the data in the datasheet shown in **FIGURE J-26**. Save and close the Positions table.

FIGURE J-26

Positions	
PositionDescription ⁻	PositionID ⁻
Center	C
Forward	F
Guard	G
*	

d. Open the Players table in Design View, click the Position field, then choose Lookup Wizard using the Data Type list arrow.

e. Choose the "I want the lookup field to get the values..." option, choose Table: Positions, choose both fields, choose PositionDescription for an ascending sort order, do not hide the key column, choose PositionID as the field that uniquely identifies the row, accept the Position label, click the Enable Data Integrity check box, finish the Lookup Wizard, then click Yes to save the table. Close the Players table.

f. Repeat Step c creating a **ClassRanks** table instead of a Positions table using the field names and data shown in **FIGURE J-27**. The ClassRankDescription and ClassRankID fields are both Short Text fields. The SortOrder field is a Number field. Make the ClassRankID field the primary key field, then close the ClassRanks table.

FIGURE J-27

ClassRanks		
ClassRankDescription ⁻	ClassRankID ⁻	SortOrder ⁻
Freshman	Fr	1
Sophomore	So	2
Junior	Jr	3
Senior	Sr	4
*		0

g. Repeat Step d by using the Lookup Wizard with the YearInSchool field in the Players table to look up data in the ClassRanks table. Choose all three fields, choose the SortOrder field for an ascending sort order, do not hide the key column, choose ClassRankID as the field that uniquely identifies the row, accept the YearInSchool label, click the Enable Data Integrity check box, finish the Lookup Wizard, then click Yes to save the table.

h. Click the Lookup tab and change the Column Widths property to 1;1;0 to hide the SortOrder field, then save the Players table.

i. Open the Players table datasheet to test the drop-down lists for the YearInSchool and Position fields.

j. Open the Relationships window, click the All Relationships button to make sure you're viewing all relationships, and resize field lists as needed to show all fields. The final Relationships window should look like **FIGURE J-28**.

FIGURE J-28

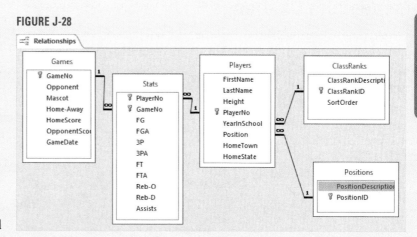

k. Create a Relationship report with the default name **Relationships for Basketball-J**.

l. Save and close the Relationships window, close the Basketball-J.accdb database, then exit Access.

Independent Challenge 2

You have been asked to create a query that displays employees as well as their manager in the same datasheet. Because each employee, regardless of title and rank, is entered as a record in the Employees table, you know that you will need to relate each record in the Employees table to another record in the same table to show the employee–manager relationship. You will work in the Northwind2 database to learn how to join a table to itself in order to answer this challenge.

a. Start Access, open the Northwind2.mdb database from the location where you store your Data Files, enable content if prompted, and click OK when prompted with the splash screen.

b. Click the CREATE tab, click the Query Design button, double-click Employees, double-click Employees a second time, click Close, right-click the Employees_1 field list, click Properties to open the Property Sheet for the Employee_1 field list, select Employees_1 in the Alias text box, type **Managers**, press [Enter], then close the Property Sheet.

c. Drag the EmployeeID field from the Managers field list and drop it on the ReportsTo field in the Employees table because each employee record reports to another employee whose EmployeeID value has been entered in the ReportsTo field. By creating this relationship using the primary key field of the Managers table, one record in the Managers table can be related to many records in the Employees table.

d. In the Managers field list, double-click the LastName field, then double-click the FirstName field.

e. In the Employees field list, double-click the LastName field, then double-click the FirstName field.

f. Add an ascending sort order on both LastName fields, as shown in **FIGURE J-29**.

g. Display the query datasheet, then widen each column to display all data. The datasheet shows that three employees report to Buchanan and five report to Fuller.

h. Save the query as **ManagerList**, close the query, then close the Northwind2 database and exit Access.

FIGURE J-29

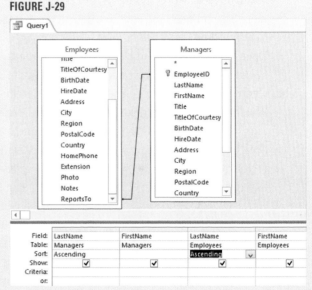

Independent Challenge 3

As the manager of a regional real estate information system, you've been asked to enhance the database to keep track of offers for each real estate listing. To do this, you will need to create a new table to track the offers, and relate it to the rest of the database in an appropriate one-to-many relationship.

a. Start Access, open the RealEstate-J.accdb database from the location where you store your Data Files, and enable content if prompted.

b. Create a table named **Offers** with the fields, data types, descriptions, and primary key shown in **FIGURE J-30**.

FIGURE J-30

Field Name	Data Type	Description
OfferID	AutoNumber	primary key field
ListingNo	Number	foreign key field to Listings table
OfferDate	Date/Time	date of offer
OfferAmount	Currency	dollar value of the offer
Buyer	Short Text	last name or company name of entity making the offer
Accepted	Yes/No	was offer accepted? Yes or No
AcceptanceDate	Date/Time	date the offer was accepted

Analyzing Database Design Using Northwind

Independent Challenge 3 (continued)

c. Use the Lookup Wizard on the ListingNo field in the Offers table to connect the Offers table to the Listings table. Select all the fields from the Listings table; sort in ascending order on the Type, Area, then SqFt fields; hide the key column; accept the ListingNo label for the lookup field; enable data integrity; and finish the wizard. Save the table when prompted.

d. In Table Design View, on the Lookup tab (Field Properties) for the ListingNo field, change the value for the Column Heads property from No to Yes.

e. In Table Design View, on the Lookup tab (Field Properties) for the ListingNo field, change the value for the List Rows property from 16 to **100**.

f. Save the table, click Yes when asked to check the data, then display it in Datasheet View.

g. Enter the record shown in the first row of **FIGURE J-31**, using the new combo box for the ListingNo field as shown.

h. Close the Offers table, close the RealEstate-J.accdb database, then exit Access.

FIGURE J-31

OfferID	ListingNo	OfferDate	OfferAmour	Buyer	Accepted	AcceptanceL	Click to Add
1	New	1/2/2015	$140,000.00	Student Last Name	✔	1/3/2015	
* (Ne							

Type	Area	SqFt	LakeFt	BR	Bath	Garage	Pool	Asking	RealtorNo	ListingDate
Cabin	Horseshoe Ber	1200	102	4	3	2	No	$150,000.00	2	3/1/2014
Cabin	Kimberling City	1350	50	2	2	2	No	$127,900.00	5	1/4/2014
Cabin	Kimberling City	1900	80	3	1	0	No	$111,900.00	8	4/1/2014
Log Cabin	Cape Fair	2000	300	3	2	0	No	$189,900.00	4	5/1/2014
Mobile Home	Galena	1200	120	3	2	0	No	$120,000.00	6	5/1/2014
New	Ridgedale	2900	180	3	2.5	2	No	$135,000.00	1	1/31/2014
New	Ridgedale	3000	65	2	3	0	No	$129,000.00	1	1/5/2014
Patio Home	Kimberling City	2200	0	2	2	1	Yes	$139,900.00	4	7/1/2014
Ranch	Branson	2700	85	4	3	2	No	$189,900.00	4	4/1/2003

Independent Challenge 4: Explore

An Access database can help record and track your job search efforts. In this exercise, you work with a database that tracks employers and job positions to better normalize and present the data.

a. Start Access, open the JobSearch-J.accdb database from the location where you store your Data Files, and enable content if prompted.

b. Open both the Employers and Positions tables in Datasheet View to review the data. One employer may offer many positions, so the tables are related by the common EmployerID field. You decide to add Lookup properties to the EmployerID field in the Positions table to better identify each employer in this view.

c. Close both table datasheets, open the Relationships window, right-click the join line between the Employers and Positions tables, then click Delete. Click Yes to confirm you want to delete the relationship. Before you can start the Lookup Wizard on the EmployerID field in the Positions table, all existing relationships to that field must be deleted.

d. Save and close the Relationships window, then open the Positions table in Design View.

e. Start the Lookup Wizard for the EmployerID field to look up values in the Employers table. Select all fields, sort in ascending order on the CompanyName field, hide the key column, select EmployerID if asked to select the field containing the value you want to store, use the EmployerID label, enable data integrity, finish the wizard, then save the table.

f. Display the Positions table in Datasheet View, then test the new Lookup properties on the EmployerID field by changing the EmployerID for both of the "Professor" positions to **JCCC**.

g. Close the Positions table, then start a new query in Query Design View. Add both the Employers and Positions tables.

h. Add the CompanyName field from the Employers table, and the Title and CareerArea fields from the Positions table.

i. Modify the join line to include all records from Employers, then view the datasheet.

j. Save the query with the name **EmployerPositions**, then close it.

k. Close the JobSearch-J.accdb database, then exit Access.

Access 2013

Visual Workshop

Start Access, open the Dives-J.accdb database from the location where you store your Data Files, and enable content if prompted. Add Lookup properties to the DiveMasterID field of the DiveTrips table to achieve the result shown in **FIGURE J-32**, which looks up every field from the DiveMasters table for the lookup list and sorts the information on the LName field. Hide the key column, accept the DiveMasterID label, and enforce referential integrity. But in order to use the Lookup Wizard, first you'll have to delete the existing relationship between the DiveMasters and DiveTrips tables. Once you've finished reestablishing the relationship with the Lookup Wizard, you'll also want to modify the Lookup properties of the DiveMasterID field so that Column Heads is set to **Yes** and List Rows is set to **100**. The final DiveTrips datasheet with Lookup properties applied to the DiveMasterID field will look like **FIGURE J-32**.

FIGURE J-32

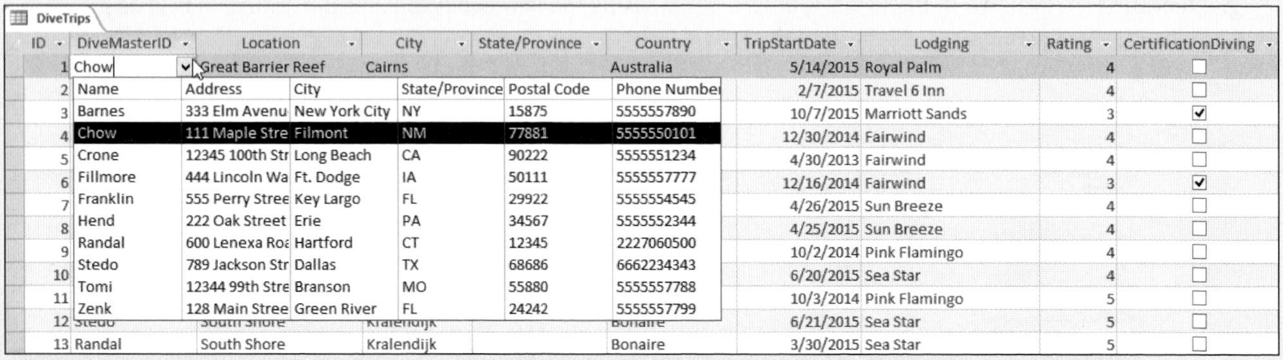

Creating Advanced Queries

CASE > You use advanced query techniques to help Jacob Thomas handle the requests for information about data stored in the Education database.

Unit Objectives

After completing this unit, you will be able to:

- Query for top values
- Create a parameter query
- Modify query properties
- Create a Make Table query
- Create an Append query

- Create a Delete query
- Create an Update query
- Specify join properties
- Find unmatched records

Files You Will Need

Education-K.accdb   Basketball-K.accdb
Seminar-K.accdb   Chocolate-K.accdb

Microsoft® product screenshots used with permission from Microsoft® Corporation.

Query for Top Values

Learning
Outcomes
• Apply Top Values
criteria
• Apply the Totals
row

After you enter a large number of records into a database, you may want to select only the most significant records by choosing a subset of the highest or lowest values from a sorted query. Use the **Top Values** feature in Query Design View to specify a number or percentage of sorted records that you want to display in the query's datasheet. **CASE** ▶ *Employee attendance at continuing education classes has grown at Quest Specialty Travel. To help plan future classes, Jacob Thomas wants a listing of the top five classes, sorted in descending order by the number of attendees for each class. You can create a summary query to find and sort the total number of attendees for each class, then use the Top Values feature to find the five most attended classes.*

STEPS

1. **Start Access, open the Education-K.accdb database, enable content if prompted, click the CREATE tab, then click the Query Design button in the Queries group**
   You need fields from both the Enrollments and Courses tables.

TROUBLE
If you add a table's field list to Query Design View twice by mistake, click the title bar of the extra field list, then press [Delete].

2. **Double-click Enrollments, double-click Courses, then click Close in the Show Table dialog box**
   Query Design View displays the field lists of the two related tables in the upper pane of the query window.

3. **Double-click EnrollmentID in the Enrollments field list, double-click Description in the Courses field list, then click the View button ▦ to switch to Datasheet View**
   The datasheet shows 404 total records. You want to know how many people took each course, so you need to group the records by the Description field and count the EnrollmentID field.

4. **Click the View button ⟨⟩ to switch to Query Design View, click the Totals button in the Show/Hide group, click Group By for the EnrollmentID field, click the Group By list arrow, then click Count**
   Sorting is required in order to find the top values.

QUICK TIP
You must sort the records to get the highest (or lowest) values at the "top" before the Top Values feature makes sense.

5. **Click the EnrollmentID field Sort cell, click the EnrollmentID field Sort list arrow, then click Descending**
   Your screen should look like **FIGURE K-1**. Choosing a descending sort order lists the courses with the highest count value (the most attended courses) at the top of the datasheet.

6. **Click the Top Values list arrow in the Query Setup group, then click 5**
   The number or percentage specified in the Top Values list box determines which records the query returns, starting with the first record on the sorted datasheet. This is why you *must sort* your records before applying the Top Values feature. See **TABLE K-1** for more information on Top Values options.

7. **Click ▦ to display the resulting datasheet, then use the ✛ pointer to widen the first column to show the complete field name**
   Your screen should look like **FIGURE K-2**. The datasheet shows the seven most attended continuing education courses. The query selected the top seven, rather than the top five courses because there is a three-way tie for fifth place. Three courses that had 17 enrollments are all tied for fifth place, so each of those courses is listed in the datasheet.

8. **Click the Save button ▤ on the Quick Access toolbar, type TopCourses, click OK, then close the datasheet**
   As with all queries, if you enter additional enrollment records into this database, the count statistics in the TopCourses query are automatically updated.

FIGURE K-1: Designing a summary query for top values

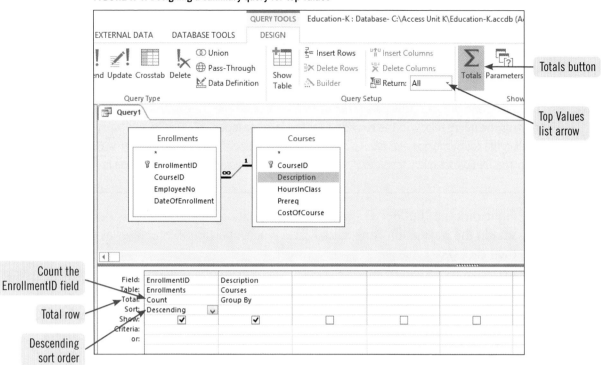

FIGURE K-2: Top Values datasheet

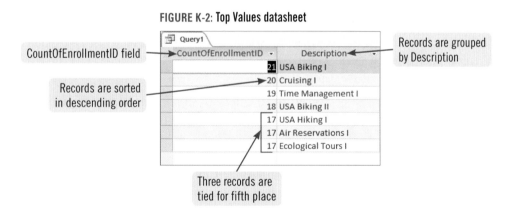

TABLE K-1: Top Values options

action	displays
Click 5, 25, or 100 in the Top Values list	Top 5, 25, or 100 records
Enter a number, such as 10, in the Top Values box	Top 10, or whatever value is entered, records
Click 5% or 25% in the Top Values list	Top 5 percent or 25 percent of records
Enter a percentage, such as 10%, in the Top Values text box	Top 10 percent, or whatever percentage is entered, of records
Click All	All records

Access 2013

Create a Parameter Query

Learning
Outcomes
• Enter parameter
  criteria
• Apply the Like
  operator

A **parameter query** displays a dialog box that prompts you for field criteria. Your entry in the dialog box determines which records appear on the final datasheet, just as if you had entered that criteria directly in the query design grid. You can also build a form or report based on a parameter query. When you open the form or report, the parameter dialog box opens. The entry in the dialog box determines which records the query selects in the recordset for the form or report. **CASE** ▶ *You want to create a query to display the courses for an individual department that you specify each time you run the query. To do so, you copy the TopCourses query then modify it to remove the Top Values option and include parameter prompts.*

STEPS

1. **Right-click the** TopCourses query **in the Navigation Pane, click** Copy**, right-click a blank spot in the Navigation Pane, click** Paste**, type** DepartmentParameter **as the Query Name, then click** OK

   You modify the DepartmentParameter query to remove the top values and to include the parameter prompt.

2. **Right-click** DepartmentParameter**, click** Design View **on the shortcut menu, click the** Show Table button **in the Query Setup group, double-click** Employees**, then click** Close

   The Employees table contains the Department field needed for this query.

3. **Drag the** title bar of the Courses field list **to the left, then drag the** title bar of the Enrollments field list **to the right so that the relationship lines do not cross behind a field list**

   You are not required to rearrange the field lists of a query, but doing so can help clarify the relationships between them.

4. **Double-click the** EDepartment **field in the Employees field list, click the** Top Values list arrow **in the Query Setup group, click** All**, delete the** Descending sort order **in the** EnrollmentID field**, then click the** View button ⊞ **to display the datasheet**

   The query now counts the EnrollmentID field for records grouped by course description as well as by employee department. Because you only want to query for one department at a time, however, you need to add parameter criteria to the Department field.

QUICK TIP
To enter a long crite-
rion, right-click the
Criteria cell, then
click Zoom.

5. **Click the** View button ⊠ **to return to Query Design View, click the** EDepartment field Criteria cell**, type** [Enter department:]**, then click** ⊞ **to display the Enter Parameter Value dialog box, as shown in** FIGURE K-3

   In Query Design View, you must enter parameter criteria within [square brackets]. The parameter criterion you enter appears as a prompt in the Enter Parameter Value dialog box. The entry you make in the Enter Parameter Value dialog box is used as the final criterion for the field that contains the parameter criterion. You can combine logical operators such as greater than (>) or less than (<) as well as wildcard characters such as an asterisk (*) with parameter criteria to create flexible search options. See **TABLE K-2** for more examples of parameter criteria.

QUICK TIP
Query criteria are
not case sensitive, so
"marketing,"
"Marketing," and
"MARKETING" all
yield the same
results.

6. **Type** Marketing **in the Enter department: text box, then click** OK

   Only those records with "Marketing" in the Department field are displayed, a portion of which are shown in **FIGURE K-4**.

7. **Save and close the DepartmentParameter query**

FIGURE K-3: Using parameter criteria for the EDepartment field

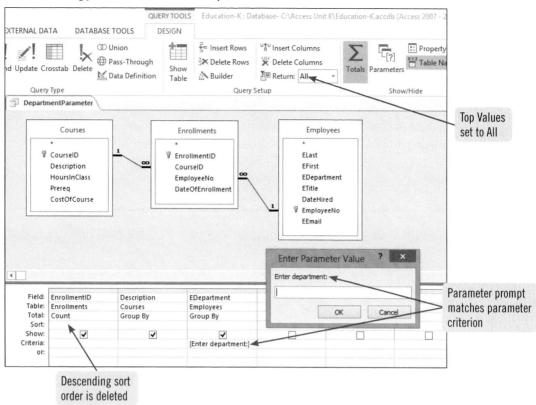

Top Values set to All

Parameter prompt matches parameter criterion

Descending sort order is deleted

FIGURE K-4: Datasheet for parameter query when EDepartment field equals Marketing

EDepartment field equals Marketing

TABLE K-2: Examples of parameter criteria

field data type	parameter criteria	description
Date/Time	>=[Enter start date:]	Searches for dates on or after the entered date
Date/Time	>=[Enter start date:] and <=[Enter end date:]	Prompts you for two date entries and searches for dates on or after the first date and on or before the second date
Short Text	Like [Enter the first character of the last name:] & "*"	Searches for any name that begins with the entered character
Short Text	Like "*" & [Enter any character(s) to search by:] & "*"	Searches for words that contain the entered characters anywhere in the field

Modify Query Properties

Learning
Outcomes
• Modify the
Description
property
• Define the
Recordset Type
property
• Create a backup

Properties are characteristics that define the appearance and behavior of items in the database, such as objects, fields, sections, and controls. You can view the properties for an item by opening its Property Sheet. **Field properties**, those that describe a field, can be changed in either Table Design View or Query Design View. If you change field properties in Query Design View, they are modified for that query only (as opposed to changing the field properties in Table Design View, which affects that field's characteristics throughout the database). Query objects also have properties that you might want to modify to better describe or protect the information they provide. **CASE** *You want to modify the query and field properties of the DepartmentParameter query to better describe and present the data.*

STEPS

1. **Right-click the** DepartmentParameter **query in the Navigation Pane, then click** Object Properties

    The DepartmentParameter Properties dialog box opens, providing information about the query and a text box where you can enter a description for the query.

2. **Type** Counts enrollments per course description and prompts for department, **then click** OK

    The **Description** property allows you to better document the purpose or author of a query. The Description property also appears on **Database Documenter** reports, a feature on the DATABASE TOOLS tab that helps you create reports with information about the database.

TROUBLE
The title bar of the
Property Sheet
always indicates
which item's proper-
ties are shown. If it
shows anything other
than "Query
Properties," click a
blank spot beside the
field lists to display
query properties.

3. **Right-click the** DepartmentParameter **query in the Navigation Pane, click** Design View **on the shortcut menu, click the** Property Sheet button **in the Show/Hide group, then click a blank spot in the upper pane to show Query Properties in the Property Sheet**

    The Property Sheet for the query is shown in **FIGURE K-5**. It shows a complete list of the query's properties, including the Description property that you modified earlier. The **Recordset Type** property determines if and how records displayed by a query are locked and has two common choices: Snapshot and Dynaset. **Snapshot** locks the recordset (which prevents it from being updated). **Dynaset** is the default value and allows updates to data. Because a summary query's datasheet summarizes several records, you cannot update the data in a summary query regardless of the Recordset Type property value. For regular Select queries, you can specify Snapshot in the Recordset Type property to give users read (but not write) access to that datasheet.

    To change the field name, you modify the field's **Caption** property in the Property Sheet for field prop-erties. When you click a property in a Property Sheet, a short description of the property appears in the status bar. Press [F1] to open Access Help for a longer description of the selected property.

4. **Click the** EnrollmentID **field, click the** Caption property **in the Property Sheet, type** Total Enrollment, **click the** View button **■, type** Personnel **as the parameter value, then click** OK

    The Total Enrollment Caption clarifies the first column of data, as shown in **FIGURE K-6**, which displays a portion of the datasheet.

QUICK TIP
To add a description
to a table, form, or
other object, close it,
right-click it in the
Navigation Pane,
then click View
Properties on the
shortcut menu.

5. **Save and close the DepartmentParameter query**

    The next few lessons work with action queries that modify data. In preparation for these lessons, you create a backup. A **backup** is a copy of the database that you could use if an error occurs in the current database that cannot be fixed. Businesses typically back up their database files each night.

6. **Click the** FILE tab, **click** Save As, **click** Back Up Database, **click the** Save As button, **navigate to the location where you store your Data Files, and click** Save

    A copy of the database has been placed in the selected folder with the name Education-K_*current date*.accdb.

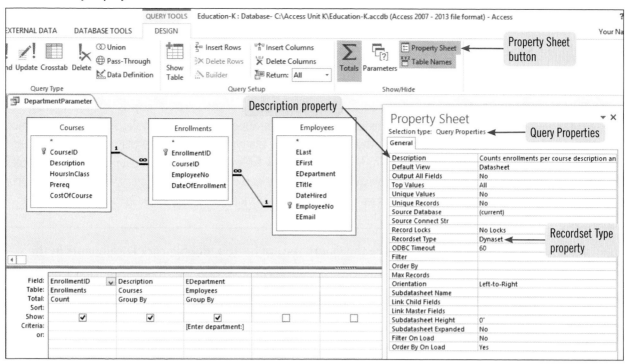

Creating an Alias

The **Alias** property renames a field list in Query Design View. An Alias doesn't change the actual name of the underlying object, but it can be helpful when you are working with a database which uses technical or outdated names for tables and queries. To create an alias, right-click the field list in Query Design View, click Properties on the shortcut menu, and then modify the Alias property.

Create a Make Table Query

Learning
Outcomes
• Define action
  queries
• Create a Make
  Table query

A **Select query** selects fields and records that match specific criteria and displays them in a datasheet. Select queries start with the SQL keyword **SELECT** and have many variations, such as summary, crosstab, top values, and parameter queries. Another very powerful type of query is the action query. Unlike Select queries that only *select* data, an **action query** *changes* all of the selected records when it is run. Access provides four types of action queries: Delete, Update, Append, and Make Table. See **TABLE K-3** for more information on action queries. A **Make Table query** is a type of action query that creates a new table of data for the selected datasheet. The location of the new table can be the current database or another Access database. Sometimes a Make Table query is used to back up data. **CASE** *You decide to use a Make Table query to archive the first quarter's records for the year 2015 that are currently stored in the Enrollments table.*

STEPS

1. **Click the CREATE tab, click the Query Design button, double-click Enrollments in the Show Table dialog box, click Close, then close the Property Sheet if it is open**

   Given you cannot undo the changes made by an action query, it's a good idea to create a backup copy of the database before running an action query. You created a backup copy of the database in the last step of the previous lesson.

2. **Double-click the * (asterisk) at the top of the Enrollments field list**

   Adding the asterisk to the query design grid includes in the grid all of the fields in that table. Later, if you add new fields to the Enrollments table, they are also added to this query.

   QUICK TIP
   Access automatically adds pound signs (#) around the date criteria.

3. **Double-click the DateOfEnrollment field to add it to the second column of the query grid, click the DateOfEnrollment field Criteria cell, type >=1/1/15 and <=3/31/15, click the DateOfEnrollment field Show check box to uncheck it, then use the resize pointer ↔ to widen the DateOfEnrollment column to view the entire Criteria entry, as shown in FIGURE K-7**

   Before changing this query into a Make Table query, it is always a good idea to run the query as a Select query to view the selected data.

4. **Click the View button 🗔 to switch to Datasheet View, click any entry in the DateOfEnrollment field, then click the Descending button in the Sort & Filter group**

   Sorting the records in descending order based on the values in the DateOfEnrollment field allows you to confirm that only records in the first quarter of 2015 appear in the datasheet.

5. **Click the View button ⬚ to return to Design View, click the Make Table button in the Query Type group, type ArchiveEnrollments in the Table Name text box, then click OK**

   The Make Table query is ready, but action queries do not change data until you click the Run button. All action query icons include an exclamation point in their buttons to remind you that they *change* data when you run them and you must *run* the queries for the action to occur. To prevent running an action query accidentally, use the Datasheet View button 🗔 to *view* the selected records, and use the Run button only when you are ready to *run* the action.

   TROUBLE
   If you do not see 154 records when viewing the datasheet, return to Design View and compare your query with **FIGURE K-7**.

6. **Click the View button 🗔 to double-check the records you have selected, click the View button ⬚ to return to Query Design View, click the Run button to execute the make table action, click Yes when prompted that you are about to paste 154 rows, then save the query with the name MakeArchiveEnrollments and close it**

   When you run an action query, Access prompts you with an "Are you sure?" message before actually updating the data. The Undo button cannot undo changes made by action queries.

   QUICK TIP
   Double-clicking an action query in the Navigation Pane runs the query.

7. **Double-click the ArchiveEnrollments table in the Navigation Pane to view the new table's datasheet as shown in FIGURE K-8, then close the ArchiveEnrollments table**

FIGURE K-7: Creating a Make Table query

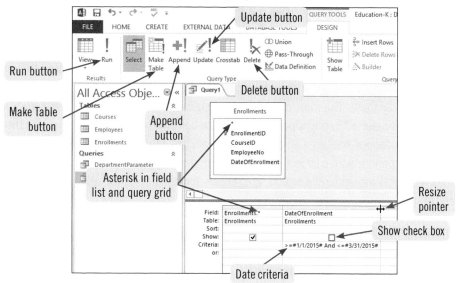

FIGURE K-8: ArchiveEnrollments table

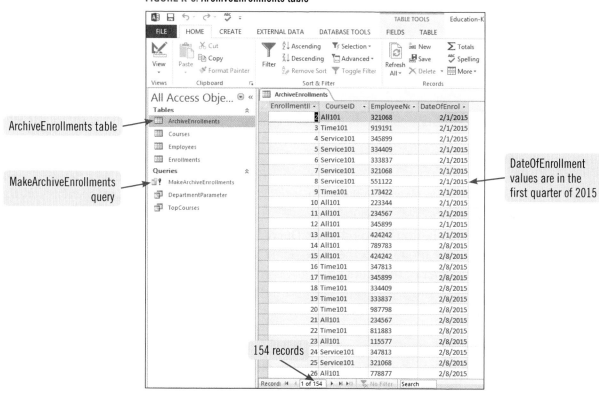

TABLE K-3: Action queries

action query	query icon	description	example
Delete		Deletes a group of records from one or more tables	Remove products that are discontinued or for which there are no orders
Update		Makes global changes to a group of records in one or more tables	Raise prices by 10 percent for all products
Append		Adds a group of records from one or more tables to the end of another table	Append the employee address table from one division of the company to the address table from another division of the company
Make Table		Creates a new table from data in one or more tables	Export records to another Access database or make a backup copy of a table

Create an Append Query

An **Append query** is an action query that adds selected records to an existing table. The existing table is called the **target table**. The Append query works like an export feature because the records are copied from one location and pasted in the target table. The target table can be in the current database or in any other Access database. The most difficult part of creating an Append query is making sure that all of the fields you have selected in the Append query match fields with the same data types in the target table. For example, you cannot append a Short Text field from one table to a Number field in another table. If you attempt to append a field to an incompatible field in the target table, an error message appears and you are forced to cancel the append process. **CASE** *You use an Append query to append the records with a DateOfEnrollment value in April 2015 from the Enrollments table to the ArchiveEnrollments table.*

STEPS

1. **Click the CREATE tab, click the Query Design button, double-click Enrollments in the Show Table dialog box, then click Close**

2. **Double-click the title bar in the Enrollments table's field list, then drag the highlighted fields to the first column of the query design grid**

   Double-clicking the title bar of the field list selects all of the fields, allowing you to add them to the query grid very quickly. To successfully append records to a table, you need to identify how each field in the query is connected to an existing field in the target table. Therefore, the technique of adding all of the fields to the query grid by using the asterisk does not work when you append records, because using the asterisk doesn't list each field in a separate column in the query grid.

3. **Click the DateOfEnrollment field Criteria cell, type Between 4/1/15 and 4/30/15, use ↔ to widen the DateOfEnrollment field column to view the criteria, then click the View button ▦ to display the selected records**

   The datasheet should show 106 records with an April date in the DateOfEnrollment field. **Between...and** criteria select all records between the two dates, including the two dates. Between...and operators work the same way as the >= and <= operators.

4. **Click the View button ☑ to return to Query Design View, click the Append button in the Query Type group, click the Table Name list arrow in the Append dialog box, click ArchiveEnrollments, then click OK**

   The **Append To row** appears in the query design grid, as shown in **FIGURE K-9**, to show how the fields in the query match fields in the target table, ArchiveEnrollments. Now that you are sure you selected the right records and set up the Append query, you're ready to click the Run button to append the selected records to the table.

5. **Click the Run button in the Results group, click Yes to confirm that you want to append 106 rows, then save the query with the name AppendArchiveEnrollments and close it**

6. **Double-click the ArchiveEnrollments table in the Navigation Pane, click any entry in the DateOfEnrollment field, then click the Descending button in the Sort & Filter group**

   The 106 April records are appended to the ArchiveEnrollments table, which previously had 154 records for a new total of 260 records, as shown in **FIGURE K-10**.

7. **Save and close the ArchiveEnrollments table**

FIGURE K-9: Creating an Append query

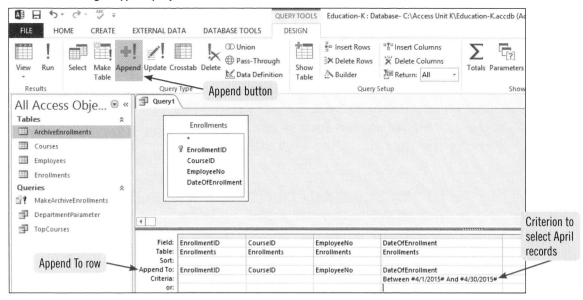

FIGURE K-10: ArchiveEnrollments table with appended records

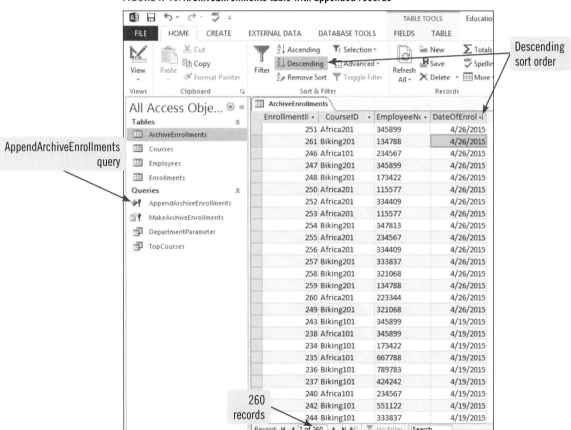

1900 versus 2000 dates

If you type only two digits of a date, Access assumes that the digits 00 through 29 are for the years 2000 through 2029. If you type 30 through 99, Access assumes the years refer to 1930 through 1999. If you want to specify years outside these ranges, you must type all four digits of the year.

Create a Delete Query

A **Delete query** deletes selected records from one or more tables. Delete queries delete entire records, not just selected fields within records. If you want to delete a field from a table, you open Table Design View, click the field name, then click the Delete Rows button. As in all action queries, you cannot reverse the action completed by the Delete query by clicking the Undo button. **CASE** ▶ *Now that you have archived the first four months of Enrollments records for 2015 in the ArchiveEnrollments table, you want to delete the same records from the Enrollments table. You can use a Delete query to accomplish this task.*

STEPS

1. **Click the CREATE tab, click the Query Design button, double-click Enrollments in the Show Table dialog box, then click Close**

2. **Double-click the * (asterisk) at the top of the Enrollments table's field list, then double-click the DateOfEnrollment field**

   Using the asterisk adds all fields from the Enrollments table to the first column of the query design grid. You add the DateOfEnrollment field to the second column of the query design grid so you can enter limiting criteria for this field.

3. **Click the DateOfEnrollment field Criteria cell, type Between 1/1/15 and 4/30/15, then use ↔ to widen the DateOfEnrollment field column to view the criteria**

   Before you run a Delete query, be sure to check the selected records to make sure you selected the same 260 records that you previously added to the ArchiveEnrollments table.

4. **Click the View button 📊 to confirm that the datasheet has 260 records, click the View button ◩ to return to Design View, then click the Delete button in the Query Type group**

   Your screen should look like **FIGURE K-11**. The **Delete row** now appears in the query design grid. You can delete the selected records by clicking the Run button.

5. **Click the Run button, click Yes to confirm that you want to delete 260 rows, then save the query with the name DeleteEnrollments and close it**

6. **Double-click the Enrollments table in the Navigation Pane, click any entry in the DateOfEnrollment field, then click the Ascending button in the Sort & Filter group**

   The records should start in May, as shown in **FIGURE K-12**. The Delete query deleted all records from the Enrollments table with dates between 1/1/2015 and 4/30/2015.

7. **Save and close the Enrollments table**

FIGURE K-11: Creating a Delete query

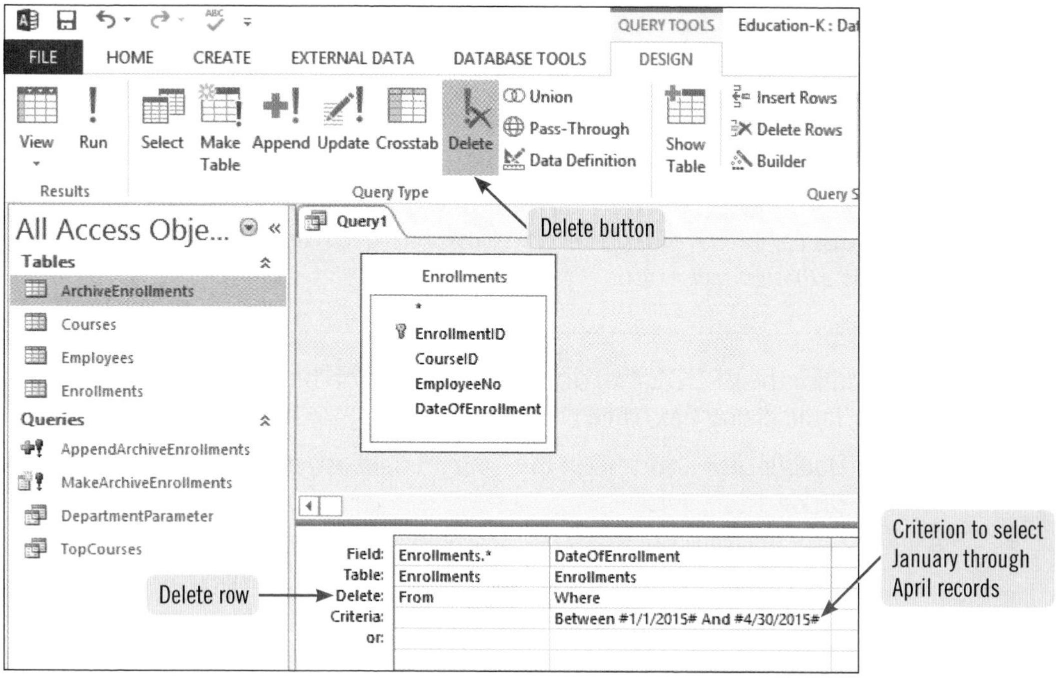

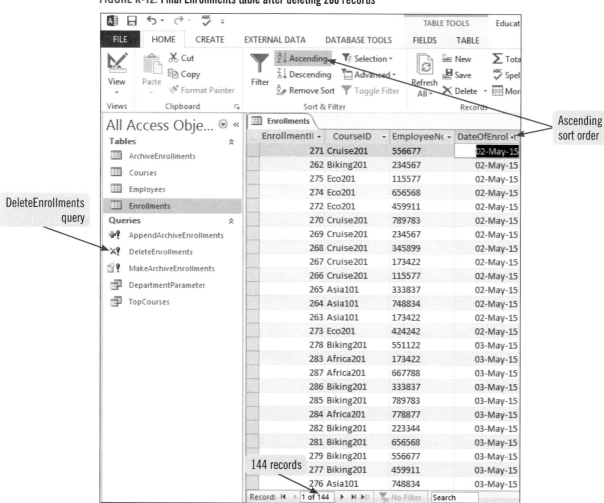

FIGURE K-12: Final Enrollments table after deleting 260 records

Create an Update Query

Learning Outcomes
• Create an Update query
• Hide and restore objects

An **Update query** is a type of action query that updates the values in a field. For example, you might want to increase the price of a product in a particular category by 10 percent. Or you might want to update information such as assigned sales representative, region, or territory for a subset of customers. **CASE** ▸ *Jacob Thomas has just informed you that the cost of continuing education is being increased by $20 for each class effective immediately. You can create an Update query to quickly calculate and update the new course costs.*

STEPS

1. Click the CREATE tab, click the Query Design button, double-click Courses in the Show Table dialog box, then click Close

2. Double-click CourseID in the Courses field list, double-click Description, then double-click CostofCourse

   Every action query starts as a Select query. Always review the datasheet of the Select query before initiating any action that changes data to double-check which records are affected.

3. Click the View button ▦ to display the query datasheet, note that the values in all three of the Africa courses are $450, then click the View button ⬚ to return to Design View

   After selecting the records you want to update and reviewing the values in the CostOfCourse field, you're ready to change this Select query into an Update query.

4. Click the Update button in the Query Type group

   The **Update To row** appears in the query design grid. To add $20 to the values in the CostOfCourse field, you need to enter the appropriate expression in the Update To cell for the CostOfCourse field.

5. Click the Update To cell for the CostOfCourse field, then type 20+[CostOfCourse]

   Your screen should look like **FIGURE K-13**. The expression adds 20 to the current value of the CostOfCourse field, but the CostOfCourse field is not updated until you run the query.

6. Click the View button ▦ to see the datasheet, click the View button ⬚ to return to Design View, click the Run button, then click Yes to confirm that you want to update 32 rows

   When you view the datasheet of an Update query, only the field being updated appears on the datasheet. To view all fields in the query, change this query back into a Select query, then view the datasheet.

7. Click the Select button in the Query Type group, then click ▦ to display the query datasheet, as shown in FIGURE K-14

   The Africa records have been updated from $450 to $470. All other CostOfCourse values have increased by $20 as well.

TROUBLE
If you double-click an action query in the Navigation Pane, you initiate that action.

8. Click ⬚ to return to Design View, click the Update button in the Query Type group to switch this query back to an Update query, save the query with the name UpdateCost, then close it

   Often, you do not need to save action queries because after the data has been updated, you generally won't use the same query again. Also, it is sometimes dangerous to leave action queries in the Navigation Pane because if you double-click an action query, you run that action (as opposed to opening its datasheet). When you double-click a Select query, you open the query's datasheet. You can keep an action query in the Navigation Pane but hide it using the **Hidden property**.

9. Right-click the UpdateCost query in the Navigation pane, click Object Properties, click the Hidden check box, then click OK

FIGURE K-13: Setting up an Update query

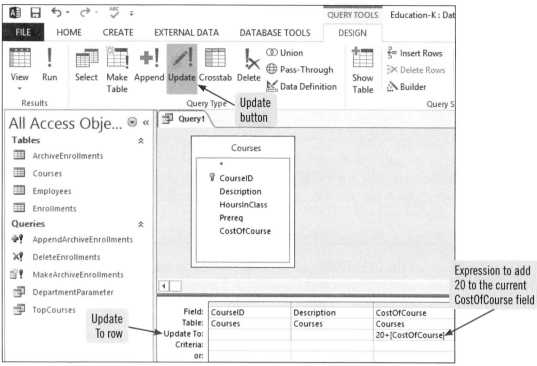

FIGURE K-14: Updated CostOfCourse values

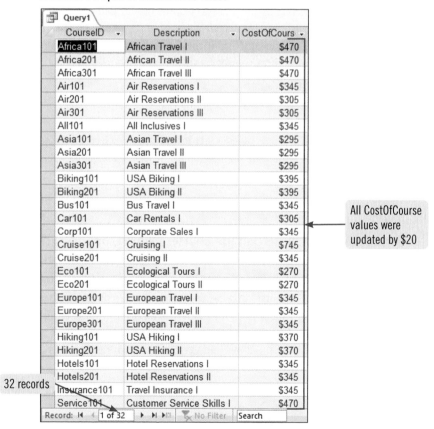

Restoring hidden objects

To view hidden objects, right-click a blank spot in the Navigation Pane, and then choose Navigation Options. In the Navigation Options dialog box, check the Show Hidden Objects check box, then click OK.

Specify Join Properties

Learning
Outcomes
• Create a left join
• Define left and
  right joins

When you use the Relationships window to define table relationships, the tables are joined in the same way in Query Design View. If referential integrity is enforced on a relationship, a "1" appears next to the field that serves as the "one" side of the one-to-many relationship, and an infinity symbol (∞) appears next to the field that serves as the "many" side. The "one" field is the primary key field for its table, and the "many" field is called the foreign key field. If no relationships have been established in the Relationships window, Access automatically creates **join lines** in Query Design View if the linking fields have the same name and data type in two tables. You can edit table relationships for a query in Query Design View by double-clicking the join line. **CASE** *Jacob Thomas asks what courses have been created that have never been attended. You can modify the join properties of the relationship between the Enrollments and Courses table to find this answer.*

STEPS

1. **Click the CREATE tab, click the Query Design button, double-click Courses, double-click Enrollments, then click Close**

   Because the Courses and Enrollments tables have already been related with a one-to-many relationship with referential integrity enforced in the Relationships window, the join line automatically appears in Query Design View.

   TROUBLE
   Double-click the middle portion of the join line, not the "one" or "many" symbol, to open the Join Properties dialog box.

2. **Double-click the one-to-many join line between the field lists**

   The Join Properties dialog box opens and displays the characteristics for the join, as shown in **FIGURE K-15**. The dialog box shows that option 1 is selected, the default join type, which means that the query displays only records where joined fields from *both* tables are equal. In **SQL (Structured Query Language)**, this is called an **inner join**. This means that if the Courses table has any records for which there are no matching Enrollments records, those courses do not appear in the resulting datasheet.

3. **Click the 2 option button**

   By choosing option 2, you are specifying that you want to see *all* of the records in the Courses table (the "one," or parent table), even if the Enrollments table (the "many," or child table) does not contain matching records. In SQL, this is called a **left join**. Option 3 selects all records in the Enrollments (the "many," or child table) even if there are no matches in the Courses table. In SQL, this is called a **right join**.

4. **Click OK**

   The join line's appearance changes, as shown in **FIGURE K-16**. With the join property set, you add fields to the query grid.

5. **Double-click CourseID in the Courses field list, double-click Description in the Courses field list, double-click EnrollmentID in the Enrollments field list, click the EnrollmentID Criteria cell, type Is Null, then click the View button ▦ to display the datasheet**

   The query finds 14 courses that currently have no matching records in the Enrollments table, as shown in **FIGURE K-17**. These courses contain a null (nothing) value in the EnrollmentID field. To select these records, you had to change the join property between the tables to include *all* records from the Courses table because the default join type, the inner join, requires a matching record in *both* tables to display a record in the resulting datasheet.

6. **Save the query with the name CoursesWithoutEnrollments, then close it**

FIGURE K-15: Join Properties dialog box

Default join (inner join)

Selects parent records even if they have no matching child records (left join)

Selects child records even if they have no matching parent records (right join)

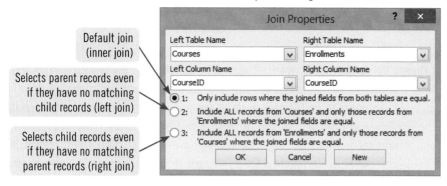

Join Properties

Left Table Name
Courses

Right Table Name
Enrollments

Left Column Name
CourseID

Right Column Name
CourseID

⦿ 1: Only include rows where the joined fields from both tables are equal.

○ 2: Include ALL records from 'Courses' and only those records from 'Enrollments' where the joined fields are equal.

○ 3: Include ALL records from 'Enrollments' and only those records from 'Courses' where the joined fields are equal.

OK   Cancel   New

FIGURE K-16: Left join between tables

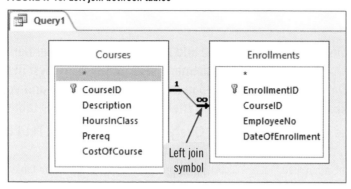

Left join symbol

FIGURE K-17: Courses without matching enrollments

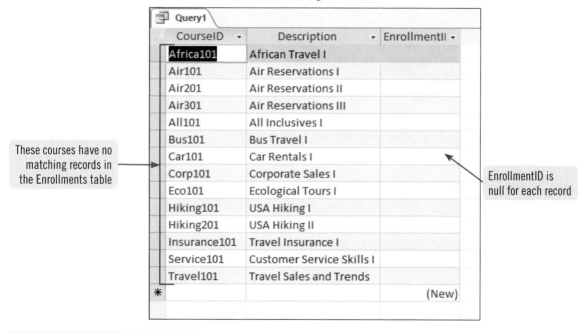

These courses have no matching records in the Enrollments table

EnrollmentID is null for each record

CourseID	Description	EnrollmentI
Africa101	African Travel I	
Air101	Air Reservations I	
Air201	Air Reservations II	
Air301	Air Reservations III	
All101	All Inclusives I	
Bus101	Bus Travel I	
Car101	Car Rentals I	
Corp101	Corporate Sales I	
Eco101	Ecological Tours I	
Hiking101	USA Hiking I	
Hiking201	USA Hiking II	
Insurance101	Travel Insurance I	
Service101	Customer Service Skills I	
Travel101	Travel Sales and Trends	
*		(New)

Null and zero-length string values

The term **null** describes a field value that does not exist because it has never been entered. In a datasheet, null values look the same as a zero-length string value but have a different purpose. A **zero-length string** value is a *deliberate* entry that contains no characters. You enter a zero-length string by typing two quotation marks ("") with no space between them. A null value, on the other hand, indicates *unknown* data.

By using null and zero-length string values appropriately, you can later query for the records that match one or the other condition. To query for zero-length string values, enter two quotation marks ("") as the criterion. To query for null values, use **Is Null** as the criterion. To query for any value other than a null value, use **Is Not Null** as the criterion.

Find Unmatched Records

Learning
Outcomes
• Use the Find
  Unmatched Query
  Wizard
• Describe the Find
  Duplicates Query
  Wizard

Another way to find records in one table that have no matching records in another is to use the **Find Unmatched Query Wizard**. In other words, the Find Unmatched Query Wizard creates an outer join between the tables in the query so that *all* records are selected in one table even if there is no match in the other table. Sometimes you inherit a database in which referential integrity was not imposed from the beginning, and unmatched records exist in the "many" table (orphan records). Or sometimes you want to find records in the "one" table that have no matching child records in the "many" table. You could use the Find Unmatched Query Wizard to create a query to answer either of these questions. **CASE** *Jacob Thomas wonders if there are any employees who have never enrolled in a class. You can use the Find Unmatched Query Wizard to create a query to answer this question.*

STEPS

1. **Open the Employees table, and add a new record with *your* name in the ELast and EFirst fields, Operations in the EDepartment field, Business Analyst in the ETitle field, 1/1/15 in the DateHired field, 93-93-93 in the EmployeeNo field, and *your* school email address in the EEmail field, press [Enter], then close the Employees table**

2. **Click the CREATE tab, click the Query Wizard button, click Find Unmatched Query Wizard, then click OK**

   The Find Unmatched Query Wizard starts, prompting you to select the table or query that may contain no related records.

3. **Click Table: Employees, then click Next**

   You want to find which employees have no enrollments, so you select the Enrollments table as the related table.

4. **Click Table: Enrollments, then click Next**

   The next question asks you to identify which field is common to both tables. Because the Employees table is already related to the Enrollments table in the Relationships window via the common EmployeeNo field, those fields are already selected as the matching fields, as shown in **FIGURE K-18**.

5. **Click Next**

   You are prompted to select the fields from the Employees table that you want to display in the query datasheet.

6. **Click the Select All Fields button** `>>`

7. **Click Next, type EmployeesWithoutEnrollments, click Finish, then resize the columns of the datasheet to view all data**

   The final datasheet is shown in **FIGURE K-19**. One existing employee plus the record you entered in Step 1 have not yet enrolled in any class.

8. **Save and close the EmployeesWithoutEnrollments query, then close the Education-K. accdb database**

Reviewing referential integrity

Recall that you can establish, or enforce, **referential integrity** between two tables when joining tables in the Relationships window. Referential integrity applies a set of rules to the relationship that ensures that no orphaned records currently exist, are added to, or are created in the database. A table has an **orphan record** when information in the foreign key field of the "many" table doesn't have a matching entry in the primary key field of the "one" table. The term "orphan" comes from the analogy that the "one" table contains **parent records**, and the "many" table contains **child records**. Referential integrity means that a Delete query would not be able to delete records in the "one" (parent) table that has related records in the "many" (child) table.

Creating Advanced Queries

FIGURE K-18: Using the Find Unmatched Query Wizard

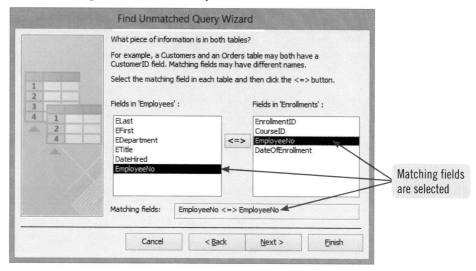

FIGURE K-19: Employees without matching Enrollments records

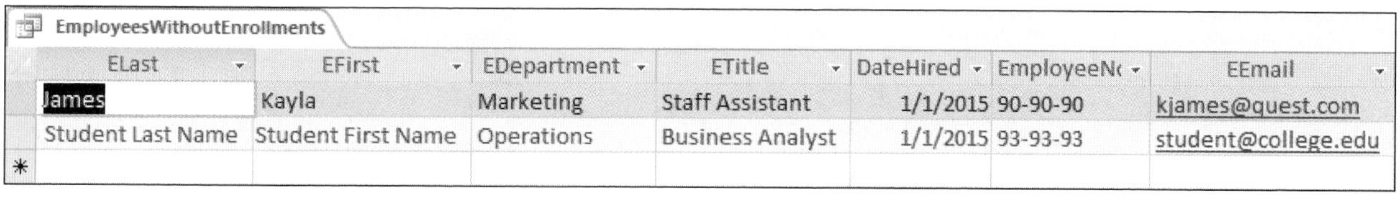

ELast	EFirst	EDepartment	ETitle	DateHired	EmployeeN	EEmail
James	Kayla	Marketing	Staff Assistant	1/1/2015	90-90-90	kjames@quest.com
Student Last Name	Student First Name	Operations	Business Analyst	1/1/2015	93-93-93	student@college.edu

EmployeesWithoutEnrollments

Find Duplicates Query Wizard

The Find Duplicates Query Wizard is another query wizard that is only available from the New Query dialog box. As you would suspect, the **Find Duplicates Query Wizard** helps you find duplicate values in a field, which can assist in finding and correcting potential data entry errors. For example, if you suspect that the same customer has been entered with two different names in your Customers table, you could use the Find Duplicates Query Wizard to find records with duplicate values in the Street or Phone field. After you isolated the records with the same values in a field, you could then edit incorrect data and delete redundant records.

Practice

Put your skills into practice with SAM! If you have a SAM account, go to www.cengage.com/sam2013 to access SAM assignments for this unit.

Concepts Review

Identify each element of the Query Design View shown in FIGURE K-20.

FIGURE K-20

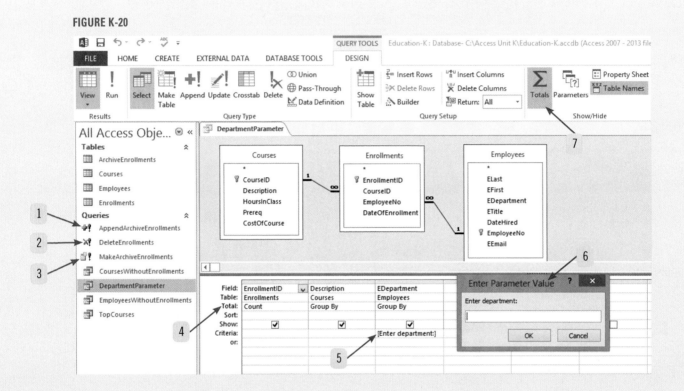

Match each term with the statement that best describes it.

8. **Null**
9. **Parameter**
10. **Top Values query**
11. **Inner join**
12. **Action query**
13. **Properties**

a. Characteristics that define the appearance and behavior of items within the database

b. Displays only a number or percentage of records from a sorted query

c. Displays a dialog box prompting you for criteria

d. Means that the query displays only records where joined fields from both tables are equal

e. Makes changes to data

f. A field value that does not exist

Select the best answer from the list of choices.

14. Which join type selects all records from the "one" (parent) table?
- **a.** Inner
- **b.** Left
- **c.** Central
- **d.** Right

15. Which of the following is a valid parameter criterion entry in the query design grid?
- **a.** >=[Type minimum value here:]
- **b.** >=Type minimum value here:
- **c.** >=(Type minimum value here:)
- **d.** >={Type minimum value here: }

16. You *cannot* use the Top Values feature to:
- **a.** Select the bottom 10 percent of records.
- **b.** Show the top 30 records.
- **c.** Display a subset of records.
- **d.** Update a field's value by 5 percent.

17. Which of the following is *not* an action query?
- **a.** Union query
- **b.** Delete query
- **c.** Make Table query
- **d.** Append query

18. Which of the following precautions should you take before running a Delete query?
- **a.** Check the resulting datasheet to make sure the query selects the right records.
- **b.** Understand the relationships between the records you are about to delete in the database.
- **c.** Have a current backup of the database.
- **d.** All of the above

19. When querying tables in a one-to-many relationship with referential integrity enforced, which records appear (by default) on the resulting datasheet?
- **a.** Only those with matching values in both tables.
- **b.** All records from both tables will appear at all times.
- **c.** All records from the "one" table, and only those with matching values from the "many" side.
- **d.** All records from the "many" table, and only those with nonmatching values from the "one" side.

20. Which of the following is *not* a type of Select query?
- **a.** Crosstab
- **b.** Update
- **c.** Summary
- **d.** Parameter

Skills Review

1. Query for top values.
- **a.** Start Access, then open the Seminar-K.accdb database from the location where you store your Data Files. Enable content if prompted.
- **b.** Create a new query in Query Design View with the EventName field from the Events table and the RegistrationFee field from the Registration table.
- **c.** Add the RegistrationFee field a second time, then click the Totals button. In the Total row of the query grid, Group By the EventName field, Sum the first RegistrationFee field, then Count the second RegistrationFee field.
- **d.** Sort in descending order by the summed RegistrationFee field.
- **e.** Enter **3** in the Top Values list box to display the top three seminars in the datasheet, then view the datasheet.
- **f.** Save the query as **Top3Revenue**, then close the datasheet.

2. Create a parameter query.
- **a.** Create a new query in Query Design View with the AttendeeLastName field from the Attendees table, the RegistrationDate field from the Registration table, and the EventName field from the Events table.
- **b.** Add the parameter criteria **Between [Enter Start Date:] and [Enter End Date:]** in the Criteria cell for the RegistrationDate field.
- **c.** Specify an ascending sort order on the RegistrationDate field.
- **d.** Click the Datasheet View button, then enter **5/1/15** as the start date and **5/31/15** as the end date to find everyone who has attended a seminar in May 2015. You should view five records.
- **e.** Save the query as **RegistrationDateParameter**, then close it.

Skills Review (continued)

3. Modify query properties.

   a. Right-click the RegistrationDateParameter query in the Navigation Pane, click Object Properties, then add the following description: **Prompts for a starting and ending registration date. Created by Your Name.**

   b. Close the RegistrationDateParameter Properties dialog box, then open the RegistrationDateParameter query in Query Design View.

   c. Right-click the RegistrationDate field in the query grid, then click Properties on the shortcut menu to open the Property Sheet for the Field Properties. Enter **Date of Registration** for the Caption property, change the Format property to Medium Date, then close the Property Sheet.

   d. View the datasheet for records between **1/1/15** and **1/31/15**, then widen the fields as needed to view the caption and the Medium Date format applied to the RegistrationDate field.

   e. Change Pham to *your* last name, then print the RegistrationDateParameter datasheet if requested by your instructor.

   f. Save and close the RegistrationDateParameter query.

4. Create a Make Table query.

   a. Create a new query in Query Design View, add the Registration table, then select all the fields from the Registration table by double-clicking the Registration field list's title bar and dragging the selected fields to the query design grid.

   b. Enter **<=3/31/15** in the Criteria cell for the RegistrationDate field to find those records in which the RegistrationDate is on or before 3/31/2015.

   c. View the datasheet. It should display 23 records.

   d. In Query Design View, change the query into a Make Table query that creates a new table in the current database. Give the new table the name **BackupRegistration**.

   e. Run the query to paste 23 rows into the BackupRegistration table.

   f. Save the Make Table query with the name **MakeBackupRegistration**, then close it.

   g. Open the BackupRegistration table, view the 23 records to confirm that the Make Table query worked correctly, then close the table.

5. Create an Append query.

   a. Create a new query in Query Design View, add the Registration table, and select all the fields from the Registration table by double-clicking the Registration field list's title bar and dragging the selected fields to the query design grid.

   b. Enter **>=4/1/15 and <=4/30/15** in the Criteria cell for the RegistrationDate field to find those records in which the RegistrationDate is in April 2015.

   c. View the datasheet, which should display one record.

   d. In Query Design View, change the query into an Append query that appends records to the BackupRegistration table.

   e. Run the query to append the one record into the BackupRegistration table.

   f. Save the Append query with the name **AppendBackupRegistration**, then close it.

   g. Open the BackupRegistration table to confirm that it now contains the additional April record for a total of 24 records, then close the table.

6. Create a Delete query.

   a. Create a new query in Query Design View, add the Registration table, and select all the fields from the Registration table by double-clicking the Registration field list's title bar and dragging the selected fields to the query design grid.

   b. Enter **<5/1/15** in the Criteria cell for the RegistrationDate field to find those records in which the RegistrationDate is before May 1, 2015.

   c. View the datasheet, which should display 24 records, the same 24 records you added to the BackupRegistration table.

   d. In Query Design View, change the query into a Delete query.

   e. Run the query to delete 24 records from the Registration table.

   f. Save the query with the name **DeleteRegistration**, then close it.

   g. Open the Registration table in Datasheet View to confirm that it contains only five records, all with RegistrationDate values greater than or equal to 5/1/2015, then close the table.

Skills Review (continued)

7. Create an Update query.

   a. Create a query in Query Design View, add the Registration table, then add the RegistrationFee field in the query grid.

   b. Sort the records in descending order on the RegistrationFee field, then view the datasheet, which should display five records. Note the values in the RegistrationFee field.

   c. In Query Design View, change the query to an Update query, then enter **[RegistrationFee]*2** in the RegistrationFee field Update To cell to double the RegistrationFee value in each record.

   d. Run the query to update the five records.

   e. Save the query with the name **UpdateRegistrationFee**, then close it.

   f. Open the Registration table to confirm that the RegistrationFee for the five records has doubled, then close it.

8. Specify join properties.

   a. Create a new query in Query Design View with the following fields: AttendeeFirstName and AttendeeLastName from the Attendees table, and EventID and RegistrationFee from the Registration table.

   b. Double-click the join line between the Attendees and Registration tables to open the Join Properties dialog box. Click the 2 option button to include *all* records from Attendees and only those records from Registration where the joined fields are equal.

   c. View the datasheet, add *your* first and last name as a new, last record, but do not enter anything in the EventID or RegistrationFee fields for your record.

   d. In Query Design View, add **Is Null** criteria to either field from the Registration table to select only those names who have never registered for an event.

   e. Save this query as **PeopleWithoutRegistrations**, then view and close the query.

9. Find unmatched queries.

   a. Start the Find Unmatched Query Wizard.

   b. Select the Events table, then the Registration table to indicate that you want to view the Events records that have no related records in the Registration table.

   c. Specify that the two tables are related by the EventID field.

   d. Select all of the fields from the Events table in the query results.

   e. Name the query **EventsWithoutRegistrations**, then view the results. Change one of the entries in the Location field to **Your Name College**, as shown in **FIGURE K-21**.

   f. If requested by your instructor, print the EventsWithoutRegistrations query, then close the query, close the Seminar-K.accdb database, and exit Access.

FIGURE K-21

Event I ▾	Event Name ▾	Location ▾	Start Date ▾	Available Sp ▾
1	Estate Planning	Student Name College	5/1/2015	100
5	Wealth Management	Millen Civic Center	5/5/2015	25
6	Planning for College	Greenfield High School	5/6/2015	25
7	Live Debt Free	Wells Fargo Center	5/7/2015	75
* (New)				

Independent Challenge 1

As the manager of a college women's basketball team, you want to create several queries using the Basketball-K database.

a. Start Access, then open the Basketball-K.accdb database from the location where you store your Data Files. Enable content if prompted.

b. Create a query in Query Design View with the FirstName and LastName fields from the Players table, the FG (field goal), 3P (three pointer), and FT (free throw) fields from the Stats table, and the Opponent and GameDate fields from the Games table.

c. Enter **Between [Enter start date:] and [Enter end date:]** in the Criteria cell for the GameDate field.

d. View the datasheet for all of the records between **12/1/14** and **12/31/14**. It should display 18 records.

e. Save the query with the name **StatsParameter**, change Lindsey Swift's name to *your* name, then print the datasheet if requested by your instructor.

f. In Query Design View of the StatsParameter query, insert a new calculated field named **TotalPoints** between the FT and Opponent fields with the expression **TotalPoints:[FG]*2+[3P]*3+[FT]**, then sort the records in descending order on the TotalPoints field.

g. Apply the 25% Top Values option, and view the datasheet for all of the records between **1/1/15** and **1/31/15**. It should display five records.

h. Use the Save Object As feature to save the revised query as **StatsParameterTopValues**. Print the datasheet if requested by your instructor, then close it.

i. Create a new query in Query Design View with the Opponent, Mascot, CycloneScore, and OpponentScore fields from the Games table, then add a new calculated field as the last field with the following field name and expression: **WinRatio:[CycloneScore]/[OpponentScore]**

j. View the datasheet to make sure that the WinRatio field calculates properly, and widen all columns as necessary to see all of the data. Because the CycloneScore is generally greater than the OpponentScore, most values are greater than 1.

k. In Query Design View, change the Format property of the WinRatio field to Percent and the Decimal Places property to **0**. View the datasheet, a portion of which is shown in FIGURE K-22.

l. Save the query as **WinPercentage**, change the first opponent's name (Northern Iowa) and mascot to *your* name and a mascot of your choice, print the WinPercentage datasheet if requested by your instructor, then close the WinPercentage query.

m. Close the Basketball-K.accdb database, then exit Access.

FIGURE K-22

Opponent	Mascot	CycloneScor	OpponentSc	WinRatio
Northern Iowa	Panthers	81	65	125%
Creighton	Bluejays	106	60	177%
Northern Illinois	Huskies	65	60	108%
Louisiana Tech	Red Raiders	69	89	78%
Drake	Bulldogs	80	60	133%
Northern Iowa	Panthers	38	73	52%
Buffalo	Bulls	50	55	91%
Oklahoma	Sooners	53	60	88%
Texas	Longhorns	57	60	95%
Kansas	Jayhawks	74	58	128%
Colorado	Buffaloes	90	84	107%

Independent Challenge 2

As the manager of a college women's basketball team, you want to enhance the Basketball-K database by creating several action queries.

a. Start Access, then open the Basketball-K.accdb database from the location where you store your Data Files. Enable content if prompted.

b. Create a new query in Query Design View, and select all the fields from the Stats table by double-clicking the field list's title bar and dragging the selected fields to the query design grid.

c. Add criteria to find all of the records with the GameNo field equal to **1**, **2**, or **3**, then view the datasheet. It should display 26 records.

d. In Query Design View, change the query to a Make Table query to paste the records into a table in the current database called **StatsForGames123**.

e. Run the query to paste the 26 rows, save the query with the name **MakeStatsBackup**, then close it.

f. Open the datasheet for the StatsForGames123 table to confirm that it contains 26 records, then close it.

g. In Query Design View, create another new query that includes all of the fields from the Stats table by double-clicking the field list's title bar and dragging the selected fields to the query design grid.

h. Add criteria to find all of the statistics for those records with the GameNo field equal to **4** or **5**, then view the datasheet. It should display 12 records.

i. In Query Design View, change the query to an Append query to append the records to the StatsForGames123 table.

j. Run the query to append the 12 rows, save it with the name **AppendStatsBackup**, then close it.

k. Open the StatsForGames123 table to confirm that it now contains 38 records (26 original records plus 12 appended records), print it if requested by your instructor, then close it.

l. Right-click the StatsForGames123 table in the Navigation Pane, click Rename, then edit the name to **StatsForGames12345**.

m. Close the Basketball-K.accdb database, then exit Access.

Independent Challenge 3

As the manager of a college women's basketball team, you want to query the Basketball-K database to find specific information about each player.

  a. Start Access, then open the Basketball-K.accdb database from the location where you store your Data Files. Enable content if prompted.

  b. Create a query in Query Design View using the Players and Stats tables. Resize the field lists to view all of the fields in each table.

  c. Double-click the join line to open the Join Properties dialog box, then change the join properties to option 2 to include *all* records from Players and only those from Stats where the joined fields are equal.

  d. Add the FirstName and LastName fields from the Players table and the Assists field from the Stats table.

  e. Type **Is Null** in the Criteria cell for the Assists field, as shown in **FIGURE K-23**, then view the datasheet to find those players who have never recorded an Assist value in the Stats table. It should display one record.

  f. Change the last name to *your* last name.

  g. Print the datasheet if requested by your instructor, save the query as **NoAssists**, then close the query.

  h. Close Basketball-K.accdb, then exit Access.

FIGURE K-23

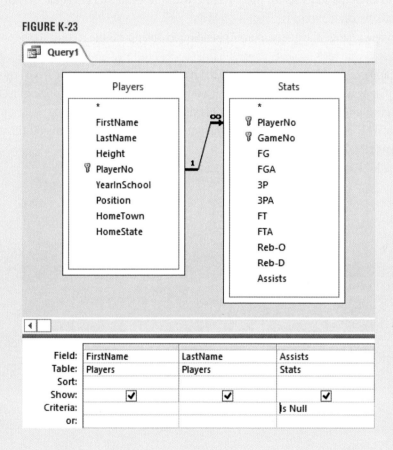

Independent Challenge 4: Explore

(*Note*: *To complete this Independent Challenge, make sure you are connected to the Internet.*)

One way to use Access to support your personal interests is to track the activities of a club or hobby. For example, suppose you belong to a culinary club that specializes in cooking with chocolate. The club collects information on international chocolate factories and museums and asks you to help build a database to organize the information.

a. Start Access, then open the Chocolate-K.accdb database from the location where you store your Data Files. Enable content if prompted.

b. Open the Countries table, then add two more country records, allowing the CountryID field to automatically increment because it is an AutoNumber data type. Close the Countries table.

c. Create a query in Query Design View with the Country field from the Countries table, and the PlaceName, City, and State fields from the ChocolatePlaces query.

d. Name the query **PlacesOfInterest**, double-click the join line between the Countries and ChocolatePlaces tables, then choose the 2 option that includes *all* records from the Countries table.

e. Save the PlacesOfInterest query and view the datasheet. Expand each column to show all of the data.

f. Print the PlacesOfInterest query if requested by your instructor, then close it.

g. Using the Internet, research a chocolate-related place of interest (a factory or museum) for one of the countries you entered in Step b.

h. Open the Countries table, and use the subdatasheet for the country you selected to enter the data for the chocolate-related place of interest. Enter **F** for factory or **M** for museum in the FactoryorMuseum field.

i. Close the Countries table, and open the PlacesOfInterest query in Design View. Modify the link line to option 1, so that records that have a match in both tables are selected.

j. Save and open the PlacesOfInterest query in Datasheet View, as shown in **FIGURE K-24**, and print the resulting datasheet if requested by your instructor. Note that the last record will show the unique data you entered.

k. Close Chocolate-K.accdb, then exit Access.

FIGURE K-24

Country	PlaceName	City	State
Germany	Lindt factory	Aachen	
Germany	Imhoff Stollwerk Chocolate Museum	Cologne	
Switzerland	Lindt factory	Kilchberg	
Switzerland	Museum del Cioccolato Alprose	Caslano	Canton Ticino
Switzerland	Nestle	Broc	Canton Fribourg
France	Lindt Factory	Oloron	
France	Atelier Musee du Chocolat, Biarritz	Biarritz	
Italy	Lindt Factory	Induno	
Italy	Lindt Factory	Luserna	
Italy	Museo Storico della Perugina	Perugia	
Italy	Museo del Cioccolato Antia Norba	Norma	Latina Province
Austria	Lindt Factory	Gloggnitz	
USA	Lindt Factory	San Leandro	CA
USA	Lindt Factory	Stratham	NH
Belgium	Musee du Cacao et du Chocolat	Brussels	
Great Britian	Cadbury World	Bourneville	
Japan	Shiroi Koibito Park	Sapporo	

Visual Workshop

As the manager of a college women's basketball team, you want to create a query from the Basketball-K.accdb database with the fields from the Players, Stats, and Games tables as shown. The query is a parameter query that prompts the user for a start and end date using the GameDate field from the Games table. FIGURE K-25 shows the datasheet where the start date of **11/13/14** and end date of **11/16/14** are used. Also note that the records are sorted in ascending order first by GameDate, and then by LastName. The TotalRebounds field is calculated by adding the Reb-O (rebounds offense) and Reb-D (rebounds defense) values. Save and name the query **Rebounds**, then print the datasheet if requested by your instructor. Be sure to change one player's name to *your* name if you haven't previously done this to identify your printout.

FIGURE K-25

GameDate	FirstName	LastName	Reb-O	Reb-D	TotalRebounds
11/13/2014	Kristen	Czyenski	2	2	4
11/13/2014	Denise	Franco	2	3	5
11/13/2014	Theresa	Grant	1	3	4
11/13/2014	Megan	Hile	1	2	3
11/13/2014	Amy	Hodel	5	3	8
11/13/2014	Ellyse	Howard	1	2	3
11/13/2014	Jamie	Johnson	0	1	1
11/13/2014	Student First Name	Student Last Name	1	2	3
11/13/2014	Morgan	Tyler	4	6	10
11/16/2014	Kristen	Czyenski	3	2	5
11/16/2014	Denise	Franco	5	3	8
11/16/2014	Sydney	Freesen	2	3	5
11/16/2014	Theresa	Grant	3	3	6
11/16/2014	Megan	Hile	1	5	6
11/16/2014	Amy	Hodel	1	4	5
11/16/2014	Ellyse	Howard	3	3	6
11/16/2014	Sandy	Robins	0	1	1
11/16/2014	Student First Name	Student Last Name	2	2	4
11/16/2014	Morgan	Tyler	3	6	9
11/16/2014	Abbey	Walker	2	4	6

Creating Advanced Queries

Creating Advanced Reports

CASE Jacob Thomas, coordinator of training at Quest Specialty Travel, wants to enhance existing reports to more professionally and clearly present the information in the Education-L database.

Unit Objectives

After completing this unit, you will be able to:

- Apply advanced formatting
- Control layout
- Set advanced print layout
- Create multicolumn reports

- Use domain functions
- Create charts
- Modify charts
- Apply chart types

Files You Will Need

Education-L.accdb   Basketball-L.accdb
RealEstate-L.accdb

Apply Advanced Formatting

Learning
Outcomes
• Set margins
• Remove a layout
• Apply the Format
  property

You use Print Preview to see how a report will fit on paper and to make overall layout modifications such as changes to margins and page orientation. You use Layout and Design Views to modify the layout and characteristics of individual controls on a report. For example, the **Format property** provides several ways to format dates and numbers. Dates may be formatted as **Medium Date** (19-Jun-16), **Short Date** (6/19/2016), or **Long Date** (Friday, June 19, 2016). Numbers may be formatted as **Currency** ($7), **Percent** (700%), or **Standard** (7). **CASE** *You review the Departmental Summary Report to identify and correct formatting and page layout problems.*

STEPS

1. **Start Access, open the Education-L.accdb database from the location where you store your Data Files, enable content if prompted, then double-click DeptSummary in the Navigation Pane**

   Double-clicking a report in the Navigation Pane opens it in Report View, which doesn't show margins and page breaks. Switch to Print Preview to see how the report will look on paper.

2. **Right-click the Departmental Summary Report tab, then click Print Preview**

   Print Preview shows that data is cut off on the right side of the report. You fix this problem by modifying the margins and page orientation.

3. **Click the Margins button in the Page Size group, click the Narrow option, click the Page Setup button in the Page Layout group, select 0.25 in the Left margin box, then type 0.5, as shown in FIGURE L-1**

   The Narrow margin option set all four margins to 0.25". To customize individual margin settings, you use the Page Setup dialog box.

4. **Click OK, then click the Landscape button in the Page Layout group**

   Now that the report fits nicely on the printed page, you want to make some modifications to the controls themselves. You want to widen the text box that contains the name expression and format the Cost fields to show a currency symbol.

5. **Right-click the Departmental Summary Report tab, click Design View, click the =[ELast]&", "&[EFirst] text box, then use ◄─► to drag the right edge to the right to widen the text box**

   Many of the controls are grouped together in a report table layout, which means that resizing one control resizes the entire group. To modify an individual control in the group, you must first remove the layout.

6. **Click the Undo button 🔄 on the Quick Access toolbar, click the ARRANGE tab, click Remove Layout in the Table group, then use ◄─► to drag the right edge of the name expression text box to the right to widen it to about the 4" mark**

   Your last improvement will be to modify the Format property of the four text boxes that display Cost information in the last column of the report to include a currency symbol, $.

7. **Click the CostOfCourse text box in the Detail section, press and hold [Shift], click the three =Sum([CostOfCourse]) text boxes in the footer sections, release [Shift], click the DESIGN tab, click the Property Sheet button, click the Format property list arrow, click Currency, right-click the DeptSummary tab, click Print Preview, then scroll and zoom to the bottom of the last page of the report, as shown in FIGURE L-2**

   The report is more professional and informative with the Cost values formatted as Currency.

8. **Save and close the report**

Creating Advanced Reports

FIGURE L-1: Page Setup dialog box

FIGURE L-2: Applying the Currency format

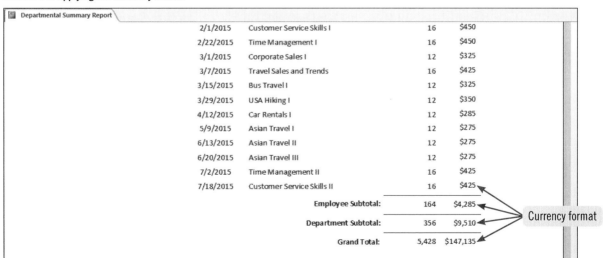

Control Layout

When you create a report using the Report button or Report Wizard, sometimes controls are automatically grouped together in a table layout. A **table layout** is a way of connecting controls together so that when you move or resize them in Layout or Design View, the action you take on one control applies to all controls in the layout. The different types of layouts are described in **TABLE L-1**. Another important report modification skill is your ability to open and close various header and footer sections. **CASE** ▶ *Jacob Thomas asks you to modify the CourseListing report to improve its format.*

STEPS

1. **Right-click the** CourseListing report **in the Navigation Pane, then click** Layout View

   Controls that are grouped together in the same layout can be resized easily in Layout View.

2. **Click** Africa101, **use** ←→ **to drag the** right edge **of the column to the left, click** African Travel I, **use** ←→ **to drag the** right edge **of the column to the left, and continue** resizing the columns **so that they all fit within the right border of the report, as shown in** FIGURE L-3

   Controls in the same layout move to provide space for the control you are moving. This report contains no title or page numbers. You add controls and open report sections in Design View.

3. **Right-click the** CourseListing tab, **then click** Design View

   You want to add a title to the Report Header section. Before you can add a label for the report title to the Report Header section, you must open it.

4. **Right-click the** Detail section bar, **click** Report Header/Footer, **click the** Label button Aa **on the DESIGN tab, click at the** 1" mark **in the Report Header section, type** Course Listing Report, **press [Enter], click the** HOME tab, **click the** Font Color list arrow $\underline{A}$ ▼ **in the Text Formatting group, then click** Automatic (black) **to make the title more visible**

   You also want to add page numbers to the Page Footer section. You can open the Page Footer section and insert the page number at the same time.

5. **Click the** DESIGN tab, **click the** Page Numbers button **in the Header/Footer group, click the** Page N of M option button, **click the** Bottom of Page [Footer] option button, **click the** Alignment list arrow, **click** Right **in the Page Numbers dialog box, as shown in** FIGURE L-4, **then click** OK

   The Page N of M option creates the expression in the text box on the right side of the Page Footer, as shown in **FIGURE L-5**. This expression displays the current page number and total pages in the Page Footer. Because neither the Page Header nor Report Footer sections have any controls, you close them.

6. **Use** ⬍ **to drag the** bottom edge of the report **up to close the Report Footer section, then use** ⬍ **to drag the** top edge of the Detail section **up to close the Page Header section**

7. **Right-click the** CourseListing report tab, **click** Print Preview, **then zoom and navigate back and forth to observe the Report Header on page one and the Page Footer on pages one and two**

   Always review your reports in Print Preview to see the contents of the Page Header and Page Footer sections as well as to see how the report fits on a printed piece of paper.

8. **Save and close the CourseListing report**

FIGURE L-3: Resizing columns in a layout

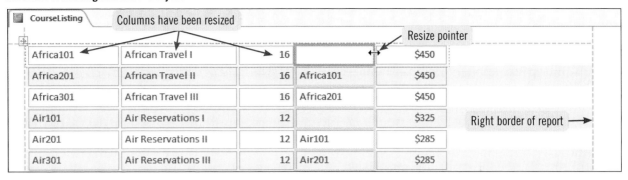

FIGURE L-4: Page Numbers dialog box

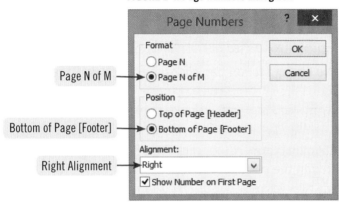

FIGURE L-5: Opening sections in Design View

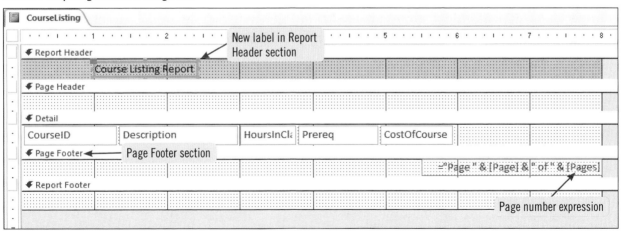

TABLE L-1: Layouts

layout	description
Stacked	Labels are positioned to the left of the text box; most often used in forms
Tabular	Labels are positioned across the top in the Page Header section forming columns of data with text boxes positioned in the Detail section; most often used in reports

Set Advanced Print Layout

Setting advanced print layout in a report means controlling print options such as where page breaks occur and how report sections span multiple pages. **CASE** ▶ *In the Departmental Summary Report, Jacob asks you to print each person's information on a separate page, and to repeat the EDepartment Header information at the top of each page.*

STEPS

1. **Right-click the DeptSummary report in the Navigation Pane, click Design View, double-click the EDepartment Header section bar to open its Property Sheet, double-click the Repeat Section property to change the property from No to Yes, then double-click the Force New Page property to change the property from None to Before Section, as shown in FIGURE L-6**

   The controls in the EDepartment Header section will now repeat at the top of every page.

QUICK TIP

If you want to include your name on the report, enter it as a label in the Page Footer section.

2. **Click the EmployeeNo Footer section bar, click the Force New Page property list arrow, then click After Section**

   Access will format the report with a page break after each EmployeeNo Footer. This means each employee's records will start printing at the top of a new page.

3. **Right-click the DeptSummary report tab, click Print Preview, then use the navigation buttons to move through the pages of the report**

   Previewing multiple pages helps you make sure that the department name repeats at the top of every page and that each employee starts on a new page.

4. **Navigate to page 2, then click the top of the page if you need to zoom in, as shown in FIGURE L-7**

   To print only page 2 of the report, you use the Print dialog box.

5. **Click the Print button on the PRINT PREVIEW tab, click the From box, enter 2, click the To box, enter 2, then if requested by your instructor to create a printout, click OK, but if not, click Cancel**

   Only page 2 of the 30+ page report is sent to the printer.

6. **Save and close the DeptSummary report**

FIGURE L-6: Working with section properties in Report Design View

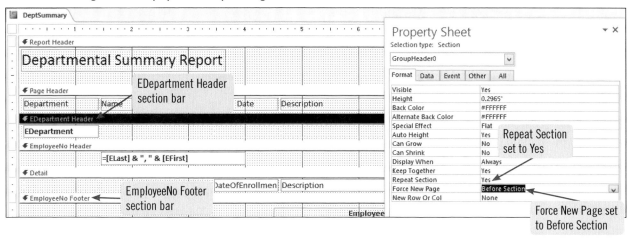

FIGURE L-7: Previewing the final Departmental Summary Report

Create Multicolumn Reports

Learning
Outcomes
• Modify a report
  for multiple
  columns
• Set column layout

A **multicolumn report** repeats information in more than one column on the page. To create multiple columns, you use options in the Page Setup dialog box. **CASE** *Jacob asks you to create a report that shows employee names sorted in ascending order for each course. A report with only a few fields is a good candidate for a multicolumn report.*

STEPS

1. **Click the CREATE tab, click the Report Wizard button, click the Tables/Queries list arrow, click Table: Courses, double-click Description, click the Tables/Queries list arrow, click Table: Employees, double-click EFirst, double-click ELast, click Next, click Next to view the data by Courses, click Next to bypass adding any more grouping levels, click the first sort list arrow, click ELast, click Next, click the Stepped option button, click the Landscape option button, click Next, type Attendance List for the title, click Finish, then click the Last Page button ▶| on the navigation bar**

   The initial report is displayed in Print Preview as a 17- or 18-page report. This report would work well as a multicolumn report because only three fields are involved. You also decide to combine the first and last names into a single expression.

2. **Right-click the report, click Design View, close the Property Sheet or Field List if it is open, click the ELast label, press [Delete], click the EFirst label, press [Delete], click the ELast text box, press [Delete], click the EFirst text box, press [Delete], click the Page expression text box in the Page Footer section, press [Delete], click the =Now() text box in the Page Footer section, press [Delete], then drag the right edge of the report as far to the left as possible**

   When designing a multicolumn report, Report Design View should display the width of only the first column. Your next task is to add a new text box to the Detail section with an expression that contains both the first and last names.

3. **Click the Text Box button |abl| in the Controls group, click at about the 1″ mark of the Detail section to insert a new text box control, then delete the accompanying Text9 label**

TROUBLE
Do not forget to
enter a space after
the comma so the
expression creates
Dawson, Ron versus
Dawson,Ron.

4. **Click the Unbound text box to select it, click Unbound, type =[ELast]&", "&[EFirst], press [Enter], widen the new control to about 2″ wide, right-click the Attendance List report tab, then click Print Preview**

   With the information clearly presented in a single, narrow column, you're ready to specify that the report print multiple columns.

5. **Click the Page Setup button, click the Columns tab, double-click 1 in the Number of Columns box, type 3, then click the Down, then Across option button, as shown in FIGURE L-8**

   The content of the report is now set to print in three newspaper-style columns. The Column Size Width value is based on 0.25″ left and right margins, which leaves room for three, 3″ columns. The Height value is based on the Height property of the Detail section.

QUICK TIP
You must use Print
Preview to view
report columns.
Report View doesn't
display multiple
columns.

6. **Click OK**

   The final Attendance List report is shown in **FIGURE L-9**. By specifying that the report is three columns wide, the number of pages in the report is significantly reduced.

7. **Save and close the Attendance List report**

Creating Advanced Reports

FIGURE L-8: Page Setup dialog box

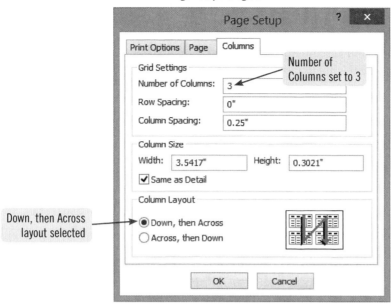

FIGURE L-9: Attendance List report in three columns

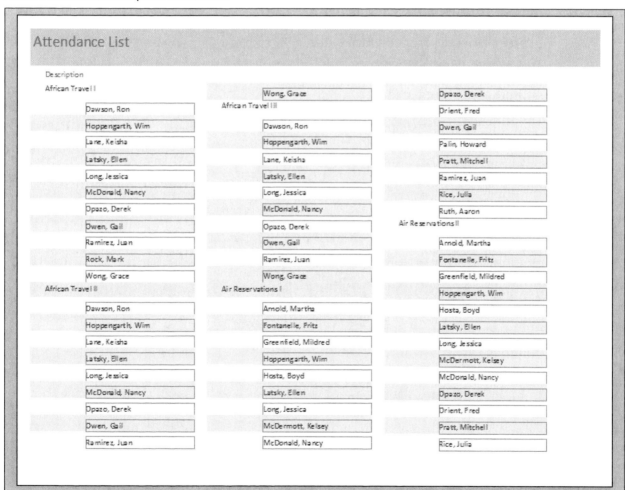

Use Domain Functions

Learning
Outcomes
• Describe domain
functions
• Create an expression
with DLookup

Domain functions, also called domain aggregate functions, are used in an expression to calculate a value based on a field that is not included in the Record Source property for the form or report. All Domain functions start with a "D" for "domain" such as DSum, DAvg, or DCount. The DSum, DAvg, and DCount functions perform the same calculations as their Sum, Avg, and Count function counterparts. The **DLookup** function returns or "looks up" a value from a specified domain. All domain functions have two required arguments: the field that is used for the calculation or "look up" and the domain. The **domain** is the table or query that contains the field. A third optional argument allows you to select records from the domain based on criteria you specify. **CASE** *Jacob asks you to add a standard disclaimer to the bottom of every report. This is an excellent opportunity to use the DLookup function.*

STEPS

1. **Click the CREATE tab, click the Table Design button, then build a new table with the fields, data types, and primary key field, as shown in FIGURE L-10**

   With the design of the Disclaimers table established, you add two records of standard text used at Quest Specialty Travel.

   TROUBLE
   Widen the StandardText column as needed to view all text.

2. **Save the table as Disclaimers, click the View button 🖽, then enter the two records shown in FIGURE L-11**

   The first disclaimer is used with any report that contains employee information for Quest Specialty Travel, QST. The second is added to all internal reports that do not contain employee information. With the data in place, you're ready to use the DLookup function on a report to insert standard text.

3. **Save and close the Disclaimers table, right-click the Attendance List report in the Navigation Pane, then click Design View**

   You can now add a text box using the DLookup function in an expression to return the correct disclaimer.

4. **Click the Text Box button ⌷ab⌷, click the Page Footer section, delete the Text11 label, click Unbound, type the expression =DLookup("[StandardText]","Disclaimers", "[StandardID]=1"), press [Enter], then widen the text box to about 3"**

   The expression is too wide to be completely displayed in Design View, but you must switch to Print Preview to see if it works anyway.

   TROUBLE
   If you see an #Error message in the Page Footer, return to Report Design View and double-check your expression.

5. **Display the report in Print Preview and zoom and scroll to the Page Footer to view the result of the DLookup function, as shown in FIGURE L-12**

   By entering standard company disclaimers in one table, the same disclaimer text can be consistently added to each report.

6. **Save and close the Attendance List report, double-click the Disclaimers table to open its datasheet, change QST to Quest Specialty Travel in the first record for the StandardID of 1, close the Disclaimers table, right-click the Attendance List report, then click Print Preview**

   When the StandardText field is changed in the Disclaimers table, all reports that reference that value using the DLookup function in an expression are automatically updated as well.

7. **Close the Attendance List report**

FIGURE L-10: Disclaimers table

Disclaimers table

Primary key field

FIGURE L-11: Records in the Disclaimers table

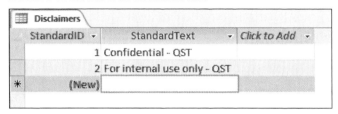

FIGURE L-12: Standard disclaimer in Report Footer section created with DLookup expression

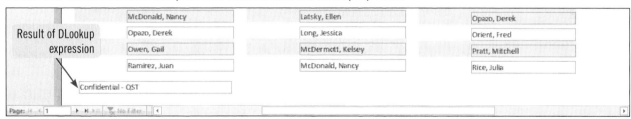

Result of DLookup expression

Adding page numbers or the date and time to a report

You can quickly add page numbers to a report by clicking the Page Numbers button on the DESIGN tab of the ribbon. The Page Numbers dialog box prompts you for a page number format and whether you want to insert the information into the Page Header or Page Footer section. To quickly add the current date and time to the report, click the Date and Time button on the DESIGN tab. Several date and time formats are available. Date and time information is always inserted on the right side of the Report Header section.

Create Charts

Charts, also called graphs, are visual representations of numeric data that help users see comparisons, patterns, and trends in data. Charts can be inserted on a form or report. Access provides a **Chart Wizard** that helps you create the chart. Common **chart types** that determine the presentation of data on the chart, such as column, pie, and line, are described in TABLE L-2. **CASE** ▸ *Jacob wants you to create a chart of the total number of course enrollments by department.*

STEPS

1. **Click the CREATE tab, click the** Query Design button, **double-click** Employees, **double-click** Enrollments, **then click** Close

   The first step in creating a chart is to select the data that the chart will graph and collect those fields and records in one query object.

2. **Double-click** EDepartment **in the Employees field list, double-click** EnrollmentID **in the Enrollments field list, save the query with the name** DepartmentEnrollments, **then close it**

   Charts can be added to forms or reports.

3. **Click the CREATE tab, click the** Report Design button, **click the** More button ⬇ **in the Controls group on the DESIGN tab, click the** Chart button 📊, **then click in the** Detail section **of the report**

   The Chart Wizard starts by asking which table or query holds the fields you want to add to the chart, then asks you to select a chart type.

4. **Click the** Queries option button, **click** Next **to choose the DepartmentEnrollments query, click the** Select All Fields button >> , **click** Next, **click** Next **to accept Column Chart, then drag the** EnrollmentID field **from the Series area to the Data area, as shown in** FIGURE L-13

   The **Data area** determines what data the chart graphs. If you drag a Number or Currency field to the Data area, the Chart Wizard automatically sums the values in the field. For Text or AutoNumber fields (such as EnrollmentID), the Chart Wizard automatically counts the values in that field.

5. **Click** Next, **type** Department Enrollment Totals **as the chart title, click** Finish, **use** ↖ **to drag the** lower-right corner **of the chart to fill the Detail section, right-click the** Report1 **tab, then click** Print Preview

   When charts are displayed in Design View or Layout View, they appear as a generic Microsoft chart placeholder. The chart in Print Preview should look similar to FIGURE L-14. The chart is beginning to take shape, but some of the labels on the x-axis may not have room to display all of their text depending on the size of the chart. You enhance this chart in the next lesson.

Using the Blank Report button versus the Report Design button

Access provides several buttons on the CREATE tab to create a new report. The Blank Report button creates a new, blank report in Layout View. The Report Design button creates a new, blank report in Design View. The only difference between these two buttons is the initial view presented when you start building a new report. The same is true for Blank Form button, which creates a new, blank form in Layout View, and the Form Design button, which creates a new, blank form in Design View.

FIGURE L-13: Choosing the chart areas

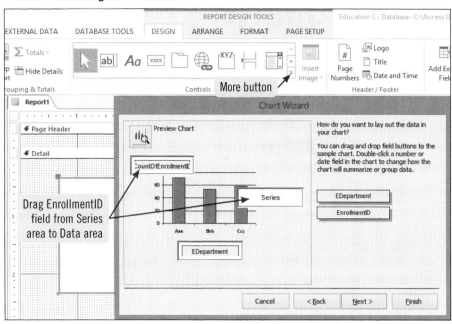

FIGURE L-14: Initial Department Enrollment Totals column chart

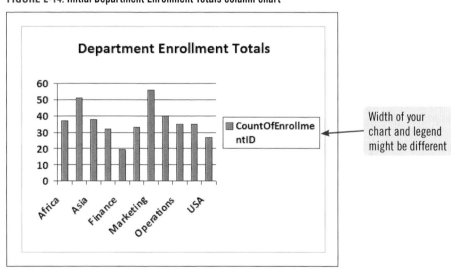

TABLE L-2: Common chart types

chart type	chart icon	used to show most commonly	example
Column		Comparisons of values (vertical bars)	Each vertical bar represents the annual sales for a different product for the year 2016
Bar		Comparisons of values (horizontal bars)	Each horizontal bar represents the annual sales for a different product for the year 2016
Line		Trends over time	Each point on the line represents monthly sales for one product for the year 2016
Pie		Parts of a whole	Each slice represents total quarterly sales for a company for the year 2016
Area		Cumulative totals	Each section represents monthly sales by representative, stacked to show the cumulative total sales effort for the year 2016

Access 2013

Modify Charts

You modify charts in Design View of the form or report that contains the chart. Modifying a chart is challenging because Design View doesn't always show you the actual chart values, but instead, displays a chart placeholder that represents the embedded chart object. To modify the chart, you modify the chart elements and chart areas within the chart placeholder. To view the changes as they apply to the real data you are charting, return to either Form View for a form or Print Preview for a report. See **TABLE L-3** for more information on chart areas. **CASE** ▶ *You want to resize the chart, change the color of the bars, and remove the legend to better display the values on the x-axis.*

STEPS

1. **Right-click the** report, **then click** Design View

   To make changes to chart elements, you open the chart in Edit mode by double-clicking it. Use **Edit mode** to select and modify individual chart elements, such as the title, legend, bars, or axes. If you double-click the edge of the chart placeholder, you open the Property Sheet for the chart instead of opening the chart itself in Edit mode.

2. **Double-click the** chart

   The hashed border of the chart placeholder control indicates that the chart is in Edit mode, as shown in **FIGURE L-15**. The Chart Standard and Chart Formatting toolbars also appear when the chart is in Edit mode. They may appear on one row instead of stacked. Because only one series of bars counts the enrollments, you can describe the data with the chart title and don't need a legend.

   TROUBLE
   If you make a mistake, use the Undo button ↺ on the Chart Standard toolbar.

3. **Click the** legend **on the chart, then press [Delete] to remove it**

   Removing the legend provides more room for the x-axis labels.

   TROUBLE
   If you don't see the Fill Color button ◇ ▾ on the Chart Formatting toolbar, drag the left edge of the toolbars to position them on two rows to show all buttons.

4. **Click any** periwinkle bar **(the first color in the set of four) to select all bars of that color, click the** Fill Color button arrow ◇ ▾ **on the Chart Formatting toolbar, then click the** Bright Green box

   Clicking any bar selects all bars in that data series as evidenced by the sizing handle in each of the bars. The bars change to bright green in the chart placeholder.

   You also decide to shorten the department names in the database so they will better fit on the x-axis. Data changed in the database automatically updates all reports, including charts, that are based on that data.

5. **Click** outside the hashed border **to return to Report Design View, double-click the** Employees table **in the Navigation Pane, change the two instances of Information Systems to IS in the EDepartment field, then close the Employees table**

   Preview the updated chart.

   TROUBLE
   If you are prompted that the report width is greater than the page width, return to Report Design View and resize the chart and the right edge of the report to fit within a width of 8".

6. **Save the report as** DepartmentChart, **then display it in Print Preview**

   The final chart is shown in **FIGURE L-16**.

FIGURE L-15: Editing a chart placeholder

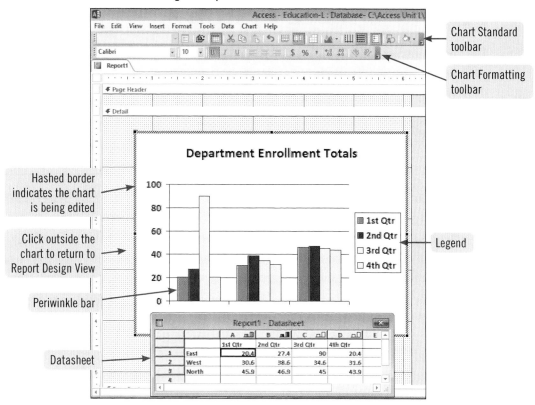

Chart Standard toolbar

Chart Formatting toolbar

Hashed border indicates the chart is being edited

Click outside the chart to return to Report Design View

Periwinkle bar

Legend

Datasheet

FIGURE L-16: Final Department Enrollment Totals column chart

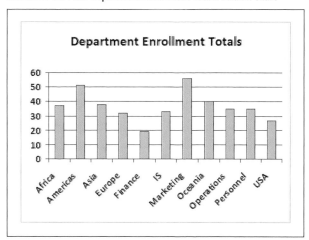

TABLE L-3: Chart areas

chart area	description
Data	Determines what field the bars (lines, wedges, etc.) on the chart represent
Axis	The x-axis (horizontal axis) or y-axis (vertical axis) on the chart
Series	Displays the legend when multiple series of data are graphed

Apply Chart Types

Learning
Outcomes
• Apply different
  chart types
• Describe 3-D chart
  types

The Chart Wizard provides 20 different chart types. While column charts are the most popular, you can also use line, area, and pie charts to effectively show some types of data. Three-dimensional effects can be used to enhance the chart, but those effects can also make it difficult to compare the sizes of bars, lines, and wedges, so choose a three-dimensional effect only if it does not detract from the point of the chart. **CASE** ▶ *You change the existing column chart to other chart types and sub-types to see how the data is presented.*

STEPS

1. **Right-click the** chart, **click** Design View, **then double-click the** chart placeholder

   You must open the chart in Edit mode to change the chart type.

2. **Click** Chart **on the menu bar, then click** Chart Type

   The Chart Type dialog box opens, as shown in **FIGURE L-17**. All major chart types plus many chart sub-types are displayed. A button is available to preview any choice before applying that chart sub-type.

3. **Click the** Clustered column with a 3-D visual effect button **(second row, first column in the Chart sub-type area), click and hold the** Press and Hold to View Sample button, **click the** 3-D Column button **(third row, first column in the Chart sub-type area), then click and hold the** Press and Hold to View Sample button

   A Sample box opens, presenting a rough idea of what the final chart will look like. Although 3-D charts appear more interesting than 2-D chart types, the samples do not show the data more clearly, so you decide to preview other 2-D chart types.

4. **Click the** Bar Chart type **in the Chart type list, click and hold the** Press and Hold to View Sample button, **click the** Line Chart type **in the Chart type list, click and hold the** Press and Hold to View Sample button, **click the** Pie Chart type **in the Chart type list, click and hold the** Press and Hold to View Sample button, **click the** Default formatting check box, **then click and hold the** Press and Hold to View Sample button

   Because this chart only has one set of values that represent 100 percent of all enrollments, the data fits a pie chart.

5. **Click** OK **to accept the pie chart type, click** Chart **on the menu bar, click** Chart Options, **click the** Data Labels tab, **click the** Percentage check box, **then click** OK

   With the modifications made to change the chart into a pie chart, you view it in Print Preview to see the final result.

6. **Click outside the hashed border to return to Report Design View, click the** Label button **in the Controls group, click above the pie chart, type** Enrollment % by Department, **press [Enter], then display the report in Print Preview**

   The same departmental data, expressed as a pie chart, is shown in **FIGURE L-18**.

7. **Save and close the DepartmentChart report, close the Education-L.accdb database, then exit Access**

FIGURE L-17: Chart Type dialog box

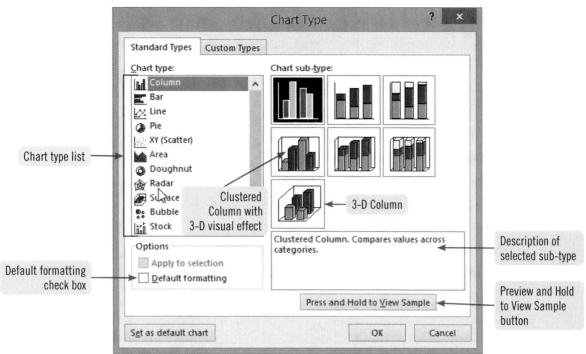

Chart type list

Clustered Column with 3-D visual effect

3-D Column

Description of selected sub-type

Default formatting check box

Preview and Hold to View Sample button

FIGURE L-18: Department Enrollment Totals pie chart

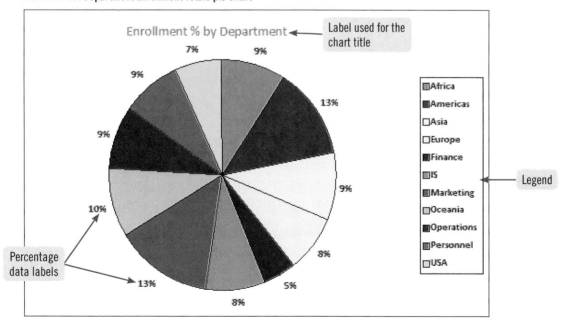

Label used for the chart title

Legend

Percentage data labels

Practice

Concepts Review

Identify each element of Report Design View shown in FIGURE L-19.

FIGURE L-19

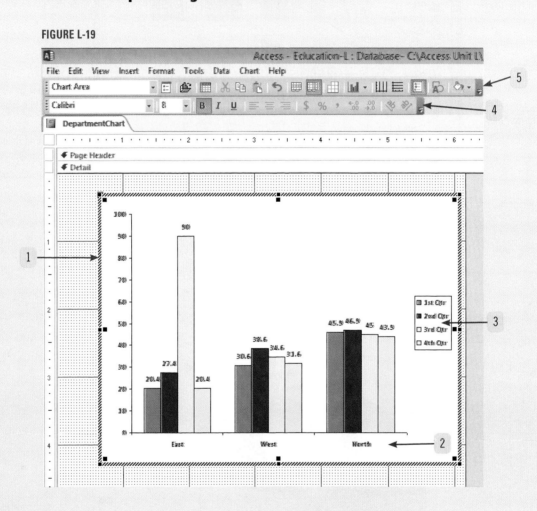

Match each term with the statement that best describes its function.

6. **Table layout**

7. **Charts**

8. **Domain functions**

9. **Chart types**

10. **Data area**

11. **Edit mode**

a. Visual representations of numeric data

b. A way of connecting controls together so that when you move or resize them in Layout or Design View, the action you take on one control applies to all controls

c. Calculate a value based on a field that is not included in the Record Source property for the form or report

d. Used to select and modify individual chart elements, such as the title, legend, bars, or axes

e. Determines what data is graphed on the chart

f. Determine the presentation of data on the chart, such as column, pie, and line

Select the best answer from the list of choices.

12. **Which button aligns the edges of two or more selected controls?**
    - **a.** Align Right button on the ARRANGE tab
    - **b.** Align Right button on the DESIGN tab
    - **c.** Align button on the ARRANGE tab
    - **d.** Align button on the DESIGN tab

13. **To set a page break before a Group Header section on a report, you would modify the properties of the:**
    - **a.** Report.
    - **b.** Detail section.
    - **c.** Group Header section.
    - **d.** Page Footer section.

14. **Which control layout is common for reports?**
    - **a.** Stacked
    - **b.** Datasheet
    - **c.** Tabular
    - **d.** Gridlines

15. **Which dialog box allows you to specify the number of columns you want to view in a report?**
    - **a.** Print
    - **b.** Page Setup
    - **c.** Columns
    - **d.** Property Sheet

16. **Which type of chart is best to show an upward sales trend over several months?**
    - **a.** Column
    - **b.** Line
    - **c.** Pie
    - **d.** Scatter

Skills Review

1. **Apply advanced formatting.**
   a. Start Access, then open the RealEstate-L.accdb database from the location where you store your Data Files. Enable content if prompted. Change the name of Sara Johnson in the Realtors table to your name, then close the table.
   b. Preview the AgencyListings report, noting the format for the SqFt and Asking fields.
   c. In Report Design View, change the Format property for the SqFt text box in the Detail section to **Standard** and change the Decimal Places property to **0**.
   d. In Report Design View, change the Format property for the Asking text box in the Detail section to **Currency** and change the Decimal Places property to **0**.
   e. Preview the report to make sure your SqFt values appear with commas, the Asking values appear with dollar signs, and no decimal places are shown.
   f. Change the top and bottom margins to **0.5"** and the left margin to **0.35"** and then save the AgencyListings report.

2. **Control layout.**
   a. Open the AgencyListings report in Design View.
   b. Open the Group, Sort, and Total pane, then open the AgencyName Footer section.
   c. Add a text box in the AgencyName Footer below the SqFt text box in the Detail section with the expression **=Sum([SqFt])**. Modify the new label to have the caption **Subtotals:**.
   d. Add a text box in the AgencyName Footer below the Asking text box in the Detail section with the expression **=Sum([Asking])**. Delete the extra label in the AgencyName Footer section.
   e. Format the =Sum([SqFt]) text box with **Standard** Format and **0** Decimals Places, format the =Sum([Asking]) text box with **Currency** Format and **0** Decimal Places, and then resize and align the text boxes under the fields they subtotal so that Print Preview looks similar to the portion of the report shown in FIGURE L-20.
   f. Insert the Page N of M page number format into the left side of the Page Footer.
   g. Print preview several pages of the report, and work in Report Design View to remove extra space so that a blank page doesn't print between pages as needed. Save the AgencyListings report.

3. **Set advanced print layout.**
   a. Open the AgencyListings report in Design View.
   b. Modify the AgencyName Footer section to force a new page after that section prints.

FIGURE L-20

Kirkpatrick	555-111-9900					
		4	Cabin	Horseshoe Bend	1,200	$150,000
		12	Ranch	Greenview	2,200	$395,613
		8	Two Story	Shell City	1,800	$138,000
		5	Ranch	Ridgedale	2,500	$199,000
		7	Two Story	Ozark Mountain	3,000	$276,000
			Subtotals:		28,115	$2,359,512

c. Preview the report to make sure each agency prints on its own page.

d. Close and save the AgencyListings report.

4. Create multicolumn reports.

a. Use the Report Wizard to create a report with the AgencyName field from the Agencies table, the RFirst and RLast fields from the Realtors table, and the Type field from the Listings table. Be sure to select the fields from the table objects.

b. View the data by Listings, add AgencyName as the grouping level, sort the records in ascending order by RLast, use a Stepped layout and a Landscape orientation, and use **Inventory** as the report title.

c. In Report Design View, delete the RLast and RFirst labels and text boxes.

d. Delete the page expression in the Page Footer section, delete the Type label in the Page Header section, and delete the AgencyName label in the Page Header section. Move the Type field in the Detail section to the left, just below the AgencyName text box.

e. Add a new text box to the right of the Type control in the Detail section with the following expression: **=[RLast]&", "&[RFirst]**

f. Delete the label for the new text box, then widen the =[RLast]&", "&[RFirst] text box in the Detail section to be about 2" wide. Drag the right edge of the report as far as you can to the left so that the report is approximately 5" wide.

g. Preview the report, and use the Page Setup dialog box to change the Number of Columns setting to **2** and the column layout to Down, then Across. The report should look like **FIGURE L-21**.

h. Save and close the Inventory report.

5. Use domain functions.

a. Create a new table named **Legal** with two new fields: **LegalID** with an AutoNumber data type and **LegalText** with a Long Text data type. Make LegalID the primary key field.

b. Add one record to the table with the following entry in the LegalText field: **The information in the listing has not been verified by an independent inspection.** Widen the column of the LegalText field as needed. Note the value of the LegalID field for the first record (probably 1), then save and close the Legal table.

FIGURE L-21

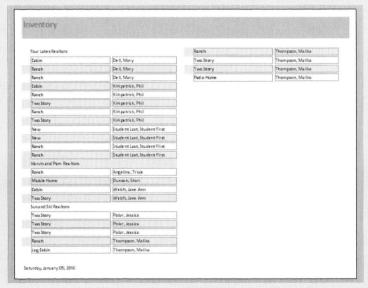

c. Open the ListingReport in Design View, open the Report Footer section, then use a DLookup function in an expression in a text box in the Page Footer section to look up the LegalText field in the Legal table as follows: **=DLookup("[LegalText]","Legal","LegalID=1")**. Delete the accompanying label. (Note that the number in the expression must match the value of the LegalID field for the first record that you created in Step b.)

d. Preview the report, then review the Report Footer. Switch back and forth between Report Design View and Print Preview to fix and widen the text box to be as wide as needed so that it clearly displays the entire expression, then save and close the ListingReport.

6. Create charts.

a. Open the Inventory query in Query Design View, then add criteria to select only the **Ranch** (in the Type field) records.

b. Save the query with a new name as **RanchHomes**, then close it.

c. Start a new report in Report Design View.

d. Insert a chart in the Detail section based on the RanchHomes query.

e. Choose the RLast and Asking fields for the chart, choose a Column Chart, make sure the SumOfAsking field appears in the Data area, and move the RLast field from the Axis to the Series area.

f. Title the chart **Ranch Inventory**, then preview the report to view the chart.

g. Save the report with the name **RanchInventoryReport**.

7. Modify charts.

a. Return to Report Design View for RanchInventoryReport, double-click the chart to open it in Edit mode.

b. Double-click the y-axis values to open the Format Axis dialog box, click the Number tab, then choose the **Currency** format from the Category list, entering **0** for the Decimal Places.

c. Change the color of the periwinkle bars to red.

d. Click the By Column button on the Chart Standard toolbar to switch the position of the fields in the x-axis and legend, and then remove the legend.

e. Return to Report Design View, then switch to Print Preview. Resize the chart as necessary so it looks like **FIGURE L-22**.

8. Apply chart types.

a. Save and close RanchInventoryReport, then copy and paste it with the name **RanchInventoryReportBar**.

b. Open RanchInventoryReportBar in Design View, open the chart in Edit mode, then change the chart type to a Clustered Bar.

c. Switch between Report Design View and Print Preview, resizing the chart and changing the font sizes as needed so that all of the labels on each axis are displayed clearly.

d. Print RanchInventoryReportBar if requested by your instructor, then save and close it.

e. Close the RealEstate-L.accdb database, and exit Access 2013.

FIGURE L-22

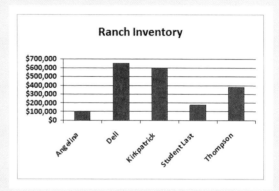

Independent Challenge 1

As the manager of a college women's basketball team, you want to enhance a form within the Basketball-L.accdb database to chart the home versus visiting team scores. You will build on your report creation skills to do so.

a. Start Access, then open the database Basketball-L.accdb from the location where you store your Data Files. Enable content if prompted.

b. Open and then maximize the GameInfo form. Navigate through several records as you observe the Home and Visitor scores.

c. Open the form in Form Design View, then insert a chart on the right side of the form based on the Games table. Choose the CycloneScore and OpponentScore fields for the chart. Choose a Column Chart type.

d. Add the OpponentScore field to the Data area so that both SumOfCycloneScore and SumOfOpponentScore appear in the Data area, double-click the SumOfCycloneScore field, select None as the summarize option, double-click the SumOfOpponentScore field, then select None as the summarize option.

e. Click Next and choose GameNo as the Form Field and as the Chart Field so that the chart changes from record to record showing the HomeScore versus the OpponentScore in the chart.

f. Title the chart **Scores**, and do not display a legend.

g. Open the form in Form View, and view the record for GameNo 3, as shown in **FIGURE L-23**. If requested by your instructor, print this record. To insert your name on the print-out, add it as a label to the Form Header section.

h. Save the GameInfo form, close it, close the Basketball-L. accdb database, and exit Access 2013.

FIGURE L-23

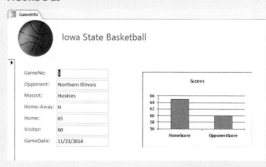

Independent Challenge 2

As the manager of a college women's basketball team, you want to build a report that shows a graph of total points per player per game.

a. Start Access, then open the database Basketball-L.accdb from the location where you store your Data Files. Enable content if prompted.

b. Open the PlayerStatistics report, and study the structure. Notice that this report has the total points per player in the last column. You want to graph these values for the entire season. Open the PlayerStatistics report in Report Design View.

c. Double-click the edge of the far-right text box in the Detail section, and click the Data tab in the Property Sheet to study the Control Source property. The expression =[FT]+([FG]*2)+([3P]*3) adds one-point free throws [FT] to two-point field goals [FG] to three-point three-pointers [3P] to find the player's total contribution to the score. You will calculate the total point value in the underlying query instead of on the report to make it easier to graph.

d. Click the report selector button, then click the Build button for the Record Source property, which currently displays the PlayerStats query. In the first blank column, add a new field with the following expression: **TotalPts:[FT]+([FG]*2)+([3P]*3)**.

e. Save and close the PlayerStats query, then return to Design View for the PlayerStatistics report. Open the Property Sheet for the GameNo Footer section. On the Format tab, change the Force New Page property to After Section.

f. Drag the bottom edge of the Report Footer section down so the height of the Report Footer section is about 3 inches, then insert a chart just below the existing controls in the Report Footer section.

g. In the Chart Wizard, choose the PlayerStats query to create the chart, choose the LastName and TotalPts fields for the chart, and choose the Column Chart type.

h. Use SumOfTotalPts in the Data area and the LastName field in the Axis area (which should be the defaults). Choose <No Field> for both the Report Fields and Chart Fields, and title the chart **Player Total Points**.

i. Widen the chart placeholder and report to be about 6" wide in Report Design View, delete the legend, then save and preview the report. The chart should look like **FIGURE L-24**.

j. Save the PlayerStatistics report, add your name as a label to the Report Header section, print the first and last pages if requested by your instructor, then close the report.

k. Close the Basketball-L.accdb database, and exit Access 2013.

FIGURE L-24

Independent Challenge 3

As the manager of a college women's basketball team, you want to create a multicolumn report from the Basketball-L.accdb database to summarize total points per game per player.

a. Start Access, then open the database Basketball-L.accdb from the location where you store your Data Files. Enable content if prompted.

b. Open the PlayerStats query in Design View. In the first blank column, add a new field with the following expression (if it has not already been added): **TotalPts:[FT]+([FG]*2)+([3P]*3)**.

c. Save and close the PlayerStats query.

d. Use the Report Wizard to create a new report from the PlayerStats query with the fields **Opponent**, **GameDate**, **LastName**, and **TotalPts**. View the data by Games, do not add any more grouping levels, then sort the records in descending order by TotalPts.

e. Click the Summary Options button, then click the Sum check box for the TotalPts field.

f. Choose a Stepped layout and a Landscape orientation. Title the report **Point Production**, and preview it.

g. Delete the long text box with the Summary expression in the GameNo Footer section. Delete the LastName and TotalPts labels from the Page Header section.

Independent Challenge 3 (continued)

h. Delete the page expression in the Page Footer section, then move the TotalPts and LastName text boxes in the Detail section to the left, just below the Opponent and GameDate text boxes in the GameNo Header section. Move any other text boxes to the left so that no control extends beyond the 4" mark on the horizontal ruler.

i. Drag the right edge of the report to the left, so that it is no wider than 4", then right-align the values within the text boxes with the subtotal for total points in the GameNo Footer and the Report Footer sections and also right-align the right edges of these two text boxes.

j. Move and right-align the Sum and Grand Total labels closer to the text boxes they describe.

k. Preview the report, and in the Page Setup dialog box, set the report to 2 columns, and specify that the column layout go down, then across.

l. In Design View, add a horizontal line across the bottom of the GameNo Footer section to separate the records from game to game.

FIGURE L-25

m. For the GameNo Footer section, change the New Row Or Col property to After Section.

n. Preview the Point Production report. It should structurally look like **FIGURE L-25**. Print the first page of the report if requested by your instructor, adding your name as a label to the Report Header section if needed for the printout.

o. Close the Point Production report, close the Basketball-L. accdb database, then exit Access.

Independent Challenge 4: Explore

In your quest to become an Access database consultant, you want to know more about the built-in Microsoft Access templates and what you can learn about report design from these samples. In this exercise, you explore the reports of the Desktop task management database.

a. Start Access 2013, then select the Desktop task management template. Name the database **TaskManagement**, save it in the location where you store your Data Files, then enable content if prompted.

b. Close the Getting Started window and expand the Navigation Pane (if it is not expanded) to review the objects in the database.

c. Open the Contacts table and add your school name in the Company field and your name in the Last Name and First Name fields. Fill in the rest of the record with fictitious but realistic data.

d. Add a second record in the Contacts table with your professor's information in the Last Name and First Name fields, using fictitious but realistic data in the rest of the record.

e. Expand the subdatasheet for your record and enter two task records with the titles **Research Paper** and **Web Site Survey**. Do not change or enter data in any of the rest of the fields, then close the Contacts table.

f. Preview each of the predeveloped reports going back and forth between Print Preview and Report Design View to study and learn about any new features or techniques these reports offer that you want to explore further.

g. Open the Contact Address Book in Print Preview and notice that the contacts are grouped by the first letter of their last name. To see how this was done, open the report in Design View and then open the Group, Sort, and Total Pane. Click the More button to reveal the characteristics of the Group on File As group. Click the list arrow for the "by first character" option to see more grouping options.

h. If requested by your instructor, print the Contact Address Book report, close the TaskManagement.accdb database, and exit Access 2013.

Visual Workshop

As the manager of a college women's basketball team, you need to create a report from the Basketball-L.accdb database that lists information about each game played and subtracts the OpponentScore from the HomeScore field to calculate the number of points by which the game was won or lost in the Win/Loss column. Use the Report Wizard to start the report. Base it on all the fields in the Games table, and sort the records in ascending order on the GameDate field. Use a Tabular layout and a Landscape orientation, and name the report **Iowa State Basketball**. Use Report Layout and Design View to move, resize, align, modify, and add controls as necessary to match **FIGURE L-26**. (*Hint*: You must add a text box that calculates the Win/Loss value for each game.) If requested to print the report, add your name as a label to the Report Header section before printing.

FIGURE L-26

Iowa State Basketball

GameDate	Opponent	Mascot	Home-Away	Our Score	Opponent	Win/Loss
11/13/2014	Northern Iowa	Panthers	A	81	65	16
11/16/2014	Creighton	Bluejays	H	106	60	46
11/23/2014	Northern Illinois	Huskies	H	65	60	5
11/30/2014	Louisiana Tech	Red Raiders	A	69	89	-20
12/11/2014	Drake	Bulldogs	H	80	60	20
12/19/2014	Northern Iowa	Panthers	A	38	73	-35
12/29/2014	Buffalo	Bulls	H	50	55	-5
1/1/2015	Oklahoma	Sooners	A	53	60	-7
1/4/2015	Texas	Longhorns	H	57	60	-3
1/8/2015	Kansas	Jayhawks	H	74	58	16

Creating Macros

CASE Kayla Green, the network administrator at Quest Specialty Travel, has identified several Access tasks that are repeated on a regular basis. She has asked you to help her automate these processes with macros.

Unit Objectives

After completing this unit, you will be able to:

- Understand macros
- Create a macro
- Modify actions and arguments
- Assign a macro to a command button

- Use If statements
- Work with events
- Create a data macro
- Troubleshoot macros

Files You Will Need

Technology-M.accdb
Basketball-M.accdb

Patients-M.accdb
Chocolate-M.accdb

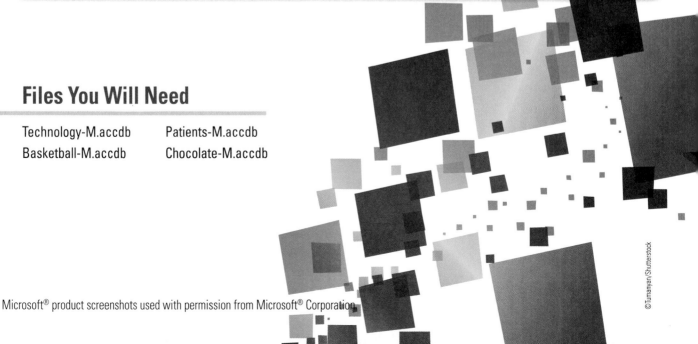

Understand Macros

Learning Outcomes
• Describe the benefits of macros
• Define macro terminology
• Describe Macro Design View components

A **macro** is a database object that stores actions to complete Access tasks. Repetitive Access tasks such as printing several reports, or opening and maximizing a form, are good candidates for a macro. Automating routine tasks by using macros builds efficiency, accuracy, and flexibility into your database. **CASE** *You decide to study the major benefits of using macros, macro terminology, and the components of the Macro Design View before building your first macro.*

DETAILS

The major benefits of using macros include the following:

- Saving time by automating routine tasks
- Increasing accuracy by ensuring that tasks are executed consistently
- Improving the functionality and ease of use of forms by using macros connected to command buttons
- Ensuring data accuracy in forms by using macros to respond to data entry errors
- Automating data transfers such as collecting data from Excel
- Helping users by responding to their interactions within a form

Macro terminology:

- A **macro** is an Access object that stores a series of actions to perform one or more tasks.
- **Macro Design View** is the window in which you create a macro. **FIGURE M-1** shows Macro Design View with an OpenForm action. See **TABLE M-1** for a description of the Macro Design View components.
- Each task that you want the macro to perform is called an **action**. A macro may contain one or more actions.
- **Arguments** are properties of an action that provide additional information on how the action should execute.
- A **conditional expression** is an expression resulting in either a true or false answer that determines whether a macro action will execute. Conditional expressions are used in If statements.
- An **event** is something that happens to a form, window, toolbar, or control—such as the click of a command button or an entry in a field—that can be used to initiate the execution of a macro.
- A **submacro** is a collection of actions within a macro object that allows you to name and create multiple, separate macros within a single macro object.

FIGURE M-1: Macro Design View with OpenForm action

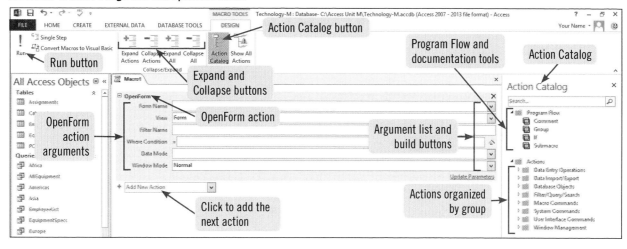

TABLE M-1: Macro Design View components

component	description
Action Catalog	Lists all available macro actions organized by category. Use the Search box to narrow the number of macro actions to a particular subject.
If statement	Contains conditional expressions that are evaluated as either true or false. If true, the macro action is executed. If false, the macro action is skipped. If statements in Access 2013 may contain Else If and Else clauses.
Comment	Allows you to document the macro with explanatory text.
Arguments	Lists required and optional arguments for the selected action.
Run button	Runs the selected macro.
Expand and Collapse buttons	Allows you to expand or collapse the macro actions to show or hide their arguments.

Create a Macro

Learning Outcomes
- Create a macro
- Describe macro actions

In Access, you create a macro by choosing a series of actions in Macro Design View that accomplishes the job you want to automate. Therefore, to become proficient with Access macros, you must be comfortable with macro actions. Some of the most common actions are listed in **TABLE M-2**. When you create a macro in other Microsoft Office products such as Word or Excel, you create Visual Basic for Applications (VBA) statements. In Access, macros do not create VBA code, though after creating a macro, you can convert it to VBA if desired. **CASE** ► Kayla observes that users want to open the AllEquipment report from the Employees form, so she asks you to create a macro to help automate this task.

STEPS

TROUBLE
If you do not enable content, your macros will not run.

1. **Start** Access, open the Technology-M.accdb database **from the location where you store your Data Files, enable content if prompted, click the** CREATE tab, **then click the** Macro button

   Macro Design View opens, ready for you to choose your first action.

TROUBLE
If you choose the wrong macro action, click the Delete button ✕ in the upper-right corner of the macro action block and try again.

2. **Click the** Action list arrow, **type** op **to quickly scroll to the actions that start with the letters** op, **then scroll and click** OpenReport

   The OpenReport action is now the first action in the macro, and the arguments that further define the OpenReport action appear in the action block. The **action block** organizes all of the arguments for a current action and is visually highlighted with a rectangle and gray background. You can expand or collapse the action block to view or hide details by clicking the Collapse/Expand button to the left of the action name or the Expand and Collapse buttons on the DESIGN tab in Macro Design View.

   The **OpenReport action** has three required arguments: Report Name, View, and Window Mode. View and Window Mode have default values, but the word *Required* is shown in the Report Name argument, indicating that you must select a choice. The Filter Name and Where Condition arguments are optional as indicated by their blank boxes.

QUICK TIP
Hover over any macro action or argument to see a ScreenTip of information about that item.

3. **Click the** Report Name argument list arrow, **then click** AllEquipment

   All of the report objects in the Technology-M.accdb database appear in the Report Name argument list, making it easy to choose the report you want.

4. **Click the** View argument list arrow, **then click** Print Preview

   Your screen should look like **FIGURE M-2**. Macros can contain one or many actions. In this case, the macro has only one action.

5. **Click the** Save button 🔲 **on the Quick Access toolbar, type** PreviewAllEquipmentReport **in the Macro Name text box, click** OK, **right-click the** PreviewAllEquipmentReport **macro tab, then click** Close

   The Navigation Pane lists the PreviewAllEquipmentReport object in the Macros group.

QUICK TIP
To print Macro Design View, click the FILE tab, click Print, click the Print button, then click OK in the Print Macro Definition dialog box.

6. **Double-click the** PreviewAllEquipmentReport macro **in the Navigation Pane to run the macro**

   The AllEquipment report opens in Print Preview.

7. **Close the AllEquipment report**

FIGURE M-2: Macro Design View with OpenReport action

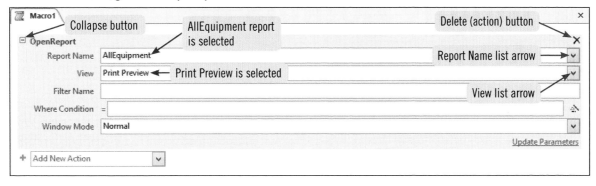

TABLE M-2: Common macro actions

subject area	macro action	description
Data Entry Operations	DeleteRecord	Deletes the current record
	SaveRecord	Saves the current record
Data Import/Export	ImportExportSpreadsheet*	Imports or exports the spreadsheet you specify
	ImportExportText*	Imports or exports the text file you specify
	EMailDatabaseObject	Sends the specified database object through Outlook with specified email settings
Database Objects	GoToControl	Moves the focus (where you are currently typing or clicking) to a specific field or control
	GoToRecord	Makes a specified record the current record
	OpenForm	Opens a form in Form View, Design View, Print Preview, or Datasheet View
	OpenReport	Opens a report in Design View or Print Preview, or prints the report
	OpenTable	Opens a table in Datasheet View, Design View, or Print Preview
	SetValue*	Sets the value of a field, control, or property
Filter/Query/Search	ApplyFilter	Restricts the number of records that appear in the resulting form or report by applying limiting criteria
	FindRecord	Finds the first record that meets the criteria
	OpenQuery	Opens a select or crosstab query; runs an action query
Macro Commands	RunCode	Runs a Visual Basic function (a series of programming statements that do a calculation or comparison and return a value)
	RunMacro	Runs a macro or attaches a macro to a custom menu command
	StopMacro	Stops the currently running macro
System Commands	Beep	Sounds a beep tone through the computer's speaker
	PrintOut*	Prints the active object, such as a datasheet, report, form, or module
	SendKeys*	Sends keystrokes directly to Microsoft Access or to an active Windows application
User Interface Commands	MessageBox	Displays a message box containing a warning or an informational message
	ShowToolbar*	Displays or hides a given toolbar
Window Management	CloseWindow	Closes a window
	MaximizeWindow	Enlarges the active window to fill the Access window

*Must click Show All Actions button on Ribbon for these actions to appear.

Modify Actions and Arguments

Learning
Outcomes
• Modify macro
  actions
• Modify macro
  arguments

Macros can contain as many actions as necessary to complete the process that you want to automate. Each action is evaluated in the order in which it appears in Macro Design View, starting at the top. Whereas some macro actions open, close, preview, or export data or objects, others are used only to make the database easier to use. **MessageBox** is a useful macro action because it displays an informational message to the user. **CASE** ▶ *You add a MessageBox action to the PreviewAllEquipmentReport macro to display a descriptive message in a dialog box.*

STEPS

1. **Right-click the PreviewAllEquipmentReport macro in the Navigation Pane, then click Design View on the shortcut menu**

   The PreviewAllEquipmentReport macro opens in Macro Design View.

2. **Click the Add New Action list arrow, type me to quickly scroll to the actions that start with the letters *me*, then click MessageBox**

   Each action has its own arguments that further clarify what the action does.

3. **Click the Message argument text box in the action block, then type Click the Print button to print this report**

   The Message argument determines what text appears in the message box. By default, the Beep argument is set to "Yes" and the Type argument is set to "None."

4. **Click the Type argument list arrow in the action block, then click Information**

   The Type argument determines which icon appears in the dialog box that is created by the MessageBox action.

5. **Click the Title argument text box in the action block, then type To print this report. . .**

   Your screen should look like **FIGURE M-3**. The Title argument specifies what text is displayed in the title bar of the resulting dialog box. If you leave the Title argument empty, the title bar of the resulting dialog box displays "Microsoft Access."

6. **Save the macro, then click the Run button in the Tools group**

   If your speakers are turned on, you should hear a beep, then the message box appears, as shown in **FIGURE M-4**.

7. **Click OK in the dialog box, close the AllEquipment report, then save and close Macro Design View**

FIGURE M-3: Adding the MessageBox action

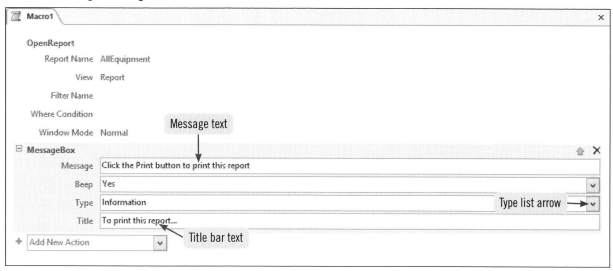

FIGURE M-4: Dialog box created by MessageBox action

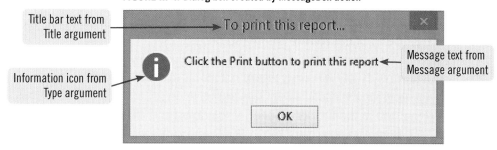

Assigning a macro to a key combination

You can assign a key combination such as [Shift][Ctrl][L] to a macro by creating a macro with the name **AutoKeys**. Enter the key combination as the submacro name. Use + for Shift, % for Alt, and ^ for Ctrl. Enclose special keys such as F3 in {curly braces}. For example, to assign a macro to [Shift][Ctrl][L], use +^L as the submacro name. To assign a macro to [Shift][F3], use +{F3} as the submacro name. Any key combination assignments you make in the AutoKeys macro override those that Access has already specified. Therefore, check the Keyboard Shortcuts information in the Microsoft Access Help system to make sure that the AutoKey assignment that you are creating doesn't override an existing Access quick keystroke that may be used for another purpose.

Assign a Macro to a Command Button

Learning
Outcomes
• Tie a command
  button to a macro
• Describe trusted
  folders and files

Access provides many ways to run a macro: clicking the Run button in Macro Design View, assigning the macro to a command button, or assigning the macro to a ribbon or shortcut menu command. Assigning a macro to a command button on a form provides a very intuitive way for the user to access the macro's functionality. **CASE** ▸ *You decide to modify the Employees form to include a command button that runs the PreviewAllEquipmentReport macro.*

STEPS

QUICK TIP
Be sure the Use
Control Wizards but-
ton 🔲 is selected.
To find it, click the
More button ▼ in
the Controls group
on the DESIGN tab.

1. **Right-click the Employees form in the Navigation Pane, click Design View, expand the Form Footer about 0.5", click the Button button xxxx in the Controls group, then click the left side of the Form Footer section**

   The **Command Button Wizard** starts, presenting you with 28 actions on the right organized within six categories on the left. For example, if you want the command button to open a report, you choose the OpenReport action in the Report Operations category. In this case, you want to run the PreviewAllEquipmentReport macro, which not only opens a report, but also presents a message. The Miscellaneous category contains an action that allows you to run an existing macro.

2. **Click Miscellaneous in the Categories list, click Run Macro in the Actions list, as shown in FIGURE M-5, click Next, click PreviewAllEquipmentReport, click Next, click the Text option button, select Run Macro, type All Equipment Report, then click Next**

   The Command Button Wizard asks you to give the button a meaningful name. When assigning names, a common three-character prefix for command buttons is **cmd**.

3. **Type cmdAllEquipment, click Finish, then click the Property Sheet button in the Tools group to open the Property Sheet for the command button**

   The new command button that runs a macro has been added to the Employees form in Form Design View. You work with the Property Sheet to change the text color to differentiate it from the button color as well as to examine how the macro was attached to the command button.

4. **Click the Format tab in the Property Sheet, scroll down and click the Fore Color list arrow, click Text Dark, then click the Event tab in the Property Sheet, noting that the On Click property contains [Embedded Macro]**

   The PreviewAllEquipmentReport macro was attached to the **On Click property** of this command button. In other words, the macro is run when the user clicks the command button. To make sure that the new command button works as intended, you view the form in Form View and test the command button.

5. **Close the Property Sheet, click the View button 📄 to switch to Form View, click the All Equipment Report command button in the Form Footer section, click OK in the message box, then close the AllEquipment report**

   The Employees form with the new command button should look like FIGURE M-6. It's common to put command buttons in the Form Footer so that users have a consistent location to find them.

6. **Save and close the Employees form**

FIGURE M-5: Adding a command button to run a macro

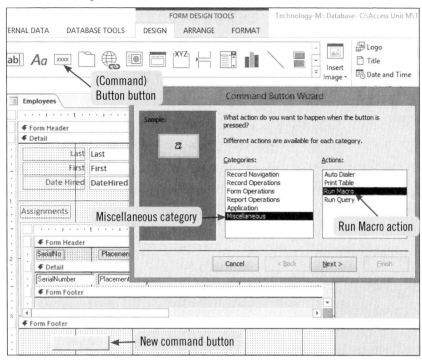

FIGURE M-6: Employees form with new command button

Using a trusted database and setting up a trusted folder

A **trusted database** allows you to run macros and VBA. By default, a database is not trusted. To trust a database, click the Enable Content button on the Security Warning bar each time you open a database. To permanently trust a database, store the database in a **trusted folder**. To create a trusted folder, open the Options dialog box from the FILE tab, click the Trust Center, click the Trust Center Settings button, click the Trusted Locations option, click the Add new location button, then browse to and choose the folder you want to trust.

Use If Statements

An **If statement** allows you to run macro actions based on the result of a conditional expression. A **conditional expression** is an expression such as [Price]>100 or [StateName]="MO" that results in a true or false value. If the condition evaluates true, the actions that follow the If statement are executed. If the condition evaluates false, the macro skips those actions. When building a conditional expression that refers to a value in a control on a form or report, use the following syntax: [Forms]![*formname*]![*controlname*] or [Reports]![*reportname*]![*controlname*]. Separating the object type (Forms or Reports) from the object name and from the control name by using [square brackets] and exclamation points (!) is called **bang notation**. **CASE** ▶ *At Quest Specialty Travel, everyone who has been with the company longer than five years is eligible to take their old PC equipment home as soon as it has been replaced. You use a conditional macro to help evaluate and present this information in a form.*

STEPS

1. **Click the CREATE tab, click the Macro button, click the Action Catalog button in the Show/Hide group to toggle on the Action Catalog window if it is not already visible, double-click If in the Program Flow area, then type the following in the If box:**
   [Forms]![Employees]![DateHired]<Date()-(5*365)
   The conditional expression shown in **FIGURE M-7** says, "Check the value in the DateHired control on the Employees form and evaluate true if the value is earlier than 5 years from today. Evaluate false if the value is not earlier than 5 years ago."

2. **Click the Add New Action list arrow in the If block, then scroll and click SetProperty**
   The **SetProperty** action has three arguments: Control Name, Property, and Value, which set the control, property, and value of that property.

3. **Click the Control Name argument text box in the Action Arguments pane, type LabelPCProgram, click the Property argument list arrow, click Visible, click the Value Property argument, then type True**
   Your screen should look like **FIGURE M-8**. The **Control Name** argument for the label is set to LabelPCProgram, which must match the **Name property** in the Property Sheet of the label that will be modified. The **Property argument** determines what property is being modified for the LabelPCProgram control. In this case, you are modifying the Visible property. The **Value argument** determines the value of the **Visible property**. For properties such as the Visible property that have only two choices in the Property Sheet, Yes or No, you enter a value of False for No and True for Yes.

4. **Save the macro with the name 5YearsPC, then close Macro Design View**
   Test the macro using the Employees form.

5. **In the Navigation Pane, double-click the Employees form to open it**
   The record for Juan Ramirez, hired 8/5/2005, appears. Given that Juan has worked at Quest much longer than 5 years, you anticipate that the macro will display the label when it is run.

6. **Click the DATABASE TOOLS tab, click the Run Macro button, verify that 5YearsPC is in the Macro Name text box, then click OK**
   After evaluating the DateHired field of this record and determining that this employee has been working at Quest Specialty Travel longer than five years, the LabelPCProgram label's Visible property was set to Yes, as shown in **FIGURE M-9**. The LabelPCProgram label's **Caption property** is "Eligible for PC Program!"

7. **Navigate through several records and note that the label remains visible for each employee even though the hire date may not be longer than 5 years ago**
   Because the macro only ran once, the label's Visible property remains Yes regardless of the current data in the DateHired field. You need a way to rerun or trigger the macro to evaluate the data in the DateHired field for each employee.

8. **Close the Employees form**

FIGURE M-7: Using an If statement to set a control's Visible property

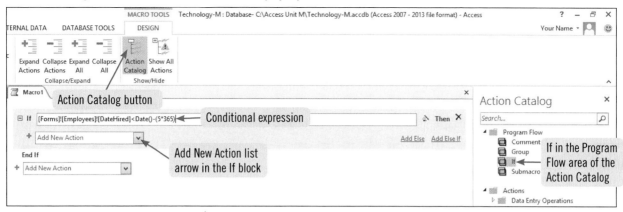

FIGURE M-8: Entering arguments for the SetProperty action

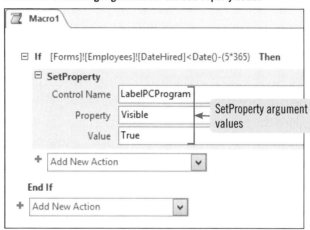

FIGURE M-9: Running the 5YearsPC macro

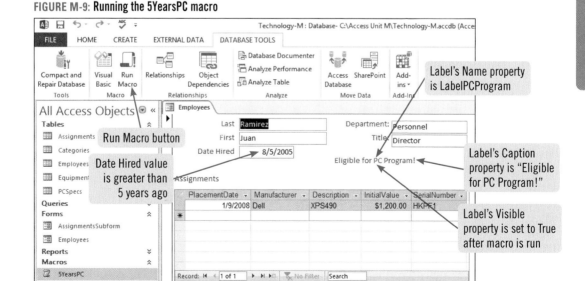

Work with Events

An **event** is a specific activity that occurs within the database, such as clicking a command button, moving from record to record, editing data, or opening or closing a form. Events can be triggered by the user or by the database itself. By assigning a macro to an appropriate event rather than running the macro from the DATABASE TOOLS tab or command button, you further automate and improve your database. **CASE** *You need to modify the 5YearsPC macro so that it evaluates the DateHired field to display or hide the label as you move from record to record.*

STEPS

1. **Right-click the 5YearsPC macro in the Navigation Pane, click Design View on the shortcut menu, click anywhere in the If block to activate it, then click the Add Else link in the lower-right corner of the If block**

   The **Else** portion of an If statement allows you to run a different set of macro actions if the conditional expression evaluates False. In this case, you want to set the Value of the Visible property to False if the conditional expression evaluates False (if the DateHired is less than five years from today's date) so that the label does not appear if the employee is not eligible for the PC program.

   TROUBLE
   If your screen doesn't match **FIGURE M-10**, use the Undo button ↩ to try again.

2. **Right-click the SetProperty action block, click Copy, right-click the Else block, click Paste, select True in the Value property, then type False, as shown in FIGURE M-10**

   With the second action edited, the macro will now turn the label's Visible property to True (Yes) *or* False (No), depending on DateHired value. To make the macro run each time you move to a new employee record, you attach the macro to the event that is triggered as you move from record to record.

3. **Save and close the 5YearsPC macro, right-click the Employees form in the Navigation Pane, click Design View, then click the Property Sheet button**

   All objects, sections, and controls have a variety of events to which macros can be attached. Most event names are self-explanatory, such as the **On Click event** (which occurs when that item is clicked).

   TROUBLE
   Be sure you are viewing the Property Sheet for the form. If not, choose Form from the Selection Type list near the top of the Property Sheet.

4. **Click the Event tab in the Property Sheet, click the On Current list arrow, then click 5YearsPC**

   Your Property Sheet should look like **FIGURE M-11**. Because the **On Current event** occurs when focus moves from one record to another, the 5YearsPC macro will automatically run each time you move from record to record in the form. Test your new macro by moving through several records in Form View.

5. **Close the Property Sheet, click the View button 🖳 to switch to Form View, then click the Next record button ▶ in the navigation bar for the main form several times while observing the Eligible for PC Program! label**

   For every DateHired value that is earlier than five years before today's date, the Eligible for PC Program! label is visible. If the DateHired is less than five years before today's date, the label is hidden.

6. **Save and close the Employees form**

FIGURE M-10: Adding an Else portion to an If block

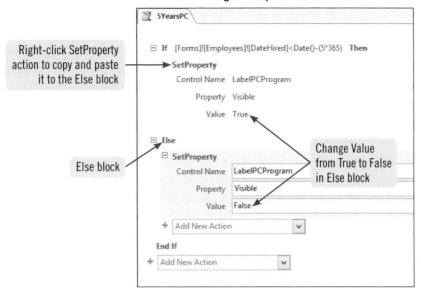

Right-click SetProperty action to copy and paste it to the Else block

Else block

Change Value from True to False in Else block

FIGURE M-11: Attaching a macro to the On Current event of the form

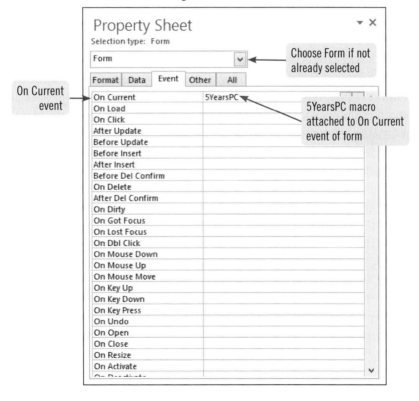

On Current event

Choose Form if not already selected

5YearsPC macro attached to On Current event of form

Create a Data Macro

Learning Outcomes
- Describe the use of data macros
- Create a data macro

A **data macro** allows you to embed macro capabilities directly in a table to add, change, or delete data based on conditions you specify. Data macros are a new feature of Access 2013. Data macros are managed directly from within tables, and do not appear in the Macros group in the Navigation Pane. You most often run a data macro based on a table event, such as modifying data or deleting a record, but you can run a data macro separately as well, similar to how you run a regular macro. **CASE** ▶ *Quest Specialty Travel grants 10 days of regular vacation to all employees except for those in the Africa and Asia departments, who receive 15 days due to the extra travel requirements of their positions. Kayla asks you to figure out an automatic way to assign each employee the correct number of vacation days based on their department. A data macro will work well for this task.*

STEPS

1. **Double-click the Employees table in the Navigation Pane, then observe the Vacation field throughout the datasheet**

   Currently, the Vacation field contains the value of 10 for each record, or each employee.

2. **Right-click the Employees table tab, click Design View on the shortcut menu, click the Create Data Macros button in the Field, Record & Table Events group, click After Insert, then click the Action Catalog button in the Show/Hide group if the Action Catalog window is not already open**

   In this case, you chose the After Insert event, which is run after a new record is entered. See TABLE M-3 for more information on table events. Creating a data macro is very similar to creating a regular macro. You add the logic and macro actions needed to complete the task at hand.

   QUICK TIP
   You can also drag a block or action from the Action Catalog to Macro Design View.

3. **Double-click ForEachRecord in the Action Catalog to add a For Each Record In block, click the For Each Record In list arrow, click Employees in the list, click the Where Condition text box, type [Department]="Africa" or [Department]="Asia", double-click the EditRecord data block in the Action Catalog, double-click the SetField data action in the Action Catalog, click the Name box in the SetField block, type Vacation, click the Value box in the SetField block, then type 15, as shown in FIGURE M-12**

   The Default value for the Vacation field is set to 10 in Table Design View of the Employees table so all existing records should have a value of 10 in the Vacation field. Test the new data macro by adding a new record.

   TROUBLE
   Be sure to tab to a completely new record to trigger the data macro attached to the After Insert event.

4. **Click the Close button, click Yes when prompted to save changes, click the View button 🔲 to display the datasheet, click Yes when prompted to save changes, click the New button in the Records group, enter the new record, as shown in FIGURE M-13, except do not enter a Vacation value, then press [Tab] to move to a new record**

   The macro is triggered by the After Insert event of the record, and the Vacation field is automatically updated to 15 for the new record and all other records with Asia or Africa in the Department field, as shown in FIGURE M-13.

5. **Right-click the Employees table tab, then click Close on the shortcut menu**

   Data is automatically saved when you move from record to record or close a database object.

Creating Macros

FIGURE M-12: Creating a data macro

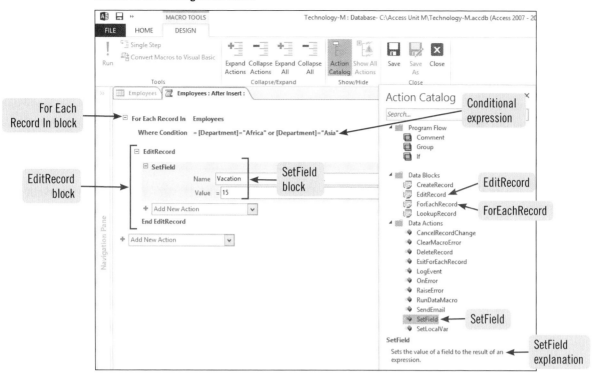

FIGURE M-13: Running a data macro

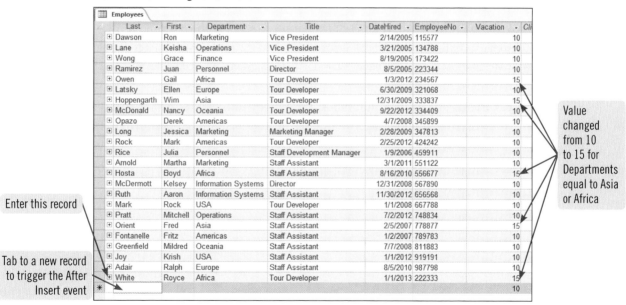

TABLE M-3: Table events

table event	runs...
After Insert	...after a new record has been inserted into the table
After Update	...after an existing record has been changed
After Delete	...after an existing record has been deleted
Before Delete	...before a record is deleted, to help the user validate or cancel the deletion
Before Change	...before a record is changed, to help the user validate or cancel the edits

Troubleshoot Macros

Learning
Outcomes
• Single step a
macro
• Describe debugg-
ing techniques

When macros don't run properly, Access supplies several tools to debug them. **Debugging** means determining why the macro doesn't run correctly. It usually involves breaking down a dysfunctional macro into smaller pieces that can be individually tested. For example, you can **single step** a macro, which means to run it one action at a time to observe the effect of each specific action in the Macro Single Step dialog box. **CASE** ▶ *You use the PreviewAllEquipmentReport macro to learn debugging techniques.*

STEPS

1. **Right-click the PreviewAllEquipmentReport macro, click Design View on the shortcut menu, click the Single Step button in the Tools group, then click the Run button**

   The screen should look like **FIGURE M-14**, with the Macro Single Step dialog box open. This dialog box displays information including the macro's name, the action's name, and the action's arguments. From the Macro Single Step dialog box, you can step into the next macro action, halt execution of the macro, or continue running the macro without single stepping.

2. **Click Step in the Macro Single Step dialog box**

   Stepping into the second action lets the first action run and pauses the macro at the second action. The Macro Single Step dialog box now displays information about the second action.

3. **Click Step**

   The second action, the MessageBox action, is executed, which displays the message box.

4. **Click OK, then close the AllEquipment report**

5. **Click the DESIGN tab, then click the Single Step button to toggle it off**

   Another technique to help troubleshoot macros is to use the built-in prompts and Help system provided by Microsoft Access. For example, you may have questions about how to use the optional Filter Name argument for the OpenReport macro action.

6. **Click the OpenReport action block, then point to the Filter Name argument to view the ScreenTip that supplies information about that argument, as shown in FIGURE M-15**

   The Access 2013 Macro Design View window has been improved with interactive prompts.

7. **Save and close the PreviewAllEquipmentReport macro, close the Technology-M.accdb database, then exit Access**

FIGURE M-14: Single stepping through a macro

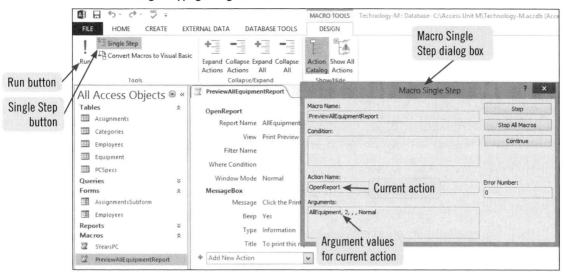

FIGURE M-15: Viewing automatic prompts

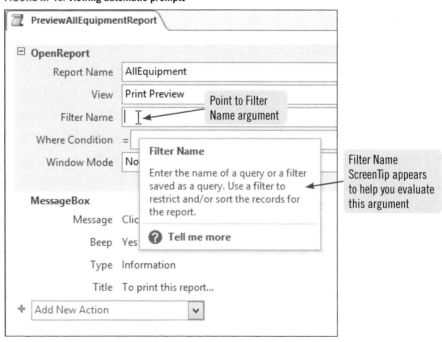

Practice

Put your skills into practice with SAM! If you have a SAM account, go to www.cengage.com/sam2013 to access SAM assignments for this unit.

Concepts Review

Identify each element of Macro Design View shown in FIGURE M-16.

FIGURE M-16

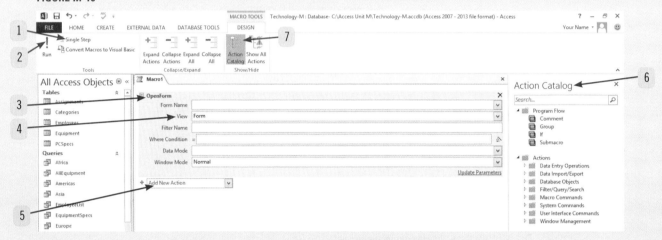

Match each term with the statement that best describes its function.

8. Macro
9. Action
10. Argument
11. Event
12. Debugging
13. Conditional expression

a. Specific action that occurs within the database, such as clicking a button or opening a form
b. Part of an If statement that evaluates as either true or false
c. Individual step that you want the Access macro to perform
d. Access object that stores one or more actions that perform one or more tasks
e. Provides additional information to define how an Access action will perform
f. Determines why a macro doesn't run properly

Select the best answer from the list of choices.

14. **Which of the following is *not* a major benefit of using a macro?**
    a. To make the database more flexible or easy to use
    b. To ensure consistency in executing routine or complex tasks
    c. To redesign the relationships among the tables of the database
    d. To save time by automating routine tasks

15. **Which of the following best describes the process of creating an Access macro?**
    a. Open Macro Design View and add actions, arguments, and If statements to accomplish the desired task.
    b. Use the single step recorder to record clicks and keystrokes as you complete a task.
    c. Use the macro recorder to record clicks and keystrokes as you complete a task.
    d. Use the Macro Wizard to determine which tasks are done most frequently.

16. **Which of the following would *not* be a way to run a macro?**
    a. Double-click a macro action within the Macro Design View window.
    b. Click the Run Macro button on the DATABASE TOOLS tab.
    c. Assign the macro to a command button on a form.
    d. Assign the macro to an event of a control on a form.

17. **Which of the following is *not* a reason to run a macro in single step mode?**
    a. You want to observe the effect of each macro action individually.
    b. You want to debug a macro that isn't working properly.
    c. You want to run only a few of the actions of a macro.
    d. You want to change the arguments of a macro while it runs.

18. **Which of the following is *not* true of conditional expressions in If statements in macros?**
    a. Macro If statements provide for Else and Else If clauses.
    b. Conditional expressions allow you to skip over actions when the expression evaluates as false.
    c. Conditional expressions give the macro more power and flexibility.
    d. More macro actions are available when you are also using conditional expressions.

19. **Which example illustrates the proper syntax to refer to a specific control on a form?**
    a. [Forms] ! [*formname*] ! [*controlname*]
    c. {Forms} ! {formname} ! (controlname)
    b. Forms ! formname. controlname
    d. (Forms) ! (formname) ! (controlname)

20. **Which event is executed every time you move from record to record in a form?**
    a. Next Record
    c. New Record
    b. On Current
    d. On Move

Skills Review

1. **Understand macros.**
    a. Start Access, then open the Basketball-M.accdb database from the location where you store your Data Files. Enable content if prompted.
    b. Open the PrintMacroGroup macro in Macro Design View, then record your answers to the following questions on a sheet of paper:
       • What is the name of the first submacro?
       • How many macro actions are in the first submacro?
       • What arguments does the first action in the first submacro contain?
       • What values were chosen for these arguments?
    c. Close Macro Design View for the PrintMacroGroup object.

2. **Create a macro.**
    a. Start a new macro in Macro Design View.
    b. Add the OpenQuery action.
    c. Select PlayerStats as the value for the Query Name argument.
    d. Select Datasheet for the View argument.
    e. Select Edit for the Data Mode argument.
    f. Save the macro with the name **ViewPlayerStats**.
    g. Run the macro to make sure it works, close the PlayerStats query, then close the ViewPlayerStats macro.

3. **Modify actions and arguments.**
    a. Open the ViewPlayerStats macro in Macro Design View.
    b. Add a MessageBox action as the second action of the query.
    c. Type **We had a great season!** for the Message argument.
    d. Select Yes for the Beep argument.
    e. Select Warning! for the Type argument.
    f. Type **Iowa State Cyclones** for the Title argument.
    g. Save the macro, then run it to make sure the MessageBox action works as intended.
    h. Click OK in the dialog box created by the MessageBox action, close the PlayerStats query, then close the ViewPlayerStats macro.
    i. Open the PrintMacroGroup macro object in Design View.
    j. Modify the View argument for the OpenReport object of the PlayerStatistics submacro from Print to **Print Preview**.

Skills Review (continued)

k. Modify the Message argument for the MessageBox object of the PlayerStatistics submacro to read **Click the Print button to send this report to the printer.**

l. Save and close the PrintMacroGroup macro.

4. Assign a macro to a command button.

a. In Design View of the PlayerEntryForm, use the Command Button Wizard to add a command button below the existing Print Current Record button. The new button should run the PlayerStatistics submacro in the PrintMacroGroup macro (PrintMacroGroup.PlayerStatistics).

b. The text on the button should read **View Player Statistics**.

c. The meaningful name for the button should be **cmdPlayerStatistics**.

d. Test the command button in Form View, click OK in the message box, then close the PlayerStats report.

e. Save and close the PlayerEntryForm.

5. Use If statements.

a. Start a new macro in Macro Design View, and open the Action Catalog window if it is not already open.

b. Double-click If in the Action Catalog window to add an If block to the macro.

c. Enter the following condition in the If box: **[Forms]![GameSummaryForm]![CycloneScore]> [OpponentScore]**.

d. Add the SetProperty action to the If block.

e. Type **VictoryLabel** in the Control Name box for the SetProperty action.

f. Select Visible for the Property argument for the SetProperty action.

g. Enter **True** for the Value argument for the SetProperty action to indicate Yes.

h. Click the Add Else link in the lower-right corner of the If block.

i. Copy the existing SetProperty action, then paste it under the Else clause.

j. Modify the Value property from True to **False** for the second SetProperty action.

k. Save the macro with the name **VictoryCalculator**, compare it with **FIGURE M-17**, make any necessary adjustments, then close Macro Design View.

6. Work with events.

a. Open the GameSummaryForm in Form Design View.

b. Open the Property Sheet for the form.

c. Assign the VictoryCalculator macro to the On Current event of the form.

d. Close the Property Sheet, save the form, then open the GameSummaryForm in Form View.

e. Navigate through the first four records. The Victory label should be visible for the first three records, but not the fourth.

f. Add your name as a label in the Form Footer section to identify your printouts, print the third and fourth records if requested by your instructor, then save and close the GameSummaryForm.

FIGURE M-17

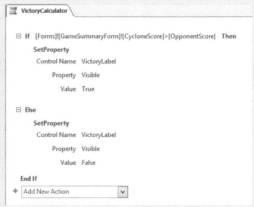

7. Create a data macro.

a. Open the Games table in Table Design View.

b. Add a field named **RoadWin** with a Yes/No data type and the following Description: **Enter Yes if the Home-Away field is Away and the CycloneScore is greater than the OpponentScore**.

c. Save the Games table and switch to Datasheet View to note that the RoadWin check box is empty (No) for every record.

d. Switch back to Table Design View, then create a data macro based on the After Insert event.

e. Insert a ForEachRecord data block, and specify **Games** for the For Each Record In argument.

f. The Where Condition should be: **[Home-Away]="A" and [CycloneScore]>[OpponentScore]**.

g. Add an EditRecord data block in the For Each Record In block, and a SetField data action. Be careful to add the EditRecord block *within* the For Each Record Block.

Skills Review (continued)

h. Enter **RoadWin** in the Name argument and **Yes** in the Value argument, as shown in **FIGURE M-18**.

i. Save and close the data macro, save the Games table, switch to Datasheet View, then test the new data macro by entering a new record in the Games table as follows:

Opponent: **Tulsa**

Mascot: **Hurricanes**

Home-Away: **A**

CycloneScore: **100**

OpponentScore: **50**

GameDate: **3/1/2015**

FIGURE M-18

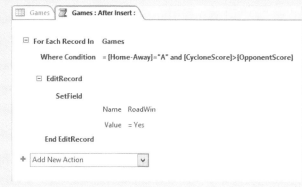

j. Tab to a new record. Six records where the Home-Away field is set to "A" and the CycloneScore is greater than the OpponentScore should be checked. Close the Games table.

8. Troubleshoot macros.

a. Open the PrintMacroGroup in Macro Design View.

b. Click the Single Step button, then click the Run button.

c. Click Step twice to step through the two actions of the submacro, PlayerStatistics, then click OK in the resulting message box.

d. Close the PlayerStats report.

e. Return to Macro Design View of the PrintMacroGroup macro, and click the Single Step button on the DESIGN tab to toggle off this feature.

f. Save and close the PrintMacroGroup macro, close the Basketball-M.accdb database, then exit Access.

Independent Challenge 1

As the manager of a doctor's clinic, you have created an Access database called Patients-M.accdb to track insurance claim reimbursements. You use macros to help automate the database.

a. Start Access, then open the database Patients-M.accdb from the location where you store your Data Files. Enable content if prompted.

b. Open Macro Design View of the CPT Form Open macro. (CPT stands for Current Procedural Terminology, which is a code that describes a medical procedure.) If the Single Step button is toggled on, click it to toggle it off.

c. On a separate sheet of paper, identify the macro actions, arguments for each action, and values for each argument.

d. In two or three sentences, explain in your own words what tasks this macro automates.

e. Close the CPT Form Open macro.

f. Open the Claim Entry Form in Form Design View.

g. In the Form Footer of the Claim Entry Form are several command buttons. Open the Property Sheet of the Add CPT Code button, then click the Event tab.

h. On your paper, write the event to which the CPT Form Open macro is assigned.

i. Open the Claim Entry Form in Form View, then click the Add CPT Code button in the Form Footer.

j. On your paper, write the current record number that is displayed for you.

k. Close the Patients-M.accdb database, then exit Access.

Independent Challenge 2

As the manager of a doctor's clinic, you have created an Access database called Patients-M.accdb to track insurance claim reimbursements. You use macros to help automate the database.

a. Start Access, then open the database Patients-M.accdb from the location where you store your Data Files. Enable content if prompted.

b. Start a new macro in Macro Design View, and open the Action Catalog window if it is not already open.

Independent Challenge 2 (continued)

c. Double-click the Submacro entry in the Program Flow folder to add a submacro block.

d. Type **Preview Date of Service Denied Report** as the first submacro name, then add the OpenReport macro action.

e. Select Date of Service Report - Denied for the Report Name argument, then select Print Preview for the View argument of the OpenReport action.

f. Double-click the Submacro entry in the Program Flow folder to add another submacro block.

g. Type **Preview Date of Service Fixed Report** as a new submacro name, then add the OpenReport macro action.

h. Select Date of Service Report - Fixed for the ReportName argument, then select Print Preview for the View argument of the second OpenReport action.

i. Save the macro with the name **Preview Group**, then close Macro Design View.

j. Using the Run Macro button on the DATABASE TOOLS tab, run the Preview Group.Preview Date of Service Denied Report macro to test it, then close Print Preview.

k. Using the Run Macro button on the DATABASE TOOLS tab, run the Preview Group.Preview Date of Service Fixed Report macro to test it, then close Print Preview.

l. Open the Preview Group macro in Macro Design View, then click the Collapse buttons to the left of the Submacro statements to collapse the two submacro blocks.

m. Create two more submacros, one that previews Monthly Claims Report - Denied and the other that previews Monthly Claims Report - Fixed. Name the two macros **Preview Monthly Denied Report** and **Preview Monthly Fixed Report**, as shown in FIGURE M-19.

n. Save and close the Preview Group macro.

o. In Design View of the Claim Line Items Subform, add four separate command buttons to the Form Footer to run the four submacros in the Preview Group macro. Use the captions and meaningful names of **Date Denied** and **cmdDateDenied**, **Date Fixed** and **cmdDateFixed**, **Monthly Denied** and **cmdMonthlyDenied**, and **Monthly Fixed** and **cmdMonthlyFixed** to correspond with the four submacros in the Preview Group macro.

p. Change the font color on the new command buttons to black.

q. Select all four new command buttons and use the Size/Space and Align commands on the ARRANGE tab to precisely size, align, and space the buttons equally in the Form Footer section.

r. Save and close the Claim Line Items Subform, then open the Claim Entry Form in Form View, as shown in FIGURE M-20. Test each of the new command buttons to make sure it opens the correct report.

s. Close the Claim Entry Form, close the Patients-M.accdb database, then exit Access

FIGURE M-19

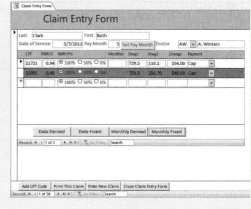

FIGURE M-20

Independent Challenge 3

As the manager of a doctor's clinic, you have created an Access database called Patients-M.accdb to track insurance claim reimbursements. You use macros to help automate the database.

a. Start Access, then open the Patients-M.accdb database from the location where you store your Data Files. Enable content if prompted.

b. Start a new macro in Macro Design View, then add an If statement.

Independent Challenge 3 (continued)

c. Enter the following in the If box: **[Forms]![CPT Form]![RBRVS]=0**.

d. Select the SetProperty action for the first action in the If block.

e. Enter the following arguments for the SetProperty action: Control Name: **ResearchLabel**, Property: **Visible**, and Value: **True**.

f. Click the Add Else link.

g. Select the SetProperty action for the first action of the Else clause.

h. Enter the following arguments for the SetProperty action: Control Name: **ResearchLabel**, Property: **Visible**, and Value: **False**.

i. Save the macro with the name **Research**, as shown in **FIGURE M-21**, then close Macro Design View.

j. Open the CPT Form in Form Design View, then open the Property Sheet for the form.

k. Assign the Research macro to the On Current event of the form.

l. Close the Property Sheet, save the form, then open the CPT Form in Form View.

m. Use the Next record button to move quickly through all 64 records in the form. Notice that the macro displays Research! only when the RBRVS value is equal to zero.

n. Save and close the CPT Form, then close the Patients-M.accdb database.

FIGURE M-21

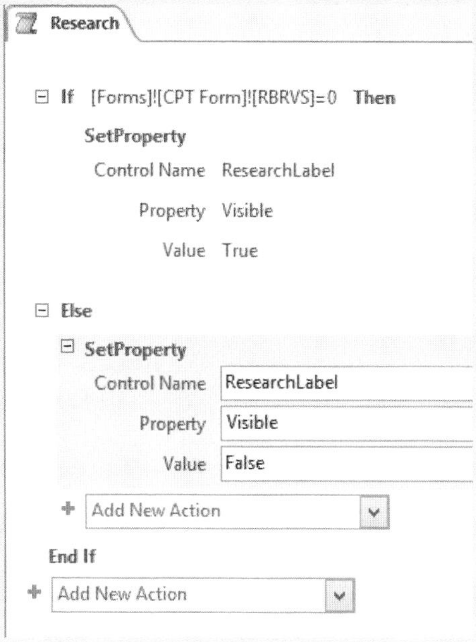

Independent Challenge 4: Explore

You are collecting information on international chocolate factories, museums, and stores in an Access database. You tie the forms together with macros attached to command buttons.

a. Open the Chocolate-M.accdb database from the location where you store your Data Files, enable content if prompted, then open the Countries form in Form View. The database option to show overlapping windows versus tabbed documents has been set. Overlapping windows allows you to restore and size windows.

b. Click the New (blank) record button for the main form, then type **Poland** in the Country text box.

c. In the subform for the Poland record, enter **Cadbury-Wedel Polska** in the Name field, **F** in the Type field (F for factory), **Praga** in the City field, and **Lodz** in the StateProvince field. Close the Countries form. If you want the windows of this database to be maximized when you open them, you can accomplish this with a macro attached to the On Load event of the form.

d. Open Macro Design View for a new macro, then add the MaximizeWindow action. Save the macro with the name **Maximize**, then close it. The Maximize macro helps you maximize windows if a database option is set to Overlapping Windows. To see this setting, click the FILE tab, click Options, click Current Database, and then view the settings in the Document Window Options section. When Tabbed Documents is selected, the windows are automatically maximized and tabs are provided at the top of each window to help you navigate between them. When Overlapping Windows is selected, however, windows can be any size.

e. Open the Countries form in Design View, add the Maximize macro to the On Load event of the Countries form, then open the Countries form in Form View to test it.

f. Save and close the Countries form.

g. Add the Maximize macro to the On Load event of the Places of Interest report, then open the Places of Interest report in Print Preview to test it.

h. Save and close the Places of Interest report.

i. Close the Chocolate-M.accdb database, then exit Access.

Visual Workshop

As the manager of a doctor's clinic, you have created an Access database called Patients-M.accdb to track insurance claim reimbursements. Develop a new macro called **Query Group** with the actions and argument values shown in FIGURE M-22. Run both macros to test them by using the Run Macro button on the DATABASE TOOLS tab, and debug the macros if necessary.

FIGURE M-22

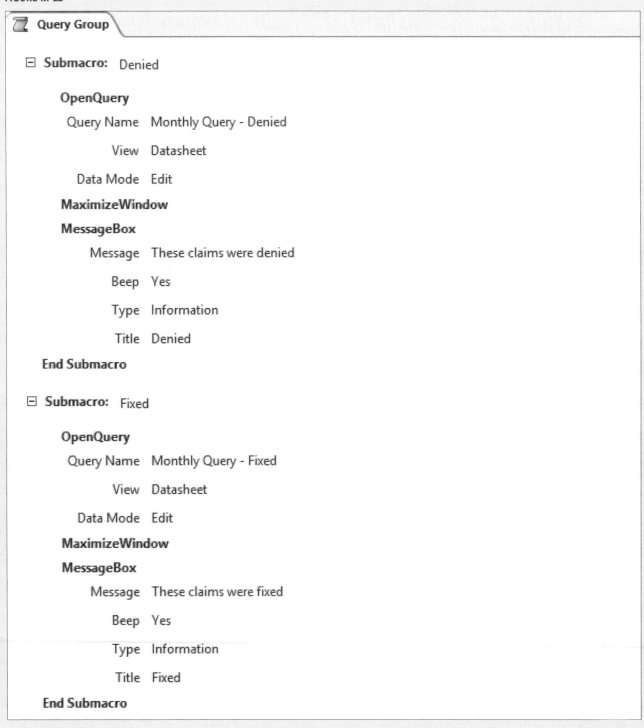

Creating Modules and VBA

CASE You want to learn about VBA and create modules to enhance the capabilities of the Technology-N database for Quest Specialty Travel.

Unit Objectives

After completing this unit, you will be able to:

- Understand modules and VBA
- Compare macros and modules
- Create functions
- Use If statements

- Document procedures
- Build class modules
- Modify sub procedures
- Troubleshoot modules

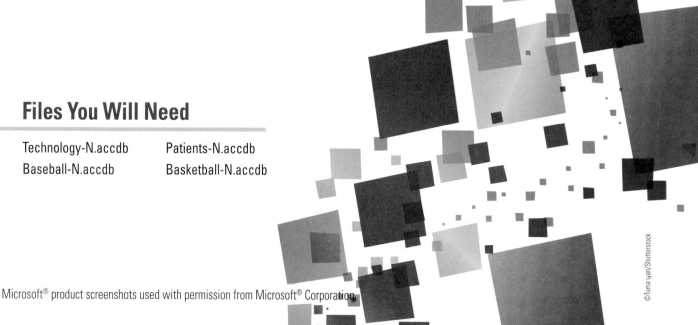

Files You Will Need

Technology-N.accdb   Patients-N.accdb
Baseball-N.accdb   Basketball-N.accdb

Microsoft® product screenshots used with permission from Microsoft® Corporation

© Tuna Iyan/Shutterstock

Understand Modules and VBA

Learning
Outcomes
• Define VBA terms
• Describe Visual
  Basic Editor
  components

Access is a robust and easy-to-use relational database program. Access provides user-friendly tools, such as wizards and Design Views, to help users quickly create reports and forms that previously took programmers hours to build. You may, however, want to automate a task or create a new function that goes beyond the capabilities of the built-in Access tools. Within each program of the Microsoft Office suite, a programming language called **Visual Basic for Applications (VBA)** is provided to help you extend the program's capabilities. In Access, VBA is stored within modules. A **module** is an Access object that stores Visual Basic for Applications (VBA) programming code. VBA is written in the **Visual Basic Editor (VBE)**, shown in **FIGURE N-1**. The components and text colors of the VBE are described in **TABLE N-1**. An Access database has two kinds of modules. **Standard modules** contain global code that can be executed from anywhere in the database. Standard modules are displayed as module objects in the Navigation Pane. **Class modules** are stored within the form or report object itself. Class modules contain VBA code used only within that particular form or report. **CASE** ▶ *Before working with modules, you ask some questions about VBA.*

DETAILS

The following questions and answers introduce the basics of Access modules:

* **What does a module contain?**

  A module contains VBA programming code organized in procedures. A procedure contains several lines of code, each of which is called a **statement**. Modules can also contain **comments**, text that helps explain and document the code.

* **What is a procedure?**

  A **procedure** is a series of VBA statements that performs an operation or calculates an answer. VBA has two types of procedures: functions and subs. **Declaration statements** precede procedure statements and help set rules for how the statements in the module are processed.

* **What is a function?**

  A **function** is a procedure that returns a value. Access supplies many built-in functions, such as Sum, Count, Pmt, and Now, that can be used in an expression in a query, form, or report to calculate a value. You might want to create a new function, however, to help perform calculations unique to your database. For example, you might create a new function called Commission to calculate the sales commission using a formula unique to your business.

* **What is a sub?**

  A **sub** (also called **sub procedure**) performs a series of VBA statements to manipulate controls and objects. Subs are generally executed when an event occurs, such as when a command button is clicked or a form is opened.

* **What are arguments?**

  Arguments are constants, variables, or expressions passed to a procedure that the procedure needs in order to execute. For example, the full syntax for the Sum function is Sum(*expr*), where *expr* represents the argument for the Sum function, the field that is being summed. In VBA, arguments are declared in the first line of the procedure. They are specified immediately after a procedure's name and are enclosed in parentheses. Multiple arguments are separated by commas.

* **What is an object?**

  In VBA, an **object** is any item that can be identified or manipulated, including the traditional Access objects (table, query, form, report, macro, and module) as well as other items that have properties, such as controls, sections, and existing procedures.

* **What is a method?**

  A **method** is an action that an object can perform. Procedures are often written to invoke methods in response to user actions. For example, you could invoke the GoToControl method to move the focus to a specific control on a form in response to the user clicking a command button.

FIGURE N-1: Visual Basic Editor (VBE) window for a standard module

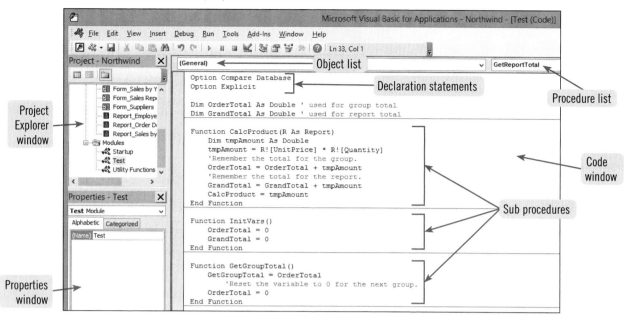

TABLE N-1: Components and text colors for the Visual Basic Editor window

component or color	description
Visual Basic Editor, VBE	Comprises the entire Microsoft Visual Basic program window that contains smaller windows, including the Code window and Project Explorer window
Code window	Contains the VBA for the project selected in the Project Explorer window
Project Explorer window	Displays a hierarchical list of the projects in the database; a **project** can be a module object or a form or report object that contains a class module
Declaration statements	Includes statements that apply to every procedure in the module, such as declarations for variables, constants, user-defined data types, and external procedures in a dynamic-link library
Object list	In a class module, lists the objects associated with the current form or report
Procedure list	In a standard module, lists the procedures in the module; in a class module, lists events (such as Click or Dblclick)
Blue	Indicates a VBA keyword; blue words are reserved by VBA and are already assigned specific meanings
Black	Indicates normal text; black words are the unique VBA code developed by the user
Red	Indicates syntax error text; a red statement indicates that it will not execute correctly because of a syntax error (perhaps a missing parenthesis or a spelling error)
Green	Indicates comment text; any text after an apostrophe is considered documentation, or a comment, and is therefore ignored in the execution of the procedure

Compare Macros and Modules

Learning
Outcomes
• Contrast macros
  and modules
• Define VBA
  keywords

Both macros and modules help run your database more efficiently and effectively. Creating a macro or a module requires some understanding of programming concepts, an ability to follow a process through its steps, and patience. Some tasks can be accomplished by using an Access macro or by writing VBA. Guidelines can help you determine which tool is best for the task. **CASE** *You compare Access macros and modules by asking more questions.*

DETAILS

The following questions and answers provide guidelines for using macros and modules:

• **For what types of tasks are macros best suited?**

   Macros are an easy way to handle common, repetitive, and simple tasks such as opening and closing forms, positioning a form to enter a new record, and printing reports.

• **Which is easier to create, a macro or a module, and why?**

   Macros are generally easier to create because Macro Design View is more structured than the VBE. The hardest part of creating a macro is choosing the correct macro action. But once the action is selected, the arguments associated with that macro action are displayed, eliminating the need to learn any special programming syntax. To create a module, however, you must know a robust programming language, VBA, as well as the correct **syntax** (rules) for each VBA statement. In a nutshell, macros are simpler to create, but VBA is more powerful.

• **When must I use a macro?**

   You must use macros to make global, shortcut key assignments. **AutoExec** is a special macro name that automatically executes when the database first opens.

• **When must I use a module?**

   1. You must use modules to create unique functions. Macros cannot create functions. For instance, you might want to create a function called Commission that calculates the appropriate commission on a sale using your company's unique commission formula.
   2. Access error messages can be confusing to the user. But using VBA procedures, you can detect the error when it occurs and display your own message.
   3. Although Access 2013 macros have been enhanced to include more powerful If-Then logic, VBA is still more robust in the area of programming flow statements with tools such as nested If statements, Case statements, and multiple looping structures. Some of the most common VBA keywords, including If...Then, are shown in **TABLE N-2**. VBA keywords appear blue in the VBE code window.
   4. VBA code may declare **variables**, which are used to store data that can be used, modified, or displayed during the execution of the procedure.
   5. VBA may be used in conjunction with SQL (Structured Query Language) to select, update, append, and delete data.

   Class modules, like the one shown in **FIGURE N-2**, are stored as part of the form or report object in which they are created. If you develop forms and reports in one database and copy them to another, the VBA class module automatically travels with the object that stores it.

FIGURE N-2: Visual Basic Editor window for a class module

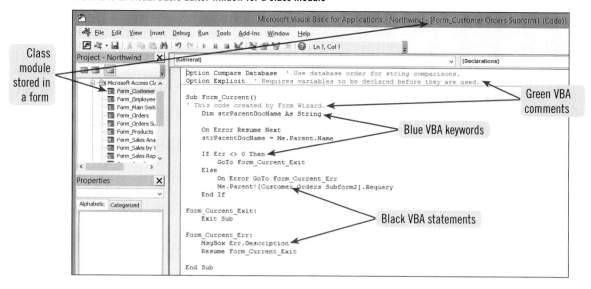

TABLE N-2: Common VBA keywords

statement	explanation
Function	Declares the name and arguments that create a new function procedure
End Function	When defining a new function, the End Function statement is required as the last statement to mark the end of the VBA code that defines the function
Sub	Declares the name for a new Sub procedure; **Private Sub** indicates that the Sub is accessible only to other procedures in the module where it is declared
End Sub	When defining a new sub, the End Sub statement is required as the last statement to mark the end of the VBA code that defines the sub
If...Then	Executes code (the code follows the Then statement) when the value of an expression is true (the expression follows the If statement)
End If	When creating an If...Then...Else clause, the End If statement is required as the last statement
Const	Declares the name and value of a **constant**, an item that retains a constant value throughout the execution of the code
Option Compare Database	A declaration statement that determines the way string values (text) will be sorted
Option Explicit	A declaration statement that specifies that you must explicitly declare all variables used in all procedures; if you attempt to use an undeclared variable name, an error occurs at **compile time**, the period during which source code is translated to executable code
Dim	Declares a **variable**, a named storage location that contains data that can be modified during program execution
On Error GoTo	Upon an error in the execution of a procedure, specifies the location (the statement) where the procedure should continue
Select Case	Executes one of several groups of statements called a **Case** depending on the value of an expression; use the Select Case statement as an alternative to using **ElseIf** in **If...Then...Else** statements when comparing one expression with several different values
End Select	When defining a new Select Case group of statements, the End Select statement is required as the last statement to mark the end of the VBA code

Create Functions

Learning
Outcomes
• Create a custom
  function
• Use a custom
  function

Access supplies hundreds of functions such as Sum, Count, IIf, First, Last, Date, and Hour. However, you might want to create a new function to calculate a value based on your company's unique business rules. You would create the new function in a standard module so that it can be used in any query, form, or report throughout the database. **CASE** *Quest Specialty Travel allows employees to purchase computer equipment when it is replaced. Equipment that is less than a year old will be sold to employees at 75 percent of its initial value, and equipment that is more than a year old will be sold at 50 percent of its initial value. Kayla Green, network administrator, asks you to create a new function called EmpPrice that determines the employee purchase price of replaced computer equipment.*

STEPS

TROUBLE

If you do not enable content, your VBA will not run.

1. **Start Access, open the Technology-N.accdb database from the location where you store your Data Files, enable content if prompted, click the CREATE tab, then click the Module button in the Macros & Code group**

   Access automatically inserts the Option Compare Database declaration statement in the Code window. You will create the new EmpPrice function one step at a time.

QUICK TIP

The Option Explicit statement appears if the Require Variable Declaration option is checked in the VBA Options dialog box. To view the default settings, click Options on the VBA Tools menu.

2. **Type Function EmpPrice(StartValue), then press [Enter]**

   This statement creates a new function named EmpPrice, and states that it contains one argument, StartValue. VBA automatically adds the blue **End Function** statement, a required statement to mark the end of the function. The insertion point is positioned between the statements so that you can enter more VBA statements to further define how the new EmpPrice function will calculate.

3. **Press [Tab], type EmpPrice = StartValue * 0.5, then press [Enter]**

   Your screen should look like **FIGURE N-3**. The EmpPrice= statement explains how the EmpPrice function will calculate. The function will return a value that is calculated by multiplying the StartValue by 0.5. It is not necessary to indent statements, but indenting code between matching Function/End Function, Sub/End Sub, or If/End If statements enhances the program's readability. When you press [Enter] at the end of a VBA statement, Access automatically adds spaces as appropriate to enhance the readability of the statement.

4. **Click the Save button on the Standard toolbar, type basFunctions in the Save As dialog box, click OK, then click the upper Close button in the upper-right corner of the VBE window to close the Visual Basic Editor**

   It is common for VBA programmers to use three-character prefixes to name objects and controls. This makes it easier to identify that object or control in expressions and modules. The prefix **bas** is short for Basic and applies to global modules. Naming conventions for other objects and controls are listed in **TABLE N-3** and used throughout the Technology-N.accdb database. You can use the new function, EmpPrice, in a query, form, or report.

5. **Click the Queries bar in the Navigation Pane to expand the Queries section if it is collapsed, right-click the qryEmpPricing query in the Navigation Pane, then click Design View on the shortcut menu**

   You use the new EmpPrice function in the query to determine the employee purchase price of replaced computer equipment.

QUICK TIP

Field names used in expressions are not case sensitive, but they must exactly match the spelling of the field name as defined in Table Design View.

6. **Click the blank Field cell to the right of the InitialValue field, type Price:EmpPrice ([InitialValue]), then click the View button to switch to Datasheet View**

   Your screen should look like **FIGURE N-4**. In this query, you created a new field called Price that uses the EmpPrice function. The value in the InitialValue field is used for the StartValue argument of the new EmpPrice function. The InitialValue field is multiplied by 0.5 to create the new Price field.

7. **Save then close the qryEmpPricing query**

Creating Modules and VBA

FIGURE N-3: Creating the EmpPrice function

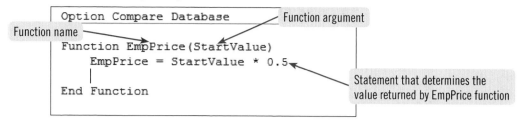

```
Option Compare Database
                                    Function argument
Function name
Function EmpPrice(StartValue)
    EmpPrice = StartValue * 0.5
                                    Statement that determines the
                                    value returned by EmpPrice function
End Function
```

FIGURE N-4: Using the EmpPrice function in a query

ELast	Manufacture	Description	PlacementDat	InitialValue	Price
Joy	Micron	Transtrek4000	7/7/2014	$2,000.00	1000
Joy	Micron	Transtrek4000	7/7/2015	$2,000.00	1000
Dawson	Micron	Prosignet403	7/14/2014	$1,800.00	900
Rock	Micron	Prosignet403	7/30/2014	$1,800.00	900
McDermott	Micron	Prosignet403	7/30/2014	$1,800.00	900
Garmin	Micron	Prosignet403	7/30/2014	$1,800.00	900
Rice	Micron	Prosignet403	1/8/2014	$1,700.00	850
Boyd	Micron	Prosignet403	8/13/2014	$1,700.00	850
McDonald	Micron	Prosignet403	8/13/2015	$1,700.00	850
Long	Micron	Prosignet403	8/13/2014	$1,700.00	850
Orient	Compaq	Centuria9099	6/13/2015	$1,500.00	750
Greenfield	Compaq	Centuria9099	6/13/2015	$1,500.00	750

qryEmpPricing

Calculated field, Price, uses EmpPrice custom function

TABLE N-3: Three-character prefix naming conventions

object or control type	prefix	example
Table	tbl	tblProducts
Query	qry	qrySalesByRegion
Form	frm	frmProducts
Report	rpt	rptSalesByCategory
Macro	mcr	mcrCloseInventory
Module	bas	basRetirement
Label	lbl	lblFullName
Text Box	txt	txtLastName
Combo box	cbo	cboStates
Command button	cmd	cmdPrint

© 2014 Cengage Learning

Access 2013

Use If Statements

If...Then...Else logic allows you to test logical conditions and execute statements only if the conditions are true. If...Then...Else code can be composed of one or several statements, depending on how many conditions you want to test, how many possible answers you want to provide, and what you want the code to do based on the results of the tests. **CASE** ▶ *You need to add an If statement to the EmpPrice function to test the age of the equipment, and then calculate the answer based on that age. You want to modify the EmpPrice function so that if the equipment is less than one year old, the StartValue is multiplied by 75% (0.75) rather than by 50% (0.5).*

STEPS

1. **Scroll down the Navigation Pane, right-click the basFunctions module, then click Design View**

   To determine the age of the equipment, the EmpPrice function needs another argument, the purchase date of the equipment.

2. **Click just before the right parenthesis in the Function statement, type , (a comma), press [Spacebar], type DateValue, then press [↓]**

   Now that you established another argument, you can work with the argument in the definition of the function.

QUICK TIP
Indentation doesn't affect the way the function works, but does make the code easier to read.

3. **Click to the right of the right parenthesis in the Function statement, press [Enter], press [Tab], then type If (Now()–DateValue) >365 Then**

   The expression compares whether today's date, represented by the Access function **Now()**, minus the DateValue argument value is greater than 365 days (1 year). If true, this indicates that the equipment is older than one year.

4. **Indent and type the rest of the statements exactly as shown in FIGURE N-5**

   The **Else** statement is executed only if the expression is false (if the equipment is less than 365 days old). The **End If** statement is needed to mark the end of the If block of code.

TROUBLE
If a compile or syntax error appears, open the VBE window, compare your function with **FIGURE N-5**, then correct any errors.

5. **Click the Save button 🖫 on the Standard toolbar, close the Visual Basic window, right-click the qryEmpPricing query in the Navigation Pane, then click Design View on the shortcut menu**

   Now that you've modified the EmpPrice function to include two arguments, you need to modify the calculated Price field expression, too.

6. **Right-click the Price field in the query design grid, click Zoom on the shortcut menu, click between the right square bracket and right parenthesis, then type ,[PlacementDate]**

   Your Zoom dialog box should look like **FIGURE N-6**. Both of the arguments used to define the EmpPrice function in the VBA code are replaced with actual field names that contain the data to be analyzed. Field names must be typed exactly as shown and surrounded by square brackets. Commas separate multiple arguments in the function.

7. **Click OK in the Zoom dialog box, then click the View button 🖽 to display the datasheet**

TROUBLE
The new calculated Price field is based on the current date on your computer, so your results may vary.

8. **Click any entry in the PlacementDate field, then click the Ascending button in the Sort & Filter group, as shown in FIGURE N-7**

   The EmpPrice function now calculates one of two different results, depending on the age of the equipment determined by the date in the PlacementDate field.

9. **Save and then close the qryEmpPricing query**

FIGURE N-5: Using an If…Then…Else structure

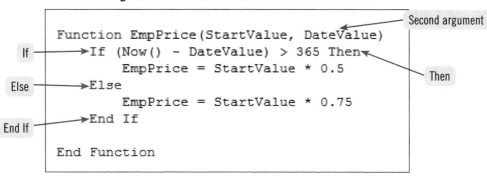

FIGURE N-6: Using the Zoom dialog box for long expressions

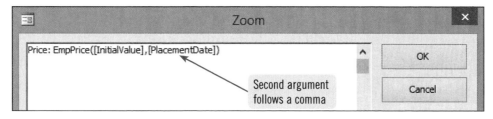

FIGURE N-7: Price field is calculated at 50% or 75% based on the age of equipment

ELast	Manufacturer	Description	PlacementDate	InitialValue	Price
Ramirez	Dell	XPS490	1/9/2008	$1,200.00	600
Dawson	Compaq	Deskpro99	3/13/2013	$1,800.00	1350
Greenfield	Compaq	Deskpro89	4/8/2013	$2,200.00	1650
Rock	Compaq	Deskpro2099	5/8/2013	$1,700.00	1275
Joy	Dell	Inspiron609	6/8/2013	$3,200.00	2400
Adair	Micron	Transtrek4000	12/30/2013	$1,900.00	1425
Rice	Micron	Prosignet403	1/8/2014	$1,700.00	1275
Arnold	Lexmark	Optra2000	1/13/2014	$2,000.00	1500
Orient	Lexmark	Optra2000	1/13/2014	$2,000.00	1500

InitialValue * 50%

InitialValue * 75%

Sort in ascending order on PlacementDate

Document Procedures

Learning
Outcomes
• Add VBA
comments
• Use the VBE
toolbar

Comment lines are statements in the code that document the code; they do not affect how the code runs. At any time, if you want to read or modify existing code, you can write the modifications much more quickly if the code is properly documented. Comment lines start with an apostrophe and are green in the VBE. **CASE** ▶ *You decide to document the EmpPrice function in the basFunctions module with descriptive comments. This will make it easier for you and others to follow the purpose and logic of the function later.*

STEPS

QUICK TIP
You can also create comments by starting the statement with the Rem statement (for remark).

TROUBLE
Be sure to use an ' (apostrophe) and not a " (quotation mark) to begin the comment line.

1. **Right-click the** basFunctions module **in the Navigation Pane, then click** Design View
   The VBE window for the basFunctions module opens.

2. **Click the** blank line between the Option Compare Database and Function statements, **press [Enter], type** 'This function is called EmpPrice and has two arguments, **then press [Enter]**
   As soon as you move to another line, the comment statement becomes green.

3. **Type** 'Created by *Your* Name on *Today's* Date, **then press [Enter]**
   You can also place comments at the end of a line by entering an apostrophe to mark that the next part of the statement is a comment.

4. **Click to the** right of Then at the end of the If statement, **press [Spacebar], type** 'Now( ) returns today's date, **then press [↓]**
   This comment explains that the Now() function returns today's date. All comments are green, regardless of whether they are on their own line or at the end of an existing line.

5. **Click to the** right of 0.5, **press [Spacebar] three times, then type** 'If > 1 year, multiply by 50%

6. **Click to the** right of 0.75, **press [Spacebar] twice, type** 'If < 1 year, multiply by 75%, **then press [↓]**
   Your screen should look like **FIGURE N-8**. Each comment will turn green as soon as you move to a new statement.

7. **Click the** Save button 💾 **on the Standard toolbar, click** File **on the menu bar, click** Print **if requested by your instructor, then click** OK
   TABLE N-4 provides more information about the Standard toolbar buttons in the VBE window.

8. **Click** File **on the menu bar, then click** Close and Return to Microsoft Access

FIGURE N-8: Adding comments to a module

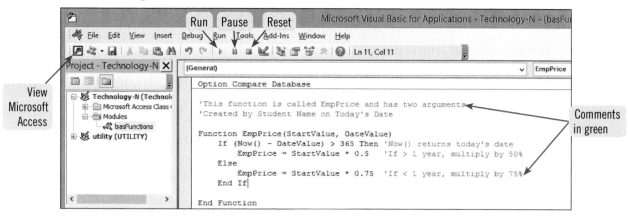

TABLE N-4: Standard toolbar buttons in the Visual Basic window

button name	button	description
View Microsoft Access		Switches from the active Visual Basic window to the Access window
Insert Module		Opens a new module or class module Code window, or inserts a new procedure in the current Code window
Run Sub/UserForm		Runs the current procedure if the insertion point is in a procedure, or runs the UserForm if it is active
Break		Stops the execution of a program while it's running and switches to Break mode, which is the temporary suspension of program execution in which you can examine, debug, reset, step through, or continue program execution
Reset		Resets the procedure
Project Explorer		Displays the Project Explorer, which displays a hierarchical list of the currently open projects (set of modules) and their contents
Object Browser		Displays the Object Browser, which lists the defined modules and procedures as well as available methods, properties, events, constants, and other items that you can use in the code

Build Class Modules

Class modules are contained and executed within specific forms and reports. Class modules most commonly run in response to an **event**, a specific action that occurs as the result of a user action. Common events include clicking a command button, editing data, and closing a form. **CASE** ▸ *You examine an existing class module and create sub procedures connected to events that occur on the form.*

1. **Double-click the frmEmployees form in the Navigation Pane to open it in Form View, then click the Branch of Service combo box list arrow to review the choices**

   The Branch of Service combo box provides a list of the branches of the armed services. For a choice to make sense, however, an employee would first need to be a veteran. You'll set the Visible property for the Branch of Service combo box to True if the Veteran check box is checked and False if the Veteran check box is not checked.

2. **Right-click the Employees form tab, click Design View on the shortcut menu, double-click the edge of the Veteran check box to open its Property Sheet, click the Event tab in the Property Sheet, click the After Update property, click the Build button ⋯ , then click Code Builder and OK if the Choose Builder dialog box appears**

   The class module for the frmEmployees form opens. Because you opened the VBE window from within a specific event of a specific control on the form, the **stub**, the first and last lines of the sub procedure, were automatically created. The procedure's name in the first line, chkVeteran_AfterUpdate, contains *both* the name of the control, chkVeteran, as well as the name of the event, AfterUpdate, that triggers this procedure. (Recall that the **Name property** of a control is found on the Other tab in the control's property sheet. The **After Update property** is on the Event tab.) A sub procedure that is triggered by an event is often called an **event handler**.

3. **Enter the statements shown in FIGURE N-9**

   When you use three-character prefixes for all controls and objects in your database, it enhances the meaning and readability of your VBA. In this case, the name of the sub procedure shows that it runs on the AfterUpdate event of the chkVeteran control. (The sub runs when the Veteran check box is checked or unchecked.) The If structure contains VBA that makes the cboBranchOfService control either visible or not visible based on the value of the chkVeteran control. To test the sub procedure, you switch to Form View.

4. **Save the changes and close the VBE window, click the View button ▦ to switch to Form View, click the Veteran check box for the first record several times to observe what happens on the After Update event, then navigate through several records**

   By clicking the Veteran check box in the first record, you triggered the procedure that responds to the After Update event of the Veteran check box. However, you also want the procedure to run every time you move from record to record. The **On Current** event of the form is triggered when you navigate through records.

5. **Right-click the Employees form tab, click Design View on the shortcut menu, click the Form Selector button ▪ , click the Event tab in the Property Sheet, click the On Current event property in the Property Sheet, click the Build button ⋯ , click Code Builder and OK if the Choose Builder dialog box appears, then copy or retype the If structure from the chkVeteran_AfterUpdate sub to the Form_Current sub, as shown in FIGURE N-10**

   By copying the same If structure to a second sub procedure, you've created a second event handler. Now, the cboBranchOfService combo box will either be visible or not based on two different events: updating the chkVeteran check box or moving from record to record. To test the new sub procedure, you switch to Form View.

6. **Save the changes and close the VBE window, click ▦ to switch to Form View, then navigate to the fifth record for Gail Owen to test the new procedures**

   Now, as you move from record to record, the Branch of Service combo box should be visible for those employees with the Veteran check box selected, and not visible if the Veteran check box is not selected.

7. **Click the Branch of Service combo box list arrow, click Army, as shown in FIGURE N-11, then save and close the frmEmployees form**

Creating Modules and VBA

FIGURE N-9: Creating an event handler procedure

```
Private Sub chkVeteran_AfterUpdate()
If chkVeteran.Value = True Then
    cboBranchOfService.Visible = True
Else
    cboBranchOfService.Visible = False
End If
End Sub
```

FIGURE N-10: Copying the If structure to a new event-handler procedure

Copy If structure from chkVeteran_AfterUpate sub to Form_Current sub

```
Private Sub chkVeteran_AfterUpdate()
If chkVeteran.Value = True Then
    cboBranchOfService.Visible = True
Else
    cboBranchOfService.Visible = False
End If
End Sub


Private Sub Form_Current()
If chkVeteran.Value = True Then
    cboBranchOfService.Visible = True
Else
    cboBranchOfService.Visible = False
End If
End Sub
```

FIGURE N-11: Branch of Service combo box is visible when the Veteran check box is checked

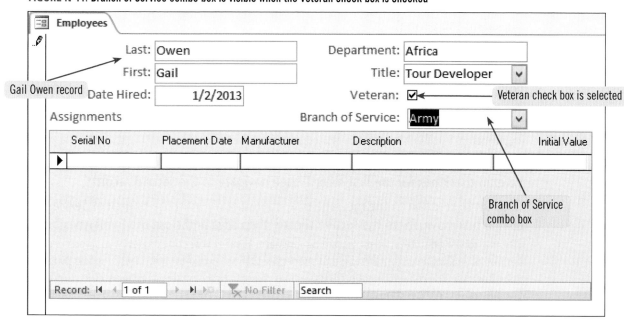

Modify Sub Procedures

Learning Outcomes
• Attach procedures to events
• Use IntelliSense technology

Sub procedures can be triggered on any event in the Property Sheet such as **On Got Focus** (when the control gets the focus), **After Update** (after a field is updated), or **On Dbl Click** (when the control is double-clicked). Not all items have the same set of event properties. For example, a text box control has both a Before Update and After Update event property, but neither of these events exists for a label or command button because those controls are not used to update data. **CASE** ▶ *Kayla Green asks if there is a way to require a choice in the Branch of Service combo box if the Veteran check box is checked. You use VBA sub procedures to handle this request.*

STEPS

QUICK TIP

If you select the Always use event procedures check box in the Object Designers section of the Access Options dialog box, you bypass the Choose Builder dialog box and go directly to the VBE.

1. **Right-click the** frmEmployees form, **click** Design View **on the shortcut menu, click the** Before Update property **in the Property Sheet, click the** Build button ▒ **, click** Code Builder **and** OK **if the Choose Builder dialog box appears, then enter the code in** FIGURE N-12 **into the Form_BeforeUpdate stub**

   Test the procedure.

2. **Close the VBE window, click the** View button ▤ **to switch to Form View, click the** Veteran check box **as needed to select it in the first record, then navigate to the second record**

   Given the chkVeteran control is selected but the cboBranchOfService combo box is null, the MsgBox statement produces the message shown in FIGURE N-13.

TROUBLE

Be sure you modified the chkVeteran_ AfterUpdate sub and not the Form_ Current sub.

3. **Click** OK, **navigate back to the first record, then click the** Veteran check box **to uncheck it**

   The code produces the correct message, but you want the code to place the focus in the cboBranchOfService combo box to force the user to choose a branch of service when this condition occurs.

   DoCmd is a VBA object that supports many methods to run common Access commands, such as closing windows, opening forms, previewing reports, navigating records, setting focus, and setting the value of controls. As you write a VBA statement, visual aids that are part of **IntelliSense technology** help you complete it. For example, when you type the period (.) after the DoCmd object, a list of available methods appears. Watching the VBA window carefully and taking advantage of all IntelliSense clues as you complete a statement can greatly improve your accuracy and productivity in writing VBA.

TROUBLE

Be sure to type a period (.) after DoCmd.

4. **Right-click the** Employees form tab, **click** Design View, **click the** View Code button **in the Tools group, click after the** MsgBox statement, **press** [Enter], **then type** DoCmd. **(including the period)**

   Your sub procedure should look like FIGURE N-14.

5. **Type** GoToControl, **press the** [Spacebar] **noting the additional IntelliSense prompt, then type** "cboBranchOfService", **as shown in** FIGURE N-15

   IntelliSense helps you fill out each statement, indicating the order of arguments needed for the method to execute. If IntelliSense displays more than one argument, the current argument is listed in bold. Optional arguments are listed in [square brackets]. Test the new procedure.

6. **Close the VBE window, click the** View button ▤ **to switch to Form View, click the** Veteran check box **for the first record, then navigate to the second record**

7. **Click** OK **to respond to the message box, choose** Navy **from the Branch of Service combo box, navigate to the second record, then save and close the Employees form**

   VBA is a robust and powerful programming language. It takes years of experience to appreciate the vast number of objects, events, methods, and properties that are available. With only modest programming skills, however, you can create basic sub procedures that greatly help users work more efficiently and effectively in forms.

Creating Modules and VBA

FIGURE N-12: Form_BeforeUpdate sub

```
Private Sub Form_BeforeUpdate(Cancel As Integer)
If chkVeteran.Value = True Then
    If IsNull(cboBranchOfService.Value) Then
        MsgBox "Please select a Branch of Service"
    End If
End If
End Sub
```
Form_BeforeUpdate sub

FIGURE N-13: Message produced by MsgBox statement

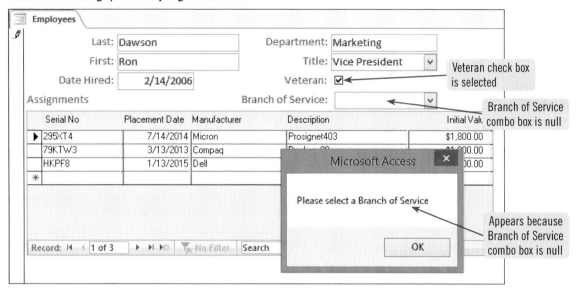

Veteran check box is selected

Branch of Service combo box is null

Appears because Branch of Service combo box is null

FIGURE N-14: IntelliSense technology prompts you as you write VBA statements

```
Private Sub Form_BeforeUpdate(Cancel As Integer)
If chkVeteran.Value = True Then
    If IsNull(cboBranchOfService.Value) Then
        MsgBox "Please select a Branch of Service"
        DoCmd.
    End If        ◦ AddMenu
End If             ◦ ApplyFilter
End Sub            ◦ Beep
                  ◦ BrowseTo
Private Sub       ◦ CancelEvent
If chkVetera      ◦ ClearMacroError
    cboBranc      ◦ Close
Else
```
IntelliSense list

FIGURE N-15: New DoCmd statement

```
Private Sub Form_BeforeUpdate(Cancel As Integer)
If chkVeteran.Value = True Then
    If IsNull(cboBranchOfService.Value) Then
        MsgBox "Please select a Branch of Service"
        DoCmd.GoToControl "cboBranchOfService"
    End If
End If
End Sub
```
New DoCmd statement

Troubleshoot Modules

Access provides several techniques to help you **debug** (find and resolve) different types of VBA errors. A **syntax error** occurs immediately as you are writing a VBA statement that cannot be read by the Visual Basic Editor. This is the easiest type of error to identify because your code turns red when the syntax error occurs. **Compile-time errors** occur as a result of incorrectly constructed code and are detected as soon as you run your code or select the Compile option on the Debug menu. For example, you may have forgotten to insert an End If statement to finish an If structure. **Run-time errors** occur as incorrectly constructed code runs and include attempting an illegal operation such as dividing by zero or moving focus to a control that doesn't exist. When you encounter a run-time error, VBA will stop executing your procedure at the statement in which the error occurred and highlight the line with a yellow background in the Visual Basic Editor. **Logic errors** are the most difficult to troubleshoot because they occur when the code runs without obvious problems, but the procedure still doesn't produce the desired result. **CASE** *You study debugging techniques using the basFunctions module.*

STEPS

1. **Right-click the basFunctions module in the Navigation Pane, click Design View, click to the right of the End If statement, press the [Spacebar], type *your* name, then press [↓]**
   Because the End If *your* name statement cannot be resolved by the Visual Basic Editor, the statement immediately turns red and an error message box appears.

2. **Click OK in the error message box, delete *your* name, then press [↓]**
   Another VBA debugging tool is to set a **breakpoint**, a bookmark that suspends execution of the procedure at that statement to allow you to examine what is happening.

QUICK TIP
Click the gray bar to
the left of a statement
to toggle a break-
point on and off.

3. **Click the If statement line, click Debug on the menu bar, then click Toggle Breakpoint**
   Your screen should look like **FIGURE N-16**.

4. **Click the View Microsoft Access button [icon] on the Standard toolbar, then double-click the qryEmpPricing query in the Navigation Pane**
   When the qryEmpPricing query opens, it immediately runs the EmpPrice function. Because you set a breakpoint at the If statement, the statement is highlighted, indicating that the code has been suspended at that point.

QUICK TIP
Pointing to an
argument in the
Code window
displays a ScreenTip
with the argument's
current value.

5. **Click View on the menu bar, click Immediate Window, type ? DateValue, then press [Enter]**
   Your screen should look like **FIGURE N-17**. The **Immediate window** is an area where you can determine the value of any argument at the breakpoint.

6. **Click Debug on the menu bar, click Clear All Breakpoints, click the Continue button [icon] on the Standard toolbar to execute the remainder of the function, then save and close the basFunctions module**
   The qryEmpPricing query's datasheet should be visible.

7. **Close the qryEmpPricing datasheet, close the Technology-N.accdb database, then exit Access**

FIGURE N-16: Setting a breakpoint

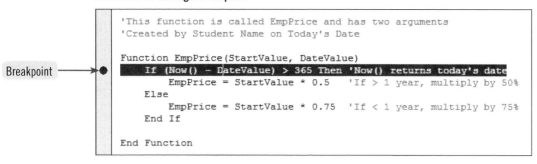

Breakpoint ●→

```
'This function is called EmpPrice and has two arguments
'Created by Student Name on Today's Date

Function EmpPrice(StartValue, DateValue)
    If (Now() - DateValue) > 365 Then 'Now() returns today's date
        EmpPrice = StartValue * 0.5    'If > 1 year, multiply by 50%
    Else
        EmpPrice = StartValue * 0.75  'If < 1 year, multiply by 75%
    End If

End Function
```

FIGURE N-17: Stopping execution at a breakpoint

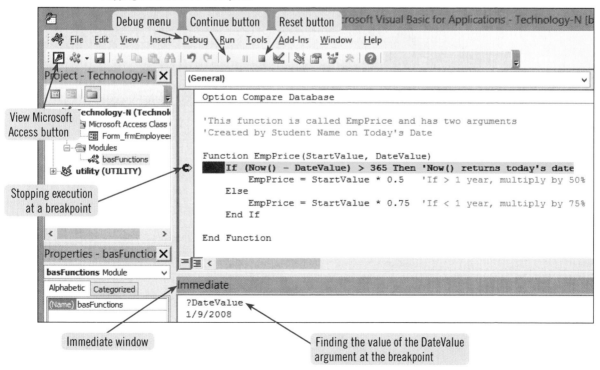

Practice

Concepts Review

Identify each element of the Visual Basic window shown in FIGURE N-18.

FIGURE N-18

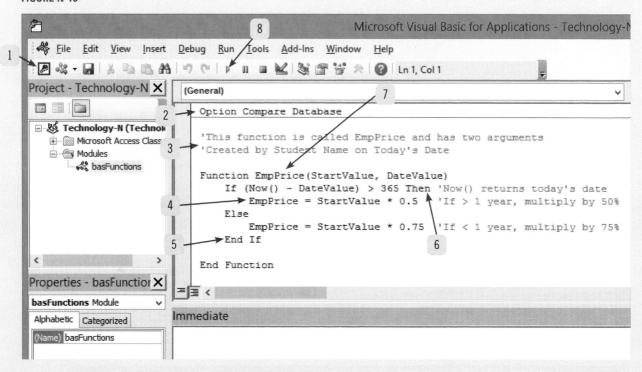

Match each term with the statement that best describes its function.

9. **Visual Basic for Applications (VBA)**
10. **Debugging**
11. **If...Then...Else statement**
12. **Class modules**
13. **Breakpoint**
14. **Function**
15. **Module**
16. **Procedure**
17. **Arguments**

a. Allows you to test a logical condition and execute commands only if the condition is true
b. The programming language used in Access modules
c. A line of code that automatically suspends execution of the procedure
d. A process to find and resolve programming errors
e. A procedure that returns a value
f. Constants, variables, or expressions passed to a procedure to further define how it should execute
g. Stored as part of the form or report object in which they are created
h. The Access object where VBA code is stored
i. A series of VBA statements that performs an operation or calculate a value

Skills Review

1. Understand modules and VBA.

a. Start Access, then open the Baseball-N.accdb (not the Basketball-N.accdb) database from the location where you store your Data Files. Enable content if prompted.
b. Open the VBE window for the basFunctions module.

Skills Review (continued)

   c. Record your answers to the following questions on a sheet of paper:
- What is the name of the function defined in this module?
- What are the names of the arguments defined in this module?
- What is the purpose of the End Function statement?
- Why is the End Function statement in blue?
- Why are some of the lines indented?

2. Compare macros and modules.

   a. If not already opened, open the VBE window for the basFunctions module.

   b. Record your answers to the following questions on a sheet of paper:
- Why was a module rather than a macro used to create this procedure?
- Why is VBA generally more difficult to create than a macro?
- Identify each of the VBA keywords or keyword phrases, and explain the purpose for each.

3. Create functions.

   a. If not already opened, open the VBE window for the basFunctions module.

   b. Create a function called **TotalBases** below the End Function statement of the BattingAverage function by typing the VBA statements shown in **FIGURE N-19**.

FIGURE N-19

```
Function TotalBases(SingleValue, DoubleValue, TripleValue, HRValue)
    TotalBases = (SingleValue + 2 * DoubleValue + 3 * TripleValue + 4 * HRValue)
End Function
```

   In baseball, total bases is a popular statistic because it accounts for the power of each hit. In the TotalBases function, each hit is multiplied by the number of bases earned (1 for single, 2 for double, 3 for triple, and 4 for home run).

   c. Save the basFunctions module, then close the VBE window.

   d. Use Query Design View to create a new query using the PlayerFName and PlayerLName fields from the tblPlayers table, and the AtBats field from the tblPlayerStats table.

   e. Create a calculated field named **Batting** in the next available column by carefully typing the expression as follows: **Batting: BattingAverage([1Base],[2Base],[3Base],[4Base],[AtBats])**. (*Hint*: Use the Zoom dialog box to enter long expressions.)

   f. Create a second calculated field named **Bases** in the next available column by carefully typing the expression as follows: **Bases: TotalBases([1Base],[2Base],[3Base],[4Base])**. (*Hint*: Use the Zoom dialog box to enter long expressions.)

   g. View the datasheet, change Doug Schaller to *your* first and last name, save the query with the name **qryStats**, then close qryStats.

4. Use If statements.

   a. Open the VBE window for the basFunctions module, then modify the BattingAverage function to add the If structure shown in **FIGURE N-20**. The If structure prevents the error caused by attempting to divide by zero. The If structure checks to see if the AtBatsValue argument is equal to 0. If so, the BattingAverage function is set to 0. Else, the BattingAverage function is calculated.

FIGURE N-20

```
Function BattingAverage(SingleValue, DoubleValue, TripleValue, HRValue, AtBatsValue)
If AtBatsValue = 0 Then
    BattingAverage = 0
Else
    BattingAverage = (SingleValue + DoubleValue + TripleValue + HRValue) / AtBatsValue
End If
End Function


Function TotalBases(SingleValue, DoubleValue, TripleValue, HRValue)
    TotalBases = (SingleValue + 2 * DoubleValue + 3 * TripleValue + 4 * HRValue)
End Function
```

Skills Review (continued)

b. Save the basFunctions module, then close the VBE window.

c. Open the qryStats datasheet, then change the AtBats value to **0** for the first record and press [Tab] to test the If statement. The Batting calculated field should equal 0.

d. Close the datasheet.

5. Document procedures.

a. Open the VBE window for the basFunctions module, and add the two statements above the End Function statement for the BattingAverage function, as shown in **FIGURE N-21**. The statements use the Format function to format the calculation as a number with three digits to the right of the decimal point. The comments help clarify the statement.

b. Add a comment at the end of the VBA code that identifies *your* name and today's date, as shown in **FIGURE N-21**.

FIGURE N-21

```
Function BattingAverage(SingleValue, DoubleValue, TripleValue, HRValue, AtBatsValue)
If AtBatsValue = 0 Then
    BattingAverage = 0
Else
    BattingAverage = (SingleValue + DoubleValue + TripleValue + HRValue) / AtBatsValue
End If
'Format as a number with three digits to the right of the decimal point
BattingAverage = Format(BattingAverage, "0.000")
End Function


Function TotalBases(SingleValue, DoubleValue, TripleValue, HRValue)
    TotalBases = (SingleValue + 2 * DoubleValue + 3 * TripleValue + 4 * HRValue)
End Function

'Created by Your Name on Today's Date
```

c. Save the changes to the basFunctions module, print the module if requested by your instructor, then close the VBE window.

d. Open the qryStats query datasheet and change the AtBats value to **3** for the first record and press [Tab] to observe how the value in the Batting calculated field changes and how it is now formatted with three digits to the right of the decimal point due to the VBA statement you added to the BattingAverage function.

e. Print the qryStats datasheet if requested by your instructor, then close it.

6. Build class modules.

a. Open frmPlayerEntry in Form View, then move through several records to observe the data.

b. Switch to Design View, and on the right side of the form, select the Print Current Record button.

c. Open the Property Sheet for the button, click the Event tab, click the On Click property, then click the Build button to open the class module.

d. Add a comment to the last line to show *your* name and the current date. Save the module, print it if requested by your instructor, then close the VBE window.

7. Modify sub procedures.

a. Open the frmPlayerEntry form in Form View, move through a couple of records to observe the txtSalary text box (currently blank), then switch to Design View.

b. The base starting salary in this league is $30,000. You will add a command button with VBA to help enter the correct salary for each player. Use the Button button to add a command button below the txtSalary text box, then cancel the Command Button Wizard if it starts.

c. Open the Property Sheet for the new command button, then change the Caption property on the Format tab to **Base Salary**. Change the Name property on the Other tab to **cmdBaseSalary**.

d. On the Event tab of the Property Sheet, click the On Click property, click the Build button, then click Code Builder if prompted. The stub for the new cmdBaseSalary_Click sub is automatically created for you.

e. Enter the following statement between the Sub and End Sub statements:
txtSalary.Value = 30000

    f. Save the changes, then close the VBE window.

    g. Close the Property Sheet, then save and open the frmPlayerEntry form in Form View.

    h. Click the Base Salary command button for the first player, move to the second record, then click the Base Salary command button for the second player.

    i. Save, then close the frmPlayerEntry form.

8. Troubleshoot modules.

    a. Open the VBE window for the basFunctions module.

    b. Click anywhere in the If AtBatsValue = 0 Then statement in the BattingAverage function.

    c. Click Debug on the menu bar, then click Toggle Breakpoint to set a breakpoint at this statement.

    d. Save the changes, then close the VBE window and return to Microsoft Access.

    e. Open the qryStats query datasheet. This action will attempt to use the BattingAverage function to calculate the value for the Batting field, which will stop and highlight the statement in the VBE window where you set a breakpoint.

    f. Click View on the menu bar, click Immediate Window (if not already visible), delete any previous entries in the Immediate window, type **?AtBatsValue**, then press [Enter]. At this point in the execution of the VBA, the AtBatsValue should be 3, the value for the first record.

    g. Type **?SingleValue**, then press [Enter]. At this point in the execution of the VBA code, the SingleValue should be 1, the value for the first record. (*Hint*: You can resize the Immediate window taller by dragging the top edge.)

    h. Click Debug on the menu bar, click Clear All Breakpoints, then click the Continue button on the Standard toolbar. Close the VBE window.

    i. Return to the qryStats query in Datasheet View.

    j. Close the qryStats query, close the Baseball-N.accdb database, then exit Access.

Independent Challenge 1

As the manager of a doctor's clinic, you have created an Access database called Patients-N.accdb to track insurance claim reimbursements and general patient health. You want to modify an existing function within this database.

    a. Start Access, then open the Patients-N.accdb database from the location where you store your Data Files. Enable content if prompted.

    b. Open the basBodyMassIndex module in Design View, and enter the **Option Explicit** declaration statement just below the existing Option Compare Database statement.

    c. Record your answers to the following questions on a sheet of paper:

       • What is the name of the function in the module?

       • What are the function arguments?

       • What is the purpose of the Option Explicit declaration statement?

    d. Edit the BMI function by adding a comment below the last line of code with *your* name and today's date.

FIGURE N-22

```
Option Compare Database
Option Explicit

'A healthy BMI is in the range of 21-24

Function BMI(weight, height)

If height = 0 Then
    BMI = 0
Else
    BMI = (weight * 0.4536) / (height * 0.0254) ^ 2
End If

End Function

'Student Name - Today's Date
```

    e. Edit the BMI function by adding a comment above the Function statement with the following information: **'A healthy BMI is in the range of 21-24**.

    f. Edit the BMI function by adding an If clause that checks to make sure the height argument is not equal to 0. The final BMI function code should look like **FIGURE N-22**.

    g. Save the module, print it if requested by your instructor, then close the VBE window.

Independent Challenge 1 (continued)

h. Create a new query that includes the following fields from the tblPatients table: **PtLastName**, **PtFirstName**, **PtHeight**, **PtWeight**.

i. Create a calculated field with the following field name and expression: **BodyMassIndex: BMI([PtWeight], [PtHeight])**. (*Hint:* Use the Zoom dialog box for long expressions.)

j. Save the query as **qryPatientBMI**, view the qryPatientBMI query datasheet, then test the If statement by entering **0** in the PtHeight field for the first record. Press [Tab] to move to the BodyMassIndex field, which should recalculate to 0.

k. Edit the first record to contain *your* last and first names, print the datasheet if requested by your instructor, then close the qryPatientBMI query.

l. Close the Patients-N.accdb database, then exit Access.

Independent Challenge 2

As the manager of a doctor's clinic, you have created an Access database called Patients-N.accdb to track insurance claim reimbursements. You want to study the existing sub procedures stored as class modules in the Claim Entry Form.

a. Start Access, then open the Patients-N.accdb database from the location where you store your Data Files. Enable content if prompted.

b. Open frmClaimEntryForm in Form View, then switch to Design View.

c. Open the VBE window to view this class module, then record your answers to the following questions on a sheet of paper:
- What are the names of the sub procedures in this class module? (*Hint:* Be sure to scroll the window to see the complete contents.)
- What Access functions are used in the PtFirstName_AfterUpdate sub?
- How many arguments do the functions in the PtFirstName_AfterUpdate sub have?
- What do the functions in the PtFirstName_AfterUpdate sub do? (*Hint:* You may have to use the Visual Basic Help system if you are not familiar with the functions.)
- What is the purpose of the On Error command? (*Hint:* Use the Visual Basic Help system if you are not familiar with this command.)

d. Use the Property Sheet of the form to create an event-handler procedure based on the On Load property. The statement will be one line using the Maximize method of the VBA DoCmd object, which will maximize the form each time it is loaded.

e. Save the changes, close the VBE window and the Claim Entry Form, then open frmClaimEntryForm in Form View to test the new sub.

f. Close frmClaimEntryForm, close the Patients-N.accdb database, then exit Access.

Independent Challenge 3

As the manager of a doctor's clinic, you have created an Access database called Patients-N.accdb to track insurance claim reimbursements that are fixed (paid at a predetermined fixed rate) or denied (not paid by the insurance company). You want to enhance the database with a class module.

a. Start Access, then open the Patients-N.accdb database from the location where you store your Data Files. Enable content if prompted.

b. Open frmCPT in Form Design View.

c. Use the Command Button Wizard to add a command button in the Form Header section. Choose the Add New Record action from the Record Operations category.

d. Accept **Add Record** as the text on the button, then name the button **cmdAddRecord**.

Independent Challenge 3 (continued)

e. Use the Command Button Wizard to add a command button in the Form Header section to the right of the existing Add Record button. (*Hint*: Move and resize controls as necessary to put two command buttons in the Form Header section.)

f. Choose the Delete Record action from the Record Operations category.

g. Accept **Delete Record** as the text on the button, and name the button **cmdDeleteRecord**.

h. Size the two buttons to be the same height and width, and align their top edges. Move them as needed so that they do not overlap.

i. Save and view frmCPT in Form View, then click the Add Record command button.

j. Add a new record (it will be record number 65) with a CPTCode value of **999** and an RBRVS value of **1.5**.

k. To make sure that the Delete Record button works, click the record selector for the new record you just entered, click the Delete Record command button, then click Yes to confirm the deletion. Close frmCPT.

l. In Design View of the frmCPT form, open the Property Sheet for the Delete Record command button, click the Event tab, then click the Build button beside [Embedded Macro]. The Command Button Wizard created the embedded macro that deletes the current record. You can convert macro objects to VBA code to learn more about VBA. To convert an embedded macro to VBA, you must first copy and paste the embedded macro actions to a new macro object. (*Hint*: You can widen the property sheet by dragging the left edge.)

m. Press [Ctrl][A] to select all macro actions, then press [Ctrl][C] to copy all macro actions to the Clipboard.

n. Close the macro window, then save and close frmCPT.

o. On the CREATE tab, open Macro Design View, then press [Ctrl][V] to paste the macro actions to the window.

p. Click the Convert Macros to Visual Basic button, click Yes when prompted to save the macro, click Convert, then click OK when a dialog box indicates the conversion is finished.

q. Save and close all open windows with default names. Open the Converted Macro-Macro1 VBE window. Add a comment as the last line of code in the Code window with *your* name and the current date, save the module, print it if requested by your instructor, then close the VBE window.

r. Close the Patients-N.accdb database, then exit Access.

Independent Challenge 4: Explore

(*Note: To complete this Independent Challenge, make sure you are connected to the Internet.*)

Learning a programming language is sometimes compared with learning a foreign language. Imagine how it would feel to learn a new programming language if English wasn't your primary language, or if you had another type of accessibility challenge. Advances in technology are helping to break down many barriers to those with vision, hearing, mobility, cognitive, and language issues. In this challenge, you explore the Microsoft Web site for resources to address these issues.

a. Go to www.microsoft.com/enable, then print that page. Explore the Web site.

b. After exploring the Web site for products, demos, tutorials, guides, and articles, write a two-page, double-spaced paper describing five types of accessibility solutions that might make a positive impact on someone you know. Refer to your acquaintances as "my friend," "my cousin," and so forth as appropriate. Do not include real names.

c. Use bold headings for the five types of accessibility solutions to make those sections of your paper easy to find and read. Be sure to spell and grammar check your paper.

Visual Workshop

As the manager of a college basketball team, you are helping the coach build meaningful statistics to compare the relative value of the players in each game. The coach has stated that one offensive rebound is worth as much to the team as two defensive rebounds, and would like you to use this rule to develop a "rebounding impact statistic" for each game. Open the Basketball-N.accdb (not the Baseball-N.accdb) database, enable content if prompted, and use FIGURE N-23 to develop a new function in a standard module. Name the new function **ReboundImpact** in a new module called **basFunctions** to calculate this statistic. Include *your* name and the current date as a comment in the last row of the function.

FIGURE N-23

```
Function ReboundImpact(OffenseValue As Integer, DefenseValue As Integer) As Integer
    ReboundImpact = (OffenseValue * 2) + DefenseValue
End Function

'Student Name - Today's Date
```

Create a query called **qryRebounds** with the fields shown in FIGURE N-24. Note that the records are sorted in ascending order on GameNo and LastName. The **ReboundPower** field is created using the following expression: **ReboundImpact([Reb-O],[Reb-D])**. Enter *your* first and last name instead of Kristen Czyenski, and print the datasheet if requested by your instructor.

FIGURE N-24

GameNo	FirstName	LastName	Reb-O	Reb-D	ReboundPower
1	Student First	Student Last	2	2	6
1	Denise	Franco	2	3	7
1	Theresa	Grant	1	3	5
1	Megan	Hile	1	2	4
1	Amy	Hodel	5	3	13
1	Ellyse	Howard	1	2	4
1	Jamie	Johnson	0	1	1
1	Lindsey	Swift	1	2	4
1	Morgan	Tyler	4	6	14
2	Student First	Student Last	3	2	8
2	Denise	Franco	5	3	13

Administering the Database

CASE Kayla Green is the network administrator at Quest corporate headquarters. You have helped Kayla develop a database to document Quest computer equipment. You use Access to create a navigation form. You also examine several administrative issues, such as setting passwords, changing startup options, and analyzing database performance to protect, improve, and enhance the database.

Unit Objectives

After completing this unit, you will be able to:

- Create a navigation form
- Compact and repair a database
- Change startup options
- Analyze database performance

- Set a database password
- Back up a database
- Convert a database
- Split a database

Files You Will Need

Technology-O.accdb   RealEstate-O.accdb
Basketball-O.accdb   MusicStore-O.accdb
Patients-O.accdb

Create a Navigation Form

Learning Outcomes
- Create a navigation form
- Add tabs to a navigation form

A **navigation form** is a special Access form that provides an easy-to-use database interface that is also Web compatible. Being **Web compatible** means that the form can be opened and used with Internet Explorer when the database is published to a SharePoint server. A **SharePoint server** is a special type of Microsoft Web server that allows people to share and collaborate on information using only a browser such as Internet Explorer. Navigation forms can be used with any Access database, however, even if you don't publish it to a SharePoint server. **CASE** ▶ *You create a navigation form to easily access forms and reports in the Technology-O database.*

STEPS

1. **Start Access, open the** Technology-O.accdb database **from the location where you store your Data Files, enable content if prompted, click the** CREATE tab**, click the** Navigation button **in the Forms group, click the** Horizontal Tabs option**, then close the Field List window**

   The new navigation form opens in Layout View. Horizontal Tabs is a **navigation system style** that determines how the navigation buttons are displayed on the form. Other navigation system styles include vertical tabs on the left or right, or both horizontal and vertical tabs.

2. **Click the** Queries collapse button ⮝ **to close that section of the Navigation Pane, then drag the** frmEmployees form **from the Navigation Pane to the** first tab**, which displays [Add New]**

   The frmEmployees form is added as the first tab, as shown in **FIGURE O-1**, and a new tab with [Add New] is automatically created as well. The second and third tabs will display reports.

3. **Click the** Reports expand button ⮟ **to expand that section of the Navigation Pane, drag the** rptAllEquipment report **from the Navigation Pane to the** second tab**, which displays [Add New], then drag** rptPCs **to the** third tab**, which also displays [Add New]**

   With the objects in place, you rename the tabs to be less technical.

4. **Double-click the** frmEmployees tab**, edit it to read** Employees**, double-click the** rptAllEquipment tab**, edit it to read** All Equipment**, double-click the** rptPCs tab**, edit it to read** PCs**, then click the** View button 🖼 **to display the form in Form View, as shown in FIGURE O-2**

   Test, save, and close the new navigation form.

5. **Click the** All Equipment tab**, click the** Employees tab**, click the** Save button 💾 **on the Quick Access toolbar, type** frmNavigation**, click** OK**, then close frmNavigation**

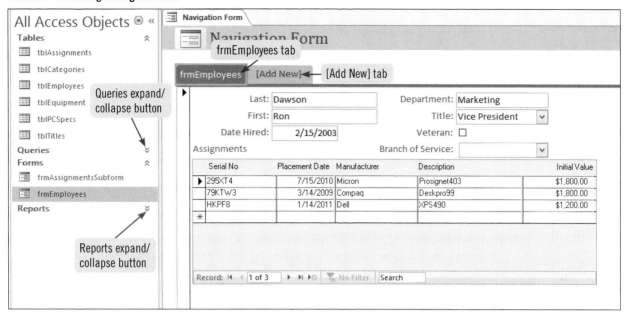

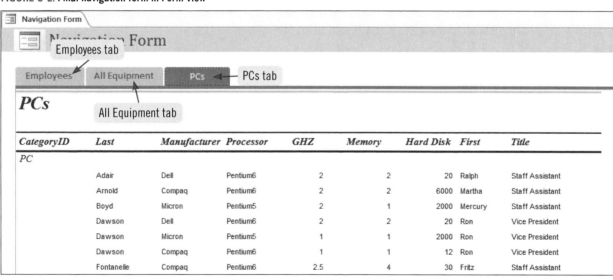

Setting navigation options

You can change the way the Navigation Pane appears by clicking the title bar of the Navigation Pane and choosing a different way to organize the objects (e.g., by Object Type, Created Date, or Custom Groups) in the upper portion of the menu. The lower portion of the menu lets you display only one object type (e.g., Tables, Queries, Forms, Reports, or All Access Objects). Right-click the Navigation Pane for more options on the shortcut menu, including Navigation Options, which allows you to create custom groups within the Navigation Pane.

Access 2013

Compact and Repair a Database

Learning
Outcomes
• Compact and
repair a database
• Apply Access
options

Compacting and repairing a database is a process that Access 2013 uses to reorganize the parts of a database to eliminate wasted space on the disk storage device, which also helps prevent data integrity problems. You can compact and repair a database at any time, or you can set a database option to automatically compact and repair the database when it is closed. **CASE** *You and Kayla Green decide to compact and repair the Technology database, and then learn about the option to automatically compact and repair the database when it is closed.*

STEPS

1. **Click the DATABASE TOOLS tab on the Ribbon, then click the Compact and Repair Database button**

   Access closes the database, completes the compact and repair process, and reopens the database automatically.

   Compacting and repairing a database can reduce the size of the database by 10, 50, or even 75 percent because the space occupied by deleted objects and deleted data is not reused until the database is compacted. Therefore, it's a good idea to set up a regular schedule to compact and repair a database. You decide to change Access options to automatically compact the database when it is closed.

2. **Click the FILE tab on the Ribbon, then click Options**

   The Compact on Close feature is in the Current Database category of the Access Options dialog box.

3. **Click the Current Database category, then click the Compact on Close check box**

   Your screen should look like **FIGURE O-3**. Now, every time the database is closed, Access will also compact and repair it. This helps you keep the database as small and efficient as possible and protects your database from potential corruption. The Access Options dialog box provides many important default options and techniques to customize Access, which are summarized in **TABLE O-1**.

4. **Click OK to close the Access Options dialog box, then click OK when prompted to close and reopen the current database**

Trusting a database

Trusting a database means to identify the database file as one that is safe to open. Trusted databases automatically enable all content, including all macros and VBA in modules, and, therefore, do not present the Enable Content message when they are opened. To trust a database, click the FILE tab, click Options, click Trust Center on the left, click the Trust Center Settings button, then use the Trusted Documents or Trusted Locations options to either trust an individual database file or an entire folder. To trust the folder, click Trusted Locations, click Add new location, click Browse to locate the folder to trust, select the desired folder, click the Subfolders of this location are also trusted check box to also trust subfolders, and then click OK to move through the dialog boxes and complete the process.

FIGURE O-3: Setting the Compact on Close option

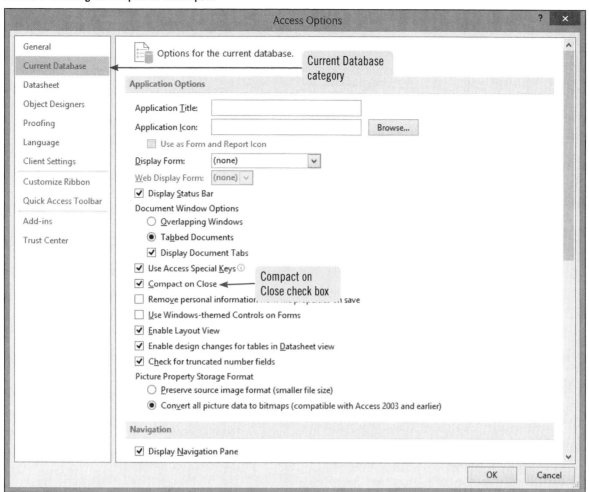

TABLE O-1: Access options

category	description
General	Sets default interface, file format, default database folder, and username options
Current Database	Provides for application changes, such as whether the windows are overlapping or tabbed, the database compacts on close, and Layout View is enabled; also provides Navigation Pane, Ribbon, toolbar, and AutoCorrect options
Datasheet	Determines the default gridlines, cell effects, and fonts of datasheets
Object Designers	Determines default Design View settings for tables, queries, forms, and reports; also provides default error-checking options
Proofing	Sets AutoCorrect and Spelling options
Language	Sets Editing, Display, and Help languages
Client Settings	Sets defaults for cursor action when editing, display elements, printing margins, date formatting, and advanced record management options
Customize Ribbon	Provides an easy-to-use interface to modify the buttons and tabs on the Ribbon
Quick Access Toolbar	Provides an easy-to-use interface to modify the buttons on the Quick Access toolbar
Add-ins	Provides a way to manage **add-ins**, software that works with Access to add or enhance functionality
Trust Center	Provides a way to manage trusted publishers, trusted locations, trusted documents, macro settings, and other privacy and security settings

Change Startup Options

Learning
Outcomes
• Set the Application
  Title startup option
• Set the Display
  Form startup option
• Describe
  command-line
  options

Startup options are a series of commands that execute when the database is opened. You manage the default startup options using features in the Current Database category of the Access Options dialog box. More startup options are available through the use of **command-line options**, a special series of characters added to the end of the pathname (for example, C:\My Documents\Quest.accdb /excl), which execute a command when the file is opened. See **TABLE O-2** for information on common startup command-line options. **CASE** *You want to view and set database properties and then specify that the frmEmployees form opens when the Technology-O.accdb database is opened.*

STEPS

1. **Click the FILE tab, click Options, then click Current Database if it is not already selected**

   The startup options are in the Application Options area of the Current Database category.

2. **Click the Application Title text box, then type Quest Specialty Travel**

   The Application Title database property value appears in the title bar instead of the database filename.

QUICK TIP
The Enable Layout
View check box
allows or removes the
ability to work with
forms and reports in
Layout View. Some
database designers
do not use this view,
and therefore may
decide to disable it.

3. **Click the Display Form list arrow, then click frmEmployees**

   See **FIGURE O-4**. You test the Application Title and Display Form database properties.

4. **Click OK to close the Access Options dialog box, click OK when prompted, close the Technology-O.accdb database, then reopen the Technology-O.accdb database and enable content if prompted**

   The Technology-O.accdb database opens with the new application title, followed by the frmEmployees form, as shown in **FIGURE O-5**. If you want to open an Access database and bypass startup options, press and hold [Shift] while the database opens.

5. **Close the frmEmployees form**

TABLE O-2: Startup command-line options

option	effect
/excl	Opens the database for exclusive access
/ro	Opens the database for read-only access
/pwd *password*	Opens the database using the specified *password* (applies to Access 2002–2003 and earlier version databases only)
/repair	Repairs the database (in Access 2000 and 2002, compacting the database also repairs it; if you choose the Compact on Close command, you don't need the /repair option)
/convert *target database*	Converts a previous version of a database to an Access 2000 database with the *target database* name
/x *macro*	Starts Access and runs the specified *macro*
/wrkgrp *workgroup information file*	Starts Access using the specified *workgroup information file* (applies to Access 2002–2003 and earlier version databases only)

© 2014 Cengage Learning

FIGURE O-4: Setting startup options

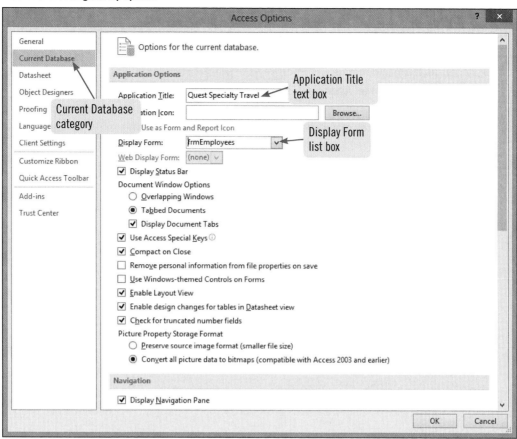

FIGURE O-5: Display Form and Application Title startup options are in effect

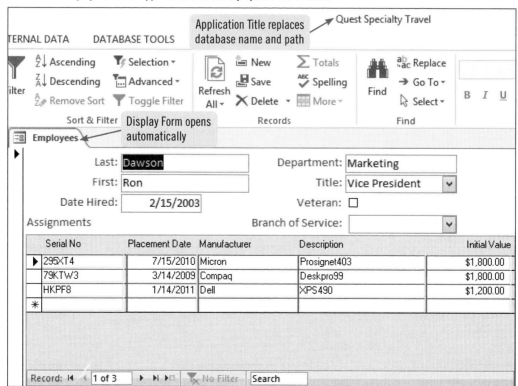

Analyze Database Performance

Learning
Outcomes
• Use the
  Performance
  Analyzer
• Describe
  performance tips

Access databases are typically used by multiple people and for extended periods. Therefore, spending a few hours to secure a database and improve its performance is a good investment. Access provides a tool called the **Performance Analyzer** that studies the structure and size of your database and makes a variety of recommendations on how you can improve its performance. With adequate time and Access skills, you can alleviate many performance bottlenecks by using software tools and additional programming techniques to improve database performance. You can often purchase faster processors and more memory to accomplish the same goal. See **TABLE O-3** for tips on optimizing the performance of your computer. **CASE** ▶ *You use the Performance Analyzer to see whether Access provides any recommendations on how to easily maintain peak performance of the Technology-O.accdb database.*

STEPS

1. **Click the DATABASE TOOLS tab, click the Analyze Performance button in the Analyze group, then click the All Object Types tab**

   The Performance Analyzer dialog box opens, as shown in **FIGURE O-6**. You can choose to analyze selected tables, forms, other objects, or the entire database.

2. **Click the Select All button, then click OK**

   The Performance Analyzer examines each object and presents the results in a dialog box, as shown in **FIGURE O-7**. The key shows that the analyzer gives four levels of advice regarding performance: recommendations, suggestions, ideas, and items that were fixed.

3. **Click each line in the Analysis Results area, then read each description in the Analysis Notes area**

   The lightbulb icon next to an item indicates that this is an idea. The Analysis Notes section of the Performance Analyzer dialog box gives you additional information regarding the specific item. All of the Performance Analyzer's ideas should be considered, but they are not as important as recommendations and suggestions.

4. **Click Close to close the Performance Analyzer dialog box**

Viewing object dependencies

Click any object in the Navigation Pane, click the DATABASE TOOLS tab, then click the Object Dependencies button in the Relationships group to view object dependencies. **Object dependencies** appear in the Object Dependencies task pane and display "Objects that depend on me" (the selected object). For example, before deleting a query you might want to select it to view its object dependencies to determine if any other queries, forms, or reports depend on that query. The Object Dependencies task pane also allows you to view "Objects that I depend on." For a selected query, this option would show you what tables are used in the query.

FIGURE O-6: Performance Analyzer dialog box

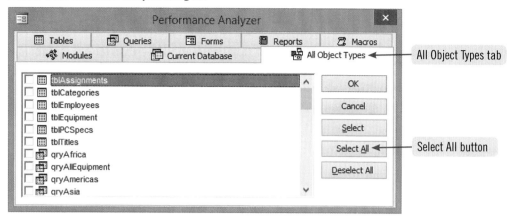

All Object Types tab

Select All button

FIGURE O-7: Performance Analyzer results

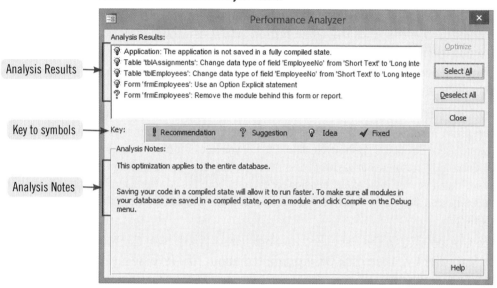

Analysis Results

Key to symbols

Analysis Notes

TABLE O-3: Tips for optimizing performance

degree of difficulty	tip
Easy	To free memory and other computer resources, close all applications that you don't currently need
Easy	If they can be run safely only when you need them, eliminate memory-resident programs, such as complex screen savers, email alert programs, and virus checkers
Easy	If you are the only person using a database, open it in Exclusive mode
Easy	Use the Compact on Close feature to regularly compact and repair your database
Moderate	Add more memory to your computer; once the database is open, memory is generally the single most important determinant of overall performance
Moderate	If others don't need to share the database, load it on your local hard drive instead of the network's file server (but be sure to back up local drives regularly, too)
Moderate	Split the database so that the data is stored on the file server, but other database objects are stored on your local (faster) hard drive
Moderate to difficult	If you are using disk compression software, stop doing so or move the database to an uncompressed drive
Moderate to difficult	Run Performance Analyzer on a regular basis, examining and appropriately acting on each recommendation, suggestion, and idea
Moderate to difficult	Make sure that all PCs are running the latest versions of Windows and Access; this might involve purchasing more software or upgrading hardware to properly support these robust software products

Set a Database Password

Learning
Outcomes
• Open the database
  in Exclusive mode
• Set a password
  and encryption

A **password** is a combination of uppercase and lowercase letters, numbers, and symbols that the user must enter to open the database. Setting a database password means that anyone who doesn't know the password cannot open the database. Other ways to secure an Access database are listed in TABLE O-4. **CASE** You apply a database password to the Technology-O.accdb database to secure its data.

STEPS

1. **Click the FILE tab, then click Close**

   The Technology-O.accdb database closes, but the Access application window remains open. To set a database password, you must open the database in Exclusive mode using the Open dialog box.

TROUBLE
You cannot use the Recent list to open a database in Exclusive mode.

2. **Click Open Other Files, navigate to the location where you store your Data Files, click Technology-O.accdb, click the Open button arrow, as shown in FIGURE O-8, click Open Exclusive, then enable content if prompted**

   Exclusive mode means that you are the only person who has the database open, and others cannot open the file during this time.

QUICK TIP
It's always a good idea to back up a database before creating a database password.

3. **Click the FILE tab, click Info, then click the Encrypt with Password button**

   Encryption means to make the data in the database unreadable by other software. The Set Database Password dialog box opens, as shown in FIGURE O-9. If you lose or forget your password, it cannot be recovered. For security reasons, your password does not appear as you type; for each keystroke, an asterisk appears instead. Therefore, you must enter the same password in both the Password and Verify text boxes to make sure you haven't made a typing error. Passwords are case sensitive, so, for example, Cyclones and cyclones are different.

QUICK TIP
Check to make sure the Caps Lock light is not on before entering a password.

4. **Type Go!3000!ISU in the Password text box, press [Tab], type Go!3000!ISU in the Verify text box, click OK, then click OK if prompted about row-level security**

   Passwords should be easy to remember, but not as obvious as your name, the word *password*, the name of the database, or the name of your company. **Strong passwords** are longer than eight characters and use the entire keyboard, including uppercase and lowercase letters, numbers, and symbols. Microsoft provides an online tool to check the strength of your password. Go to www.microsoft.com and search for password checker.

5. **Close, then reopen Technology-O.accdb**

   The Password Required dialog box opens.

6. **Type Go!3000!ISU, then click OK**

   The Technology-O.accdb database opens, giving you full access to all of the objects. To remove a password, you must exclusively open a database, just as you did when you set the database password.

7. **Click the FILE tab, click Close, click Open Other Files, navigate to the location where you store your Data Files, click Technology-O.accdb, click the Open button arrow, click Open Exclusive, type Go!3000!ISU in the Password Required dialog box, then click OK**

8. **Click the FILE tab, click Info, click the Decrypt Database button, type Go!3000!ISU, then click OK**

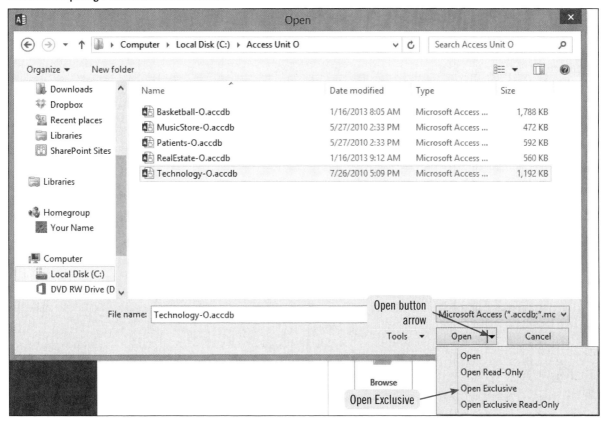

TABLE O-4: Methods to secure an Access database

method	description
Password	Restricts access to the database, and can be set at the database, workgroup, or VBA level
Encryption	Makes the data indecipherable to other programs
Startup options	Hides or disables certain functions when the database is opened
Show/hide objects	Shows or hides objects in the Navigation Pane; a simple way to prevent users from unintentionally deleting objects is to hide them in the Navigation Pane by checking the Hidden property in the object's Property Sheet
Split a database	Separates the back-end data and the front-end objects (such as forms and reports) into two databases that work together; splitting a database allows you to give each user access to only those front-end objects they need as well as add security measures to the back-end database that contains the data

Back Up a Database

Backing up a database refers to making a copy of it in a secure location. Backups are important to protect those who rely on a database from the problems created when the database is corrupted, stolen, or otherwise compromised. Database threats and solutions are summarized in **TABLE O-5**. Backups can be saved on an external hard drive, the hard drive of a second computer, or a Web server such as SkyDrive. Because most users are familiar with saving and copying files to hard drives, the new technology streamlines the effort of backing up a database. **CASE** ▶ *Kayla Green asks you to review the methods of backing up the database.*

STEPS

1. **Click the FILE tab, click Save As, click the Save Database As option if it is not selected, click Back Up Database, then click the Save As button, as shown in FIGURE O-10**

   The Save As dialog box is shown in **FIGURE O-11**. When using the Back Up Database option, the current date is automatically added to the database filename. However, any copy of the entire database with any filename also serves as a valid backup of the database. The **Save Database As** option saves the *entire* database, including all of its objects to a completely new database file. The **Save Object As** option saves only the *current object* (table, query, form, report, macro, or module).

   The Save As window shown in **FIGURE O-10** allows you to save the database in an older 2000 database format (.mdb file extension), a database template file (.accdt file extension), or an executable database (.accde file extension).

   The Save As dialog box shown in **FIGURE O-11** allows you to save the database to external locations such as an FTP (File Transfer Protocol) server, Dropbox folder, SkyDrive folder, or SharePoint site. Your locations will vary based on the resources available to you on the computer you are using.

2. **Navigate to the location where you store your Data Files, then click Save**

   A copy of the Technology-O.accdb database is saved in the location you selected with the name Technology-O-*currentdate*.accdb. Yet another way to make a backup copy of an Access database is to use your Windows skills to copy and paste the database file in a File Explorer or Windows Explorer window. If you choose this backup method, however, make sure the database and Access are closed before copying the database file.

   Although you can open and work in a backup database file just as you would any other file, a better way to recover data from a backup is to copy and paste the backup file to first create a production database with the name and in the location you desire, and then open and work in the copy. To copy only certain objects from a backup database to a production database, use the Access button in the Import & Link group of the EXTERNAL DATA tab to select and import specific objects from the backup database.

Using portable storage media

Technological advancements continue to make it easier and less expensive to store large files on portable storage devices. A few years ago, 3.5-inch disks with roughly 1 **MB** (**megabyte**, a million bytes) of storage capacity were common. Today, 3.5-inch disks have been replaced by a variety of inexpensive, high-capacity storage media that work with digital devices, such as digital cameras, cell phones, tablet computers, and personal digital assistants (PDAs). **Secure digital (SD) cards** are quarter-sized devices that slip directly into a computer and typically store around 32 **GB** (**gigabyte**, a million bytes or a thousand megabytes).

CompactFlash (CF) cards are slightly larger, and store more data, around 16 GB to 32 GB. **USB (Universal Serial Bus) drives** (which plug into a computer's USB port) are also popular. USB drives are also called thumb drives, flash drives, and travel drives. USB devices typically store 2 GB to 64 GB of information.

Larger still are **external hard drives**, sometimes as small as the size of a cell phone, that store anywhere from 20 GB to about 2 **TB** (**terabyte**, a trillion bytes or a thousand gigabytes) of information and connect to a computer using either a USB or FireWire port.

FIGURE O-10: Save As options

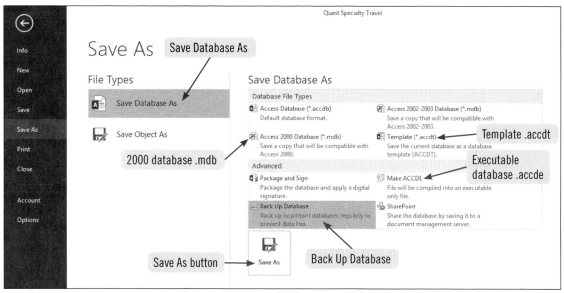

FIGURE O-11: Save As dialog box to back up a database

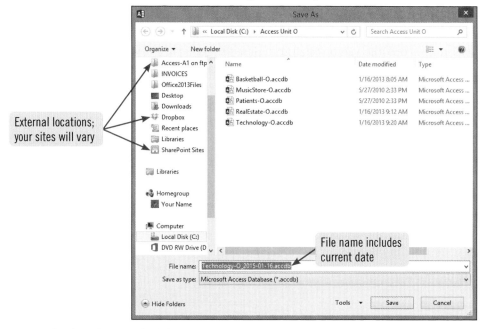

TABLE O-5: Database threats and solutions

incident	what can happen	appropriate actions
Virus	Viruses can cause a wide range of harm, from profane messages to corrupted files	Purchase the leading virus-checking software for each machine, and keep it updated
Power outage	Power problems such as construction accidents, **brownouts** (dips in power often causing lights to dim), and **spikes** (surges in power) can damage the hardware, which may render the computer useless	Purchase a **UPS** (uninterruptible power supply) to maintain constant power to the file server Purchase a **surge protector** (power strip with surge protection) for each user
Theft or intentional damage	Computer thieves or other scoundrels steal or vandalize computer equipment	Place the file server in a room that can be locked after-hours Use network drives for user data files, and back them up on a daily basis Use off-site storage for backups Set database passwords and encrypt the database so that files that are stolen cannot be used; use computer locks for equipment that is at risk, especially laptops

Convert a Database

Learning
Outcomes
• Convert a
database to a
previous version
• Define database
formats and file
extensions

When you **convert** a database, you change the database file into one that can be opened in a previous version of Access. In Access 2013, the default file format is Access 2007, a database format that can be shared between users of Access 2007, 2010, or 2013. To open a current database in Access 2000, 2002 (also called Access XP), or Access 2003, however, you first need to convert it to a previous file format such as an Access 2000 database format. Access 2000 was the default file format for Access 2000, 2002, and 2003. **CASE** *The Training Department asks you to convert the Technology-O.accdb database to a version that they can open and use in early versions of Access.*

STEPS

1. **Click the** FILE **tab, click** Save As, **click** Access 2000 Database, **click the** Save As button, **then click** Yes **to close open objects**

   To back up or convert a database, you must make sure that no other users are currently working with it. Because you are the sole user of this database, it is safe to start the conversion process. The Save As dialog box opens, prompting you for the name of the database.

   TROUBLE
   If you do not see
   the extensions on
   the filenames, open
   Windows Explorer
   or File Explorer. For
   Windows 8, click the
   View tab, and click
   the File name exten-
   sions check box. For
   Windows 7, click the
   Organize button,
   click Folder and
   search options, click
   the View tab, and
   uncheck the Hide
   extensions for known
   file types check box.

2. **Navigate to the location where you store your Data Files, then type** Technology-O-2000.mdb **in the File name text box, as shown in** FIGURE O-12

   Because Access 2000, 2002, and 2003 all work with Access 2000 databases equally well, you decide to convert this database to an Access 2000 version database to allow for maximum backward compatibility. Recall that Access 2013 databases have an **.accdb** file extension, but Access 2000 and 2002–2003 databases have the **.mdb** file extension.

   You may occasionally see two other database extensions, .ldb for older databases and .laccdb for newer databases. The **.ldb** and **.laccdb** files are temporary files that keep track of record-locking information when the database is open. They help coordinate the multiuser capabilities of an Access database so that several people can read and update the same database at the same time.

3. **Click** Save, **then click** OK

   A copy of the database with the name Technology-O-2000.mdb is saved to the location you specified and is opened in the Access window. You can open and use Access 2000 and 2002–2003 databases in Access 2013 just as you would open and use an Access 2007 database. Each database version has its advantages, however, which are summarized in TABLE O-6.

4. **Close the database**

FIGURE O-12: Save As dialog box for Access 2000 file format

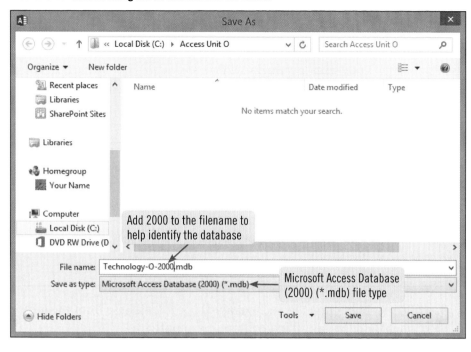

TABLE O-6: Differences between database file formats

database file format	file extension	Access version(s) that can read this file	benefits
2000	.mdb	2000, 2002, 2003, 2007, 2010, and 2013	Most versatile if working in an environment where multiple versions of Access are still in use
2002–2003	.mdb	2002, 2003, 2007, 2010, and 2013	Provides some advanced technical advantages for large databases over the Access 2000 file format
2007	.accdb	2007, 2010, and 2013	Supports the Attachment data type Supports multivalued fields Provides excellent integration with SharePoint and Outlook Provides more robust encryption

Split a Database

As your database grows, more people will want to use it, which creates the need for higher levels of database connectivity. **Local area networks (LANs)** are installed to link multiple PCs so they can share hardware and software resources. After a LAN is installed, a shared database is generally stored on a **file server**, a centrally located computer from which every user can access the database via the network. To improve the performance of a database shared among several users, you might **split** the database into two database files: the **back-end database**, which contains the actual table objects and is stored on the file server, and the **front-end database**, which contains the other database objects (forms and reports, for example). The front-end database is stored on each user's computer and links to the back-end database tables. You can also customize the objects contained in each front-end database. Therefore, front-end databases not only improve performance, but also add a level of customization and security. **CASE** ▶ *You split the Technology-O.accdb database into two databases in preparation for the new LAN being installed in the Information Systems Department.*

STEPS

1. **Start Access, then open the** Technology-O.accdb database **from the location where you store your Data Files, enabling content if prompted**

2. **Close the frmEmployees form, click the** DATABASE TOOLS tab, **click the** Access Database **button in the Move Data group, read the dialog box, then click** Split Database

   Access suggests the name of Technology-O_be.accdb for the back-end database in the Create Back-end Database dialog box.

3. **Navigate to the location where you store your Data Files, click** Split, **then click** OK

   Technology-O.accdb has now become the front-end database, which contains all of the Access objects except for the tables, as shown in **FIGURE O-13**. The tables have been replaced with links to the physical tables in the back-end database.

4. **Point to several linked** table icons **to read the path to the back-end database, right-click any of the** linked table icons, **then click** Linked Table Manager

   The Linked Table Manager dialog box opens, as shown in **FIGURE O-14**. This allows you to select and manually update tables. This is useful if the path to the back-end database changes and you need to reconnect the front-end and back-end database.

5. **Click** Cancel

   Linked tables work just like regular physical tables, even though the data is physically stored in another database.

6. **Close the Technology-O.accdb database and exit Access**

FIGURE O-13: Front-end database with linked tables

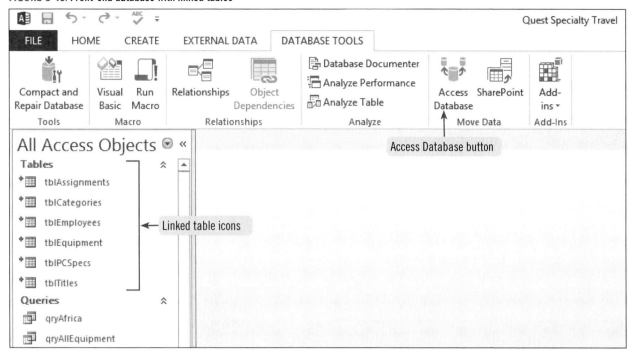

FIGURE O-14: Linked Table Manager dialog box

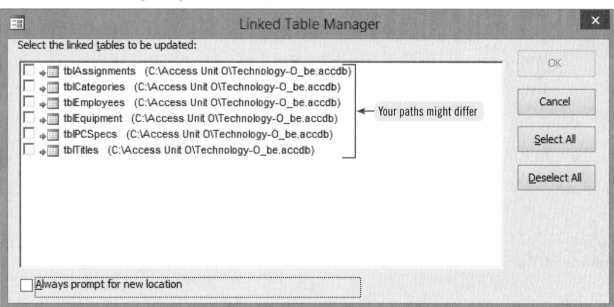

Databases and client/server computing

Splitting a database into a front-end and back-end database that work together is an excellent example of client/server computing. **Client/server computing** can be defined as two or more information systems cooperatively processing to solve a problem. In most implementations, the **client** is defined as the user's PC and the **server** is defined as the shared file server, minicomputer, or mainframe computer. The server usually handles corporate-wide computing activities, such as data storage and management, security, and connectivity to other networks. Within Access, client computers generally handle those tasks specific to each user, such as storing all of the queries, forms, and reports used by a particular user. Effectively managing a client/server network in which many front-end databases link to a single back-end database is a tremendous task, but the performance and security benefits are worth the effort.

Practice

Put your skills into practice with SAM! If you have a SAM account, go to www.cengage.com/sam2013 to access SAM assignments for this unit.

Concepts Review

Identify each element of the Access Options dialog box in FIGURE O-15.

FIGURE O-15

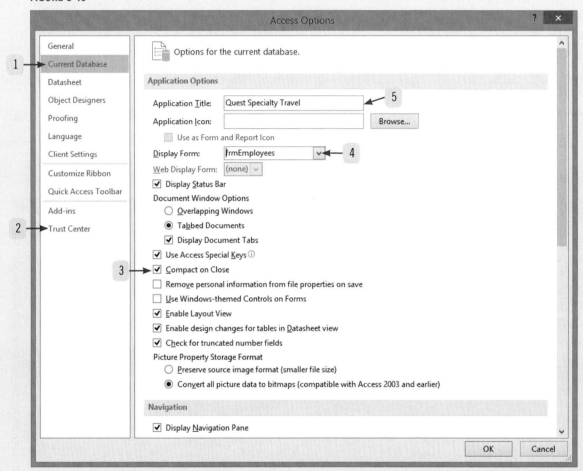

Match each term with the statement that best describes its function.

6. **Exclusive mode**
7. **Back-end database**
8. **Encrypting**
9. **Performance Analyzer**
10. **Navigation form**

a. Scrambles data so that it is indecipherable when opened by another program
b. Studies the structure and size of your database, and makes a variety of recommendations on how you can improve its speed
c. Contains database tables
d. Provides an easy-to-use database interface
e. Means that no other users can have access to the database file while it's open

Select the best answer from the list of choices.

11. **Changing a database file so that a previous version of Access can open it is called:**
    a. Splitting.
    b. Analyzing.
    c. Converting.
    d. Encrypting.

12. **Which is *not* a strong password?**
    a. 1234$College=6789
    b. password
    c. 5Matthew14?
    d. Lip44Balm*!

13. **Power outages can be caused by which of the following?**
    a. Surges
    b. Spikes
    c. Construction accidents
    d. All of the above

14. **Which character precedes a command-line option?**
    a. ^
    b. /
    c. @
    d. !

15. **Client/server computing is defined as:**
    a. Analyzing the performance of the database.
    b. Two or more information systems cooperatively processing to solve a problem.
    c. Creating an easy-to-use interface for a database application.
    d. Making sure that the database is encrypted and secure.

16. **Compacting and repairing a database does *not* help with which issue?**
    a. Eliminating wasted space
    b. Preventing data integrity problems
    c. Making the database as small as possible
    d. Identifying unused database objects

17. **Which of the following is *not* an item that you can "trust"?**
    a. Database table
    b. Database file
    c. Folder that stores the database
    d. You can trust all of the above.

18. **Which of the following is *not* a reason to create a backup?**
    a. Improve performance of the database
    b. Safeguard information should a natural disaster destroy the database
    c. Minimize damage caused by an incident that corrupts data
    d. Protect against theft

19. **Why might you split a database?**
    a. To make access to the database more secure
    b. To customize the front-end databases
    c. To improve performance
    d. All of the above

20. **Which phrase best defines a SharePoint server?**
   a. A special type of Microsoft Web server
   b. An online learning management system
   c. An academic wiki Web site
   d. A UNIX-based Web server

Skills Review

1. Create a navigation form.
   a. Start Access, open the Basketball-O.accdb database from the location where you store your Data Files, and enable content if prompted.
   b. Create a navigation form using the Vertical Tabs, Left style.
   c. Close the Field List.
   d. Add the frmGameInfo form, the frmGameSummaryForm, and the frmPlayerInformationForm to the tabs.
   e. Rename the tabs **Game Info**, **Game Summary**, and **Player Information**.
   f. Display the form in Form View, then test each tab.
   g. Save the form with the name **frmNavigation**, then close it.

2. Compact and repair a database.
   a. Compact and repair the database using an option on the DATABASE TOOLS tab.
   b. Open the Access Options dialog box, and check the Compact on Close option in the Current Database category.

3. Change startup options.
   a. Open the Access Options dialog box.
   b. Type **Iowa State Cyclones** in the Application Title text box, click the Display Form list arrow, click the frmNavigation form, then apply the changes.
   c. Close the Basketball-O.accdb database, then reopen it to check the startup options. Notice the change in the Access title bar.
   d. Close the frmNavigation form that automatically opened when the database was opened.

4. Analyze database performance.
   a. On the DATABASE TOOLS tab, click the Analyze Performance button.
   b. On the All Object Types tab, select all objects, then click OK.
   c. Read each of the ideas and descriptions, then close the Performance Analyzer and the database.

5. Set a database password.
   a. Open the Basketball-O.accdb database in Exclusive mode.
   b. Set the database password to **b*i*g*1*2**. (*Hint*: Check to make sure the Caps Lock light is not on because passwords are case sensitive.) Click OK if prompted about row level locking.
   c. Close the Basketball-O.accdb database, but leave Access open.
   d. Reopen the Basketball-O.accdb database to test the password. Close the Basketball-O.accdb database.
   e. Reopen the Basketball-O.accdb database in Exclusive mode. Type **b*i*g*1*2** as the password.
   f. Unset the database password.
   g. Close the frmNavigation form.

6. Back up a database.
   a. Click the FILE tab, click Save As, then use the Back Up Database option to save a database backup with the name **Basketball-O-*currentdate*.accdb** in the location where you store your Data Files.

Skills Review (continued)

7. Convert a database.

    a. Click the FILE tab, click Save As, and save the database backup as an Access 2000 database with the name **Basketball-O-2000.mdb** in the location where you store your Data Files.

    b. Notice that the frmNavigation no longer works correctly because the navigation form is a feature that is only compatible with Access 2007 database file formats. Close frmNavigation.

    c. Open the Access Options dialog box.

    d. Click the Display Form list arrow, select (none), then apply the changes.

    e. If the Navigation Pane displays only Tables, click the arrow to the right of Tables in the Navigation Pane title bar, and then click All Access Objects.

    f. Close the Basketball-O-2000.mdb database and click OK if prompted about a collating sequence.

8. Split a database.

    a. Start Access, open the Basketball-O.accdb database from the location where you store your Data Files, and enable content if prompted.

    b. Close frmNavigation.

    c. On the DATABASE TOOLS tab, click the Access Database button and split the database.

    d. Name the back-end database with the default name, **Basketball-O_be.accdb**, and save it in the location where you store your Data Files.

    e. Point to the linked table icons to observe the path to the back-end database.

    f. Close the Basketball-O.accdb database and exit Access.

Independent Challenge 1

As the manager of a doctor's clinic, you have created an Access database called Patients-O.accdb to track insurance claims. You want to set a database password and encrypt the database, as well as set options to automatically compact the database when it is closed.

    a. Start Access. Open Patients-O.accdb in Exclusive mode from the location where you store your Data Files. Enable content if prompted.

    b. Encrypt the database with a password.

    c. Enter **4-your-health** in the Password text box and the Verify text box, then click OK. Click OK if prompted about row level locking.

    d. Close the Patients-O.accdb database, but leave Access running.

    e. Reopen the Patients-O.accdb database, enter **4-your-health** as the password, then click OK.

    f. In the Access Options dialog box, check the Compact on Close option.

    g. Close the database and Access.

Independent Challenge 2

As the manager of a doctor's clinic, you have created an Access database called Patients-O.accdb to track insurance claims. You want to analyze database performance.

    a. Open the Patients-O.accdb database from the location where you store your Data Files, and enable content if prompted.

    b. Enter **4-your-health** as the password if prompted.

    c. Use the Analyze Performance tool on the DATABASE TOOLS tab to analyze all objects.

    d. Click each item in the Performance Analyzer results window, and read the Analysis Notes in the Performance Analyzer dialog box.

Independent Challenge 2 (continued)

e. Click Close in the Performance Analyzer dialog box and apply the first suggestion by double-clicking the basBodyMassIndex module. Choose Debug on the menu bar, then Compile. Save and close the VBE and run the Performance Analyzer again.

f. Click each item in the Performance Analyzer results window, and read the Analysis Notes in the Performance Analyzer dialog box.

g. Click Close in the Performance Analyzer dialog box and apply the third suggestion by double-clicking the basBodyMassIndex module. Enter **Option Explicit** as the second declaration statement, just below the Option Compare Database statement. Save and close the VBE and run the Performance Analyzer again.

h. Click each item in the Performance Analyzer results window, and read the Analysis Notes in the Performance Analyzer dialog box.

i. Click Close in the Performance Analyzer dialog box and consider the second suggestion by opening the tblClaimLineItems table in Datasheet View. The suggestion was to change the Data Type of the Diag1 field from Short Text to Number with a Field Size property value of Double. Given those values represent codes and not quantities, Short Text is a better description of the data and you will not implement this suggestion. Close the tblClaimLineItems table.

j. Run the Performance Analyzer for all objects again. To implement the first suggestion, close the Performance Analyzer dialog box, click the FILE tab, click Save As, click Make ACCDE, then click the Save As button. Save the Patients-O.accde file to the location where you save your Data Files. An accde file is a database file that can be used just like an accdb file, but many of the objects cannot be modified in Design View.

k. Close the Patients-O.accde database, then close Access.

Independent Challenge 3

As the manager of a residential real estate listing service, you have created an Access database called RealEstate-O.accdb to track properties that are for sale. You want to analyze how the compact and repair feature affects a database.

a. Open File Explorer (Windows 8) or Windows Explorer (Windows 7), then open the folder that contains your Data Files.

b. Change the view to Details. (In Windows 8, click the Details button on the right side of the status bar. In Windows 7, click the More Options button in the upper-right corner of the window, then click Details. Record the Size value for the RealEstate-O.accdb database.

c. Double-click RealEstate-O.accdb to open it, right-click the frmListingsEntryForm, and then click Delete.

d. Close the RealEstate-O.accdb database and return to File Explorer or Windows Explorer. Record the Size value for the RealEstate-O.accdb database.

e. Double-click RealEstate-O.accdb to open it, click the DATABASE TOOLS tab, then click the Compact and Repair Database button.

f. Close the RealEstate-O.accdb database and return to File Explorer or Windows Explorer. Record the Size value for the RealEstate-O.accdb database.

Administering the Database

Independent Challenge 4: Explore

Microsoft provides extra information, templates, files, and ideas at a Web site called Tools on the Web. You have been given an opportunity to intern with an Access consultant and are considering this type of work for your career. As such, you know that you need to be familiar with all of the resources on the Web that Microsoft provides to help you work with Access. In this exercise, you explore the Tools on the Web services.

a. Start Access, but do not open any databases.

b. Click the Microsoft Access Help button.

c. Click the What's new in Access link to open a page similar to the one shown in **FIGURE O-16**.

d. Click the link to watch the video about What's New in Access 2013.

e. After the video is finished, scroll through the Access Help window to read the article.

f. In a Word document, create a one-page, double-spaced article to summarize your understanding of an Access app. Include an example of where, how, and why you would apply an Access app in the real world.

g. Close Access and any open Access Help windows.

FIGURE O-16

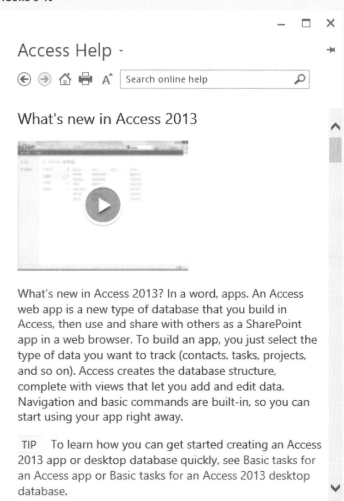

Visual Workshop

As the manager of a music store, you have created an Access database called MusicStore-O.accdb that tracks musical instrument rentals to schoolchildren. Use the Performance Analyzer to generate the results shown in FIGURE O-17 by analyzing all object types. Save the database as an ACCDE file, but do not implement the other ideas. In a Word document, explain why implementing the last three ideas might not be appropriate.

FIGURE O-17

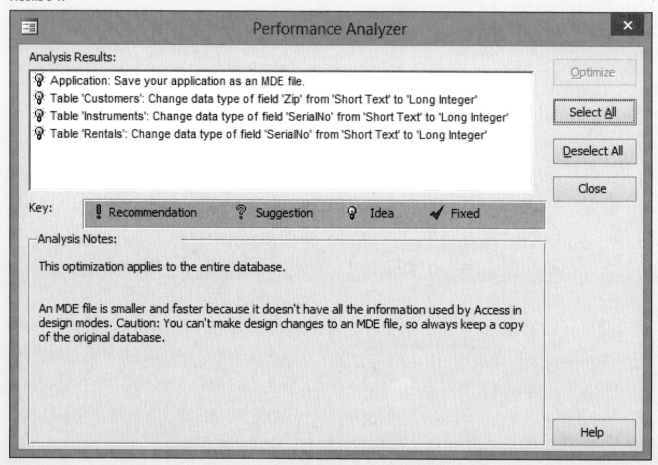

Access and the Web

CASE Kayla Green is the network administrator at Quest corporate headquarters. Kayla asks about ways that Access can participate with Web technologies. You work with Kayla to explore and use the Web technologies that complement an Access database.

Unit Objectives

After completing this unit, you will be able to:

- Create a hyperlink field
- Create a hyperlink control
- Use HTML tags to format text
- Export to HTML and XML

- Import from HTML and XML
- Save and share a database with SkyDrive
- Understand Access Web apps
- Create an Access Web app

Files You Will Need

QuestTravel-P.accdb
Vail.docx
Newsletter.docx
NewCustomers.html
NewTours.xml
NewTours.xsd
Basketball-P.accdb
Cavalier.png

NextSeason.html
NewPlayers.xml
NewPlayers.xsd
Unit P Skills Review
Question 7.docx
Patients-P.accdb
MusicStore-P.accdb

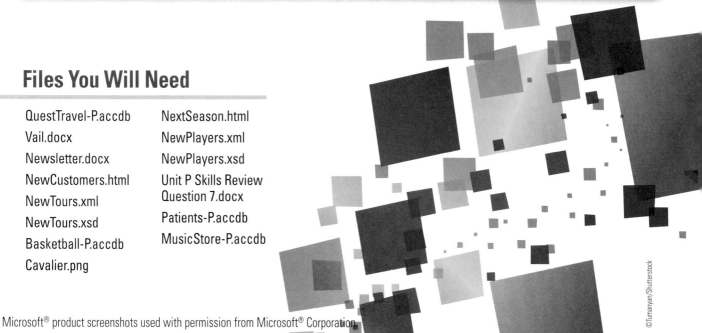

Create a Hyperlink Field

Learning
Outcomes
• Create a hyperlink
field
• Enter hyperlink
data for a Web
page or file

A **hyperlink field** is a field with the **Hyperlink** data type. Use the Hyperlink data type when you want to store a link to a Web page or file. The file can be located on the Internet, on your company's local area network, or on your own computer. **CASE** ▸ *You create two hyperlink fields to store linked information about each tour record in the Tours table. The first hyperlink field will link to a Web page that provides information about the tour location. The second hyperlink field will link to a Word document that contains a tour flyer.*

STEPS

1. **Start Access, open the** QuestTravel-P.accdb database **from the location where you store your Data Files, enable content if prompted, then double-click the** Tours table **to open it in Datasheet View**

   You can add new fields in either Datasheet View or Design View.

2. **Click the** *Click to Add* **placeholder to the right of the Price field, click** Hyperlink **in the drop-down list, type** WebPage **as the new field name, then press** [Enter]

   The new WebPage field will store a hyperlink to the Web page address for that tour. Before you enter those values, you will create another hyperlink field to link to a local Word document that contains a flyer for the tour.

3. **Click the** *Click to Add* **placeholder to the right of the WebPage field if the placeholder is not selected, click** Hyperlink, **type** Flyer, **press** [Enter], **then click the WebPage field for the first record**

   The Tours datasheet should look like **FIGURE P-1**. With the new hyperlink fields in place, you'll use them to further describe the Vail Biking Tour record. Hyperlink values such as Web page addresses may be typed directly in the field.

4. **Click the** WebPage field **for the Vail Biking Tour record (TourNo 5), type** www.vail.com, **then press** [Enter]

   To store the link to a local Word document, you browse for the file.

TROUBLE
If you do not see the
Hyperlink option on
the shortcut menu,
click in the Flyer field
to switch to Edit
mode (you will see
the blinking insertion
point in the field),
then redo Step 5.

5. **Right-click the** Flyer field **for the Vail Biking Tour record (TourNo 5), click** Hyperlink, **click** Edit Hyperlink, **browse for the** Vail.docx file **in the location where you store your Data Files, click the** Vail.docx **file, as shown in FIGURE P-2, then click** OK **in the Edit Hyperlink dialog box**

   The Edit Hyperlink dialog box lets you link to an existing file, Web page, or email address. Test your hyperlinks.

6. **Click the** www.vail.com hyperlink, **close the browser to return to Access, click the** Vail. docx hyperlink, **click** Yes **if prompted about a security concern, then close Word to return to Access**

   Note that your mouse pointer becomes a **hyperlink pointer** 🖑 and displays the path to the resource when you hover over a hyperlink. Also note that the hyperlink changes colors, from blue to purple, once the hyperlink has been visited, as shown in **FIGURE P-3**.

7. **Right-click the** Tours table tab, **then click** Close

   Hyperlink fields store paths to files and Web pages, not the files or Web pages themselves. If the location of the hyperlink file or database changes, the Hyperlink value must be changed in the Edit Hyperlink dialog box to reflect the new path as well.

FIGURE P-1: Creating hyperlink fields

FIGURE P-2: Edit Hyperlink dialog box

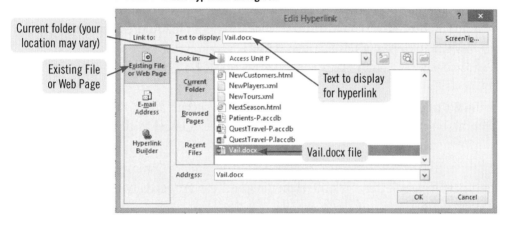

FIGURE P-3: Tours datasheet with visited hyperlinks

Create a Hyperlink Control

A **hyperlink control** is a control on a form that when clicked, works like a hyperlink to redirect the user to a Web page or file. You can convert a label control into a hyperlink label by modifying the label's **Hyperlink Address property**. Command button and image controls can also be used as hyperlinks. **CASE** *Kayla asks you to create hyperlinks to quickly open the QST newsletter (a Word document) as well as the www.mapquest.com Web site from the Tour Entry form. You will create a hyperlink command button for each link.*

STEPS

1. **Right-click the** TourEntry form **in the Navigation Pane, then click** Design View
   You will add two new hyperlink controls in the Form Header, just to the left of the existing command buttons.

2. **Click the** Button button ⌧ **in the Controls group, click at about the 4.5" mark on the horizontal ruler in the Form Header section, then click** Cancel **to close the Command Button Wizard**
   You work with the command button's Property Sheet to modify it into a hyperlink control.

3. **Click the** Property Sheet button **to toggle open the Property Sheet if it is closed, click the** Format tab **in the Property Sheet if it is not already selected, select** Command19 **in the Caption property, type** Mapquest, **click the** Hyperlink Address property, **type** http://www.mapquest.com, **then press** [Enter]
   The command button's Property Sheet should look like **FIGURE P-4**. Now you will add another command button hyperlink for the newsletter.

4. **Click the** Button button ⌧ **in the Controls group, click at about the 3" mark on the horizontal ruler in the Form Header section, then click** Cancel **to close the Command Button Wizard**

5. **In the Property Sheet for the new command button, select** Command20 **in the Caption property, type** Newsletter, **click the** Hyperlink Address property, **type** newsletter.docx, **then press** [Enter]
   With the new hyperlink command buttons in place, you will align them for a more professional look.

6. **Click the** Property Sheet button **to close the Property Sheet, drag a selection box through all four command buttons in the Form Header section, click the** ARRANGE tab **on the Ribbon, click the** Align button, **then click** Top **to align the top edges of the four buttons, as shown in** FIGURE P-5
   Test the hyperlinks in Form View.

7. **Right-click the** TourEntry form tab, **click** Form View, **click the** Newsletter link, **click** Yes **if prompted about unsafe content, close Word to return to Access, click the** Mapquest link, **close your browser to return to Access, as shown in** FIGURE P-6, **close the TourEntry form, then click** Yes **when prompted to save it**

Access and the Web

FIGURE P-4: Property Sheet for hyperlink command button

Property Sheet for Command Button control

Format tab

Caption property

Hyperlink Address property

FIGURE P-5: Aligning new command buttons

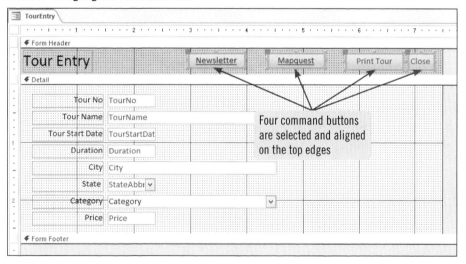

Four command buttons are selected and aligned on the top edges

FIGURE P-6: TourEntry form with hyperlink command buttons

New hyperlink command buttons

Use HTML Tags to Format Text

Learning
Outcomes
• Apply the Rich
  Text format
• Apply HTML
  formatting tags
• Apply HTML line
  break tags

HTML is the language used to describe content in a traditional Web page. HTML stands for **Hypertext Markup Language**. HTML **tags** are the codes used to identify or "mark up" the content in the page. Tags are entered into an HTML file in <angle brackets> and many HTML tags are used in pairs to mark the beginning and end of the content they identify. For example, you would use the <b> tag to mark where bold starts. The same tag with a slash, </b>, marks where bold ends. See **TABLE P-1** for more examples of common HTML tags you can use with the Rich Text format. **Rich Text** is a Text Format property that allows you to mix formatting of text displayed by a text box on a form or a report. With a little bit of HTML knowledge, you can transform a large block of text on a report into a paragraph with multiple formatting embellishments. **CASE** ▶ *Kayla has asked you to review the CustomerInvoice report. She wants you to format the payment disclaimer paragraph so it is more readable. You will use HTML tags to format the text.*

STEPS

1. **Double-click the** Switchboard form **to open it in Form View, click the** FIND Customer Invoice combo box arrow, **click the** Alman, Jacob entry, **click the** Preview Invoice command button **to open the Customer Invoice report in Print Preview, then click the report to zoom in on it**

   You want to better format the sentences in the large text box that starts with "Thank you for your order."

2. **Right-click the** CustomerInvoice tab, **then click** Design View **to open the report in Design View**

   The first step in formatting text in a text box is to change the Text Format property to Rich Text.

3. **Click the** large text box **in the Detail section to select it, click the** Property Sheet button **to open the Property Sheet for the text box if it is not already visible, click the** Data tab **in the Property Sheet if it is not already selected, click the** Text Format property, **click the** Text Format list arrow, **then click** Rich Text

   With the Text Format property set to Rich Text, you can mark up the text with HTML tags.

4. **Edit the text box entry, as shown in** FIGURE P-7

   Note that all HTML tags are surrounded by <angle brackets>. The beginning of the text to be formatted is marked with an **opening tag** such as <b> for start bold. The end of the text to be formatted is marked with a **closing tag**, which is identified with a forward slash such as </b> for end bold. **Empty tags**, those that are a single tag and not paired, end with a forward slash such as <br/> for line break.

5. **Save and close the CustomerInvoice report**

   Test the new Rich Text box with HTML formatting tags.

6. **On the Switchboard form, click the** FIND Customer Invoice combo box arrow, **click the** Alman, Jacob entry, **click the** Preview Invoice command button **to open the CustomerInvoice report in Print Preview, then click the report to zoom in**

   The final report should look like **FIGURE P-8**.

7. **Close the CustomerInvoice report, and then close the Switchboard form**

FIGURE P-7: Using HTML tags to format Rich Text

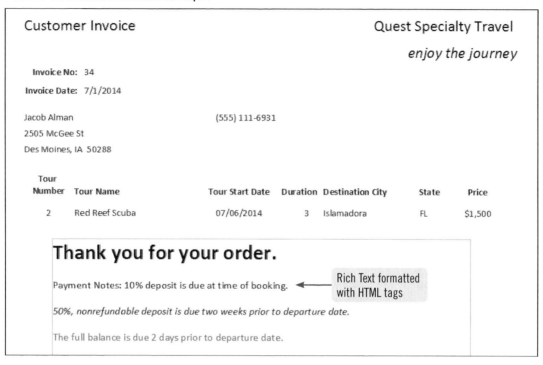

="\<font size=6>\Thank you for your order.\</font>\ \
\
Payment Notes: 10% deposit is due at time of booking. \
\
\<i>50%, nonrefundable deposit is due two weeks prior to departure date.\</i>\
\
 \<font color=red>The full balance is due 2 days prior to departure date.\</font>"

HTML tags must be entered precisely as shown

FIGURE P-8: Formatted CustomerInvoice report

Customer Invoice

Quest Specialty Travel

enjoy the journey

Invoice No: 34

Invoice Date: 7/1/2014

Jacob Alman   (555) 111-6931
2505 McGee St
Des Moines, IA 50288

Tour Number	Tour Name	Tour Start Date	Duration	Destination City	State	Price
2	Red Reef Scuba	07/06/2014	3	Islamadora	FL	$1,500

Thank you for your order.

Payment Notes: 10% deposit is due at time of booking.

50%, nonrefundable deposit is due two weeks prior to departure date.

The full balance is due 2 days prior to departure date.

Rich Text formatted with HTML tags

TABLE P-1: Common HTML tags

HTML tag	description	example
p	paragraph	\<p>The p tag marks the beginning and ending of a paragraph of text. \</p>
br	Marks a line break	\ (*Note*: The br tag is not a paired tag. One single tag creates the line break. Non-paired tags are also called empty tags.)
b	Marks the beginning and end of **bold** text	We **appreciate**\ your business.
i	Marks the beginning and end of *italic* text	Product may be returned for a full refund \<i>*within 30 days.*\</i>
code	Marks the beginning and end of `monospaced` text	\<code>`Terms and Conditions`\</code>
font	Identifies the color, font face, and size of the marked content	\<font color=red>Merry Christmas!\</font> \<font font_family=Arial>Purchase Order\</font> \<font size=16>Inventory Report\</font>

© 2014 Cengage Learning

HTML 5

HTML 5 is the latest version of HTML as defined by the leading international standards committee on fundamental Web technologies, the **W3C**, or **World Wide Web Consortium**, at www.w3c.org. HTML 5 has **deprecated** (retired due to new, better technologies) the HTML font tag in favor of a much more powerful, flexible, and productive way to define Web page formatting and presentation called **CSS, Cascading Style Sheets**. Therefore, it would not be appropriate or professional to use the HTML font tag in traditional Web page development. Given there is no current way to apply CSS technology to a Rich Text control in an Access form or report, however, the HTML formatting tags such as the font tag still have a meaningful role for this situation.

Export to HTML and XML

Learning
Outcomes
• Export data
  to HTML
• Export data
  to XML
• Compare HTML
  and XML files

Given the widespread use of the Web to share information, you may want to export Access data to a format that works well with existing Web technologies. For example, you might want to view data stored in an Access database using a common browser such as Internet Explorer. Access allows you to export data to two common Web-related formats: HTML and XML. Recall that HTML files are Web pages that use HTML tags to mark up content stored in the file. **XML**, short for **Extensible Markup Language**, is a language used to mark up structured data so that the data can be more easily shared between different computer programs. The process of exporting a report to an HTML or XML file is very similar. **CASE** *You use Access export features to export data to both an HTML file as well as an XML file to compare and better understand them.*

STEPS

1. **Click the Customers table in the Navigation pane, click the EXTERNAL DATA tab, click the More button in the Export group, then click HTML Document**

   The Export - HTML Document dialog box opens, prompting you for a name and location of the HTML file it is about to create, as shown in **FIGURE P-9**.

2. **Click the Export data with formatting and layout check box, click the Open the destination file after the export option is complete check box, click Browse, navigate to the location where you store your Data Files, click Save in the File Save dialog box, click OK in the Export - HTML Document dialog box, click OK in the HTML Output Options dialog box, then click Close if prompted**

   The Web page created by the export process automatically opens in the program that is associated with the HTML file extension, which is probably your default browser, such as Internet Explorer or Firefox. If you were to look at the HTML in this Web page, you would see a mixture of tags used to structure as well as format this data. Although mixing structure and formatting works well if you need to distribute the Web page for people to read, it creates problems when you want to pass the data to another program. XML files address this issue by separating the data from the presentation (formatting) of the data.

3. **Close the window with the Customers.html file to return to Access, click Close in the Export - HTML Document dialog box if it is not already closed, click the Tours table if it is not already selected, click the XML File button in the Export group, click Browse, navigate to the location where you store your Data Files, click Save in the File Save dialog box, click OK, click OK in the Export XML dialog box, then click Close in the Export - XML File dialog box**

   The Export - XML File dialog box doesn't have an option to automatically open the exported XML file, but you can find and double-click the Tours.xml to review its contents.

4. **Start File Explorer, navigate to the location where you store your Data Files, then double-click the Tours.xml file to open it**

   Tours.xml opens in the program associated with the .xml file extension, which is probably Notepad, as shown in **FIGURE P-10**. Note that the XML file uses markup tags to identify content similarly to how an HTML file uses markup tags. An XML file, therefore, is often a better choice when your goal is to share structured data because it separates the raw data into one file (**XML**), a description of the data's characteristics into another file (**XSD**), and a description of how the data should be formatted into a third file (**XSL**).

5. **Close the Tours.xml file and return to Access**

   The decision on which file format to choose when exporting Access data is dictated by the needs of the person or program that is receiving the file. Simply realize that you can export Access data just as easily to an HTML or XML file format as you previously experienced with other common file formats, such as Excel and PDF in Unit I.

FIGURE P-9: Export - HTML Document dialog box

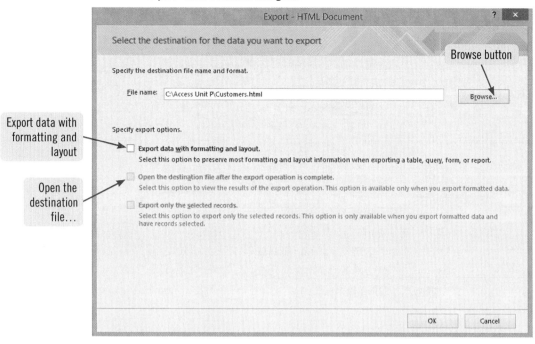

Export data with formatting and layout

Open the destination file...

Browse button

FIGURE P-10: Tours.xml file

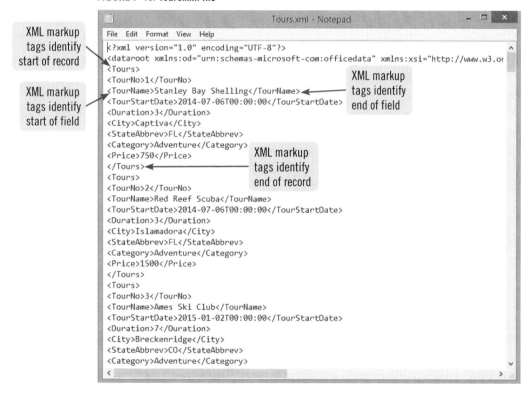

XML markup tags identify start of record

XML markup tags identify start of field

XML markup tags identify end of field

XML markup tags identify end of record

XML, XSD, and XSL files

When you export data as an XML file, you are prompted to export two helper files, XSD and XSL. The **XSD** file stores the schema of data stored in the XML file. The **schema** of the data is a description of the fields and their properties. The **XSL** file describes how to display an XML file. Therefore, if you're using the XML file to pass data from one computer application to another, the XSD file provides information about the data types and properties that can be used to describe and ensure the integrity of the data. The XSL file isn't used to pass data from one computer to another, but if you want a human to open and be able to easily read an XML file, include an XSL file in the export.

Import from HTML and XML

Learning
Outcomes
• Import data
from HTML
• Import data
from XML

Importing brings data into the database from an external file. You can import data directly from an HTML file provided the data is structured in the HTML file with HTML table tags so that Access knows where each field and record starts and stops. If the data is stored in an XML file, it is by definition already structured into fields and records with XML tags. **CASE** ➤ *You use Access import features to import new customer data from an HTML file that the Marketing Department created. You also import new tour data from an XML file that the Information Systems Department created.*

STEPS

1. **Start** File Explorer**, navigate to the location where you store your Data Files, then double-click the** NewCustomers.html file **to open it**

   The NewCustomers.html file opens in the program associated with viewing HTML files, which is probably a browser such as Internet Explorer, as shown in **FIGURE P-11**. View the HTML stored in the page to see how the data is structured.

   > **TROUBLE**
   > The View source option in Internet Explorer is named View Page Source in Firefox.

2. **Right-click the** NewCustomers.html file **in the browser, then click** View source **on the shortcut menu**

   The NewCustomers.html file opens in the program associated with creating and editing HTML files, which may be a text editor program such as Notepad or the Original Source window, as shown in **FIGURE P-12**. Note that HTML table tags separate the data using HTML **tr** tags to separate the records and **td** tags to separate each field. HTML table tags are further described in **TABLE P-2**.

   > **TROUBLE**
   > Be sure to click the More button in the *Import & Link* group on the Ribbon and not the *Export* group.

3. **Close all windows that display the NewCustomers.html file to return to Access, click the** EXTERNAL DATA tab **on the Ribbon, click the** More button **in the Import & Link group, click** HTML Document**, click** Browse**, navigate to the location of your Data Files, click** NewCustomers.html**, click** Open**, click** OK **in the Get External Data - HTML Document dialog box, click the** First Row Contains Column Headings check box**, click** Next**, click** Next **to accept the default field options for each field, click the** No primary key option button**, click** Next**, type** NewCustomers**, click** Finish**, then click** Close **if prompted**

   The records in the NewCustomers.html file are imported to a new Access table named NewCustomers. That gives you the ability to view the imported data in Access to make sure the import was successful and then use an Append query to combine the records from the imported table to an existing table.

4. **Double-click the** NewCustomers table **to make sure the import process was successful, then right-click the** NewCustomers tab **and click** Close **to close the table**

   Confident that the data in the HTML file was successfully imported into the Access database as a new table, you import the XML file.

   > **TROUBLE**
   > Be sure to click the XML File button in the *Import & Link* group on the Ribbon and not the *Export* group.

5. **Click the** XML File button **in the Import & Link group, click** Browse**, navigate to the location of your Data Files, click** NewTours.xml**, click** Open**, click** OK **in the Get External Data – XML File dialog box, click** OK **in the Import XML dialog box, click** Close **in the Get External Data - XML File dialog box, then double-click the** NewTours table **to make sure that the data imported successfully**

   The NewTours.xml data imported successfully. Switch to Design View to see more information about each field.

6. **Right-click the** NewTours tab**, then click** Design View

   The TourNo and Duration fields are identified as Number fields, the NewTourStartDate field with a Date/Time data type, and the Price field has a Currency data type. The import process made these intelligent choices because of the information about the fields stored in the schema file, the XSD file.

7. **Right-click the** NewTours tab**, then click** Close

FIGURE P-11: NewCustomers.html file opened in a browser

<table>
<caption>Customers</caption>

FName	LName	Street	City	State	Zip	Phone	FirstContact
Marcus	Welby	39411 Oakmont Rd	Texarama City	TX	84144	(333) 444-1934	List
Todd	Grant	9303 Monrovia St	Fisher	IA	30988	(333) 111-8931	List
Stan	Lovelace	3900 Meriam St	Austin	TX	84103	(333) 111-3081	List
Fritz	Arnold	55 Main Dr	Lemonwood	OK	88914	(333) 999-9101	List
Stewart	Baker	10 Cherry St	Overton	OK	88031	(333) 999-7009	List
Kelly	Sanders	500 W 10th St	Oklahoma City	OK	84103	(333) 999-3809	List
Tom	Cardwell	222 W 20th St	Oklahoma City	OK	84103	(333) 999-3809	List
Samuel	Adams	88 8th St	Wellman	OK	88910	(333) 999-8409	List
Harrison	Barnes	33 W. 303 Ter	Stillwater	OK	88913	(333) 333-9871	List
Boo	Palo	11 Memory Lane	Texarcana	TX	84143	(333) 333-0401	List

← HTML table

FIGURE P-12: NewCustomers.html tags

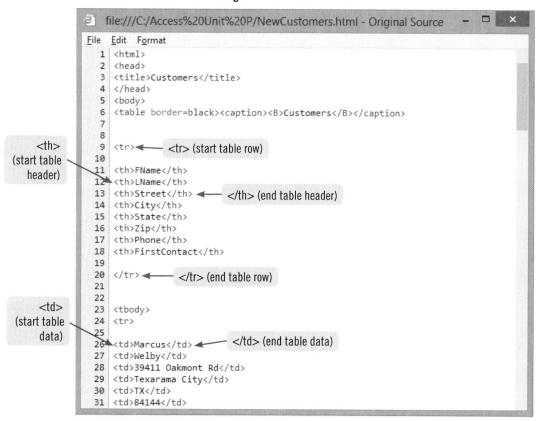

```
file:///C:/Access%20Unit%20P/NewCustomers.html - Original Source

File   Edit   Format
 1  <html>
 2  <head>
 3  <title>Customers</title>
 4  </head>
 5  <body>
 6  <table border=black><caption><B>Customers</B></caption>
 7
 8
 9  <tr>          ← <tr> (start table row)
10
11  <th>FName</th>       <th>
12  <th>LName</th>       (start table
13  <th>Street</th>   ← </th> (end table header)   header)
14  <th>City</th>
15  <th>State</th>
16  <th>Zip</th>
17  <th>Phone</th>
18  <th>FirstContact</th>
19
20  </tr>         ← </tr> (end table row)
21
22
23  <tbody>
24  <tr>
25
26  <td>Marcus</td>   ← </td> (end table data)
27  <td>Welby</td>
28  <td>39411 Oakmont Rd</td>
29  <td>Texarama City</td>
30  <td>TX</td>
31  <td>84144</td>
```

<th> (start table header)

<td> (start table data)

TABLE P-2: HTML table tags

tag	description
<table> </table>	Marks the beginning and end of the entire table
<tr> </tr>	Marks the beginning and end of a table row (a table row in HTML becomes a table record in Access)
<th> </th>	Marks the beginning and end of a table header entry (a table header entry in HTML becomes a field name in Access)
<td> </td>	Marks the beginning and end of a table data entry (a table data entry in HTML becomes a field value in Access)

Access 2013

Save and Share a Database with SkyDrive

Learning
Outcomes
• Create a SkyDrive
folder
• Save a database to
SkyDrive
• Share a database
from SkyDrive

SkyDrive is a cloud-based storage and file-sharing service provided by Microsoft. Saving files to SkyDrive means that you can access those files from any computer connected to the Internet. You can also share the file with other people or create **shared folders** in your SkyDrive to organize shared files. SkyDrive is particularly helpful to students who work on many different computers. The shared file and folder feature is very useful to anyone who works on group projects where the same file or files need to be constantly accessible to several team members. **CASE** ▶ *Kayla Green asks you to create a folder on your SkyDrive to save and share the QuestTravel-P database.*

STEPS

TROUBLE
You must be signed in to your Microsoft account to access your SkyDrive. See the "Working in the Cloud" appendix. If you do not see the SkyDrive in Step 1, continue to Step 2 to access it directly and sign in.

1. **Click the FILE tab on the Ribbon, click Save As, click the Save As button, click SkyDrive in your Favorites section or navigate to your SkyDrive, and then click Save**

   A copy of the QuestTravel-P.accdb database can be saved to your personal SkyDrive if it is available in the Save As dialog box. The SkyDrive works just like your hard drive but is available to you on any computer connected to the Internet.

2. **Close the QuestTravel-P database and Access 2013, start Internet Explorer or another browser, type skydrive.com in the Address box, then press [Enter]**

   The contents of your SkyDrive appear. From here, you can upload, delete, move, download, or copy files, similarly to how you work with files on your local computer. You want to share the QuestTravel-P database with your instructor. You decide to first create a folder for the database. That way, your SkyDrive will stay more organized.

QUICK TIP
You can use SkyDrive to create Word, Excel, PowerPoint, and OneNote files. See the "Working in the Cloud" appendix.

3. **Click the Create button, click Folder, type Quest Shared Files as the new folder name, then press [Enter] to create the folder, as shown in FIGURE P-13**

   Now you're ready to open the Quest Shared Files folder, then upload the QuestTravel-P database file into it.

QUICK TIP
Icons look like tiles if you are using Windows 8 and traditional Icons if you are using Windows 7.

4. **Click the Quest Shared Files folder to open it, click the Upload button, navigate to the location where you store your Data Files, click QuestTravel-P.accdb, then click Open in the Choose File to Upload dialog box**

   See **FIGURE P-14**. With the QuestTravel-P database stored in an appropriate folder on the SkyDrive, you're now ready to invite your instructor to share it.

TROUBLE
Depending on your operating system, you may be asked to complete a security check.

5. **Click the Sharing button, enter the email address of your instructor, enter Quest Unit P as the personal message, click Share, then click Done or Close**

   To review the share permissions, right-click the QuestTravel-P tile and click Sharing on the shortcut menu. A list of the individuals who have permission to view and or edit the file is listed on the left, and you can modify the permissions or delete people from the list. You can also share the entire folder, which automatically shares all files stored in that folder.

6. **Close the skydrive.com browser window**

FIGURE P-13: Creating a Quest Shared Files folder

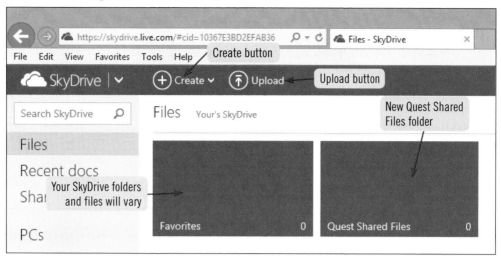

FIGURE P-14: SkyDrive with new file and folder

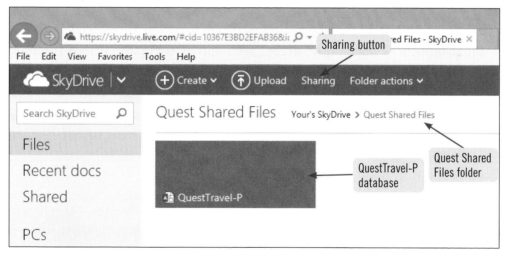

Understand Access Web Apps

Learning
Outcomes
• Describe the
advantages and
disadvantages of
an Access Web app
• Define the software
requirements for
an Access Web app

An **Access Web app** is a special type of Access database that is stored on a SharePoint 2013 server and allows users to enter and edit data using a common browser. An Access Web app is saved with the extension of **.accdw**. See TABLE P-3 for a description of the software requirements to create and use an Access Web app, which include SharePoint 2013, SQL Server 2012, Access 2013, and a browser. FIGURE P-15 shows how those software tools are used to develop and use an Access Web app. **CASE** ► *Kayla Green asks you review the benefits of and requirements for an Access Web app.*

DETAILS

Advantages of building an Access Web app over a traditional desktop application include the following:

* **Access is not required for the user**

  A copy of Microsoft Access on each client computer is no longer required for each user. An Access Web app is available to any user with a current browser.

* **A local connection to the database is not required for each user**

  An Access Web app is available to any user with an Internet connection.

* **Access Web app data is stored in a back-end SQL Server database**

  Storing data in SQL Server tables versus embedded Access tables provides these benefits:
  * **User-level security**: The data is more secure because it can be password protected at a user level.
  * **Scalabilility**: Much larger amounts of data can be stored and managed.
  * **Performance**: More people can be reliably working with the application with very fast response times.

Disadvantages of building an Access Web app as compared with a traditional desktop application include the following:

* **Complexity**

  Access Web apps require several technical prerequisites. See TABLE P-3 for a listing of the software requirements to create, modify, and use an Access Web app. See TABLE P-4 for a short listing of helpful Access Web app resources.

* **Less robust development tools**

  The tools used to develop Access Web apps are not as mature as those you use to create traditional desktop applications. For example, the objects in an Access Web app do not provide a full set of development tools in Design View as compared with their desktop counterparts. Also, VBA, Visual Basic for Applications, is not available to extend or enhance an Access Web app.

* **Traditional desktop databases cannot be easily upgraded to Access Web apps**

  Although the data from a traditional Access database can be easily imported into an SQL Server database, other objects such as forms and reports cannot be transferred from traditional databases to Web app applications.

  In conclusion, Access Web apps are a powerful new tool to deploy Access database applications across the Internet. By marrying the fast, easy application developments of Microsoft Access with the power, speed, and ubiquity of SQL Server and the Internet, Access Web apps provide a fast way to deploy secure relational database applications across the Internet.

FIGURE P-15: Software required to develop and use an Access Web app

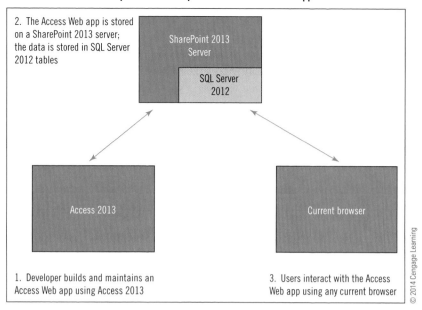

2. The Access Web app is stored on a SharePoint 2013 server; the data is stored in SQL Server 2012 tables

SharePoint 2013 Server

SQL Server 2012

Access 2013

Current browser

1. Developer builds and maintains an Access Web app using Access 2013

3. Users interact with the Access Web app using any current browser

© 2014 Cengage Learning

TABLE P-3: Software required to create, modify, and use an Access Web app

software	description
SharePoint 2013	An Access Web app is deployed to a file server loaded with SharePoint 2013. **SharePoint** is a Microsoft software product that is loaded on a file server to help a company organize and share files and data across its business. SharePoint 2013 can be purchased separately and is also included in the Microsoft Office 365 Small Business Premium and Office 365 Enterprise plans.
SQL Server 2012	**SQL Server** is a Microsoft software product used to store and manage a relational database. All Access Web apps use SQL Server 2012 to manage the data. No tables are created or managed by Access.
Access 2013	Access is required to make modifications to Access Web apps.
Web browser	A browser is required for users to view and enter data into an Access Web app.
Other	See the white paper article titled "Office 2013 - Access Services Setup for an On-Premises Installation" found at www.microsoft.com/en-us/download/details.aspx?id=30445 (or search for *Access Services Setup* on microsoft.com) for a full description of the software requirements for Access Web apps.

TABLE P-4: Reference material for Access Web apps

type of resource	title	author	location
Article	How to: Create and Customize a Web App in Access 2013	Microsoft	http://msdn.microsoft.com/en-us/library/office/jj249372.aspx or search for this article by title on microsoft.com
YouTube, Article, and Blog	Get Started with Access 2013 Web Apps	Microsoft	http://blogs.office.com/b/microsoft-access/archive/2012/07/30/get-started-with-access-2013.aspx or search for this article by title on microsoft.com
YouTube, Article, and Blog	4 Ways to Create Business Apps with Access 2013	Microsoft	http://blogs.office.com/b/microsoft-access/archive/2012/08/20/4-ways-to-create-access-apps.aspx or search for this article by title on microsoft.com
Article	What's New for Access 2013 Developers	Microsoft	http://msdn.microsoft.com/en-us/library/office/jj250134.aspx or search for this article by title on microsoft.com
YouTube	Creating and Using an Access Web App	Lisa Friedrichsen	Search for this Lisa Friedrichsen video on YouTube
YouTube	Modify an Access Web App	Lisa Friedrichsen	Search for this Lisa Friedrichsen video on YouTube

© 2014 Cengage Learning

Access 2013

Create an Access Web App

If you have access to a SharePoint 2013 server that is configured to support Access Web apps, you can quickly create an Access Web app using Access 2013. Setup issues require that you have a SharePoint 2013 server location (a Web address) where you will store the Access Web app, and a username and password that has already been given permission to save files on the SharePoint server. **CASE** *Kayla asks you to explore the possibility of using an Access Web app to allow employees to track customer comments, concerns, and issues. You explore how this would be started using Access 2013, and then read the rest of the process from the Microsoft Web site.*

STEPS

1. **Start Access 2013, click the** Issue tracking database template, **then click** OK **if prompted with an error message about not being able to connect to a server**

   The Issue tracking Web app template information window opens, as shown in **FIGURE P-16**, to provide a quick preview of what types of tables the template will create (Issues, Customers, and Employees) and what the List View for the Issues table will look like. Note that SharePoint is required and that you can customize the Web app after it is created. You are also prompted for an App Name and Web Location.

2. **Type** Customer Feedback **as the App Name, enter the** Web location of your SharePoint 2013 server **in the Web Location box, click** Create, **then enter** *your* **username and password when prompted**

   Access and SharePoint work together to create the Web app. Three tables—Issues, Customers, and Employees—are created automatically. Two **views** (called forms in a traditional desktop database) of each table, named **List** and **Datasheet**, are also automatically created to give you a fast way to quickly enter and edit data.

3. **Close Access 2013, open** Internet Explorer **or another browser, enter the** Web location **for your new Access Web app, then enter** *your* **username and password when prompted**

4. **Click the** Customers table **in the left panel, enter** *your* **name and fictitious but realistic data for the rest of the record, click the** Save button, **then click the** Datasheet button **to observe your new record in that view**

   At this point, you could continue to enter data into one of the three tables using either the List or Datasheet views created by the Issue tracking Web app template. To modify the interface (the views), however, you have to download the Web app and open it in Access 2013.

5. **Go to** http://msdn.microsoft.com/en-us/library/office/jj249372.aspx **or go to** www.microsoft.com **and search for** how to create a web app in Access 2013

6. **Read the Microsoft article about how to create and customize an Access Web app, as shown in** FIGURE P-17

7. **Close your browser, then close Access 2013**

FIGURE P-16: Issue tracking Web app template information window

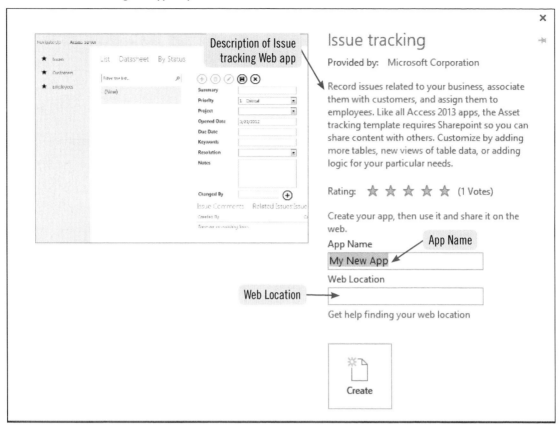

FIGURE P-17: How to: Create and Customize a Web App in Access 2013 article

How to: Create and customize a web app in Access 2013

Office 2013 | 45 out of 74 rated this helpful - Rate this topic
Published: July 16, 2012

Learn how to use the schema templates built into Access 2013 to jump-start creating an Access 2013 app, explore the features of the app, and then customize the app.

Applies to: *Access 2013*

In this article
Introduction
Prerequisites for building an app with Access 2013
Create the app
Explore the app
Customize the app
Conclusion
Additional resources

Practice

Put your skills into practice with SAM! If you have a SAM account, go to www.cengage.com/sam2013 to access SAM assignments for this unit.

Concepts Review

Identify each element of Form Design View in FIGURE P-18.

FIGURE P-18

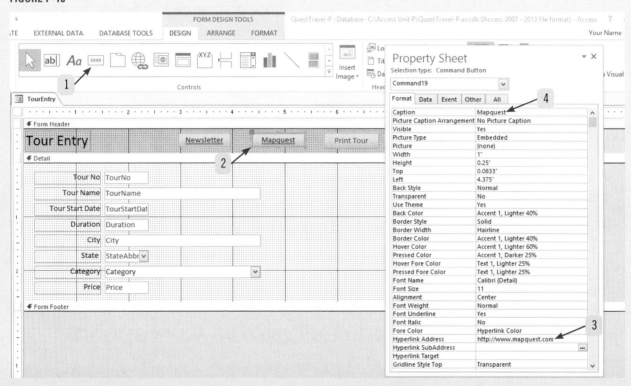

Match each term with the statement that best describes its function.

5. SQL Server
6. Hyperlink data type
7. Access Web app
8. HTML
9. XML
10. SkyDrive

a. The language used to describe content in a traditional Web page
b. A cloud-based storage and file-sharing service
c. Used to store a link to a Web page or file
d. A language used to mark up structured data
e. A Microsoft relational database management program
f. A special type of Access database that is stored on a SharePoint 2013 server

Select the best answer from the list of choices.

11. **If you wanted to create a field that stored email addresses, which data type would work best?**
    a. Short Text
    b. Long Text
    c. Hyperlink
    d. Memo

12. **Which of the following is *not* used to work with Access Web apps?**
    a. SharePoint Server 2013
    b. SQL Server 2012
    c. Access 2013
    d. All are used.

13. **Where is an Access Web app stored?**
    a. On a SharePoint server
    b. In the Data Files folder on your local hard drive
    c. In a SkyDrive folder
    d. In the Downloads folder on your local hard drive

14. **What is the purpose of an .accdw file?**
    a. To help you connect an Access Web app to your SkyDrive
    b. To allow you to modify the Access Web app in Access 2013
    c. To store Access Web app data in Access tables
    d. To sync your local hard drive to a shared SkyDrive

15. **Which HTML tags would you use to identify the start and end of a paragraph?**
    a. <p> </p>
    b.
    c.
    d. <start text> </end text>

16. **Which of the following form controls is *not* a common candidate for a hyperlink?**
    a. Combo box
    b. Label
    c. Command button
    d. Image

17. **What are forms called in an Access Web app?**
    a. Tables
    b. Reports
    c. Layouts
    d. Views

18. **Where is data stored in an Access Web app?**
    a. Access tables
    b. SQL Server tables
    c. SkyDrive folders
    d. XML files

19. **Which of the following is *not* a reason to use SkyDrive?**
    a. To access to your files from any computer connected to the Internet
    b. To share files with others
    c. To deploy an Access Web app
    d. To eliminate the problems associated with losing a flash drive

20. **HTML tags are also called:**
    a. Elements.
    b. Properties.
    c. Selectors.
    d. Attributes.

Skills Review

1. Create a hyperlink field.
   a. Start Access, open the Basketball-P.accdb database from the location where you store your Data Files, and enable content if prompted.
   b. Open the tblGames table and add two fields each with a Hyperlink data type, **SchoolWebSite** and **Logo**.
   c. Save the tblGames table and switch to Datasheet View. Enter a new record with *your* school name in the Opponent field and **Cavaliers** in the Mascot field. Enter the Web page address for *your* school's home page in the SchoolWebSite field. Browse for the file named **Cavalier.png** in the location where you store your Data Files, then insert it in the Logo field.
   d. Click both hyperlinks to test that they locate and display the desired resource. The SchoolWebSite hyperlink should open a browser that takes you to the home page for your school. The Cavalier.png hyperlink should display the Cavalier.png image.
   e. Close the tblGames table.

 2. Create a hyperlink control.
   a. Open the frmPlayerInformation form in Form Design View, then open the Form Header section by dragging the top edge of the Detail section down about 0.5".
   b. Add a command button to the left side of the Form Header section, then cancel the Command Button Wizard.

Skills Review (continued)

c. Open the Property Sheet for the new command button and make these property modifications:

Caption: **NCAA**

Hyperlink Address: **http://www.ncaa.org**

d. Add a second command button to the right side of the Form Header section, then cancel the Command Button Wizard.

e. In the Property Sheet for the new command button, make these property modifications:

Caption: **Player Statistics**

Hyperlink Address: Click the Build button, click Object in This Database on the left, expand the Reports section on the right, click rptPlayerStatistics, then click OK. (*Note*: You can also directly type **Report rptPlayerStatistics** in the Hyperlink SubAddress property.)

f. Save the frmPlayerInformation form, test both of the new command buttons in Form View, close the NCAA Web page, close the rptPlayerStatistics report, then close the frmPlayerInformation form.

3. **Use HTML tags to format text.**

a. Right-click the rptCodeOfConduct report, then click Print Preview to review the Player Code of Conduct. Although this is an unbound report (it does not display data from the database and the Record Source property is blank), you want to keep the information in the Basketball-P database.

b. Switch to Report Design View, select the text box that contains the code of conduct text, then change the Text Format property to **Rich Text**.

c. Use HTML tags to format the report as follows:

- Increase the size of the Player Code of Conduct title with the font tag: **<font size=8>**Player Code of Conduct**</font>**
- Increase the size of four introductory phrases with the font tags:
  - **<font size=6>** As a college player, I recognize that: **</font>**
  - **<font size=6>** I therefore pledge that: **</font>**
  - **<font size=6>** I understand that: **</font>**
  - **<font size=6>** The consequences for any such behavior could be: **</font>**
- Add two line breaks to create spaces between the lines with two line break tags at the end of every line: **

**
- Format Player Name in red, bold text with the font tags: **<font color=red>**Player Name**</font>**

d. Save and preview the rptCodeOfConduct report, as shown in **FIGURE P-19**.

FIGURE P-19

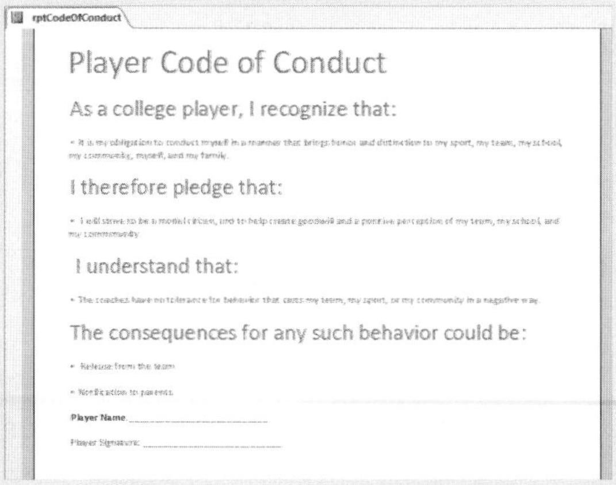

e. Close the rptCodeOfConduct report.

4. **Export to HTML and XML.**

a. Select the tblPlayers table in the Navigation Pane, then export it to an HTML document named **Players.html** in the location where you store your Data Files.

b. Select the qryFieldGoalStats query, then export it to an XML document named **FieldGoals.xml** in the location where you store your Data Files. Export both the XML and XSD files.

5. **Import from HTML and XML.**

a. Import the NextSeason.html file into the database. The first row does not contain column headings.

b. In the Import HTML Wizard, use the Field Name box in the Field Options area to rename Field1 through Field4: **Opponent**, **Mascot**, **HomeOrAway**, and **GameDate**. Let Access add the primary key, then import the data to a new table named **tblNextSeason**.

c. Import the NewPlayers.xml file into the database.

d. After Access imports the data into a table named tblPlayers1, rename the tblPlayers1 table to **tblNewPlayers**.

Skills Review (continued)

6. Save and share a database with SkyDrive.

  a. Save the Basketball-P.accdb database to your SkyDrive using the Save As option on the FILE tab, or going directly to the SkyDrive through a browser (see Step b).

  b. Open Internet Explorer or another browser, then go to **www.skydrive.com**.

  c. Create a new folder named **UnitP** on your SkyDrive, then upload the Basketball-P.accdb database to the Basketball folder.

  d. Share the UnitP folder with your instructor using your instructor's email address. Type **Unit P Exercises** for the message.

  e. Close the browser, close the Basketball-P.accdb database, then exit Access 2013.

7. Understand Access Web apps.

  a. Start Word 2013 and open the Unit P Skills Review Question 7.docx document from the location where you store your Data Files.

  b. Complete the header information to identify your name, the current date, the class, and the instructor's name.

  c. Respond to the following three instructions in the document using complete sentences, proper grammar, and spelling.

    1. Briefly describe the difference between the purpose for an Access Web app and an Access traditional desktop database.

    2. Briefly describe the different software requirements for an Access Web app and an Access traditional desktop database.

    3. Why do you think Microsoft uses the word desktop to describe traditional Access databases?

  d. Save the document, close it, then close Word 2013.

8. Create an Access Web app.

  a. Start Access 2013 and click the Contacts Access Web App template. (*Note*: If you do not have access to a SharePoint server, watch a video that demonstrates Step 8 by going to www.youtube.com or www.microsoft.com and searching for a video that shows how to create an Access Web app.)

  b. Enter **Alumni Contacts** as the App Name, enter your SharePoint server Web location, then click Create.

  c. Enter *your* username and password as prompted.

  d. Click the Contacts table icon on the left, click the Navigation Pane button, then double-click the Contacts table.

  e. Add a field named **Pledge** with a Currency data type to the end of the field list, then save and close the table.

  f. Click the Launch App button to view the Access Web app in your browser. Enter *your* information in the First Name, Last Name, and Email fields. Enter realistic but fictitious information in the other fields. Enter **5000** in the Pledge field, then click the Save button.

  g. Close the browser, then close Access 2013.

Independent Challenge 1

As the manager of a doctor's clinic, you have created an Access database called Patients-P.accdb to track patient visits. You need to create two hyperlink fields to reference the patient's employer and insurance company. You also want to add some hyperlink command buttons to a form to link the form to medical reference guides on the Web.

  a. Start Access 2013, then open the Patients-P.accdb database from the location where you store your Data Files. Enable content if prompted.

  b. Open the tblPatients table in Design View. Add the following two new fields at the bottom of the list, each with the Hyperlink data type: **Employer**, **Insurance**.

  c. Save the tblPatients table, then switch to Datasheet View. Enter **www.iastate.edu** for the Employer field in the first record for PatientSequence 20. Enter **www.welmark.com** for the Insurance field for PatientSequence 20.

  d. Enter *your* school's Web site address in the Employer field for the second record for PatientSequence 21. Research and enter the Web site address for a common health insurance company in your state in the Insurance field.

  e. Test all four hyperlinks to make sure they work correctly, close all browser windows to return to Access, then save and close the tblPatients table.

Independent Challenge 1 (continued)

f. Open frmClaimEntryForm in Design View, then add a command button to the upper-right corner of the Form Header. The Hyperlink Address property for the button should match the value of the Web Page address value in the Insurance field for the first record you previously entered in the tblPatients table. Be sure to include http:// as the first part of the Hyperlink Address property for the button. The Caption property should be **Welmark**.

g. Add a second command button to the upper-right corner of the Form Header section. The Hyperlink Address property for the button should match the value of the Web Page address value in the Insurance field for the second record you previously entered in the tblPatients table. The Caption property should refer to the name of the company that the Web address references. Be sure to include http:// as the first part of the Hyperlink Address property for the button. **FIGURE P-20** shows how the command buttons look for the Welmark and Blue KC insurance companies. The Caption for your second command button will vary based on the insurance company you chose in Step d.

FIGURE P-20

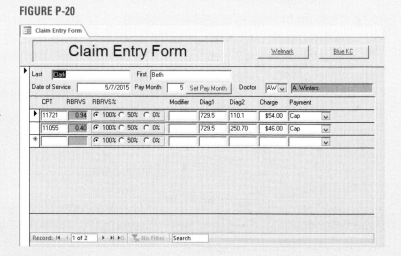

h. Save frmClaimEntryForm, then test both of your new hyperlink command buttons.

i. Close all browser windows and return to Access, close the Patients-P database, then close Access 2013.

Independent Challenge 2

As the manager of a doctor's clinic, you have created an Access database called Patients-P.accdb. You are in the process of expanding the database to include information about employees. One of the first documents a new employee must read and sign is the Employee Pledge, which you have partially completed and stored as an Access report. Your employer wants you to format certain words with red and bold text. You use a Rich Text format and HTML tags to format the pledge.

a. Open the Patients-P.accdb database from the location where you store your Data Files, then enable content if prompted.

b. In the Navigation Pane, double-click the rptPledge report to open it in Report View. Open the rptPledge report in Report Design View, select the large text box in the Detail section, open the Property Sheet, then change the Text Format property on the Data tab to **Rich Text**.

c. Use HTML tags as follows to format and space the following phrases with red, bold text and line breaks:
To the best of my ability, I pledge to:**

**

arrive and begin work **<font color=red>**on time**</font>

**

focus on my work and the **<font color=red>**patients**</font>** while on the job**

**

maintain a **<font color=red>**positive attitude**</font>

**

continue to **<font color=red>**learn and improve**</font>

**

be **<font color=red>**honest and trustworthy **</font>

**

treat everyone with **<font color=red>**respect

**</font>

**

limit all personal communication to a minimum while on the job**

**

follow the law and regulations**

**

**** not complain about the job I agreed to take

**

**

Signature: _____ **

**

Independent Challenge 2 (continued)

FIGURE P-21

d. Save and preview the rptPledge report, as shown in **FIGURE P-21**. Switch between Report Design View and Print Preview as needed to perfect the report.

e. Close the rptPledge report, close the Patients-P database, then close Access 2013.

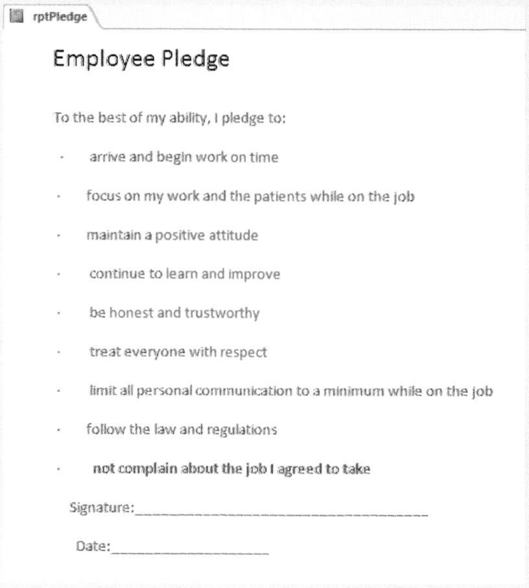

Independent Challenge 3

In this exercise, you will create a SkyDrive folder and share all of the databases you used to complete the end-of-unit exercises for Unit P with your instructor.

a. Open File Explorer, then open the folder that contains your completed Data Files to review them.

b. Open a browser window, then open your SkyDrive folder by going to **www.skydrive.com**.

c. If you completed all steps of the Skills Review, you have already created a SkyDrive folder named UnitP and shared it with your instructor. If that is the case, add the Patients-P.accdb database to the shared UnitP folder.

d. If you have not completed all of the steps of the Skills Review, complete Skills Review Step 6 to create the shared SkyDrive UnitP folder with the Basketball-P.accdb database. After you have completed Independent Challenges 1 and 2, add the Patients-P.accdb database to the shared UnitP folder.

e. After you have completed Independent Challenge 4, add the Web Based Benefits document to the shared UnitP folder.

f. After you have completed the Visual Workshop, add the MusicStore-P.accdb file to the shared UnitP folder.

g. Close File Explorer and the browser window that displays your SkyDrive.

Independent Challenge 4: Explore

Developing software solutions in a proprietary technology such as Microsoft Access is a simpler, faster solution for the developer because he or she only has to work with one software product for both developing and using the application Access. As soon as an application is deployed to the Internet, the work becomes more difficult because multiple software products are typically involved. To create and deploy an Access Web app, for example, the developer needs Access 2013, SharePoint 2013, SQL Server 2012, and a Web browser. However, there are also many benefits to making your application Web accessible. In this exercise, you'll research the Web to document five benefits of Web-based applications.

a. Using a browser and your favorite search engine, search for **benefits of Web-based applications**.

b. In a Word document, create a table with *your* name and the current date on the first line. Below your name, create a table with three columns and six rows. Enter these column headings in the first row: **Benefit**, **Description**, **Source**.

c. Complete the table with five more rows that identify and describe five benefits of a Web-based application over a traditional desktop Access database application. In the first column, identify the benefit. In the second column, briefly describe the benefit using one to two sentences. In the third column, copy and paste the Web address of the source you are citing for that benefit. The five benefits should reference at least three different sources.

d. Save your document with the name **Web Based Benefits** to the location where you save your Data Files, and then close Word.

Visual Workshop

As the manager of a music store, you have created an Access database called MusicStore-P.accdb, which tracks musical instrument rentals to schoolchildren. You need to provide parents a list of current rentals posted as a Web page, a portion of which is shown in FIGURE P-22. To create this page, create a query using all four tables in the database to select the fields in the order shown in the Web page. Note that the records are sorted by SchoolName and then by LastName. Save the query with the name **CurrentRentals**. Export the CurrentRentals query with the name **CurrentRentals.html** to the location where you store your Data Files. Do not select the Export data with formatting and layout check box. Open the CurrentRentals.html file in a browser to make sure that the export was successful.

FIGURE P-22

CurrentRentals			
Blackbob School Elementary	Eagan	7714	Clarinet
Blackbob School Elementary	Eagan	55442	Viola
Blackbob School Elementary	Eagan	7715	Clarinet
Blackbob School Elementary	Eagan	90	Bass
Blackbob School Elementary	Jupiter	89	Bass
Blackbob School Elementary	Jupiter	12999	Trumpet
Blackbob School Elementary	Shering	12997	Trumpet
Blackbob School Elementary	Shering	1234570	Cello
Blue Eye Elementary	Andrews	9988776	Violin
Blue Eye Elementary	Scott	12998	Trumpet
Blue Eye Elementary	Scott	55443	Viola
Blue Eye Elementary	Thompson	1234569	Cello
Blue Eye Elementary	Thompson	1234567	Cello
Blue Eye Elementary	Thompson	888335	Saxophone
Naish Middle School	Douglas	888334	Saxophone
Naish Middle School	Douglas	9988775	Violin
Naish Middle School	Friend	7713	Clarinet

Office 2013 **Appendix**

Working in the Cloud

CASE ▶ In your job for the Vancouver branch of Quest Specialty Travel, you travel frequently, you often work from home, and you also collaborate online with colleagues and clients. You want to learn how you can use SkyDrive with Office 2013 to work in the Cloud so that you can access and work on your files anytime and anywhere. (*Note*: SkyDrive and Office Web Apps are dynamic Web pages, and might change over time, including the way they are organized and how commands are performed. The steps and figures in this appendix reflect these pages at the time this book was published.)

Unit Objectives

After completing this unit, you will be able to:

- Understand Office 2013 in the Cloud
- Work Online
- Explore SkyDrive
- Manage Files on SkyDrive
- Share Files
- Explore Office Web Apps
- Complete a Team Project

Files You Will Need

WEB-1.pptx
WEB-2.docx

Understand Office 2013 in the Cloud

The term **cloud computing** refers to the process of working with files and apps online. You may already be familiar with Web-based e-mail accounts such as Gmail and outlook.com. These applications are **cloud-based**, which means that you do not need a program installed on your computer to run them. Office 2013 has also been designed as a cloud-based application. When you work in Office 2013, you can choose to store your files "in the cloud" so that you can access them on any device connected to the Internet. **CASE** ➤ *You review the concepts related to working online with Office 2013.*

DETAILS

- ## How does Office 2013 work in the Cloud?

  When you launch an Office application such as Word or Excel, you might see your name and maybe even your picture in the top right corner of your screen. This information tells you that you have signed in to Office 2013, either with your personal account or with an account you are given as part of an organization such as a company or school. When you are signed in to Office and click the FILE tab in any Office 2013 application such as Word or Excel, you see a list of the files that you have used recently on your current computer and on any other connected device such as a laptop, a tablet or even a Windows phone. The file path appears beneath each filename so that you can quickly identify its location as shown in **FIGURE WEB-1**. Office 2013 also remembers your personalized settings so that they are available on all the devices you use.

- ## What are roaming settings?

  A **roaming setting** is a setting that travels with you on every connected device. Examples of roaming settings include your personal settings such as your name and picture, the files you've used most recently, your list of connected services such as Facebook and Twitter, and any custom dictionaries you've created. Two particularly useful roaming settings are the Word Resume Reading Position setting and the PowerPoint Last Viewed Slide setting. For example, when you open a PowerPoint presentation that you've worked on previously, you will see a message similar to the one shown in **FIGURE WEB-2**.

- ## What is SkyDrive?

  SkyDrive is an online storage and file sharing service. When you are signed in to your computer with your Microsoft account, you receive access to your own SkyDrive, which is your personal storage area on the Internet. On your SkyDrive, you are given space to store up to 7 GB of data online. A SkyDrive location is already created on your computer as shown in **FIGURE WEB-3**. Every file you save to SkyDrive is synced among your computers and your personal storage area on SkyDrive.com. The term **synced** (which stands for synchronized) means that when you add, change or delete files on one computer, the same files on your other devices are also updated.

- ## What are Office Web Apps?

  Office Web Apps are versions of Microsoft Word, Excel, PowerPoint, and OneNote that you can access online from your SkyDrive. An Office Web App does not include all of the features and functions included with the full Office version of its associated application. However, you can use the Office Web App from any computer that is connected to the Internet, even if Microsoft Office 2013 is not installed on that computer.

- ## How do SkyDrive and Office Web Apps work together?

  You can create a file in Office 2013 using Word, Excel, PowerPoint, or OneNote and then save it to your SkyDrive. You can then open the Office file saved to SkyDrive and edit it using your Office 2013 apps. If you do not have Office 2013 installed on the computer you are using, you can edit the file using your Web browser and the corresponding Office Web App. You can also use an Office Web App to create a new file, which is saved automatically to SkyDrive while you work and you can download a file created with an Office Web App and work with the file in the full version of the corresponding Office application.

FIGURE WEB-1: FILE tab in Microsoft Excel

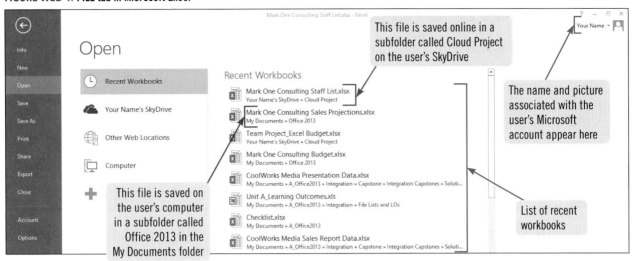

FIGURE WEB-2: PowerPoint Last Viewed Slide setting

FIGURE WEB-3: Saving a Word file on SkyDrive

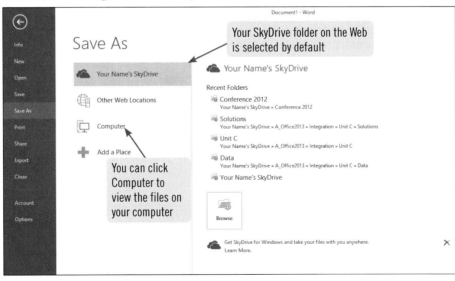

Work Online

When you work on your own computer, you are usually signed in to your Microsoft account automatically. When you use another person's computer or a public computer, you will be required to enter the password associated with your Microsoft account to access files you have saved on Windows SkyDrive. You know you are signed in to Windows when you see your name and possibly your picture in the top right corner of your screen. *Note*: To complete the steps below, you need to be signed in to your Microsoft account. If you do not have a Microsoft account, see "Getting a Microsoft account" in the yellow box. **CASE** *You explore the settings associated with your account, learn how to switch accounts, and sign out of an account.*

STEPS

1. **Sign in to Windows, if necessary, launch Word, click** Blank document**, then verify that your name appears in the top right corner of your screen**

2. **Click the** list arrow **to the right of your name, as shown in** FIGURE WEB-4**, then click** About me **and sign in if prompted**

   Internet Explorer opens and your Profile page appears. Here, you can add or edit your contact information and information about your workplace. You can also change the name and picture that appear in the top right corner of your window.

3. **Click the** list arrow **next to Profile in the top left corner of your screen, above the picture**

   The tiles representing the services your Windows account is connected to appear as shown in **FIGURE WEB-5**. Note that if you have connected your Microsoft account to accounts in other services such as Facebook, LinkedIn, or outlook.com, you will see these connections in the appropriate app. For example, your connections to Facebook and LinkedIn appear in the People app.

4. **Click a blank area below the apps tiles, click** Your Name **in the top right corner, then click** Account settings

   Either you are taken directly to the Microsoft account screen or, depending on your security settings, a Sign in screen appears. To make changes to your account, you might need to enter the password associated with your account. You can also choose to sign in with a different Microsoft account. Once you sign in, you can change the information associated with your account such as your name, email address, birth date, and password. You can also choose to close your Microsoft account, which deletes all the data associated with it.

5. **Click the** Close button ▢×▢ **in the upper right corner of the window to remove the Sign-in window, click** Close all tabs **to return to Word, then click the** list arrow ▾ **next to Your Name in the top right corner of the Word window**

   To sign out of your account, you can click Sign Out at the top of the Accounts dialog box that appears when you click Account Settings. When you are working on your own computers, you will rarely need to sign out of your account. However, if you are working on a public computer, you may want to sign out of your account to avoid having your files accessible to other users.

6. **Click** Switch account

   You can choose to sign into another Microsoft account or to an account with an organization.

7. **Click the** Close button ▢×▢

   You are returned to a blank document in Word.

8. **Exit Word**

FIGURE WEB-4: Viewing Windows account options in Word

FIGURE WEB-5: Connected services associated with a Profile

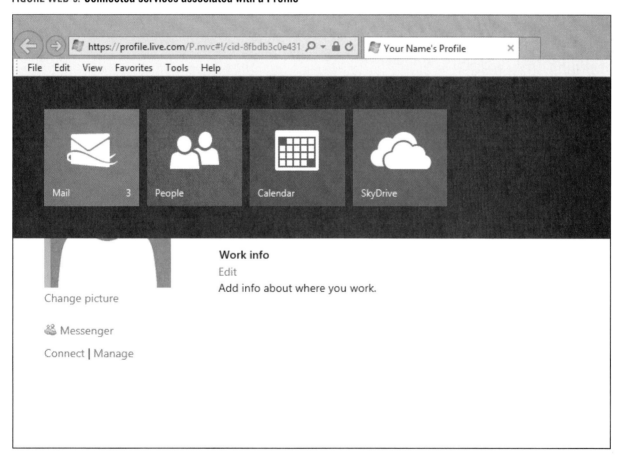

Getting a Microsoft account

If you have been working with Windows and Office 2013, you might already have a Microsoft account, which was previously referred to as a Windows Live ID. You also have an account if you use outlook.com (formerly Hotmail), SkyDrive, Xbox LIVE, or have a Windows Phone. A Microsoft account consists of an email address and a password. If you wish to create a new Microsoft account, go to https://signup.live.com/ and follow the directions provided.

Explore SkyDrive

Learning Outcomes
• Save a file to SkyDrive
• Create a folder on SkyDrive

SkyDrive works like the hard drive on your computer. You can save and open files from SkyDrive, create folders, and manage your files. You can access the files you save on SkyDrive from any of your connected devices and from anywhere you have a computer connection. **CASE** ▸ *You open a PowerPoint presentation, save the file to your SkyDrive, then create a folder.*

STEPS

1. **Start PowerPoint, then open the file** WEB-1.pptx **from the location where you store your Data Files**

2. **Click the** FILE **tab, click** Save As, **then click** Your Name's SkyDrive **(top selection) if it is not already selected**

3. **Click the** Browse button
   The Save As dialog box opens, showing the folders stored on your SkyDrive. You may have several folders already stored there or you may have none.

4. **Click** New folder, **type** Cengage, **then press** [Enter]

5. **Double-click** Cengage, **select** WEB-1.pptx **in the File name text box, type** WEB-QST Vancouver 1 **as shown in** FIGURE WEB-6, **then click** Save
   The file is saved to the Cengage folder on the SkyDrive that is associated with your Microsoft account. The PowerPoint window reappears.

6. **Click the** FILE **tab, click** Close, **click the** FILE **tab, then click** Open
   WEB-QST Vancouver 1.pptx appears as the first file listed in the Recent Presentations list, and the path to your Cengage folder on your SkyDrive appears beneath it.

7. **Click** WEB-QST Vancouver 1.pptx **to open it, then type your name where indicated on the title slide**

8. **Click** Slide 2 **in the Navigation pane, select** 20% **in the third bullet, type** 30%, **click the** FILE **tab, click** Save As, **click** Cengage **under Current Folder, change the file name to** WEB-QST Vancouver 2, **then click** Save

9. **Exit PowerPoint**
   A new version of the presentation is saved to the Cengage folder that you created on SkyDrive.

How to disable default saving to Skydrive

You can specify how you want to save files from Office 2013 applications. By default, files are saved to locations you specify on your SkyDrive. You can change the default to be a different location. In Word, PowerPoint, or Excel, click the FILE tab, then click Options. Click Save in the left sidebar, then in the Save section, click the Save to Computer by default check box, as shown in **FIGURE WEB-7**. Click OK to close the PowerPoint Options dialog box. The Save options you've selected will be active in Word, PowerPoint, and Excel, regardless of which application you were using when you changed the option.

FIGURE WEB-6: Saving a presentation to SkyDrive

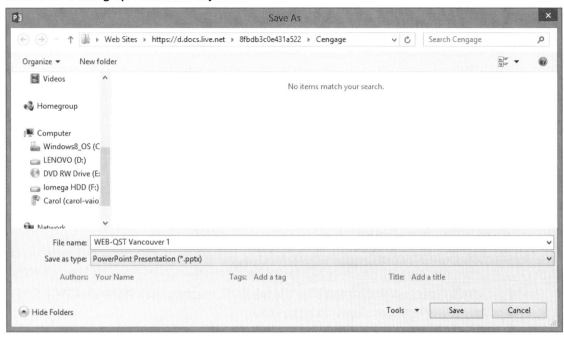

FIGURE WEB-7: Changing the default Save location in PowerPoint

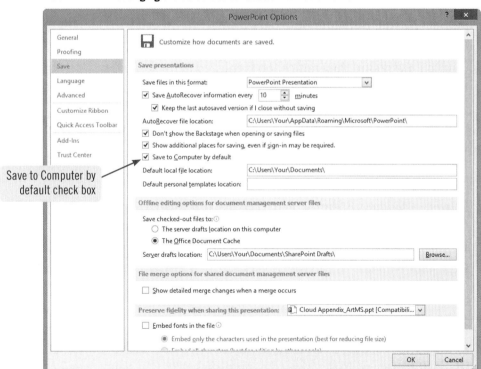

Manage Files on SkyDrive

**Learning
Outcomes**
• Access SkyDrive
  from Internet
  Explorer
• Rename, Delete,
  and Move files
  in SkyDrive

You are automatically connected to SkyDrive when you sign into your Microsoft account and launch an Office 2013 application. You can also access SkyDrive through your Web browser or from the SkyDrive App in Windows 8. When you start the SkyDrive App, you can upload and download files, create folders, and delete files. You can also download the SkyDrive app to your tablet or other mobile device so you can access files wherever you have an Internet connection. When you access SkyDrive from Internet Explorer, you can do more file management tasks, including renaming and moving files. **CASE** *You explore how to work with SkyDrive from your Web browser and from the SkyDrive App.*

STEPS

1. **Launch Internet Explorer or another Web browser, type** skydrive.com **in the Address box, then press [Enter]**

   If you are signed in to your Microsoft account, your SkyDrive opens. If you are not signed in, the login page appears where you can enter the email address and password associated with your Microsoft account.

2. **Sign in if necessary, click the blue tile labeled** Cengage, **then right-click** WEB-QST Vancouver 1.pptx **as shown in** FIGURE WEB-8

   You can open the file in the PowerPoint Web App or in PowerPoint, download the file to your computer, share it, embed it, and perform other actions such as renaming and deleting.

3. **Click** Download, **click** Open **in the bar at the bottom of the screen, then click** Enable Editing

   The presentation opens in PowerPoint where you can save it to your computer hard drive or back to SkyDrive.

4. **Click the** DESIGN **tab, click the** More button ⏷ **in the Themes group, select the** Wisp **theme, click the** FILE **tab, click** Save As, **click** Computer, **click** Browse, **navigate to a location on your computer or on an external drive such as a USB flash drive, click** Save, **then exit PowerPoint**

5. **Launch PowerPoint, then notice the files listed in the left pane under Recent**

   The file you just saved to your computer or external drive appears first and the file saved to the Cengage folder on SkyDrive appears second.

6. **Click the second listing, notice that the file is not updated with the Wisp design, then exit PowerPoint**

   When you download a file from SkyDrive, changes you make are not saved to the version on SkyDrive. You can also access SkyDrive from your Windows 8 screen by using the SkyDrive app.

TROUBLE
If prompted, enter
your log in informa-
tion in the Add your
Microsoft account
screen. Note that
you can only com-
plete steps 7 to 9 if
you are working on
Windows 8.

7. **Show the Windows 8 Start screen, click the** SkyDrive **tile, open the Cengage folder, right-click** WEB-QST Vancouver 1, **view the buttons on the taskbar as shown in** FIGURE WEB-9, **click the** Delete **button on the taskbar, then click** Delete

8. **Right-click** WEB-QST Vancouver 2, **click the** New Folder **button on the taskbar, type** Illustrated, **then click** Create folder

   You can rename and move files in SkyDrive through Internet Explorer.

9. **Move the mouse pointer to the top of the screen until it becomes the hand pointer, drag to the bottom of the screen to close the SkyDrive App, click the** Internet Explorer **tile on the Start screen, go to** skydrive.com, **right-click** WEB-QST Vancouver 2 **on the SkyDrive site, click** Move to, **click the** ⟩ **next to Cengage, click** Illustrated, **then click** Move

FIGURE WEB-8: **File management options on SkyDrive**

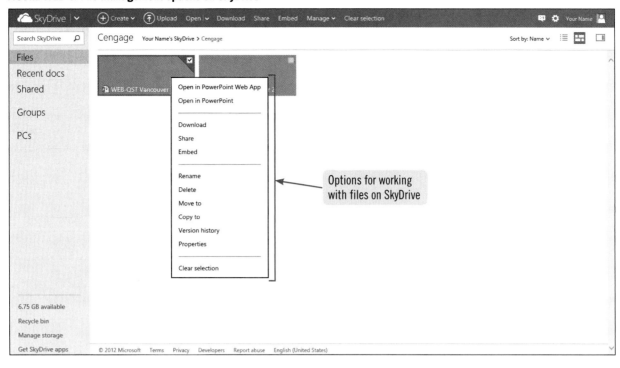

FIGURE WEB-9: **File management options on SkyDrive App**

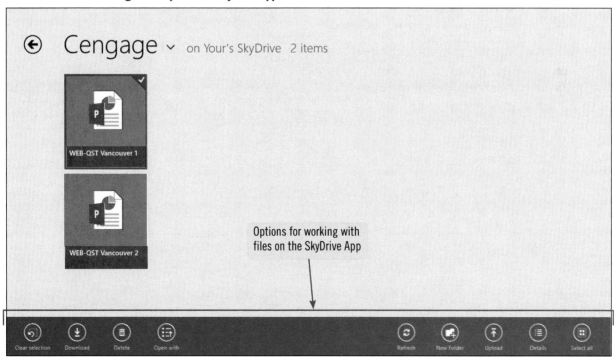

Cloud

Share Files

Learning Outcome
- Share a file from SkyDrive

One of the great advantages of working with SkyDrive is that you can share your files with others. Suppose, for example, that you want a colleague to review a presentation you created in PowerPoint and then add a new slide. You can, of course, e-mail the presentation directly to your colleague who can then make changes and e-mail the presentation back. Alternatively, you can share the PowerPoint file directly from SkyDrive. Your colleague can edit the file using the PowerPoint Web App or the full version of PowerPoint, and then you can check the updated file on SkyDrive. In this way, you and your colleague are working with just one version of the presentation that you both can update. **CASE** *You have decided to share files in the Illustrated folder that you created in the previous lesson with another individual. You start by sharing files with your partner and your partner can share files with you.*

STEPS

TROUBLE
If you cannot find a partner, you can email the file to yourself.

1. **Identify a partner with whom you can work, and obtain his or her e-mail address; you can choose someone in your class or someone on your e-mail list, but it should be someone who will be completing these steps when you are**

2. **Right-click the Illustrated folder, then click Sharing as shown in** FIGURE WEB-10

3. **Type the e-mail address of your partner**

4. **Click in the Include a personal message box, then type Here's the presentation we're working on together as shown in** FIGURE WEB-11

5. **Verify that the Recipients can edit check box is selected, then click Share**

   Your partner will receive a message advising him or her that you have shared the WEB-QST Vancouver 2.pptx file. If your partner is completing the steps at the same time, you will receive an e-mail from your partner.

TROUBLE
If you do not receive a message, your partner has not yet completed the steps to share the folder.

6. **Check your e-mail for a message advising you that your partner has shared a folder with you**

   The subject of the e-mail message will be "[Name] has shared documents with you."

7. **If you have received the e-mail, click the Show content link that appears in the warning box, if necesary, then click WEB-QST Vancouver 2.pptx in the body of the e-mail message**

   The PowerPoint presentation opens in the Microsoft PowerPoint Web App. You will work in the Web App in the next lesson.

Co-authoring documents

You can work on a document, presentation, or workbook simultaneously with a partner. First, save the file to your SkyDrive. Click the FILE tab, click Share, then click Invite People. Enter the email addresses of the people you want to work on the file with you and then click Share. Once your partner has received, opened, and started editing the document, you can start working together. You will see a notification in the status bar that someone is editing the document with you. When you click the notification, you can see the name of the other user and their picture if they have one attached to their Windows account. When your partner saves, you'll see his or changes in green shading which goes away the next time you save. You'll have an opportunity to co-author documents when you complete the Team Project at the end of this appendix.

FIGURE WEB-10: **Sharing a file from SkyDrive**

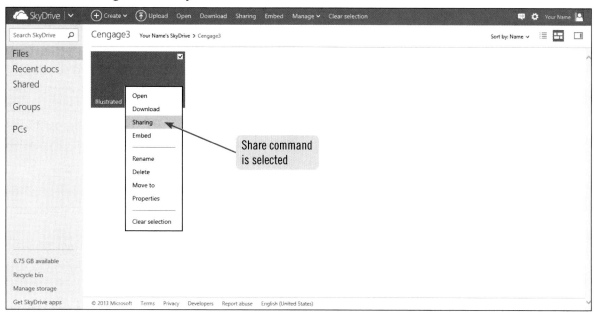

FIGURE WEB-11: **Sharing a file with another person**

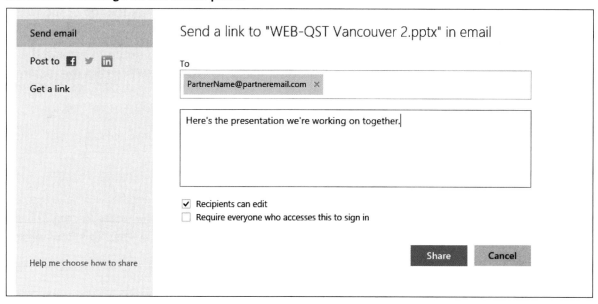

Cloud

Explore Office Web Apps

Learning Outcomes
• Edit a presentation with PowerPoint Web App
• Open a presentation from PowerPoint Web App

As you have learned, a Web App is a scaled-down version of an Office program. Office Web Apps include Word, Excel, PowerPoint, and OneNote. You can use the Office Web Apps to create and edit documents even if you don't have Office 2013 installed on your computer and you can use them on other devices such as tablets and smartphones. From SkyDrive, you can also open the document in the full Office application if the application is installed on the computer you are using. **CASE** *You use the PowerPoint Web App and the full version of PowerPoint to edit the presentation.*

STEPS

1. **Click EDIT PRESENTATION, then click Edit in PowerPoint Web App**

   Presentations opened using the PowerPoint Web App have the same look and feel as presentations opened using the full version of PowerPoint. However, like all of the Office Web Apps, the PowerPoint Web App has fewer features available than the full version of PowerPoint.

2. **Review the Ribbon and its tabs to familiarize yourself with the commands you can access from the PowerPoint Web App**

   TABLE WEB-1 summarizes the commands that are available.

TROUBLE
You need to click the text first, click it again, then drag to select it.

3. **Click Slide 3, click the text Hornby Island, click it again and select it, then type Tofino so the bullet item reads Tofino Sea Kayaking**

4. **Click outside the text box, click the DESIGN tab, then click the More Themes list arrow ▼ to show the selection of designs available**

   A limited number of designs are available on the PowerPoint Web App. When you want to use a design or a command that is not available on the PowerPoint Web App, you open the file in the full version of PowerPoint.

5. **Click on a blank area of the slide, click OPEN IN POWERPOINT at the top of the window, then click Yes in response to the message**

6. **Click the DESIGN tab, click the More button ▼ in the Themes group to expand the Themes gallery, select the Quotable design as shown in FIGURE WEB-12, click the picture on Slide 1, then press [Delete]**

7. **Click the Save button 🖫 on the Quick Access toolbar**

   The Save button includes a small icon indicating you are saving to SkyDrive and not to your computer's hard drive or an external drive.

8. **Click the Close button ✕ to exit PowerPoint**

   You open the document again to verify that your partner made the same changes.

9. **Launch PowerPoint, click WEB-QST Vancouver 2.pptx at the top of the Recent list, verify that the Quotable design is applied and the picture is removed, then exit PowerPoint**

Exploring other Office Web Apps

Three other Office Web Apps are Word, Excel, and OneNote. You can share files on SkyDrive directly from any of these applications using the same method you used to share files from PowerPoint. To familiarize yourself with the commands available in an Office Web App, open the file and then review the commands on each tab on the Ribbon. If you want to perform a task that is not available in the Web App, open the file in the full version of the application.

FIGURE WEB-12: Selecting the Quotable design

TABLE WEB-1: Commands on the PowerPoint Web App

tab	category/group	options
FILE	Info	• Open in PowerPoint (also available on the toolbar above the document window)
		• Previous Versions
	Save As	• Where's the Save Button?: In PowerPoint Web App, the presentation is being saved automatically so there is no Save button
		• Download: use to download a copy of the presentation to your computer
	Print	• Create a printable PDF of the presentation that you can then open and print
	Share	• Share with people - you can invite others to view and edit your presentation
		• Embed - include the presentation in a blog on Web site
	About	• Try Microsoft Office, Terms of Use, and Privacy and Cookies
	Help	• Help with PowerPoint questions, Give Feedback to Microsoft, and modify how you can view the presentation (for example, text only)
	Exit	• Close the presentation and exit to view SkyDrive folders
HOME	Clipboard	• Cut, Copy, Paste, Format Painter
	Delete	• Delete a slide
	Slides	• Add a new slide, duplicate a slide, hide a slide
	Font	• Change the font, size, style, and color of selected text
	Paragraph	• Add bullets and numbering, indent text, align text, and change text direction
	Drawing	• Add text boxes and shapes, arrange them on the slide, apply Quick Styles, modify shape fill and outline, and duplicate a shape
INSERT	Slides	• Add new slides with selected layout
	Images	• Add pictures from your computer, online pictures, or screen shots
	Illustrations	• Add shapes, SmartArt, or charts
	Links	• Add links or actions to objects
	Text	• Add comments, text boxes, headers and footers, and other text elements
	Comments	• Add comments
DESIGN	Themes	• Apply a limited number of themes to a presentation and apply variants to a selected theme
		• Apply variants to a selected theme
ANIMATIONS	Animation	• Apply a limited number of animation effects to a slide element and modify existing timings
TRANSITIONS	Transitions to This Slide	• Apply a limited number of transition effects to slides and chose to apply the effect to all slides
VIEW	Presentation Views	• You can view the slide in Editing View, Reading View, Slide Show View, and Notes View and you can show any comments made by users who worked on PowerPoint using the full version

Team Project

Introduction

From SkyDrive, you can easily collaborate with others to produce documents, presentations, and spreadsheets that include each user's input. Instead of emailing a document to colleagues and then waiting for changes, you can both work on the document at the same time online. To further explore how you can work with SkyDrive and Office 2013, you will work with two other people to complete a team project. The subject of the team project is the planning of a special event of your choice, such as a class party, a lecture, or a concert. The special event should be limited to a single afternoon or evening.

Follow the guidelines provided below to create the files required for the team project. When you have completed the project, the team will submit a Word document containing information about your project, as well as three files related to the project: a Word document, a PowerPoint presentation, and an Excel workbook.

Project Setup

As a team, work together to complete the following tasks.

a. Share email addresses among all three team members.

b. Set up a time (either via email, an online chat session, Internet Messaging, or face to face) when you will get together to choose your topic and assign roles.

c. At your meeting, complete the table below with information about your team and your special event.

Team Name (last name of one team member or another name that describes the project.)
Team Members
Event type (for example, party, lecture, concert, etc.)
Event purpose (for example, fundraiser for a specific cause, celebrate the end of term, feature a special guest, etc.)
Event location, date, and time
Team Roles indicate who is responsible for each of the following three files (one file per team member)
Word document:
Excel workbook:
PowerPoint presentation:

Document Development

Individually, complete the tasks listed below for the file you are responsible for. You need to develop appropriate content, format the file attractively, and then be prepared to share the file with the other team members.

Word Document

The Word document contains a description of your special event and includes a table listing responsibilities and a time line. Create the Word document as follows:

1. Create a Cloud Project folder on your SkyDrive, then create a new Word document and save it as **Cloud Project_ Word Description** to the Cloud Project folder.

Document Development (continued)

2. Include a title with the name of your project and a subtitle with the names of your team members. Format the title with the Title style and the subtitle with the Subtitle style.

3. Write a paragraph describing the special event—its topics, purpose, the people involved, etc. You can paraphrase some of the information your team discussed in your meeting.

4. Create a table similar to the table shown below and then complete it with the required information. Include up to ten rows. A task could be "Contact the caterers" or "Pick up the speaker." Visualize the sequence of tasks required to put on the event.

Task	Person Responsible	Deadline

5. Format the table using the table style of your choice.

6. Save the document to your SkyDrive. You will share the document with your team members and receive feedback in the next section.

Excel Workbook

The Excel workbook contains a budget for the special event. Create the Excel workbook as follows:

1. Create a new Excel workbook and save it as **Cloud Project_Excel Budget** to the Cloud Project folder on your SkyDrive.

2. Create a budget that includes both the revenues you expect from the event (for example, ticket sales, donations, etc.) and the expenses. Expense items include advertising costs (posters, ads, etc.), food costs if the event is catered, transportation costs, etc. The revenues and expenses you choose will depend upon the nature of the project.

3. Make the required calculations to total all the revenue items and all the expense items.

4. Calculate the net profit (or loss) as the revenue minus the expenses.

5. Format the budget attractively using fill colors, border lines, and other enhancements to make the data easy to read.

6. Save the workbook to your SkyDrive. You will share the workbook with your team members and receive feedback in the next section.

PowerPoint Presentation

The PowerPoint presentation contains a presentation that describes the special event to an audience who may be interested in attending. Create the PowerPoint presentation as follows:

1. Create a new PowerPoint presentation and save it as **Cloud Project_PowerPoint Presentation** to the Cloud Project folder on your SkyDrive.

2. Create a presentation that consists of five slides including the title slide as follows:
   a. Slide 1: Title slide includes the name of the event and your team members
   b. Slide 2: Purpose of the party or event
   c. Slide 3: Location, time, and cost
   d. Slide 4: Chart showing a breakdown of costs (to be supplied when you co-author in the next section)
   e. Slide 5: Motivational closing slide designed to encourage the audience to attend; include appropriate pictures

3. Format the presentation attractively using the theme of your choice.

4. Save the presentation to your SkyDrive. You will share the presentation with your team members and receive feedback.

Co-Authoring on Skydrive

You need to share your file, add feedback to the other two files, then create a final version of your file. When you read the file created by the other two team members, you need to add additional data or suggestions. For example, if you created the Excel budget, you can provide the person who created the PowerPoint presentation with information about the cost break-down. If you created the Word document, you can add information about the total revenue and expenses contained in the Excel budget to your description. You decide what information to add to each of the two files you work with.

1. Open the file you created.
2. Click the **FILE tab**, click **Share**, then click **Invite People**.
3. Enter the email addresses of the other two team members, then enter the following message: **Here's the file I created for our team project. Please make any changes, provide suggestions, and then save it. Thanks!** See FIGURE WEB-13.

FIGURE WEB-13

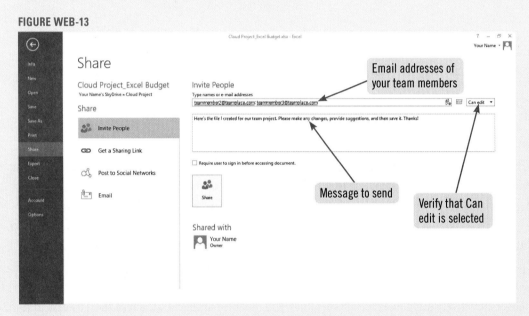

4. Click the **Share button**.
5. Allow team members time to add information and comments to your file. Team members should save frequently. When the file is saved, it is saved directly to your SkyDrive. Note that you can work together on the document or you can work separately. You can also choose to make changes with the full version of the Office 2013 applications or with the Office Web Apps. When someone is working on your file, you will see their user name on the status bar.
6. Decide which changes you want to keep, make any further changes you think are needed to make the document as clear as possible, then save a final version.

Project Summary

When you are pleased with the contents of your file and have provided feedback to your team members, assign a team member to complete the following tasks and then complete your portion as required.

1. Open **WEB-2.docx** from the location where you save your Data Files, then save it to your Cloud Project folder on your SkyDrive as **Cloud Project_Summary**.
2. Read the directions in the document, then enter your name as Team Member 1 and write a short description of your experience working with SkyDrive and Office 2013 to complete the team project.
3. Share the file with your team members and request that they add their own names and descriptions.
4. When all team members have finished working on the document, save all the changes.
5. Make sure you store all four files completed for the project in the Cloud Project appendix on your SkyDrive, then submit them to your instructor on behalf of your team.

Glossary

.accdb The file extension for the Access 2007–2013 database file format.

.accdw The file extension for an Access Web App file.

.jpg The file extension for a JPEG file.

.laccdb The file extension for a temporary file that keeps track of record-locking information when a .accdb database is open. It helps coordinate the multiuser capabilities of an Access database so that several people can read and update the same database at the same time.

.ldb The file extension for a temporary file that keeps track of record-locking information when a .mdb database is open. It helps coordinate the multiuser capabilities of an Access database so that several people can read and update the same database at the same time.

.mdb The file extension for the Access 2000–2003 database file format.

Access Web App A special type of Access database that is stored on a SharePoint 2013 server and allows users to enter and edit data using a common browser.

Accessories Simple Windows application programs (apps) that perform specific tasks, such as the Calculator accessory for performing calculations. Also called Windows accessories.

Action Each task that you want a macro to perform.

Action block In Macro Design View, the area of the window that organizes all of the arguments for a current action.

Action query A query that changes all of the selected records when it is run. Access provides four types of action queries: Delete, Update, Append, and Make Table.

Active window The window you are currently using; if multiple windows are open, the window with the darker title bar.

Add-in Software that works with Access to add or enhance functionality.

Address A sequence of drive and folder names that describes a folder's or file's location in the file hierarchy; the highest hierarchy level is on the left, with lower hierarchy levels separated by the symbol to its right.

Address bar In a window, the area just below the title bar that shows the file hierarchy, or address of the files that appear in the file list below it; the address appears as a series of links you can click to navigate to other locations on your computer.

Adobe Reader software A software program provided free of charge by Adobe Systems for reading PDF files.

After Update A property that specifies an action to perform after an object or control is updated.

Aggregate function A function such as Sum, Avg, and Count used in a summary query to calculate information about a group of records.

Alias A property that renames a field list in Query Design View.

Alignment command A command used in Layout or Design View for a form or report to either left-, center-, or right-align a value within its control, or to align the top, bottom, right, or left edge of the control with respect to other controls.

Allow Multiple Values property A field property that allows you to store multiple values in one field, which is called a multivalued field.

Allow Value List Edits The Lookup field property that determines whether users can add to or edit the list of items.

Allow Zero Length A field property that does not allow zero-length strings (""), which are intentional "nothing" entries, such as a blank Phone Number field for an employee who does not provide a home phone number.

Alternate Back Color property A property that determines the alternating background color of the selected section in a form or report.

Anchoring A layout positioning option that allows you to tie controls together so you can work with them as a group.

AND criteria Criteria placed in the same row of the query design grid. All criteria on the same row must be true for a record to appear on the resulting datasheet.

App An application program; Windows 8 apps are designed to occupy the full screen and are available on the Start screen and at the Windows store. Desktop apps, such as Microsoft Office, open in resizable windows, and are available from many software companies.

App window The window that opens after you start an app, showing you the tools you need to use the program and any open program documents.

Append To add records to an existing table.

Append Only A field property available for Memo or Long Text fields in Access 2007 databases. When enabled, the property allows users to add data to a Memo or Long Text field, but not change or remove existing data.

Append query An action query that adds selected records to an existing table, and works like an export feature because the records are copied from one location and a duplicate set is pasted within the target table.

Append To row When creating an Append query, a row that appears in the query design grid to show how the fields in the query match fields in the target table.

Application Part An object template that creates objects such as tables and forms.

Application program Any program that lets you work with files or create and edit files such as graphics, letters, financial summaries, and other useful documents, as well as view Web pages on the Internet and send and receive e-mail. Also called an app.

Argument Information that a function uses to create the final answer. Multiple arguments in a function are separated by commas. All of the arguments for a function are surrounded by a single set of parentheses. For example, the IIf function has three arguments: IIf(logical test, value if true, value if false). In a macro, an argument provides additional information on how to carry out an action. In VBA, a constant, variable, or expression passed to a procedure that the procedure needs in order to execute.

Asterisk (*) A wildcard character used to search for any number of characters in query criteria.

Attachment A field data type for adding one or more files to a record such as images.

Attachment field A field that allows you to attach an external file such as a Word document, PowerPoint presentation, Excel workbook, or image file to a record.

AutoExec A special macro name that automatically executes when a database opens.

AutoKeys A macro designed to be assigned a key combination (such as [Shift][Ctrl][L]).

AutoNumber A field data type in which Access enters a sequential integer for each record added into the datasheet. Numbers cannot be reused even if the record is deleted.

Avg function A built-in Access function used to calculate the average of the values in a given field.

Back up (*verb*) To create a duplicate copy of a database that is stored in a secure location.

Back-end database Part of a split database that contains the table objects and is stored on a file server that all users can access.

Background image An image that fills an entire form or report, appearing "behind" the other controls.

Backstage view Appears when then FILE tab is clicked. The navigation bar on the left side contains commands to perform actions common to most Office programs, such as opening a file, saving a file, and closing the file.

Backup (*noun*) A copy of the database.

Backward-compatible Software feature that enables documents saved in an older version of a program to be opened in a newer version of the program.

Bang notation A format that separates the object type from an object name and from a control name by using [square brackets] and exclamation points (!).

Between... and Criteria Criteria that selects all records between the two dates, including the two dates. Between...and criteria work the same way as the >= and <= operators.

Blog Web log, or a personal commentary on a website.

Border A window's edge; you can drag to resize the window.

Border Style A form property that determines the appearance of the outside border of the form.

Bound control A control used in either a form or report to display data from the underlying field; used to edit and enter new data in a form.

Breakpoint A VBA debugging tool that works like a bookmark to suspend execution of the procedure at that statement so you can examine what is happening.

Brown-out A power problem caused by a dip in power, often making the lights dim.

Button A small rectangle you can click in order to issue a command to an application program.

Byte A field size that allows entries only from 0 to 255.

Calculated field A field created in Query Design View that results from an expression of existing fields, Access functions, and arithmetic operators. For example, the entry Profit: [RetailPrice]-[WholesalePrice] in the field cell of the query design grid creates a calculated field called Profit that is the difference between the values in the RetailPrice and WholesalePrice fields.

Calculation A new value that is created by entering an expression in a text box on a form or report.

Calendar Picker A pop-up calendar from which you can choose dates for a date field.

Canvas In the Paint accessory, the area in the center of the app window that you use to create drawings.

Caption A field property that determines the default field name at the top of the field column in datasheets as well as in labels on forms and reports.

Caption property A property that specifies the text to display in place of the value of the Name property for an object, control, or field.

Cascade Delete Related Records A relationship option that means that if a record in the "one" side of a one-to-many relationship is deleted, all related records in the "many" table are also deleted.

Cascade Update Related Fields A relationship option that means that if a value in the primary key field (the field on the "one" side of a one-to-many relationship) is modified, all values in the foreign key field (the field on the "many" side of a one-to-many relationship) are automatically updated as well.

Cascading Style Sheets (CSS) A powerful, flexible, and productive way to define web page formatting and layout.

Case In VBA, a programming structure that executes one of several groups of statements depending on the value of an expression.

Case sensitive An application program's (app's) ability to differentiate between uppercase and lowercase letters; usually used to describe how an operating system evaluates passwords that users type to gain entry to user accounts.

CCur function A built-in Access function used to convert an expression to Currency.

Charms bar A set of buttons that appear on the right side of the Windows 8 screen that let you find and send information, change your machine settings, and turn off your computer. When you display the Charms bar, the time and date appear on the left side of the screen.

Chart A visual representation of numeric data that helps users see comparisons, patterns, and trends in data. Also called a graph.

Chart type A category of chart layouts that determines the presentation of data on the chart such as column, pie, and line.

Chart Wizard A wizard that guides you through the steps of creating a chart in Access.

Check box A box that turns an option on when checked or off when unchecked.

Child record A record contained in the "many" table in a one-to-many relationship.

Child table The "many" table in a one-to-many relationship.

Class module An Access module that is contained and executed within specific forms and reports.

Click To quickly press and release the left button on the pointing device; also called single-click.

Client In client/server computing, the user's PC.

Client/server computing Two or more information systems cooperatively processing to solve a problem.

Clipboard A temporary Windows storage area that holds the selections you copy or cut.

Close button In a Windows title bar, the rightmost button; closes the open window, app, and/or document.

Closing tag In HTML, the tag used to mark the end of text to be identified or formatted, such as </b> for end bold.

Cloud computing Work done in a virtual environment using data, applications, and resources stored on servers and accessed over the Internet or a company's internal network rather than on users' computers.

Cloud storage File storage locations on the World Wide Web, such as Windows SkyDrive or Dropbox.

Cloud-based Refers to applications that are stored online, or "in the cloud," and not installed on your computer.

cmd The common three-character prefix for command buttons.

Code window Contains the VBA for the project selected in the Project Explorer window.

Column separator The thin line that separates the field names to the left or right.

Combo box A bound control used to display a list of possible entries for a field in which you can also type an entry from the keyboard. It is a "combination" of the list box and text box controls.

Combo Box Wizard A bound control used to display a list of possible entries for a field in which you can also type an entry from the keyboard.

Command An instruction to perform a task, such as opening a file or emptying the Recycle Bin.

Command button An unbound control used to provide an easy way to initiate an action. In Windows, a button you click to issue instructions to modify application program (app) objects.

Command Button Wizard A wizard that organizes 28 of the most common command button actions within six categories.

Command-line option A special series of characters added to the end of the path to the file (for example, C:\Quest.accdb /excl), and execute a special command when the file is opened.

Comma-separated values (CSV) A text file where fields are delimited, or separated, by commas.

Comment Text in a module that helps explain and document the code.

Comment line In VBA, a statement in the code that documents the code; it does not affect how the code runs.

Compact and repair To reorganize the pieces of the database to eliminate wasted space on the disk storage device, which also helps prevent data integrity problems.

Compact Flash (CF) card A card about the size of a matchbook that you can plug into your computer to store data. Current compact flash cards store anywhere from 128MB to about 4GB of data.

Compatibility The ability of different programs to work together and exchange data.

Compile time The period during which source code is translated to executable code.

Compile-time error In VBA, an error that occurs as a result of incorrectly constructed code and is detected as soon as you run your code or select the Compile option on the Debug menu.

Conditional expression An expression resulting in either a true or false answer that determines whether a macro action will execute. Conditional expressions are used in VBA If statements.

Conditional formatting Formatting that is based on specified criteria. For example, a text box may be conditionally formatted do display its value in red if the value is a negative number.

Constant In VBA, an value that doesn't change throughout the execution of the code.

Control Any element on a form or report such as a label, text box, line, or combo box. Controls can be bound, unbound, or calculated.

Control Box A form property that determines whether a control box (which provides access to menu commands that let you close or minimize a form, for example) are displayed in a form.

Control Name A property that specifies the name of a control on a form or report.

Control Source property A property of a bound control in a form or report that determines the field to which the control is connected.

Convert To change the database file into one that can be opened in another version of Access.

Copy To make a duplicate copy of a file, folder, or other object that you want to store in another location.

Criteria Entries (rules and limiting conditions) that determine which records are displayed when finding or filtering records in a datasheet or form, or when building a query.

Criteria syntax Rules by which criteria need to be entered. For example, text criteria syntax requires that the criteria are surrounded by quotation marks (" "). Date criteria are surrounded by pound signs (#).

Crosstab query A query that represents data in a cross-tabular layout (fields are used for both column and row headings).

Crosstab Query Wizard A wizard used to create crosstab queries and which helps identify fields that will be used for row and column headings, and fields that will be summarized within the datasheet.

Crosstab row A row in the query design grid used to specify the column and row headings and values for the crosstab query.

CSV *See* comma-separated values.

Currency A number format provided by the Format property that displays numbers with a currency symbol.

Current record The record that has the focus or is being edited.

Data area When creating a chart, the area in the Chart Wizard that determines what data the chart graphs.

Data macro A type of macro that allows you to embed macro capabilities directly in a table to add, change, or delete data based on conditions you specify.

Data type A required property for each field that defines the type of data that can be entered in each field. Valid data types include AutoNumber, Short Text, Number, Currency, Date/Time, and Long Text.

Database administration The task of making a database faster, easier, more secure, and more reliable.

Database designer The person responsible for building and maintaining tables, queries, forms, and reports.

Database Documenter A feature on the DATABASE TOOLs tab that helps you create reports containing information about the database.

Database template A tool that can be used to quickly create a new database based on a particular subject such as assets, contacts, events, or projects.

Database user The person primarily interested in entering, editing, and analyzing the data in the database.

Datasheet A spreadsheet-like grid that displays fields as columns and records as rows.

Datasheet View A view that lists the records of the object in a datasheet. Tables, queries, and most form objects have a Datasheet View.

Date function A built-in Access function used to display the current date on a form or report; enter the Date function as Date().

Debug To determine why a macro or program doesn't run correctly.

Declaration statement A type of VBA statement that precedes procedure statements and helps set rules for how the statements in the module are processed.

Default In an app window or dialog box, a value that is automatically set; you can change the default to any valid value.

Default View property A form property that determines whether a subform automatically opens in Datasheet or Continuous Forms view.

Delete query An action query that deletes selected records from one or more tables.

Delete row When creating a Delete query, a row that appears in the query design grid to specify criteria for deleting records.

Delimited text file A text file that typically stores one record on each line, with the field values separated by a common character such as a comma, tab, or dash.

Delimiter A common character, such as a comma, tab, or dash.

Deprecate To retire the usage of some type of technology in the current standard. For example, the font tag has been deprecated in the latest HTML standards.

Description A query property that allows you to better document the purpose or author of a query.

Design View A view in which the structure of the object can be manipulated. Every Access object (table, query, form, report, macro, and module) has a Design View.

Desktop apps Application programs (apps), such as Microsoft Office, that open in resizeable windows that you can move and resize to view alongside other app windows; also called traditional apps.

Desktop database A traditional Access database available to users who work with Access on their computers over a local area network. Desktop database templates are identified by the word *desktop* in the template name.

Device A hardware component that is part of your computer system, such as a disk drive, a pointing device, or a touch screen device.

Dialog box In Access, a special form used to display information or prompt a user for a choice. In Windows, a window with controls that lets you tell Windows how you want to complete an application program's (app's) command.

Dialog box launcher An icon you can click to open a dialog box or task pane from which to choose related commands.

Dim A VBA keyword that declares a variable.

DLookup A domain function that returns, or "looks up," a value from a specified table or query.

DoCmd A VBA object that supports many methods to run common Access commands such as closing windows, opening forms, previewing reports, navigating records, and setting the value of controls.

Domain The recordset (table or query) that contains the field used in a domain function calculation.

Domain function A function used in an expression to calculate a value based on a field that is not included in the Record Source property for a form or report. Also called domain aggregate function.

Double-click To quickly press and release or click the left button on the pointing device twice.

Drag To point to an object, press and hold the left button on the pointing device, move the object to a new location, and then release the left button.

Drag and drop To use a pointing device to move or copy a file or folder directly to a new location instead of using the Clipboard.

Drive A physical location on your computer where you can store files.

Drive name A name for a drive that consists of a letter followed by a colon, such as C: for the hard disk drive.

Dropbox A free online storage site that lets you transfer files that can be retrieved by other people you invite. *See also* Cloud storage.

Dynaset A property value for the Recordset Type query property that allows updates to data in a recordset.

Edit List Items button A button you click to add items to the combo box list in Form View.

Edit mode When working with Access records, the mode in which Access assumes you are trying to edit a particular field, so keystrokes such as [Ctrl][End], [Ctrl][Home], [←], and [→] move the insertion point within the field. When working with charts, a mode that lets you select and modify individual chart elements such as the title, legend, bars, or axes.

Edit record symbol A pencil-like symbol that appears in the record selector box to the left of the record that is currently being edited in either a datasheet or a form.

Else The part of an If statement that allows you to run a different set of actions if the conditional expression evaluates False.

ElseIf In VBA, a keyword that executes a statement depending on the value of an expression.

Empty tag In HTML, a single, unpaired tag that ends with a forward slash, such as <br/> for line break.

Enabled property A control property that determines whether the control can have the focus in Form View.

Encryption To make the data in the database unreadable by tools other than opening the Access database itself, which is protected by a password.

End Function In VBA, a required statement to mark the end of the code that defines the new function.

End If In VBA, a statement needed to mark the end of the If block of code.

End Select When defining a new Select Case group of VBA statements, the End Select statement is required as the last statement to mark the end of the VBA code.

End Sub When defining a new sub in VBA, the End Sub statement is required as the last statement to mark the end of the VBA code that defines the sub.

Error indicator An icon that automatically appears in Design View to indicate some type of error. For example, a green error indicator appears in the upper-left corner of a text box in Form Design View if the text box Control Source property is set to a field name that doesn't exist.

Event A specific activity that happens in a database, such as the click of a command button or an entry in a field, that can be used to initiate the execution of a macro or VBA procedure.

Event handler A procedure that is triggered by an event. Also called an event procedure.

Exclusive mode A mode indicating that you are the only person who has the database open, and others cannot open the file during this time.

Export To copy Access information to another database, spreadsheet, or file format.

Expression A combination of values, functions, and operators that calculates to a single value. Access expressions start with an equal sign and are placed in a text box in either Form Design View or Report Design View.

Expression Builder A dialog box that helps you evaluate and create expressions.

Extensible Markup Language (XML) A programming language in which data can be placed in text files and structured so that most programs can read the data.

External hard drive A device that plugs into a computer using either a USB or FireWire port and stores anywhere from 20 to 900 GB of information.

Field In a table, a field corresponds to a column of data, a specific piece or category of data such as a first name, last name, city, state, or phone number.

Field list A list of the available fields in the table or query that the field list represents. Also, a pane that opens in Access and lists the database tables and the fields they contain.

Field name The name given to each field in a table.

Field Properties pane The lower half of Table Design View, which displays field properties.

Field property A property that helps define a field.

Field selector In Query Design View, the thin gray bar above a field name in the query grid.

Field selector button The button to the left of a field in Table Design View that indicates which field is currently selected.

Field Size property A field property that determines the number of characters that can be entered in a field.

File A stored collection of data; in Access, the entire database and all of its objects are in one file.

File Explorer A Windows accessory that allows you to navigate your computer's file hierarchy and manage your files and folders.

File extension A three- or four-letter sequence, preceded by a period, at the end of a filename that identifies the file as a particular type of document; for example, documents in the Rich Text Format have the file extension .rtf.

File hierarchy The tree-like structure of folders and files on your computer.

File list A section of a window that shows the contents of the folder or drive currently selected in the Navigation pane.

File management The ability to organize folders and files on your computer.

Filename A unique, descriptive name for a file that identifies the file's content.

Filter A way to temporarily display only those records that match given criteria.

Filter By Form A way to filter data that allows two or more criteria to be specified at the same time.

Filter By Selection A way to filter records for an exact match.

Find Duplicates Query Wizard A wizard used to create a query that determines whether a table contains duplicate values in one or more fields.

Find Unmatched Query Wizard A wizard that guides you through the steps of creating a query that finds records in one table that do not have matching records in a related table.

First normal form (1NF) The first degree of normalization, in which a table has rows and columns with no repeating groups.

Focus The property that indicates which field would be edited if you were to start typing.

Folder An electronic container that helps you organize your computer files, like a cardboard folder on your desk; it can contain subfolders for organizing files into smaller groups.

Folder name A unique, descriptive name for a folder that helps identify the folder's contents.

Force New Page A property that forces a report section to start printing at the top of a new page.

Foreign key field In a one-to-many relationship between two tables, the foreign key field is the field in the "many" table that links the table to the primary key field in the "one" table.

Form An Access object that provides an easy-to-use data entry screen that generally shows only one record at a time.

Form Header The section of a form that appears at the beginning of a form and typically displays the form title.

Form section A location in a form that contains controls. The section in which a control is placed determines where and how often the control prints.

Form View View of a form object that displays data from the underlying recordset and allows you to enter and update data.

Form Wizard An Access wizard that helps you create a form.

Format A property that provides ways to format text, dates, and numbers.

Format Painter A tool you can use when designing and laying out forms and reports to copy formatting characteristics from one control to another.

Format property A field property that controls how information is displayed and printed.

Formatting Enhancing the appearance of information through font, size, and color changes.

Forum Electronic gathering place where anyone can add questions and answers on computer issues.

FROM A SQL keyword that determines how tables are joined.

Front-end database Part of a split database that contains the database objects other than tables (queries, forms, reports, macros, and modules), and which links to the back-end database tables.

Function A special, predefined formula that provides a shortcut way to make a calculation. Sum, Count, and IIF are examples of built-in Access functions. You can create custom functions using VBA.

Gallery A visual collection of choices you can browse through to make a selection. Often available with Live Preview.

Gesture An action you take with your fingertip directly on the screen, such as tapping or swiping, to make a selection or perform a task.

Get External Data – Excel Spreadsheet A dialog box used to import data from an external file into an Access database.

Gigabyte (GB or G) One billion bytes (or one thousand megabytes).

Graphic image See Image.

Grouping A way to sort records in a particular order, as well as provide a section before and after each group of records.

Groups Each tab on the Ribbon is arranged into groups to make features easy to find.

Hard disk A built-in, high-capacity, high-speed storage medium for all the software, folders, and files on a computer. Also called a hard drive.

Hidden A property you can apply to an object to hide the object in the Navigation Pane.

Highlighted Describes the changed appearance of an item or other object, usually a change in its color, background color, and/or border; often used for an object on which you will perform an action, such as a desktop icon.

HTML 5 the latest version of HTML as defined by the leading international standards committee on fundamental Web technologies, the W3C, www.w3c.org.

Hyperlink Address property A control property that allows the control to behave like a hyperlink.

Hyperlink control A control on a form that when clicked, works like a hyperlink to redirect the user to a web page or file.

Hyperlink data type A data type for fields that store a link to a web page, file, or email address.

Hyperlink field A field with the Hyperlink data type.

Hyperlink pointer A mouse pointer that looks like a pointing hand when it is positioned over a hyperlink.

Hypertext Markup Language (HTML) The language used to describe content in a traditional web page.

Icon A small image that represents an item, such as the Recycle Bin on your computer; you can rearrange, add, and delete desktop icons.

If statement A statement in a macro that allows you to run macro actions based on the result of a conditional expression.

If...Then In VBA, a logical structure that executes code (the code that follows the Then statement) when the value of an expression is true (the expression follows the If statement).

If...Then...Else In VBA, a logical structure that allows you to test logical conditions and execute statements only if the conditions are true. If...Then...Else code can be composed of one or several statements, depending on how many conditions you want to test, how many possible answers you want to provide, and what you want the code to do based on the results of the tests.

Image A nontextual piece of information such as a picture, piece of clip art, drawn object, or graph. Because images are graphical (and not numbers or letters), they are sometimes referred to as graphical images.

Immediate window In the Visual Basic Editor, a pane where you can determine the value of any argument at the breakpoint.

Import To quickly convert data from an external file into an Access database. You can import data from one Access database to another—or from many other data sources such as files created by Excel, SharePoint, Outlook, or text files in an HTML, XML, or delimited text file format.

Import Spreadsheet Wizard A wizard that guides you through the steps of importing data from Excel into an Access database.

Inactive window An open window you are not currently using; if multiple windows are open, the window(s) with the dimmed title bar.

Index A field property that keeps track of the order of the values in the indexed field as data is being entered and edited. Therefore, if you often sort on a field, the Index property should be set to Yes as this theoretically speeds up the presentation of the sorted data later (because the index has already been created).

Indexed property A field property used to improve database performance when a field is often used for sorting.

Infinity symbol The symbol that indicates the "many" side of a one-to-many relationship.

Inner join A type of relationship in which a query displays only records where joined fields from *both* tables are equal. This means that if a parent table has any records for which there are no matching records in the child table, those records do not appear in the resulting datasheet.

Input Mask A field property that provides a visual guide for users as they enter data.

Insertion point A blinking vertical line that appears when you click in a text box; indicates where new text will be inserted.

Integrate To incorporate a document and parts of a document created in one program into another program; for example, to incorporate an Excel chart into a PowerPoint slide, or an Access report into a Word document.

IntelliSense technology In VBA, visual aids that appear as you write a VBA statement to help you complete it.

Interface The look and feel of a program; for example, the appearance of commands and the way they are organized in the program window.

Is Not Null An operator you use to query for any value other than a null value; it finds all records in which any entry has been made in the field.

Is Null An operator you use to query for null values; it finds all records in which no entry has been made in the field.

Join line The line identifying which fields establish the relationship between two related tables. Also called a link line.

JPEG (Joint Photographic Experts Group) Acronym for Joint Photographic Experts Group, which defines the standards for the compression algorithms that allow image files to be stored in an efficient compressed format. JPEG files use the .jpg filename extension.

Junction table A table created to establish separate one-to-many relationships to two tables that have a many-to-many relationship.

Key symbol The symbol appearing to the left of a primary key field.

Keyword A descriptive word or phrase you enter to obtain a list of results that include that word or phrase.

Label control An unbound control that displays text to describe and clarify other information on a form or report.

Label Wizard A report wizard that precisely positions and sizes information to print on a vast number of standard business label specifications.

Landscape orientation A way to print or view a page that is 11 inches wide by 8.5 inches tall.

Launch To open or start a program on your computer.

Layout The general arrangement in which a form displays the fields in the underlying recordset. Layout types include Columnar, Tabular, and Datasheet. Columnar is most popular for a form, and Datasheet is most popular for a subform. In Windows, an arrangement of files or folders in a window, such as Large icons or Details. There are eight layouts available.

Layout View An Access view that lets you make some design changes to a form or report while you are browsing the data.

Left function An Access function that returns a specified number of characters, starting with the left side of a value in a Text field.

Left outer join A type of relationship in which a query displays all of the records in the "one" table, regardless of whether they have matching records in the "many" table. Also called a left join.

Len function Built-in Access function used to return the number of characters in a field.

Library A window that shows files and folders stored in different storage locations; default libraries in Windows 8 include the Documents, Music, Pictures, and Videos libraries.

Like operator An operator used in a query to find values in a field that match the pattern you specify.

Limit to List A combo box control property that allows you to limit the entries made by that control to those provided by the combo box list.

Line A graphical element that can be added to a report to highlight information or enhance its clarity.

Link To connect an Access database to data in an external file such as another Access database; an Excel or other type of spreadsheet; a text file; an HTML file; or an XML file. In Windows, text or an image that you click to display another location, such as a Help topic, a Web site, or a device.

Link Child Fields A subform property that determines which field serves as the "many" link between the subform and main form.

Link line The line identifying which fields establish the relationship between two related tables.

Link Master Fields A subform property that determines which field serves as the "one" link between the main form and the subform.

Link Spreadsheet Wizard A wizard that guides you through the steps of linking to a spreadsheet.

List box A bound control that displays a list of possible choices for the user. Used mainly on forms. In Windows, a box that displays a list of options from which you can choose (you may need to scroll and adjust your view to see additional options in the list).

List Rows A control property that determines how many items can be displayed in a list, such as in a combo box.

Live Preview A feature that lets you point to a choice in a gallery or palette and see the results in the document or object without actually clicking the choice.

Live tile Updated, "live" content that appears on some apps' tiles on the Windows Start screen, including the Weather app and the News app.

Load To copy and place an app into your computer's memory in preparation for use.

Local area network (LAN) A type of network installed to link multiple PCs together so they can share hardware and software resources.

Lock screen The screen that appears when you first start your computer, or after you leave it unattended for a period of time, before the sign-in screen.

Locked property A control property that specifies whether you can edit data in a control in Form View.

Log in To select a user account name when a computer starts up, giving access to that user's files. Also called sign in.

Logic error In VBA, an error that occurs when the code runs without obvious problems, but the procedure still doesn't produce the desired result.

Logical view The datasheet of a query is sometimes called a logical view of the data because it is not a copy of the data, but rather, a selected view of data from the underlying tables.

Long Date A date format provided by the Format property that displays dates in the following format: Friday, June 19, 2016.

Long Integer The default field size for a Number field.

Lookup field A field that has Lookup properties.

Lookup properties Field properties that allow you to supply a drop-down list of values for a field.

Lookup table A table that contains one record for each field value and supplies the values for a foreign key field in another table.

Lookup Wizard A wizard used in Table Design View that allows one field to "look up" values from another table or entered list. For example, you might use the Lookup Wizard to specify that the Customer Number field in the Sales table display the Customer Name field entry from the Customers table.

Macro An Access object that stores a collection of keystrokes or commands.

Macro Design View An Access window in which you create and modify macros.

Mail merge A way to export Access data by merging it to a Word document. Data from an Access table or query is combined into a Word form letter, label, or envelope to create mass mailing documents.

Main document In a mail merge, the document used to determine how the letter and Access data are combined. This is the standard text that will be consistent for each letter created in the mail merge process.

Main form A form that contains a subform control.

Main report A report that contains a subreport control.

Make Table query An action query that creates a new table of data for a selected datasheet. The location of the new table can be the current database or another Access database.

Many-to-many relationship The relationship between two tables in an Access database in which one record of one table relates to many records in the other table and vice versa. You cannot directly create a many-to-many relationship between two tables in Access. To relate two tables with such a relationship, you must establish a third table called a junction table that creates separate one-to-many relationships with the two original tables.

Maximize button On the right side of a window's title bar, the center button of three buttons; used to expand a window so that it fills the entire screen. In a maximized window, this button changes to a Restore button.

Maximized window A window that fills the desktop.

Medium Date A date format provided by the Format property that displays dates in the dd-Mmm-yy format, such as 19-Jun-16.

Megabyte (MB or M) One million bytes (or one thousand kilobytes).

Menu A list of related commands.

Merge field A code in the main document of a mail merge that is replaced with the values in the field that the code represents when the mail merge is processed.

MessageBox A macro action that displays an informational message to the user.

Method An action that an object can perform. Procedures are often written to invoke methods in response to user actions.

Microsoft Community Website A Microsoft Help feature that lets you search forums (electronic gathering places where anyone can add questions and answers on computer issues), Microsoft help files, and even on-screen video demonstrations about selected topics. (Formerly the Microsoft Answers website.)

Microsoft Excel The spreadsheet program in the Microsoft Office suite.

Microsoft SkyDrive A Microsoft Web site where you can obtain free file storage space, using your own account, that you can share with others; you can access SkyDrive from a laptop, tablet computer, or smartphone.

Microsoft Windows 8 An operating system.

Microsoft Word The word-processing program in the Microsoft Office suite.

Microsoft Word Mail Merge Wizard A wizard that guides you through the steps of preparing to merge Access data with a Word document.

Min Max Buttons A form property that determines whether Minimize and Maximize buttons are displayed in a form.

Minimize button On the right side of a window's title bar, the leftmost button of three buttons; use to reduce a window so that it only appears as an icon on the taskbar.

Minimized window A window that is visible only as an icon on the taskbar.

Module An Access object that stores Visual Basic for Applications (VBA) programming code that extends the functions of automated Access processes.

Mouse pointer A small arrow or other symbol on the screen that you move by manipulating the pointing device; also called a pointer.

Move To change the location of a file, folder, or other object by physically placing it in another location.

Multicolumn report A report that repeats the same information in more than one column on the page.

Multifield primary key A primary key that is composed of two or more fields. For example, an OrderID value can be listed multiple times in the Order Details table, and a ProductID value can be listed multiple times in the Order Details table. But the combination of a particular OrderID value plus a ProductID value should be unique for each record.

Multiuser A characteristic that means more than one person can enter and edit data in the same Access database at the same time.

Multivalued field A field that allows you to make more than one choice from a drop-down list.

My Documents folder The folder on your hard drive used to store most of the files you create or receive from others; might contain subfolders to organize the files into smaller groups.

Name property The property that determines that name of a control or object that is used when you want to work with that control or object in VBA.

Navigate down To move to a lower level in your computer's file hierarchy.

Navigate up To move to a higher level in your computer's file hierarchy.

Navigation Buttons A form property that determines whether a navigation bar is displayed in a form.

Navigation buttons Buttons in the lower-left corner of a datasheet or form that allow you to quickly navigate between the records in the underlying object as well as add a new record.

Navigation form A special Access form that provides an easy-to-use database interface to navigate between the objects of the database.

Navigation mode A mode in which Access assumes that you are trying to move between the fields and records of the datasheet (rather than edit a specific field's contents), so keystrokes such as [Ctrl][Home] and [Ctrl][End] move you to the first and last field of the datasheet.

Navigation Pane A pane in the Access program window that provides a way to move between objects (tables, queries, forms, reports, macros, and modules) in the database.

Navigation system style In a navigation form, a style that determines how the navigation buttons will be displayed on the form.

Normalize To structure data for a relational database.

Northwind.mdb A fully developed relational database in an Access 2000 file format that illustrates many advanced database techniques you can apply to your own development needs.

Notification area An area on the right side of the Windows 8 taskbar that displays the current time as well as icons representing apps; displays pop-up messages when a program on your computer needs your attention.

Now() An Access function that displays today's date.

Null A field value that means that a value has not been entered for the field.

Null entry The state of "nothingness" in a field. Any entry such as 0 in a numeric field or a space in a text field is not null. It is common to search for empty fields by using the Null criterion in a filter or query. The Is Not Null criterion finds all records where there is an entry of any kind.

Object A table, query, form, report, macro, or module in a database. In VBA, any item that can be identified or manipulated is an objective, including the traditional Access objects (table, query, form, report, macro, module) as well as other items that have properties such as controls, sections, and existing procedures.

Object dependency Indicates whether an object depends on the selected object or whether the selected object depends on other objects and displayed in the Object Dependencies task pane.

Object list In a VBA class module, lists the objects associated with the current form or report.

ODBC *See* open database connectivity

On Click A property of a control such as a command button that triggers an event when the control is clicked.

On Current An event that occurs when focus moves from one record to another in a form.

On Dbl Click An Access event that is triggered by a double-click.

On Error GoTo Upon an error in the execution of a procedure, the On Error GoTo statement specifies the location (the statement) where the procedure should continue.

On Got Focus An Access event that is triggered when a specified control gets the focus.

One-to-many line The line that appears in the Relationships or query design window and shows which field is duplicated between two tables to serve as the linking field. The one-to-many line displays a "1" next to the field that serves as the "one" side of the relationship and displays an infinity symbol next to the field that serves as the "many" side of the relationship when referential integrity is specified for the relationship. Also called the one-to-many join line.

One-to-many relationship The relationship between two tables in an Access database in which a common field links the tables together. The linking field is called the primary key field in the "one" table of the relationship and the foreign key field in the "many" table of the relationship.

Online collaboration The ability to incorporate feedback or share information across the Internet or a company network or intranet.

Open database connectivity (ODBC) A collection of standards that govern how Access connects to other sources of data.

Opening tag In HTML, the tag used to mark the beginning of text to be identified or formatted, such as <b> for start bold.

OpenReport action A macro action that opens a specified report.

Operating system A program that manages the complete operation of your computer and lets you interact with it.

Option button A bound control used to display a limited list of mutually exclusive choices for a field, such as "female" or "male" for a gender field in form or report. In Windows, a small circle in a dialog box that you click to select only one of two or more related options.

Option Compare Database A VBA declaration statement that determines the way string values (text) will be sorted.

Option Explicit A VBA declaration statement that specifies that you must explicitly declare all variables used in all procedures; if you attempt to use an undeclared variable name, an error occurs at compile time.

Option group A bound control placed on a form that is used to group together several option buttons that provide a limited number of values for a field.

Option Value An option button property that determines the value entered into a field when the option button is selected.

OR criteria Criteria placed on different rows of the query design grid. A record will appear in the resulting datasheet if it is true for any single row.

ORDER BY A SQL keyword that determines how records in the query result are sorted.

Orphan record A record in the "many" table of a one-to-many relationship that doesn't have a matching entry in the linking field of the "one" table.

Padding The space between controls.

Parameter criteria Text entered in [square brackets] that prompts the user for an entry each time the query is run.

Parameter query A query that displays a dialog box to prompt users for field criteria. The entry in the dialog box determines which records appear on the final datasheet, similar to criteria entered directly in the query design grid.

Parameter report A report that prompts you for criteria to determine the records to use for the report.

Parent record A record contained in the "one" table in a one-to-many relationship.

Parent table The "one" table in a one-to-many relationship.

Password A combination of uppercase and lowercase letters, numbers, and symbols that when entered correctly, allow you to open a database (Access) or a user account (Windows).

Paste To place a copied item from the Clipboard to a location in a document.

Path An address that describes the exact location of a file in a file hierarchy; shows the folder with the highest hierarchy level on the left and steps through each hierarchy level toward the right. Locations are separated by small triangles or by backslashes.

Percent A number format provided by the Format property that displays numbers with a percent symbol.

Performance Analyzer An Access tool that studies the structure and size of your database and makes a variety of recommendations on how you can improve its performance.

Photos app A Windows 8 app that lets you view and organize your pictures.

Picture A form and report property that determines which image is displayed in the form or report (if any).

Pixel (picture element) One pixel is the measurement of one picture element on the screen.

Pmt function Built-in Access function used to calculate the monthly payment on a loan; enter the Pmt function as Pmt([Rate],[Term],[Loan]).

Point To position the tip of the mouse pointer over an object, option, or item.

Pointer *See* Mouse pointer.

Pointing device A device that lets you interact with your computer by controlling the movement of the mouse pointer on your computer screen; examples include a mouse, trackball, touchpad, pointing stick, on-screen touch pointer, or a tablet.

Pointing device action A movement you execute with your computer's pointing device to communicate with the computer; the five basic pointing device actions are point, click, double-click, drag, and right-click.

Portable Document Format (PDF) A file format developed by Adobe Systems that has become the standard format for exchanging documents.

Portrait orientation A way to print or view a page that is 8.5 inches wide by 11 inches tall.

Power button The physical button on your computer that turns your computer on.

Preview pane A pane on the right side of a window that shows the actual contents of a selected file without opening an app; might not work for some types of files.

Previewing Prior to printing, seeing onscreen exactly how the printout will look.

Primary key field A field that contains unique information for each record. A primary key field cannot contain a null entry.

Print Preview An Access view that shows you how a report or other object will print on a sheet of paper.

Private Sub A statement that indicates that a sub procedure is accessible only to other procedures in the module where it is declared.

Procedure A series of VBA statements that performs an operation or calculates an answer. VBA has two types of procedures: functions and subs.

Procedure list In a VBA standard module, lists the procedures in the module; in a class module, lists events (such as Click or Dblclick).

Program A set of instructions written for a computer, such as an operating system program or an application program; also called an application or an app.

Project In VBA, a module object or a form or report object that contains a class module.

Project Explorer window In the Visual Basic Editor, a window you use to switch between objects that can contain VBA code.

Property A characteristic that defines the appearance and behavior of items in the database such as objects, fields, sections, and controls. You can view the properties for an item by opening its Property Sheet. In a macro, an argument that determines what property is being modified.

Property Sheet A window that displays an exhaustive list of properties for the chosen control, section, or object within the Form Design View or Report Design View.

Property Update Options A Smart Tag that applies property changes in one field to other objects of the database that use the field.

Query An Access object that provides a spreadsheet-like view of the data, similar to that in tables. It may provide the user with a subset of fields and/or records from one or more tables. Queries are created when the user has a "question" about the data in the database.

Query Datasheet View The view of a query that shows the selected fields and records as a datasheet.

Query design grid The bottom pane of the Query Design View window in which you specify the fields, sort order, and limiting criteria for the query.

Query Design View The window in which you develop queries by specifying the fields, sort order, and limiting criteria that determine which fields and records are displayed in the resulting datasheet.

Question mark (?) A wildcard character used to search for any single character in query criteria.

Quick Access toolbar A small toolbar on the left side of a Microsoft application window's title bar, containing icons that you click to quickly perform common actions, such as saving a file.

RAM (Random Access Memory) The storage location that is part of every computer, that temporarily stores open apps and document data while a computer is on.

Read-only An object property that indicates whether the object can read and display data, but cannot be used to change (write to) data.

Record A row of data in a table.

Record Selectors A form property that determines whether record selectors are displayed in a form.

Record Source A property of a form or report that identifies the table or query containing the data to display.

Recordset Type A property that determines if and how records displayed by a query are locked. The Recordset Type settings are Snapshot and Dynaset.

Recycle Bin A desktop object that stores folders and files you delete from your hard drive(s) and enables you to restore them.

Referential integrity A set of Access rules that govern data entry and help ensure data accuracy.

Relational database software Software such as Access that is used to manage data organized in a relational database.

Relationship report A printout of the Relationships window that shows how a relational database is designed and includes table names, field names, primary key fields, and one-to-many relationship lines.

Removable storage Storage media that you can easily transfer from one computer to another, such as DVDs, CDs, or USB flash drives.

Report An Access object that creates a professional printout of data that may contain such enhancements as headers, footers, and calculations on groups of records.

Report Design View An Access view that allows you to work with a complete range of report, section, and control properties.

Report Wizard An Access wizard that helps you create a report.

Restore Down button On the right side of a maximized window's title bar, the center of three buttons; use to reduce a window to its last non-maximized size. In a restored window, this button changes to a Maximize button.

Ribbon Appears below the title bar in every Office program window, and displays commands you're likely to need for the current task.

Rich Text A Text Format property that allows you to mix formatting of text displayed by a text box on a form or a report.

Rich Text Format (RTF) A file format for exporting data to a text file that can be opened and edited in Word. Also, the file format that the WordPad app uses to save files.

Right function Built-in Access function used to return the specified number of characters from the end of a field value.

Right outer join A type of relationship in which a query selects all records in the "many" table even if there are no matches in the "one" table. Also called a right join.

Right-click To press and release the right button on the pointing device; use to display a shortcut menu with commands you issue by left-clicking them.

Roaming setting A computer setting, such as your account name or picture, that you can access from any connected device.

Row Source A property that defines the values to display in a list, such as in a Lookup field or combo box.

RTF *See* Rich Text Format.

Ruler A vertical or horizontal guide that appears in Form and Report Design View to help you position controls.

Run a query To open a query and view the fields and records that you have selected for the query presented as a datasheet.

Run-time error In VBA, an error that occurs as incorrectly constructed code runs and includes attempting an illegal operation such as dividing by zero or moving focus to a control that doesn't exist. When you encounter a run-time error, VBA will stop executing your procedure at the statement in which the error occurred and highlight the line with a yellow background in the Visual Basic Editor.

Save As command A command on the FILE tab that saves the entire database (and all objects it contains) or only the current object with a new name.

Save Database As An Access command that saves an entire database including all of its objects to a completely new database file.

Save Object As An Access command that allows you to save the current object, such as a table, query, form, report, macro, or module with a new name.

Saved Exports An option provided in Access that lets you quickly repeat the export process by saving the export steps.

Saved Imports An option provided in Access that lets you quickly repeat the import process by saving the import steps.

Schema A description of the fields and their properties stored in XML data.

Screen capture An electronic snapshot of your screen, as if you took a picture of it with a camera, which you can paste into a document.

ScreenTip A small box containing informative text that appears when you position the mouse over an object; identifies the object when you point to it.

Scroll To adjust your view to see portions of the app window that are not currently in a window.

Scroll arrow In Windows, a button at each end of a scroll bar for adjusting your view in a window in small increments in that direction.

Scroll Bars A form property that determines whether vertical, horizontal, or both scroll bars are displayed in a form.

Scroll box In Windows, a box in a scroll bar that you can drag to display a different part of a window.

Scrub the database To remove and fix orphan records.

Search Tools tab A tab that appears in the File Explorer window after you click the Search text box; lets you specify a specific search location, limit your search, repeat previous searches, save searches, and open a folder containing a found file.

Second normal form (2NF) The second degree of normalization, in which redundant data from an original table is extracted, placed in a new table, and related to the original table.

Section A location in a form or report that contains controls. The section in which a control is placed determines where and how often the control prints.

Secure digital (SD) card A small device that slips directly into a computer, and typically stores around 256 MB.

SELECT A SQL keyword that determines what fields a query selects.

Select To change the appearance of an item by clicking, double-clicking, or dragging across it, to indicate that you want to perform an action on it.

Select Case In VBA, executes one of several groups of Case statements depending on the value of an expression.

Select pointer The mouse pointer shape that looks like a white arrow pointing toward the upper-left corner of the screen.

Select query The most common type of query that retrieves data from one or more linked tables and displays the results in a datasheet.

Server In client/server computing, the shared file server, mini, or mainframe computer. The server usually handles corporate-wide computing activities such as data storage and management, security, and connectivity to other networks.

SetProperty A macro action that allows you to manipulate the property value of any control on a form.

Shared folder A folder created online, such as on SkyDrive, which you allow others to open and access.

SharePoint server A server computer that runs Microsoft SharePoint, software that allows an organization to host Web pages on an intranet.

Short Date A date format provided by the Format property that displays dates in the mm/dd/yyyy format, such as 6/19/2016.

Shortcut An icon that acts as a link to an app, file, folder, or device that you use frequently.

Shortcut menu A menu of context-appropriate commands for an object that opens when you right-click that object.

Shut down To exit the operating system and turn off your computer.

Sign in To select a user account name when a computer starts up, giving access to that user's files. Also called log in.

Simple Query Wizard An Access wizard that prompts you for information it needs to create a new query.

Single step To run a macro one line (one action) at a time to observe the effect of each specific action in the Macro Single Step dialog box.

Single-click *See* Click.

Sizing handles Small squares at each corner of a selected control in Access. Dragging a handle resizes the control. Also known as handles.

SkyDrive A cloud-based storage and file-sharing service provided by Microsoft. Saving files to SkyDrive means that you can access those files from any computer connected to the Internet.

Smart Tag A button that provides a small menu of options and automatically appears under certain conditions to help you work with a task, such as correcting errors. For example, the AutoCorrect Options button, which helps you correct typos and update properties, and the Error Indicator button, which helps identify potential design errors in Form and Report Design View, are Smart Tags.

Snap feature For desktop application programs, the Windows 8 feature that lets you drag a window to the left or right side of the screen, where it "snaps" to fill that half of the screen; also, for Windows 8 apps, the feature that lets you position one of two open apps so it occupies one- or two-thirds of the screen.

Snapshot A property value for the Recordset Type query property that locks the recordset (which prevents it from being updated).

Sort To reorder records in either ascending or descending order based on the values of a particular field. In Windows, to change the order of, such as the order of files or folders in a window, based on criteria such as date, file size, or alphabetical by filename.

Spike A surge in power, which can cause damage to the hardware.

Spin box A text box with up and down arrows; you can type a setting in the text box or click the arrows to increase or decrease the setting.

Splash screen A special form used to announce information. A splash screen is often set to automatically appear when you open a database.

Split To separate the tables into one database and the other database objects into another.

Split form A form split into two panes; the upper pane allows you to display the fields of one record in any arrangement, and the lower pane maintains a datasheet view of the first few records.

SQL (Structured Query Language) A language that provides a standardized way to request information from a relational database system.

SQL Server A Microsoft software product used to store and manage a relational database. All Access Web apps use SQL Server 2012 to manage the data.

SQL View A query view that displays the SQL code for the query.

Standard A number format provided by the Format property that displays numbers with no symbols or decimal places.

Standard module A type of Access module that contains global code that can be executed from anywhere in the database. Standard modules are displayed as module objects in the Navigation Pane.

Start screen The screen you see after you sign in to Windows 8; contains controls, such as tiles, that let you interact with the Windows 8 operating system.

Startup option One of a series of commands that execute when the database is opened.

Statement A single line of code within a VBA procedure.

Strong password A password longer than eight characters that uses a combination of uppercase and lowercase letters, numbers, and symbols.

Stub In the Visual Basic window, the first and last lines of an event handler procedure.

Sub (sub procedure) A procedure that performs a series of VBA statements, but it does not return a value and cannot be used in an expression like a function procedure. You use subs to manipulate controls and objects. They are generally executed when an event occurs, such as when a command button is clicked or a form is opened.

Subdatasheet A datasheet that is nested within another datasheet to show related records. The subdatasheet shows the records on the "many" side of a one-to-many relationship.

Subfolder A folder within another folder.

Subform A form placed within a form that shows related records from another table or query. A subform generally displays many records at a time in a datasheet arrangement.

Submacro A collection of actions within a macro object that allows you to name and create multiple, separate macros within a single macro object.

Subquery A query based on another query's field list.

Subreport A control that displays a report within another report.

Suite A group of programs that are bundled together and share a similar interface, making it easy to transfer skills and program content among them.

Sum function A mathematical function that totals values in a field.

Summary query A query used to calculate and display information about records grouped together.

Summary report A report that calculates and displays information about records grouped together.

Surge protector A power strip with surge protection.

Switchboard A special Access form that provides command buttons to help users navigate throughout a database.

Synced Short for synchronized; refers to when you add, change, or delete files on one computer and the same files on your other devices are also updated.

Syntax Rules for entering information such as query criteria or property values. In VBA, rules that govern how to write programming statements so that they execute properly.

Syntax error In VBA, an error that occurs immediately as you are writing a VBA statement that cannot be read by the Visual Basic Editor. Syntax errors are displayed in a red text color.

Tab A page in an application program's Ribbon, or in a dialog box, that contains a group of related commands and settings.

Tab control An unbound control used to create a three-dimensional aspect to a form so that other controls can be organized and shown in Form View by clicking the "tabs."

Tab Index property A form property that indicates the numeric tab order for all controls on the form that have the Tab Stop property set to Yes.

Tab order property A form property that determines the sequence in which the controls on the form receive the focus when the user presses [Tab] or [Enter] in Form view.

Tab Stop property A form property that determines whether a field accepts focus.

Table A collection of records for a single subject, such as all of the customer records; the fundamental building block of a relational database because it stores all of the data.

Table Design View A view of a table that provides the most options for defining fields.

Table layout A way of connecting controls together so that when you move or resize them in Layout or Design View, the action you take on one control applies to all the controls in the layout.

Tag In HTML, the codes used to identify or "mark up" the content in a web page. Also called an HTML element.

Target table The table to which an Append query adds records.

Taskbar The horizontal bar at the bottom of the Windows 8 desktop; displays icons representing apps, folders, and/or files on the left, and the Notification area, containing the date and time and special program messages, on the right.

td An HTML table data tag that separates each field of data in a table.

Template A sample file, such as a database provided within the Microsoft Access program.

Terabyte (TB) One triillion bytes (or one thousand gigabytes).

Text Align property A control property that determines the alignment of text within the control.

Text box The most common type of control used to display field values.

Theme A predefined set of colors, fonts, line and fill effects, and other formats that can be applied to an Access database and give it a consistent, professional look.

Third normal form (3NF) The third degree of normalization, in which calculated fields (also called derived fields) such as totals or taxes are removed. Strive to create databases that adhere to the rules of third normal form.

Tile A shaded rectangle on the Windows 8 Start screen that represents an app. *See also* App and Application program.

Toolbar In an application program, a set of buttons, lists, and menus you can use to issue program commands.

Top Values A feature in Query Design View that lets you specify a number or percentage of sorted records that you want to display in the query's datasheet.

Total row Row in the query design grid used to specify how records should be grouped and summarized with aggregate functions.

Touch pointer A pointer on the screen for performing pointing operations with a finger if touch input is available on your computer.

tr An HTML table row tag that separates each record in a table.

Traditional apps Application programs (apps), such as Microsoft Office, that open in windows that you can move and resize to view alongside other app windows; also called desktop apps.

Trusted database A database that allows you to run macros and VBA.

Trusted folder A folder specified as a trusted location for storing files.

Unbound control A control that does not change from record to record and exists only to clarify or enhance the appearance of the form, using elements such as labels, lines, and clip art.

Update query An action query that updates the values in a field.

Update To row When creating an Update query, a row that appears in the query design grid to specify criteria or an expression for updating records.

UPS (Uninterruptible Power Supply) A device that provides constant power to other devices, including computers.

USB (Universal Serial Bus) drive A device that plugs into a computer's USB port to store data. USB drives are also called thumb drives, flash drives, and travel drives. USB devices typically store 1 GB to 10 GB of information.

User account A special area in a computer's operating system where users can store their own files and preferences.

User interface A collective term for all the ways you interact with a software program.

Utility project A VBA project containing code that helps Access with certain activities such as presenting the Zoom dialog box. It automatically appears in the Project Explorer window when you use the Access features that use this code.

Validation Rule A field property that helps eliminate unreasonable entries by establishing criteria for an entry before it is accepted into the database.

Validation Text A field property that determines what message appears if a user attempts to make a field entry that does not pass the validation rule for that field.

Value argument In a macro, the argument that determines the value of a property or field.

Value field A numeric field, such as Cost, that can be summed or averaged.

Variable In VBA, a named location that stores data that can be used, modified, or displayed during the execution of the procedure.

VBA *See* Visual Basic for Applications.

VBE *See* Visual Basic Editor.

View Each Access object has different views for different purposes. For example, you work with data in Datasheet View. You modify the design of the object in Layout and Design Views. You preview a printout in Print Preview. In an Access Web App, the equivalent to a form in a traditional desktop database.

Visible property A property that determines whether a control such as a label is visible in a form or report.

Visual Basic Editor (VBE) Comprises the entire Microsoft Visual Basic program window that contains smaller windows, including the Code window and Project Explorer window.

Visual Basic for Applications (VBA) A programming language provided within each program of the Microsoft Office suite to help you extend the program's capabilities. In Access, VBA code is stored within modules.

Watermark A background picture applied to a form or report.

Web app An Access database published to a SharePoint server and which is available to users to interact with using a Web browser.

Wildcard A special character used in criteria to find, filter, and query data. The asterisk (*) stands for any group of characters. For example, the criteria I* in a State field criterion cell would find all

records where the state entry was IA, ID, IL, IN, or Iowa. The question mark (?) wildcard stands for only one character.

Window A rectangular-shaped work area that displays an app or a collection of files, folders, and Windows tools.

Window control icons The set of three buttons on the right side of a window's title bar that let you control the window's state, such as minimized, maximized, restored to its previous open size, or closed.

Windows 8 apps Apps (application programs) for Windows 8 that have a single purpose, such as Photos, News, or SkyDrive.

Windows 8 UI The Windows 8 user interface. *See also* User interface.

Windows accessories Application programs (apps), such as Paint or WordPad, that come with the Windows 8 operating system.

Windows desktop An electronic work area that lets you organize and manage your information, much like your own physical desktop.

Windows Search The Windows feature that lets you look for files and folders on your computer storage devices; to search, type text in the Search text box in the title bar of any open window, or click the Office button and type text in the Search programs and files text box.

Windows Website A link in the Windows Help app that lets you find Windows 8 resources such as blogs, video tours, and downloads.

Word wrap A feature in word processing programs that determines when a line of text extends into the right margin of the page and automatically forces the text to the next line without you needing to press Enter.

World Wide Web Consortium (W3C) The leading international standards committee on fundamental Web technologies.

XML Short for Extensible Markup Language, a language used to mark up structured data so that the data can be more easily shared between different computer programs.

XML file A text file containing XML tags that identify field names and data. *See also* Extensible Markup Language (XML).

XPS file A structured XML file that can be exchanged and read with Word, similar to a PDF file.

XSD A file that stores the schema of data stored in an XML file.

XSL A file that describes how to display the data in an XML file.

Zero-length string A deliberate entry that contains no characters. You enter a zero-length string by typing two quotation marks ("") with no space between them.

Zooming in A feature that makes a printout appear larger but shows less of it on screen at once; does not affect the actual size of the printout.

Zooming out A feature that shows more of a printout on screen at once but at a reduced size; does not affect the actual size of the printout.

Index

SPECIAL CHARACTERS

< (left angle bracket), AC 39, AC 143, AC 272
> (right angle bracket), AC 39, AC 143, AC 272
( ) (parentheses), AC 88
! (exclamation point), AC 330
(pound sign), AC 38, AC 115, AC 116, AC 120, AC 276
' (apostrophe), AC 354
* (asterisk), AC 36, AC 37, AC 115, AC 145, AC 147, AC 272, AC 276, AC 280
+ (plus sign), AC 147
– (minus sign), AC 147
/ (forward slash), AC 147
= (equal sign), AC 39, AC 64, AC 88, AC 143
? (question mark), AC 36, AC 37, AC 115, AC 145
^ (caret), AC 147
_ (underscore), AC 115
[ ] (square brackets), AC 64, AC192

A

About command, PowerPoint Web App, CL 13
.accdb (Access 2007-2013) file extension, AC 123, AC 246, AC 382, AC 383
.accdw file extension, AC 406
Access
   creating, modifying, and using Web apps, AC 407
   Excel compared, AC 2, AC 3
   filename and file extension, OFF 8
   options for customizing, AC 372, AC 373
   overview, OFF 2, OFF 3
Access 2007-2013 (.accdb) file extension, AC 123, AC 246, AC 382, AC 383
Access 2002 or 2002-2003 (.mdb) file extension, AC 123, AC 246, AC 382, AC 383
Access button, AC 222
Access Options dialog box, AC 219
action(s), macros, AC 322, AC 324, AC 325
   modifying, AC 326–327
action blocks, AC 324
Action Catalog, Macro Design View, AC 323
action queries, AC 276, AC 277
active window, WIN 12
Add-ins category, Access Options dialog box, AC 373
address(es), WIN 26

Address bar, WIN 6, WIN 26
   navigating file hierarchy, WIN 31
Adobe Reader software, AC 232
Advanced button, AC 37
After Delete event, AC 335
After Insert event, AC 335
After Update event, AC 335, AC 358
After Update property, AC 356
aggregate functions, AC 148, AC 149
   domain, AC 306–307
Alias property, AC 275
Align button, AC 168
Align Left button, AC 90, AC 93
Align Right button, AC 90, AC 93
aligning
   control edges, AC 168–169
   controls in reports, AC 90, AC 91
Allow Multiple Values property, AC 113, AC 246
Allow Value List Edits property, AC 112, AC 113
Allow Zero Length property, AC 250
Alternate Back Color property, AC 92
Alternate Row Color button, AC 93
anchoring controls, AC 67, AC 168
AND criteria, AC 38–39, AC 142–143
Animation command, PowerPoint Web App, CL 13
ANIMATIONS tab, PowerPoint Web App, CL 13
apostrophes ('), comment lines, AC 354
app(s), WIN 4
   desktop (traditional), WIN 4, WIN 8
   launching, OFF 4–5
   searching for, WIN 8
   starting, WIN 8–9
   Web. See Web apps
Append Only property, AC 251
Append queries, AC 277, AC 278–279
Append To row, AC 278
appending records, AC 222
application(s)
   cloud-based, CL 2
   Web. See Web apps
Application Parts, AC 220–221
application programs. See app(s); Web apps
ApplyFilter action, AC 325
area charts, AC 309

arguments, macros, AC 322
    Macro Design View, AC 323
    modifying, AC 326–327
    VBA, AC 346
arithmetic operators, AC 147
ARRANGE tab, Align button, AC 168
Ascending button, AC 35
asterisk (*)
    Input Mask property, AC 115
    multiplication operator, AC 147
    wildcard character, AC 36, AC 37, AC 145, AC 272,
        AC 276, AC 280
Attachment controls, forms, AC 164
Attachment data type, AC 7
Attachment fields, AC 122–123
Auto Order option, Tab Order dialog box, AC 66
AutoExec macro, AC 348
Autofilter arrow, AC 117
AutoKeys, AC 327
AutoNumber data type, AC 7
AutoNumber field, AC 8, AC 14
Avg function, AC 104, AC 148, AC 149
axes, charts, AC 311

B

<b> tag, AC 399
Back Color property, AC 92
back-end databases, AC 384
Background Color or Shape Fill button, AC 93
background images, AC 69
[Backspace] key, WIN 28
Backstage view, OFF 6, OFF 7
backup copies, AC 274, WIN 36
backward compatibility, OFF 11
bang notation (!), AC 330
bar charts, AC 309
bas prefix, AC 350, AC 351
Beep action, AC 325
Before Change event, AC 335
Before Delete event, AC 335
Between...and criteria, AC 278
Between...And operator, AC 143
black text color, VBE, AC 347
blank fields, searching for, AC 39
Blank Form tool, AC 56
Blank Report button, AC 308
blogs, WIN 16
blue text color, VBE, AC 347
Bold button, AC 93
border, WIN 12
Border Style property, AC 256
bound controls, AC 61, AC 63

 tag, AC 399

Break button, AC 355
breakpoints, AC 360, AC 361
Build button, AC 164, AC 170
buttons, WIN 6. *See also specific buttons*
    command. *See* command buttons
    groups, WIN 10, WIN 11
    option. *See* option buttons
    power, WIN 2
    toggle, forms, AC 63
    toolbar, Visual Basic window, AC 355
Byte field property, AC 117

C

Calculated data type, AC 7
calculated fields, AC 146–147
calculations
    forms, AC 64–65
    reports, AC 88, AC 89
Calendar Picker, AC 16
Caption property, AC 115, AC 250, AC 274, AC 298, AC 330
caret (^), exponentiation operator, AC 147
Cascade Delete Related Fields, AC 221, AC 247
Cascade Update Related Fields, AC 221, AC 247
cascading style sheets (CSSs), AC 399
case sensitivity, WIN 2
    search text, WIN 16
cbo prefix, AC 351
Center button, AC 90
Center command, AC 93
CF (CompactFlash) cards, AC 380
Charms bar, WIN 4, WIN 5
chart(s)
    creating, AC 308–309
    modifying, AC 310–311
chart areas, AC 311
chart type(s), AC 308, AC 309
    applying, AC 312–313
Chart Type dialog box, AC 312, AC 313
Chart Wizard, AC 308
check boxes, WIN 14
    forms, AC 63
child records, AC 286
child tables, AC 111
class modules, AC 346, AC 356–357
clicking, WIN 7
client(s), AC 385
Client Settings category, Access Options dialog box, AC 373
client/server computing, AC 385
Clipboard (Office). *See* Office Clipboard
Clipboard (Windows), OFF 13, WIN 36
Clipboard command, PowerPoint Web App, CL 13
Close button, WIN 10
CloseWindow action, AC 325

closing tags, AC 398
cloud computing, AC 15, OFF 9
  definition, CL 2
  SkyDrive. *See* SkyDrive
cloud storage, WIN 35
cloud-based applications, CL 2
  Office Web Apps. *See* Office Web Apps
cmd prefix, AC 328, AC 351
code tag, AC 399
code window, VBE, AC 347
Collapse button, Macro Design View, AC 323
color, text, VBE, AC 347
column(s)
  datasheets, adjusting width automatically, AC 140
  datasheets, resizing and moving, AC 17
  subforms, adjusting width automatically, AC 166
column charts, AC 309
Columnar layout, forms, AC 167
combo box(es), AC 54, AC 55, AC 63
  data entry, AC 170–171
  finding records, AC 172–173
  list boxes compared, AC 170, AC 171
  prefix naming convention, AC 351
Combo Box Wizard, AC 170
command(s), WIN 6. *See also specific commands*
  Send to menu, WIN 36
command button(s), WIN 14
  assigning macros to, AC 328–329
  forms, AC 63, AC 174–175
  prefix naming convention, AC 351
Command Button Wizard, AC 174, AC 175, AC 328
command-line options, AC 374
comma-separated values (CSVs), AC 222
comment(s)
  Macro Design View, AC 323
  modules, AC 346
comment line(s), AC 354–355
Comments command, PowerPoint Web App, CL 13
Comments table, AC 8, AC 9
Compact On Close feature, AC 372, AC 373
CompactFlash (CF) cards, AC 380
compacting databases, AC 372, AC 373
comparison operators, AC 39, AC 143
compatibility, OFF 2
Compatibility Mode, OFF 11
compile-time errors, AC 360
conditional expressions, macros, AC 322, AC 330
conditional formatting
  data bars, AC 195
  reports, AC 194–195
Conditional Formatting Rules Manager dialog box, AC 194, AC 195
Const statement, VBA, AC 349
control(s). *See* form controls; report controls;
  specific types of controls
Control Box property, AC 256

control icons, WIN 10, WIN 11
Control Source property, AC 64
ControlName argument, AC 330
/convert option, AC 374
converting databases, AC 382–383
copying
  Access data to other applications, AC 229
  files, WIN 36–37
  items using Office Clipboard, OFF 5
count(s), reports, AC 88, AC 89
Count function, AC 104, AC 149
CREATE tab
  Blank Report button, AC 308
  Report Design button, AC 308
criteria, queries, AC 32
  AND, AC 38–39, AC 142–143
  OR, AC 40–41, AC 144–145
  parameter, AC 192, AC 193
  parameter queries, AC 272, AC 273
  wildcard characters, AC 145
criteria syntax, AC 38
crosstab queries, AC 150–151
Crosstab Query Wizard, AC 150
Crosstab row, query grid, AC 150
CSS (cascading style sheets), AC 399
CSVs (comma-separated values), AC 222
Currency data type, AC 7
Currency fields, modifying, AC 116, AC 117
Currency format, AC 298
Current Database category, Access Options dialog box,
  AC 219, AC 373
Current record text box, AC 14
Customize Quick Access Toolbar button, OFF 12, WIN 11
Customize Ribbon category, Access Options dialog box, AC 373
customizing Access, options, AC 372, AC 373
Cut command, WIN 38, WIN 39
cutting items, Office Clipboard, OFF 5

D

data, charts, AC 311
data bars, conditional formatting, AC 195
data entry, AC 14–15
data entry combo boxes, AC 170–171
data macros, AC 334–335
Data tab, Property Sheet, AC 64
data type(s), AC 6, AC 7
  selecting, AC 108
Data Type field, AC 11
database(s)
  analyzing performance, AC 376–377
  back-end, AC 384
  backing up, AC 380–381
  compacting, AC 372, AC 373

converting, AC 382–383
creating, AC 6–7
desktop, AC 218
file formats, AC 382, AC 383
file types, AC 122, AC 123
front-end, AC 384
multiuser, AC 14
overview, AC 4–5
passwords, AC 378–379
relational. *See* relational database(s)
relationships. *See* relationship(s)
repairing, AC 372, AC 373
saving, AC 380–381
saving with SkyDrive, AC 404, AC 405
scrubbing, AC 111
securing, methods, AC 379
sharing with SkyDrive, AC 404, AC 405
splitting, AC 379, AC 384–385
terminology, AC 9
threats and solutions for, AC 381
trusted, AC 329
trusting, AC 372
database designers, AC 54
Database Documenter, AC 274
database templates, AC 218–219
database users, AC 54
database wizards. *See* database templates
datasheet(s), AC 6
deleting objects, AC 148
filtering data, AC 36–37
finding data, AC 34, AC 35
formatting, AC 42–43
freezing and unfreezing fields, AC 31
hiding and unhiding fields, AC 31
printing, AC 42
renaming objects, AC 148
resizing and moving columns, AC 17
sorting data, AC 34, AC 35
Datasheet category, Access Options dialog box, AC 373
Datasheet layout, forms, AC 167
Datasheet View, AC 6
creating tables, AC 8
modifying fields, AC 249
date(s)
formatting, AC 298
1900 vs. 2000, AC 279
reports, AC 307
date criteria, AC 276
DATE function, AC 147
Date/Time data type, AC 7
Date/Time fields, modifying, AC 118–119
dBase, linking, importing, and exporting to Access, AC 227
debugging
macros, AC 336–337
modules, AC 360–361

Decimal Places field property, AC 117
declaration statements
VBA, AC 346
VBE, AC 347
default, WIN 28
Default Value property, Short Text fields, AC 115
Default View property, AC 166
Delete command, PowerPoint Web App, CL 13
Delete File dialog box, WIN 42, WIN 43
Delete queries, AC 277, AC 280–281
Delete row, AC 280
DeleteRecord action, AC 325
deleting. *See also* removing
fields from query design grid, AC 139
files, WIN 42, WIN 43
objects in datasheets, AC 148
records in one-to-many relationship, AC 221
tables, AC 108
tables in queries, AC 33
delimited text files, AC 222
delimiters, AC 222
deprecated tags, AC 399
Descending button, AC 35
Description property, AC 274
DESIGN tab
Insert Rows button, AC 144
Page Numbers button, AC 307
PowerPoint Web App, CL 13
Single Step button, AC 336
Use Control Wizards button, AC 328
Design View. *See* Form Design View; Query Design View; Report Design View; Table Design View
desktop
navigating, WIN 4–5
saving files to, OFF 8
desktop apps, WIN 4, WIN 8
desktop databases, AC 218
Detail section, AC 68, AC 84
forms, AC 173
reports, AC 191
dialog box(es), AC 258, AC 259, WIN 13, WIN 14.
See also specific dialog boxes
controls, WIN 14
dialog box launcher, OFF 6, OFF 7
Dim statement, VBA, AC 349
displaying. *See also* viewing
fields, AC 146
long entries in field cells, AC 146
DLookup function, AC 306
DoCmd statement, AC 358, AC 359
document(s), OFF 12. *See also* file(s)
co-authoring, CL 10
HTML, linking, importing, and exporting to Access, AC 227
main, mail merge, AC 230, AC 231
Document Recovery task pane, OFF 15

document window, OFF 6, OFF 7
documenting code, AC 354–355
domain(s), AC 306
domain functions (domain aggregate functions), AC 306–307
Double field property, AC 117
double-clicking, WIN 6, WIN 7
  fields in field lists, AC 138
drag and drop method, WIN 43
  copying Access data to other applications, AC 229
dragging, WIN 7
  fields to query design grid, AC 138
Drawing command, PowerPoint Web App, CL 13
drives
  hard, external, AC 380
  USB, AC 380, WIN 28
DropBox, WIN 35
duplicate values, finding, AC 287
Dynaset value, AC 274

E

Edit Hyperlink dialog box, AC 394, AC 395
Edit List Items button, AC 112
Edit mode, AC 310
  keyboard shortcuts, AC 17
  switching to Navigation mode from, AC 14
Edit Relationships dialog box, AC 12, AC 13, AC 110, AC 111, AC 247
editing data, AC 16–17
  split forms, AC 56, AC 57
editing files, WIN 34, WIN 35
elements, AC 398
Else portion of If statements, AC 332, AC 333
email attachments, linking, importing, and exporting to Access, AC 227
EMailDatabase Object action, AC 325
empty tags, AC 398
Enable Layout View check box, AC 374
Enabled property, AC 177
encryption, databases, AC 379
End Function statement, AC 350
  VBA, AC 349
End If statement, VBA, AC 349
End Select statement, VBA, AC 349
End Sub statement, VBA, AC 349
Enter Parameter Value dialog box, AC 193
equal sign (=)
  expressions in controls, AC 64, AC 88
  greater than or equal to operator, AC 39
  less than or equal to operator, AC 39
error correction, WIN 28. See also troubleshooting
error indicator, AC 84
Error Indicator Smart Tag, AC 119

event(s)
  class modules, AC 356
  macros, AC 322, AC 332–333
event handler, AC 356
Excel
  Access compared, AC 2, AC 3
  exporting data to, AC 226–227
  filename and file extension, OFF 8
  importing data from, AC 222–223
  linking, importing, and exporting to Access, AC 227
  linking data to, AC 224–225
  Office Web App, CL 12
  overview, OFF 2, OFF 3
/excl option, AC 374
exclamation point (!), bang notation, AC 330
exclusive mode, AC 378
Exit command, PowerPoint Web App, CL 13
exiting Windows 8, WIN 18–19
Expand button, Macro Design View, AC 323
Export - HTML Document dialog box, AC 400, AC 401
exporting, AC 226–227
  Access data to other applications, AC 229
  file formats supported, AC 227
  to HTML and XML, AC 400–401
  to PDF files, AC 232–233
expression(s), AC 146
  calculations in reports, AC 88
  field names, AC 146
  forms, AC 64, AC 65
Expression Builder dialog box, AC 252
Extensible Markup Language (XML), AC 222, AC 232
EXTERNAL DATA tab
  Access button, AC 222
  Saved Exports button, AC 226
  Saved Imports button, AC 222
external hard drives, AC 380

F

field(s), AC 6, AC 9. See also specific types of fields
  adding to forms, AC 60–61
  AutoNumber, AC 8, AC 14
  blank, searching for, AC 39
  calculated, AC 146–147
  deleting from query design grid, AC 139
  displaying, AC 146
  dragging to query design grid, AC 138
  field lists, double-clicking, AC 138
  foreign key, AC 8, AC 12, AC 106
  freezing and unfreezing in datasheets, AC 31
  hiding and unhiding in datasheets, AC 31
  hyperlink, AC 394–395
  Long Text fields, AC 251
  Lookup, AC 112–113

merge, AC 230, AC 231
modifying in Datasheet View, AC 249
multivalued, AC 113
primary key, AC 8
properties, AC 11
reordering in Table Design View, AC 122
Field List, AC 60, AC 164
field lists
queries, AC 32
resizing, AC 138
tables, AC 12
field names, AC 6
expressions, AC 146
field properties, AC 114–115, AC 250–251, AC 274
Field Properties pane, AC 114
field selector(s), AC 139
queries, AC 34
Tab Order dialog box, AC 66
field selector button, AC 114, AC 250
Field Size property
Number fields, AC 117
Short Text fields, AC 114, AC 115
FIELDS tab
modifying fields, AC 249
Table Datasheet View, AC 117
file(s), OFF 10, OFF 11, WIN 4. *See also*
database(s); document(s)
attached, opening, AC 122, AC 123
blank, creating, OFF 8
copying, WIN 36–37
creating, OFF 8, OFF 9
definition, OFF 8
deleting, WIN 42, WIN 43
editing, WIN 34, WIN 35
exploring, WIN 30–31
integrating, OFF 2
moving, WIN 38, WIN 39, WIN 43
names, OFF 8
opening, OFF 10, OFF 11, WIN 34, WIN 35
PDF. *See* PDF (Portable Document Format) files
planning organization, WIN 27
recovering, OFF 15
renaming, WIN 38, WIN 39
restoring, WIN 42, WIN 43
saving. *See* saving files; saving files to SkyDrive
searching for, WIN 8, WIN 40, WIN 41
selecting, WIN 43
sharing, SkyDrive, CL 10–11
text. *See* text files
views, WIN 32–33
XML, linking, importing, and exporting to Access, AC 227
XPS, linking, importing, and exporting to Access, AC 227
XSD, AC 400, AC 401
File Explorer, WIN 26, WIN 27
search results, WIN 39, WIN 40

file extensions, AC 122, AC 123, AC 246, AC 382,
AC 383, AC 406, OFF 8, WIN 28
file hierarchy, WIN 26, WIN 27
navigating, WIN 31
File list, WIN 26
navigating file hierarchy, WIN 31
file management, SkyDrive, CL 8–9
file servers, AC 384
FILE tab, CL 2, CL 3, OFF 7
PowerPoint Web App, CL 13
file types, databases, AC 122, AC 123
filter(s), queries vs., AC 37
Filter button, AC 37
Filter by Form, AC 36, AC 37
Filter by Selection, AC 36
filtering data, AC 36–37
Find and Replace dialog box, AC 34, AC 35
Find button, AC 35
Find Duplicates Query Wizard, AC 151, AC 287
Find Unmatched Query Wizard, AC 151, AC 286–287
finding. *See also* searching
blank fields, AC 39
data in tables or datasheets, AC 34, AC 35
duplicate values, AC 287
records, combo boxes, AC 172–173
unmatched records, AC 286–287
FindRecord action, AC 325
First function, AC 149
first normal form (1NF), AC 245
focus, AC 14
folders, WIN 4
exploring, WIN 30–31
new, creating, WIN 36
searching for, WIN 40, WIN 41
shared, AC 404
trusted, AC 329
views, WIN 32–33
Font Color button, AC 93
Font command, PowerPoint Web App, CL 13
font tag, AC 399
foreign key(s), specifying data types, AC 109
foreign key fields, AC 12, AC 106
form(s), AC 4, AC 5, AC 53–69, AC 163–179, AC 256–257
adding fields, AC 60–61
aligning control edges, AC 168–169
Attachment controls, AC 164
calculations, AC 64–65
combo boxes. *See* combo box(es)
command buttons, AC 174–175
controls. *See* form controls
definition, AC 54
expressions, AC 64, AC 65
Form Design View, AC 164–165
Form Wizard, AC 54–55
images, AC 68–69

Layout View, AC 58–59
layouts, AC 166, AC 167
limiting access, AC 177
linking with subforms, AC 167
main, AC 166
option groups, AC 176–177
prefix naming convention, AC 351
sections, AC 68, AC 69, AC 172, AC 173
split, AC 56–57
startup, AC 219, AC 256, AC 257
subforms, AC 164, AC 166–167
tab controls, AC 178–179
tab order, AC 66–67
form controls, AC 54, AC 55
aligning edges, AC 168–169
anchoring, AC 168
bound, AC 61, AC 63
conditional formatting, AC 194–195
labels, AC 164
layout, AC 67
list, AC 63
margins, AC 168
modifying, AC 62–63
multiple, selecting, AC 168
padding, AC 168
properties, AC 62
resizing, AC 168, AC 169
text boxes, AC 164
unbound, AC 61, AC 63
Form Design tool, AC 56
Form Design View, AC 55
Form Footer section, AC 68, AC 173
Form Header section, AC 68, AC 69, AC 172
form sections, AC 68, AC 69, AC 172, AC 173
form selector button, AC 164
Form tool, AC 56
Form View, AC 54, AC 55
Form Wizard, AC 54–55, AC 56
Format Painter, AC 198, AC 199
Format property, AC 298
Date/Time fields, AC 118, AC 119
Short Text fields, AC 115
formatting
datasheets, AC 42–43
dates, AC 298
numbers, AC 298
reports. See formatting reports
formatting reports, AC 92–93
advanced formatting, AC 298–299
conditional formatting, AC 194–195
Format Painter, AC 198, AC 199
themes, AC 198, AC 199
forums, WIN 16
forward slash (/), division operator, AC 147
freezing fields in datasheets, AC 31

frm prefix, AC 351
FROM keyword, AC 140, AC 141
front-end databases, AC 384
functions, AC 88, AC 146, AC 147
aggregate, AC 148, AC 149
creating, AC 350–351
domain (domain aggregate functions), AC 306–307
summary reports, AC 204–205
VBA, AC 346

G

GB (gigabyte), AC 380
General category, Access Options dialog box, AC 373
gestures, WIN 2
Get External Data - Excel Spreadsheet dialog box,
   AC 222, AC 224, AC 225
gigabyte (GB), AC 380
Go To button, AC 35
GoToControl action, AC 325
GoToRecord action, AC 325
graph(s). See chart(s)
graphic images, inserting in forms, AC 68–69
graphics tablet, WIN 7
greater than operator (>), AC 39, AC 143, AC 272
greater than or equal to operator (>=), AC 39,
   AC 143
green text color, VBE, AC 347
group(s), OFF 6
buttons, WIN 10, WIN 11
Group, Sort, and Total pane, AC 86, AC 87
Group Footer section, reports, AC 84, AC 191
Group Header section, reports, AC 84, AC 191
grouping records, AC 86–87

H

hard drives, external, AC 380
Help and Support, WIN 16–17
Help button, OFF 14
Help command, PowerPoint Web App, CL 13
Help window, OFF 14, OFF 15
hidden apps, WIN 4
hidden objects, restoring, AC 283
Hidden property, AC 282
hiding fields in datasheets, AC 31
highlighting, WIN 6
HOME tab, PowerPoint Web App, CL 13
HTML (Hypertext Markup Language), AC 398
exporting to, AC 400, AC 401
HTML 5, AC 399
importing from, AC 402, AC 403
linking, importing, and exporting documents to Access, AC 227
tags. See HTML tags

HTML tags, AC 398–399
  deprecating, AC 399
  tables, AC 403
Hyperlink Address property, AC 396
hyperlink controls, AC 396–397
Hyperlink data type, AC 7
hyperlink fields, AC 394–395
hyperlink pointers, AC 394
Hypertext Markup Language. *See* HTML (Hypertext Markup Language); HTML tags

I

<i> tag, AC 399
icons, WIN 4
  control, WIN 10, WIN 11
  selecting, WIN 6
If statements, AC 330–331, AC 352–353
  Macro Design View, AC 323
If...Then statement, VBA, AC 349
If...Then...Else logic, AC 352–353
Illustrations command, PowerPoint Web App, CL 13
images, inserting in forms, AC 68–69
Images command, PowerPoint Web App, CL 13
Import Spreadsheet Wizard, AC 222, AC 223
ImportExportSpreadsheet action, AC 325
ImportExportText action, AC 325
importing
  from another database, AC 222
  data from Excel, AC 222–223
  file formats supported, AC 227
  from HTML and XML, AC 402–403
In operator, AC 143
inactive window, WIN 12
index(es), AC 250
Indexed property, AC 250
infinity symbol, AC 12
Info command, PowerPoint Web App, CL 13
inner joins, AC 254, AC 255, AC 284
Input Mask property, Short Text fields, AC 114, AC 115
Input Mask Wizard, AC 114
Insert Module button, AC 355
Insert Picture dialog box, AC 68
Insert Rows button, AC 144
INSERT tab, PowerPoint Web App, CL 13
insertion point, OFF 8
Integer field property, AC 117
integrating files, OFF 2
IntelliSense technology, AC 358
intentional damage, databases, AC 381
interface, OFF 2
Is Not Null criterion, AC 39, AC 143, AC 285
Is Null criterion, AC 285
Is Null operator, AC 250
Italic button, AC 93

J

join(s)
  inner, AC 254, AC 255, AC 284
  left, AC 284, AC 285
  left outer, AC 254, AC 255
  right, AC 284
  right outer, AC 254, AC 255
join lines, AC 32, AC 284
join properties, AC 284–285
Join Properties dialog box, AC 254, AC 255, AC 284, AC 285
Joint Photographic Experts Group (JPEG), AC 122
.jpg file extension, AC 122
junction tables, AC 107, AC 246

K

key combinations, assigning macros, AC 327
key fields, AC 9. *See also* foreign key fields; primary key fields
key symbols, AC 108
keyboard, navigating file hierarchy, WIN 31
keywords, WIN 16
  VBA, AC 349

L

.laccdb file extension, AC 382
label(s)
  controls, AC 164
  forms, AC 63
  prefix naming convention, AC 351
label controls, AC 54, AC 55
Label Wizard, AC 94–95
landscape orientation, AC 80
  changing to portrait, AC 81
Language category, Access Options dialog box, AC 373
Last function, AC 149
launching apps, OFF 4–5
layout(s), WIN 32
  controls on forms, AC 67
  forms, AC 166, AC 167
  print, reports, AC 302–303
  tables, AC 59, AC 300–301
Layout View
  forms, AC 55, AC 56, AC 58–59
  reports, AC 82–83, AC 90, AC 91
lbl prefix, AC 351
.ldb file extension, AC 382
left angle bracket (<)
  less than operator, AC 39, AC 272
  less than or equal to operator, AC 39
  not equal to operator, AC 39
LEFT function, AC 147
left joins, AC 284, AC 285
left outer joins, AC 254, AC 255

LEN function, AC 147
less than operator (<), AC 39, AC 143, AC 272
less than or equal to operator (<=), AC 39, AC 143
libraries, WIN 38
Library Tools Manage tab, WIN 42
Like operator, AC 143
Limit To List property, AC 112, AC 113, AC 171
line(s)
    join, AC 32, AC 284
    reports, AC 196–197
line charts, AC 309
line controls, forms, AC 63
link(s), WIN 16
Link Child Fields property, AC 167
link lines, AC 32, AC 284
Link Master Fields property, AC 167
Link Spreadsheet Wizard, AC 224
Linked Table Manager dialog box, AC 384, AC 385
linking, AC 224–225
    file formats supported, AC 227
    forms and subforms, AC 167
Links command, PowerPoint Web App, CL 13
list(s), redesigning into relational databases, AC 106, AC 107
list boxes, WIN 14
    combo boxes compared, AC 170, AC 171
    forms, AC 63
Live Preview, OFF 6, OFF 7
live tile, WIN 4
local area networks (LANs), AC 384
lock screen, WIN 2, WIN 3
Locked property, AC 177
logging in, WIN 2
logic errors, AC 360
logical operators, AC 272
logical view, AC 28, AC 138
Long date format, AC 298
long entries, displaying in field cells, AC 146
Long Integer Number field property, AC 116, AC 117
Long Text data type, AC 7
Long Text fields, AC 251
Lookup fields, AC 112–113
Lookup properties
    removing, AC 112
    setting, AC 112, AC 113
Lookup Wizard, AC 7, AC 112, AC 113

M

macro(s), AC 321–337
    actions. See action(s), macros
    arguments. See arguments, macros
    assigning to command buttons, AC 328–329
    assigning to key combinations, AC 327
    conditional expressions, AC 322, AC 330

    creating, AC 324–325
    data, AC 334–335
    definition, AC 322
    events, AC 322, AC 332–333
    If statements, AC 330–331
    modifying actions and arguments, AC 326–327
    modules compared, AC 348–349
    prefix naming convention, AC 351
    submacros, AC 322
    troubleshooting, AC 336–337
Macro Design View, AC 322, AC 323
    printing, AC 324
Macro Single Step dialog box, AC 336
Mail Merge task pane, AC 230
mailing labels, AC 94–95
main document, mail merge, AC 230, AC 231
main form, AC 166
main report, AC 200
Make Table queries, AC 276–277
many-to-many relationships, AC 107, AC 246
margins, controls, AC 67, AC 168
Max function, AC 148, AC 149
Maximize button, WIN 10
MaximizeWindow action, AC 325
MB (megabyte), AC 380
mcr prefix, AC 351
.mdb (Access 2002 or 2002-2003) file extension,
    AC 123, AC 246, AC 382, AC 383
Medium Date format, AC 298
megabyte (MB), AC 380
menus, WIN 10, WIN 13, WIN 14
    shortcut, WIN 17
merge fields, AC 230, AC 231
merging Access data with Word, AC 230–231
MessageBox action, AC 325, AC 326, AC 327
methods, VBA, AC 346
Microsoft Access. See Access
Microsoft accounts, OFF 9
    new, creating, CL 5
    signing in to, CL 4
    signing out of, CL 4
Microsoft Answers website, WIN 16
Microsoft Community website, WIN 16
Microsoft Excel. See Excel
Microsoft Office. See also Access; Excel; PowerPoint; Word
    benefits, OFF 2
    launching apps, OFF 4–5
    moving between programs, OFF 4
    user interface, OFF 6
Microsoft Office 365, OFF 3
Microsoft Office 365 Home Premium edition, OFF 3
Microsoft PowerPoint. See PowerPoint
Microsoft SkyDrive, WIN 35
Microsoft Word. See Word
Microsoft Word Mail Merge Wizard, AC 230

Min function, AC 148, AC 149
Min Max Buttons property, AC 256
Minimize button, WIN 10
minus sign (–), subtraction operator, AC 147
modifying properties, queries, AC 274–275
modules, AC 346–347
   class, AC 346, AC 356–357
   comments, AC 346
   macros compared, AC 348–349
   prefix naming convention, AC 351
   standard, AC 346
   statements, AC 346
   troubleshooting, AC 360–361
More Forms tool, AC 56
mouse, WIN 7
   scroll wheels, WIN 16
mouse pointer, WIN 6
   shapes, AC 58
moving
   controls in reports, AC 90, AC 91
   datasheet columns, AC 17
   files, WIN 38, WIN 39, WIN 43
   objects, WIN 13
   Property Sheet, AC 64
multicolumn reports, AC 304–305
multifield primary keys, AC 246
multiple windows, WIN 12–13
multiuser databases, AC 14
multivalued fields, AC 113

N

Name property, AC 66, AC 330, AC 356
   fields, AC 11
naming conventions, prefixes, AC 351
navigating
   desktop, WIN 4–5
   down, WIN 26
   file hierarchy, WIN 31
   Navigation pane, WIN 26, WIN 31
   Open dialog box, WIN 35
   setting navigation options, AC 371
   start screen, WIN 4–5
   up, WIN 26
   windows, WIN 12
navigation buttons, AC 14
Navigation Buttons property, AC 256
navigation forms, AC 370–371
Navigation mode
   keyboard shortcuts, AC 15
   switching to Edit mode from, AC 14
Navigation pane, AC 4, WIN 26, WIN 31
navigation system styles, AC 370
Navigation tool, AC 56

normalizing data, AC 244–245
Northwind, AC 246
not equal to operator (<>), AC 39, AC 143
Not operator, AC 143
Notepad, WIN 9
Now() function, AC 352
null entries, AC 250
null field value, AC 285
Null operator, AC 143
number(s), formatting, AC 298
Number data type, AC 7
Number fields, modifying, AC 116, AC 117

O

object(s), AC 4, AC 9. *See also specific objects*
   read-only, AC 80
   renaming, AC 8
   VBA, AC 346
Object Browser button, AC 355
object dependencies, AC 376
Object Designers category, Access Options dialog box, AC 373
object lists, VBE, AC 347
ODBC (Open Database Connectivity), AC 224
   linking, importing, and exporting databases to
      Access, AC 227
Office. *See* Microsoft Office
Office Clipboard, OFF 5
   copying Access data to other applications, AC 229
Office Web Apps, CL 2, CL 12–13
OLE Object data type, AC 7
On Click event, AC 332
On Current event, AC 332, AC 333
On Dbl Click event, AC 358
On Error GoTo statement, VBA, AC 349
On Got Focus event, AC 358
1NF (first normal form), AC 245
OneNote, Office Web App, CL 12
one-to-many join lines, AC 138
one-to-many line, AC 12, AC 110
one-to-many relationships, AC 10, AC 12–13, AC 106, AC 109
   creating, AC 110–111
   records, AC 221
online, definition, AC 218
online collaboration, OFF 2, OFF 9
Open as Copy option, Open dialog box, OFF 10
Open Database Connectivity. *See* ODBC (Open Database
   Connectivity)
Open dialog box, OFF 10, OFF 11, WIN 34, WIN 35
OpenForm action, AC 325
opening
   attached files, AC 122, AC 123
   files, OFF 10, OFF 11, WIN 34, WIN 35
   Property Sheets for reports, AC 152

opening tags, AC 398
OpenQuery action, AC 325
Open-Read-Only option, Open dialog box, OFF 10
OpenReport action, AC 324, AC 325
OpenTable action, AC 325
operating systems, WIN 2
option buttons, WIN 14
  forms, AC 63
    Option Group Wizard, AC 176
Option Compare Database statement, VBA, AC 349
Option Explicit statement, AC 350
  VBA, AC 349
option groups, forms, AC 63, AC 176–177
Option Value property, AC 176
OR criteria, AC 40–41, AC 144–145
ORDER BY keyword, AC 140, AC 141
orphan records, AC 56, AC 106, AC 111, AC 286
outer joins, AC 254, AC 255
Outlook, linking, importing, and exporting to Access, AC 227

P

<p> tag, AC 399
padding, controls, AC 67, AC 168
Page Footer section, AC 84
  forms, AC 173
  reports, AC 191
Page Header section, AC 84
  forms, AC 173
  reports, AC 191
page numbers, reports, AC 307
Page Numbers button, AC 307
Page Numbers dialog box, AC 300, AC 301
page orientation, AC 80
  changing, AC 81
Page Setup dialog box, AC 298, AC 299, AC 305
Paint, WIN 9
panes, WIN 26. See also specific panes
paper orientation. See page orientation
Paragraph command, PowerPoint Web App, CL 13
parameter criteria, reports, AC 192, AC 193
parameter queries, AC 272–273
parameter reports, AC 192–193
parent records, AC 286
parent tables, AC 111
parentheses (( )), expressions, AC 88
passwords, AC 378–379, WIN 2, WIN 3
  strong, AC 378
Paste command, WIN 38, WIN 39
pasting items, Office Clipboard, OFF 5
paths, WIN 26
PDF (Portable Document Format) files
  exporting data to, AC 232–233
  linking, importing, and exporting to Access, AC 227

Percent format, AC 298
performance, tips for optimizing, AC 377
Performance Analyzer, AC 376–377
Photos app, WIN 4
Picture property, AC 258
pie charts, AC 309
pixels (picture elements), AC 90
plus sign (+), addition operator, AC 147
PMT function, AC 147
pointing, WIN 7
pointing devices, WIN 6, WIN 7
  actions, WIN 6, WIN 7
pointing stick, WIN 7
Portable Document Format files. See PDF (Portable Document Format) files
portable storage media, AC 380
portrait orientation, AC 80
  changing to landscape, AC 81
pound sign (#)
  data too wide for column, AC 116
  date criteria, AC 38, AC 120, AC 276
  Input Mask property, AC 115
power button, WIN 2
power options, WIN 19
power outages, databases, AC 381
PowerPoint
  filename and file extension, OFF 8
  Office Web App, CL 12–13
  overview, OFF 2, OFF 3
PowerPoint Last Viewed Slide setting, CL 2
prefix naming conventions, AC 351
Presentation Views command, PowerPoint Web App, CL 13
previewing documents, OFF 12
primary key(s), multifield, AC 246
primary key fields, AC 8, AC 10–11, AC 106
Print button, AC 42
Print command, PowerPoint Web App, CL 13
Print dialog box, WIN 14
print layout, reports, AC 302–303
Print layout view, OFF 12
Print Preview, AC 80, AC 81, AC 83
PRINT PREVIEW tab, AC 42
printing
  database content, reports, AC 80
  datasheets, AC 42
  Macro Design View, AC 324
  Relationships window, AC 12
PrintOut action, AC 325
procedure(s), VBA, AC 346
procedure lists, VBE, AC 347
programs, WIN 2. See also app(s); application(s); software; specific programs
  searching for, WIN 40, WIN 41
Project Explorer button, AC 355
Project Explorer window, VBE, AC 347

Proofing category, Access Options dialog box, AC 373
properties. *See also specific properties*
  fields, AC 11
  form controls, AC 62
Property argument, AC 330
Property Sheets, AC 62, AC 63
  Data tab, AC 64
  moving, AC 64
  reports, opening, AC 152
  title bar, AC 170
Property Update Options Smart Tag, AC 119
Publish as PDF or XPS dialog box, AC 232, AC 233
/pwd option, AC 374

Q

qry prefix, AC 351
queries, AC 4, AC 5, AC 27–43, AC 137–153
  action, AC 276, AC 277
  adding tables, AC 33, AC 148
  Append, AC 277, AC 278–279
  calculated fields, AC 146–147
  criteria. *See* criteria, queries
  crosstab, AC 150–151
  data, AC 30–31
  definition, AC 28
  Delete, AC 277, AC 280–281
  deleting tables, AC 33
  filtering data, AC 36–37
  filters vs., AC 37
  Find Duplicates, AC 287
  finding data, AC 34, AC 35
  Make Table, AC 276–277
  modifying properties, AC 274–275
  multitable, AC 138–139
  parameter, AC 272–273
  prefix naming convention, AC 351
  Query Design View, AC 32–33
  reports, AC 152–153
  running, AC 138, AC 139
  Select, AC 138, AC 276–277
  Simple Query Wizard, AC 28, AC 29
  sorting, AC 34, AC 35, AC 140, AC 141
  SQL View, AC 140, AC 141
  subqueries, AC 252–253
  summary, AC 148–149
  for top values, AC 270–271
  Update, AC 277, AC 282–283
  wildcard characters in criteria, AC 145
Query Datasheet View, AC 138
query design grid, AC 32
  deleting fields, AC 139
  dragging fields to, AC 138

Query Design View, AC 32–33, AC 138, AC 139
  adding tables to queries, AC 148
  parameter criteria, AC 193
  selecting data, AC 140, AC 141
  sorting data, AC 140, AC 141
query wizards, AC 150, AC 151
question mark (?)
  Input Mask property, AC 115
  wildcard character, AC 36, AC 145
Quick Access toolbar, OFF 6, OFF 7, WIN 10, WIN 11
  customizing, OFF 12
Quick Access Toolbar category, Access Options dialog box, AC 373

R

random access memory (RAM), WIN 28
read-only objects, AC 80
record(s), AC 8, AC 9
  appending, AC 222
  child, AC 286
  finding, combo boxes, AC 172–173
  grouping, AC 86–87
  orphan, AC 56, AC 106, AC 111, AC 286
  parent, AC 286
  referential integrity, AC 221
  sorting, AC 140, AC 141
  unmatched, finding, AC 286–287
Record Selectors property, AC 256
record source(s), AC 80, AC 164
Record Source property, AC 164, AC 190, AC 192
Recordset property, AC 274
Rectangle button, AC 194
rectangle controls, forms, AC 63
Recycle Bin, WIN 4, WIN 5
  empty, WIN 42
  restoring files, WIN 42, WIN 43
red text color, VBE, AC 347
Redo button, WIN 11
Redo command, AC 92
referential integrity, AC 12, AC 13, AC 106, AC 111, AC 286
  cascade options, AC 221, AC 247
relational database(s), AC 9, AC 105–123
  Attachment fields, AC 122–123
  Date/Time fields, AC 118–119
  foreign key fields, AC 106
  foreign keys, AC 109
  Lookup fields, AC 112–113
  many-to-many relationships, AC 107
  Number and Currency fields, AC 116–117
  one-to-many relationships, AC 106, AC 109, AC 110–111
  primary key fields, AC 106
  redesigning lists into, AC 106, AC 107
  referential integrity, AC 106, AC 111
  related tables, AC 108–109

Short Text fields, AC 114–115
    Validation Rule and Validation Text properties, AC 120–121
relational database software, AC 2–3
relationship(s), AC 246–247
    many-to-many, AC 107, AC 246
    one-to-many. *See* one-to-many relationships
Relationship report, AC 110
Relationships window, AC 110, AC 111
    printing, AC 12
Remove Single Field button, AC 28
Remove Sort button, AC 35
removing. *See also* deleting
    form layouts, AC 166
    Lookup properties, AC 112
renaming
    files, WIN 38, WIN 39
    objects in datasheets, AC 8, AC 148
    tables, AC 108
reordering fields in Table Design View, AC 122
/repair option, AC 374
repairing databases, AC 372, AC 373
Replace button, AC 35
report(s), AC 4, AC 5, AC 75–95, AC 189–205, AC 258–259
    aligning controls, AC 90, AC 91
    calculations, AC 88, AC 89
    controls. *See* report controls
    counts, AC 88, AC 89
    date and time, AC 307
    formatting. *See* formatting reports
    grouping records, AC 86–87
    Layout View, AC 82–83, AC 90, AC 91
    lines, AC 196–197
    main, AC 200
    multicolumn, AC 304–305
    opening Property Sheets, AC 152
    page numbers, AC 307
    parameter, AC 192–193
    parameter criteria, AC 192, AC 193
    prefix naming convention, AC 351
    print layout, AC 302–303
    queries, AC 152–153
    Report Design View, AC 190–191
    Report Wizard, AC 80–81
    resizing controls, AC 90, AC 91
    section properties, AC 202–203
    sections, AC 84–85, AC 191
    selecting multiple controls at a time, AC 91
    subreports, AC 200–201
    subtotals, AC 88, AC 89
    summary, AC 204–205
report controls
    aligning, AC 90, AC 91
    resizing, AC 90, AC 91
    selecting multiple controls at a time, AC 91
Report Design button, AC 308

Report Design View, AC 84, AC 85, AC 190–191
    lines, AC 197
    reports, AC 83
Report Footer section, AC 84
Report Header section, AC 84, AC 191
Report View, AC 83
Report Wizard, AC 80–81, AC 152
Required property, Short Text fields, AC 115
Reset button, AC 355
resizing
    controls in forms, AC 168, AC 169
    controls in reports, AC 90, AC 91
    datasheet columns, AC 17
    field lists, AC 138
restarting, WIN 19
Restore Down button, WIN 10
restoring
    files, WIN 42, WIN 43
    hidden objects, AC 283
Results list, WIN 29
Ribbon, OFF 6, OFF 7, WIN 6, WIN 10, WIN 11
    appearance, WIN 10
    Library Tools Manage tab, WIN 42
Rich Text, AC 398
Rich Text Format (RTF), AC 228, WIN 28
right angle bracket (>)
    greater than operator, AC 39, AC 272
    greater than or equal to operator, AC 39
    not equal to operator, AC 39
RIGHT function, AC 147
right joins, AC 284
right outer joins, AC 254, AC 255
right-clicking, WIN 7, WIN 17
/ro option, AC 374
roaming settings, CL 2
Row Source property, AC 112, AC 113, AC 170
rpt prefix, AC 351
RTF (Rich Text Format), AC 228, WIN 28
ruler, AC 84
Run button, Macro Design View, AC 323
Run Sub/UserForm button, AC 355
RunCode action, AC 325
RunMacro action, AC 325
running queries, AC 138
run-time errors, AC 360

S

Save As command, AC 32, WIN 34
    PowerPoint Web App, CL 13
Save As dialog box, AC 380, AC 381, AC 382, AC 383, OFF 8, OFF 9, OFF 10, OFF 11, WIN 28
Save button, WIN 11
Save command, WIN 34

Save Database As option, AC 380
Save Object As option, AC 380
Saved Exports button, AC 226
Saved Imports button, AC 222
SaveRecord action, AC 325
saving
   databases with SkyDrive, AC 404, AC 405
   files. *See* saving files; saving files to SkyDrive
saving files, OFF 8, OFF 9, OFF 10, OFF 11,
   WIN 28, WIN 34, WIN 35
   SkyDrive. *See* saving files to SkyDrive
saving files to SkyDrive, OFF 9
   default, disabling, CL 6, CL 7
schemas, AC 401
screen captures, OFF 13
ScreenTips, AC 324, WIN 6
scroll arrows, WIN 11
scroll bar, WIN 10, WIN 11
   parts, WIN 11
Scroll Bars property, AC 256
scroll box, WIN 11
scroll wheel, WIN 16
scrubbing the database, AC 111
SD (secure digital) cards, AC 380
search criteria, WIN 40
search text, case sensitivity, WIN 16
Search Tools tab, WIN 40
searching. *See also* finding
   for apps, WIN 8
   for files, WIN 8, WIN 40, WIN 41
   for folders, WIN 40, WIN 41
   for programs, WIN 40, WIN 41
second normal form (2NF), AC 245
section(s)
   forms, AC 55, AC 172, AC 173
   reports, AC 84–85, AC 191
section properties, reports, AC 202–203
secure digital (SD) cards, AC 380
security, limiting access to forms, AC 177
Select All button, AC 254
Select button, AC 35
Select Case statement, VBA, AC 349
SELECT keyword, AC 140, AC 141, AC 276
Select pointer, WIN 6
Select queries, AC 138, AC 276
SELECT statement, AC 170
selecting
   data types, AC 108
   date using Query Design View, AC 140, AC 141
   files, WIN 43
   icons, WIN 6
   multiple form controls, AC 168
   multiple report controls, AC 91
Selection button, AC 37
Send to command, WIN 37

Send to menu, WIN 36
SendKeys action, AC 325
series, charts, AC 311
server(s), AC 385
   client/server computing, AC 385
   file, AC 384
   SharePoint, AC 370
Set Database Password dialog box,
   AC 378, AC 379
SetProperty action, AC 330
SetValue action, AC 325
Shape Outline button, AC 93
Shapes button, WIN 13
Share command, PowerPoint Web App, CL 13
shared folders, AC 404
SharePoint servers, AC 370
SharePoint site, linking, importing, and exporting to
   Access, AC 227
SharePoint 2013, AC 407
sharing databases with SkyDrive, AC 404, AC 405
sharing files, SkyDrive, CL 10–11
Short Date format, AC 298
Short Text data type, AC 7
Short Text fields, properties, AC 114–115
shortcut keys, OFF 4
shortcut menus, WIN 17
Show Table dialog box, AC 12, AC 138
show/hide objects, securing databases, AC 379
ShowToolbar action, AC 325
Shutter Bar Open/Close button, AC 4
shutting down Windows 8, WIN 18–19
sign-in screen, WIN 2
signing in, WIN 2
Simple Query Wizard, AC 28, AC 29, AC 138
Single field property, AC 117
Single Step button, AC 336
single stepping, AC 336, AC 337
sizing handles, AC 68
SkyDrive, AC 15, CL 2, CL 6–7, WIN 35
   accessing, CL 8
   file management, CL 8–9
   saving and sharing databases, AC 404–405
   saving files to. *See* saving files to SkyDrive
   sharing files, CL 10–11
sleep, WIN 19
Slides command, PowerPoint Web App, CL 13
Smart Tags, AC 119
snapping Windows 8 apps, WIN 32
Snapshot value, AC 274
Snipping Tool, OFF 13, WIN 9
software. *See also* app(s); application(s); programs
   required to create, modify, and use Web apps,
   AC 407
Sort and filter arrow, AC 36, AC 37
Sort buttons, AC 35

sorting
    data in tables or datasheets, AC 34, AC 35
    records, AC 140, AC 141
    specifying sort order, AC 141
Sound Recorder, WIN 9
spin boxes, WIN 14
splash screen, AC 256, AC 257
split form(s), AC 56–57
Split Form tool, AC 56
splitting databases, AC 379, AC 384–385
SQL (Structured Query Language), AC 28, AC 140, AC 284
SQL Server 2013, AC 407
SQL View, AC 140, AC 141
square brackets ([ ])
    expressions in controls, AC 64
    field names in expressions, AC 146
    parameter criteria, AC192
Stacked layout, tables, AC 301
Standard format, AC 298
standard modules, AC 346
Start screen, OFF 4, OFF 5, WIN 2, WIN 3
    navigating, WIN 4–5
starting
    apps, WIN 8–9
    Windows 8, WIN 2–3
startup forms, AC 219, AC 256, AC 257
startup options, AC 374–375
    securing databases, AC 379
statements, modules, AC 346
StDev function, AC 149
Sticky Notes, WIN 9
StopMacro action, AC 325
storage media, portable, AC 380
strong passwords, AC 378
Structured Query Language (SQL), AC 28, AC 140, AC 284
stubs, AC 356
sub(s) (sub procedures)
    modifying, AC 358–359
    VBA, AC 346
Sub statement, VBA, AC 349
subdatasheets, AC 12
subfolders, WIN 26
subform(s), AC 164, AC 166–167
    linking with forms, AC 167
Subform Wizard, AC 166
submacros, AC 322
Submit button, WIN 2
subqueries, AC 252–253
subreport(s), AC 200–201
SubReport Wizard, AC 200, AC 201
subscriptions, Microsoft Office 365, OFF 3
subtotals, reports, AC 88, AC 89
suites, OFF 2
Sum function, AC 104, AC 148, AC 149

summary queries, AC 148–149
summary reports, AC 204–205
switchboards, AC 256, AC 257
switching
    between Start screen and desktop, WIN 34
    between views, AC 66
syncing, CL 2
syntax
    property values, AC 62
    query criteria, AC 38
    VBA statements, AC 348
syntax error, AC 360

T

Tab(s), WIN 6
tab(s), OFF 6, OFF 7
tab controls, forms, AC 63, AC 178–179
Tab Index property, AC 66
tab order, forms, AC 66–67
Tab Order dialog box, AC 66, AC 67
tab stop(s), AC 66
Tab Stop property, AC 66
table(s), AC 4, AC 5, AC 9, AC 248–249
    adding to queries, AC 33, AC 148
    child, AC 111
    creating, AC 8–9
    deleting, AC 108
    deleting in queries, AC 33
    HTML tags, AC 403
    junction, AC 107, AC 246
    layouts, AC 59, AC 300–301
    one-to-many relationships, AC 10, AC 12–13.
        See also one-to-many relationships
    parent, AC 111
    prefix naming convention, AC 351
    renaming, AC 108
    target, AC 278
Table Datasheet View, AC 117
Table Design View, AC 6, AC 7, AC 117
    creating tables, AC 8
    designing tables, AC 108–109
    reordering fields, AC 122
    setting Lookup properties, AC 112–113
table events, AC 335
table layout, AC 300–301
<table> </table>tags, AC 403
<table> tag, AC 403
Tabular layout
    forms, AC 167
    tables, AC 301
tags, HTML. *See* HTML tags
target table, AC 278

taskbar, WIN 4, WIN 11, WIN 13
TB (terabyte), AC 380
tbl prefix, AC 351
<td> </td>tags, AC 403
templates, AC 6, OFF 4
  Application parts, AC 220–221
  database, AC 218–219
terabyte (TB), AC 380
Text Align property, AC 62
text boxes, WIN 14
  forms, AC 54, AC 55, AC 63, AC 164
  prefix naming convention, AC 351
text color, VBE, AC 347
Text command, PowerPoint Web App, CL 13
text files
  delimited, AC 222
  linking, importing, and exporting to Access, AC 227
<th> </th>tags, AC 403
theft, databases, AC 381
themes, OFF 2
  reports, AC 198, AC 199
Themes command, PowerPoint Web App, CL 13
third normal form (3NF), AC 245
3NF (third normal form), AC 245
tiles, WIN 4
times, reports, AC 307
title bar, OFF 6, OFF 7, WIN 6
  Property Sheet, AC 170
toggle buttons, forms, AC 63
Toggle Filter button, AC 37
toolbar(s), WIN 10, WIN 28
toolbar buttons, Visual Basic window, AC 355
Top Values feature, AC 270–271
Total row
  query design grid, AC 148, AC 149
  query grid, AC 150
touch mode, enabling, OFF 15
Touch Mode button, OFF 15
touch pad, WIN 7
touch screens, WIN 2
<tr> </tr> tags, AC 403
trackball, WIN 7
traditional apps, WIN 4, WIN 8
TRANSITIONS tab, PowerPoint Web App, CL 13
Transitions to This Slide command, PowerPoint Web App, CL 13
troubleshooting
  macros, AC 336–337
  modules, AC 360–361
Trust Center category, Access Options dialog box, AC 373
trusted databases, AC 329
trusted folders, AC 329
trusting databases, AC 372
2NF (second normal form), AC 245
txt prefix, AC 351
typing errors, correcting, WIN 28

U

UI (user interface), OFF 2, WIN 4
unbound controls, AC 61, AC 63
Underline button, AC 93
underscore (_), Input Mask property, AC 115
Undo button, AC 16, AC 168, WIN 11
Undo command, AC 16, AC 92
unfreezing fields in datasheets, AC 31
unhiding fields in datasheets, AC 31
universal serial bus (USB) drives, AC 380, WIN 28
unmatched records, finding, AC 286–287
update(s), installing while exiting Windows, WIN 18–19
Update queries, AC 277, AC 282–283
Update To row, AC 282
updating records in one-to-many relationship, AC 221
USB (universal serial bus) drives, AC 380, WIN 28
USB ports, WIN 28
Use Control Wizards button, AC 328
user accounts, WIN 2
user interface (UI), OFF 2, WIN 4

V

Validation Rule expressions, AC 121
Validation Rule property, AC 120, AC 121
Validation Text property, AC 120, AC 121
Value argument, AC 330
Value field, query grid, AC 150
Var function, AC 149
variables, VBA, AC 348
VBA. *See* Visual Basic for Applications (VBA)
VBE. *See* Visual Basic Editor (VBE); Visual Basic Editor (VBE) window
view(s), AC 408, OFF 12–13, WIN 32–33.
  See also specific views
  logical, AC 138
View buttons, OFF 12
View Microsoft Access button, AC 355
VIEW tab, OFF 12
  PowerPoint Web App, CL 13
viewing, OFF 12, OFF 13. *See also* displaying
  objects organized by the table they support, AC 220
viruses, databases, AC 381
Visible property, AC 330
Visual Basic Editor (VBE), AC 346
Visual Basic Editor (VBE) window
  components and text colors, AC 347
  toolbar buttons, AC 355
Visual Basic for Applications (VBA), AC 346–347
  arguments, AC 346
  declaration statements, AC 346
  functions, AC 346
  keywords, AC 349

methods, AC 346
modules. *See* modules
objects, AC 346
procedures, AC 346
subs (sub procedures), AC 346
syntax, AC 348
variables, AC 348

W

watermarks, AC 258
Web apps, AC 218, AC 406–407
   creating, AC 408–409
   Office, CL 2, CL 12–13
   reference materials, AC 407
   software required to create, modify, and use, AC 407
Web browsers, creating, modifying, and using
   Web apps, AC 407
Web compatibility, AC 370
wildcard characters
   query criteria, AC 145, AC 272
   query design grid, AC 276, AC 280
   searching for patterns, AC 36, AC 37
windows, WIN 10–11
   active, WIN 12
   elements, WIN 10, WIN 11
   inactive, WIN 12
   multiple, WIN 12–13
   navigating, WIN 12
Windows 8
   exiting, WIN 18–19
   starting, WIN 2–3
Windows 8 apps, WIN 4, WIN 8, WIN 9
   snapping, WIN 32
Windows 8 UI, WIN 4
Windows accessories, WIN 8
Windows Clipboard, OFF 13
Windows desktop, navigating, WIN 4–5
Windows Live ID, CL 5. *See also* Microsoft accounts

Windows Media Player, WIN 9
Windows Search, WIN 40
Windows 7, starting apps, OFF 4, OFF 5
Windows website, WIN 16
Word
   linking, importing, and exporting to Access, AC 227
   merging data with, AC 230–231
   Office Web App, CL 12
   overview, OFF 2, OFF 3
   publishing data to, AC 228–229
Word Resume Reading Position setting, CL 2
word wrap feature, AC 228
working online, CL 4–5
World Wide Web Consortium (W3C), AC 399
/wrkgrp option, AC 374
W3C (World Wide Web Consortium), AC 399

X

/x option, AC 374
XML (Extensible Markup Language), AC 222, AC 232
   exporting to, AC 400, AC 401
   importing from, AC 402, AC 403
   linking, importing, and exporting files to Access, AC 227
XPS, AC 232, AC 233
   linking, importing, and exporting files to Access, AC 227
XSD files, AC 400, AC 401

Y

Yes/No data type, AC 7
Your Profile page, CL 4

Z

zero-length strings, AC 285
Zoom button, OFF 6
zooming in, OFF 6
zooming out, OFF 6